STAR TREK™
THE CLASSIC EPISODES

DEL REY

Star Trek: The Classic Episodes 1 copyright © 1967, 1968, 1969, 1971, 1972, 1973, 1974, 1975, 1977 by Paramount Pictures Corporation, Desilu Productions, Inc., and Bantam Books; copyright © 1991 by Paramount Pictures Corporation

Star Trek: The Classic Episodes 2 copyright © 1967, 1968, 1969, 1971, 1972, 1973, 1974, 1975, 1977 by Paramount Pictures Corporation, Desilu Productions, Inc., and Bantam Books; copyright © 1991 by Paramount Pictures Corporation

Star Trek: The Classic Episodes 3 copyright © 1967, 1968, 1969, 1971, 1972, 1973, 1974, 1975, 1977 by Paramount Pictures Corporation, Desilu Productions, Inc., and Bantam Books; copyright © 1991 by Paramount Pictures Corporation

All rights reserved.

Published in the United States by Del Rey, an imprint of Random House, a division of Penguin Random House LLC, New York.

DEL REY and the HOUSE colophon are registered trademarks of Penguin Random House LLC.

Star Trek: The Classic Episodes 1, *Star Trek: The Classic Episodes 2*, and *Star Trek: The Classic Episodes 3* were each originally published separately by Bantam Spectra, an imprint of Random House, a division of Penguin Random House LLC in 1991.

ISBN 9780385365246

Cover design by David Ter-Avanesyan

Printed in China

randomhousebooks.com
9 8 7 6 5 4 3 2
2016 Sterling Books Edition

CONTENTS

A Note on the Text	viii
Star Trek in the Real World	ix
The Menagerie	1

SEASON 1

Where No Man Has Gone Before	21
Charlie's Law	41
The Naked Time	56
The Enemy Within	67
What Are Little Girls Made Of?	89
Dagger of the Mind	110
The Conscience of the King	122
Balance of Terror	136
The Galileo Seven	151
Arena	174
Tomorrow is Yesterday	183
Court Martial	194

The Return of the Archons	206
Space Seed	229
A Taste of Armageddon	242
This Side of Paradise	252
The Devil in the Dark	263
Errand of Mercy	279
The City on the Edge of Forever	290
Operation Annihilate	304

SEASON 2

Amok Time	318
Who Mourns for Adonais?	328
The Changeling	348
Mirror, Mirror	365
The Apple	378
The Doomsday Machine	393
Metamorphosis	406
Journey to Babel	423
The Deadly Years	440
The Trouble with Tribbles	462
A Piece of the Action	475
The Immunity Syndrome	489
By Any Other Name	508

| The Ultimate Computer | 526 |
| Assignment: Earth | 551 |

SEASON 3

The Enterprise Incident	560
The Day of the Dove	576
For the World is Hollow and I Have Touched the Sky	596
The Tholian Web	617
Wink of an Eye	630
Let That Be Your Last Battlefield	651
The Cloudminders	666
All Our Yesterdays	684

A Note on the Text

The stories in this volume were selected from adaptations that James Blish wrote based on scripts for episodes of the original *Star Trek* television series that aired between 1966 and 1969. These adaptations were originally collected in twelve volumes published by Bantam Books between 1967 and 1975.

    The ordering of the stories in this book follows the order in which the original episodes were aired with two exceptions. "The Menagerie" appears as a "prologue" to the other stories. Aired in two parts on November 17 and November 24 in 1966, "The Menagerie" incorporated footage from "The Cage," the original pilot for *Star Trek*, which the network had rejected in 1965. "Where No Man Has Gone Before" was filmed as the second pilot for the series in 1965. An edited version of this pilot aired under the same title as the third episode of the first season on September 22, 1966.

STAR TREK IN THE REAL WORLD

Norman Spinrad

> Far too little attention has been paid to *Star Trek* as the pivotal work in the growth of SF cinema into a dominant force, and the concurrent growth of SF publishing into what it is today....
>
> The creation of the *Star Trek* concept ... was a cunning and audacious stroke of genius that changed the relation of SF to popular culture forever....
>
> *Star Trek* imprinted the imagery of science fiction on mass public consciousness, where it had never been before, opening, thereby, the languages and concerns of science fiction to a mass audience for the very first time ... so that years and a generation of Trekkies later, George Lucas could confidently begin *Star Wars* with a full-bore space chase and take the largest film audiences in history with him from the opening shot.
>
> —*Science Fiction in the Real World*, Norman Spinrad

You must pardon me for beginning this essay by quoting myself, but the above words were written long before I was asked to write this introduction; they appeared not in a piece on *Star Trek* itself but as part of a chapter on cinematic science fiction in a critical book exploring the relationship of science fiction to the wider world around us, and for purposes of this discussion, *that* is as important as the words themselves, or who happened to be the author thereof.

In science fiction, and in the real world, there has never been a phenomenon quite like *Star Trek*. One scarcely knows where to begin. Consider perhaps the most improbable event of all.

Star Trek's third and final season as a network prime-time show was nearly a decade in the past when the first test-bed model of a Space Shuttle was rolled out of the hangar.

Presiding at the roll-out ceremony of the Space Shuttle *Enterprise* was the President of the United States. Gerald Ford and his people had not planned to name the prototype Shuttle *Enterprise*; in fact there was no little derision when the notion was first broached.

That was before the letters came pouring in.

And even when the inevitable decision was finally made, the powers that be insisted that in the time-honored military tradition, this first true spaceship had been named in honor of a previous vessel, the aircraft carrier *Enterprise* of World War II fame.

Sure it was.

Nevertheless, when the Space Shuttle *Enterprise* was rolled out, there beside the President of the United States was the captain of what the whole nation knew as the real *Enterprise*, along with representatives of his bridge crew, and the music they played was the theme from *Star Trek*.

Trekkies made him do it.

Just as they had kept the show on the air in prime time for two and a half seasons after NBC had tried to cancel it after the first thirteen weeks.

By the network numbers, *Star Trek* was a flop. It never rose much above twentieth place in the weekly Nielsens. NBC decided to pull the plug and told Paramount and Gene Roddenberry that no new episodes would be ordered. After the thirteenth week, *Star Trek*, like hundreds of failed series before it, would be dead.

But Roddenberry did something utterly unprecedented. He refused to take no for an answer. He decided to fight the network, to save his show using tactics that Hollywood had never seen.

He contacted a number of well-known science fiction writers, myself among them, and asked us to join a committee to save *Star Trek*. All Gene really wanted was our permission to use our names on a letterhead, and so most of us readily agreed.

Armed with this letterhead, he hired Bjo and John Trimble, well-connected science fiction fans, to use the "writers' committee" to put together a campaign to convince science fiction fans to write letters to NBC and Paramount demanding that the show be allowed to continue.

He succeeded beyond what must have been even his own wildest expectations.

When a network received a couple of thousand letters in praise of a TV show, they sat up and took notice. If they got 5000, they were mightily impressed.

Science fiction fans dumped upward of 75,000 letters on Paramount and NBC in a few short weeks. Fans picketed the studio and the network. It became a TV news item. Dumbfounded by this totally unprecedented outpouring of public opinion, NBC capitulated.

They literally didn't know what had hit them.

Particularly since the ratings never really improved.

What did Gene Roddenberry know that the network and studio mavens didn't?

It had taken Roddenberry years to get *Star Trek* on the air. He himself had written a ninety-minute pilot that didn't sell. He didn't give up. He hired Samuel Peeples to write another script, changed Spock's makeup a bit, recast the role of Captain Kirk with William Shatner, and shot another pilot that finally sold.

Introduction

During this whole process, Roddenberry did what no other producer had ever done. He made the rounds of the science fiction conventions, made speeches, sat on panels, socialized with the writers and fans, treated the science fiction community to early screenings of both pilot films. He took the fans and the writers inside. He campaigned for support within the science fiction community, and he got it.

What Roddenberry knew that NBC and Paramount didn't was that while there were perhaps no more than ten or fifteen thousand committed science fiction fans in the United States, they were highly organized, literate, and voluble in print. Scores of science fiction conventions were held every year. Fans published hundreds of amateur "fanzines" filled with articles and letters from readers.

By tapping into this existing network, he was able to generate far more letters than there were fans. What NBC and Paramount didn't know was that those 75,000 letters were written for the most part by a comparatively small universe of committed people.

But, contrary to popular belief, network and studio heads are not *complete* idiots. When the first-season ratings didn't improve, they tried to cancel the show again, and when they were bombarded by another blizzard of letters, even they began to realize that something, in the immortal words of Mr. Spock, did not compute, especially when the second-season ratings were no better.

Roddenberry, however, had boxed them into a corner. The numbers said "cancel this show." But the continued letter-writing campaigns and the attendant well-managed publicity would have made them seem like high-handed antidemocratic monsters if they did.

They were royally pissed off. It almost seemed as if they had set out to assassinate *Star Trek* at the beginning of the third season, to make sure that the ratings would be so bad that no reasonable person could blame them for finally canceling it.

Their demographic studies told them that *Star Trek*'s main audiences were young children, teenagers, and young adults in their twenties. So they slotted the show at 10:00 P.M. on Friday night, when most of the kiddies had been put to bed, and most of the teenagers and young adults were out on weekend dates.

This time, the powers that be finally had their way. The third season's ratings were so bad that no amount of letter writing could save the show again, *Star Trek* was canceled, and no doubt they thought that was the end of it.

How wrong they were.

Network and studio heads may not be idiots, but they're not exactly Einsteins either. In the case of *Star Trek*, they failed to understand the true implications of their own numbers.

True, *Star Trek* had always been a ratings failure by network prime-time standards. But this "failure" still was watched by *twenty million people* a week for three years.

Ironically enough, the fact that Roddenberry was able to beat the system for three full seasons ended up enriching Paramount enormously. Three seasons worth of programs is what you need to sell a viable syndication package, and from the time of its cancellation as a prime-time show until the present day, for over twenty years, *Star Trek* reruns have been a staple of local syndication markets.

A show that flopped in prime time became the greatest syndication success in television history. For twenty years, it wouldn't die. It was so successful in syndication that it finally spawned a series of high-budget theatrical motion pictures. Successful films have from time to time spawned TV series, but only *Star Trek* has reversed the process.

Indeed, incredibly enough, *Star Trek* now exists in three simultaneous incarnations. You can go to a movie theater and see a *Star Trek* film, go home, turn on the tube, and catch *Star Trek: The Next Generation*, and, with a little button-pushing on your remote, probably tune in reruns of the original TV show too!

How could this possibly happen? After all, hundreds of TV series have run three seasons or more and gone into syndication, but none have taken on a life after primetime death like *Star Trek*'s. Perhaps the Hollywood powers that be should be pardoned for failing to anticipate the incredible.

How could they have known?

The conditions that created this phenomenon didn't exist when it began. Before *Star Trek*, there *was* no mass audience for science fiction.

Star Trek created it.

At the time that Gene Roddenberry began putting together the *Star Trek* project, science fiction had long languished in cultural obscurity.

The genre had been born as an offshoot of the pulp adventure magazines in the 1920's, and in the middle of the 1960's, there were a handful of science fiction magazines, none of them with a circulation much above 100,000, and less than 200 science fiction books published annually. Five thousand copies was quite a nice sale for an SF hardcover, and 100,000 sales made a paperback a big winner.

There had been a few successful major SF films like *Metropolis*, *The War of the Worlds*, and *The Day the Earth Stood Still*, and some artistically successful B-movies like *Forbidden Planet*, *This Island Earth*, and *The Power*, but generally speaking, SF films, or "sci-fi flics," as they were more generally known, were B-movies featuring tacky monsters from outer space or other venues, typified by *The Creature from the Black Lagoon* and *The Thing*, in which John W. Campbell's subtle masterpiece *Who Goes There?* was turned into a monster movie featuring James Arness as a savage carnivorous carrot.

When it came to TV, *The Twilight Zone* had been a big long-running success, though most of the episodes were only borderline SF, and *The Outer Limits*, while it had done some serious SF, had relied heavily on monsters.

True, the hard core of regular readers knew that inside the sleazy covers of those magazines and paperbacks there existed a universe of literally infinite literary possibility, that some of the finest American writers had done their best work therein for decades, that what passed for "sci-fi movies" was only a pale shadow of the real stuff.

But the general public, when it thought of science fiction at all, thought of mad scientists, crazed robots, and bug-eyed monsters, and the Hollywood powers that be viewed SF as low-budget monster movies aimed at a modest-sized cult audience.

How this situation evolved could be and has been the subject of whole books, *Science Fiction in the Real World* being one of them, and is far too complex a story to go into here, but for present purposes, the point is that by the 1960s science fiction had evolved into something largely impenetrable to anyone who was not a regular science fiction reader.

The real stuff dealt with alien civilizations, faster-than-light space travel, mutated consciousness, time travel, alternate universes, relativity theory, synthetic religions, outré biology, the frontiers of psychology, speculative science, political theory, cybernetics. And because it had been written for a limited, educated, in-group audience for so long, it had long since come to be written without compromise, without any real attempt to make it transparent to anyone unfamiliar with the conventions, imagery, and secret language.

This, in a way, was a literary strength. Most science fiction writers felt they had no chance of reaching a general audience, so they felt free to write for a theoretical ideal audience—the fans and regular readers, who understood the conventions and the special language, for whom the recondite imagery held meaning, who were generally speaking scientifically literate, who did not have to be persuaded that space travel lay in the realm of the realistic possible, who were already convinced that there must be other intelligent beings out there somewhere. This enabled science fiction writers at their best to produce work without intellectual compromise.

But this literary strength was a commercial weakness. It made much of even the best SF largely incomprehensible to a general audience. And when writers *did* try to reach a wider audience, they usually did it by watering the stuff down, by simplifying it, bringing it closer to the here and now; in a way, by patronizing the general public.

These were the conditions that Gene Roddenberry faced when he set out to do a science fiction TV series. And two further problems as well, which were interrelated.

The first problem was that the anthology series was a dead form as far as prime-time TV was concerned; that is, the series in which each episode was a self-contained story with its own cast of characters. Since science fiction is inherently a literature built around surprise, novelty, and the attendant sense of wonder, the anthology series was the ideal form for televised SF, and indeed, the only two successful SF TV series, *Twilight Zone* and *The Outer Limits*, had been anthologies.

But what the networks wanted was series that used *familiarity* to retain and build audience share, episodic series in which the same main characters appeared each week in a familiar format and setting, characters who could not really be changed by the events of each week's episode, and this would seem to be the esthetic antithesis of the central appeal of science fiction.

Then too, science fiction was *expensive* to film. Space-ships. Other worlds. Alien civilizations. No problem when you're writing short stories and novels, but when you have to build the sets, create the costumes and the makeup, do the special-effects processing, the budget becomes prohibitive when you're talking about a time when $200,000 was about the top for an hour-long show. Not to mention the problem of doing it all on a timetable that must enable you to do twenty-six episodes a season on a six-day shooting schedule for each.

The genius of Gene Roddenberry was that he was able to look at these problems, these creative restrictions, and, by making one big leap of faith, let them determine a series format that turned them into strengths.

It would be futile to attempt a science fiction anthology series. The networks weren't buying anthologies, and besides, you simply couldn't create sets, makeup, and special effects for a new science fiction setting every week at $200,000 an episode without descending to tacky sleaze. No, it had to be an episodic series, and it had to use mostly reusable standing sets. But then how could you create the sense of novelty and sense of wonder each week that was the core esthetic effect of science fiction?

The answer to that one was the solution to all the problems via the required leap of faith.

Set the whole thing aboard a single spaceship. You could then do most of your shooting on standing sets. Irwin Allen had done much the same thing with a futuristic submarine in the series *Voyage to the Bottom of the Sea*. Network executives love one-line descriptions of a new concept told in terms of old shows when it's time to pitch—"*Voyage to the Bottom of the Sea* in outer space!"

Or better yet, "Captain Cooke in outer space." A starship on a long voyage of exploration, completely out of touch with the Earth so you don't have to show the complex civilization of the far future, so that each week the same cast of characters can confront almost anything that the writers can dream up. You can set many of the stories entirely within the standing spaceship sets. You can use the same spaceship models over and over again, even a library of standard space shots and effects.

In retrospect, it all seems quite obvious, but to conceive it at all required one big leap of faith—namely that you *could* persuade a mass general audience to accept an interstellar spaceship as the setting for a TV series.

Roddenberry approached this problem from two directions, one dramatic, the other purely cinematic.

Give a general audience familiar character types and well-worn traditional character relationships they can readily understand, and they'll swallow your setting, no matter how outré, for it is character relationships that draw an audience into a story, not the physical backdrop.

So . . . The Heroic Captain—call him . . . Kirk. His sidekick, the Crusty Old Sea Doctor Bones—call him . . . McCoy. The Pragmatic Grumbling Engineer—call him . . . what else, Scotty.

Any audience will accept such characters, familiar as they are from tales of the sea, and from there it's not such a great leap to transfer them from a sailing ship to a ship of space.

As for the spaceship itself, well, seeing is believing, one picture is worth a thousand words, work off the familiar conventions, give them a spaceship they can understand, a transmogrified ship of the sea.

A bridge, of course, the main and most elaborate set, where most of the action will naturally take place. An engine room to serve as Scotty's domain. A sick bay for Dr. Bones. A captain's cabin. A wardroom that can easily be redressed into anything. A corridor set to provide a sense of the ship's complex interior.

Voilà, the starship *Enterprise*, its five-year mission to seek out new worlds and new civilizations, to boldly go where no man and no TV series has gone before!

But not quite yet *Star Trek*.

Roddenberry could have stopped there and, having cracked the basic problems, probably gotten his science fiction series on the air. But it wouldn't have been *Star Trek*, and it wouldn't have become the phenomenon that created the present mass audience for science fiction both literary and cinematic. It would have indeed been merely *Voyage to the Bottom of the Sea in Outer Space*, a good format for a successful TV series maybe, but not something that would pass into the collective popular unconscious.

But Gene Roddenberry, unlike Irwin Allen, took science fiction seriously. He wanted *Star Trek* to appeal to a naive audience, but he wanted it to have credibility with the SF cognoscenti too. He wanted it to be a genuine work of science fiction.

The original series guide, the so-called bible, makes that almost maniacally clear. Roddenberry consulted experts and the *Enterprise* was designed and even blueprinted down to the smallest niggling detail, to the point where NASA even took a look at his plans to pick up some tips on spaceship ergonomics. The ship was utterly real for Roddenberry, as I learned during the story conferences for "The Doomsday Machine."

Similarly with the details of the rest of the *Star Trek* universe. The phasers, the communicators, the shuttlecraft, the chain of command, and of course the implications of the famous Prime Directive, which by now has attained the real-world credibility of Asimov's Three Laws of Robotics. When the writers sat down to do their episodes, all of this was as predetermined as a street map of contemporary New York, and if you got something wrong, you had to change it, even if it meant altering the story to make it fit "*Star Trek* reality."

The result was that the layout, hardware, capabilities, and limitations of the *Enterprise*, the parameters of the *Star Trek* universe, remained consistent from episode to episode. Gene Roddenberry knew his ship and its universe, and if you watched enough episodes, so did you. It allowed this imaginary spaceship to become psychologically real, seemingly complex, and seemingly familiar in every detail, even though all you really ever saw was less than a dozen sets. No fictional spaceship has ever surpassed the *Enterprise* for this kind of detailed solidity, and not much on the NASA drawing boards either.

As a result, over three seasons, the *Enterprise* became as familiar as Dodge City or Gilligan's Island or Lucy Ricardo's living room to twenty million regular viewers. And over time, the reruns made it familiar to scores of millions more, to the point that by the time the Space Shuttle *Enterprise* was rolled out, an overwhelming majority of the American people were as at home on the bridge of what they psychologically regarded as the *real Enterprise*, the one commanded by the James T. Kirk that half of them had known all their adult lives, as they were in their own living room.

Indeed, the *Enterprise* was an extension of the collective national living room, just as the battlefields of Viet Nam had been for eleven long years, via the magic window of the tube.

Endless TV coverage had quite literally brought Viet Nam home, given it a psychological reality that no war had ever had before, altering, over time, the national psyche, by demystifying war, leaching it of glory, revealing the reality as the grubby horror that it truly was.

So too did endless exposure to the science fiction universe of *Star Trek* via the familiar confines of the *Enterprise* demystify science fiction, imprint its imagery on the public consciousness, make an entire generation feel at home in outer space, precisely because it brought outer space into the home.

Thus did *Star Trek* create a mass general audience for science fiction. The technology of the *Enterprise* and all that it implied—faster-than-light travel, matter transmission, alien beings, human colonization of other planets—had passed into folklore, had become familiar, had become as American as apple pie, or Gerald Ford's desire not to offend the Trekkie voting bloc.

Thus was the beaming presence of Captain Kirk and the *Star Trek* theme music required to give *NASA's* new spaceship media credibility.

Thus could George Lucas open *Star Wars* with a simple type frame reading "Once upon a time, in a galaxy far, far away," cut to a space battle shot, and take the largest film audience in history with him.

Thus did major science fiction films become a Hollywood staple, indeed for a time quite dominating the industry. Thus did literary science fiction come to crash the bestseller lists, and eventually come to represent about 20 percent of all fiction published in the United States.

Star Trek opened the way.

INTRODUCTION • xvii •

* * *

Or rather, the *Star Trek* phenomenon opened the way. If the show had died after three first-run seasons and the usual few years of syndication, none of this would have happened, and the world would probably be very different. It took time, a decade of reruns, for *Star Trek* to alter the attitude of the American mass audience toward science fiction.

Josef Goebbels had declared that even the biggest lie will come to be believed if it is repeated often enough, and gone on to prove it.

If lies, why not images of the future, which, by their very nature, are neither false nor true? It was the endless repetitive exposure to *Star Trek* that did the deed.

But why didn't *Star Trek* die after the show was canceled? Easy enough to see how *Star Trek* created the mass audience for science fiction via decades of reruns, but *that audience didn't yet exist* when *Star Trek* went into syndication. How could a show that had flopped in prime time survive long enough in syndication to become the staple of popular culture that it is today? How did it create the mass public audience for *itself* in the first place?

By the time the show was finally canceled, the letter-writing campaign had already spawned *Star Trek* fan clubs and huge *Star Trek* conventions, fanzines, the whole Trekkie subculture. While there were never enough Trekkies to make the show successful in prime time, there were enough to keep the tie-ins going even after the show had died, something quite unprecedented.

Star Trek fans continued to buy books like the one you are now reading, *Star Trek* toys, games, comics. They continued to hold conventions, which actually got *bigger* after the show was canceled. They continued to publish fanzines, they started writing their own *Star Trek* stories, even whole novels. Even *Star Trek* religions sprang up.

In short, *Star Trek* transcended television. It was no longer defined as those seventy-eight episodes of a canceled TV show running over and over again. It had become a popular myth imprinted upon mass culture, as surely as Robin Hood, or Billy the Kid, or Cinderella, a modern legend, a set of mythic archetypes, the dramatic material for books, a cartoon series, a film series, a spin-off TV series, paintings, even a strange sort of underground pornographic literature.

To the point where any character in any contemporary story who finds himself in trouble can look skyward, cry "Beam me up, Scotty," and everyone will know just what he means.

Clearly then, one cannot entirely explain the *Star Trek* phenomenon by detailing the process that gave it birth and the consequences. That can tell you *how* it happened, but not *why*. Clearly one must deal with *Star Trek* as dramatic literature in order to understand the power of its appeal in the first place.

We have come a long way into this discussion without really considering Mr. Spock. Kirk, the Heroic Captain, Scotty and Bones, the loyal sidekicks, Uhura, Chekov, and

Sulu, the gallant crewpeople—these are a traditional cast of shipboard characters as old as the tale of the sea, individuated and made memorable really only by the scripts and the actors' interpretations.

But Spock is . . . something else.

Whereas the rest of the *Star Trek* format may be seen as Gene Roddenberry's clever reinterpretations and combinations of preexisting elements into a coherent and successful whole, Mr. Spock is Roddenberry's act of literary genius, a character unlike any other, a new mythic archetype, and an exceedingly complex one.

Physically, with his pointed ears and green skin, Spock evokes the image of Satan and—with his ability to mind-meld, his physical powers, and his superior intellect—certainly possesses power beyond that of mortal men.

But far from being an egoistic Faustian power-tripper, a tempter, a figment of evil, Spock, at least on the surface, *has* no ego. As a creature of pure logic, he may represent science, but with his total loyalty to the ship, his captain, his duty, he represents social virtue, not overweening intellectual pride, a kind of scientific angel in devil's clothing, a being of pure intellect serving the cause of good because it is the logical thing to do.

And that's only the surface. Beneath the surface, Spock's cold logicality is the product of his people's long and finally successful battle with their own savage nature. Vulcan dedication to pure logic is, paradoxically enough, ultimately a religious belief, not a genetic inevitable. Vulcans have *chosen* to suppress their emotional life, although not entirely, as witness their behavior when they come into sexual heat. Logical Vulcan society still seems rather ritualized and even mystical whenever we see it, and perhaps it is no accident that Vulcan features tend to evoke the orient in western eyes, with implications of Zen, Taoism, transcendent states of being achieved through spiritual discipline.

Nor is that the end of it. For Spock is half-human, though he dislikes being reminded of it, and the two halves of his being are shown to be in continual conflict. Over and over again, Spock surrenders to human emotions against his will, but almost always when these emotions represent human virtues like loyalty, empathy, compassion, rather than vices.

Surely Mr. Spock is the most complex character ever to appear in a prime-time TV series. And more than that, he is that science fictional rarity, a fully realized intelligent alien, with an inner life at least as complex as that of any human, but one that is truly *different*. A character that is, on many levels, and in Spock's own oft-repeated words, "quite fascinating."

William Shatner was hired as the star, but Kirk was never the central character in *Star Trek*, and never could be. Whether Roddenberry intended it or not, Mr. Spock is the central figure of *Star Trek*, and in the end, it is the character of Spock that has enabled *Star Trek* to transcend television, to survive, in one incarnation and another, for a quarter of a century, to pass into the collective consciousness of popular culture as surely as Superman, and take science fiction with it.

Did Roddenberry really know what he was doing when he created the character of Spock? Somehow I doubt it, for Spock, in the end, is a collaborative creation, the parameters of his character outlined by Roddenberry, interpreted by Leonard Nimoy, elaborated by the writers of the individual episodes, given additional reality by the imagination of the audience.

Spock is many things to many people. To those of a certain scientific beat, he represents not merely the intellectual but the moral and even spiritual superiority of the logical scientific viewpoint. To those of a more mystical inclination, he represents higher consciousness, mental and spiritual clarity achieved by a continuous conscious act of will. To the humanist, he epitomizes the struggle toward a balance between logic and intuition, emotion and intellect.

Finally, Mr. Spock is a sexual fantasy figure of great power and considerable complexity. Physically, he resembles Satan, Dracula, the Mysterious Dark Stranger, the Dark Side of the sexual force, the deliciously dangerous Dream Lover. Yet, unlike such Satanic sex symbols, Spock is controlled, logical, loyal, trustworthy, admirable, virtuous. As a sexual fantasy figure, Spock is like no other, allowing the frisson of dark danger, *within* the safe limits of spiritual and moral virtue; Albert Einstein in Jim Morrison's tight black leather clothing, a Mick Jagger that a girl can bring home to meet Mother.

It is the presence of this great character that in the end has elevated a canceled television series to the status of a modern myth, a contemporary legend, a new literary archetype that has entered the collective unconscious, opening thereby the way for science fiction itself.

And in the end, perhaps, this opening up of the mass public consciousness to the things of science fiction by *Star Trek* goes deeper than mere familiarization with the imagery and the formerly secret language.

For Mr. Spock, alien though he is, is admirable, not menacing, humanity's ally, not its nemesis. His friendship with Kirk represents the possibility of empathy between the Self and the Other, between our own evolving species, and the very different beings we are likely to meet when we venture out into the Final Frontier. Even McCoy, who seemingly represents humanity's conservative reticence to love the Stranger, warms up to Spock in his heart of hearts, though neither of them are about to admit it.

This positive emotional openness to the new and the strange, this empathy for the alien, defines the heart and soul of science fiction. And up until a certain stage in human evolution, this acceptance of the alien, the foreigner, the Other, ran counter to the emotional attitude of our mass culture, and perhaps it was this divergence, as much as the unfamiliar settings, bizarre imagery, and secret language, that prevented the acceptance of science fiction as part of the literary and cinematic mainstream.

Ultimately, then, *Star Trek*, despite the literary flaws of so many of its episodes, films, books, and assorted spin-offs, succeeds on a moral level. In some small (or perhaps not so small) way, it has served the cause of our spiritual evolution as a species.

Clever format, fanatically loyal fans, marketing strategies, letter-writing campaigns, all explain how *Star Trek* has survived through a quarter of a century in all its many incarnations.

But when it comes to *why Star Trek* has survived to attain a kind of permanent place in our cultural life, and why it will probably still be with us in the twenty-first century, in the end, perhaps, it can be simply said that it deserved to.

This essay was originally published in *Star Trek: The Classic Episodes 3* (Bantam, 1991).

THE MENAGERIE*

WRITER: GENE RODDENBERRY

DIRECTORS: MARC DANIELS (PART I),
ROBERT BUTLER (PART II)

FIRST AIRED: NOVEMBER 17, 24, 1966

When the distress signal from Talos IV came through, via old-fashioned radio, Captain Christopher Pike was of two minds about doing anything about it. The message said it was from survivors of the SS *Columbia*, and a library search by Spock showed that a survey ship of that name had indeed disappeared in that area—eighteen years ago. It had taken all of those years for the message, limited to the speed of light, to reach the *Enterprise*, which passed through its wave-front just slightly eighteen light-years from the Talos system. A long time ago, that had been.

In addition, Pike had his own crew to consider. Though the *Enterprise* had come out of the fighting around Rigel VIII—her maiden battle—unscarred, the ground skirmishing had not been as kind to her personnel. Spock, for example, was limping, though he was trying to minimize it, and Navigator Jose Tyler's left forearm was bandaged down to his palm. Pike himself was unhurt, but he felt desperately tired.

Nevertheless, the library also reported Talos IV to be habitable, so survivors from the *Columbia* might still be alive; and since the *Enterprise* would be passing within visual scanning distance anyhow, it wouldn't hurt to take a look. The chances of finding anything at this late date . . .

But almost at once, Tyler picked up reflections from the planet's surface whose

---

* As originally produced, this story ran in two parts. The main story, which takes place so far back in the history of the *Enterprise* that the only familiar face aboard her then was Spock, appeared surrounded by and intercut with an elaborate "framing" story, in which Spock is up for court-martial on charges of mutiny and offers the main story as an explanation of his inarguably mutinous behavior. Dramatically, this was highly effective—indeed, as I've already noted, it won a "Hugo" award in this category for that year—but told as fiction, it involves so many changes of viewpoint, as well as so many switches from present to past, that it becomes impossibly confusing. (I know—I've tried!) Hence the present version adapts only the main story, incidentally restoring to it the ending it had—never shown on television—before the frame was grafted onto it. I think the producers also came to feel that the double-plotted version had been a mistake; at least, "The Menagerie" turned out to be the only two-part episode in the entire history of the series. —J.B.

polarization and scatter pattern indicated large, rounded chunks of metal, which might easily have been parts of a spaceship's hull. Pike ordered the *Enterprise* into orbit.

"I'll want a landing party of six, counting myself. Mr. Tyler, you'll be second in command, and we'll need Mr. Spock too; both of you, see that there's a fresh dressing on your wounds. Also, Dr. Boyce, Chief Garrison and ship's geologist. Number One, you're in command of the *Enterprise* in our absence. Who seconds you now?"

"Yeoman Colt, sir."

Pike hesitated. That this left the bridge dominated by women didn't bother him; female competence to be in Star Fleet had been tested and proven before he had been born. And Pike had the utmost confidence in Number One, ordinarily the ship's helmsman and, after the Rigel affair, the most experienced surviving officer. Slim and dark in a Nile Valley sort of way, she was one of those women who always look the same between the ages of twenty and fifty, but she had a mind like the proverbial steel trap and Pike had never seen her shaken in any situation. Yeoman Colt, however, was a recent replacement, and an unknown quantity. Well, the assignment was likely to prove a routine one, anyhow.

"Very well. We'll beam down to the spot where Mr. Tyler picked up those reflections."

This proved to be on a rocky plateau, not far from an obvious encampment—a rude collection of huts, constructed out of slabs of rock, debris from a spaceship hull, scraps of canvas and other odds and ends. Several fairly old men were visible, all bearded, all wearing stained and tattered garments. One was carrying water; the others were cultivating a plot of orange vegetation. The ingenuity and resolute will which had enabled them to exist for nearly two decades on this forbidding alien world were everywhere evident.

One of them looked up in the direction of the landing party and froze, clearly unable to believe his eyes. At last he called hoarsely, "Winter! *Look!*"

A second man looked up, and reacted almost as the first had. Then he shouted; "They're men! Human!"

The sound of their voices brought other survivors out of their huts and sheds. The youngest looked to be nearly fifty, but they were tanned, hardened, in extraordinarily good health. The two groups approached each other slowly, solemnly; Pike could almost feel the intensity of emotion. He stepped forward and extended a hand.

"Captain Christopher Pike, United Spaceship *Enterprise*."

The first survivor to speak mutely accepted Pike's hand, tears on his face. At last he said, with obvious effort, "Dr. Theodore Haskins, American Continent Institute."

"They're *men*! Here to take us back!" the man called Winter said, laughing with sudden relief. "You are, aren't you? Is Earth all right?"

"Same old Earth," Pike said, smiling. "You'll see it before long."

"And you won't believe how fast you can get back," Tyler added. "The time barrier's been broken! Our new ships can . . ."

He broke off, mouth open, staring past Haskins' shoulder. Following the direction of the navigator's gaze, Pike saw standing in a hut doorway a remarkably beautiful young woman. Although her hair was uncombed and awry, her makeshift dress tattered, she looked more like a woodland nymph than the survivor of a harrowing ordeal. Motioning her forward, Haskins said, "This is Vina. Her parents are dead; she was born almost as we crashed."

There were more introductions all around, but Pike found himself almost unable to take his eyes off the girl. Perhaps it was only the contrast she made with the older men, but her young, animal grace was striking. No wonder Tyler had stared.

"No need to prolong this," Pike said. "Collect what personal effects you want to keep and we'll be off. I suggested you concentrate on whatever records you have; the *Enterprise* is amply stocked with necessities, and even some luxuries."

"Extraordinary," Haskins said. "She must be a very big vessel."

"Our largest and most modern type; the crew numbers four hundred and thirty."

Haskins shook his head in amazement and bustled off. Amidst all the activity, Vina approached Pike and drew him a little to one side.

"Captain, may I have a word?"

"Of course, Vina."

"Before we go, there is something you should see. Something of importance."

"Very well. What is it?"

"It's much easier to show than to explain. If you'll come this way . . ."

She led him to a rocky knoll some distance from the encampment, and pointed to the ground at its base. "There it is."

Pike did not know what he had expected—anything from a grave to some sort of alien artifact—but in fact he saw nothing of interest at all, and said so. Vina looked disappointed.

"The angle of the light is probably wrong," she said. "Come around to this side."

They changed places, so that his back was to the knoll, hers to the encampment. As far as Pike could tell, this made no difference.

"I don't understand," he said.

"You will," Vina said, the tone of her voice changing suddenly. "You're a perfect choice."

Pike looked up sharply. As he did so, the girl vanished. It was not the fading dematerialization of the Transporter effect; she simply blinked out as though someone had snapped off a light. With her went all the survivors and their entire encampment, leaving nothing behind but the bare plateau and the stunned men from the *Enterprise*.

There was a hiss behind him and he spun, reaching for his phaser. A cloud of white gas was rolling toward him, through which he could see an oddly shaped portal which, perfectly camouflaged as a part of the rock, had noiselessly opened to reveal the top of a lift shaft. He had an instant's impression of two occupants—small, slim, pale, human-like creatures with large elongated heads, in shimmering metallic robes; one of them was holding a small cylinder which was still spitting the white spray.

In the same instant, the gas hit him and he was paralyzed, still conscious but unable to move anything but his eyes. The two creatures stepped forward and dragged him into the opening.

"*Captain!*" Spock's voice shouted in the distance. Then there was the sound of running, suddenly muffled as though the doors had closed again, and then the lift dropped with a hissing *whoosh* like that of a high-speed pneumatic tube. Above, and still more distantly, came the sound of a rock explosion as someone fired a phaser at full power, but the lift simply fell faster.

With it, Pike fell into unconsciousness.

He awoke clawing for his own phaser, a spongelike surface impeding his movements. The gun was gone. Rolling to his feet, he looked around, at the same time reaching next for his communicator. That was gone too; so was his jacket.

He was in a spotless utilitarian enclosure. The spongy surface turned out to belong to a plastic shape, apparently a sort of bed, with a filmy metallic-cloth blanket folded on it. There was also a free-form pool of surging water, with a small drinking container sitting on the floor next to it. A prison cell, clearly; the bars . . .

But there were no bars. The fourth wall was made up entirely of a transparent panel. Pike hurried to it and peered through. He found himself looking up and down a long corridor, faced with similar panels; but they were offset to, rather than facing each other, so that Pike could see into only small angled portions of the two nearest him on the other side.

Some sound he had made must have penetrated into the corridor, for suddenly there was a wild snarl, and in the cell—cage?—to his left, a flat creature, half anthropoid, half spider, rushed hungrily at him, only to be thrown back, its ugly fangs clattering against the transparency. Startled, Pike looked to the right; in this enclosure he could see a portion of some kind of tree. Then there was a leathery flapping, and an incredibly thin humanoid/bird creature came into view, peering curiously but shyly toward Pike's cage. The instant it saw Pike watching, it whirled and vanished.

As it did, a group of the pale, large-headed men like those who had kidnapped him came into view, coming toward him. They were lead by one who wore an authoritative-looking jeweled pendant on a short chain around his neck. They all came to a halt in front of Pike's cage, silently watching him. He studied them in turn. They were quite bald, all of them, and each had a prominent vein across his forehead.

Finally, Pike said, "Can you hear me? My name is Christopher Pike, commander of the vessel *Enterprise* of the United Federation of Planets. Our intentions are peaceful. Can you understand me?"

The large forehead vein of one of the Talosians pulsed strong and, although Pike could see no lip movement, a voice sounded in his head, a voice that sounded as though it were reciting something.

"It appears, Magistrate, that the intelligence of the specimen is shockingly limited."

Now the forehead of the creature with the pendant pulsed. "This is no surprise, since his vessel was lured here so easily with a simulated message. As you can read in its thoughts, it is only now beginning to suspect that the survivors and the encampment were a simple illusion we placed in their minds. And you will note the confusion as it reads our thought transmissions . . ."

"All right, telepathy," Pike broke in. "You can read my mind, I can read yours. Now, unless you want my ship to consider capturing me an unfriendly act . . ."

"You now see the primitive fear-threat reaction. The specimen is about to boast of his strength, the weaponry of his vessel, and so on." As Pike stepped back a pace and tensed himself, the Magistrate added, "Next, frustrated into a need to display physical prowess, the creature will throw himself against the transparency."

Pike, his act predicted in mid-move, felt so foolish that he canceled it, which made him angrier than ever. He snarled, "There's a way out of every cage, and I'll find it."

"Despite its frustration, the creature appears more adaptable than our specimens from other planets," the Magistrate continued. "We can soon begin the experiment."

Pike wondered what they meant by *that*, but it was already obvious that they were not going to pay any attention to anything he said. He began to pace. The telepathic "voices" continued behind him.

"Thousands of us are now probing the creature's thoughts, Magistrate. We find excellent memory capacity."

"I read most strongly a recent struggle in which it fought to protect its tribal system. We will begin with this, giving the specimen something more interesting to protect."

The cage vanished.

He was standing alone among rocks and strange vegetation which, on second look, proved to be vaguely familiar. Then an unmistakably familiar voice sounded behind him.

"Come. Hurry!"

He turned to see Vina, her hair long and in braids, dressed like a peasant girl of the terrestrial Middle Ages. Behind her towered a fortress which he might have taken as belonging to the same period had he not recognized it instantly. The girl pointed to it and said, "It is deserted. There will be weapons, perhaps food."

"This is Rigel VIII," Pike said slowly. "I fought in that fortress just two weeks ago. But where do you fit in?"

There was a distant bellowing sound. Vina started, then began walking rapidly toward the fortress. Pike remained where he was.

I was in a cell, a cage in some kind of zoo. I'm still *there. I just* think *I see this. They must have reached into my mind, taken the memory of somewhere I've been, something that's happened to me—except that she wasn't in it then.*

The bellowing sounded again, nearer. Pike hurried after the girl, catching up with her just inside the gateway to the fortress' courtyard. The place was a scatter of battered shields, lance staves, nicked and snapped swords; there was even a broken catapult—the debris that had been left behind after Pike's own force had breached and reduced the fortress. Breaking the Kalars' hold over their serfs had been a bloody business, and made more so by the hesitancy of Star Fleet Command over whether the whole operation was not in violation of General Order Number One. Luckily, the Kalars themselves had solved that by swarming in from Rigel X in support of their degenerate colony . . .

And that animal roar of rage behind them could only be a stray Kalar colonist, seeking revenge for the fall of his fortress and his feudalism upon anything in his path. Vina was looking desperately for a weapon amid the debris, but there was nothing here she could even lift.

Then the bellow sounded at the gateway. Vina shrank into the nearest shadow, pulling Pike with her. He was in no mood to hang back; memory was too strong. The figure at the courtyard entry was a local Kalar warrior, huge, hairy, Neanderthal, clad in cuirass and helmet and carrying a mace. It looked about, shoulders hunched.

"What nonsense," Pike said under his breath. "It was all over weeks ago . . ."

"*Hush*," Vina whispered, terrified. "You've been here—you know what he'll do to us."

"It's nothing but a damn silly illusion."

The warrior roared again, challengingly, raising tremendous echoes. Apparently he hadn't seen them yet.

"It doesn't matter *what* you call this," Vina whispered again. "You'll feel it, that's what matters. You'll feel every moment of whatever happens. I'll feel it happening too."

The warrior moved tentatively toward them. Either in genuine panic or to force Pike's hand, Vina whirled and raced for a parapet stairway behind them which lead toward the battlement above. The Kalar spotted her at once; Pike had no choice but to follow.

At the top was another litter of weapons; Vina had already picked up a spear with a head like an assegai. Pike found himself a shield and an unbroken sword. As he straightened, the girl pushed him aside. A huge round rock smashed into the rampart wall inches away from him, the force of the fragments knocking him down.

The pain was real, all right. He raised a hand to his forehead to find it bleeding.

Below, the warrior was picking up another rock from a depleted pile on the other side of the catapult.

While Pike scrambled back, Vina threw her spear, but she did it inexpertly, and in any event her strength proved insufficient for the range. Changing his mind at once, the Kalar dropped the stone and came charging up the stairs.

Pike's shield was almost torn from his arm at the first blow of the mace. His own sword clanged harmlessly against the Kalar's armor, and he was driven back by a flurry of blows.

Then there was a twanging sound. The warrior bellowed in pain and swung around, revealing an arrow driven deep into his back. Vina had found a crossbow, cocked and armed, and at that range she couldn't miss.

But the wound wasn't immediately mortal and she obviously did not know how to cock the weapon again. The Kalar, staggering, moved in upon her.

From that close, a crossbow bolt would go through almost any armor, but Pike's sword certainly wouldn't. Dropping it, he sprang forward, raised his shield high, and brought it down with all his strength on the back of the warrior's neck. The creature spun off the rampart edge and plummeted to the floor of the compound below. It struck supine and lay still.

Vina, sobbing with relief, threw herself into Pike's arms . . .

. . . and they were back in the menagerie cage.

She was now wearing her own, shorter hair, and a simple garment of the metallic Talosian material. His own bruises and exhaustion had vanished completely, along with the shield. It took him a startled moment to realize what had happened.

Vina smiled. "It's over."

"Why are you here?" he demanded.

She hesitated slightly, then smiled again. "To please you."

"Are you real?"

"As real as you wish."

"That's no answer," he said.

"Perhaps they've made me up out of dreams you've forgotten."

He pointed to her garment. "And I dreamed of you in the same metal fabric they wear?"

"I must wear something." She came closer. "Or must I? I can wear anything you wish, be anything you wish . . ."

"To make this 'specimen' perform for them? To watch how I react? Is that it?"

"Don't you have a dream, something you've wanted very badly . . ."

"Do they do more than just watch me?" he asked. "Do they *feel* with me too?"

"You can have any dream you wish. I can become anything. Any woman you ever imagined." She tried to nestle closer. "You can go anyplace, do anything—have any experience from the whole universe. Let me please you."

Pike eyed her speculatively. "You can," he said abruptly. "Tell me about them. Is there some way I can keep them from using my own thoughts against me? Ah, you're frightened. Does that mean there *is* a way?"

"You're being a fool."

He nodded. "You're right. Since you insist you're an illusion, there's not much point in this conversation."

He went over to the bed and lay down, ignoring her. It was not hard to sense her anxiety, however. Whatever her task was, she did not want to fail it.

After a while she said, "Perhaps—if you asked me something I could answer . . ."

He sat up. "How far can they control my mind?"

"That's not a—that is—" she paused. "If I tell you—will you pick some dream you've had, let me live it with you?"

Pike considered this. The information seemed worth the risk. He nodded.

"They—they can't actually make you do anything you don't want to."

"They have to try to trick me with their illusions?"

"Yes. And they can punish when you're not cooperative. You'll find out about that."

"They must have lived on the planet's surface once . . ."

"Please," she interrupted. "If I say too much . . ."

"Why did they move underground?" he pressed insistently.

"War, thousands of centuries ago," she said hurriedly. "The ones left on the surface destroyed themselves and almost their whole world too. It's taken that long for the planet to heal itself."

"And I suppose the ones who came underground found life too limited—so they concentrated on developing their mental power."

She nodded. "But they've found it's a trap. Like a narcotic. When dreams become more important than reality, you give up travel, building, creating, and even forget how to repair the machines left behind by your ancestors. You just sit living and reliving other lives in the thought records. Or probe the minds of zoo specimens, descendants of life they brought back long ago from all over this part of the galaxy."

Pike suddenly understood. "Which means they had to have more than one of each animal."

"Yes," Vina said, clearly frightened now. "Please, you said if I answered your questions . . ."

"But that was a bargain with something that didn't exist. You said you were an illusion, remember."

"*I'm a woman*," she said, angry now. "As real and human as you are. We're—like Adam and Eve. If they can . . ."

She broke off with a scream and dropped to the floor, writhing.

"Please!" she wailed. "Don't punish me—I'm trying my best with him—no, *please* . . ."

In the midst of her agony, she vanished. Pike looked up to see the creature called the Magistrate watching through the panel. Furiously, he turned his back—and noticed for the first time an almost invisible circular seam, about man-high, in the wall beside his bed. Was there a hidden panel there?

A small clink of sound behind him made him turn again. A vial of blue liquid was sitting on the floor, just inside the transparency. The Magistrate continued to watch; his mental speech said, "The vial contains a nourishing protein complex."

"Is the keeper actually communicating with one of his animals?"

"If the form and color are not appealing, it can appear as any food you wish to visualize."

"And if I prefer—" Pike began.

"To starve? You overlook the unpleasant alternative of punishment."

With the usual suddenness, Pike found himself writhing in bubbling, sulphurous brimstone in a dark place obscured by smoke. Flame licked at him from all sides. The instant agony was as real as the surprise, and a scream was wrenched from him.

It lasted only a few seconds and then he was back in the cage, staggering.

"From a fable you once heard in childhood," the Magistrate said. "You will now consume the nourishment."

"Why not just put irresistible—hunger in my mind?" Pike said, still gasping with remembered pain. "You can't—do that. You do have limitations, don't you?"

"If you continue to disobey, deeper in your mind there are things even more unpleasant."

Shakily, Pike picked up the vial and swallowed its contents. Almost simultaneously he tossed the vial aside and threw himself at the transparency. It bounced him back, of course—but the Magistrate had also stepped back a pace.

"That's very interesting," Pike said. "You were startled. Weren't you reading my mind then?"

"Now, to the female. As you have conjectured, an Earth vessel did actually crash on our planet. But with only a single survivor."

"Let's stay on the first subject. All I wanted for that moment was to get my hands around your neck. Do primitive emotions put up a block you can't read through?"

"We repaired the survivor's injuries and found the species interesting. So it became necessary to attract a mate."

"All right, we'll talk about the girl. You seem to be going out of your way to make her seem attractive, to make me feel protective."

"This is necessary in order to perpetuate the species."

"That could be done medically, artificially," Pike said. "No, it seems more important to you now that I accept her, begin to like her . . ."

"We wish our specimens to be happy in their new life."

"Assuming that's another lie, why would you want me attracted to her? So I'll feel love, a husband-wife relationship? That would be necessary only if you needed to build a family group, or even a whole human . . ."

"With the female now properly conditioned, we will continue with . . ."

"You mean properly punished!" Pike shouted. "I'm the one who's not cooperating. Why don't you punish me?"

"First an emotion of protectiveness, now one of sympathy. Excellent." The Magistrate turned and walked away down the corridor. Frustrated again, Pike turned to study the mysterious seam.

He found himself studying a tree instead. Around him, in full day, was richly planted park and forest land, with a city on the horizon. He recognized the place instantly.

Immediately to his right was tethered a pair of handsome saddle horses. To the left, Vina, in casual Earth garb, was laying out a picnic lunch on the grass.

Looking up at him, smiling, she said, "I left the thermos hooked to my saddle."

Pike went to the horses and patted them. "Tango! You old quarter-gaited devil, you! Hello, Mary Lou! No, sorry, no sugar this time . . ."

But patting his pockets automatically, he was astonished to find the usual two sugar cubes there. He fed them to the horses. The Talosians seemed to think of everything.

He unhooked the thermos, carried it to the picnic and sat down, eyeing Vina curiously. She seemed nervous.

"Is it good to be home?" she asked him.

"I've been aching to be back here. They read our minds very well."

"Please!" It was a cry of fear. Her face pleaded with him to keep silent.

"Home, everything else I want," he said. "*If* I cooperate. Is that it?"

"Have you forgotten my—headaches, darling? The doctor said when you talk strangely like this . . ."

Her voice trailed off, shaken. Pike was beginning to feel trapped again.

"Look, I'm sorry they punish you," he said. "But I can't let them hold that over our heads. They'll *own* us then."

She continued to lay out the lunch, trying to ignore him. "My, it turned out to be a beautiful day, didn't it?"

"Funny," he mused. "About twenty-four hours ago I was telling the ship's doctor how much I wanted—something not so far from what's being offered here. No responsibility, no frustrations or bruises . . . And now that I have it, I understand the doctor's answer. You either *live* life, bruises and all, or you turn your back on it and start dying. The Talosians went the second way."

"I hope you're hungry," Vina said, with false brightness. "The white sandwiches are your mother's chicken-tuna recipe."

He tried one. She was right. "Doc would be happy about part of this, at least. Said I needed a rest."

"This is a lovely place to rest."

"I spent my boyhood here. Doesn't compare with the gardens around the big cities, but I liked it better." He nodded toward the distant skyline. "That's Mojave. I was born there."

Vina laughed. "Is that supposed to be news to your wife? See—you're home! You can even stay if you want. Wouldn't it be nice showing your children where you once played?"

"These—'headaches,'" Pike said. "They'll be hereditary. Would you wish them on a child—or a whole group of children?"

"That's foolish."

"Is it? Look, first I'm made to protect you, then to feel sympathy for you—and now familiar surroundings, comfortable husband and wife feelings. They don't need all this just for passion. They're after respect, affection, mutual dependence—and something else . . ."

"They say, in the old days all this was a desert. Blowing sand, cactus . . ."

"I can't help either of us if you won't give me a chance!" Pike said sharply. "You told me once that illusions have become like a narcotic to them. They've even forgotten how to repair the machines left by their ancestors. Is that why we're so important? To build a colony of slaves who can . . ."

"Stop it, stop it! Don't you care what they do to me?"

"There's no such thing as a perfect prison," Pike said. "There's always some way out. Back in my cage, it seemed for a couple of minutes our keeper couldn't read my thoughts. Do emotions like anger block off our thought from them?"

"Don't you think," Vina said angrily, "that I've already tried things like that?"

"There's *some* way to beat them. Answer me!"

Her anger turned to tears. "Yes, they can't read—through primitive emotions. But you can't keep it up long enough I've tried!" She began to sob. "They—keep at you and—at you, year after year—probing, looking for a weakness, and tricking—and punishing and—they've won. They own me. I know you hate me for it."

Her fear, desperation, loneliness, everything that she had undergone were welling up in misery, deep and genuine. He put an arm around her. "I don't hate you. I can guess what it was like."

"It's not enough! They want you to have feelings that would build a family, protect it, work for it. Don't you understand? They read my thoughts, my desires, my dreams of what would be a perfect man. That's why they picked you. *I can't help but love you*. And they expect you to feel the same way."

Pike was shaken despite himself. The story was all too horribly likely. "If they can read my mind, they know I'm attracted to you. From the first day in the survivor's encampment. You were like a wild little animal."

"Was that the reason? Because I was like a barbarian?"

"Perhaps," Pike said, amused.

"I'm beginning to see why none of this has really worked on you," Vina said, straightening. "You've *been* home. And fighting, like on Rigel, that's not new to you either. A person's strongest dreams are about things he *can't* do."

"Maybe so. I'm no psychologist."

"Yes," she said, smiling, almost to herself. "A ship's captain, always having to be so formal, so decent and honest and proper—he must wonder what it would be like to forget all that."

The scene changed, with a burst of music and wild merriment. The transition caught him still seated. He was now on a pillowed floor at a low round table bearing a large bowl of fruit and goblets of wine. He seemed to be clad now in rich silk robes, almost like that of an Oriental potentate; near him sat a man whom he vaguely remembered as an Earth trader, similarly but less luxuriantly garbed, while on the other side was an officer in Star Fleet uniform whom he did not recognize at all. All of them were being served by women whose garb and manner strongly suggested slavery, and whose skins were the same color as Spock's. The music was coming from a quartet seated near a fountain pool.

Again he recognized the place; it was the courtyard of the Potentate of Orion. The officer leaned forward.

"Say, Pike," he said. "You used to be Captain of the *Enterprise*, didn't you?"

"Matter of fact, he was," said the trader.

"Thought so. You stopped here now and then—to check things out, so to speak."

"And then," the trader added, "sent Earth a blistering report on 'the Orion traders taking shocking advantage of the natives.'"

Both men laughed. "Funny how they are on this planet," the officer said. "They actually like being taken advantage of."

"And not just in profits, either."

The officer looked around appraisingly. "Nice place you've got here, Mr. Pike."

"It's a start," the trader said. Both laughed again. The officer patted the nearest slave girl on the rump.

"Do any of you have a green one?" he asked. "They're dangerous, I hear. Razor-sharp claws, and they attract a man like a sensation of irresistible hunger."

Up to now, the officer had simply repelled Pike, but that last phrase sounded familiar—and had been delivered with mysterious emphasis. The trader gave Pike a knowing look.

"Now and then," he said, "comes a man who tames one."

There was a change in the music; it became louder, took on a slow, throbbing rhythm. The slave girls turned hurriedly, as if suddenly anxious to excape. Looking toward the musicians, Pike saw another girl, nude, her skin green, and glistening as if it had been oiled, kneeling at the edge of the pool. Her fingertips were long, gleaming, razor-edged scimitars; her hair like the mane of a wild animal. She was staring straight at him.

One of the slaves was slow. The green girl sprang up with a sound like a spitting cat, barring her escape. A man Pike had not seen before leapt forward to intervene, raising a whip.

"Stop!" Pike shouted, breaking his paralysis. The green girl turned and looked at him again, and then he recognized her. It was Vina once more.

She came forward to the center of the rectangle and posed for a moment. Then the music seemed to reach her, the slow surging beat forcing movement out of her as a reed flute takes possession of a cobra. She threw her head back, shrieked startlingly, and began to dance.

"Where'd he find her?" said the officer's voice. Pike was unable to tear his eyes away from her.

"He'd stumbled into a dark corridor," the trader's voice said, "and then he saw flickering light ahead. Almost like secret dreams a bored sea captain might have, wasn't it? There she was, holding a torch, glistening green . . ."

"Strange looks she keeps giving you, Pike."

"Almost as if she knows something about you."

Somewhere in the back of his mind he knew that the Talosians were baiting him through these two men; but he could not stop watching the dance.

"Wouldn't you say that's worth a man's soul?" said the trader.

"It makes you believe she could be anything," said the officer. "Suppose you had all of space to choose from, and this was only one small sample . . ."

That was too much. Pike rose, growling. "Get out of my way, blast you!"

He crossed the courtyard to a curtained doorway which he seemed to recall was an exit. Brushing the curtains aside, he found himself in a corridor. It was certainly dark, and grew darker as he strode angrily along it. In the distance was a flickering light, and then, there indeed was Vina, holding aloft a torch . . .

The scene lightened and the torch vanished. Vina, her skin white, her body covered with the Talosian garment, continued to hold her empty hand aloft for a second. They were back in the cage.

Vina's face contorted in fury. She ran to the transparency and pounded on it, shouting out into the corridor.

"No! Let us finish! I could have . . ."

"What's going on here?" another woman's voice demanded. Both Pike and Vina whirled.

There were two other women in the cage: Number One, and Yeoman Colt. After so many shocks, Pike could summon no further reaction to this one.

"I might well ask you the same thing," he said numbly.

"We tried to Transport down in here," Number One said. "There was a risk we'd materialize in solid rock, but we'd already tried blasting open the top of the lift, with no luck."

"But there were six of us to start with," Yeoman Colt said. "I don't know why the others didn't make it."

"It's not fair!" Vina said to Pike. "You don't need them."

"They may be just what I need," Pike said drily, beginning to recover some of his wits. "Number One, Yeoman, hand me those phasers."

They passed the weapons over. He examined them. What he found did not particularly surprise him. "Empty."

"They were fully charged when we left," Number One said.

"No doubt. But you'll find your communicators don't work either." A thought struck him. He looked quickly toward the almost circular panel he had found before. Then, suddenly, he hurled both phasers at it.

"What good does that do?" Number One said coolly.

"Don't talk to me. Don't say anything. I'm working up a hate—filling my mind with a picture of beating their huge, misshapen heads to a pulp. Thoughts so primitive they shut everything else out. I hate them—do you understand?"

"How long can you block your thoughts?" Vina said. "A few minutes, an hour? How can that help you?"

Pike concentrated, trying to pay no attention to her. She turned on the two other women.

"He doesn't need you," she said, with jealous anger she did not have to force-feed. "He's already picked me."

"Picked you for what?" Colt asked.

Vina looked at her scornfully. "Now there's a great chance for intelligent offspring."

"'Offspring?'" Colt echoed. "As in 'children'"?

"As in he's 'Adam,'" Number One said, indicating Pike. "Isn't that it?"

"You're no better choice. They'd have better luck crossing him with a computer!"

"Shall I compute your age?" Number One said. "You were listed on that expedition as an adult crewman. Now, adding eighteen years to that . . ."

She broke off as Vina turned to the transparency. The Magistrate was back. The two crewwomen stared at him with interest.

"It's not fair," Vina said. "I did everything you asked."

The Magistrate ignored her. "Since you resist the present specimen," he said to Pike, "you now have a selection."

Pike threw himself at the impervious figure. "I'll break out, get to you somehow!" he shouted. "Is your blood red like ours? I'm going to find out!"

"Each of the two new specimens has qualities in her favor. The female you call 'Number One' has the superior mind and would produce highly intelligent offspring. Although she seems to lack emotion, this is largely a pretense. She often has fantasies involving you."

Number One looked flustered for the first time in Pike's memory, but he turned this, too, into rage at the invasion of her privacy. "All I want is to get my hands on you! Can you read these thoughts? Images of hate, killing . . ."

"The other new arrival has considered you unreachable, but is now realizing that this has changed. The factors in her favor are youth and strength, plus an unusually strong female emotion which . . ."

"You'll find my thoughts more interesting! Primitive thoughts you can't understand; emotions so ugly you can't . . ."

The pain hit him then and he went down, writhing. The images involved this time were from the torture chambers of the Inquisition. Over them, dimly, floated the Magistrate's thought, as though directed at someone else.

"Wrong thinking is punishable; right thinking will be as quickly rewarded. You will find it an effective combination."

The illusion vanished and Pike rolled weakly to a sitting position. He found the Magistrate gone, and the two crewwomen bending over him.

"No—don't—help me. Just leave me alone. Got to concentrate on hate. They can't read through it."

The hours wore on and eventually the lights went down. It seemed obvious that the Talosians intended to keep all three women penned with him. Trying to keep the hate alive became increasingly more difficult; he slammed his fist against the enclosure wall again and again, hoping the pain would help.

The women conversed in low tones for a while, and then, one by one, fell asleep, Vina on the bed, the other two on the floor leaning against it. Pike squatted against the wall nearby, no thoughts in his mind now but roaring fatigue and the effort to fight it.

Then he sensed, rather than heard movement at his side. The wall panel had opened, and a Talosian arm was reaching in for the discarded phasers. He exploded into action, grabbing the arm and heaving.

The Magistrate was almost catapulted into the room by the force of that yank. Instantly, Pike's hands were around his throat.

"Don't hurt him!" Vina cried from the bed. "They don't mean to be evil . . ."

"I've had some samples of how 'good' they are . . ."

The Talosian vanished and Pike found himself holding the neck of the snarling anthropoid-spider creature he had first seen in a cell across from his. Its fangs snapped at his face. Colt shrieked.

Pike grimly tightened his grip. "I'm still holding your neck! Stop this illusion or I'll snap it!" The spider-thing changed back into the Magistrate again. "That's better. Try one more illusion—try anything at all—I'll take one quick twist. Understand?"

He loosened his hands slightly, allowing the Magistrate to gasp for breath. The forehead vein throbbed. "Your ship. Release me or we destroy it."

"He's not bluffing," Vina said. "With illusions they can make your crew work the wrong controls, push any button it takes to destroy the ship."

"I'll gamble he's too intelligent to kill for no reason at all. On the other hand, *I've* got a reason. Number One, take a good grip on his throat for me. And at the slightest excuse . . ."

"I understand, Captain," Number One said grimly.

Freed, Pike picked up the phaser. Putting one into his belt, he adjusted the other, leveled it at the transparency, and pulled the trigger. As he expected, it didn't fire. He turned back to the Magistrate and pressed the weapon against his head.

"I'm betting," he said almost conversationally, "that you've created an illusion that this phaser is empty. That you don't know enough about your own machines, let alone ours, to dare to tamper with them. And that this one just blasted a hole in that wall which you're keeping us from seeing. Shall I test my theory on your head?"

The Magistrate closed his eyes resignedly. At once, there was a huge, jagged hole in the front of the cage.

"Q.E.D. Number One, you can let go of him now. If he acts up, I can shoot him, and he knows it. Everybody out. We're leaving!"

On the surface, only the top of the lift shaft still stood; the top of the knoll had been blasted clean off. So the Talosians had prevented the rescue party from seeing that, too.

Number One tried her communicator, but without effect. Noting the Magistrate's forehead vein throbbing again, Pike raised his phaser and said in a voice of iron, "I want contact with my ship. *Right now.*"

"No," said the Magistrate. "You are now on the surface where we intended you to be in the end. With the female of your choice, you will soon begin carefully guided lives . . ."

"Beginning with burying you."

"I see you intend to kill. I shall not prevent you; others of us will replace me. To help you reclaim the planet, our zoological gardens will furnish a variety of plant life . . ."

"Look," Pike said, "I'll make a deal with you. You and your life for the lives of these two Earthwomen."

"Since our life span is many times yours, we have time to evolve a society trained as artisans, technicians . . ."

"Do you understand what I'm saying? Give me proof our ship is all right, send these two back to it, and I'll stay here with Vina."

He felt a tug at his belt, and out of the corner of his eyes saw that Number One had pulled the spare phaser out of it. The rachet popped like firecrackers as she turned the gain control full around. The phaser began to hum, rising in both pitch and volume. The weapon was building up an overload—a force chamber explosion.

"It's wrong," Number One said, "to create a whole race of humans to live as slaves. Do you concur, Captain?"

After a moment of hesitation, Pike nodded.

"Is this a deception?" asked the Magistrate. "Do you really intend to destroy yourselves? Yes, I see that you do."

"Vina, you've got time to get back underground. But hurry. And Talosian, to show just how primitive humans are, you can go with her."

The Magistrate did not move, nor did Vina.

"No," she said. "If you all think it's this important, then I can't leave either. I suppose if they still have one human, they might try again."

"We had not believed this possible," the Magistrate said, his thoughts betraying what might have been a strange sadness. "The customs and history of your race show a unique hatred of captivity, even when pleasant and benevolent. But you prefer death. This makes you too violent and dangerous a species for our needs."

"He means," Vina said, "they can't use you. You're free to go back to your ship."

Number One turned the phaser off, and just in time, too. In the renewed silence, Pike said, "Vina, that's it. No apologies. You captured one of us, threatened us, tortured us . . ."

"Your unsuitability has condemned the Talosian race to eventual death," the Magistrate said. "Is this not sufficient? No other specimens have shown your adaptability. You were our last hope."

"Nonsense," Pike said, surprised. "Surely some form of trade, some mutual cooperation . . ."

The Magistrate shook his head. "Your race would learn our power of illusion—and destroy itself. It is important to *our* beliefs to prevent this."

"Captain," Number One said, "we have Transporter control now."

"Good. Let's go. Vina, you too."

"I—" Vina said. "I can't go with you."

Pike felt a flash of what might almost have been exasperation. "Number One, Yeoman Colt, go aloft. I'll be with you when I've gotten to the bottom of this." As they hesitated, he added, "Orders."

They shimmered and vanished. Pike swung on Vina. "Now . . ."

He stopped, astounded and horrified. Vina was changing. Her face was wrinkling. An ugly scar appeared. Her body was becoming cruelly deformed. Throughout, she looked back at Pike with bitter eyes. The change did not stop until she was old, shockingly twisted, downright ugly.

"This is the female's true appearance," the Magistrate said.

It couldn't be true. *This* was the youngster of the survivors' camp, the sturdy peasant, the wife on Earth, the green Orionese savage who had danced so . . .

"This is the truth," Vina said, in an old woman's voice. She lifted her arms. "See me as I am. They found me in the wreckage, dying, nothing but a lump of flesh. They fixed me fine. Everything works. But—*they had no guide for putting me back together.*

"Do you understand now? Do you see why I can't go with you?"

She turned and stumbled toward the lift. Pike watched her go with horror and pity. Then he turned to the Magistrate, who said; "It was necessary to convince you that her desire to stay is an honest one."

Pike looked at him with new eyes. "You have some sparks of decency in you after all. Will you give her back her illusion of beauty?"

"We will. And more. See."

At the shaft, the image of the lovely Vina was entering the lift—*accompanied by himself.* The two turned and waved. Then the lift carried them down into the bowels of Talos IV.

"She has her illusion," the Magistrate said. Was he almost smiling? "And you have reality. May you find your way as pleasant."

Spock, Number One, Jose, Colt and Boyce all crowded toward him as he stepped out of the Transporter Chamber.

"What happened to Vina?" Colt demanded.

"Isn't she—coming with us?" asked Number One.

"No," Pike said shortly. "And I agree with her reasons. Now break it up here: What is this we're running, a cadet ship? Everybody on the bridge! Navigator, I want a course!"

"Yessir!"

They scattered like flushed partridges—all except Boyce, who said, "Hold on a minute, Captain."

"What for? I feel fine."

"That's the trouble. You look a hundred per cent better."

"I am. Didn't you recommend rest and change? I've had both. I've even been—home. Now, let's get on with things."

As the *Enterprise* moved away from Talos IV, routine re-established itself quickly, and the memory of all those illusions began to fade. They had not, after all, been real experiences—most of them. But Pike could not resist stealing a quick look from Number One to Colt, wondering which of them, in other circumstances, he might have picked.

When he found them both looking at him as if with the same speculation, he turned his eyes determinedly to the viewscreen and banished the thought.

He had had plenty of practice at that, lately.

Afterword

As the reader will now see, this story constituted the original pilot film for "Star Trek," and was shown as such at the 24th World Science Fiction Convention in Cleveland, Ohio, September 1–5, 1966. Between the selling of the series and the actual television broadcast of "The Menagerie," the whole concept of the cast changed radically. Number One was moved one step down in the chain of command, becoming Uhura, while her ostensible lack of emotion and computer-like mind were transferred to Spock; Yeoman Colt became Yeoman Rand; Boyce became McCoy; Tyler became Sulu. The net effect was to make the new officers more interracial than before. The notion that the highly trained crew would ever be risked in ordinary hand-to-hand infantry combat was dropped.

Most important, perhaps, was that in the pilot film, Pike had wound up with a potentially explosive situation with two of his crewwomen which would be too complex to maintain through a long-term series of episodes. He had to be replaced, and the whole story turned into relatively ancient history; and thus was born Captain Kirk, and the framing story I have left out. All these stages are visible in the scripts I had to work from, which are heavily revised in various handwritings (and in which Pike confusingly appears from time to time as "Captain Spring" and "Captain Winter").

The only alternative would have been to reshoot the original "Menagerie" with the new cast, which would have been not only expensive, but would have produced all kinds of unwanted complexities in succeeding stories. Mr. Roddenberry obviously decided to let it stand as something that had happened way-back-when, and frame it as such. I think this was wise and I have followed his lead in this adaptation.

Ordinarily, writers should not inflict their technical problems on readers, who have every right to demand that such problems be solved before the story is published. But I sometimes get letters from "Star Trek" fans who castigate me for changing even one or two words in scripts they have memorized, or even have on tape. In this case, as in that of "The City on the Edge of Forever," there were conflicts that couldn't be resolved by slavishly following the final text and ignoring how it had evolved. In both cases, I had to make my own judgment of what would best serve the authors' intents.

—J. B.

WHERE NO MAN HAS GONE BEFORE

Writer: Samuel A. Peeples
Director: James Goldstone
First Aired: September 22, 1966

Star date 1312.5 was a memorable one for the U.S.S. *Enterprise*. It marked the day of its first venture beyond the frontier of Earth's galaxy. The screen in its Briefing Room was already showing a strange vista—thinning stars etched against a coming night of depthless darkness broken only by the milky spots of phosphorescence which defined the existence of further galaxies millions of light years distant.

Kirk and Spock, a chessboard between them, looked away from the board to fix their eyes on the screen's center. It held, invisibly, an object detected by the *Enterprise* sensors; an object that was impossibly emitting the call letters of a starship known to be missing for two centuries.

Spock said, "Your move, Captain."

"We should be intercepting that thing now," Kirk said, frowning. "The bridge said they'd call . . ."

". . . any minute now." Spock finished the sentence for him. "I'll have you checkmated in your next move, sir."

"Have I ever mentioned that you play irritating chess, Mr. Spock?"

"Irritating? Ah yes, one of your Earth's emotions, I believe."

But Kirk had seen an opening for his bishop. Pouncing on the piece, he moved it. Spock's eyebrows went up.

"Certain that you don't know what irritation is?" Kirk asked.

Spock glowered at the board. "The fact that one of my ancestors was a human female is one, sir, I cannot . . ."

"Terrible, having bad blood like that," Kirk said sympathetically. "In addition to being checkmated, it could be called intolerable."

But the voice of Lieutenant Lee Kelso was speaking from the intercom. "Bridge to Briefing Room. Object now within tractor beam range, Captain."

"No visual contact yet, Lieutenant?"

"No, sir. Can't be a vessel. Reads only about one meter in diameter. Small enough to bring it aboard—if you want to risk it."

Kirk decided to risk it. It was a curious encounter on the edge of illimitable space.

Curious—and just possibly informative. "The Transporter Room. Let's go, Mr. Spock," he said.

Scott was waiting for them at the console. "Materializer ready, sir, when you are."

"Bring it aboard," Kirk said.

The familiar hum came. And, with it, the platform's familiar shimmer, finally solidifying into the spherical shape of an old-style starship's recorder. Squatting on tripod legs, it stood about three feet in height, its metal surface seared, pockmarked. But it still identified itself by letters that read "U.S.S. *Valiant*"; and in smaller ones beneath them, "Galactic Survey Cruiser."

Kirk said, "That old-time variety of recorder could be ejected when something threatened its ship."

"In this case more probably destroyed its ship, sir," Spock said. "Look how it's burnt and pitted."

Kirk was approaching the platform when Scott said sharply, "Take care, sir! That thing's radioactive!"

Kirk stopped. "The Q signal, Mr. Scott."

Scott hit a button on his console. It beeped shrilly. As a pulsating glow enveloped the recorder, its antennae moved out and clicked into position.

"It's transmitting," Scott said.

"Interesting," said Spock. "I have a recorder monitoring . . ."

He was interrupted by Kelso's voice from the intercom. "All decks, six minutes to galaxy edge."

The galaxy's edge—where, as far as anyone knew, no man had ever gone before. Of course, there was no neat boundary to the edge of the galaxy; it just gradually thinned out. But in six minutes, the last of its stars and systems would be behind them.

"Yellow alert," Kirk said.

"Captain's orders—yellow alert, all decks," Kelso relayed it.

A moment later, an elevator slid open to emit Lieutenant Commander Gary Mitchell, now senior helmsman since Sulu had become ship's physicist. The promotion had won widespread approval—unnecessary, of course, but helpful; Mitchell was a popular officer. But during a yellow alert his normal chore was monitoring the artificial gravity system as well as the helm.

"Everything's in order, Jim," he said with a grin, as if reading Kirk's mind. "Kelso's voice sounded so nervous, I figured you'd left the bridge. Finish the game, Spock?"

"The Captain plays most illogically," the Science Officer complained. "I expected him to move his castle."

Kirk laughed, making a throat-cutting gesture for Mitchell's benefit. It was clear that the two were old, warm friends. In the bridge all three hurried to their positions. "Relieving you, Mr. Alden," Mitchell told the junior helmsman.

"Screen on," Kirk said. "Lieutenant Kelso, how far now to the galaxy edge?"

"Four minutes to our jumping-off point, sir."

"Alert off, Lieutenant Kelso." He turned to Mitchell. "Neutralize warp, Commander. Hold this position."

As the heavy throb of the ship's powerful engines eased, the bridge elevator opened. First to step out of it was Dr. Elizabeth Dehner, tall, slim, in her mid-twenties, a potentially beautiful woman if she had cared to be one, which she didn't. Other professional personnel followed her—senior physician, Dr. Piper, physicist Sulu, Engineering Chief Scott. Turning to Mitchell, Kirk said, "Address intercraft."

"Intercraft open, sir."

Kirk seized his speaker. "This is the Captain speaking. The object we encountered is a ship's disaster recorder, apparently ejected from the U.S.S. *Valiant* almost two hundred years ago. Mr. Spock is now exploring its memory banks. We hope to learn how the *Valiant* got this far, whether it probed out of the galaxy and what destroyed the vessel. As soon as we have those answers, we'll begin our own probe. All decks stand by." He paused a moment. "All department heads, check in, as per rota."

"Astro Sciences standing by, Captain," Sulu said.

"Engineering divisions ready as always," Scott's voice said cheerfully. Nothing, not even the awesome void now before them, could check his Gaelic self-assurance for long.

"Life Sciences ready, sir," Dr. Piper's voice reported. He was temporary—McCoy was on a special study leave—and rather an elderly man for Starfleet service, but he seemed to be a competent enough physician. "Request permission to bring to the bridge my special assistant, Dr. Dehner."

Elizabeth Dehner had joined the expedition at the Aldebaran colony; Kirk had not yet had much chance to talk to her, and now was not the time. But she might be interested in the abyss now opening before them all. "Granted."

The two appeared within a minute. Kirk said, "Dr. Dehner, you're a psychiatrist, I'm told, assigned to study crew reactions under extreme conditions."

"Quite correct, Captain."

Kirk gestured at the screen. "There's an extreme condition. Millions upon millions of light years of absolutely nothing, except a few molecules of ionized gas."

Spock called from his station. "Getting something from the recorder now, Captain."

But Dr. Elizabeth Dehner had more to say. "Sir, I shall be interested, too, in how the *Valiant*'s crew reacted to disaster."

Kirk eyed her curiously. Mitchell also appraised her, a little smile on his handsome face. "You want to improve the breed, Doctor?"

"I've heard that's more your own specialty, Commander," she said icily.

"Sock!" Mitchell murmured to Kelso. "It's a walking refrigerator, by gum!" She overheard him. A flush crept up and over her composed features.

Coded electronic beeps were sounding from the listening device Spock had applied to the recorder. He looked up as Kirk joined him. "Decoding memory banks," he said. "Captain's log now—reports the *Valiant* encountered a magnetic space storm that swept it back into this direction."

Kirk nodded. "The old impulse engines weren't strong enough to resist a thing like that."

Spock was leaning closer to his listener. "The storm flung it past this point . . . about a half light year out of the galaxy . . . they were thrown clear of the storm . . . then they seem to have headed back into the galaxy." He made a control adjustment. "I'm not getting it all. It sounds as though the ship were struggling with some unknown force."

The beeps grew louder. Interpreting, Spock said, "Confusion now . . . orders and counterorders . . . emergency power drains . . . repeated urgent requests for information from the ship's computer records." He stopped to look up at Kirk again. "They want to know everything there is to know about ESP in human beings!" He shook his head. "Odd, that. Very odd indeed."

"Extrasensory perception!" Kirk was incredulous. But he motioned to Elizabeth Dehner. "Dr. Dehner, what do you know about ESP?"

She went to the computer station. "In tests I've taken, my ESP rated rather high."

Kirk said, "I asked what you *know* about ESP."

She spoke with the pomp of the pendant. "It is a fact some people can sense future events, read the backs of playing cards and so on. But the Esper ability is always quite limited . . ."

Spock broke in. "Severe damage—no, make that severe injuries." His face was strained with listening concentration. "Seven crewmen dead . . . no, make that *six*—one crewman recovered." He looked up at Kirk once more. "It's the casualties that appear to have stimulated the interest in extrasensory perception. Interest is the wrong word. It seems to be driving them frantic."

Bent to the listener again, he suddenly stiffened. "No, this must be garbled. I'm getting something about 'Destruct.'" Frowning, he removed the earphone. "I must have read it incorrectly. It sounded as though the Captain had ordered the destruction of his own ship!"

Kirk turned questioningly to the department heads.

"You heard," he said. "Comments?"

Piper shrugged. "The only fact we have for sure is that the *Valiant* was destroyed."

"The fact," Kirk said, "which is the best argument to continue *our* probe. Other vessels will be heading out here some day—and they'll have to know what they'll be facing."

He strode back to his command chair. "Commander Mitchell, ahead, warp-factor one," he said. "We are leaving the galaxy."

As the *Enterprise* moved past the last stars, the bridge alarm light flashed. All eyes turned to the large viewing screen. Against the blackness of deep space a wispy pattern of colors was building up ahead of the ship.

Spock said, "Force field of some kind."

Mitchell said, "Whatever it is, we're coming up on it fast."

Kirk said nothing. Though distance from the phenomenon made certain judgment dangerous, it seemed to be some variety of impalpable barrier. Its colors were growing brighter, extending, interweaving into what appeared to be a flaring, multicolored, massive curtain of pure energy. It might have been a monstrous space version of Earth's Aurora Borealis. And it was sending the bridge alarm siren into shrieks of warning.

He stared at it, hard-jawed. Its colors, radiating from the screen, rippled across the strained faces around him.

The auroral colors were blazing now. Suddenly, with a muted crackle, a circuit shorted.

"Field intensity rising..." Spock began.

As he spoke, the bridge lights died. For several seconds Kirk didn't notice their loss, the radiance from the screen had simultaneously become so brilliant that hands were rising instinctively to shield dazzled eyes.

Then a blinding whip of pure white light shot from the screen. At the same moment, an entire instrument panel went out in a shower of sparks and smoke. Another promptly shorted, with an angry crackle. The whole bridge seemed to be hazed in flying sparks. Elizabeth Dehner screamed and fell to the deck, writhing as if in the grip of some uncontrollable energy. Once down, she kept on screaming. The dial needles on Kirk's command board whirled.

"*Helmsman!*"

But the sparks had invaded Mitchell, too. Jerking like a marionette pulled by a madman's strings, he staggered to his feet and then went rigid. With a last galvanic convulsion, he toppled to the deck, inert, unconscious. His body rolled as the ship shuddered.

The confusion mounted, shock after shock, now joined by the mindless hysteria of the alarm siren. Kirk and Spock clung to their chairs; most of the others had been jolted out of theirs.

In the end, discipline triumphed while technology failed all around them. Painfully, inch by inch, Kirk dragged himself back to his command control panel. Kelso crawled over to his. Spock, stepping over the crumpled Mitchell, took over his helmsman's station. But the battering continued. Wrenched metal screeched as the *Enterprise* fought to hold itself together.

"*Lateral power!*" Kirk shouted. "*Crash speed. Take her out of this!*"

Spock and Kelso wrestled with controls. Power returned to the shaking ship. The bridge lights glimmered back on. The alarm siren quieted. But many of the instrument panels were dead with their circuits. Smoke from one still drifted through the bridge.

Kirk got to his feet. "Take damage reports, Mr. Spock."

Spock relayed the order to the ship's crew—and Piper lifted Elizabeth's head. Clinging to his arm, she climbed shakily to her feet. "Something hit me like an electrical charge," she whispered. Piper left her to go to Mitchell.

"Well?" Kirk asked.

"He's alive. Appears to be in shock."

Spock made his damage report. "Our main engines are out, Captain. We're on emergency power cells. Casualties—seven dead."

A moment prolonged itself. Then Kirk said, "Perhaps we are fortunate."

"Commander Mitchell is moving, sir," Spock said.

Kirk dropped to a knee beside his senior helmsman. "Gary! How do you feel?"

Mitchell's arm covered his eyes as though the screen's radiance still dazzled them. "Jim? Weak as a kitten—but better now. I think I'll live."

He moved the arm from his eyes. Their blue had turned into a gleaming metallic silver.

No amount of technical resourcefulness could repair the damage suffered by the crippled *Enterprise*. Moving now on impulse power alone, its dim bridge lights gave everybody the measure of the havoc. Kirk, considering his burned-out engines, remembered the burned recorder ejected by the *Valiant*. Had it survived the onslaught by that merciless radiation? If it had, what happened afterwards?

On his computer station screen, Spock was busily flashing the names of certain members of the ship's personnel. Among them were those of Elizabeth Dehner and Gary Mitchell. Noting them, Kirk gave Spock a sober look. Spock hastily flashed off Elizabeth's name as she approached them.

"Autopsy report, Captain," she said. "Each case showed damage to the body's neural circuits—an area of the brain burned out."

"And you?" Kirk said. "Feeling all right now?"

"Much better. And Commander Mitchell is, too, except for the eyes. We're trying to find a reason for those. And why, of all the people in the crew, only certain ones were affected."

Spock spoke quietly. "I think we have found that answer."

"You said that tests show you have a high degree of extrasensory perception, Doctor," Kirk reminded her. "The others who were affected have it, too. Gary Mitchell has the highest ESP rating of all."

She was clearly puzzled. "I suppose it's conceivable the Esper ability attracted some force." Then she shrugged. "But if you're suggesting there's something dangerous in that..."

Spock interrupted. "Before the *Valiant* was destroyed, its Captain was frantically searching for ESP information on his crew members."

"Espers are merely people who have flashes of—well, *insight*," she said.

"Aren't there also those who seem able to see through solid objects?" Spock asked. "Or can cause fires to start spontaneously?"

The question irritated her. "ESP is nothing more than a sort of sixth sense. There's nothing about it that can make a person dangerous!"

"I take it you're speaking of *normal* ESP power, Doctor," Spock said.

"Perhaps you know of another kind!" she flared.

Kirk intervened. "Do you know for sure, Doctor, that there *isn't* another kind?"

An angry disdain sharpened her voice. "I have work to do," she said. "You must excuse me." She left them to move quickly to the elevator.

In Sickbay, Mitchell, propped up against pillows, was sufficiently recovered to use his reading viewer. The eyes that followed its turning pages were as gleamingly silver as quicksilver. Kirk, entering, watched him read for a long moment. Without looking up, Mitchell snapped off the reading viewer to say, "Hello, Jim."

He hadn't even been obliged to turn his head to identify his caller. For some reason this realization troubled Kirk. He sat down in the chair beside the bed. "Hey, you look worried," Mitchell said.

Kirk forced a smile. "I've been worried about you since that girl on Deneb IV."

Mitchell nodded reminiscently. "She was a nova, that one," he said. "But there's nothing to worry about. Except for the eyes, I'm fine." He grinned his charming grin. "They kind of stare back at me when I'm shaving."

"Vision all right?"

"Twenty-twenty."

"Nothing else, Gary?"

Mitchell looked up curiously at Kirk's tone. "Like what, for instance?"

"Do you—feel any different in yourself?"

"In a way, I feel better than I ever felt before in my life." He paused. "It actually seems to have done me some good."

"Oh. How?"

Mitchell gestured toward the reading viewer. "I'm getting a chance to bone up on some of that long-hair stuff you like. Man, I remember you at the Academy! A stack of books with legs! The first thing I heard from upper classmen was 'Watch out for Lieutenant Kirk! In his class you either *think*—or you sink.'"

"Oh, come on," Kirk said. "I wasn't that bad."

"You weren't *what*?" Mitchell laughed. "Do you remember almost washing me out?"

"I sort of leaned on cadets I liked," Kirk said.

"Man, if I hadn't aimed that little blond lab technician at you . . ."

"You *what*?" Kirk stared at him. "You mean you actually *planned* that?"

"You wanted me to *think*, didn't you? So I *thought*. I outlined her whole campaign for her."

Kirk found it hard to return the grin. "Gary, I almost married her!"

"I sort of lean, too, on people I like. She said you came through great."

Kirk, remembering, struggled with his dismay. He repeated, "Gary, I almost *married* her."

"Better be good to me," Mitchell said. He pointed again to the reading viewer. "I'm getting even better ideas from *that*."

Kirk looked at the tape on the viewer. "Spinoza?"

"That's one," Mitchell said. "Once you get into him, he's simple. Childish, almost. By the way, I don't agree with him at all."

"No?" Kirk said. "Go on."

"Go on where? So I'm finally doing some reading." The cold, silver glitter of his eyes made an uncomfortable contrast with the easy warmth of his manner. His white teeth flashed again in the charming grin. "I'm saying I'm fine! When do I go back on duty?"

Kirk hesitated. "I want Dr. Dehner to keep you under observation for a while yet."

Mitchell groaned. "With almost a hundred women on board, you choose *that* one to hang around me!"

"Think of it as a challenge," Kirk said.

The silver eyes fixed on him. "That's not so friendly, James, my friend. Didn't I say you'd better be good to me?"

The mutually gauging moment passed. Finally Mitchell shook his head in mock resignation. Then he pointedly turned back to the reading viewer. Kirk, more troubled than before, didn't speak, either, as he got to his feet and left Sickbay.

Behind him, Mitchell increased the speed of the viewer's turning pages. He read fast—a man locking facts into his mind with an incredible rapidity.

An image of the turning pages was showing on Spock's library computer screen. When Kirk joined him, they were turning so quickly that their movement was blurred. Spock said, "He's reading faster with every passing second. Is that Gary Mitchell? The slowpoke reader we used to know?"

Kirk took three paces away from the screen and returned. "Put a twenty-four hour watch on Sickbay. The fullest possible range of examinations and tests."

The results gave joy to the heart of Piper. "Perfect—perfect," he murmured as he completed his final checkup. "Such perfect health is rare." He tapped the body function panel as though it were hard to credit the veracity of its readings.

"Great in all departments, right?" said Mitchell. Bored, he spoke to Elizabeth. "Too bad psychiatry isn't an exact science, eh, Doctor? Be nice to have a dial that showed the level of a patient's sanity."

"I am aware that you don't particularly like me, Commander," she said. "But since I'm assigned here, can we make the best of it?"

"I've got nothing against you, Doctor."

"Or against the 'walking refrigerator'?"

He was openly startled. "Sorry about that." All his charm went into the three words.

"Women professionals do tend to overcompensate," she said. "Now let's talk about you. How do you feel? Tell me everything."

"Everything about what? Everyone seems worried because I don't have a fever or something." He pointed to the body function panel. "Now old Piper's gone, maybe I can make you happy by changing those readings . . ."

The panel's normal levels altered into abnormal ones. Elizabeth stared at them and back at Mitchell. Slightly shaken himself, he said, "Now the normal readings again . . ."

The levels dropped back to normal.

"How did you do that?" Elizabeth demanded.

"I'm not sure. I—just thought of making it happen. Then it happened." He eyed the panel. "It's not the instruments. It's me. Something I do inside. Hey, watch this . . ."

All the panel's levels plummeted to zero.

Elizabeth grabbed his hand. "Stop it!" she cried. "Stop it now!"

The gauge needles quivered. Rising swiftly up from the "death" indication, they came to rest at normal.

Mitchell stared at them, too. He had paled; and Elizabeth, appalled, said, "For twenty-two seconds you were *dead*! No life function at all!"

Mitchell suddenly realized she was holding his hand. Reddening, she tried to pull hers away but he held it fast. "Hang on a minute, baby. I'm scared. There've been other things, too. Like going halfway through the ship's library in hardly a day. What's happened to me?"

"Do you remember everything you read that quickly?"

He nodded. She took a tape from his bedside table. "On any tape? How about this one? Do you remember page 387?"

"Sure," he said. "It's *The Nightingale Woman* written by Tarbolde on a Canopus planet back in 1996. It begins, 'My love has wings, Slender, feathered things, With grace in upswept curve and tapered tip—'" He stopped, amused. "Funny you should pick that one."

"Why?"

"It's one of the most passionate love poems of the last couple of centuries."

She pulled her hand from his. He watched her do it, smiling. "How do *you* feel?" he asked.

"What? Oh, you mean that electrical blast! It just knocked me down. That's all."

"You're very sure?"

She wasn't sure of anything in the presence of this man with the silver eyes so bright upon her. But somehow, she suspected that she'd given herself away. She was glad when the knock came at the door. It was Kelso. "I was on my coffee break," he told them, "and thought I'd just check up on Gary here."

"It's OK, Lee," Mitchell said. "Come on in."

It was Kelso's first full view of the changed eyes. They disconcerted him. Mitchell laughed. "Don't let my gorgeous orbs throw you, chum. The lady doctor here likes them, don't you, beautiful Doctor?"

Surprised, Kelso said, "Oh. Yeah. Sure."

"How goes the repair work?"

"The main engines are gone." Kelso's face grew somber. "And they'll stay gone, too, unless we can find some way of re-energizing them."

Mitchell frowned. "You'd better check on the starboard impulse packs. The points have decayed to lead." At Kelso's look of amazement, he said, "I'm not joking, pal. So wipe the shock off your face. You activate those packs—and you'll blow up the whole impulse deck!"

The hardness in his voice got through to Kelso. "Sure," he said hastily. "I'll get on to them right away. I—I just wanted to say I'm glad you're all right."

Mitchell glared angrily after him. "The fool! He's seen those rotten points a hundred times but is too dumb to notice their condition!"

"How did *you* know about them?" Elizabeth asked.

The arrogance was suddenly gone. "I don't know. Maybe the image of what he saw was still in his mind and I—I could see it in his mind." The silver eyes were looking up at her out of a bewildered, very frightened face.

In the Briefing Room, Kelso was pointing to the fused tip in a starboard impulse pack. "It made no sense at all that he'd know about this," he said to Kirk. "But naturally I took a look at the packs anyway. And he's right! This point's burned out just as he described it!"

Each in turn, the Science Department heads examined the piece of metal on the Briefing Room table. Elizabeth opened the door. "Sorry I'm late, Captain. I became so interested in observing Gary—Commander Mitchell—that I . . ."

Spock said, "The subject under discussion is not Commander Mitchell, Doctor. We are concerned with what he is mutating into."

Her face tightened with anger. "I know Vulcans lack human feeling, but to talk like that about a man you've worked next to for years . . ."

"That's enough, Doctor!" Kirk said.

"No, it isn't!" she cried. "I understand you least of all! Gary's told me you've been friends ever since he joined the service! You even asked him to join your first command!"

Kirk kept his voice level. "It is my duty, Doctor, to note the reports, observations, even speculations on any subject which affects the safety of this ship." He nodded toward Spock. "And it is my Science Officer's duty to see that I'm provided with them. Go ahead, Mr. Spock."

Spock addressed Elizabeth. "Has he shown any evidence of unusual powers to you?"

She didn't mention the tricks he'd played with the body function panel. Instead, she chose to say, "He can control certain autonomic reflexes. He reads very fast; and retains more than most of us consider usual."

Kirk spoke sharply. "Repeat what you just told us, Mr. Scott."

"About an hour ago," Scott said, "the bridge controls started going crazy. Levers shifted all by themselves. Buttons were pressed without fingers to press them. Instrument readings wavered from safety points to danger ones."

"And on my monitor screen," Spock said, "I saw the Commander smile each time it happened. He treated the confusion he caused as though this ship and its crew were toys created for his amusement."

"Is that correct, Dr. Dehner?" Kirk queried. "Does he show abilities of that magnitude?"

"I've seen some such indications," she said.

Piper spoke up. "And you didn't think that worth the concern of the Captain?"

"No one's been hurt!" she protested. "Don't any of you understand? A mutated superior man could be a wonderful asset to the race—the forerunner of a new and better kind of human being!"

Kirk, looking at her exalted face, thought, *Idealism gone rampant again! My God!* He turned with relief to Sulu.

"If you want the mathematics on this, sir," Sulu said, "the Commander's ability is increasing geometrically. It's like owning a penny that doubles every day. In a month you'd be a millionaire."

Spock said, "In less time than that, Mitchell will attain powers we can neither understand nor cope with. What happens when we're not only useless to him—but actual annoyances?"

Elizabeth, about to speak, decided for silence. Kirk glanced around the table. "There'll be no discussion of this with the crew. Thank you. That's all."

The room emptied of everyone but Spock. Kirk turned to see his Science Officer inspecting him, creases of worry in his forehead. He spoke with careful deliberateness. "We will never reach an Earth base with Mitchell aboard, sir. You heard the mathematics of it. In a month he'll have as much in common with us as we'd have with a ship full of white mice."

His own anxiety oppressing him, Kirk snapped, "I need recommendations, Mr. Spock—not vague warnings."

"Recommendation number one. The planet, Delta-Vega, is only a few light days away from here. It has a lithium-cracking station. If we could adapt some of its power packs to our engines . . ."

"And if we can't, we'll be trapped in orbit there. We haven't the power to blast back out of it."

"It's the only possible way to get Mitchell off this ship, sir."

"If you mean strand him there, I won't do it. The station is fully automated. There's not a soul on the whole planet. Even ore ships call there only once every twenty years."

"Then you have only one other choice," Spock said. "Kill Mitchell while you can."

"*Get out of here!*" Kirk yelled.

Imperturbable, Spock repeated, "That's your only other choice. Assuming you take it while you still have time."

Kirk slammed his fist on the table. "Will you try for one moment to *feel*? We're talking about Gary Mitchell!"

"The Captain of the *Valiant* probably felt as you do, sir. But he waited too long to make his decision. I think we have both guessed that."

Kirk groped for a chair. Spock turned one around for him. He sank down in it, his face in his hands. After a moment, he removed them. Nodding to Spock, he said, "Set course for Delta-Vega."

Mitchell's powers were indeed expanding. And he'd begun to exult in exerting them. Lying in his Sickbay bed, he suddenly decided to snap his fingers. The lights flicked off. He waved a hand—and the lights blazed back. He sat up on the bed's edge, eyeing other portions of his room. He pointed a finger at a table. It soared into the air, teetered insanely on one leg and dropped quietly back into place.

"I am thirsty!" he abruptly announced to nobody.

Across the room, a metal cup on the water dispenser slid under the spigot. Water flowed from it. The filled cup lifted, and floating through the air, settled into Mitchell's outstretched hand. He was sipping from it when Kirk, with Spock and Elizabeth, came in.

"I feel great," Mitchell told them. "So don't bother to inquire into my state of health. Sometimes I think there's nothing I can't do. And some people believe that makes a monster of me, don't they?"

"Are you reading all our thoughts, Gary?" Kirk asked.

"Just in flashes so far—mostly strong thoughts like fear. For instance, you, Jim. You're worried about the safety of this ship."

"What would you do in my place?"

"Just what Mr. Spock is thinking—kill me while you can." Lifting his hand, he pointed a finger at Kirk. A bolt of radiance shot from it—and stunned, Kirk toppled over. Spock leaped at Mitchell—but before he could touch him, he, too, had crashed to the floor.

Elizabeth seized Mitchell's arm. "Stop it, Gary!"

He looked down at Kirk who was struggling back to his feet. "Sure, I know a lot," he said. "I know you're orbiting Delta-Vega, Jim. I can't let you maroon me there. I may not want to leave the ship, not yet. I may want another place. I'm not sure what kind of world I can use."

"*Use?*" Elizabeth said, shocked by the word's implications.

"Yes, beautiful Doctor. I don't get it all yet, but if I keep on growing, I'll be able to do things a god can do."

Spock sprang up. He struck Mitchell with a force that knocked him from the bed. He started to rise and Kirk landed a hard, fast blow on his jaw. His legs gave way. Groggy, he sprawled, supporting himself by his hands and knees. Breathing heavily, Kirk whirled to Elizabeth. "I want him unconscious for a while."

She took a hypogun from her medical case. Gas hissed as she touched Mitchell's shoulder with it. He subsided, spread-eagled, at their feet.

But another shot was required. This time Piper administered it in the Transporter Room where its technicians were preparing the beam-down to the surface of Delta-Vega. But the torpor induced by the second shot lasted for less time than the unconsciousness caused by the first one. Mitchell came out of it to begin to struggle so fiercely that he pulled himself free of the combined hold of Kirk and Spock. "Fools!" he said thickly. "Soon I will squash you all like crawling insects!"

Piper moved quickly in for a third shot. Mitchell slumped again. Dragging at him, Kirk and Spock rushed him over to the Transporter platform. The other members of the landing party hastened to their positions on it. Mitchell was swaying back onto his feet when Kirk shouted, "*Energize!*"

They materialized before the lithium-cracking plant.

From what could be seen of Delta-Vega's surface, it was a genuinely alien planet. Its soil was dust of a muddy blue color, and the vegetation that sprouted from it was brassy, scaled and knobbed like crocodile skin. Black boulders, their fissures filled with the blue dust, abounded—the only familiar aspect of the landscape. In the distance, a mountain of the black rock shouldered up against the horizon. But Kirk's concerns were other than the weird phenomena of the uninhabited planet. The hypos had finally got to Mitchell. Spock and Communications Officer Alden were supporting him into the building's entrance.

"Can we make it, Lee?" Kirk asked Kelso.

"If we can bypass the fuel bins without blowing ourselves up, we can make it, Captain." Kelso was gazing up at the installation. It was enormous, stretching its huge towers, metallic vats, its strangely coiling ells of complex instrumentation in all directions. Elizabeth stooped to touch a scaly flowerlike growth. It was burning hot.

"And not a soul on this planet but us?" she said.

Kirk answered her briefly. "Just us, Doctor. Lee, let's find the control room of this place."

They couldn't miss it. Doorless, it faced them in the building's central hall. Except for its contour, its size, the steady drone of its automated mechanisms, it bore some resemblance to the *Enterprise* bridge. Its walls were ranked by the same type of instrument panels, the same arrangements of meters, switches and dials. Kelso and Communications Officer Alden went at once to work selecting panels for later beam-up to the *Enterprise* Engineering section. A detail of other crewmen busied themselves with the thick electronic cables that would be needed to interlink the panels left to maintain the cracking planet's operation.

Kirk watched thoughtfully. "Those fuel bins, Lee. They could be detonated from here. A destruct switch?"

Kelso looked up, surprised. "I guess a destruct switch could be wired into this panel, sir."

"Do it," Kirk said.

Kelso stared at him. Then he nodded—and Spock spoke from the doorless entrance. "Mitchell's regained full consciousness, Captain. Perhaps you'd better come."

He had been confined in a maximum security room, one made escape-proof not by bars and bolts but by the invisible fence of a force field. He was pacing the room like a caged tiger. Outside, Piper, Elizabeth beside him, held his hypogun at the ready. Near them, an *Enterprise* security guard, phaser in hand, kept his eyes on the furious tiger.

"I want only one medical officer here at any one time," Kirk said. "The other will monitor him on the dispensary screen."

"I'd like my turn now," Elizabeth said. "I want to try and talk to him."

Piper nodded, handing her the hypogun. As he left, Kirk, pressing a button, tested the force field. It crackled sharply. Mitchell stopped pacing. Eyeing Kirk across the barrier, he said, "My friend, James Kirk. Remember the rodent things on Dimorus, the poisoned darts they threw? I took one meant for you . . ."

"And almost died. I remember," Kirk said.

"Then why be afraid of me now, Jim?"

"Gary, you have called us insects to be squashed if we got in your way."

"I was drugged then!"

"And before that, you said you'd kill a mutant like yourself were you in my place."

"Kill me then! Spock is right! And you're a fool not to do it!"

Elizabeth cried, "Gary, you don't mean that!"

He spoke directly to her. "In time, beautiful Doctor, you will understand, in time. Humans cannot survive if a race of true Espers like me is born. That's what Spock knows—and what that fool there," he nodded toward Kirk, "is too sentimental to know." He moved toward the force field sealing off his security room. As he neared it, there was a screech of high voltage. A spray of sparks flew up, scattered and died.

Spock and the guard had drawn their phasers. But Mitchell continued to push against the force field. For a moment his whole body glowed red. But through the brightness Kirk saw that the old human blueness of his eyes had replaced the silver. Then the force field flung him away. He staggered backward and fell on the room's bunk. He sank down on it, his face in his hands, groaning.

Kirk said, "His eyes returned to normal."

"Fighting the force field drained his strength." Spock studied the swaying figure on the bunk. "He could be handled now, Captain."

"Handled," Mitchell said. He looked up. His eyes were shining with so bright a silver that the room seemed lit with silver. "I grow stronger with every passing second. I thought you knew that, Spock."

Kirk snapped his communicator open. "Put full energy on this force field, Lieutenant Kelso."

There was a louder hum as power poured into the force field. A visible radiance began to gather around it.

Mitchell rose from the bunk. He rose from it to smile at Kirk from the other side of his barricade.

But if he remained Kirk's rankling thorn of anxiety, there was good news from the *Enterprise*. In its Engine Room a charred control panel had been successfully replaced by one beamed up from the cracking station. More new panels were required. So Kelso was still busy with the heavy cables he was using for the connecting link among the station's remaining panels.

Over his communicator, Scott said, "It fits like a glove, Captain. Did Mr. Spock get that phaser rifle we beamed down?"

At Kirk's surprised look, Spock moved the heavy weapon from the wall he'd laid it against. Kirk shook his head in a wordless sadness before he answered Scott. "Affirmative, Scotty. Landing party out."

"Mitchell tried to break through the force field again," Spock said tonelessly. "And his eyes changed faster. Nor did he show any signs of weakness this time."

"Dr. Dehner feels he isn't that dangerous," Kirk said. "What makes you right and a trained psychiatrist wrong?"

"Because she *feels*," Spock said. "Her feelings for Mitchell weaken the accuracy of her judgment. Mine tell me we'll be lucky if we can repair the ship and get away from him before he becomes very dangerous indeed."

"Captain!" Kelso called. Wearily Kirk crossed over to him. He looked at the sheathed switch Kelso had attached to a panel. It had been painted red. "Direct to the power bins," Kelso said. "From here a man could blow up the whole valley, Captain."

"Lee," Kirk said. "Lee, if Mitchell gets out—at your discretion, positioned here, you'll be the last chance. Lee, if he gets out—I want you to hit that switch."

The full meaning of Kirk's words struck Kelso dumb. If he hit the red switch, he'd go where the valley went. He looked at the switch and back into Kirk's eyes. After a moment, he managed a very sober, "Yes, sir."

In other circumstances, regeneration of the *Enterprise* engines would have been cause for rejoicing. The ship was ready for takeoff. The working detail of crewmen had been transported back up to it. But Mitchell's condition had worsened.

Now his skin tones had altered. What had once been ruddy flesh had a silvery cast, suggesting solid metal. He stood, arms folded across his chest, looking at them across the force field. If he noticed Spock's phaser rifle, he gave no sign of it.

"He's been like this for hours," Elizabeth said.

A silver man. "Have Dr. Piper meet us in the control room with Kelso," Kirk said. "We'll all beam up to the ship together."

"That's risky, sir," Spock said. "If we take our eyes off him . . ."

"Kelso will be on the destruct switch until the last minute." Kirk gestured to the silent figure behind the force field. "I think he knows that."

Elizabeth said, "I'm staying with him."

Kirk spoke flatly. "You'll leave with the ship, Doctor."

"I can't," she said. "I'm sorry."

Kirk's communicator beeped. "Kirk here," he said.

"The station seems to be running fine, sir," Kelso said. "Even without its quota of panels. The cables have done the job. Fission chamber three checks."

Behind him one of the cables stirred. It began to crawl toward him, snakelike. Slithering, silent, it lifted from the floor, twisting itself into loops. Abruptly, but still silently, a loop rose high into the air—and dropped over Kelso's head. A noose, flexible, inexorable, it tightened around his neck. Helplessly, Kelso tore at it, choking. Then he fell to the floor.

Mitchell smiled into Kirk's eyes. There was something ghastly in the movement of his silver lips. But Elizabeth saw only the smile.

"You see?" she cried to Kirk. *"He's not evil!"*

"You will leave with the ship, Doctor," Kirk repeated.

Mitchell spoke. "You should have killed me when you could, James. Compassion and command are an idiot's mixture."

Kirk grabbed Spock's phaser rifle. Mitchell's hand made a gesture that included them both. Flame blazed from it. As they collapsed, Mitchell walked to the force field. He brushed it as one brushes aside a flimsy curtain. A single spark flared briefly. He passed through the portal to stand face to face with Elizabeth. Taking her hand, he led her back into his room and over to a wall mirror. "Look at yourself, beautiful Doctor," he said.

She screamed. Then she flung her hands over her face to shut out the sight of her silver eyes.

Kirk wavered slowly back into consciousness. Pale, drained-looking, Piper was stooping over him. "Whatever it was, Captain, it affected me, too. Swallow this capsule." He paused. "Kelso's dead. Strangled. At least Spock is still alive."

"Dr. Dehner?" Kirk whispered.

"She's gone with Mitchell. That capsule will restore your strength in a minute or so. I must insert one in Spock's mouth. He's still unconscious and . . ."

"What direction did they take?" Kirk asked.

"Toward the rock mountain."

Kirk struggled to his knees. He reached for the phaser rifle he had dropped. As he checked it, he said, "As soon as Mr. Spock recovers, you will both immediately transport up to the *Enterprise*."

Piper looked up from his work of massaging the capsule down Spock's throat. "Captain, you're not—" he began.

"Where," Kirk continued inflexibly, "if you have not received a signal from me in twelve hours, you will proceed at maximum warp to the nearest Earth base. You will inform it that this entire planet is to be subjected to a lethal concentration of neutron radiation."

The capsule was working. He found he was able to stand. "No protest on this, Doctor Piper! It's an order!"

He slung the rifle over his shoulder and walked out of the cracking station.

The approach to the rock mountain's craggy escarpments made harsh going for Mitchell and Elizabeth. The sharp black stones and slithery blue sand which composed the terrain of Delta-Vega had not been created for pleasant afternoon strolls. As a sudden breeze blew sand into her face, Elizabeth panted, "It—it would take a miracle to survive here."

"Sit down," Mitchell said. "I'll make one."

He made a gesture. The blue sand around them darkened into the rich brown of loam. It shifted to give way to an upswing of bubbling water. The scaly, brass-colored vegetation turned green. From a patch of it, the leafy trunk of a peach tree rose up. Fruit hung from its boughs. Mitchell bent to drink from the spring.

When she had quenched her thirst, he said, "You'll share this power, too. As you develop, you'll feel like me, able to make a world into anything you want it to be. Soon we will fully control our bodies. We'll never grow old. You're woman enough now to like that. Always young, as beautiful as you desire to be . . ."

He suddenly stiffened.

"What's wrong?" she asked anxiously.

"A visitor," he said. "A very foolish visitor."

"Who is it?"

"You'll enjoy playing God, Elizabeth."

A splinter of unnameable fear jabbed her. He laughed at the look on her face. "Blasphemy scares you?" He flung his arms wide, the silver hands outspread. "Let there be food! Give me Kaferian apples, world, my world!"

A squat, odd-shaped tree appeared, heavy with huge red fruit. Mitchell, detaching an apple from it, bit into it, its rich yellow juice running down his silver chin. "Whenever we'd stop at that planet, I'd stock up on these," he said. "What is *your* wish? Just speak it."

Her answer came in the form of a slow, thoughtful question. "How much have I changed, Gary?"

But he wasn't listening. He had turned to concentrate his gaze on the still unseen figure of Kirk clambering over boulders, the heavy weight of the phaser rifle on his shoulder.

Mitchell spoke. "Can you hear me, James? You can't see me, I know. So let me comfort you. You're on the right path. You'll see me soon. Soon enough."

Kirk stopped. He had heard the words. How, he didn't know. He started to unlimber the rifle when he realized that Mitchell wasn't there. He resumed climbing.

"It's Captain Kirk," Elizabeth said as though speaking to herself. "In my mind I can see him."

"Go and meet him," Mitchell said. "Talk to him. Now that you're changing, you've got to discover how unimportant they are."

Hesitating, she stepped forward. Kirk sensed the presence on the shallow cliff above him, grabbed his rifle—and recognized the girl. Climbing up to her, he saw the hard silver of her eyes for the first time.

"Yes," she said. "It just took a little longer for it to happen to me."

Kirk lowered the rifle. "You've got to help me stop it, Dr. Dehner. Before it goes too far with you, too."

"I've already gone far enough to—to realize what he's doing is right. It's right for us."

"And for humans?" Kirk said. "You're still partly human—or you wouldn't be with him."

She looked away from him. Without certainty, she said, "Earth is—really unimportant. Before long, we'll be where it would take millions of years of learning for humans to reach."

"How will *he* learn if he skips over those millions of years?" Kirk said. "You don't know. You can't know. *He won't have lived through them!*"

"*Please*," she said. "Go back while you can!"

"You heard him joke about compassion. Above all a god needs compassion, Elizabeth."

"Go back!" she shouted.

"You were a psychiatrist," Kirk said. "You know the savage we all keep buried—the primitive self we dare not expose. But he'll dare to expose his! In God's name, Doctor, make your prognosis!"

Her face was tortured. Then she whispered, "He's coming!"

But he was already here. He ignored Kirk to speak to the girl. "I'm disappointed in you, Elizabeth. You still have doubts."

Whipping up his rifle, Kirk fired it at him. A fiery beam lanced out of it and struck him full in the chest. Its redness faded. Mitchell raised a finger. The rifle tore from Kirk's grasp to clatter on the stones beside him.

Time passed. Then Mitchell broke the silence. "I have been meditating," he said. "I have been reflecting upon the death of an old friend. His death and his honorable burial."

Kirk turned. Behind him, brown earth was scooping itself out into the neat shape of a grave. Elizabeth stared at Mitchell in unbelief. Trembling, she looked back at the grave. At its head stood a tidy, white military cross bearing the inscription "James R. Kirk. C-1277.1 to 1313.7."

A grinding sound came from overhead. Kirk looked up. A huge, rectangular rock slab was detaching itself from the cliff wall. It wobbled for a moment. Then it teetered into position directly above the grave.

Elizabeth screamed. "No, Gary, no!"

"You still like what you're seeing?" Kirk asked her.

"Time to pray, Captain," Mitchell said.

"To you?" Kirk said. "Not to both of you?"

The silver finger pointed at him. He was struck to his knees by the flash that darted from it. He remained on his knees, his eyes on the girl. "This is a jealous god, Elizabeth. In the end there will be one of you."

"Your last chance, Kirk!"

Elizabeth tensed. Sparks suddenly crackled between her and Mitchell. He reeled, recovered—and extended a silver hand toward her. A storm of sparks broke from it. She staggered, moaning with pain. But the energy drain had told on Mitchell. For a single second his eyes went blue. Then they were impervious silver once more. And once more the silver hand was extended toward the girl. A fiery mantle of sparks engulfed her. She crumpled. "Hurry," she whispered to Kirk. "There's—so little time."

The second outlay of energy had been expensive. Realizing his weakness, Mitchell turned to run. Kirk hurled himself forward and made a grab for his legs. A booted foot caught him in the chest. Then Mitchell seized a jagged rock. Kirk dodged the blow and closed with him.

"Gary, listen! For this moment you are human again . . ."

"It's gone now!" On a new surge of power, Mitchell smashed Kirk down with a silver fist.

He hit the ground hard, almost falling into the open grave. Then Mitchell was on him. In dizzy changes his face turned from silver to flesh. The silver won. Wrestling with him, Kirk could feel his whole body transforming itself into metal. He wrenched himself free, and had reached the rifle when Mitchell ripped an edge section of rock from the outcropping above them. It brushed his shoulder at the same moment he fired the rifle.

The beam missed Mitchell. But it struck the soft blue sand beneath the overhanging slab of rock that was to be his tombstone. It toppled and fell toward the grave.

"Gary!" Kirk shouted. "Look out!"

It was too late. Stumbling backward, Mitchell tripped. The rock slab hit him, tumbling him into the grave. A cloud of blue dust rose. When it settled, it had filled the letters etched into the broken white military cross.

Kirk kneed himself over to Elizabeth. The silver had gone from her eyes. "It's—all over, isn't it?" The voice was so weak that he had to stoop to hear it. Her head lolled over Kirk's arm. She was dead.

He got to his feet, a lonely stranger on a strange planet in a strange galaxy. But his communicator was familiar.

He spoke into it, his voice very tired. "Kirk to *Enterprise*. Come in, *Enterprise*."

It was almost as strange to be back in his command chair. He'd been a far way. The magnetic space storm—Delta-Vega—Mitchell's death—Kelso's—were they all events that had occurred in a dream? The new control panels around him were blinking as steadily as though they were the old ones. It was good to see Spock just standing there beside him.

"Ready to leave orbit, sir," Scott called from Kelso's old position.

"*Engage*," Kirk said. He switched on his Captain's log. "Add to official casualties, Dr. Elizabeth Dehner. Be it noted that she gave her life in performance of her duty. And Lieutenant Commander Gary Mitchell. The same notation."

He looked at Spock. "After all, he didn't ask for what happened to him. I want his service record to end that way."

Spock's Mephisto features were tranquil. "I felt for him, too, sir, strange to say."

Kirk eyed him speculatively. "Watch yourself, Mr. Spock," he said. "Your compassion is showing."

CHARLIE'S LAW

(aired as "CHARLIE X")

WRITER: D. C. FONTANA (STORY BY GENE RODDENBERRY)

DIRECTOR: LAWRENCE DOBKIN

FIRST AIRED: SEPTEMBER 15, 1966

Though as Captain of the starship *Enterprise* James Kirk had the final authority over four hundred officers and crewmen, plus a small and constantly shifting population of passengers, and though in well more than twenty years in space he had had his share of narrow squeaks, he was firmly of the opinion that no single person ever gave him more trouble than one seventeen-year-old boy.

Charles Evans had been picked up from a planet called Thasus after having been marooned there for fourteen years, the sole survivor of the crash of his parents' research vessel. He was rescued by the survey ship *Antares*, a transport about a tenth of the size of the *Enterprise*, and subsequently transferred to Kirk's ship, wearing hand-me-down clothes and carrying all the rest of his possessions in a dufflebag.

The offers of the *Antares* who brought him aboard the *Enterprise* spoke highly of Charlie's intelligence, eagerness to learn, intuitive grasp of engineering matters—"He could run the *Antares* himself if he had to"—and his sweetness of character; but it struck Kirk that they were almost elbowing each other aside to praise him, and that they were in an unprecedented hurry to get back to their own cramped ship, without even so much as begging a bottle of brandy.

Charlie's curiosity had certainly been obvious from those first moments, though he showed some trepidation, too—which was not surprising, considering his long and lonely exile. Kirk assigned Yeoman Rand to take him to his quarters. It was at this point that Charlie stunned her and everyone else present by asking Kirk honestly:

"Is that a girl?"

Leonard McCoy, the ship's surgeon, checked Charlie from top to toe and found him in excellent physical condition: no traces of malnutrition, of exposure, of hardship of any sort; truly remarkable for a boy who'd had to fend for himself on a strange world from the age of three. On the other hand, it was reasonable to suppose that fourteen years later, Charlie would either be in good shape, or dead; he would have had to come to terms with his environment within the first few years.

Charlie was not very communicative about this puzzle, though he asked plenty of questions himself—he seemed earnestly to want to know all the right things to do, and even more urgently, to be liked, but the purport of some of McCoy's questions apparently baffled him.

No, nobody had survived the crash. He had learned English by talking to the memory banks on the ship; they still worked. No, the Thasians hadn't helped him; there were no Thasians. At first he had eaten stores from the wreck; then he had found some other . . . things, growing around.

Charlie then asked to see the ship's rule book. On the *Antares*, he said, he hadn't done or said all the right things. When that happened, people got angry; he got angry, too. He didn't like making the same mistake twice.

"I feel the same way," McCoy told him. "But you can't rush such matters. Just keep your eyes open, and when in doubt, smile and say nothing. It works very nicely."

Charlie returned McCoy's grin, and McCoy dismissed him with a swat on the rump, to Charlie's obvious astonishment.

McCoy brought the problem up again on the bridge with Kirk and his second-in-command, Mr. Spock. Yeoman Rand was there working on a duty roster, and at once volunteered to leave; but since she had seen as much of Charlie as anyone had, Kirk asked her to stay. Besides, Kirk was fond of her, though he fondly imagined that to be a secret even from her.

"Earth history is full of cases where a small child managed to survive in a wilderness," McCoy went on.

"I've read some of your legends," said Spock, who was native to a nonsolar planet confusingly called Vulcan. "They all seem to require a wolf to look after the infants."

"What reason would the boy have to lie, if there *were* Thasians?"

"Nevertheless there's some evidence that there were, at least millennia ago," Spock said. "The first survey reported some highly sophisticated artifacts. And conditions haven't changed on Thasus for at least three million years. There might well be *some* survivors."

"Charlie says there aren't," Kirk said.

"His very survival argues that there are. I've checked the library computer record on Thasus. There isn't much, but one thing it does say: 'No edible plant life.' He simply had to have had some kind of help."

"I think you're giving him less credit than he deserves," McCoy said.

"For the moment let's go on that assumption," Kirk said. "Mr. Spock, work out a briefing program for young Charlie. Give him things to do—places to be. If we keep him busy until we get to Colony Five, experienced educators will take him over, and in the meantime, he should leave us with relative calm aboard . . . Yeoman Rand, what do you think of our problem child?"

"Wellll," she said. "Maybe I'm prejudiced. I wasn't going to mention this, but . . .

he followed me down the corridor yesterday and offered me a vial of perfume. My favorite, too; I don't know how he knew it. There's none in the ship's stores, I'm sure of that."

"Hmm," McCoy said.

"I was just going to ask him where he got it, when he swatted me on the rump. After that I made it my business to be someplace else."

There was an outburst of surprised laughter, quickly suppressed.

"Anything else?" Kirk said.

"Nothing important. Did you know that he can do card tricks?"

"Now, where would he have learned that?" Spock demanded.

"I don't know, but he's very good. I was playing solitaire in the rec room when he came in. Lieutenant Uhura was playing 'Charlie is my darling' and singing, and at first he seemed to think she was mocking him. When he saw she didn't mean it personally, he came over to watch me, and he seemed to be puzzled that I couldn't make the game come out. So he made it come out for me—without even touching the cards, I'd swear to that. When I showed I was surprised, he picked up the cards and did a whole series of tricks with them, good ones. The best sleight-of-hand I've ever seen. He said one of the men on the *Antares* taught him how. He was enjoying all the attention, I could tell that, but I didn't want to encourage him too much myself. Not after the swatting incident."

"He got *that* trick from me, I'm afraid," McCoy said.

"No doubt he did," Kirk said. "But I think I'd better talk to him, anyhow."

"Fatherhood becomes you, Jim," McCoy said, grinning.

"Dry up, Bones. I just don't want him getting out of hand, that's all."

Charlie shot to his feet the moment Kirk entered his cabin; all his fingers, elbows, and knees seemed to bend the wrong way. Kirk had barely managed to nod when he burst out: "I didn't do anything!"

"Relax, Charlie. Just wanted to find out how you're getting along."

"Fine. I . . . I'm supposed to ask you why I shouldn't—I don't know how to explain it."

"Try saying it straight out, Charlie," Kirk said. "That usually works."

"Well, in the corridor . . . I talked to . . . when Janice . . . Yeoman Rand was . . ." Abruptly, setting his face, he took a quick step forward and slapped Kirk on the seat. "I did that and she didn't like it. She said you'd explain it to me."

"Well," Kirk said, trying hard not to smile, "it's that there are things you can do with a lady, and things you can't. Uh, the fact is, there's no right way to hit a lady. Man to man is one thing, man to woman is something else. Do you understand?"

"I don't know. I guess so."

"If you don't, you'll just have to take my word for it for the time being. In the meantime, I'm having a schedule worked out for you, Charlie. Things to do, to help you learn all the things you missed while you were marooned on Thasus."

"That's very nice, for you to do that for me," Charlie said. He seemed genuinely pleased. "Do you like me?"

That flat question took Kirk off guard. "I don't know," he said equally flatly. "Learning to like people takes time. You have to watch what they do, try to understand them. It doesn't happen all at once."

"Oh," Charlie said.

"Captain Kirk," Lieutenant Uhura's voice broke in over the intercom.

"Excuse me, Charlie . . . Kirk here."

"Captain Ramart of the *Antares* is on D channel. Must speak to you directly."

"Right. I'll come up to the bridge."

"Can I come too?" Charlie said as Kirk switched out.

"I'm afraid not, Charlie. This is strictly ship's business."

"I won't disturb anybody," Charlie said. "I'll stay out of the way."

The boy's need for human company was touching, no matter how awkwardly he went about it. There were many years of solitude to be made up for. "Well, all right," Kirk said. "But only when you have my permission. Agreed?"

"Agreed," Charlie said eagerly. He followed Kirk out like a puppy.

On the bridge, Lieutenant Uhura, her Bantu face intent as a tribal statue's, was asking the microphone: "Can you boost your power, *Antares*? We are barely reading your transmission."

"We are at full output, *Enterprise*," Ramart's voice said, very distant and hashy. "I must speak with Captain Kirk at once."

Kirk stepped up to the station and picked up the mike. "Kirk here, Captain Ramart."

"Captain, thank goodness. We're just barely in range. I've got to warn—"

His voice stopped. There was nothing to be heard from the speaker now but stellar static—not even a carrier wave.

"See if you can get them back," Kirk said.

"There's nothing to get, Captain," Lieutenant Uhura said, baffled. "They aren't transmitting any more."

"Keep the channel open."

Behind Kirk, Charlie said quietly: "That was an old ship. It wasn't very well constructed."

Kirk stared at him, and then swung toward Spock's station.

"Mr. Spock, sweep the transmission area with probe sensors."

"I've got it," Spock said promptly. "But it's fuzzy. Unusually so even for this distance."

Kirk turned back to the boy. "What happened, Charlie? Do you know?"

Charlie stared back at him, with what seemed to be uneasy defiance. "I don't know," he said.

"The fuzzy area is spreading out," Spock reported. "I'm getting some distinct pips now along the edges. Debris, undoubtedly."

"But no *Antares*?"

"Captain Kirk, that *is* the *Antares*," Spock said quietly. "No other interpretation is possible. Clearly, she blew up."

Kirk continued to hold Charlie's eye. The boy looked back.

"I'm sorry it blew up," Charlie said. He seemed uneasy, but nothing more than that. "But I won't miss them. They weren't very nice. They didn't like me. I could tell."

There was a long, terribly tense silence. At last Kirk carefully unclenched his fists.

"Charlie," he said, "one of the first things you're going to have to get rid of is that damned cold-bloodedness. Or self-centeredness, or whatever it is. Until that gets under control, you're going to be less than half human."

And then, he stopped. To his embarrassed amazement, Charlie was crying.

"He what?" Kirk said, looking up from his office chair at Yeoman Rand. She was vastly uncomfortable, but she stuck to her guns.

"He made a pass at me," she repeated. "Not in so many words, no. But he made me a long, stumbling speech. He wants me."

"Yeoman, he's a seventeen-year-old boy."

"Exactly," the girl said.

"All this because of a swat?"

"No, sir," she said. "Because of the speech. Captain, I've seen that look before; *I'm not seventeen*. And if something isn't done, sooner or later I'm going to have to hold Charlie off, maybe even swat him myself, and not on the fanny, either. That wouldn't be good for him. I'm his first love and his first crush and the first woman he ever saw and . . ." She caught her breath. "Captain, that's a great deal for anyone to have to handle, even one item at a time. All at once, it's murder. And he doesn't understand the usual put-offs. If I have to push him off in a way he does understand, there may be trouble. Do you follow me?"

"I think so, Yeoman," Kirk said. He still could not quite take the situation seriously. "Though I never thought I'd wind up explaining the birds and the bees to anybody, not at my age. But I'll send for him right now."

"Thank you, sir." She went out. Kirk buzzed for Charlie. He appeared almost at once, as though he had been expecting something of the sort.

"Come in, Charlie, sit down."

The boy moved to the chair opposite Kirk's desk and sat down, as if settling into a bear trap. As before, he beat Kirk to the opening line.

"Janice," he said. "Yeoman Rand. It's about her, isn't it?"

Damn the kid's quickness! "More or less. Though it's more about you."

"I won't hit her like that any more. I promised."

"There's more to it than that," Kirk said. "You've got some things to learn."

"Everything I do or say is wrong," Charlie said desperately. "I'm in the way. Dr. McCoy won't show me the rules. I don't know what I am or what I'm supposed to be, or even *who*. And I don't know why I hurt so much inside all the time—"

"I do, and you'll live," Kirk said. "There's nothing wrong with you that hasn't gone haywire inside every human male since the model came out. There's no way to get over it, around it, or under it; you just have to live through it, Charlie."

"But, it's like I'm wearing my insides outside. I go around bent over all the time. Janice—Yeoman Rand—she wants to give me away to someone else. Yeoman Lawton. But she's just a, just a, well, she doesn't even smell like a girl. Nobody else on the ship is like Janice. I don't want anybody else."

"It's normal," Kirk said gently. "Charlie, there are a million things in the universe you can have. There are also about a hundred million that you can't. There's no fun in learning to face that, but you've got to do it. That's how things are."

"I don't like it," Charlie said, as if that explained everything.

"I don't blame you. But you have to hang on tight and survive. Which reminds me: the next thing on your schedule is unarmed defense. Come along to the gym with me and we'll try a few falls. Way back in Victorian England, centuries ago, they had a legend that violent exercise helped keep one's mind off women. I've never known it to work, myself, but anyhow let's give it a try."

Charlie was incredibly clumsy, but perhaps no more so than any other beginner. Ship's Officer Sam Ellis, a member of McCoy's staff, clad like Kirk and Charlie in work-out clothes, was patient with him.

"That's better. Slap the mat when you go down, Charlie. It absorbs the shock. Now, again."

Ellis dropped of his own initiative to the mat, slapped it, and rolled gracefully up onto his feet. "Like that."

"I'll never learn," Charlie said.

"Sure you will," Kirk said. "Go ahead."

Charlie managed an awkward drop. He forgot to slap until almost the last minute, so that quite a thud accompanied the slap.

"Well, that's an improvement," Kirk said. "Like everything else, it takes practice. Once more."

This time was better. Kirk said, "That's it. Okay, Sam, show him a shoulder roll."

Ellis hit the mat, and was at once on his feet again, cleanly and easily.

"I don't want to do that," Charlie said.

"It's part of the course," Kirk said. "It's not hard. Look." He did a roll himself. "Try it."

"No. You were going to teach me to fight, not roll around on the floor."

"You have to learn to take falls without hurting yourself before we can do that. Sam, maybe we'd better demonstrate. A couple of easy throws."

"Sure," Ellis said. The two officers grappled, and Ellis, who was in much better shape than the Captain, let Kirk throw him. Then, as Kirk got to his feet, Ellis flipped him like a poker chip. Kirk rolled and bounced, glad of the exercise.

"See what I mean?" Kirk said.

"I guess so," Charlie said. "It doesn't look hard."

He moved in and grappled with Kirk, trying for the hold he had seen Ellis use. He was strong, but he had no leverage. Kirk took a counter-hold and threw him. It was not a hard throw, but Charlie again forgot to slap the mat. He jumped to his feet flaming mad, glaring at Kirk.

"*That* won't do," Ellis said, grinning. "You need a lot more falls, Charlie."

Charlie whirled toward him. In a low, intense voice, he said: "Don't laugh at me."

"Cool off, Charlie," Ellis said, chuckling openly now. "Half the trick is in not losing your temper."

"*Don't laugh at me!*" Charlie said. Ellis spread out his hands, but his grin did not quite go away.

Exactly one second later, there was a pop like the breaking of the world's largest light bulb. Ellis vanished.

Kirk stared stupefied at the spot where Ellis had been. Charlie, too, stood frozen for a moment. Then he began to move tentatively toward the door.

"Hold it," Kirk said. Charlie stopped, but he did not turn to face Kirk.

"He shouldn't have laughed at me," Charlie said. "That's not nice, to laugh at somebody. I was trying."

"Not very hard. Never mind that. What happened? What did you do to my officer?"

"He's gone," Charlie said sullenly.

"That's no answer."

"He's gone," Charlie said. "That's all I know. I didn't want to do it. He made me. He laughed at me."

And suppose Janice has to slap him? And ... there was the explosion of the *Antares* ... Kirk stepped quickly to the nearest wall intercom and flicked it on. Charlie turned at last to watch him. "Captain Kirk in the gym," Kirk said. "Two men from security here, on the double."

"What are you going to do with me?" Charlie said.

"I'm sending you to your quarters. And I want you to stay there."

"I won't let them touch me," Charlie said in a low voice. "I'll make them go away too."

"They won't hurt you."

Charlie did not answer, but he had the look of a caged animal just before it turns at last upon its trainer. The door opened and two security guards came in, phaser pistols holstered. They stopped and looked to Kirk.

"Go with them, Charlie. We'll talk about this later, when we've both cooled off. You owe me a long explanation." Kirk jerked his head toward Charlie. The guards stepped to him and took him by the arms.

Or, tried to. Actually, Kirk was sure that they never touched him. One of them simply staggered back, but the other was thrown violently against the wall, as though he had been caught in a sudden hurricane. He managed to hold his footing, however, and clawed for his sidearm.

"No!" Kirk shouted.

But the order was way too late. By the time the guard had his hand levelled at the boy, he no longer had a weapon to hold. It had vanished, just like Sam Ellis. Charlie stared at Kirk, his eyes narrowed and challenging.

"Charlie," Kirk said, "you're showing off. Go to your quarters."

"No."

"Go with the guards, or I'll pick you up and carry you there myself." He began to walk steadily forward. "That's your only choice, Charlie. Either do as I tell you, or send me away to wherever you sent the phaser, and Sam Ellis."

"Oh, all right," Charlie said, wilting. Kirk drew a deep breath. "But tell them to keep their hands to themselves."

"They won't hurt you. Not if you do as I say."

Kirk called a general council on the bridge at once, but Charlie moved faster: by the time Kirk's officers were all present, there wasn't a phaser to be found anywhere aboard ship. Charlie had made them all "go away." Kirk explained what had happened, briefly and grimly.

"Given this development," McCoy said, "it's clear Charlie wouldn't have needed any help from any putative Thasians. He could have magicked up all his needs by himself."

"Not necessarily," Spock said. "All we know is that he can make things vanish—not make them appear. I admit that that alone would have been a big help to him."

"What are the chances," Kirk said, "that he's a Thasian himself? Or at least, something really unprecedented in the way of an alien?"

"The chance is there," McCoy said, "but I'd be inclined to rule it out. Remember I checked him over. He's ostensibly human, down to his last blood type. Of course, I could have missed something, but he was hooked to the body-function panel, too; the machine would have rung sixteen different kinds of alarms at the slightest discrepancy."

"Well, he's inhumanly powerful, in any event," Spock said. "The probability is that he was responsible for the destruction of the *Antares*, too. Over an enormous distance—well beyond phaser range."

"Great," McCoy said. "Under the circumstances, how can we hope to keep him caged up?"

"It goes further than that, Bones," Kirk said. "We can't take him to Colony Five, either. Can you imagine what he'd do in an open, normal environment—in an undisciplined environment?"

Clearly, McCoy hadn't. Kirk got up and began to pace.

"Charlie is an adolescent boy—probably human, but totally inexperienced with other human beings. He's short-tempered because he wants so much and it can't come fast enough for him. He's full of adolescent aches. He wants to be one of us, to be loved, to be useful. But . . . I remember when I was seventeen that I wished for the ability to remove the things and people that annoyed me, neatly and without fuss. It's a power fantasy most boys of that age have. Charlie doesn't have to wish. *He can do it.*

"In other words, in order to stay in existence, gentlemen, we'll have to make damn sure we don't annoy him. Otherwise—pop!"

"Annoyance is relative, Captain," Spock said. "It's all going to depend on how Charlie is feeling minute by minute. And because of his background, or lack of it, we have no ways to guess what little thing might annoy him next, no matter how carefully we try. He's the galaxy's most destructive weapon, and he's on a hair trigger."

"No," Kirk said. "He's not a weapon. He *has* a weapon. That's a difference we can use. Essentially, he's a child, a child in a man's body, trying to be a whole man. His trouble isn't malice. It's innocence."

"And here he is," McCoy said with false heartiness. Kirk swung his chair around to see Charlie approaching from the elevator, smiling cheerfully.

"Hi," said the galaxy's most destructive weapon.

"I thought I confined you to your quarters, Charlie."

"You did," Charlie said, the grin fading. "But I got tired of waiting around down there."

"Oh, all right. You're here. Maybe you can answer a few questions for us. Were you responsible for what happened to the *Antares*?"

"Why?"

"Because I want to know. Answer me, Charlie."

Breaths were held while Charlie thought it over. Finally, he said: "Yes. There was a warped baffle plate on the shielding of their Nerst generator. I made it go away. It would have given sooner or later anyhow."

"You could have told them that."

"What for?" Charlie said reasonably. "They weren't nice to me. They didn't like me. You saw them when they brought me aboard. They wanted to get rid of me. They don't any more."

"And what about us?" Kirk said.

"Oh, I need you. I have to get to Colony Five. But if you're not nice to me, I'll think of something else." The boy turned abruptly and left, for no visible reason.

McCoy wiped sweat off his forehead. "What a chance you took."

"We can't be walking on eggs every second," Kirk said. "If every act, every question might irritate him, we might as well pretend that none of them will. Otherwise we'll be utterly paralyzed."

"Captain," Spock said slowly, "do you suppose a force field might hold him? He's too smart to allow himself to be lured into a detention cell, but we just might rig up a field at his cabin door. All the lab circuitry runs through the main corridor on deck five, and we could use that. It's a long chance, but—"

"How long would the work take?" Kirk said.

"At a guess, seventy-two hours."

"It's going to be a long seventy-two hours, Mr. Spock. Get on it." Spock nodded and went out.

"Lieutenant Uhura, raise Colony Five for me. I want to speak directly to the Governor. Lieutenant Sulu, lay me a course away from Colony Five—not irrevocably, but enough to buy me some time. Bones—"

He was interrupted by the sound of a fat spark, and a choked scream of pain from Uhura. Her hands were in her lap, writhing together uncontrollably. McCoy leapt to her side, tried to press the clenched fingers apart.

"It's . . . all right," she said. "I think. Just a shock. But there's no reason for the board to be charged like that—"

"Probably a very good reason," Kirk said grimly. "Don't touch it until further orders. How does it look, Bones?"

"Superficial burns," McCoy said. "But who knows what it'll be next time?"

"I can tell you that," Sulu said. "I can't feed new coordinates into this panel. It operates, but it rejects the course change. We're locked on Colony Five."

"I'm in a hurry," Charlie's voice said. He was coming out of the elevator again, but he paused as he saw the naked fury on Kirk's face.

"I'm getting tired of this," Kirk said. "What about the transmitter?"

"You don't need all that subspace chatter," Charlie said, a little defensively. "If there's any trouble, I can take care of it myself. I'm learning fast."

"I don't want your help," Kirk said. "Charlie, for the moment there's nothing I can do to prevent your interference. But I'll tell you this: you're quite right, I don't like you. I don't like you at all. Now beat it."

"I'll go," Charlie said, quite coolly. "I don't mind if you don't like me now. You will pretty soon. I'm going to make you."

As he left, McCoy began to swear in a low whisper.

"Belay that, Bones, it won't help. Lieutenant Uhura, is it just outside communications that are shorted, or is the intercom out too?"

"Intercom looks good, Captain."

"All right, get me Yeoman Rand . . . Janice, I have a nasty one for you—maybe the nastiest you've ever been asked to do. I want you to lure Charlie into his cabin. . . . That's right. We'll be watching—but bear in mind that if you make him mad, there won't be much we can do to protect you. You can opt out if you want; it probably won't work anyhow."

"If it doesn't," Yeoman Rand's voice said, "it won't because *I* didn't try it."

They watched, Spock's hand hovering over the key that would activate the force field. At first, Janice was alone in Charlie's cabin, and the wait seemed very long. Finally, however, the door slid aside, and Charlie came into the field of the hidden camera, his expression a mixture of hope and suspicion.

"It was nice of you to come here," he said. "But I don't trust people any more. They're all so complicated, and full of hate."

"No, they're not," Janice said. "You just don't make enough allowance for how *they* feel. You have to give them time."

"Then . . . you do like me?"

"Yes, I like you. Enough to try to straighten you out, anyhow. Otherwise I wouldn't have asked to come here."

"That was very nice," Charlie said. "I can be nice, too. Look. I have something for you."

From behind his back, where it had already been visible to the camera, he produced the single pink rosebud he had been carrying and held it out. There had been no roses aboard ship, either; judging by that and the perfume, he could indeed make things appear as well as disappear. The omens did not look good.

"Pink *is* your favorite color, isn't it?" Charlie was saying. "The books say all girls like pink. Blue is for boys."

"It was . . . a nice thought, Charlie. But this isn't really the time for courting. I really need to talk to you."

"But you asked to come to my room. The books all say that means something important." He reached out, trying to touch her face. She moved instinctively away, trying to circle for the door, which was now on remote control, the switch for it under Spock's other hand; but she could not see where she was backing and was stopped by a chair.

"No. I said I only wanted to talk and that's what I meant."

"But I only wanted to be nice to you."

She got free of the chair somehow and resumed sidling. "That's a switch on Charlie's Law," she said.

"What do you mean? What's that?"

"Charlie's Law says everybody better be nice to Charlie, or else."

"That's not true!" Charlie said raggedly.

"Isn't it? Where's Sam Ellis, then?"

"I don't know where he is. He's just gone. Janice, I only *want* to be nice. They won't let me. None of you will. I can give you anything you want. Just tell me."

"All right," Janice said. "Then I think you had better let me go. That's what I want now."

"But you said . . ." The boy swallowed and tried again. "Janice, I . . . love you."

"No you don't. You don't know what the word means."

"Then show me," he said, reaching for her.

Her back was to the door now, and Spock hit the switch. The boy's eyes widened as the door slid back, and then Janice was through it. He charged after her, and the other key closed.

The force field flared, and Charlie was flung back into the room. He stood there for a moment like a stabled stallion, nostrils flared, breathing heavily. Then he said:

"All right. All right, then."

He walked slowly forward. Kirk swung the camera to follow him. This time he went through the force field as though it did not exist. He advanced again on Janice.

"Why did you do that?" he said. "You won't even let me try. None of you. All right. From now on I'm not trying. I won't keep any of you but the ones I need. I don't need you."

There came the implosion sound again. Janice was gone. Around Kirk, the universe turned a dull, aching gray.

"Charlie," he said hoarsely. The intercom carried his voice to Charlie's cabin. He looked blindly toward the source.

"You too, Captain," he said. "What you did wasn't nice either. I'll keep you a while. The *Enterprise* isn't quite like the *Antares*. Running the *Antares* was easy. But if you try to hurt me again, I'll make a lot of other people go away . . . I'm coming up to the bridge now."

"I can't stop you," Kirk said.

"I know you can't. Being a man isn't so much. I'm not a man and I can do anything. You can't. Maybe I'm the man and you're not."

Kirk cut out the circuit and looked at Spock. After a while the First Officer said:

"That was the last word, if ever I heard it."

"It's as close as I care to come to it, that's for sure. Did that field react at all, the second time?"

"No. He went through it as easily as a ray of light. Easier—I could have stopped a light ray if I'd known the frequency. There seems to be very little he can't do."

"Except run the ship—and get to Colony Five by himself."

"Small consolation."

They broke off as Charlie entered. He was walking very tall. Without a word to anyone, he went to the helmsman's chair and waved to Sulu to get out of it. After a brief glance at Kirk, Sulu got up obediently, and Charlie sat down and began to play with the controls. The ship lurched, very slightly, and he snatched his hands back.

"Show me what to do," he told Sulu.

"That would take thirty years of training."

"Don't argue with me. Just show me."

"Go ahead, show him," Kirk said. "Maybe he'll blow us up. Better than letting him loose on Colony Five—"

"Captain Kirk," Lieutenant Uhura broke in. "I'm getting something from outside; subspace channel F. Ship to ship, I think. But it's all on instruments; I can't hear it."

"There's nothing there," Charlie said, his voice rough. "Just leave it alone."

"Captain?"

"I am the captain," Charlie said. Yet somehow, Kirk had the sudden conviction that he was frightened. And somehow, equally inexplicably, he knew that the *Enterprise* had to get that call.

"Charlie," he said, "are you creating that message—or are you blocking one that's coming in?"

"It's my game, Mr. Kirk," Charlie said. "You have to find out. Like you said—that's how the game is played." He pushed himself out of the chair and said to Sulu, "You can have it now. I've locked on course for Colony Five again."

He could have done nothing of the sort in that brief period; not, at least, with his few brief stabs at the controls. Probably, his original lock still held unchanged. But either way, it was bad enough; Colony Five was now only twelve hours away.

But Charlie's hands were trembling visibly. Kirk said:

"All right, Charlie, that's the game—and the game is over. I don't think you can handle any more. I think you're at your limit and you can't take on one more thing. But you're going to have to. Me."

"I could have sent you away before," Charlie said. "Don't make me do it now."

"You don't dare. You've got my ship. I want it back. And I want my crew back whole, too—if I have to break your neck to do it."

"Don't push me," Charlie whispered. *"Don't push me."*

At the next step forward, a sleet-storm of pain threw Kirk to the deck. He could not help crying out.

"I'm sorry," Charlie said, sweating. "I'm sorry—"

The subspace unit hummed loudly, suddenly, and then began to chatter in intelligible code. Uhura reached for the unscrambler.

"Stop that!" Charlie screamed, whirling. "I said, stop it!"

The pain stopped; Kirk was free. After a split-second's hesitation to make sure he was all there, he lunged to his feet. Spock and McCoy were also closing in, but Kirk was closer. He drew back a fist.

"Console is clear," Sulu's voice said behind him. "Helm answers."

Charlie dodged away from Kirk's threat, whimpering. He never had looked less like the captain of anything, even his own soul. Kirk held back his blow in wonder.

Pop!

Janice Rand was on the bridge, putting out both hands to steady herself. She was white-faced and shaken, but otherwise unharmed.

Pop!

"That was a hell of a fall, Jim," Sam Ellis' voice said. "Next time, take it a little—hey, what's all this?"

"Message is through," Lieutenant Uhura's voice said dispassionately. "Ship off our starboard bow. Identifies itself as from Thasus."

With a cry of animal panic, Charlie fell to the deck, drumming on it with both fists.

"Don't listen, don't listen!" he wailed. "No, no please! I can't live with them any more."

Kirk watched stolidly, not moving. The boy who had been bullying and manipulating them for so long was falling apart under his eyes.

"You're my friends. You *said* you were my friends. Remember—when I came aboard?" He looked up piteously at Kirk. "Take me home, to Colony Five. That's all I want . . . It's really all I want!"

"Captain," Spock said in an emotionless voice. "Something happening over here. Like a transporter materialization. Look."

Feeling like a man caught in a long fall of dominoes, Kirk jerked his eyes toward Spock. There was indeed something materializing on the bridge, through which Spock himself could now be seen only dimly. It was perhaps two-thirds as tall as a man, roughly oval, and fighting for solidity. It wavered and changed, and colors flowed through it. For a moment it looked like a gigantic human face; then, like nothing even remotely human; then, like a distorted view of a distant but gigantic building. It did not seem able to hold any state very long.

Then it spoke. The voice was deep and resonant. It came, not from the apparition, but from the subspace speaker; but like the apparition, it wavered, blurred, faded, blared, changed color, as if almost out of control.

"We are sorry for this trouble," it said. "We did not realize until too late that the human boy was gone from us. We searched a long time to find him, but space travel is a long-unused skill among us; we are saddened that his escape cost the lives of those aboard the first ship. We could not help them because they were exploded in this frame; but we have returned your people and your weapons to you, since they were only intact in the next frame. Now everything else is as it was. There is nothing to fear; we have him in control."

"No," Charlie said. He was weeping convulsively. Clambering to his knees, he grappled Kirk by a forearm. "I won't do it again. Please, I'll be nice. I won't ever do it again. I'm sorry about the *Antares*, I'm sorry. Please let me go with you, please!"

"Whee-oo," McCoy said gustily. "Talk about the marines landing—!"

"It's not that easy," Kirk said, looking steadily at the strange thing—a Thasian?—before him. "Charlie destroyed the other ship and will have to be punished for it. But thanks to you, all the other damage is repaired—and he is a human being. He belongs with his own people."

"You're out of your mind," McCoy said.

"Shut up, Bones. He's one of us. Rehabilitation might make him really one of us, reunite him to his own people. We owe him that, if he can be taught not to use his power."

"We gave him the power," the apparition said, "so that he could live. It cannot be taken back or forgotten. He will use it; he cannot help himself. He would destroy you and your kind, or you would be forced to destroy him to save yourselves. We alone offer him life."

"Not at all," Kirk said. "You offer him a prison—not even a half-life."

"We know that. But that damage was done long ago; we can do now only what little best is left. Since we are to blame, we must care for him. Come, Charles Evans."

"Don't let them!" Charlie gasped. "Don't let them take me! Captain—*Janice!* Don't you understand, I *can't even touch them*—"

The boy and the Thasian vanished, in utter silence. The only remaining sound was the dim, multifarious humming surround of the *Enterprise*.

And the sound of Janice Rand weeping, as a woman weeps for a lost son.

THE NAKED TIME

Writer: John D. F. Black
Director: Marc Daniels
First Aired: September 29, 1966

Nobody, it was clear, was going to miss the planet when it did break up. Nobody had even bothered to name it; on the charts it was just ULAP-G42821DB, a coding promptly shorted by some of the *Enterprise*'s junior officers to "La Pig."

It was not an especially appropriate nickname. The planet, a rockball about 10,000 miles in diameter, was a frozen, windless wilderness, without so much as a gnarled root or fragment of lichen to relieve the monotony from horizon to purple horizon. But in one way the name fitted: the empty world was too big for its class.

After a relatively short lifetime of a few hundred million years, stresses between its frozen surface and its shrinking core were about to shatter it.

There was an observation station on La Pig, manned by six people. These would have to be got off, and the *Enterprise*, being in the vicinity, got the job. After that, the orders ran, the starship was to hang around and observe the breakup. The data collected would be of great interest to the sliderule boys back on Earth. Maybe some day they would turn the figures into a way to break up a planet at will, people and all.

Captain Kirk, like most line officers, did not have a high opinion of the chairborne arms of his service.

It turned out, however, that there was nobody at all to pick up off La Pig. The observation station was wide open, and the ice had moved inside. Massive coatings of it lay over everything—floors, consoles, even chairs. The doors were frozen open, and all the power was off.

The six members of the station complement were dead. One, in heavy gear, lay bent half over one of the consoles. On the floor at the entrance to one of the corridors was the body of a woman, very lightly clad and more than half iced over. Inspection, however, showed that she had been dead before the cold had got to her; she had been strangled.

In the lower part of the station were the other four. The engineer sat at his post with all the life-support system switches set at OFF, frozen there as though he hadn't given a damn. There was still plenty of power available; he just hadn't wanted it on any more. Two of the others were dead in their beds, which was absolutely normal and expectable considering the temperature. But the sixth and last man had died while taking a shower—fully clothed.

"There wasn't anything else to be seen," Mr. Spock, the officer in charge of the transporter party, later told Captain Kirk. "Except that there were little puddles of water here and there that hadn't frozen, though at that temperature they certainly should have, no matter what they might have held in solution. We brought back a small sample for the lab. The bodies are in our morgue now, still frozen. As for the people, I think maybe this is a job for a playwright, not an official investigation."

"Imagination's a useful talent in a police officer," Kirk commented. "At a venture, I'd guess that something volatile and highly toxic got loose in the station. One of the men got splattered and rushed to the shower hoping to sluice it off, clothes and all. Somebody else opened all the exit ports in an attempt to let the stuff blow out into the outside atmosphere."

"And the strangled woman?"

"Somebody blamed her for the initial accident—which was maybe just the last of a long chain of carelessnesses, and maybe irritating behavior too, on her part. You know how tempers can get frayed in small isolated crews like this."

"Very good, Captain," Spock said. "Now what about the engineer shutting off the life systems?"

Kirk threw up his hands. "I give up. Maybe he saw that nothing was going to work and decided on suicide. Or more likely I'm completely wrong all down the line. We'd better settle in our observation orbit. Whatever happened down there, apparently the books are closed."

For the record, it was just as well that he said "apparently."

Joe Tormolen, the crewman who had accompanied Mr. Spock to the observation station, was the first to show the signs. He had been eating all by himself in the recreation room—not unusual in itself, for though efficient and reliable, Joe was not very sociable. Nearby, Sulu, the chief pilot, and Navigator Kevin Riley were having an argument over the merits of fencing as exercise, with Sulu of course holding the affirmative. At some point in the discussion, Sulu appealed to Joe for support.

For answer, Joe flew into a white fury, babbling disconnectedly but under high pressure about the six people who had died on La Pig, and the unworthiness of human beings in general to be in space at all. At the height of this frenzied oration, Joe attempted to turn a steak knife on himself.

The resulting struggle was protracted, and because Sulu and Riley naturally misread Joe's intentions—they thought he was going to attack one of them with the knife—Joe succeeded in wounding himself badly. All three were blood-smeared by the time he was subdued and hauled off to sick bay; at first arrival, the security guards couldn't guess which of the three scuffling figures was the hurt one.

There was no time to discuss the case in any detail; La Pig was already beginning to break up, and Sulu and Riley were needed on the bridge as soon as they could wash up. As the breakup proceeded, the planet's effective mass would change, and perhaps even its center of gravity—accompanied by steady, growing distortion of its extensive magnetic field—so that what had been a stable parking orbit for the *Enterprise* at one moment would become unstable and fragment-strewn the next. The changes were nothing the computer could predict except in rather general orders of magnitude; human brains had to watch and compensate, constantly.

Dr. McCoy's report that Joe Tormolen had died consequently did not reach Kirk for twenty-four hours, and it was another four before he could answer McCoy's request for a consultation. By then, however, the breakup process seemed to have reached some sort of inflection point, where it would simply pause for an hour or so; he could leave the vigil to Sulu and Riley for a short visit to McCoy's office.

"I wouldn't have called you if Joe hadn't been one of the two men down on La Pig," McCoy said directly. "But the case is odd and I don't want to overlook the possibility that there's some connection."

"What's odd about it?"

"Well," McCoy said, "the suicide attempt itself was odd. Joe's self-doubt quotient always rated high, and he was rather a brooding, introspective type; but I'm puzzled about what could have brought it to the surface this suddenly and with this much force.

"And Jim, he shouldn't have died. He had intestinal damage, but I closed it all up neatly and cleaned out the peritoneum; there was no secondary infection. He died anyhow, and I don't know of what."

"Maybe he just gave up," Kirk suggested.

"I've seen that happen. But I can't put it on a death certificate. I have to have a proximate cause, like toxemia or a clot in the brain. Joe just seemed to have a generalized circulatory failure, from no proximate cause at all. And those six dead people on La Pig are not reassuring."

"True enough. What about that sample Spock brought back?"

McCoy shrugged. "Anything's possible, I suppose—but as far as we can tell, that stuff's just water, with some trace minerals that lower its freezing point a good deal. We're handling it with every possible precaution, it's bacteriologically clean—which means no viruses, either—and very nearly chemically pure. I've about concluded that it's a blind alley, though of course I'm still trying to think of new checks to run on it; we all are."

"Well, I'll keep an eye on Spock," Kirk said. "He was the only other man who was down there—though his metabolism's so different that I don't know what I'll be looking for. And in the meantime, we'll just have to hope it was a coincidence."

He went out. As he turned from the door, he was startled to see Sulu coming down a side corridor, not yet aware of Kirk. Evidently he had just come from the gym, for his velour shirt was off, revealing a black tee-shirt, and he had a towel around his neck. He was carrying a fencing foil with a tip protector on it under his arm, and he looked quite pleased with himself—certainly nothing like a man who was away from his post in an alert.

He swung the foil so that it pointed to the ceiling, then let it slip down between his hands so that the capped end was directly before his face. After a moment's study, he took the cap off. Then he took the weapon by the hilt and tested its heft.

"Sulu!"

The pilot jumped back and hit lightly in the guard position. The point of the foil described small circles in the air between the two men.

"Aha!" Sulu said, almost gleefully. "Queen's guard or Richelieu's man? Declare yourself!"

"Sulu, what's this? You're supposed to be on station."

Sulu advanced one pace with the crab-step of the fencer.

"You think to outwit me, eh? Unsheathe your weapon!"

"That's enough," Kirk said sharply. "Report yourself to sick bay."

"And leave you the bois? Nay, rather—"

He made a sudden lunge. Kirk jumped back and snatched out his phaser, setting it to "stun" with his thumb in the same motion, but Sulu was too quick for him. He leapt for a recess in the wall where there was an access ladder to the 'tween-hulls catwalks, and vanished up it. From the vacated manhole his voice echoed back:

"Cowarrrrrrrrrrrd!"

Kirk made the bridge on the double. As he entered, Uhura was giving up the navigator's position to another crewman and moving back to her communications console. There was already another substitute in Sulu's chair. Kirk said, "Where's Riley?"

"Apparently he just wandered off," Spock said, surrendering the command chair to Kirk in his turn. "Nobody but Yeoman Harris here saw him go."

"Symptoms?" Kirk asked the helmsman.

"He wasn't violent or anything, sir. I asked where Mr. Sulu was and he began to sing, 'Have no fear, Riley's here.' Then he said he was sorry for me that I wasn't an Irishman—in fact I am, sir—and said he was going for a turn on the battlements."

"Sulu's got it too," Kirk said briefly. "Chased me with a sword on level two, corridor three, then bolted between the hulls. Lieutenant Uhura, tell Security to locate and confine them both. I want every crewman who comes in contact with them medically checked."

"Psychiatrically, I would suggest, Captain," Spock said.

"Explain."

"This seizure, whatever it is, seems to force buried self-images to the surface. Tormolen was a depressive; it drove him down to the bottom of his cycle and below it, so he suicided. Riley fancies himself a descendant of his Irish kings. Sulu at heart is an eighteenth-century swashbuckler."

"All right. What's the present condition of the planet?"

"Breaking faster than predicted," Spock said. "As of now we've got a 2 per cent fall increment."

"Stabilize." He turned to his own command board, but the helmsman's voice jerked his attention back.

"Sir, the helm doesn't answer."

"Fire all ventral verniers then. We'll rectify orbit later."

The helmsman hit the switch. Nothing happened.

"Verniers also dead, sir."

"Main engines: warp one!" Kirk rasped.

"That'll throw us right out of the system," Spock observed, as if only stating a mild inconvenience.

"Can't help that."

"No response, sir," the helmsman said.

"Engine room, acknowledge!" Spock said into the intercom. "Give us power. Our controls are dead."

Kirk jerked a thumb at the elevator. "Mr. Spock, find out what's going on down there."

Spock started to move, but at the same time the elevator door slid aside, and Sulu was advancing, foil in hand. "Richelieu!" he said. "At last!"

"Sulu," Kirk said, "put down that damned—"

"For honor, Queen and France!" Sulu lunged directly at Spock, who in sheer unbelief almost let himself be run through. Kirk tried to move in but the needlepoint flicked promptly in his direction. "Now, foul Richelieu—"

He was about to lunge when he saw Uhura trying to circle behind him. He spun; she halted.

"Aha, fair maiden!"

"Sorry, neither," Uhura said. She threw a glance deliberately over Sulu's left shoulder; as he jerked in that direction, Spock's hand caught him on the right shoulder with the Vulcanian nerve pinch. Sulu went down on the deck like a sack of flour.

Forgetting his existence instantly, Kirk whirled on the intercom. "Mr. Scott! We need power! Scott! Engine room, acknowledge!"

In a musical tenor, the intercom said indolently: "You rang?"

"Riley?" Kirk said, trying to repress his fury.

"This is Capt. Kevin Thomas Riley of the Starship *Enterprise*. And who would I have the honor of speakin' to?"

"This is Kirk, dammit."

"Kirk who? Sure and I've got no such officer."

"Riley, this is Captain Kirk. Get out of the engine room, Navigator. Where's Scott?"

"Now hear this, cooks," Riley said. "This is your captain and I'll be wantin' double portions of ice cream for the crew. Captain's compliments, in honor of St. Kevin's Day. And now, your Captain will render an appropriate selection."

Kirk bolted for the elevator. Spock moved automatically to the command chair. "Sir," he said, "at our present rate of descent we have less than twenty minutes before we enter the planet's exosphere."

"All right," Kirk said grimly. "I'll see what I can do about that monkey. Stand by to apply power the instant you get it."

The elevator doors closed on him. Throughout the ship, Riley's voice began to bawl: "I'll take you home again, Kathleen." He was no singer.

It would have been funny, had it not been for the fact that the serenade had the intercom system completely tied up; that the seizure, judging by Joe Tormolen, was followed by a reasonless death; and that the *Enterprise* itself was due shortly to become just another battered lump in a whirling, planet-sized mass of cosmic rubble.

Scott and two crewmen were outside the engine room door, running a sensor around its edge, as Kirk arrived. Scott looked quickly at the Captain, and then back at the job.

"Trying to get this open, sir," he said. "Riley ran in, said you wanted us on the bridge, then locked us out. We heard you talking to him on the intercom."

"He's cut off both helm and power," Kirk said. "Can you by-pass him and work from the auxiliary?"

"No, Captain, he's hooked everything through the main panel in there." Scott prodded one of the crewmen. "Get up to my office and pull the plans for this bulkhead here. If we've got to cut, I don't want to go through any circuitry." The crewman nodded and ran.

"Can you give us battery power on the helm, at least?" Kirk said. "It won't check our fall but at least it'll keep us stabilized. We've got maybe nineteen minutes, Scotty."

"I heard. I can try it."

"Good." Kirk started back for the bridge.

"And tears be-dim your loving eyes . . ."

On the bridge, Kirk snapped, "Can't you cut off that noise?"

"No, sir," Lieutenant Uhura said. "He can override any channel from the main power panels there."

"There's one he can't override," Kirk said. "Mr. Spock, seal off all ship sections. If this is a contagion, maybe we can stop it from spreading, and at the same time—"

"I follow you," Spock said. He activated the servos for the sector bulkheads. Automatically, the main alarm went off, drowning Riley out completely. When it quit, there was a brief silence. Then Riley's voice said:

"Lieutenant Uhura, this is Captain Riley. You interrupted my song. That was petty of you. No ice cream for you."

"Seventeen minutes left, sir," Spock said.

"Attention crew," Riley's voice went on. "There will be a formal dance in the ship's bowling alley at 1900 hours. All personnel will have a ball." There was a skirl of gleeful laughter. "For the occasion all female crewmen will be issued one pint of perfume from ship's stores. All male crewmen will be raised one pay grade to compensate. Stand by for further goodies."

"Any report on Sulu before the intercom got blanketed?" Kirk said.

"Dr. McCoy had him in sick bay under heavy tranquilization," Lieutenant Uhura said. "He wasn't any worse then, but all tests were negative . . . I got the impression that the surgeon had some sort of idea, but he was cut off before he could explain it."

"Well, Riley's the immediate problem now."

A runner came in and saluted. "Sir, Mr. Scott's compliments and you have a jump circuit from batteries to helm control now. Mr. Scott has resumed cutting into the engine room. He says he should have access in fourteen minutes, sir."

"Which is just the margin we have left," Kirk said. "And it'll take three minutes to tune the engines to full power again. Captain's compliments to Mr. Scott and tell him to cut in any old way and not worry about cutting any circuits but major leads."

"Now hear this," Riley's voice said. "In future all female crew members will let their hair hang loosely down over their shoulders and will use restraint in putting on makeup. Repeat, women should not look made up."

"Sir," Spock said in a strained voice.

"One second. I want two security guards to join Mr. Scott's party. Riley may be armed."

"I've already done that," Spock said. "Sir—"

". . . Across the ocean wide and deep . . ."

"Sir, I feel ill," Spock said formally. "Request permission to report to sick bay."

Kirk clapped a hand to his forehead. "Symptoms?"

"Just a general malaise, sir. But in view of—"

"Yes, yes. But you can't *get* to sick bay; the sections are all sealed off."

"Request I be locked in my quarters, then, sir. I can reach those."

"Permission granted. Somebody find him a guard." As Spock went out, another dismaying thought struck Kirk. Suppose McCoy had the affliction now, whatever it was? Except for Spock and the now-dead Tormolen, he had been exposed to it longest, and Spock could be supposed to be unusually resistant. "Lieutenant Uhura, you might as well abandon that console, it's doing us no good at the moment. Find yourself a length of telephone cable and an eavesdropper, and go between hulls to the hull above the sick bay. You'll be able to hear McCoy but not talk back; get his attention, and answer him, by prisoners' raps. Relay the conversation to me by pocket transmitter. Mark and move."

"Yes, *sir.*"

Her exit left the bridge empty except for Kirk. There was nothing he could do but pace and watch the big screen. Twelve minutes.

Then a buzzer went off in Kirk's back pocket. He yanked out his communicator.

"Kirk here."

"Lieutenant Uhura, sir. I've established contact with Doctor McCoy. He says he believes he has a partial solution, sir."

"Ask him what he means by partial."

There was an agonizing wait while Uhura presumably spelled out this message by banging on the inner hull. The metal was thick; probably she was using a hammer, and even so the raps would come through only faintly.

"Sir, he wants to discharge something—some sort of gas, sir—into the ship's ventilating system. He says he can do it from sick bay and that it will spread rapidly. He says it worked on Lieutenant Sulu and presumably will cure anybody else who's sick—but he won't vouch for its effect on healthy crew members."

"That sounded like typical McCoy caution, but—ask him how he feels himself."

Another long wait. Then: "He says he felt very ill, sir, but is all right now, thanks to the antidote."

That might be true and it might not. If McCoy himself had the illness, there would be no predicting what he might actually be preparing to dump into the ship's air. On the other hand, to refuse him permission wouldn't necessarily stop him, either. If only that damned singing would stop! It made thinking almost impossible.

"Ask him to have Sulu say something; see if he sounds sane to you."

Another wait. Only ten minutes left now—three of which would have to be used for tune-up. And no telling how fast McCoy's antidote would spread, or how long it would need to take hold, either.

"Sir, he says Lieutenant Sulu is exhausted and he won't wake him, under the discretion granted him by his commission."

McCoy had that discretion, to be sure. But it could also be the cunning blind of a deranged mind.

"All right," Kirk said heavily. "Tell him to go ahead with it."

"Aye aye, sir."

Uhura's carrier wave clicked out and Kirk pocketed his transceiver, feeling utterly helpless. Nine minutes.

Then, Riley's voice faltered. He appeared to have forgotten some of the words of his interminable song. Then he dropped a whole line. He tried to go on, singing "La, la, la," instead, but in a moment that died away too.

Silence.

Kirk felt his own pulse, and sounded himself subjectively. Insofar as he could tell, there was nothing the matter with him but a headache which he now realized he had had for more than an hour. He strode quickly to Uhura's console and rang the engine room.

There was a click from the g.c. speakers, and Riley's voice said hesitantly: "Riley here."

"Mr. Riley, this is Kirk. Where are you?"

"Sir, I . . . I seem to be in the engine room. I'm . . . off post, sir."

Kirk drew a deep breath. "Never mind that. Give us power right away. Then open the door and let the chief engineer in. Stand out of the way when you do it, because he's trying to cut in with a phaser at full power. Have you got all that?"

"Yes, sir. Power, then the door—and stand back. Sir, what's this all about?"

"Never mind now, just do it."

"Yes, sir."

Kirk opened the bulkhead override. At once, there was the heavy rolling sound of the emergency doors between the sections opening, like a stone being rolled back from a tomb. Hitting the general alarm button, Kirk bawled: "All officers to the bridge! Crash emergency, six minutes! Mark and move!"

At the same time, the needles on the power board began to stir. Riley had activated the engines. A moment later, his voice, filled with innocent regret, said into the general air:

"Now there won't be a dance in the bowling alley tonight."

Once a new orbit around the disintegrating mass of La Pig had been established, Kirk found time to question McCoy. The medico looked worn down to a nubbin, and small wonder; his had been the longest vigil of all. But he responded with characteristic indirection.

"Know anything about cactuses, Jim?"

"Only what everybody knows. They live in the desert and they stick you. Oh yes, and some of them store water."

"Right, and that last item's the main one. Also, cactuses that have been in museum cases for fifty or even seventy years sometimes astonish the museum curators by sprouting. Egyptian wheat that's been in tombs for thousands of years will sometimes germinate, too."

Kirk waited patiently. McCoy would get to the point in his own good time.

"Both those things happen because of a peculiar form of storage called *bound water*. Ordinary mineral crystals like copper sulfate often have water hitched to their molecules, loosely; that's water-of-crystallization. With it, copper sulfate is a pretty blue gem, though poisonous; without it, it's a poisonous green powder. Well, organic molecules can bind water much more closely, make it really a part of the molecule instead of just loosely hitched to it. Over the course of many years, that water will come out of combination and become available to the cactus or the grain of wheat as a liquid, and then life begins all over again."

"An ingenious arrangement," Kirk said. "But I don't see how it nearly killed us all."

"It was in that sample of liquid Mr. Spock brought back, of course—a catalyst that *promoted* water-binding. If it had nothing else to bind to, it would bind even to itself. Once in the bloodstream, the catalyst began complexing the blood-serum. First it made the blood more difficult to extract nutrients from, beginning with blood sugar, which starved the brain—hence the psychiatric symptoms. As the process continued, it made the blood too thick to pump, especially through the smaller capillaries—hence Joe's death by circulatory collapse.

"Once I realized what was happening, I had to figure out a way to poison the catalysis. The stuff was highly contagious, through the perspiration, or blood, or any other body fluid; and catalysts don't take part in any chemical reaction they promote, so the original amount was always present to be passed on. I think this one may even have multiplied, in some semi-viruslike fashion. Anyhow, the job was to alter the chemical nature of the catalyst—poison it—so it wouldn't promote that reaction any more. I almost didn't find the proper poison in time, and as I told Lieutenant Uhura through the wall, I wasn't sure what effect the poison itself would have on healthy people. Luckily, none."

"Great Galaxy," Kirk said. "That reminds me of something. Spock invalided himself off duty just before the tail end of the crisis and he's not back. Lieutenant Uhura, call Mr. Spock's quarters."

"Yes, sir."

The switch clicked. Out of the intercom came a peculiarly Arabic howl—the noise of the Vulcanian musical instrument Spock liked to practice in his cabin, since nobody else on board could stand to listen to it. Along with the noise, Spock's rough voice was crooning:

"Alab, wes-craunish, sprai pu ristu,

Or en r'ljiik majiir auooo—"

Kirk winced. "I can't tell whether he's all right or not," he said. "Nobody but another Vulcanian could. But since he's not on duty during a crash alert, maybe your antidote did something to him it didn't do to us. Better go check him."

"Soon as I find my earplugs."

McCoy left. From Spock's cabin, the voice went on:

"Rijii, bebe, p'salku pirtu,

Fror om—"

The voice rose toward an impassioned climax and Kirk cut the circuit. Rather than that, he would almost rather have "I'll take you home again, Kathleen," back again.

On the other hand, if Riley had sounded like that to Spock, maybe Spock had needed no other reason for feeling unwell. With a sigh, Kirk settled back to watch the last throes of La Pig. The planet was now little better than an irregularly bulging cloud of dust, looking on the screen remarkably like a swelling and disintegrating human brain.

The resemblance, Kirk thought, was strictly superficial. Once a planet started disintegrating, it was through. But brains weren't like that.

Given half a chance, they pulled themselves together.

Sometimes.

THE ENEMY WITHIN

WRITER: RICHARD MATHESON
DIRECTOR: LEO PENN
FIRST AIRED: OCTOBER 6, 1966

THE PLANET'S DESERT TERRAIN HAD YIELDED AN INTERESTING ROUNDUP OF mineral and animal specimens, and Kirk was busy checking the containers for beam-up to the *Enterprise* when a gust of icy wind blew a spray of sand in his face. Beside him, Sulu, holding a meek doglike creature on a leash, shivered.

"Temperature's beginning to drop, Captain."

"Gets down to 250 degrees below at nightfall," Kirk said. He blinked the sand out of his eyes, stooped to pat Sulu's animal—and wheeled at the sound of a shout. Geological technician Fisher had fallen from the bank where he'd been working. From shoulders to feet his jumpsuit was smeared with a sticky, yellowish ore.

"Hurt yourself?" Kirk asked.

Fisher winced. "Cut my hand, sir."

It was a jagged, ugly cut. "Report to Sickbay," Kirk said.

Obediently Fisher removed his communicator from his belt. In the *Enterprise* Transporter Room, Scott, receiving his request for beam-up, said, "Right. Locked onto you." He turned to Transporter technician Wilson at the console. "Energize!" he ordered.

But as Fisher sparkled into shape on the platform, the console flashed a warning red light. "Coadjustor engagement," Scott said hastily. Wilson threw a switch. The red light faded.

Materialized, Fisher stepped off the platform.

"What happened?" Wilson asked.

"Took a flop," Fisher told him.

Wilson eyed the yellowish splatterings on his jumpsuit. Some lumps of the stuff had fallen from it to the platform's floor.

"Took a flop onto what?" Wilson asked.

"I don't know—some kind of soft ore."

Scott had reached for a scanner device. He ran it over the jumpsuit. "That ore's magnetic," he said. "Decontaminate your uniform, Fisher."

"Yes, sir."

Frowning, Scott examined the console. "It acted like a burnout," he grumbled to Wilson. "I don't like it."

Kirk's voice broke in on his concentration. "Captain Kirk, ready for beam-up."

"Just a moment, Captain." Scott tested the console again. "Seems to be OK now," he told Wilson. "But we can do with a double check. Get me a synchronic meter." Returning to his speaker, he said, "All right, Captain. Locked onto you." Then he activated the Transporter.

There was an unfamiliar whine in its humming. Hurriedly dialing it out, Scott decided to warn Kirk he was delaying the beam-up. But the process had already begun. The engineer looked anxiously toward the platform. In its dazzle Kirk stood on it, dazed-looking, unusually pale. As he stepped from it, his legs almost buckled. Scott ran to him. "What's wrong, Captain? Let me give you a hand."

"Just a little dizzy, that's all," Kirk said. "I'm sure it's nothing serious." He glanced around him. "You're not leaving the Transporter Room untended to look after me, are you?"

"No, sir. Wilson's just gone for a tool."

The door closed behind them. More sparkle appeared on the platform. A figure took shape on it. When it had gathered solidity, it could be seen as a perfect double of Kirk. Except for its eyes. They were those of a rabid animal just released from a cage.

It looked around it, tense, as though expecting attack.

Wilson opened the door. Immediately sensing that tension, "Captain," he said, "are you all right?"

His reply was a hoarse growl. The double glanced around it again seeking some means of escape. It licked its dry lips. Then it saw the door Wilson had left open.

Out in the corridor Kirk was saying, "I can manage now. You'd better get back to the Transporter Room, Scotty."

"Yes, sir."

"Thanks for the help."

"I wish you'd let Dr. McCoy give you a look-over, Captain."

"All right, Engineer. I'll have him check my engines."

He didn't have far to go. At the next cross passage he collided with McCoy. "I think we need a control signal at this cor—" McCoy broke off to stare at Kirk. "What's happened to you?"

"I don't know," Kirk said.

"You look like you ran into a wall."

"Is that your official diagnosis?"

"Never mind my diagnosis! Go and lie down. I have a malingerer to be treated. Then I'll come and check you."

"If you can find me," Kirk said—and moved on down the corridor. McCoy followed his going with puzzled eyes. Then he hastened on back to the waiting Fisher in Sickbay.

The soiled jumpsuit had been discarded. McCoy cleaned the cut hand. "Like to get off duty, wouldn't you?" he said. "Take a little vacation."

Fisher grinned. And McCoy, swabbing the wound, lifted his head at the sound of the opening door.

The double spoke at once. "*Brandy*," it said.

The demand, the manner, the whole bearing of replica Kirk was uncharacteristic of the real one. Fisher's presence put a brake on McCoy's amazement. He decided to ignore the demand. "Don't go running back to work now," he told Fisher. "Keep the bandage moist with this antiseptic. Take the bottle along with you."

"Yes, sir." Fisher held up his swathed hand, smiling at the double. "It isn't too bad, Captain."

The remark was ignored. McCoy turned to the double standing in the doorway and gestured to it to enter the office. "Sit down, Jim," he said. "I think we'd better . . ."

He stopped. The double had gone to the locked liquor cabinet, its nails clawing at it. "*I said brandy*," it said.

McCoy stared, dumbfounded. The double was snarling now at its failure to pry open the cabinet's door. Nervous, uneasy, McCoy tried again. "Sit down, Jim."

A shudder passed through the double. A savage whisper broke from it. "*Give me the brandy!*"

"What is the *matter* with—" McCoy began. The clawing hands were lifting with the clear intention of smashing the cabinet's glass.

"Jim!" McCoy shouted.

The double whirled, crouched for a leap, its fists clenching. Instinctively McCoy recoiled from the coming blow. Then he recovered himself. "All right, I'll give you the brandy. Sit down!" But he didn't give the brandy. As he unlocked the cabinet door, he was shouldered aside—and the double, seizing a bottle of liquor, made for the door.

"Drink it in *your quarters*, Jim! I'll see you there in a . . ."

The door slammed shut.

McCoy, striding over to his viewing screen, flicked it on. Spock's face appeared. "Anything peculiar happen down on that planet's surface, Mr. Spock?"

The cool voice said, "One slight accident, Doctor, which I'm sure won't tax your miraculous healing powers."

But McCoy was too disturbed to rise to the bait. "Did it involve the Captain?"

"No."

"Well, there's something very wrong with him. He just left my office after carrying on like a wild man."

The wild man, rampaging down the corridor, suddenly had a mind to private drinking. A sign over a door declared it to be the entrance to the quarters of Yeoman Janice Rand. The double touched it, conceiving unmentionable notions—and slipped through the door. Inside, it uncorked the bottle. Tipping it up, it gulped down the brandy in deep swallows. Then it grunted in pure, voluptuous pleasure. The bite of the brandy down its throat was too seductive to resist the impulse to swallow some more. Eyes half-shut in sensual delight, its face was the face of a Kirk released from all repressions, all self-discipline and moral order.

Kirk himself had not entirely recovered from his mysterious vertigo. Alone in his quarters, he had his shirt off, and was flexing his neck and shoulder muscles to rid his head of the whirling inside it. When the knock came at his door, he said, "Yes?"

"Spock, sir."

"Come in," Kirk said, pressing the door's unlocking button.

"Dr. McCoy asked me to check on you, sir."

Shouldering back into his shirt, Kirk said, "Why you?"

"Only Dr. McCoy could answer that, Captain."

"He must have had a reason."

"One would assume so," Spock said mildly, his keen eyes on Kirk's face.

"Well, Mr. Spock? I hope you know me next time we meet."

"Dr. McCoy said you were acting like a wild man."

"McCoy said that?" Kirk paused. "He must have been joking."

"I'll get back to the bridge now," Spock said.

"I'll tell McCoy you were here."

As the door closed, Kirk, puzzled by the interchange, reached for his Captain's coat.

On Deck 12, corridors above him, his double was feeling the effects of the brandy. But at the sound of a door sliding open, it was sober enough to take hiding in the bedroom of Yeoman Rand's quarters. It watched her enter. When she had placed her tricorder on a table, it stepped forward into her full sight.

It was not Kirk's custom to visit the bedrooms of attractive female members of his crew. Janice was shaken by his appearance in hers. She decided to smile. "This is an unexpected pleasure, sir," she said gamely.

The smile faltered at the suggestive leer she received. "Is there something I can—?" Then she tensed. The double had come so close to her she could smell the brandy on its breath. She flushed at such male nearness, fought back an uprush of embarrassed apprehension and said, "Is there—can I do something for you, Captain?"

"You bet you can," the double grinned. "But Jim will do here, Janice."

Neither the words nor the tone fitted the image of Kirk that existed in the mind of Janice Rand. She had never seen him anything but coolly courteous toward women members of his crew. Since the day she had joined it, she had thought of him as the unobtainable but most desirable man she'd ever met. However, that was her own secret. It just wasn't possible that he *was* obtainable, not Captain James T. Kirk of the Starship *Enterprise*. And by a twenty-year-old, obscure yeoman named Janice Rand. He'd been drinking, of course; and when men drank . . . Nevertheless, of all the women on the ship, this handsomest man in the world had sought her out; and by some miraculous quirk of circumstance seemed to be finding her worthy of his sexual interest. She suddenly felt that she, along with her uniform, had gone transparent.

"I—Captain, this isn't—" she stammered.

"You're too much woman not to know," the double said. "I've been mad for you since the day you joined the ship. We both know what's been inside us all this time. We can't say no to it—not any more, not when we're finally alone, just you and me. Just try to deny it—after this . . ."

It swept her into its arms, kissing her hard on the lips. For a moment she was immobilized by the shock. Then she pulled back. "*Please*, Captain. You—we . . ."

The handsome face tightened with anger. She was kissed again harshly; and with a little moan, she tried to pull free. She was jerked closer. Now the kisses pressed against her throat, her neck.

"You're—hurting me," she whispered.

"Then don't fight me. You know you don't want to."

She stared into what she thought were Kirk's eyes. In some shameful way it was true. She *didn't* want to fight the Captain's kisses. Only how dare he presume to know it?

"Shall I make that an order, Yeoman Rand?"

This time the kiss on her mouth was openly brutal. Janice, infuriated by exposure of a truth she wanted neither to know herself nor be known to anyone else, began to fight in earnest. She scratched the double across its handsome face. It pulled back; and she dashed for the door. She was grabbed as it opened—but out in the corridor, Fisher, returning to his room with the antiseptic liquid he'd forgotten, had seen the struggling pair.

"*On your way!*" It was Kirk's command voice.

Relief surged through Janice. *The Captain had implicated himself in this disgraceful scene.* If there was penalty to pay in loss of his crew's respect, he'd have only himself to blame. She screamed, "Call Mr. Spock!"

Fisher gaped at her. "*Call Mr. Spock!*" she screamed again. Fisher broke into a run. The double tightened its hold on her. Then, realizing how the witness menaced it, it rushed out into the corridor.

Fisher made it to a wall intercom. "This is Fisher of Geology! Come to Deck 12, Section . . ."

The double caught him in midsentence. Fisher was spun around to take a smashing right to his jaw. It was his turn to scream. "Help! Section 3!"

The scream came through to the bridge. Spock bolted for the elevator, shouting "Take over!" to navigator Farrell.

Deck 12 was deserted. Spock hesitated. Then, starting down the corridor, he slowed his run to a wary walk, his sharp Vulcan eyes searching. After a moment, he stooped to run a finger along a dark streak on the flooring. When he looked at the finger, it was red, wet with blood.

Its trail of drops led to the quarters of Yeoman Rand. He opened the door. She was sitting on a chair, her uniform disheveled, her eyes blank, stunned. Near her, Fisher lay on the floor. She didn't speak as Spock bent down to him. His face was a mass of mangled flesh and blood.

"Who did this to you?" Spock asked.

Fisher's torn lips moved. "Captain Kirk," he whispered. Then he subsided into unconsciousness.

Kirk asked his question very quietly. "And Yeoman Rand says I assaulted her?"

"Yes, sir," Spock said. "And technician Fisher also accuses you of assault upon her and himself."

"I've been here in my quarters for the past half hour," Kirk said.

Spock held up the nearly empty brandy bottle.

"What's that?" Kirk said.

"The bottle of brandy Dr. McCoy says you took from his office cabinet. I found it in Yeoman Rand's room with Fisher."

"McCoy says *I* took that brandy?" The whirling in Kirk's head had come back. He shut his eyes against its wheeling stars. Then he rose. "Let's find out what's going on in this ship." He moved past Spock into the corridor.

The elevator door closed behind them—and the double, a darker shadow in the shadows of a cross passage, slipped quietly out into the corridor. Panting, it pried at the door of Kirk's quarters. It got it open. Inside, the lock on the panel of the sleeping compartment caught its eye. It depressed the unlocking button. It relocked the panel behind it and fell across the bed, sighing with exhaustion. Then it buried the replica of Kirk's face in a pillow to shut out the sights and sounds of a world that hated it.

In Sickbay, Yeoman Rand was saying, "Then he kissed me—and said we—that he was the Captain and could order me to—" Her eyes were on her cold hands, safer to look at than Kirk's face. She had addressed her words to Spock.

"Go on," Kirk said.

She looked at him now. "I—I didn't know what to do. When you started talking about—us—about the feeling we've been—hiding all this time . . ."

"The feeling you and I have been hiding, Yeoman Rand?" Kirk said. "Do I understand you correctly?"

"Yes, sir." In desperation she twisted around to McCoy. "He *is* the Captain, Doctor! I couldn't just—" Her face tightened. "I couldn't *talk* to you!" she burst out at Kirk. "I had to fight you, scratch your face and kick and . . ."

"Yeoman Rand," Kirk said. He went over to her, pretending not to notice how she shrank from his approach. "Look at me! Look at my face! Do you see any scratches on it?"

"No, sir," she whispered.

"I have been in my quarters, Yeoman. How could I have been with you and in my own quarters at one and the same time?"

She wrung her hands. "But—" Her voice broke. "I know what happened. And it *was* you. I—I don't want to get you into trouble. I wouldn't even have mentioned it if technician Fisher hadn't seen you, too, and . . ."

"Yeoman," Kirk said, "it wasn't *me!*"

She began to cry. She looked very small, very young in her rumpled uniform. Kirk reached out a compassionate hand to her shoulder—but she shied away from his touch as though it might burn her.

Spock said, "You can go now, Yeoman."

Sobbing, she got to her feet. As she reached the door, Kirk said, "Yeoman." She stopped. "*It was not me,*" he repeated. But she went on out the door without looking back.

Spock broke the silence. "Captain, there is an impostor aboard this ship."

It was to be expected from Spock. Faith to the end—that was Spock. Kirk pulled his uniform collar away from his neck as though it were choking him. After a moment he went to the door of Sickbay's treatment room where McCoy had gone back to work on the battered Fisher. He was busy, of course; too busy with Fisher to look at him. But the prone Fisher looked at him from the sheeted table—and in his eyes there was open scorn.

The intercom buzzed; and Scott said, "Captain, can we see you in the Transporter Room for a minute?"

Kirk took the scalding memory of Fisher's look with him. If Spock hadn't silently joined him, he wondered if he'd have found the courage to respond to Scott's call. Had he, too, heard the interesting details of his Captain's recent activities? But Scott's total concern seemed to be the still defective Transporter. He looked up from the console as Kirk entered. "It's a complete breakdown, Captain." He turned his head to say to his technicians, "Continue circuit testing." The meek, doglike creature collected from the planet was lying beside the console. Scott pointed to it. "We beamed this animal up to the ship, sir, and . . ."

"And what?" Kirk said.

Scott paused. "The animal is here. But it's also over there in that specimen case."

He left the console to go over to the case with Kirk and Spock. A fierce growl greeted them. Scott cautiously lifted the lid. The beast inside bared its teeth, its lips flecked with the foam of its fury. Scott hastily dropped the lid over its leap at them.

"It appears to be the twin of the other animal," Spock said slowly. "Except for the difference in temperament, they might be one and the same."

Scott had hurried back to the console to pick up the quiet creature. Stroking it, he said, "A few seconds after they sent this one up through the Transporter, that duplicate of it appeared on the platform. If this had happened to a man—it's some kind of opposite."

The intentness on Kirk's face was naked. Scott went on. "One beast gentle like this—and one savage, wolfish, this one and *that* one—some kind of ferocious *opposite*. Captain, till we know what's gone wrong with the Transporter, we dare not use it to beam up the landing party!"

"Oh, my God . . ."

The whisper was wrenched from Kirk by the force of sudden revelation. It was no impostor who was loose on the *Enterprise*. What was loose on it was his own counterpart—the dark, brutish aspect of human nature which every mortal carries within him from birth to the grave. His Cain was roaming the *Enterprise* in a mindless, murderous search for a vengeance that would appease the bitterness of years of denial—the years it had spent as a prisoner of conscience, of duty, of responsibility. Somehow it had got free from its embodiment in him, and wearing his face, using his voice, wandering his ship, had found its release.

He gradually became conscious of Spock's eyes. The Vulcan had taken the lamb-gentle animal into his arms. Something in the way he held it stilled the turmoil in Kirk's soul. He was able to speak.

"Do you know what caused the animal to divide in two, Scotty?"

"We think we do, sir. When Fisher came up, his clothes were splashed with some soft, yellowish stuff. He said it was ore. Some of it fell on the Transporter platform. When we scanned it, we found it contained unknown magnetic elements. Maybe it caused an overload. We can't tell—not yet."

"Is the Transporter working at all?"

"Yes, sir. But to use it to bring up the landing party—they might all be duplicated like you—" He caught himself. "Like the animal, Captain."

So Scott *had* heard. "How long will it take to locate the trouble?"

"Can't say, sir."

Kirk fought for calm, for reason. "We can't just leave those four men down there. They'll freeze to death. At night that planet's temperature sinks to 250 degrees below zero."

"We're doing everything we can, Captain!"

Kirk looked at the Transporter platform. What was the secret it refused to divulge? He'd emerged from it whole, unsplit, a thousand times. Why not this last time? *What had happened?* When and how had he been divided in two halves like a one-celled organism reproducing itself? The whirling in his head was back once more. And the platform looked back at him, empty, its secret still withheld.

Spock had come to stand beside him. "About this double of yours, Captain."

Kirk started like a man aroused from nightmare. "Yes, we've got to find him. Search parties, Mr. Spock—we've got to organize search parties."

"We can't risk killing it," Spock said. "We have no data—no way of knowing the effect of its death on you."

So Spock understood. "Yes, that's right," Kirk said. "We don't know that—but the men must be armed. All men to be armed with phasers locked to the stun setting. He's to be taken without—if anyone fires to kill, he won't die—it's not the way to get rid of him..."

Spock noted the breaks between thoughts and words. They were disjointed, disorganized. No, there was no doubt. This Kirk was not the integrated, decisive Kirk he knew.

"It will be difficult to order the search parties to capture a being who so closely resembles you, Captain."

"Tell them—" Kirk looked at him helplessly. "I'd better make an announcement to the entire crew—tell them what's happened as well as I can. It's a good crew—they deserve to be told."

"I must object, sir," Spock said. "You are the Captain of this ship. You cannot afford to appear vulnerable in the eyes of your crew. It is your damnable fate to have to seem perfect to them. I'm sorry, sir. Yet that is the fact. They lose their confidence in you—and you lose your command."

Kirk pressed his forehead between his hands. "I know that, Mr. Spock. Why did I forget it?" He turned away, then stopped without looking back. "If you see me slipping again, your order is to *tell* me so."

"Yes, Captain."

His back stiff, Kirk walked out of the Transporter Room. In the bridge he touched the back of his command chair before he took his position in it. Command—no weakness, no fault, no hesitation. Bracing himself for the front of perfection, he flicked on his intercom. "This is the Captain speaking. There is an impostor aboard this ship—a man who looks exactly like me and is pretending to *be* me. The man is dangerous. Utmost caution is to be observed. All crew members are to arm themselves. The impostor may be identified by scratches on his face."

The message reached the double. It sat up quickly on Kirk's bed. "Repeat," came the voice from the intercom. "The impostor may be identified by scratches on his face. Search parties will report to Mr. Spock for assignment. All hand phasers will be set to stun force. The impostor is not to be injured. Repeat. The impostor is not to be injured."

The double touched the scratches on its face. Then it got up to go to the mirror and stare at its reflection. "Impostor!" it muttered to itself. *"I'm Kirk!"* it shouted at Kirk's image on the intercom viewing screen. A gust of fury shook it. It seized a metal box from the dresser and hurled it at the screen. The sound of crashing glass frightened it. "I'm Kirk," it whimpered to its reflection in the mirror. The scratches showed red, unhealed. To examine them more closely, it pushed aside a jar of medicated cream. The loosened lid fell off. The double dug its fingers into the cream, looked once more at the scratches and began to rub the cream into them. It made them feel better. It also hid the weals. The double grunted with satisfaction. It was dabbing more of the concealing cream into the cuts when it heard running sounds from the corridor outside.

When the sounds had gone, it unlocked the door. Moving out into the working area of Kirk's quarters, it slid its entrance panel half open. Wilson, carrying some Transporter equipment, was hurrying down the corridor.

"Wilson!" the double called. "Come here!"

Wilson came.

"Give me your weapon belt!"

"Yes, sir."

As he handed over the belt, Wilson saw the smeared cream on its face. But his suspicion came too late. The double had the phaser out of the belt. It struck him on the jaw with its butt. When Wilson fell, it stooped to pound his jaw with the heavy butt. Then it dragged him into Kirk's cabin. The bloody phaser still in hand, it nodded to itself—and walked casually out into the corridor.

Down on the planet's surface it was growing dark. Sulu and his three crewmen were gathering rocks to erect a wall against the rising wind. Frost had already whitened the dismal landscape as far as they could see.

Over his communicator, Kirk said, "Mr. Sulu, how is the rock shelter coming?"

"It's a compliment to these rocks, sir, to call them a shelter. It's down to 50 below zero now, Captain."

They were not equipped with thermal clothing. It was hard to say, "Kirk out." He might better have said, "Kirk down and out." That was the truth. In his command chair, he had to steady himself against another attack of vertigo. "We've got to get those men up!" he said to Spock. But Spock was taking a report from one of his search parties. "Deck 5 Sections 2 and 3 completely covered now, sir. Result, negative. Proceeding to Sections 4 and 5."

"Acknowledged," Spock said and flicked off his audio—but only to flick it on again to another intercom call.

"Search party number eight, sir. Transporter technician Wilson has just been found crawling out of the Captain's cabin. He's been badly beaten. He says the impostor attacked him, called him by his name and took his phaser."

The Enemy Within

"Get him to Sickbay," Spock said. "Then continue your search."

"We must locate this—this opposite of mine before he—" Kirk broke off. "But how, Spock, how?"

"It is apparent, sir, that it possesses your knowledge of the ship, its crew and devices. That being so, perhaps we can foresee its next move. Knowing how this ship is constructed, where would *you* go to elude a mass search, Captain?"

For the first time since his disaster, Kirk spoke without hesitation. "The lower level. The Engineering deck. Let's go!"

In the elevator Spock removed his phaser from his belt. Without looking at Kirk, he said, "I'm setting this, not to the kill cycle, but to the stun one, sir. What about your phaser?" Kirk took the hint; and Spock said, "The thing is dangerous. Don't you think we'll need some help if we find it?"

The torture of indecision was back. Finally Kirk said, "No. If we find him, I don't want anyone else around but you." He had stepped out of the elevator when Spock called, "*Captain!*"

Kirk turned.

Spock said, "You ordered me to tell you . . ."

"I said *no*, Mr. Spock. No one but you."

The lower level of the Engineering deck held the vast complex that powered the *Enterprise*. It was a cavern of shadows, broken by glints of gleaming machinery, its passageways narrowing, widening, narrowing again to crisscross other passages. The droning hum of its huge nuclear energizers reverberated against its metal walls. Suddenly, as he rounded a dynamo, Spock realized he was alone. He turned to retrace his steps in hope of locating Kirk again.

Kirk, unaware he had lost Spock, looked at the phaser he held at the ready. The sight of it repelled him. A suicide weapon was what it was. The life it would fell was part of his own. He replaced the phaser in his belt.

And his Cain saw him do it. Crouched between two power generators, the double had heard his approaching footsteps. Its features tensed with its curious mixture of fear and ferocity. Its phaser aimed, it moved away from its shelter for a full confrontation.

Kirk stopped dead. As he recognized his own face in the Other's face, a chill passed over him. This nameless Thing belonged to him more utterly than any name his parents had given him. The two Kirks stared at each other in a kind of trance. Then, as though he were drawn by a power as unknown as it was powerful, Kirk stepped toward his double. It raised its phaser.

Kirk spoke. His voice sounded strange in his own ears. It was solemn with the prophetic tone of a mystic suddenly endowed with an incontrovertible truth. "You must not hurt me," he said. "You must not kill me. You can live only as long as I live."

Uncertainty flickered over the double's face; and Kirk, in a kind of dream, knew he was seeing the reflection of his own new uncertainty.

Then the hesitation faded. "*I don't need you!*" the double said. "I don't have to believe what you say. So I *can* kill you!"

Its finger was on the kill trigger. Leaping, the momentum of his leap lending force to his clenched fist, Spock lunged from behind the generator to land it, hammerlike, on the double's chin. It fell. Its phaser fired, the beam striking a machine unit behind Kirk. It flared into glow and collapsed.

Spock looked down at the sprawled double. "I fear," he said, "that the ministrations of Dr. McCoy will be needed."

The fear was well-founded. Consciousness was reluctant to return to the double. Each in his different way anxious, Kirk and Spock watched McCoy as he stooped over the still figure in its bed. McCoy worked silently. After a moment, Kirk went to the viewing screen. Turning it on to Engineering, he said, "What about those Transporter circuits, Scotty? They're all checked through now, aren't they?"

"Yes, sir. And we thought we'd corrected the trouble. But now something else has gone wrong."

"*What?*" Kirk demanded.

"We don't know, sir. We're working on it. Is that all, Captain?"

Once more Kirk was unable to rally either a yes or a no. There was an uncomfortable pause. Finally Scott said, "Then I'd better get back to work, sir."

It would be darker on the planet. Kirk cried out, "Find out what's wrong, Scott! And fix it in God's name! Four human lives are depending on that Transporter!"

Scott said stiffly, "We're doing our best, sir."

Kirk leaned his forehead against the frame of the viewing screen. "I know, Scotty. You always do your best. Keep me posted, will you?"

"Yes, sir." The voice had relaxed.

Over at the bed, McCoy had completed his examination. "How is—he?" Kirk asked.

"Pulse and blood pressure high," McCoy said. He glanced at Spock. "Probably due to that sock on the chin."

"It was necessary, Doctor."

"This—creature will be recovering consciousness soon. As I have no idea at all about its mental state, I can't give it a tranquilizer. I think we'd better bind it."

He looked at Kirk for authorization. Kirk was suddenly oppressed by a sense of suffocation. The heavy tonnage of command responsibility seemed to be crushing him. He shook his head to try and clear it of the dizziness. "Yes," he said, "all right. I just wish someone would tell me what's the matter with *me*."

"You are losing the power of decision, Captain," Spock said.

"What?"

McCoy was busy binding the double but not so busily that he couldn't direct a glare at Spock. But the Vulcan continued, cool and unruffled. "Judging from my observations," he said, "you are rapidly losing your capacity for action. There's hesitation in time of crises—loss of perception. Captain, you refuse to defend yourself. You refused to demand adequate assistance when we went down to the Engineering level whereas you should have placed yourself in guarded isolation until the impostor was captured." He paused. "You have dismissed men for less hesitation, less passivity in the face of danger."

"Make your point, Spock!" shouted McCoy.

"Point?"

"You *have* one, I presume," McCoy said.

"I am analyzing, Doctor; not point-making."

"It's the Captain's guts you're analyzing! Are you aware of that, Mr. Spock?"

"Vituperation, Doctor?"

Composed, unmoved, Spock went on. "The dichotomies inherent in the human mind are multiple," he said. "The problem of command, for instance, highly pertinent in this case. Command is a balance between positive and negative energies—an equilibrium of the forces generated by each of these energies. The proof?"

He turned to Kirk. "Your negative energy was removed from you by that duplication process. Thus, the power of command has begun to fail you. Things remaining as they are, how long can you continue to function as Captain of this ship? Finally unable to decide anything at all, will you . . ."

McCoy broke in. "Jim, give him a command! Tell him to get lost!"

"If I seem emotionally insensitive to the agony of your ordeal, Captain, please understand. It's the way I am."

"That's for damned sure!" yelled McCoy.

"*Gentlemen*," Kirk said. In the end, always in the end, one's pain remained a private matter. The scene, however dismal, was always enacted alone. He smiled wryly at them. "I may be losing my ability to command but it hasn't entirely disappeared. Until it does, you will both kindly knock it off."

The intercom on McCoy's desk whirred. Kirk flicked it on. "Kirk here."

"Engineering, sir. We've just located that new trouble with the Transporter. Its Ionizer Unit has been mangled. Looks as if a phaser beam had hit it."

The double's phaser beam had hit it, the double, that separated part of himself. If his crewmen died their lonely death on the subarctic planet beneath him, it would be he, Kirk, their trusted Captain who had killed them.

He got up to walk to the door. "If I'm needed," he said, "I'll be in the Briefing Room."

They had lit a fire down on the planet. Black night was spreading toward them from its horizon. And the stealthy fronds of frost were creeping over the rocks of the rock shelter where the abandoned crewmen huddled together for warmth. Sulu, his lips cracked and sore, had to hold his hands over the fire before his fingers could manipulate his communicator. "Can you give us a status report, *Enterprise*? It's fallen to 90 degrees below zero down here."

"This is the Captain, Mr. Sulu. We have located the trouble. It shouldn't be much longer."

"Think you could rig up a cord, sir, and lower us down a pot of coffee?"

"I'll see what I can do about that," Kirk said.

"Rice wine will do, sir, if you're short of coffee."

"I'll check the commissariat for rice wine, Mr. Sulu." And once more it had to be "Kirk out."

He watched his hand reach out to the intercom button. He was afraid to call Scott. He pressed the button. "That mangled unit, Scotty. Status report."

"Nothing much of it left, sir."

"How bad is it?"

"We can't repair it in less than a week."

A week. One hundred and sixty-eight hours. Death by cold was said to be preceded by sleep. Alone in the Briefing Room, Kirk realized that imagination had become his mortal enemy. It showed him the planet's surface under the deadly grip of its incredible cold, its night ominous with the coming sleep of death as the blood in his men's veins turned to ice. They'd be moving slowly now if they could move at all . . .

Reality endorsed imagination. Sulu was slowed to a crawl as he elbowed himself to the dying warmth to check his phaser. He fired it at another boulder. It burst into glow. The others inched toward it; and Sulu made his frost-blackened lips say, "That rice wine is taking too long. I'm giving Room Service another call."

Nobody spoke as he opened his communicator. "*Enterprise*, this is Sulu."

"Kirk here, Mr. Sulu."

"Hot line direct to the Captain again. Are we that far gone, sir?"

Kirk struck the Briefing Room table with his fist. "Everybody but you's got the afternoon off. I'm watching the store. How is it down there?"

"Lovely," Sulu said. "We're using our phasers to heat the rocks. One phaser's quit on us. Three are still operational. Any chance of getting us aboard before the skiing season opens down here?"

The ice—maybe it would be merciful, quick. *Think*. But he couldn't think. His thoughts like comets that would not be stayed flashed through his mind—and were gone . . .

He felt no surprise to see Spock quietly lift the speaker he had dropped.

"This is Spock, Mr. Sulu. You will hold out a little longer. *Hold out*. Survival procedures, Mr. Sulu."

"As per your training program, Mr. Spock."

"Yes, Mr. Sulu."

Kirk reached for the speaker. "Sulu—just don't drift, don't lose—awareness. Sulu, beware of sleep . . ."

As Spock said, "Spock out," Kirk felt an irresistible impulse to return to Sickbay. He wasn't entirely composed of that atavism that had destroyed the Ionizer Unit. He was Captain James T. Kirk of the Starship *Enterprise*, too—and he was going back to Sickbay. Courage was doing what you were afraid to do.

The consciousness that had come back to the double was a thing of howling panic. It was thrusting madly against the net of cords that held it, the force of its screams swelling the veins of its neck. As he watched the writhing body on the bed, it seemed to Kirk that he could taste the acid of its frenzy in his mouth. How he knew what he knew he didn't know; but he knew that the double was feeling some ultimate terror it had met in the black labyrinth of its Cain fate.

"It should be calming down," McCoy said, laying a hypodermic aside. "This tranquilizer should be working now." He threw a worried glance at the body function panel. All its readings showed a dangerous peak.

The tormented body on the bed strained again at its bonds. A shudder shook it. Then, suddenly, it collapsed, its head lolling like a broken doll's.

"What's happened?" Kirk cried. The readings on the body-function panel were rapidly falling.

"The tranquilizer was a mistake," McCoy said. "Its system has rejected it."

"He's not—*dying*?" Kirk said.

McCoy spoke tonelessly. "Yes, it is."

"No," Kirk whispered. "No." He reached for McCoy's arm. "I can't survive without him and he can't survive without me."

McCoy shook his head; and the double moaned. "Afraid, afraid," it said.

Kirk went to it. "Help me," it wept. "I am afraid—so afraid."

Kirk took its hand. McCoy started forward. "Jim, you'd better not . . ."

Kirk stooped over the bed. "Don't be afraid. This is my hand. Feel it. Hold on to it. That's it. Hang on to my hand. I won't let you go."

"Afraid," whimpered the double painfully.

Some strength rose up from unknown depths in Kirk. It was as though he had lived through just such a scene before. The words that came to him seemed familiar. "You must hold on to me because we've been pulled apart. Come back! No, you're letting go! Hold on to me. Tight! Tighter!"

He lifted the sheet to wipe the sweat from its forehead. "I'm pulling you back to me. We need each other! That's it. *Tight!* We have to hang on—together . . ."

McCoy, at the body-function panel, looked around, astounded. But all Kirk saw were the tragic eyes fixed on his in abject dependence. "No fear," he said. "You can come back. You are not afraid. *You are not afraid.* Be back with me. Be back, be back, be back . . ."

McCoy touched his shoulder. "Jim, it *is* back."

Kirk stumbled over to McCoy's desk, slumping into its chair. "Now *you* can use some brandy," McCoy said.

He gagged on the drink. Eyes shut, he said, "I must take him back—into myself. I don't want to, Bones—a brutish, mindless wolf in human shape. But I must. He is me, *me*!"

"Jim, don't take this so hard," McCoy said. "We are all part wolf and part lamb. We need both parts. Compassion is reconciliation between them. It is human to be both lamb and wolf."

"Human?" Kirk asked bitterly.

"Yes, *human*. Some of his wolfishness makes you the man you are. God forbid that I should ever agree with Spock—but he was right! Without the strength of the wolf in you, you could not command this ship! And without the lamb in you, your discipline would be harsh and cruel. Jim, you just used the lamb to give life back to that dying wolf . . ."

The double was listening, concentrated.

The intercom buzzed. Drained, Kirk said, "Kirk here."

"Spock, sir. Will you come to the Transporter Room? We think we may have found an answer."

"I'm on my way," Kirk said. He turned to McCoy. "Thanks, Bones. And keep your fingers crossed."

"Tell Mr. Spock I'm shaking all my rattles to invoke good spirits."

But as the door closed behind Kirk, there came a cry from the bed. *"No!"* The startled McCoy went to the bed. The double was sitting up. It said quietly, "No. *Everything is under control right now.*"

In the Transporter Room, Wilson was holding the mild doglike creature.

"What's that answer you think you've found?" Kirk asked.

"A way to make the Transporter safe, sir," Scott said. "We have attached some temporary bypass and leader circuits to compensate for the velocity variation. There shouldn't be more than a five-point difference in speed balance."

"Our suggestion is that we send the two animals through the Transporter," Spock said.

So that was the answer—hope that amendment in the Transporter would somehow rejoin the two halves of the animal as it had somehow cut them apart. It was hoped that his dying men could be beamed home to the *Enterprise* without risk of the fatal division. Hope. Well, without it, you couldn't live.

"All right," Kirk said. "Go ahead."

Spock took the hypodermic from the top of the Transporter console. He nodded at Scott. The Chief Engineer went to the specimen case and lifted its lid. "I'll grab it by the scruff of its neck and hold it as still as I can." He reached into the case. The snarling beast twisted and writhed against Scott's grip on its neck.

"Don't hurt it!" Kirk cried.

Injecting the shot, Spock said, "It's painless, Captain, quick. The animal will lose consciousness for only the few, necessary moments." The snarls subsided. Spock took the creature from Scott and carried it to the Transporter platform where Wilson was waiting with the other one. They laid them on the platform, side by side. Scott, at the console, said, "If this doesn't work—" He broke off at Spock's signal. He turned a dial. The platform flared into glow. The two animals vanished and the glow faded.

"Energize to reverse," Spock said.

Scott twisted a dial. The platform flared into light again. The two animals reappeared—and the light dimmed.

Spock ran to the console. He made some adjustment of dials. "Again," he said to Scott. The process was repeated. The energizing dial was reversed. The platform broke into dazzle. As it shaped itself into substance, McCoy came in.

One animal lay on the platform.

"It's dead," Kirk said.

"Not so fast, Jim," McCoy said.

Kirk waited while he checked the limp body for heart-beat. There was none. Into the silence Spock said, "The shock—the shock of reabsorption . . ."

Kirk stumbled out of the Transporter Room.

Later, in Sickbay, McCoy gave tentative support to Spock's diagnosis of the cause of the death. Straightening up from the table that held the dead beast, he said, "Maybe it *was* the shock of reabsorption that killed it. But it would take a post mortem before we could even approach certainty."

"Why shock?" Kirk asked.

"We're only guessing, Jim."

"Yes, I know. But you've both used the word shock."

"The consequence of instinctive fear," Spock said. "The animal lacked the ability to understand the process of reabsorption. Its fear was so great it induced shock. Other conditions that cause shock are not apparent." He was carefully examining the creature. "You yourself can see, sir, that the body is quite undamaged."

Kirk was groping for some answer of his own. "*He*—in that bed in there—felt great fear." He turned to McCoy. "You saw him feel it. But he survived it. He *survived* it!"

"Just by a hairsbreadth," McCoy reminded him. "I can hear it coming, Jim. You want to take this double of yours through the Transporter with you—you and it, *with* it. No, Jim, *no*!"

"Four of my men are freezing to death," Kirk said.

"But there isn't one genuine shred of evidence to prove this animal died of fear! Shock? Yes. But fear? That's mere theory!"

"Based on the laws of probability," Spock said.

"Probability be hanged!" McCoy shouted. "It's Jim's life that's at stake! And all of a sudden you're an expert on fear! That's a base emotion, Mr. Spock. What do you know about it?"

"I must remind you, Doctor, that I am half human," Spock said. "I am more aware than you of what it means to live with a divided spirit—of the suffering involved in possession of two separate selves. I survive it daily."

"That may be—but a piece of machinery is the problem. What do the laws of probability say about the Transporter? Is it reliable? You don't know! It's just more theory, more hopeful guesswork!"

Kirk said, "I am going through the Transporter with him."

McCoy threw up his arms in a gesture of hopelessness. "You've got more guts than brains, Jim! Use your head, for God's sake!"

"I'm getting my four men back on this ship," Kirk said. "And we can't risk using that Transporter until we know whether this animal died of fear—or mechanical malfunction in the Transporter."

"I want to save the men, too, Jim! But you're more vital to this ship than four crew members. That's the brutal truth—and you know it!"

Listening, Kirk felt his weakened will sink to its final depth of hesitation. "I have to—try. I must be allowed to try. If I don't try, their death is sure. So will mine be. I shall look alive, Bones. But I shall live as a half man. What good to this ship is a half man Captain?"

"Jim, do me one favor. Before you decide, let me run an autopsy on this animal."

"Delay is too expensive," Kirk said.

"At least give Spock more time to test the Transporter. And let me get the lab started on the autopsy." McCoy gathered up the dead animal in a sheet. "Wait, Jim, please wait." He hurried out of Sickbay.

Spock said, "I'll put the Transporter through another check-out cycle as soon as the Doctor returns."

Kirk whirled on him. "I don't need nursemaids, Mr. Spock!"

"As soon as the Doctor returns." The six words too many, Spock thought. The weakened will had finally steeled itself to decision only to meet doubt, argument, pressure. Those last six words had been a mistake.

"If you will excuse me, Captain," he said.

Kirk nodded. He watched Spock go. Half human, Spock—but you never came to the end of his aware humanity. Gratitude heartened him to do what he had to do. He was turning toward Sickbay's bed section when Sulu's voice sounded from the wall speaker.

"Kirk here, Mr. Sulu."

The voice was a whisper. "Captain—the rocks are cold—no phasers left—one of us is unconscious—we can't hold out much longer." The communicator crackled. "Captain—the cold is freezing the communicator—no time left—no time . . ."

The whisper fell silent. There was another crackle from the dead communicator. Kirk sank down on the double's bed. Four lives at risk on the fatal planet—two lives at risk in the Transporter process. There was no alternative.

The double spoke fearfully. "What are you going to do?"

Kirk didn't answer. He began to untie the cords of the restraining net over the bed. The double reached out and touched the phaser at his belt. "You don't need that," it said. "I'm not going to fight you any more. What are you going to do?"

"We are going through the Transporter together," Kirk said.

The double tensed. Then it controlled itself. "If that's what you want," it said.

"It's what I have to want," Kirk said. He untied the last cord, stepped back and raised his phaser. Staggering, the double got up. Then it leaned back against the bed for support. "I feel so weak," it said. "I'll be glad when this is over."

"Let's go," Kirk said.

The double moved toward the door; but on its first step it faltered, groaning. It tried again, staggered again—and Kirk instinctively reached out to help it. It saw its chance. Lunging, it drove its shoulder into Kirk, knocking him backward. The phaser dropped. It stooped for it. Recovering his balance, Kirk shouted, "No, no, you can't . . ."

The phaser butt crashed into the side of his head. He fell back on the bed. The double paused to finger the scratches on its face. McCoy's medication covered them. It smiled to itself. Then it began to strap Kirk into the bed. "I'm *you*," it told him.

Swaggering, it walked out into the corridor. At its end the elevator door slid open. Janice Rand was standing inside it. At once it tempered its swagger to a quiet walk.

"How are you, Yeoman Rand?"

"Captain," the girl said nervously.

It smiled at her. "Is that a question? No, I am not the impostor. Are you feeling better?"

"Yes, sir. Thank you."

"Good."

Maybe it was her opportunity, Janice thought. She'd done this man a grave injustice. "Captain" she said, "I've wanted to apologize. If I caused you . . ."

She got Kirk's own grin. "That's a big word—'if.' I understand, Yeoman. I hope you do. I owe you, I think, a personal explanation."

"No," she said. "It's I who owe you . . ."

"Let's call it a clarification, then," the double said. "I trust your discretion. There was no impostor, not really. The Transporter malfunctioned. It seems to have created a duplicate of me. It's hard to understand because we haven't yet determined what went wrong. But what we *do* know I'll explain to you later. You're entitled to that. All right?"

Bewildered, she nodded. "All right, sir."

The elevator door opened. Politely, the double stepped back, gesturing her forward. As the elevator moved on up to the bridge deck, it shouted with laughter. Slamming its hand against the elevator wall, it yelled, "*My* ship! Mine—all mine!"

The sight of Kirk's command chair intoxicated it. As it settled back into it, a frowning Farrell spoke from the navigation console. "No word from Mr. Sulu, Captain."

It ignored the comment; and Spock, hurrying over to the command chair, said, "Captain, I couldn't find you in the Transporter Room."

"I changed my mind," the double said. "Take your station, Mr. Spock." It didn't look at the Vulcan.

Spock walked slowly back to his computer. It was a very sudden change of mind for a mind that had struggled so valiantly for decision.

"Prepare to leave orbit, Mr. Farrell!"

If the order had commanded activation of the Destruct unit, its impact could not have been more devastating. Farrell stared in stark unbelief. The double became abruptly aware that every eye in the bridge was fixed on it.

"Captain—" Farrell began.

"I gave you an order, Mr. Farrell."

"I know, sir, but what—what about . . . ?"

"*They can't be saved. They're dead now.*" Its voice rose. "Prepare to leave orbit, Mr. Farrell!"

"Yes, sir." Farrell's hand was moving toward a switch when the elevator opened. Kirk and McCoy stepped out of it. There were badly covered scratches on Kirk's face but the hand that held the phaser was steady. The double leaped from the command chair. "There's the impostor," it shouted. "Grab him!"

Nobody moved.

"You are the impostor," McCoy said.

"Don't believe him!" the double shrieked. "Take them both! Grab them!"

Kirk, McCoy beside him, walked on toward the command chair. Spock, reaching out a hand, halted McCoy, shaking his head. McCoy nodded—and Kirk moved on, alone.

"You want me dead, don't you? You want this ship all to yourself! But it's *mine*!"

Farrell had jumped from his chair. Spock touched his shoulder. "This is the Captain's private business," he said.

Kirk maintained his slow advance toward the maddened thing. It backed up, slow step by slow step, screaming.

"I am Captain Kirk, you ship of pigs! All right, let the liar destroy you all! He's already killed four of you! I run this ship! I own it. I own you—all of you!"

Kirk fired his phaser. The double crumpled to the deck, stunned.

"Spock, Bones," he said quietly. "Quickly, please."

Kirk had already taken up his position on the Transporter platform when they laid the unconscious body at his feet.

"You'll have to hold it, Captain," Spock said.

Kirk sat down on the platform. He lifted the drooping head to his shoulder, an arm around the flaccid waist. Then he looked up.

"Mr. Spock..."

"Yes, sir."

"If this doesn't work..."

"Understood, sir."

"Jim!" McCoy burst out. "Jim, don't do it! Not yet! In God's name, wait!"

"The console, Mr. Spock," Kirk said.

Spock's half-human part had taken him over. This could be good-bye to Kirk. At the console, he bowed his head over his treacherously shaking hands. When he lifted it, his face was calm, impassive.

"I am energizing, sir."

He saw Kirk draw the double closer to him. In the glow that lit the platform, he knew that he was seeing the embrace of an acknowledged, irrevocable brotherhood. Unfaltering, Spock reversed the console's controls. The hum of dematerialization rose. There was dazzle—and silence.

McCoy ran to the platform. Kirk stood on it, alone.

"Jim—Jim?" McCoy cried.

"Hello, Bones," Kirk said. He walked off the empty platform and over to the console. "Mr. Spock," he said, "let's get those men of ours up and aboard."

Spock swallowed. "Yes, Captain. At once, sir."

It wasn't done at once. It was twenty minutes before the Transporter platform surrendered its burden of the four bodies to the eager hands awaiting them.

McCoy rose from his last examination. "They'll make it, Jim. Those rocks they heated saved their lives. They're all suffering from severe frostbite—but I think they'll make it."

The pallor of Kirk's face suddenly struck him. "How do *you* feel, Jim?"

There was a new sadness in Kirk's smile. "What's that old expression? 'Sadder but wiser.' I feel sadder, Bones, but much less wise."

"Join the human race, Jim," McCoy said.

There was a sense of quiet thanksgiving as Kirk entered the bridge. His first move was over to Spock at the computer station. "You know, of course," he said, "I could never have made it without you."

"Thank you, Captain. What do you plan to tell the crew?"

"The truth, Mr. Spock—that the impostor was put back where he belongs."

Janice Rand approached him. "I just wanted to say, Captain, how—glad I am that..."

"Thank you, Yeoman." Kirk returned to his command chair. The girl watched him go. Spock watched the girl.

"That impostor," he said, "had some very interesting qualities. And he certainly resembled the Captain. You agree, I'm sure, Yeoman Rand."

She had flushed scarlet. But she met his quizzical eyes with courage. "Yes, Mr. Spock. The impostor had some exceedingly interesting qualities."

WHAT ARE LITTLE GIRLS MADE OF?

WRITER: ROBERT BLOCH
DIRECTOR: JAMES GOLDSTONE
FIRST AIRED: OCTOBER 20, 1966

That day the efficiency of the *Enterprise* bridge personnel was a real tribute to their professionalism. For a human drama was nearing its climax among them, the closer they came to the planet Exo III.

Its heroine was the starship's chief nurse, Christine Chapel. She stood beside Kirk at his command chair, her eyes on the main viewing screen where the ice-bound planet was slowly rotating. Touched by the calm she was clearly struggling to maintain, he said, "We're now entering standard orbit, Nurse."

A flicker of her nervous anticipation passed over her face. "I know he's alive down there, Captain," she said.

Kirk said, "Five years have passed since his last message." It seemed only decent to remind this brave, loving, though perhaps vainly hoping woman of that sinister fact. But she answered him with firm certainty. "I know, sir. But Roger is a very determined man. He'd find some way to live."

Uhura spoke from her panel. "Beginning signals to surface, Captain."

"Run it through all frequencies, Lieutenant." Kirk rose to go and check the library computer screen. Spock, concentrated on it, said, "Ship's record banks show little we don't already know. Gravity of the planet one point one of Earth, sir. Atmosphere within safety limits."

"But surface temperatures are close to a hundred degrees below zero," Kirk said.

Spock, too, was conscious of the woman who was patiently awaiting her moment of truth. He lowered his voice. "It may have been inhabited once, but the sun in this system has been steadily fading for half a million years." He hit a switch. "Now for Doctor Korby, the hero of our drama, Captain . . ."

Onto the computer screen flashed a small photograph of a distinguished-looking man in his vital mid-forties. There was a printed caption beneath it and Spock read it aloud. "Doctor Roger Korby, often called the 'Pasteur of archaeological medicine.' His translation of medical records salvaged from the Orion ruins revolutionized immunization techniques . . ."

"Those records were required reading at the Academy, Mr. Spock. I've always wanted to meet him." Kirk paused. Then, he, too, lowered his voice. "Any chance at all that he could still be alive?"

Grave-faced, Spock shook his head. He switched off the photograph; and Uhura, as though confirming his negative opinion, called, "No return signal, Captain. Not on any frequency."

"One more try, Lieutenant." Kirk returned to the waiting woman who had heard Uhura's report. She said, "His last signal told about finding underground caverns . . ."

Her implication was only too obvious. Korby had sheltered in the caverns so deeply no signal could reach him. He was safe. He *was* still alive. Kirk, remembering how it is to be tortured by a hopeless hope, said gently, "Christine, since that last signal, two expeditions have failed to find him."

Uhura, making her second report, called, "I've run all frequencies twice now, Captain. There's no—" A blast of static crackled from all the bridge speakers. It subsided—and a male voice, strong, resonant spoke. "This is Roger Korby," it said. "Come in, *Enterprise*. Repeating, this is Roger Korby . . ."

Christine swayed. Reaching for the support of Kirk's command chair, she whispered, "That's—his voice . . ."

It spoke again. "Do you read me, *Enterprise*? This is Doctor Roger Korby, standing by . . ."

Kirk seized his speaker. "*Enterprise* to Korby. Thank you. We have your landing coordinates pinpointed. Preparing to beam down a party." He smiled up at Christine. "It may interest you to know that we have aboard this vessel—"

Korby's voice interrupted. "I have a rather unusual request, Captain. Can you beam down alone, just yourself? We've made discoveries of such a nature that this extraordinary favor must be required of you."

Astounded, Kirk took refuge in silence. Spock joined him, torn between his respect for the great scientist and the unprecedented demand. Cocking a brow, he said, "Odd. To say the least . . ."

"The man who's asked this is Roger Korby," Kirk said.

Spock spoke to Christine. "You're quite certain you recognized the voice?"

She laughed out of her great joy. "Have you ever been engaged to be married, Mr. Spock? Yes, it's Roger."

Kirk made his decision. Hitting the speaker button, he said, "Agreed, Doctor. However, there will be *two* of us." He nodded to Christine, passing the speaker to her.

"Hello, Roger," she said.

There was a long pause. Then the unbelieving voice came. "Christine . . . ?"

"Yes, Roger. I'm up here."

"Darling, how . . . what are you . . ." The voice poured excited enthusiasm through the speaker. "Yes, by all means, ask the Captain to bring you with him! I had no idea, no hope . . . Darling, are you all right? It's almost too much to credit . . ."

"Yes, Roger," she said. "Everything's all right. Now everything is just fine."

The anxious tension on the bridge had given way to a sympathetic delight. Kirk, feeling it, too, recovered his speaker. "We're on our way, Doctor. Be with you soon, both of us. Kirk out."

He made for the bridge elevator, followed by the radiant Christine.

They materialized in a rock cave. It was primitive, unfurnished. Beyond its rough entrance there stretched an unending snow-world; a world as white as death under its dark and brooding sky. Its horizon was jagged, peaked by mountains. In the half-twilight of the planet's dying sun, Kirk could see that they were shrouded in ice, cold, forbidding. It was a depressing arrival.

"He said he'd be waiting for us," Christine said.

Kirk also found the absence of welcome strange. He went forward to peer deeper into the cavern; and Christine, touching one of its walls, hastily withdrew her chilled fingers. Kirk, cupping his hands to his mouth called into the darkness, "Doctor Korby! Korby!" The rebounding echoes suggested a long extension of distance beyond the cavern.

He was aware of a sudden uneasiness. "I suppose it's possible," he said, "that we hit the wrong cavern entry." But the supposition didn't hold up. The beamdown coordinates had been checked with Korby in the Transporter Room. And Spock was right. Korby's request *had* been odd. He detached his communicator from his belt. "Captain to *Enterprise*."

"Spock here, sir."

"Beam down a couple of security men," Kirk said.

"Any problems, Captain?"

"Some delay in meeting us, Mr. Spock. Probably nothing at all. Kirk out." He motioned to Christine to join him at a wall to leave the cave's center open for the beam-down. "Getting up here to us may be taking more time than the Doctor estimated," he told her. "The corridors of this place may go deeper than we know."

She said, "Thank you, Captain. I'm trying not to worry."

He felt distinct relief when crewmen Matthews and Rayburn sparkled into materialization. Spock had seen to it that they were both fully armed. "Maintain your position here in this cave, Rayburn." Turning to Matthews, he added, "Nurse Chapel and I are going to investigate a little further. You'll go with us."

They found the narrow passageway that led out of the cave. They found it by groping along a wall. It slanted downward. The inky blackness ahead of them endorsed what the echoes had suggested. The passageway could divide itself into many unseen and distant directions.

The light grew still dimmer. Abruptly, Kirk halted. "Stop where you are," he told the others. He stooped for a stone and flung it into what he'd sensed lay right before him—an abyss. They could hear the stone rebounding from rock walls. Then there was silence—absolute. Christine had clutched at Kirk's arm when a light beam suddenly blazed at them, blinding them in its searchlight glare. Kirk jerked his phaser out. As he shielded his eyes with his left hand, a figure stepped in front of the light, a featureless shadow.

Christine hurried forward. "Roger!"

Kirk grabbed at her. "Careful! That drop-down . . ."

The figure stepped to what must have been a light-switch panel. The glare faded to a fainter light that revealed the rather ordinary face of a middle-aged man. Christine stared at him in mixed surprise and disappointment. It wasn't Korby. Kirk adjusted his phaser setting and stepped up beside her just as recognition broke into her face.

"Why, it's Doctor Brown!" she exclaimed. "He's Roger's assistant!" Identifying the man for Kirk, she rushed toward him, crying, "Brownie, where's Roger? Why . . . ?"

She never finished her sentence. Behind them, Matthews shrieked, "Capt—! Ahh-hhhhhhhhhhhh . . . hhh . . ."

The scream died in the depths of the abyss. Then there was only the clatter of stones dislodged by Matthews' misstep.

Sickened, Kirk pulled himself out of his shock. He went to his knees, edging himself dangerously near to the pit's rim. Pebbles were still falling from it into the blackness below. Brown joined him. "Careful . . . please be careful," he said.

Kirk rose. "Is there any path down?"

"There's no hope, Captain. It's bottomless."

Though Doctor Brown had warned of peril from the pit, he did not mention the momentary appearance of a huge, hairless nonhuman creature on the other, shadowy side of the pit. Perhaps he didn't see it. It remained only for a second before it was gone, a monstrous shadow lost in shadows. Instead, he said sympathetically, if unhelpfully, "Your man must have slipped."

"Any chance of a projection? a ledge of some kind?"

"None, Captain. We lost a man down there, too. Listen . . ." He reached for a heavy boulder and heaved it over the pit's edge. There was the same crashing of rebound—and then the same absolute silence.

"Unfortunate," Brown said. "Terribly unfortunate. Doctor Korby was detained. I came as rapidly as I could."

"Not soon enough," Kirk said.

He looked at Brown in his worn lab clothing. One learned composure in the presence of human death, if you lived with its daily threat for five years. His voice had sounded regretful. Was he regretful? Was he composed? Or was he cold, numb to feeling? Kirk could see that the weeping Christine had also sensed a certain peculiarity in Brown's response to Matthews' death.

She wiped her eyes on her uniform sleeve. "Brownie," she said suddenly, "don't you recognize me?"

"Explain," Brown said.

"You don't recognize me" she said.

"Christine, you look well," Brown said. He turned to Kirk. "My name is Brown. I am Doctor Korby's assistant. I presume you are Captain Kirk."

Something was definitely askew. Christine had already named Brown as Korby's assistant. And the man had addressed Kirk as "Captain" several times. Why did he now have to "presume" that he was Captain Kirk? Christine's uncertainty was mounting, too. Her eyes and ears insisted that Brown was indeed her old acquaintance—but the feeling of an off-kilter element in his present personality persisted. Of course, Time and harsh experience *did* make changes in people . . .

Kirk had returned to the pit's edge. "He's dead, I assure you," Brown said. "Come. Doctor Korby will be waiting." He moved over to the searchlight panel to turn a couple of switches. Lights came on further along the corridor. Kirk walked back to Christine. "You do know him well, don't you? This Brown is the Brown you remember, isn't he?"

She hesitated. "I—I suppose existing alone here for so long . . ."

Kirk reached for his phaser. Then he snapped open his communicator. "Captain Kirk to Rayburn."

"All quiet here, Captain. Any problems there, sir?"

"We've lost Matthews. An accident, apparently. Tell the *Enterprise* to have a full security party stand by."

"Yes, sir."

"And inform Mr. Spock that we will both report in at hourly intervals. If you and I lose contact—or if he fails to hear from either of us—the security force is to be beamed down immediately. Kirk out."

He heard the snap-off of Rayburn's communicator. He couldn't hear what followed it—Rayburn's choking gurgle as the hairless creature's great arm lunged from the darkness to encircle his throat.

"This way, please," Brown was saying. "The illumination is automatic from here on."

It was a long walk. Brown appeared to feel a need to install himself as the interpreter of Korby's work. He dissertated. "The doctor has discovered that this planet's original inhabitants were forced to move underground as the warmth of their sun waned. When you were his student, Christine, you often heard him say that freedom of choice produced the human spirit. The culture of Exo III proved his theory. When its people were compelled to move from light to darkness, their culture also became choiceless, mechanistic. The doctor has found elements in it that will revolutionize the universe when removed from this cavernous environment."

The prediction struck Kirk as slightly grandiose. Polite Christine said, "That's fascinating."

"I thought you'd be interested," Brown said. "We have arrived, Captain."

The place of their arrival was a large and luxurious study. Though its walls were of rock, they were so finely polished they conveyed an impression of massive grandeur. Modern taste had been sensitively superimposed on the foundations constructed by the ancient race. In their five years of underground life, Korby and his staff had clearly undertaken to make themselves comfortable. And well supplied. There were huge cabinets of gleaming scientific instruments, archaeological tools, favorite artifacts found and cherished. Odd-looking doors led out of the room into other unseen ones. In one corner was a dining area complete with tables and chairs.

One of the doors opened. A girl came in, pale, slim, dark-haired. There was a serene innocence in her face that merited the word "lovely." Her lips moved in a smile that exposed her perfect teeth.

"I'm Andrea," she said. "You must be Christine. I've always thought it was a beautiful name."

Christine was unpleasantly startled. Youthfully innocent she might be, but the girl was nevertheless a woman. And why she was serving as hostess in Korby's personal study was a question his affianced wife was obviously asking herself.

Andrea was good at her job. She turned the lovely smile to Kirk. "And you must be Captain Kirk of the starship *Enterprise*. I can't tell you how we appreciate your bringing Roger's fiancée to him."

Christine stiffened at the use of Korby's first name. "I don't remember Doctor Korby's mentioning an 'Andrea' as a member of his staff."

The smile didn't waver. "You are exactly as Roger described you. No wonder he's missed you so."

Such awareness of Korby's intimate emotions did nothing to alleviate Christine's growing resentment. Kirk, conscious of it, said, "Where is Doctor Korby?"

"Here, Captain." A strong-faced man, easily seen to be the man of the *Enterprise* photograph, had emerged from another door. Kirk was absurdly reminded of a theatrical buildup to the star's entrance. That Korby *was* the star, there was no mistaking. Kirk, himself accustomed to command, recognized the self-assurance in another commander. Korby, his hand extended, said, "I've been looking forward to meeting you."

Kirk had lost a crewman to a brutal death. He didn't like Brown. Nor had he lost his heart to Andrea. Ignoring the hand, he contented himself with saying, "And I to meeting you, sir."

"Roger . . ." Christine said.

"Christine . . . darling . . ."

She went to him. He bent to kiss her outstretched hands. Kirk, still wary, saw the honest joy in both their faces. It was a reunion that recovered two relationships—

the intellectual bond of teacher and student, the bond of physical love between man and woman. Both loves still lived after all the years apart. So much was clear as they embraced—an embrace restrained in the others' presence but a double reunion that was real.

Christine lifted her head from his shoulder. Misty-eyed, she said, "I knew I'd find you."

He drew her back. "Forgive me, Captain. It's been a long time."

"There's no need to apologize, sir."

"The captain lost a man in the caverns, Doctor," Brown said.

There was no doubt of the horror on Korby's face. He released Christine to whirl on Brown. "What? How did it happen?"

"The pit near the outer junction. The edge must have given way."

Visibly shaken, Korby was silent. Then he spoke. "Captain, what can I say? I should have been there. I know the passages so well. I am sorry—so sorry."

"It isn't your fault, Doctor." Kirk had his communicator out. "Captain to Rayburn," he said. "Rayburn, report." As he waited for Rayburn's voice, he turned back to Korby. "I'll have to call my ship on a security confirmation. If you have any cargo requirements, any special needs, I'll be glad—"

"Captain!" Korby interrupted. His face was suddenly agitated. "I should much prefer—"

It was Kirk's turn to interrupt. He spoke loudly into the communicator. "Kirk to Rayburn. *Rayburn, are you receiving me?*"

He made an adjustment on the communicator and tried again. Then he gave himself a moment. "My other man has failed to respond, Doctor. It is now necessary that I call my ship . . ."

"No communications, Captain!"

It was Brown who had shouted. In his hand he held an old-style phaser rifle. It was aimed at Kirk's heart.

Aghast, Christine said, "Roger, what . . ."

"I'm sorry, dear," Korby said. "But if they should send down more people . . ."

Kirk, appalled by the sudden turn events had taken, realized that Andrea, rushing at him, had snatched the communicator from his hand.

"Roger!" Christine cried. "This man . . . this girl . . . Why do you allow . . . ?"

"Your captain won't be harmed," Korby said hurriedly. "Christine, listen. You must admit the possibility that there are things here unknown to you but so vitally important that—"

"Doctor Korby!" Kirk shouted. "I have one man dead! Now I've got another one out of contact!"

"Take his weapon, Andrea," Korby said.

The girl began to circle Kirk to get at the phaser hung on the rear of his belt. He drew back—and Brown leveled the rifle at his forehead. Kirk grabbed for reason. "Doctor, I have a command to consider, crewmen, a starship . . ."

"This is necessary, Captain. You will understand."

Kirk moved. He jerked out his phaser; and all in the same blur of action, ducked behind a heavy desk.

"Drop that rifle!" he said to Brown.

Instead, Brown's finger reached for the trigger. Kirk fired his phaser—and Brown fell.

Christine screamed, "Captain, behind you . . . !"

Her warning came too late. The hairless ape-thing had him by the arm. Under the fierce force of the grip, he was lifted high into the air, his whole body convulsed by the arm's agony. The phaser rang on the stone floor. Like a puppet, he kicked, helpless in the immense hand—and the other one struck him in the jaw. Christine screamed again. And he was dropped to fall, limp, half-conscious in a crumpled heap.

Christine, paralyzed with horror, stared vaguely around her as though seeking some answer to the incomprehensible. Then she saw what she had to see. Brown lay on the floor near Kirk, face upturned. There was no blood on the chest where the phaser beam had struck him. Instead, a metallic tangle of twisted dials and wires protruded from it . . . the infinitely complex circuitry required to animate an android robot.

Kirk found the strength to move his eyes. Then, he, too, saw what Christine had seen.

An anxious Spock was at Uhura's panel when she finally received Kirk's signal.

"Frequency open, sir," she told him, relief in her face.

He seized the speaker. "Spock here, Captain."

The familiar voice said, "Contact established with Doctor Korby."

"We were becoming concerned, Captain. Your check-in is overdue. Nor have we heard from your security team."

"There's no problem, Mr. Spock. They're with me. Return to ship will take about forty-eight hours. Doctor Korby's records and specimens will need careful packing."

"We can send down a work detail, sir."

"Korby has ample staff here. It's just that the work is quite delicate."

Abruptly Spock asked, "Captain . . . Is everything all right down there?"

Nothing was all right down there.

Spock had received no signal from Kirk. The captain of the *Enterprise* was sitting on a bunk in a detention chamber, watching as his voice issued from the mouth of the hairless ape-thing across the room. His communicator looked like a cigarette lighter in the creature's enormous paw. Korby was supervising its performance. He wasn't enjoying it. There was real concern for Kirk in his face. But real or unreal, Korby's feelings, his work, the man himself had ceased to matter to Kirk. The hot rage he felt had burned up all save the overriding fact that a neolithic savage was masquerading as commander of the *Enterprise*.

He tensed on the bunk. The bald thing noted it; and clicking the communicator off, prepared for muscle work.

"Please be still," Korby said. "If you move or cry out, Ruk may injure you. At least wait until you and I can talk together."

The communicator snapped back on. And a yet more anxious Spock said to Ruk, "Acknowledge, Captain. You sound tired."

Kirk heard his exact intonation come again from the flabby lips. "It's just the excitement of what we've found out, Mr. Spock. Korby's discoveries are scientifically amazing. All under control. Stand by for regular contact, Kirk out."

Ruk closed the communicator.

"This isn't a vain display, Captain," Korby said. "You know my reputation. Trust me."

"Yes, I know your reputation," Kirk said. "The whole galaxy knows who you are and what you used to stand for."

"There's so much you must learn before you make a judgment," Korby said. He turned to Ruk. "Andrea," he said tersely.

The loose mouth opened to say sweetly, "And you must be Captain Kirk of the starship *Enterprise*."

There was horror in the sound of the girlish voice emerging from the bald grotesque across the room. Kirk's obvious repulsion pleased it. Ruk began to show off.

It was Korby's voice now, saying, "Forgive me, Captain. It's been a long time." Then it was Christine's turn. Ruk reproduced her precise emotional inflection in the words, "I knew I'd find you."

"Enough!" Korby said sharply. "You are not to mock Christine! You are never to harm her!"

"Or disobey an order from her?" Kirk said.

Korby rose to the challenge. To Ruk he said, "You will never disobey Christine's orders." He looked at Kirk. "Satisfied, Captain?" He came over to sit beside Kirk on the bunk. Ruk rose, menacing. Korby waved him back. "Give me just twenty-four hours to convince you, Captain."

"Must I be a prisoner to be convinced?"

"What would your first duty be on return to your ship? A report! Do you realize how many vital discoveries have been lost to laymen's superstitions, their ignorance?"

"Here is an ignorant layman's question for you, Doctor," Kirk said. *"Where is my man I could not contact?"*

"Ruk is programmed to protect my experiments. The logic of his machine-mind saw danger to me . . ."

"Where is my other crewman?" Kirk repeated.

Korby's voice was very quiet. "Ruk—destroyed them both, Captain. But totally against my wishes, believe me."

Kirk's fists clenched. He looked down at them; and deliberately relaxing them, swallowed. Putting interest into his voice, he said, "He's a robot, isn't he? Like Brown?"

Korby nodded to Ruk. The thing spoke heavily, dully. "More complex than Brown, much superior. The old ones made me."

Korby said, "Ruk was still tending the machinery when we arrived here. How many centuries old he is even Ruk doesn't know. With his help, with the records I could find, we built Brown."

"You've convinced me, Doctor," Kirk said. "You've convinced me that you're a very dangerous man . . ."

He pushed Korby off the bunk; and in a fast pivot, shoved him across the room at Ruk. Then he made a leap for the door. But Ruk was too quick for him. Moving with a surprising speed, the thing grabbed his arm and flung him back across the room. He struck the hard masonry of the wall, thrust against it to regain his feet—but the move was useless. He was seized and lifted, a toy in the gigantic hand.

"Careful, Ruk!" Korby shouted. "Gently!"

The vise-like grip eased. But Ruk's notion of gentleness left something to be desired. He cuffed Kirk across the head—and dropped him, unconscious.

"Where is Captain Kirk?"

Christine stopped pacing the length of Korby's study to put the question to an Andrea who'd suddenly appeared through a door. The sweetly innocent looked back at her, puzzled.

"You are concerned about the captain when you are with Roger again? I do not understand."

There was that familiar use of his name again. Christine was engulfed by a desolate sense of helplessness. She could understand nothing at all, not the man she had loved so long, his purpose nor his companions.

"Yes," she said. "I am much concerned about the captain."

With manifest sincerity, her voice wholly guileless, Andrea said, "How can you love Roger without trusting him?"

Christine didn't answer. The query had gone straight to the heart of her agony. She began her restless pacing again and Andrea said, "Why does it trouble you when I use the name 'Roger'?"

"It is sufficient that it does trouble her."

Korby had entered the study. Ruk was with him, the giant hand tight on Kirk's arm. The door hummed closed behind them; and Korby, moving to Andrea, said, "You will call me 'Doctor Korby' from now on."

She said, "Yes, Doctor Korby."

He took Christine's cold hand, smiling down into her eyes. "As you can see, dear, Captain Kirk is fine. He won't be harmed. What's at stake here simply makes it necessary to prevent his reporting to his ship. I need time to explain, to demonstrate to him—and to you. Shall we start with Andrea?"

"Yes," she said. "Do start with Andrea."

The girl spoke simply, openly. "I am like Doctor Brown—an android robot. You did not know?"

"Remarkable, isn't she?" Korby said. He looked back at Kirk. "Notice the lifelike pigmentation, the variation in skin tones." He lifted Andrea's wrist. "The flesh has warmth. There's even a pulse, physical sensation . . ."

"Remarkable, indeed," Christine said.

The bitter irony in her voice got through to Korby. He released Andrea's wrist. "Darling," he said to Christine, "all I require for my purpose are obedience and awareness . . ."

It was an unfortunate choice of words. Christine walked away from him. For a moment he lost his self-assurance. Then he followed her. "Christine. You must realize that an android robot is like a computer. It does only what I program into it. As a trained scientist yourself, you must surely see . . ."

". . . that given a mechanical assistant, constructing a mechanical 'geisha' would be easy?"

Korby suddenly reached for Christine, pulling her close to him. "Do you think I could love a machine?" he demanded.

"Did you?" she said.

"Love can't exist where all is predictable! Christine, you must listen! Love must have imperfection—moments of worship, moments of hate. Andrea is as incapable of anger and fear as she is of love. She has no meaning for me. She simply obeys orders! Watch her . . ."

He spoke to Andrea. "Kiss Captain Kirk," he said.

She kissed Kirk.

"Now strike him," Korby said.

She slapped Kirk.

"You see, Christine? All she can do is what she's told to do. She's a sterile, a computer—a thing, not a woman." He whirled to Kirk. "Have you nothing to say, Captain?"

"Yes, Doctor, I have something to say," Kirk said. "If these inventions of yours can only do what they're told to do, why did Brown attack me? Who told him to do it? For that matter, who told this thing"—he indicated Ruk—"to kill two of my men?"

Korby's face went closed, cold. Taking Christine's arm, he said, "Come with me, darling. You owe it to me." She looked at Kirk, the feeling of nightmare helplessness still heavier in her limbs. Then she went with Korby.

His laboratory was at the end of a lengthy corridor. It was spotlessly white. Cabinets of gleaming equipment shared its walls with banks of computer-like control panels. But its dominating feature was a large central turntable. It was flanked by two squat dynamos. Ruk was busy at the table. Into a scooped-out hollow in its top, he was fitting a mold of some greenish-brown stuff, roughly conformed to the height and breadth of a human body. As a cook pats dough into a bread pan, his gargantuan hands worked deftly to shape the mold into the indentation. It was when they reached for a shining, complicated mechanism suspended from the ceiling that Christine first noticed it. Then she saw there was a similar one hanging over the other side of the table. Ruk lowered the nearer device over the mold's midsection. Slowly the table began to turn.

Its opposite side slid into view. Kirk was lying on it, eyes closed, pressed down, immobile. The ceiling's other machine, descended over him, covered him from breast to thighs.

Pointing to it, Korby said proudly, "This is how we make an android robot."

With a signal to Ruk, he went over to a wall of control panels. He twisted a knob. Blue lights flashed deep, blinding, within the instrumentation that masked the alternately passing mold-form and the body of Kirk. The heavy dynamos glowed red, throbbing under impulses of power flowing to them from the control panel. When Korby made an adjustment to increase the turning speed of the table, a dizziness seized Christine. She leaned back against an equipment cabinet, her eyes shut against the vertigo. When she opened them, the blue lights were blazing, pulsating to the rhythm of a human heartbeat. And the table was spinning now, blurring the forms it held in a haze of speed so fast they appeared to be one.

Unknowingly she was wringing her hands. Korby left the panel to take them in his. "Don't be afraid for him. I promise you, he's not being harmed in any way."

She found stumbling words. "To fix a man to a table like a lab specimen on a slide . . . I don't . . . Oh, Roger, what's happened to you . . . ? I remember when I sat in your class . . ." Tears choked her. "You wouldn't even consider injuring an animal, an insect . . . Life was sacred to you . . . It was what I loved about you . . ." She was openly weeping.

He took her in his arms. "I haven't changed, Christine. This is just a harmless demonstration to convince his skeptical, military mind. Please try and understand. If I'd beamed up to his ship with Brown and the others, they would have been objects of mere curiosity, freaks—the origin of wild rumors and destructive gossip."

"You don't *know* Captain Kirk!" she cried.

He patted her shoulder. "Now is the time to watch most carefully . . ." He left her to make some new, precise adjustment on the panel. Apparently, the table had reached its maximum acceleration. It was slowing down. In mingled amazement and horror, Christine caught a glimpse of the mold-form. It had assumed detailed human shape, human skin tones. The table came to a halt before her. Its niches held two identical Kirks.

Triumphant, Korby came back to her. "Which of the two is your captain, Christine? Can you tell?"

She shook her head. "I don't . . . know. I don't know—anything any more."

"This one is your captain," Korby said. "Do you see any harm that's been done him?"

Kirk's eyes opened. Immediately aware that he couldn't move, he was struggling against the appliance that covered him when he saw Korby. His jaw muscles hardened; and he was about to speak when he decided to listen, instead. For Korby was expounding to Christine. "The android's synthetic organs are now all in place. We merely synchronized them with Kirk's autonomic nervous system, duplicating his body rhythms. Now we must duplicate his mental patterns . . ."

A glimmer of realization came to Kirk. He saw Korby move to another control panel. He saw Andrea slip into the laboratory. And Ruk had gone into a crouch at the dynamo near his feet. He sensed what Korby was going to say before he said it. "Ruk, we're ready for final synaptic fusion. Andrea, stand by the cortex circuits. This android we're making will be so perfect, it could even replace the captain. It will have the same memories, the same abilities, the same attitudes . . ."

The implications of the boast were so appalling that they stimulated Kirk to a scurry of thinking faster than any he'd ever done in his life. As Korby shouted, *"Activate the circuits!"* he contorted his face with fury. As though mumbling to himself, he muttered, "Mind your business, Mr. Spock! I'm sick of your halfbreed interference! Do you hear me? Mind your business, Mr. Spock! I'm sick of your halfbreed—"

In midsentence a spasm of agony convulsed his body. Bolts of lightning seemed to split his head. The dynamo's hum screamed to an ear-shattering roar. Then the pain, the lightning, the roar were all over. Distraught, Christine ran to him. "I'm all right," he said. "It seems to be finished."

Korby came for her. "And now, my dear, you can meet my new android."

He gave the table a rotating twist. On it lay a perfect replica of Kirk. Its eyelids fluttered. Its gaze fastened on Christine and its lips moved in Kirk's characteristic smile of recognition. It said, "Nurse Chapel, how nice to see you."

Hostess Andrea was serving a meal to Christine in the study when Korby's new android opened its door. It was wearing Kirk's uniform.

"May I join you?" it said, seating itself at the table. "The doctor tells me I'm more or less on parole now. He thought you and I might like a little time together."

Christine whispered, "Captain, what are we . . . ?"

The android also lowered its voice. "We've got to find a way to contact the ship."

"I don't know what's happened to Roger." She looked despairingly into what she thought were Kirk's eyes.

"If I gave you a direct order to betray him, would you obey it, Christine?"

She bowed her head. "Please, Captain. Don't ask me to make such a choice. I'd rather you pushed me off the precipice where Matthews died."

Andrea placed a bowl of soup before her. "Thank you," she said. "I'm not hungry."

Her table companion also pushed its bowl aside. "I'm not, either," it said. "But then I am not your captain, Nurse Chapel. We androids don't eat, you see."

She'd thought she'd had all the shocks she could take. But there was a cat-and-mouse aspect to this last one that chilled her. She'd been about to confide her heartbreak to this manufactured thing masquerading as Kirk. She pushed her chair back and rose from the table just as Korby entered the study. The real Kirk was with him—a pale, haggard Kirk clad in the kind of nondescript lab outfit which Brown had worn.

He sniffed at the smell of food. "I'm hungry," he said; and turning to Korby, added, "That's the difference between me and your androids, Doctor."

His replica got up from its chair. "The difference is your weakness, Captain, not mine."

"Eating is a human pleasure," Kirk retorted. "Sadly, it is one you will never know."

"Perhaps. But I shall never starve, either," the android said.

Kirk looked at Korby. "It is an exact duplicate?"

"In every detail."

Kirk spoke directly to the duplicate. "Tell me about Sam, Mr. Android."

The answer came promptly. "George Samuel Kirk is your brother. Only *you* call him Sam."

"He saw me off on this mission."

"Yes. With his wife and three sons."

"He said he was being transferred to Earth Colony Two Research Station."

"No. He said he *wanted* a transfer to Earth Colony Two."

Korby intervened. "You might as well try to out-think a calculating machine, Captain."

"Obviously, I can't," Kirk said. "But we do have some interesting differences."

Korby was annoyed. "Totally unimportant ones." Abruptly, he dismissed his perfect android; and seating himself at the table, motioned Kirk and Christine to chairs. "Bring food," he told Andrea. "Lots of it. The captain is hungry."

As Kirk began eating, he leaned forward. "You haven't guessed the rest, have you? Not even you, Christine. What you saw was only a machine—*only half of what I could have accomplished had I continued the process of duplication*. I could have put *you*, Captain—your very consciousness into that android." He smiled faintly. "Your very 'soul' if you prefer the term. All of you. Brown was an example. My assistant was dying. I gave him life in android form."

Intensity came into his voice. "Yes, humans converted into androids can be programmed—but for the better! Can you conceive how life would be if we could do away with jealousy, greed, hate?"

Kirk said, "That coin has an opposite side, Doctor. You might also do away with tenderness, love, respect."

Korby slammed his fist on the table. "No death! No disease, no deformities! Even fear can be programmed out to be replaced with perpetual peace! Open your mind, Captain! I'm speaking of a practical heaven, a new Paradise—and all I need is your help!"

"I thought all you needed was my 'open mind,'" Kirk said.

"I've got to get transportation to a planet with the proper raw materials. There must be several possibilities among your next stops. I'm not suggesting any diversion from your route. I myself want no suspicion aroused. I simply want to begin producing androids more carefully, selectively . . ."

Under his chair Kirk's hand had found a thong that bound its joints together. He located one end of it. "I can see your point," he said. "Any publicity about such a project could only frighten uninformed prejudice."

Korby nodded. "My androids must be widely infiltrated into human societies before their existence is revealed. Otherwise, we'd have a tidal wave of superstitious hysteria that could destroy what is right and good. Are you with me, Captain?"

Christine was staring at Korby in unbelief. Had the years of loneliness sent him mad? To advance such a cooperation to the captain of a Federation starship! But Kirk was taking it quietly. "You've created your own Kirk, Doctor. You don't need me."

"I created him to impress you, Captain, not to replace you."

"You'd better use him," Kirk said. "I am impressed—but not the way you intended." He had the thong unraveled now.

"Ruk!" Korby called. "Ruk, take the captain to his quarters!"

As the hairless Caliban approached him, Kirk sat still, his hand busy with a slipknot he was putting into the cord under his chair. When Ruk reached for his shoulder, he tensed for action. All in one fast move, he ducked under Ruk's arm, leaped for Korby; and, dropping the slipknot over his head, jerked it tight around his throat. Then he ran for the door. Ruk made a lunge for him but was halted by the sound of Korby's agonized choking. Turning, he saw Korby fall from his chair, hands clawing at the cord that was throttling him. He hesitated. Then he returned to Korby to loosen the noose.

Christine went to help him. But Korby, furious, pushed her away. "Get after—" he broke off, coughing. Clearing his throat, he tried again. "Get after him, Ruk. Stop him. I have no more use for him. You understand?"

Ruk understood. So did Christine. She heard the growl rumble in the great chest as Ruk made for the door. She followed him, calling, "Ruk! Ruk, stop!" She could see the huge android speeding down the lighted corridor toward what she thought were Kirk's quarters. Then the figure disappeared around a corner. She turned with it into an unlighted passageway, still calling, "Ruk, stop! The doctor told you to obey my orders. Stop!"

The speed of the running footsteps increased. She raced on. "Ruk, where are you? I order you not to harm him! Do you hear me? He is not to be harmed! Ruk, where are you?"

He'd vanished into the darkness. And the character of the passage had changed. Its stone floor had become uneven and she stumbled over a pebble. It flung her against a rough, unpolished rock wall. The blackness swallowed the sound of the footsteps.

But Kirk heard them pounding behind him. He'd come to the end of the passage and was clambering over rocks. He fell into a gully between two boulders. He clung to one of them, listening.

"Captain Kirk?"

It was Ruk's voice, echoing hollowly among the rocks. Kirk hauled himself up over a boulder; and began to edge forward again through the pitch blackness, groping along a wall.

"Captain Kirk . . ."

The sound of the footsteps had ceased. But he could hear Ruk's heavy breathing, somewhere close. Frantically, Kirk felt around him for some kind of weapon. A sharp stalagmite jutted up from the floor. He wrestled with it. It was immovable. Desperate now, he seized a rock and crashed it over the stalagmite's pointed end. It broke. He scrabbled around among its pieces and found a club-like shard of it.

There came a hushed whisper. "Captain Kirk? Where are you?"

Now it was Christine's voice. Kirk peered into the darkness—and was about to answer when he remembered Ruk's trick of voice imitation.

It came again—Christine's voice. "Captain Kirk, help! I've lost my way! Don't leave me here . . ."

Was it Christine? Or was it Ruk? There was no way of telling. Kirk tightened his hold on his rock weapon. It just might be Christine, lost in this labyrinth of underground pathways. He might as well answer. The suspense was as difficult to bear as any fact would be. And he had taken all the precautions it was possible to take.

"Over here, Christine," he said.

Darker than the dark, the monstrous android loomed toward him, surefooted, moving easily, swiftly. Kirk struggled for solid rock under his feet, pivoted and was swinging his arm back for the strike when the edge of the rock that held him crumbled.

The solid footing he'd struggled for bordered a chasm. It fell away beneath him as sheer and deep as the one that had lost him Matthews. His fingertip clutch on its rim was his clutch on life. He fought to maintain it against the rain of stones disturbed by the crumbled edge. One struck his head. He looked up to see Ruk leaning over it. He became aware that his fingers were weakening.

More debris loosened. The rock he clawed at cracked. As it gave way, Ruk's arm snaked down to seize one of his wrists. They exchanged a long look. Then slowly Ruk hauled him back up.

Spock saw the bridge elevator open. Kirk walked out of it and turned to stride down the corridor that led to his quarters. Spock hurried after him. "Captain!" he called. "I've just received word that you had beamed up."

Kirk was at his desk, leafing through a drawer for his command orders. "Doctor Korby has considerable cargo coming aboard, Mr. Spock. I'll have to go over our destinations schedule with him."

Spock looked at the packet in his hand. Surprised, he said, "You're going back down with the command orders, sir?"

"Mind your business, Mr. Spock!" Kirk shouted savagely. "I'm sick of your half-breed interference! Do you hear me? Mind your business, Mr. Spock! I'm sick of your halfbreed—"

Shocked, Spock stood stock-still. Kirk moved for the door. Spock, confounded, still staggered, tried again. "Are you feeling all right, Captain?"

All hardness had left Kirk's voice. He spoke quietly, his customary, courteous self. "Quite all right, thank you, Mr. Spock. I'll beam up shortly with Dr. Korby and his party." He eyed Spock, puzzled. "You look upset, Mr. Spock. Everything all right up here?"

The Vulcan looked as bewildered as he'd ever permitted himself to appear. He finally decided to compromise with a noncommittal, "No problems here, sir."

He got himself a nod, a friendly smile and Kirk's exit to the corridor. But his sense of dismayed shock persisted. He went over to the intercom button in the cabin and hit it.

"Security, this is First Officer Spock. Status of your landing party?"

"Ready and standing by, sir."

"Wait until the captain has beamed down. Then have them meet me in the Transporter Room."

He was asking for trouble with Kirk. On the other hand, trouble between them already existed.

Korby was pleased with his new android's performance. He shuffled through the command-orders packet and his android said, "I've looked them over. You'll find planet Midos V an excellent choice." It indicated a sheet among the others on Korby's desk.

"A small colony. And abundant raw materials." He rose. "You've made a good beginning, Captain Kirk."

"Thank you, Doctor," it said. "I felt quite at home on the *Enterprise*."

Down the corridor Kirk lay on the bed in his quarters, thinking, thinking. His life had been saved, but to what purpose he couldn't see. The *Enterprise* hijacked by the thing that wore his uniform . . . Some planet, perhaps the galaxy itself, doomed to be peopled by non-people . . . Humanoid life extinguished by the machines of Korby's making.

The door hummed open. Andrea entered with a tray of food. She placed it on the table.

Kirk sat up on his bunk. "Kiss me, Andrea," he said.

She kissed him. Then the cortical circuit that had obeyed a former order to kiss him activated the one connecting the kiss with a slap. She drew her hand back to strike him when Kirk seized it. "No," he said. He got up. Taking her in his arms, he gave her the most impassioned kiss in his repertoire. She liked it. But her circuitry protested. From somewhere in her came the tiny whine of a hard-pressed coil.

Panic-stricken, her responses chaotic, she pushed him away, crying, "Not you . . . not programmed for you . . ."

She went weaving, half-reeling toward the door. Kirk, alarmed, followed her, only to find Ruk standing guard in the corridor.

His eyes on Kirk, Ruk said, "To maintain your life is illogical."

"Why?" Kirk said.

Ruk didn't answer. Under the hairless scalp, his brain seemed to be fighting with a swarm of thoughts that confused him more cruelly than Andrea's terrified response to the kiss. Finally, he said. "You are no longer needed here."

"You want to kill me, Ruk? Or, as Doctor Korby calls it—turn me off?"

"You cannot be programmed. You are inferior."

"I want to live," Kirk said.

"You are from the outside," Ruk said. "You make disorder here."

"I'm not programmed. But I'll do anything, no matter how illogical to stay alive. Does that disturb you, Ruk?"

"Our place was peaceful. There was no threat to existence."

"Is existence important to you, too?"

"I am programmed to exist. Therefore, I exist."

The massive face was contorted with unaccustomed thought. Kirk felt a stab of pity. He said, "Korby speaks of you as just a machine to be turned on or turned off. That is a good thing to be, is it, Ruk?"

"You are evil. Until you came all was at peace here. That was good."

"I came in peace," Kirk said. "The only difference between us is that I have emotion. I have unpredictability. And with each human, our evil unpredictability increases. How would you like to live with thousands of unpredictable humans around you, all of them evil like me?"

Ruk was staring at him. "Yes, it was so . . . long ago. I had forgotten. The old ones here, the ones who made me, they were human . . . and evil. It is still in my memory banks . . . It became necessary to destroy them."

He turned his vast bulk slowly at the sound of footsteps. White-coated, self-assured, Korby was striding down the corridor.

Ruk lumbered toward him. "You . . . *you* brought him among us," he said heavily.

Startled, Korby looked from Kirk back to Ruk. "What?"

Ruk continued to advance on him. "You brought the inferior ones here!" His voice rose. "We had cleansed ourselves of them! You brought them and their evil back!"

"Ruk, I order you to stop! Go back! Stand away from me! You are programmed to—"

It was Korby who retreated. As Ruk made a grab for him he drew Kirk's phaser from the white coat's pocket. There was no hesitation. He fired it. Ruk was gone. Where he'd stood was a charred spot, a drift of metallic-smelling smoke.

"You didn't have to destroy him," Kirk said into the tight silence.

Korby leveled the phaser at him. "Move," he said. "Ahead of me . . ."

A tense Christine stood at the door of the study, apparently awaiting the result of Korby's visit to Kirk's quarters. At the entrance, Kirk turned to face his captor. "You were once a man with respect for all living things. How is the change in you to be explained, Doctor? If I were to tell Earth that I am your prisoner, to tell them what you have become—"

He made a grab for the phaser. But Korby used it to shove him into the study. Then the door, humming shut, caught his other hand between it and the jamb. Kirk, about to exploit his advantage, paused. Korby's wedged hand was being cruelly mashed. Yet his right hand still held the phaser in an unwavering aim at Kirk. It seemed a remarkable fortitude. When he wrenched the smashed hand free, it struck Kirk as yet more remarkable.

Then a slow horror chilled him. Christine, too, was staring at the injured hand. Instead of revealing torn and mangled flesh, the wound had exposed a fine mesh of tiny complex gears and pulsing wires. Some connection in the wires short-circuited. A wisp of smoke rose from it, leaving a smell of scorched metal.

Korby saw Christine's face. "It's still me, Christine—your Roger . . . in this android form . . . You can't imagine why—how it was with me. I was frozen, dying, my legs were gone. I had only my brain between death and life . . ." He lifted the hand. "This can be repaired, more easily than any surgeon could possibly repair it. I'm the same man that you knew and loved—a better one. There will never be any death for me . . . never . . ."

She put her hands over her face to shut out the sight of the dangle of still-pulsing wires, Korby, turning to Kirk, cried, "Imagine it, Captain! A world with no corruption, no suffering, no death . . ."

"Then why keep me alive, Doctor?" Kirk said. "I am mere flesh and blood. So I shall die. You've got yourself an immortal Kirk. Why don't you kill this mortal one—and get done with me?"

"You know that answer," Korby said. "I am still the man you described—the one with respect for all living things. I am still that man."

"You are not that man, Doctor," Kirk said. "Look at Christine . . . heartbroken, terrified. Where is your human response to her suffering?"

As the question was taken in by his computer brain, Korby looked shaken. Its whirring circuits churned to no effective answer. So it dismissed the question. Recovering his composure, he went to a speaker built into a wall. "Andrea," he said, "come to the study."

The door hummed open and Kirk laid his arm around Christine's shoulders.

"Yes, Doctor," Andrea said.

"Someone is coming down the corridor," Korby told her.

"I will find Ruk," she said.

"Ruk has been turned off. Get Brown's weapon! Fast! Deal with it. *Protect!*"

She found Brown's old-style phaser in a desk drawer and hurried out of the study.

In full uniform, Kirk's facsimile was sauntering along the corridor. Its appearance puzzled Andrea. It also interested her. She moved toward the android, lifting her face to it.

"I will kiss you," she said.

"No!" it said sharply.

A look of anger flickered over her face.

"Protect," she said. Then she pulled the trigger of the phaser rifle. She looked down at the black ash that was all that remained, sniffing curiously at the drift of smoke. "Protect," she said again—and returned to the study.

Korby was shouting wildly. "I'm the *same*! A direct transfer—*all of me*! Wholly rational . . . human but without a flaw!"

Smiling, innocent, Andrea said, "I just turned off Captain Kirk."

"She's killed your perfect android," Kirk said. "Just as you killed Ruk. Is this your perfect world? Your flawless beings? Killing, killing, killing! Aren't you flawless beings doing exactly what you most hate in humans? Killing with no more feeling than you feel when you turn off a light?"

This time the computer brain was unable to dismiss the question. Kirk extended his hand. "Give me that phaser, Doctor. If any of the human Korby remains in you, you must know that your only hope is to give me that gun."

"No! You refuse to understand! I have constructed perfect beings . . . tested them . . ." Korby's face seemed to shrivel as his brain circuits told him he'd contradicted himself. His own illogic got through to them. "I—I have proven they are perfect . . . I . . . I have . . ."

With a look of blank bafflement, he gave the phaser to Kirk. Pale as death, Christine sank down on a chair.

"Give me your rifle, Andrea," Kirk said.

"No," she said. She waved him back with the weapon. "No . . . protect . . ." She moved to Korby. "I am programmed to love you, protect you. To kiss you . . ." she lifted her face to his.

Christine moaned faintly. Stunned, she watched Korby push Andrea away. "Don't touch me," he said. "You cannot love, you machine!" But Andrea still clung to him. The phaser she held came into position between them as Korby fought to free himself from her arms. "Programmed," Andrea said. "To love you . . . to kiss you . . ."

The rifle discharged. There was a flash of light. Then that, too, was gone. All that was left was the blur of smoke, the two piles of ash on the floor.

Dry-eyed, stumbling, Christine moved to Kirk. She was shuddering uncontrollably. He held her, the heiress to a permanent legacy of disillusioned loneliness.

As the last of the smoke dissolved, the study door was wrenched open. Spock and two security crewmen, phasers drawn, entered the study.

"Captain . . ." Spock hesitated. "You're all right, sir? Nurse Chapel?"

"All right, Mr. Spock," Kirk said.

"Where is Dr. Korby?" Spock asked.

Kirk took Christine's hand. "He was never here, Mr. Spock."

He took it again when she approached his command chair in the bridge of the *Enterprise*.

"Thank you for letting me make my decision, Captain," she said. "I'm fairly certain I'm doing the right thing."

"I am, too," he said. "Maybe you can get some sleep now that your decision is made."

Neither smiled. "I'll be seeing you around," she said.

When she'd left the bridge, Spock said, "She's brave."

"That's why we need her on the *Enterprise*, Mr. Spock." He looked at the viewing screen. "Helm, steady as she goes. Nurse Chapel has decided to remain with us." But Spock still stood at the command chair. "Something bothering you, Mr. Spock?"

"Captain, I . . . must protest your using the term 'halfbreed' in reference to me."

"I didn't *use* it, Mr. Spock. I directed it toward you as a—"

"Even as an android, you might have thought of a better expression," Spock said.

Kirk eyed him gravely. "I'll remember that, Mr. Spock, when I find myself in a similar position again."

"Thank you, sir," Spock said.

DAGGER OF THE MIND

Writer: S. Bar-David
Director: Vincent McEveety
First Aired: November 3, 1966

Simon van Gelder came aboard the *Enterprise* from the Tantalus Penal Colony via transporter, inside a box addressed to the Bureau of Penology in Stockholm—a desperate measure, but not a particularly intelligent one, as was inevitable under the circumstances. He had hardly been aboard three minutes before Tristan Adams, the colony's director and chief medic, had alerted Captain Kirk to the escape ("a potentially violent case") and the search was on.

Nevertheless, in this short time van Gelder, who was six feet four and only in his early forties, was able to ambush a crewman, knock him out, and change clothes with him, acquiring a phaser pistol in the process. Thus disguised, he was able to make his way to the bridge, where he demanded asylum and managed to paralyze operations for three more minutes before being dropped from behind by one of Mr. Spock's famous nerve squeezes. He was then hauled off to be confined in sick bay, and that was that.

Or that should have been that. Standard operating procedure would have been to give the captive a routine medical check and then ship him by transporter back to Tantalus and the specialized therapeutic resources of Dr. Adams. Kirk, however, had long been an admirer of Dr. Adams' rehabilitation concepts, and had been disappointed that ship's business had given him no excuse to visit the colony himself; now the irruption of this violent case seemed to offer an ideal opportunity. Besides, there was something about van Gelder himself that intrigued Kirk; in their brief encounter, he had not struck Kirk as a common criminal despite his desperation, and Kirk had not been aware that noncriminal psychiatric cases were ever sent to Tantalus. He went to visit the prisoner in the sick bay.

Dr. McCoy had him under both restraint and sedation while running body function tests. Asleep, his face was relaxed, childlike, vulnerable.

"I'm getting bursts of delta waves from the electroencephalograph," McCoy said, pointing to the body function panel. "Highly abnormal, but not schizophrenia, tissue damage, or any other condition I'm acquainted with. After I got him here, it took a triple dose of sedation to—"

He was interrupted by a sound from the bed, a strange combination of groan and snarl. The patient was coming back to consciousness, struggling against his bonds.

"The report said he was quite talkative," Kirk said.

"But not very informative. He'd claim one thing, seem to forget, then start to claim something else . . . and yet what little I could understand seemed to have the ring of truth to it. Too bad we won't have time to study him."

"So that's the system, is it?" the man on the bed said harshly, still struggling. "Take him back! Wash your hands of him! Let somebody else worry! Damn you—"

"What's your name?" Kirk said.

"My name . . . my name . . ." Suddenly, it seemed to Kirk that he was struggling not against the restraints, but against some kind of pain. "My name is . . . is Simon . . . Simon van Gelder."

He sank back and added almost quietly: "I don't suppose you've heard of me."

"Same name he gave before," McCoy said.

"Did I?" said van Gelder. "I'd forgotten. I was Director of . . . of . . . at the Tantalus Colony. Not a prisoner . . . I was . . . assistant. Graduate of . . . of . . ." His face contorted. "And then at . . . I did graduate studies at . . . studies at . . ."

The harder the man tried to remember, the more pain he seemed to be in. "Never mind," Kirk said gently. "It's all right. We—"

"I know," van Gelder said through clenched teeth. "They erased it . . . edited, adjusted . . . subverted me! I won't . . . I won't forget it! Won't go back there! Die first! Die, die!"

He had suddenly gone wild again, straining and shouting, his face a mask of unseeing passion. McCoy stepped close and there was the hiss of a spray hypo. The shouting died down to a mutter, then stopped altogether.

"Any guess at all?" Kirk said.

"One point I don't have to guess at," McCoy said. "He doesn't want to go back to that—how did you describe it? 'More like a resort than a prison.' Evidently a cage is still a cage, no matter how you label it."

"Or else there's something drastically wrong down there," Kirk said. "Keep him secure, Bones. I'm going to do a little research."

By the time Kirk returned to the bridge, Spock was already removing a tape casette from the viewer. "I got this from our library, Captain," he said. "No doubt about it: our captive is Dr. van Gelder."

"Dr.—?"

"That's right. Assigned to Tantalus Colony six months ago as Dr. Adams' assistant. Not committed; assigned. A highly respected man in his field."

Kirk thought about it a moment, then turned to his Communications Officer.

"Lieutenant Uhura, get me Dr. Adams on Tantalus . . . Doctor? This is Captain Kirk of the *Enterprise*. Regarding your escapee—"

"Is Dr. van Gelder all right?" Adams' voice cut in with apparent concern. "And your people? No injuries? In the violent state he's in—"

"No harm to him or anyone, sir. But we thought you might be able to enlighten us about his condition. My medical officer is baffled."

"I'm not surprised. He'd been doing some experimental work, Captain. An experimental beam we'd hoped might rehabilitate incorrigibles. Dr. van Gelder felt he hadn't the moral right to expose another man to something he hadn't tried on his own person."

While Adams had been talking, McCoy had entered from the elevator and had crossed to the library-computer station, where he stood listening with Kirk and Spock. Now he caught Kirk's eye and made the immemorial throat-cutting gesture.

"I see," Kirk said into the microphone. "Please stand by a moment, Dr. Adams." Uhura broke contact, and Kirk swung to McCoy. "Explain."

"It doesn't quite ring true, Jim," the medico said. "I don't think whatever's wrong with this patient is something he did to himself. I think it was something that was done to him. I can't defend it, it's just an impression—but a strong one."

"That's not enough to go on," Kirk said, irritated in spite of himself. "You're not dealing with just any ordinary warden here, Bones. In the past twenty years, Adams has done more to revolutionize, to humanize, prisons and the treatment of prisoners than all the rest of humanity had done in forty centuries. I've been to penal colonies since they've begun following his methods. They're not 'cages' any more, they're clean, decent hospitals for sick minds. I'm not about to start throwing unsubstantiated charges against a man like that."

"Who said anything about charges?" McCoy said calmly. "Just ask questions. Propose an investigation. If something's really wrong, Adams will duck. Any harm in trying it?"

"I suppose not." Kirk nodded to Uhura, who closed the circuit again. "Dr. Adams? This is rather embarrassing. One of my officers has just reminded me that by strict interpretation of our starship regulations, I'm required to initiate an investigation of this so that a proper report—"

"No need to apologize, Captain Kirk," Adams' voice said. "In fact, I'd take it as a personal favor if you could beam down personally, look into it yourself. I'm sure you realize that I don't get too many visitors here. Oh—I would appreciate it if you could conduct the tour with a minimum staff. We're forced to limit outside contact as much as possible."

"I understand. I've visited rehab colonies before. Very well. *Enterprise* out . . . Satisfied, McCoy?"

"Temporarily," the medical officer said, unruffled.

"All right. We'll keep van Gelder here until I complete my investigation, anyway.

Find me somebody in your department with psychiatric *and* penological experience—both in the same person, if possible."

"Helen Noel should do nicely. She's an M.D., but she's written several papers on rehab problems."

"Very good. We beam down in an hour."

Though there were plenty of women among the *Enterprise*'s officers and crew, Helen Noel was a surprise to Kirk. She was young and almost uncomfortably pretty—and furthermore, though Kirk had seen her before, he had not then realized that she was part of the ship's complement. That had been back at the medical lab's Christmas party. He had had the impression then that she was simply a passenger, impressed as female passengers often were to be singled out for conversation by the Captain; and in fact, in the general atmosphere of Holiday he had taken certain small advantages of her impressionability ... It now turned out that she was, and had then been, the newest addition to the ship's medical staff. Her expression as they met in the transporter room was demure, but he had the distinct impression that she was enjoying his discomfiture.

Tantalus was an eerie world, lifeless, ravaged, and torn by a bitter and blustery climate, its atmosphere mostly nitrogen slightly diluted by some of the noble gasses—a very bad place to try to stage an escape. In this it closely resembled all other penal colonies, enlightened or otherwise. Also as usual, the colony proper was all underground, its location marked on the surface only by a small superstructure containing a transporter room, an elevator head, and a few other service modules.

Dr. Tristan Adams met them in his office: a man in his mid-forties, with broad warm features, a suspicion of old freckles at the nose, and an almost aggressively friendly manner which seemed to promise firm handshakes, humor, an ounce of brandy at the right hour, and complete candor at all times. He hardly seemed to be old enough to have accumulated his massive reputation. The office reflected the man; it was personal, untidy without being littered, furnished with an eye to comfort and the satisfaction of someone perhaps as interested in primitive sculpture as in social medicine.

With him was a young woman, tall and handsome though slightly cadaverous, whom he introduced as "Lethe." There was something odd about her which Kirk could not quite fathom: perhaps a slight lack of normal human spontaneity in both manner and voice. As if expecting just such a reaction, Adams went on:

"Lethe came to us for rehabilitation, and ended up staying on as a therapist. And a very good one."

"I love my work," the girl said, in a flat voice.

With a glance at Adams for permission, Kirk said: "And before you came here?"

"I was another person," Lethe said. "Malignant, hateful."

"May I ask what crime you committed?"

"I don't know," Lethe said. "It doesn't matter. That person no longer exists."

"Part of our treatment, Captain, is to bury the past," Adams said. "If the patient can come to terms with his memories, all well and good. But if they're unbearable, why carry them at all? Sufficient unto the day are the burdens thereof. Shall we begin the tour?"

"I'm afraid we haven't time for a complete tour," Kirk said. "Under the circumstances, I'd primarily like to see the apparatus or experiment that injured Dr. van Gelder. That, after all, is the whole point of our inquiry."

"Yes, quite. One doesn't enjoy talking about failures, but still, negative evidence is also important. If you'll just follow me—"

"One minute," Kirk said, pulling his communicator out of his hip pocket. "I'd best check in with the ship. If you'll pardon me a moment—?"

Adams nodded and Kirk stepped to one side, partly turning his back. In a moment, Spock's voice was saying softly:

"Van Gelder's no better, but Dr. McCoy has pulled a few additional bits and pieces out of his memory. They don't seem to change the situation much. He insists that Adams is malignant, the machine is dangerous. No details."

"All right. I'll check in with you at four-hour intervals. Thus far everything here seems open and aboveboard. Out."

"Ready, Captain?" Adams said pleasantly. "Good. This way, please."

The chamber in which van Gelder had allegedly undergone his mysterious and shattering conversion looked to Kirk's unsophisticated eye exactly like any other treatment room, perhaps most closely resembling a radiology theater. There was a patient on the table as Kirk, Adams, and Helen entered, seemingly unconscious; and from a small, complex device hanging from the ceiling, a narrow, monochromatic beam of light like a laser beam was fixed on the patient's forehead. Near the door, a uniformed therapist stood at a small control panel, unshielded; evidently, the radiation, whatever it was, was not dangerous at even this moderate distance. It all looked quite unalarming.

"This is the device," Adams said softly. "A neural potentiator, or damper. The two terms sound opposite to each other but actually both describe the same effect: an induced increase in neural conductivity, which greatly increases the number of cross-connections in the brain. At a certain point, as we predicted from information theory, increased connectivity actually results in the disappearance of information. We thought it would help the patient to cope better with his most troublesome thoughts and desires. But the effects are only temporary; so, I doubt that it'll be anything like as useful as we'd hoped it would be."

"Hmm," Kirk said. "Then if it's not particularly useful—"

"Why do we use it?" Adams smiled ruefully. "Hope, that's all, Captain. Perhaps we can still get some good out of it, in calming violent cases. But strictly as a palliative."

"Like tranquilizing drugs," Helen Noel suggested. "They do nothing permanent. And to continually be feeding drugs into a man's bloodstream just to keep him under control . . ."

Adams nodded vigorously. "Exactly my point, Doctor."

He turned toward the door, but Kirk was still eyeing the patient on the table. He swung suddenly on the uniformed therapist and said, "How does it operate?"

"Simply enough, it's nonselective," the therapist said. "On and off, and a potentiometer for intensity. We used to try to match the output to the patient's resting delta rhythms, but we found that wasn't critical. The brain seems to do its own monitoring, with some help from outside suggestion. For that, of course, you have to know the patient pretty well; you can't just put him on the table and expect the machine to process him like a computer tape."

"And we shouldn't be talking so much in his presence, for that very reason," Adams said, a faint trace of annoyance in his voice for the first time. "Better if further explanations waited until we're back in the office."

"I'd better ask my questions while they're fresh," Kirk said.

"The Captain," Helen said to Adams, "is an impulsive man."

Adams smiled. "He reminds me a little of the ancient skeptic who demanded to be taught all the world's wisdom while he stood on one foot."

"I simply want to be sure," Kirk said stonily, "that this is in fact where Dr. van Gelder's injury occurred."

"Yes," Adams said, "and it was his own fault, if you must know. I dislike maligning a colleague, but the fact is that Simon is a stubborn man. He could have sat in here for a year with the beam adjusted to this intensity, or even higher. Or if there simply had been someone standing at the panel to cut the power when trouble began. But he tried it alone, at full amplitude. Naturally, it hurt him. Even water can poison a man, in sufficient volume."

"Careless of him," Kirk said, still without expression. "All right, Dr. Adams, let's see the rest."

"Very well. I'd like to have you meet some of our successes, too."

"Lead on."

In the quarters which Adams' staff had assigned him for the night, Kirk called the *Enterprise*, but there was still nothing essentially new. McCoy was still trying to get past the scars in van Gelder's memory, but nothing he had uncovered yet seemed contributory. Van Gelder was exhausted; toward the end, he would say nothing but, "He empties us . . . and then fills us with himself. I ran away before he could fill me. It is so lonely to be empty . . ."

Meaningless; yet somehow it added up to something in Kirk's mind. After a while, he went quietly out into the corridor and padded next door to Helen Noel's room.

"Well!" she said, at the door. "What's this, Captain? Do you think it's Christmas again?"

"Ship's business," Kirk said. "Let me in before somebody spots me. Orders."

She moved aside, hesitantly, and he shut the door behind himself.

"Thanks. Now then, Doctor: What did you think of the inmates we saw this afternoon?"

"Why . . . I was impressed, on the whole. They seemed happy, or at least well-adjusted, making progress—"

"And a bit blank?"

"They weren't normal. I didn't expect them to be."

"All right. I'd like to look at that treatment room again. I'll need you; you must have comprehended far more of the theory than I did."

"Why not ask Dr. Adams?" she said stiffly. "He's the only expert on the subject here."

"And if he's lying about anything, he'll continue to lie and I'll learn nothing. The only way I can be sure is to see the machine work. I'll need an operator; you're the only choice."

"Well . . . all right."

They found the treatment room without difficulty. There was nobody about. Quickly Kirk pointed out the controls the therapist had identified for him, then took up the position that had been occupied by the patient then. He looked ruefully up at the device on the ceiling.

"I'm expecting you to be able to tell if that thing is doing me any harm," he said. "Adams says it's safe; that's what I want to know. Try minimum output; only a second or two."

Nothing happened.

"Well? Any time you're ready."

"I've already given you two seconds."

"Hmm. Nothing happened at all."

"Yes, something did. You were frowning; then your face went blank. When I cut the power, the frown came back."

"I didn't notice a thing. Try it again."

"How do you feel now?"

"Somewhat . . . uh, nothing definite. Just waiting. I thought we were going to try again."

"We did," Helen said. "It looks as though your mind goes so completely blank that you don't even feel the passage of time."

"Well, well," Kirk said drily. "Remarkably effective for a device Adams said he was thinking of abandoning. The technician mentioned that suggestion was involved. Try one—something harmless, please. You know, when we finally get through this, I hope we can raid a kitchen somewhere."

"It works," Helen said in a strained voice. "I gave you two seconds at low intensity and said, 'You're hungry.' And now you are."

"I didn't hear a thing. Let's give it one more try. I don't want to leave any doubt about it."

"Quite right," Adams' voice said. Kirk sat bolt upright, to find himself staring squarely into the business end of a phaser pistol. The therapist was there too, another gun held unwaveringly on Helen.

"Prisons and mental hospitals," Adams went on, smiling, almost tolerantly, "monitor every conversation, every sound—or else they don't last long. So I'm able to satisfy your curiosity, Captain. We'll give you a proper demonstration."

He stepped to the control panel and turned the potentiometer knob. Kirk never saw him hit the on-off button. The room simply vanished in a wave of intolerable pain.

As before, there was no time lapse at all; he only found himself on his feet, handing his phaser to Adams. At the same time, he knew what the pain was: it was love for Helen, and the pain of loneliness, of being without her. She was gone; all he had was the memory of having carried her to her cabin that Christmas, of her protests, of his lies that had turned into truth. Curiously, the memories seemed somewhat colorless, one-dimensional, the voices in them, monotonous; but the longing and the loneliness were real. To assuage it, he would lie, cheat, steal, give up his ship, his reputation . . . He cried out.

"She's not here," Adams said, passing Kirk's phaser to the therapist. "I'll send her back in a while and then things will be better. But first, it's time to call your vessel. It's important that they know all is well. Then perhaps we can see Dr. Noel."

Through a renewed stab of pain, Kirk got out his communicator and snapped it open. "Captain . . . to *Enterprise*," he said. He found it very difficult to speak; the message did not seem to be important.

"*Enterprise* here, Captain," Spock's voice said.

"All is well, Mr. Spock. I'm still with Dr. Adams."

"You sound tired, Captain. No problems?"

"None at all, Mr. Spock. My next call will be in six hours. Kirk out."

He started to pocket the communicator, but Adams held out his hand.

"And that, too, Captain."

Kirk hesitated. Adams reached for the control panel. The pain came back, redoubled, tripled, quadrupled; and now, at last, there came a real and blessed unconsciousness.

He awoke to the murmur of a feminine voice, and the feeling of a damp cloth being smoothed across his forehead. He opened his eyes. He was on his bed in the quarters on

Tantalus; he felt as though he had been thrown there. A hand obscured his vision and he felt the cloth again. Helen's voice said:

"Captain . . . Captain. They've taken you out of the treatment room. You're in your own quarters now. Wake up, please, please!"

"Helen," he said. Automatically, he reached for her, but he was very weak; she pushed him back without effort.

"Try to remember. He put all that in your mind. Adams took the controls away from me—do you remember the pain? And then his voice, telling you you love me—"

He lifted himself on one elbow. The pain was there all right, and the desire. He fought them both, sweating.

"Yes . . . I think so," he said. Another wave of pain. "His machine's not perfect. I remember . . . some of it."

"Good. Let me wet this rag again."

As she moved away, Kirk forced himself to his feet, stood dizzily for a moment, and then lurched forward to try the door. Locked, of course. In here, he and Helen were supposed to consolidate the impressed love, make it real . . . and forget the *Enterprise*. Not bloody likely! Looking around, he spotted an air-conditioning grille.

Helen came back, and he beckoned to her, holding his finger to his lips. She followed him curiously. He tested the grille; it gave slightly. Throwing all his back muscles into it, he bent it outward. At the second try, it came free in his hand with a slight shearing sound. He knelt and poked his head into the opening.

The tunnel beyond was not only a duct; it was a crawl-space, intended also for servicing power lines. It could be crawled through easily, at least, as far as he could see down it. He tried it, but his shoulders were too bulky.

He stood up and held out his arms to the girl. She shrank back, but he jerked his head urgently, hoping that there was nothing in his expression which suggested passion. After a moment's more hesitation, she stepped against him.

"He may be watching as well as listening," Kirk whispered. "I'm just hoping he's focused on the bed, in that case. But that tunnel has to connect with a whole complex of others. It probably leads eventually to their power supply. If you can get through it, you can black out the whole place—and cut off their sensors, so Spock could beam us down some help without being caught at it. Game to try?"

"Of course."

"Don't touch any of those power lines. It'll be a bad squeeze."

"Better than Adams' treatment room."

"Good girl."

He looked down at her. The pain was powerful, reinforced by memory and danger, and her eyes were half-closed, her mouth willing. Somehow, all the same, he managed to break away. Dropping to her knees, she squirmed inside the tunnel and vanished, and Kirk began to replace the grille.

It was bent too badly to snap it back into place; he could only force it into reasonable shape and hope that nobody would notice that it wasn't fastened. He was on his feet and pocketing the sheared rivet heads when he heard the tumblers of the door lock clicking. He swung around just in time to see the therapist enter, holding an old-style phaser pistol. The man looked around incuriously.

"Where's the girl?" he said.

"Another of you zombies took her away. If you've hurt her, I'll kill you. Time for another 'treatment'?" He took a step closer, crouching. The pistol snapped up.

"Stand back! Cross in front of me and turn right in the corridor. I won't hesitate to shoot."

"That would be tough to explain to your boss. Oh, all right, I'm going."

Adams was waiting; he gestured curtly toward the table.

"What's the idea?" Kirk said. "I'm co-operating, aren't I?"

"If you were, you wouldn't have asked," Adams said. "However, I've no intention of explaining myself to you, Captain. Lie down. Good. Now."

The potentiator beam stabbed down at Kirk's head. He fought it, feeling the emptiness increase. This time, at least, he was aware of time passing, though he seemed to be accomplishing nothing else. His very will was draining away, as though somebody had opened a petcock on his skull.

"You believe in me completely," Adams said. "You believe in me. You trust me. The thought of distrusting me is intensely painful. You believe."

"I believe," Kirk said. To do anything else was agony. "I believe in you. I trust you, I trust you! Stop, stop!"

Adams shut off the controls. The pain diminished slightly, but it was far from gone.

"I give you credit," Adams said thoughtfully. "Van Gelder was sobbing on his knees by now, and he had a strong will. I'm glad I've had a pair like you; I've learned a great deal."

"But . . . what . . . purpose? Your reputation . . . your . . . work . . ."

"So you can still ask questions? Remarkable. Never mind. I'm tired of doing things for others, that's all. I want a very comfortable old age, on my terms—and I am a most selective man. And you'll help me."

"Of course . . . but so unnecessary . . . just trust . . ."

"Trust you? Naturally. Or, trust mankind to reward me? All they've given me thus far is Tantalus. It's not enough. I know how their minds work. Nobody better."

There was the sound of the door, and then Kirk could see the woman therapist, Lethe. She said:

"Dr. Noel's gone. Nobody took her out. She just vanished."

Adams swung back to the panel and hit the switch. The beam came on, at full amplitude. Kirk's brainpan seemed to empty as if it had been dumped down a drain.

"Where is she?"

"I . . . don't know . . ."

The pain increased. "Where is she? Answer!"

There was no possibility of answering. He simply did not know, and the pain blocked any other answer but the specific one being demanded. As if realizing this, Adams backed the beam down a little.

"Where did you send her? With what instructions? *Answer!*"

The pain soared, almost to ecstasy—and at the same instant, all the lights went out but a dim safe light in the ceiling. Kirk did not have to stop to think what might have happened. Enraged by agony, he acted on reflex and training. A moment later, the therapist was sprawled on the floor and he had Lethe and Adams covered with the old-style phaser.

"No time for you now," he said. Setting the phaser to "stun," he pulled the trigger. Then he was out in the corridor, a solid mass of desire, loneliness, and fright. He had to get to Helen; there was nothing else in his mind at all, except a white line of pain at having betrayed someone he had been told to trust.

Dull-eyed, frightened patients milled about him as he pushed toward the center of the complex, searching for the power room. He shoved them out of the way. The search was like an endless nightmare. Then, somehow, he was with Helen, and they were kissing.

It did not seem to help. He pulled her closer. She yielded, but without any real enthusiasm. A moment later, there was a familiar hum behind him: the sound of a transporter materialization. Then Spock's voice said:

"Captain Kirk—what on—"

Helen broke fee. "It's not his fault. Quick, Jim, where's Adams?"

"Above," Kirk said dully. "In the treatment room. Helen—"

"Later, Jim. We've got to hurry."

They found Adams sprawled across the table. The machine was still on. Lethe stood impassively beside the controls; as they entered, backed by a full force of security guards from the ship, she snapped them off.

McCoy appeared from somewhere and bent over Adams. Then he straightened.

"Dead."

"I don't understand," Helen said. "The machine wasn't on high enough to kill. I don't think it could kill."

"He was alone," Lethe said stonily. "That was enough. I did not speak to him."

Kirk felt his ringing skull. "I think I see."

"I can't say that I do, Jim," McCoy said. "A man has to die of something."

"He died of loneliness," Lethe said. "It's quite enough. I know."

"What do we do now, Captain?" Spock said.

"I don't know . . . let me see . . . get van Gelder down here and repair him, I guess. He'll have to take charge. And then . . . he'll have to decondition me. Helen, I don't want that, I want nothing less in the world; but—"

"I don't want it either," she said softly. "So we'll both have to go through it. It was nice while it lasted, Jim—awful, but nice."

"It's still hard to believe," McCoy said, much later, "that a man could die of loneliness."

"No," Kirk said. He was quite all right now; quite all right. Helen was nothing to him but another female doctor. But—

"No," he said, "it's not hard to believe at all."

THE CONSCIENCE OF THE KING

Writer: Barry Trivers
Director: Gerd Oswald
First Aired: December 8, 1966

"A CURIOUS EXPERIENCE," Kirk said. "I've seen *Macbeth* in everything from bearskins to uniforms, but never before in Arcturian dress. I suppose an actor has to adapt to all kinds of audiences."

"This one has," Dr. Leighton said. He exchanged a glance with Martha Leighton; there was an undertone in his voice which Kirk could not fathom. There seemed to be no reason for it. The Leightons' garden, under the bright sun of the Arcturian system, was warm and pleasant; their hospitality, including last night's play, had been unexceptionable. But time was passing, and old friends or no, Kirk had to be back on duty shortly.

"Karidian has an enormous reputation," he said, "and obviously he's earned it. But now, Tom, we'd better get down to business. I've been told this new synthetic of yours is something we badly need."

"There is no synthetic," Leighton said heavily. "I want you to think about Karidian. About his voice in particular. You should remember it; you were there."

"I was where?" Kirk said, annoyed. "At the play?"

"No," Leighton said, his crippled, hunched body stirring restlessly in its lounger. "On Tarsus IV, during the Rebellion. Of course it was twenty years ago, but you couldn't have forgotten. My family murdered—and your friends. And you saw Kodos—and heard him, too."

"Do you mean to tell me," Kirk said slowly, "that you called me three light-years off my course just to accuse an actor of being Kodos the Executioner? What am I supposed to put in my log? That you lied? That you diverted a starship with false information?"

"It's not false. Karidian is Kodos."

"That's not what I'm talking about. I'm talking about your invented story about the synthetic food process. Anyhow, Kodos is dead."

"Is he?" Leighton said. "A body burned beyond recognition—what kind of evidence is that? And there are so few witnesses left, Jim: you, and I, and perhaps six or seven others, people who actually saw Kodos and heard his voice. You may have forgotten, but I never will."

Kirk turned to Martha, but she said gently: "I can't tell him anything, Jim. Once he heard Karidian's voice, it all came back. I can hardly blame him. From all accounts, that was a bloody business . . . and Tom wasn't just a witness. He was a victim."

"No, I know that," Kirk said. "But vengeance won't help, either—and I can't allow the whole *Enterprise* to be sidetracked on a personal vendetta, no matter how I feel about it."

"And what about justice?" Leighton said. "If Kodos is still alive, oughtn't he to pay? Or at least be taken out of circulation—before he contrives another massacre? Four thousand people, Jim!"

"You have a point," Kirk admitted reluctantly. "All right, I'll go this far: Let me check the ship's library computer and see what we have on *both* men. If your notion's just a wild hare, that's probably the quickest way to find out. If it isn't—well, I'll listen further."

"Fair enough," Leighton said.

Kirk pulled out his communicator and called the *Enterprise*. "Library computer . . . Give me everything you have on a man named or known as Kodos the Executioner. After that, a check on an actor named Anton Karidian."

"Working," the computer's voice said. Then: "Kodos the Executioner. Deputy Commander, forces of Rebellion, Tarsus IV, twenty terrestrial years ago. Population of eight thousand Earth colonists struck by famine after fungus blight largely destroyed food supply. Kodos used situation to implement private theories of eugenics, slaughtered fifty per cent of colony population. Sought by Earth forces when rebellion overcome. Burned body found and case closed. Biographical data—"

"Skip that," Kirk said. "Go on."

"Karidian, Anton. Director and leading man of traveling company of actors, sponsored by Interstellar Cultural Exchange project. Touring official installations for past nine years. Daughter, Lenore, nineteen years old, now leading lady of troupe. Karidian a recluse, has given notice current tour is to be his last. Credits—"

"Skip that too. Data on his pre-acting years?"

"None available. That is total information."

Kirk put the communicator away slowly. "Well, well," he said. "I still think it's probably a wild hare, Tom . . . but I think I'd better go to tonight's performance, too."

After the performance, Kirk went backstage, which was dingy and traditional, and knocked on the door with the star on it. In a moment, Lenore Karidian opened it, still beautiful, though not as bizarre as she had looked as an Arcturian Lady Macbeth. She raised her eyebrows.

"I saw your performance tonight," Kirk said. "And last night, too. I just want to . . . extend my appreciation to you and to Karidian."

"Thank you," she said, politely. "My father will be delighted, Mr. . . . . ?"

"Capt. James Kirk, the starship *Enterprise*."

That told, he could tell; that and the fact that he had seen the show two nights running. She said: We're honored. I'll carry your message to father."

"Can't I see him personally?"

"I'm sorry, Captain Kirk. He sees no one personally."

"An actor turning away his admirers? That's very unusual."

"Karidian is an unusual man."

"Then I'll talk with Lady Macbeth," Kirk said. "If you've no objections. May I come in?"

"Why . . . of course." She moved out of the way. Inside, the dressing room was a clutter of theatrical trunks, all packed and ready to be moved. "I'm sorry I have nothing to offer you."

Kirk stared directly at her, smiling. "You're being unnecessarily modest."

She smiled back. "As you see, everything is packed. Next we play two performances on Benecia, if the *Astral Queen* can get us there; we leave tonight."

"She's a good ship," Kirk said. "Do you enjoy your work?"

"Mostly. But, to play the classics in these times, when most people prefer absurd three-V serials . . . it isn't always as rewarding as it could be."

"But you continue," Kirk said.

"Oh yes," she said, with what seemed to be a trace of bitterness. "My father feels that we owe it to the public. Not that the public cares."

"They cared tonight. You were very convincing as Lady Macbeth."

"Thank you. And as Lenore Karidian?"

"I'm impressed." He paused an instant. "I think I'd like to see you again."

"Professionally?"

"Not necessarily."

"I . . . think I'd like that. Unfortunately, we must keep to our schedule."

"Schedules aren't always as rigid as they seem," Kirk said. "Shall we see what happens?"

"Very well. And hope for the best."

The response was promising, if ambiguous, but Kirk had no chance to explore it further. Suddenly his communicator was beeping insistently.

"Excuse me," he said. "That's my ship calling . . . Kirk here."

"Spock calling, Captain. Something I felt you should know immediately. Dr. Leighton is dead."

"Dead? Are you sure?"

"Absolutely," Spock's voice said. "We just had word from Q Central. He was murdered—stabbed to death."

Slowly, Kirk put the device back in his hip pocket. Lenore was watching him. Her face showed nothing but grave sympathy.

"I'll have to go," he said. "Perhaps you'll hear from me later."

"I quite understand. I hope so."

Kirk went directly to the Leightons' apartment. The body was still there, unattended except by Martha, but it told him nothing; he was not an expert in such matters. He took Martha's hand gently.

"He really died the first day those players arrived," she said, very quietly. "Memory killed him. Jim . . . do you suppose survivors ever really recover from a tragedy?"

"I'm deeply sorry, Martha."

"He was convinced the moment we saw that man arrive," she said. "Twenty years since the terror, but he was sure Karidian was the man. Is that possible, Jim? Is he Kodos, after all?"

"I don't know. But I'm trying to find out."

"Twenty years and he still had nightmares. I'd wake him and he'd tell me he still heard the screams of the innocent—the silence of the executed. They never told him what happened to the rest of his family."

"I'm afraid there's not much doubt about that," Kirk said.

"It's the not knowing, Jim—whether the people you love are dead or alive. When you know, you mourn, but the wound heals and you go on. When you don't—every dawn is a funeral. That's what killed my husband, Jim, not the knife . . . But with him, I know."

She managed a small smile and Kirk squeezed her hand convulsively. "It's all right," she said, as if she were the one who had to do the comforting. "At least he has peace now. He never really had it before. I suppose we'll never know who killed him."

"I," Kirk said, "am damn well going to find out."

"It doesn't matter. I've had enough of all this passion for vengeance. It's time to let it all rest. More than time."

Suddenly the tears welled up. "But I shan't forget him. Never."

Kirk stomped aboard ship in so obvious a white fury that nobody dared even to speak to him. Going directly to his quarters, he barked into the intercom: "Uhura!"

"Yes, Captain," the Communications Officer responded, her normally firm voice softened almost to a squeak.

"Put me through to Captain Daly, the *Astral Queen*, on orbit station. And put it on scramble."

"Yes, *sir* . . . He's on, sir."

"John, this is Jim Kirk. Can you do me a little favor?"

"I owe you a dozen," Daly's voice said. "And two dozen drinks, too. Name your poison."

"Thanks. I want you to pass up your pickup here."

"You mean strand all them actors?"

"Just that," Kirk said. "I'll take them on. And if there's any trouble, the responsibility is mine."

"Will do."

"I appreciate it. I'll explain later—I hope. Over and out . . . Lieutenant Uhura, now I want the library computer."

"Library."

"Reference the Kodos file. I'm told there were eight or nine survivors of the massacre who were actual eyewitnesses. I want their names and status."

"Working . . . In order of age: Leighton, T., deceased. Molson, E., deceased—"

"Wait a minute, I want survivors."

"These were survivors of the massacre," the computer said primly. "The deceased are all recent murder victims, all cases open. Instructions."

Kirk swallowed. "Continue."

"Kirk, J., Captain, S.S. *Enterprise*. Wiegand, R., deceased. Eames, S., deceased. Daiken, R. Communications, S.S. *Enterprise*—"

"What!"

"Daiken, R., Communications, *Enterprise*, five years old at time of Kodos incident."

"All right, cut," Kirk said. "Uhura, get me Mr. Spock . . . Mr. Spock, arrange for a pickup for the Karidian troupe, to be recorded in the log as stranded, for transfer to their destination; company to present special performance for officers and crew. Next destination to be Eta Benecia; give me arrival time as soon as it's processed."

"Aye, aye, sir. What about the synthetic food samples we were supposed to pick up from Dr. Leighton?"

"There aren't any, Mr. Spock," Kirk said shortly.

"That fact will have to be noted, too. Diverting a starship—"

"Is a serious business. Well, a black mark against Dr. Leighton isn't going to hurt him now. One more thing, Mr. Spock. I want the privacy of the Karidian company totally respected. They can have the freedom of the ship within the limits of regulations, but their quarters are off limits. Pass it on to all hands."

"Yes, sir." There was no emotion in Spock's voice; but then, there never was.

"Finally, Mr. Spock, reference Lt. Robert Daiken, in Communications. Please have him transferred to Engineering."

"Sir," Spock said, "he came up from Engineering."

"I'm aware of that. I'm sending him back. He needs more experience."

"Sir, may I suggest a further explanation? He's bound to consider this transfer a disciplinary action."

"I can't help that," Kirk said curtly. "Execute. And notify me when the Karidians come aboard."

He paused and looked up at the ceiling, at last unable to resist a rather grim smile. "I think," he said, "I shall be taking the young lady on a guided tour of the ship."

There was quite a long silence. Then Spock said neutrally:

"As you wish, sir."

At this hour, the engine room was empty, and silent except for the low throbbing of the great thrust units; the *Enterprise* was driving. Lenore looked around, and then smiled at Kirk.

"Did you order the soft lights especially for the occasion?" she said.

"I'd like to be able to say yes," Kirk said. "However, we try to duplicate conditions of night and day as much as possible. Human beings have a built-in diurnal rhythm; we try to adjust to it." He gestured at the hulking drivers. "You find this interesting?"

"Oh yes . . . All that power, and all under such complete control. Are you like that, Captain?"

"I hope I'm more of a man than a machine," he said.

"An intriguing combination of both. The power's at your command; but the decisions—"

"—come from a very human source."

"Are you sure?" she said. "Exceptional, yes; but human?"

Kirk said softly, "You can count on it."

There was a sound of footsteps behind them. Kirk turned reluctantly. It was Yeoman Rand, looking in this light peculiarly soft and blonde despite her uniform—and despite a rather severe expression. She held out an envelope.

"Excuse me, sir," she said. "Mr. Spock thought you ought to have this at once."

"Quite so. Thank you." Kirk pocketed the envelope. "That will be all."

"Very good, sir." The girl left without batting an eyelash. Lenore watched her go, seemingly somewhat amused.

"A lovely girl," she said.

"And very efficient."

"Now *there's* a subject, Captain. Tell me about the women in your world. Has the machine changed them? Made then, well, just people, instead of women?"

"Not at all," Kirk said. "On this ship they have the same duties and functions as the men. They compete equally, and get no special privileges. But they're still women."

"I can see that. Especially the one who just left. So pretty. I'm afraid she didn't like me."

"Nonsense," Kirk said, rather more bluffly than he had intended. "You're imagining things. Yeoman Rand is all business."

Lenore looked down. "You are human, after all. Captain of a starship, and yet you know so little about women. Still I can hardly blame her."

"Human nature hasn't changed," Kirk said. "Grown, perhaps, expanded . . . but not changed."

"That's a comfort. To know that people can still feel, build a private dream, fall in love . . . all that, and power too! Like Caesar—and Cleopatra."

She was moving steadily closer, by very small degrees. Kirk waited a moment, and then took her in his arms.

The kiss was warm and lingering. She was the first to draw out of it, looking up into his eyes, her expression half sultry, half mocking.

"I had to know," she whispered against the power hum. "I never kissed a Caesar before."

"A rehearsal, Miss Karidian?"

"A performance, Captain."

They kissed again, hard. Something crackled against Kirk's breast. After what seemed to be all too short a while, he took her by the shoulders and pushed her gently away—not very far.

"Don't stop."

"I'm not stopping, Lenore. But I'd better see what it was that Spock thought was so important. He had orders not to know where I was."

"I see," she said, her voice taking on a slight edge. "Starship captains tell *before* they kiss. Well, go ahead and look at your note."

Kirk pulled out the envelope and ripped it open. The message was brief, pointed, very Spock-like. It said:

SHIP'S OFFICER DAIKEN POISONED, CONDITION SERIOUS. DR. McCOY ANALYZING FOR CAUSE AND ANTIDOTE, REQUESTS YOUR PRESENCE.

SPOCK

Lenore watched his face change. At last she said, "I see I've lost you. I hope not permanently."

"No, hardly permanently," Kirk said, trying to smile and failing. "But I should have looked at this sooner. Excuse me, please; and goodnight, Lady Macbeth."

Spock and McCoy were in the sick bay when Kirk arrived. Daiken was on the table, leads running from his still, sweating form to the body function panel, which seemed to be quietly going crazy. Kirk flashed a glance over the panel, but it meant very little to him. He said: "Will he make it? What happened?"

"Somebody put tetralubisol in his milk," McCoy said. "A clumsy job; the stuff is poisonous, but almost insoluble, so it was easy to pump out. He's sick, but he has a good chance. More than I can say for you, Jim."

Kirk looked sharply at the surgeon, and then at Spock. They were both watching him like cats.

"Very well," he said. "I can see that I'm on the spot. Mr. Spock, why don't you begin the lecture?"

"Daiken was the next to last witness of the Kodos affair," Spock said evenly. "You are the last. Dr. McCoy and I checked the library, just as you did, and got the same information. We suppose you are courting Miss Karidian for more information—but the next attempt will be on you. Clearly, you and Daiken are the only survivors because you are both aboard the *Enterprise;* but if Dr. Leighton was right, you no longer have that immunity, and the attempt on Daiken tends to confirm that. In short, you're inviting death."

"I've done that before," Kirk said tiredly. "If Karidian is Kodos, I mean to nail him down, that's all. Administering justice is part of my job."

"Are you certain that's all?" McCoy said.

"No, Bones, I'm not at all certain. Remember that I was there on Tarsus—a midshipman, caught up in a revolution. I saw women and children forced into a chamber with no exit . . . and a half-made self-appointed messiah named Kodos throw a switch. And then there wasn't anyone inside any more. Four thousand people, dead, vanished—and I had to stand by, just waiting for my own turn . . . I can't forget it, any more than Leighton could. I thought I had, but I was wrong."

"And what if you decide Karidian is Kodos?" McCoy demanded. "What then? Do you carry his head through the corridors in triumph? That won't bring back the dead."

"Of course it won't," Kirk said. "But they may rest easier."

"Vengeance is mine, saith the Lord," Spock said, almost in a whisper. Both men turned to look at him in astonishment.

At last Kirk said, "That's true, Mr. Spock, whatever it may mean to an outworlder like you. Vengeance is not what I'm after. I am after justice—and prevention. Kodos killed four thousand; if he is still at large, he may massacre again. But consider this, too: Karidian is a human being, with rights like all of us. He deserves the same justice. If it's at all possible, he also deserves to be cleared."

"I don't know who's worse," McCoy said, looking from Spock to Kirk, "the human calculator or the captain-cum-mystic. Both of you go the hell away and leave me with my patient."

"Gladly," Kirk said. "I'm going to talk to Karidian, and never mind his rule against personal interviews. He can try to kill me if he likes, but he'll have to lay off my officers."

"In short," Spock said, "you *do* think Karidian is Kodos."

Kirk threw up his hands. "Of course I do, Mr. Spock," he said. "Would I be making such an idiot of myself if I didn't? But I am going to make sure. That's the only definition of justice that I know."

"I," Spock said, "would have called it logic."

* * *

Karidian and his daughter were not only awake when they answered Kirk's knock, but already half in costume for the next night's command performance which was part of the official excuse for their being on board the *Enterprise* at all. Karidian was wearing a dressing-gown which might have been the robe of Hamlet, the ghost, or the murderer king; whichever it was, he looked kingly, an impression which he promptly reinforced by crossing to a tall-backed chair and sitting down in it as if it were a throne. In his lap he held a much-worn prompter's copy of the play, with his name scrawled across it by a felt pen.

Lenore was easier to tape; she was the mad Ophelia . . . or else, simply a nineteen-year-old girl in a nightgown. Karidian waved her into the background. She withdrew, her expression guarded, but remained standing by the cabin door.

Karidian turned steady, luminous eyes on Kirk. He said, "What is it you want, Captain?"

"I want a straight answer to a straight question," Kirk said. "And I promise you this: You won't be harmed aboard this ship, and you'll be dealt with fairly when you leave it."

Karidian only nodded, as if he had expected nothing else. He was certainly intimidating. Finally Kirk said:

"I suspect you, Mr. Karidian. You know that. I believe the greatest performance of your life is the part you're acting out offstage."

Karidian smiled, a little sourly. "Each man in his time plays many parts."

"I'm concerned with only one. Tell me this: Are you Kodos the Executioner?"

Karidian looked toward his daughter, but he did not really seem to see her; his eyes were open, but shuttered, like a cat's.

"That was a long time ago," he said. "Back then I was a young character actor, touring the Earth colonies . . . As you see, I'm still doing it."

"That's not an answer," Kirk said.

"What did you expect? Were I Kodos, I would have the blood of thousands on my hands. Should I confess to a stranger, after twenty years of fleeing much more organized justice? Whatever Kodos was in those days, I have never heard it said that he was a fool."

"I have done you a favor," Kirk said. "And I have promised to treat you fairly. That's not an ordinary promise. I am the captain of this ship, and whatever justice there is aboard it is in my hands."

"I see you differently. You stand before me as the perfect symbol of our technological society: mechanized, electronicized, uniformed . . . and not precisely human. I hate machinery, Captain. It has done away with humanity—the striving of men to achieve greatness through their own resources. That's why I am a live actor, still, instead of a shadow on a three-V film."

"The lever is a tool," Kirk said. "We have new tools, but great men still strive, and don't feel outclassed. Wicked men use the tools to murder, like Kodos; but that doesn't make the tools wicked. Guns don't shoot people. Only men do."

"Kodos," Karidian said, "whoever he was, made decisions of life and death. Some had to die that others could live. That is the lot of kings, and the cross of kings. And probably of commanders, too—otherwise why should you be here now?"

"I don't remember ever having killed four thousand innocent people."

"I don't remember it either. But I do remember that another four thousand were saved because of it. Were I to direct a play about Kodos, that is the first thing I would bear in mind."

"It wasn't a play," Kirk said. "I was there. I saw it happen. And since then, all the surviving witnesses have been systematically murdered, except two . . . or possibly, three. One of my officers has been poisoned. I may be next. And here you are, a man of whom we have no record until some nine years ago—and positively identified, positively, no matter how mistakenly, by the late Dr. Leighton. Do you think I can ignore all that?"

"No, certainly not," Karidian said. "But that is your role. I have mine. I have played many." He looked down at his worn hands. "Sooner or later, the blood thins, the body ages, and finally one is grateful for a failing memory. I no longer treasure life—not even my own. Death for me will be a release from ritual. I am old and tired, and the past is blank."

"And that's your only answer?"

"I'm afraid so, Captain. Did you ever get everything you wanted? No, nobody does. And if you did, you might be sorry."

Kirk shrugged and turned away. He found Lenore staring at him, but there was nothing he could do for her, either. He went out.

She followed him. In the corridor on the other side of the door, she said in a cold whisper: "You are a machine. And with a big bloody stain of cruelty on your metal hide. You could have spared him."

"If he's Kodos," Kirk said, equally quietly, "then I've already shown him more mercy than he deserves. If he isn't, then we'll put you ashore at Eta Benecia, with no harm done."

"Who are you," Lenore said in a dangerous voice, "to say what harm is done?"

"Who do I have to be?"

She seemed to be about to answer; cold fire raged in her eyes. But at the same moment, the door slid open behind her and Karidian stood there, no longer so tall or so impressive as he had been before. Tears began to run down over her cheeks; she reached for his shoulders, her head drooping.

"Father . . . father . . ."

"Never mind," Karidian said gently, regaining a little of his stature. "It's already all over. I am thy father's spirit, doomed for a certain time to walk the night—"

"Hush!"

Feeling like six different varieties of monster, Kirk left them alone together

For the performance, the briefing room had been redressed into a small theater, and cameras were spotted here and there so that the play could be seen on intercom screens elsewhere in the ship for the part of the crew that had to remain on duty. The lights were already down. Kirk was late, as usual; he was just settling into his seat—as captain he was entitled to a front row chair and had had no hesitation about claiming it—when the curtains parted and Lenore came through them, in the flowing costume of Ophelia, white with make-up.

She said in a clear, almost gay voice: "Tonight the Karidian Players present *Hamlet*—another in a series of living plays in space—dedicated to the tradition of the classic theater, which we believe will never die. *Hamlet* is a violent play about a violent time, when life was cheap and ambition was God. It is also a timeless play, about personal guilt, doubt, indecision, and the thin line between Justice and Vengeance."

She vanished, leaving Kirk brooding. Nobody needed to be introduced to *Hamlet*; that speech had been aimed directly at him. He did not need the reminder, either, but he had got it nonetheless.

The curtains parted and the great, chilling opening began. Kirk lost most of it, since McCoy chose that moment to arrive and seat himself next to Kirk with a great bustle.

"Here we are, here we are," McCoy muttered. "In the long history of medicine no doctor has ever caught the curtain of a play."

"Shut up," Kirk said, *sotto voce*. "You had plenty of notice."

"Yes, but nobody told me I'd lose a patient at the last minute."

"Somebody dead?"

"No, no. Lieutenant Daiken absconded out of sick bay, that's all. I suppose he wanted to see the play too."

"It's being piped into sick bay!"

"I know that. Pipe down, will you? How can I hear if you keep mumbling?"

Swearing silently, Kirk got up and went out. Once he was in the corridor, he went to the nearest open line and ordered a search; but it turned out that McCoy already had one going.

Routine, Kirk decided, was not enough. Daiken's entire family had been destroyed on Tarsus . . . and somebody had tried to kill him. This was no time to take even the slightest chance; with the play going on, not only Karidian, but the whole ship was vulnerable to any access of passion . . . or vengeance.

"Red security alert," Kirk said. "Search every inch, including cargo."

Getting confirmation, he went back into the converted briefing room. He was still not satisfied, but there was nothing more he could do now.

His ears were struck by a drum beat. The stage was dim, lit only by a wash of red, and the characters playing Marcellus and Horatio were just going off. Evidently the play had already reached Act One, Scene 5. The figure of the ghost materialized in the red beam and raised its arm, beckoning to Hamlet, but Hamlet refused to follow. The ghost—Karidian—beckoned again, and the drum beat heightened in intensity.

Kirk could think of nothing but that Karidian was now an open target. He circled the rapt audience quickly and silently, making for the rear of the stage.

"Speak," Hamlet said. "I'll go no further."

"Mark me," said Karidian hollowly.

"I will."

"My hour is almost come, when I to sulphurous and tormenting flames must render up myself—"

There was Daiken, crouching in the wings. He was already leveling a phaser at Karidian.

"—and you must seek revenge—"

"Daiken!" Kirk said. There was no help for it; he had to call across the stage. The dialogues intercut.

"I am thy father's spirit, doomed for a certain term to walk the night—"

"He murdered my father," Daiken said. "And my mother."

"—And for the day confined to fast in fires, Till the foul crimes done in my days—"

"Get back to sick bay!"

"I know. I saw. He murdered them."

"—are burnt and purged away."

The audience had begun to murmur; they could hear every word. So could Karidian. He looked off toward Daiken, but the light was too bad for him to see anything. In a shaken voice, he tried to go on.

"I . . . I could a tale unfold whose lightest word—"

"You could be wrong. Don't throw your life away on a mistake."

"—would t-tear up thy soul, freeze thy young blood—"

"Daiken, give me that weapon."

"No."

Several people in the audience were standing now, and Kirk could see a few security guards moving cautiously down the sidelines. They would be too late; Daiken had a dead bead on Karidian.

Then the scenery at the back tore, and Lenore came out. Her eyes were bright and feverish, and in her hand she carried an absurdly long dagger.

"It's over!" she said in a great, theatrical voice. "Never mind, father, I'm strong!

Come, ye spirits of the air, unsex me now! Hie thee hither, that in the porches of thine ear—"

"Child, child!"

She could not hear him. She was the mad Ophelia; but the lines were Lady Macbeth's.

"All the ghost are dead. Who would have thought they had so much blood in 'em? I've freed you, father. I've taken the blood away from you. Had he not so much resembled my father as he slept, I'd have done it—"

"No!" Karidian said, his voice choked with horror. "You've left me nothing! You were untouched by what I did, you weren't even born! I wanted to leave you something clean—"

"Balsam! I've given you everything! You're safe, no one can touch you! See Banquo there, the Caesar, even he can't touch you! This castle hath a pleasant seat."

Kirk went out onto the stage, watching the security guards out of the corner of his eyes. Daiken seemed to be frozen by the action under the lights, but his gun still had not wavered.

"That's enough," Kirk said. "Come with me, both of you."

Karidian turned to him, spreading his hands wide. "Captain," he said. "Try to understand. I was a soldier in a great cause. There were things that had to be done—hard things, terrible things. You know the price of that; you too are a captain."

"Stop it, father," Lenore said, in a spuriously rational voice. "There is nothing to explain."

"There is. Murder. Flight. Suicide. Madness. And still the price is not enough; my daughter has killed too."

"For you! For you! I saved you!"

"For the price of seven innocent men," Kirk said.

"Innocent?" Lenore gave a great theatrical laugh, like a coloratura playing Medea. "Innocent! They saw! They were guilty!"

"That's enough, Lenore," Kirk said. "The play is over. It was over twenty years ago. Are you coming with me, or do I have to drag you?"

"Better go," Daiken's voice said from the wings. He stood up and came forward into the light, the gun still leveled. "I wasn't going to be so merciful, but we've had enough madness. Thanks, Captain."

Lenore spun on him. With a movement like a flash of lightning, she snatched the gun away from him.

"Stand back!" she screamed. "Stand back, everyone! The play goes on!"

"No!" Karidian cried out hoarsely. "In the name of God, child—"

"Captain Caesar! You could have had Egypt! Beware of Ides of March!"

She pointed the gun at Kirk and pulled the trigger. But fast as she was in her madness, Karidian was even quicker. The beam struck him squarely on the chest. He fell silently.

Lenore wailed like a lost kitten and dropped to her knees beside him. The security guards stampeded onto the stage, but Kirk waved them back.

"Father!" Lenore crooned. "Father! Oh proud death, what feast is toward in thine eternal cell, that thou such a prince at a shot so bloodily has struck!" She began to laugh again. "The cue, father, the cue! No time to sleep! The play! The play's the thing, wherein we'll catch the conscience of the king . . ."

Gentle hands drew her away. In Kirk's ear, McCoy's voice said: "And in the long run, she didn't even get the lines right."

"Take care of her," Kirk said tonelessly. "Kodos is dead . . . but I think she may walk in her sleep."

BALANCE OF TERROR

WRITER: PAUL SCHNEIDER
DIRECTOR: VINCENT McEVEETY
FIRST AIRED: DECEMBER 15, 1966

When the Romulan outbreak began, Capt. James Kirk was in the chapel of the starship *Enterprise*, waiting to perform a wedding.

He could, of course, have declined to do any such thing. Not only was he the only man aboard the starship empowered to perform such a ceremony—and many others even less likely to occur to a civilian—but both the participants were part of the ship's complement: Specialist (phaser) Robert Tomlinson and Spec. 2nd Cl. (phaser) Angela Martine.

Nevertheless, the thought of refusing hadn't occurred to him. Traveling between the stars, even at "relativistic" or near-light speeds, was a long-drawn-out process at best. One couldn't forbid or even ignore normal human relationships over such prolonged hauls, unless one was either a martinet or a fool, and Kirk did not propose to be either.

And in a way, nothing could be more symbolic of his function, and that of the *Enterprise* as a whole, than a marriage. Again because of the vast distances and time lapses involved, the starships were effectively the only fruitful links between the civilized planets. Even interstellar radio, which was necessarily faster, was subject to a dozen different kinds of interruptions, could carry no goods, and in terms of human contact was in every way less satisfactory. On the other hand, the starships were as fructifying as worker bees; they carried supplies, medical help, technical knowledge, news of home, and—above all—the sight and touch of other people.

It was for the same complex of reasons that there was a chapel aboard the *Enterprise*. Designed by some ground-lubber in the hope of giving offense to nobody (or, as the official publicity had put it, "to accommodate all faiths of all planets," a task impossible on the face of it), the chapel was simplified and devoid of symbols to the point of insipidity; but its very existence acknowledged that even the tightly designed *Enterprise* was a world in itself, and as such had to recognize that human beings often have religious impulses.

The groom was already there when Kirk entered, as were about half a dozen crew members, speaking *sotto voce*. Nearby, Chief Engineer Scott was adjusting a small television camera; the ceremony was to be carried throughout the intramural network, and outside the ship, too, to the observer satellites in the Romulus-Remus neutral zone. Scotty could more easily have assigned the chore to one of his staff, but doing it himself was his acknowledgment of the solemnity of the occasion—his gift to the bride, as it were. Kirk grinned briefly. Ship's air was a solid mass of symbols today.

"Everything under control, Scotty?"

"Can't speak for the groom, sir, but all's well otherwise."

"Very good."

The smile faded a little, however, as Kirk moved on toward the blankly nondenominational altar. It bothered him a little—not exactly consciously, but somewhere at the back of his conscience—to be conducting an exercise like this so close to the neutral zone. The Romulans had once been the most formidable of enemies. But then, not even a peep had been heard from them since the neutral zone had been closed around their system, fifty-odd years ago. Even were they cooking something venomous under there, why should they pick today to try it—and with a heavily armed starship practically in their back yards?

Scotty, finishing up with the camera, smoothed down his hair self-consciously; he was to give the bride away. There was a murmur of music from the intercom—Kirk could only suppose it was something traditional, since he himself was tone-deaf—and Angela came in, flanked by her bridesmaid, Yeoman Janice Rand. Scott offered her his arm. Tomlinson and his best man were already in position. Kirk cleared his throat experimentally.

And at that moment, the ship's alarm went off.

Angela went white. Since she was new aboard, she might never have heard the jarring blare before, but she obviously knew what it was. Then it was replaced by the voice of Communications Officer Uhura:

"Captain Kirk to the bridge! Captain Kirk to the bridge!"

But the erstwhile pastor was already out the door at a dead run.

Spock, the First Officer, was standing beside Lieutenant Uhura's station as Kirk and his engineer burst onto the bridge. Spock, the product of marriage between an earth woman and a father on Vulcan—not the imaginary Solar world of that name, but a planet of 40 Eridani—did not come equipped with Earth-human emotions, and Lieutenant Uhura had the impassivity of most Bantu women; but the air was charged with tension nonetheless. Kirk said: "What's up?"

"It's Commander Hansen, outpost satellite four zero two three," Spock said precisely. "They've picked up clear pips of an intruder in the neutral zone."

"Identification?"

"None yet, but the engine pattern is modern. Not a Romulan vessel, apparently."

"Excuse me, Mr. Spock," a voice said from the comm board. "I'm overhearing you. We have a sighting now. The vessel is modern—but the markings are Romulan."

Kirk shouldered forward and took the microphone from Lieutenant Uhura's hand. "This is Captain Kirk. Have you challenged it, Hansen?"

"Affirmative. No acknowledgment. Can you give us support, Captain? You are the only starship in this sector."

"Affirmative."

"We're clocking their approach visually at . . ." Hansen's voice died for a moment. Then: "Sorry, just lost them. Disappeared from our monitors."

"Better transmit your monitor picture. Lieutenant Uhura, put it on our bridge viewscreen."

For a moment, the screen showed nothing but a scan of stars, fading into faint nebulosity in the background. Then, suddenly, the strange ship was there. Superficially, it looked much like an *Enterprise*-class starship; a domed disc, seemingly coming at the screen nearly edge-on—though of course it was actually approaching the satellite, not the *Enterprise*. Its size, however, was impossible to guess without a distance estimate.

"Full magnification, Lieutenant Uhura."

The stranger seemed to rush closer. Scott pointed mutely, and Kirk nodded. At this magnification, the stripes along the underside were unmistakable: broad shadows suggesting a bird of prey with half-spread wings. Romulan, all right.

From S-4023, Hansen's voice said urgently: "Got it again! Captain Kirk, can you see—"

"We see it."

But even as he spoke, the screen suddenly turned white, then dimmed as Uhura backed it hastily down the intensity scale. Kirk blinked and leaned forward tensely.

The alien vessel had launched a torpedolike bolt of blinding light from its underbelly. Moving with curious deliberateness, as though it were traveling at the speed of light in some other space but was loafing sinfully in this one, the dazzling bolt swelled in S-4023's camera lens, as if it were bound to engulf the *Enterprise* as well.

"She's opened fire!" Hansen's voice shouted. "Our screen's failed—we're—"

The viewscreen of the *Enterprise* spat doomsday light throughout the control room. The speaker squawked desperately and went dead.

"Battle stations," Kirk told Uhura, very quietly. "General alarm. Mr. Spock, full ahead and intercept."

Nobody had ever seen a live Romulan. It was very certain that "Romulan" was not their name for themselves, for such fragmentary evidence as had been pieced together from wrecks, after they had erupted from the Romulus-Remus system so bloodily a good seventy-five years ago, suggested that they'd not even been native to the planet, let alone a race that could have shared Earthly conventions of nomenclature. A very few bloated bodies recovered from space during that war had proved to be humanoid, but of the hawklike Vulcanite type rather than the Earthly anthropoid. The experts had guessed that the Romulans might once have settled on their adopted planet as a splinter group from some mass migration, thrown off, rejected by their less militaristic fellows as they passed to some more peaceful settling, to some less demanding kind of new world. Neither Romulus nor Remus, twin planets whirling around a common center in a Trojan relationship to a white-dwarf sun, could have proved attractive to any race that did not love hardships for their own sakes.

But almost all this was guesswork, unsupported either by history or by interrogation. The Vulcanite races who were part of the Federation claimed to know nothing of the Romulans; and the Romulans themselves had never allowed any prisoners to be taken—suicide, apparently, was a part of their military tradition—nor had they ever taken any. All that was known for sure was that the Romulans had come boiling out of their crazy little planetary system on no apparent provocation, in primitive, clumsy cylindrical ships that should have been clay pigeons for the Federation's navy and yet in fact took twenty-five years to drive back to their home world—twenty-five years of increasingly merciless slaughter on both sides.

The neutral zone, with its sphere of observer satellites, had been set up around the Romulus-Remus system after that, and for years had been policed with the utmost vigilance. But for fifty years nothing had come out of it—not even a signal, let alone a ship. Perhaps the Romulans were still nursing their wounds and perfecting their grievances and their weapons—or perhaps they had learned their lesson and given up—or perhaps they were just tired, or decadent. . . .

Guesswork. One thing was certain now. Today, they had come out again—or one ship had.

The crew of the *Enterprise* moved to battle stations with a smooth efficiency that would hardly have suggested to an outsider that most of them had never heard a shot fired in anger. Even the thwarted bridal couple was at the forward phaser consoles, as tensely ready now to launch destruction as they had been for creation only a few hours before.

But there was nothing to fire at in the phaser sights yet. On the bridge, Kirk was in the captain's chair, Spock and Scott to either side of him. Sulu was piloting; Second Officer Stiles navigating. Lieutenant Uhura, as usual, was at the comm board.

"No response from satellites four zero two three, two four or two five," she said. "No trace to indicate any are still in orbit. Remaining outposts still in position. No sightings of intruding vessel. Sensor readings normal. Neutral zone, zero."

"Tell them to stay alert and report anything abnormal."

"Yes, sir."

"Entering four zero two three's position area," Sulu said.

"Lieutenant Uhura?"

"Nothing, sir. No, I'm getting a halo effect here now. Debris, I'd guess—metallic, finally divided, and still scattering. The radiant point's obviously where the satellite should be; I'm running a computer check now, but—"

"But there can't be much doubt about it," Kirk said heavily. "They pack a lot more punch than they did fifty years ago—which somehow doesn't surprise me much."

"What *was* that weapon, anyhow?" Stiles whispered.

"We'll check before we guess," Kirk said. "Mr. Spock, put out a tractor and bring me in some of that debris. I want a full analysis—spectra, stress tests, X-ray diffusion, microchemistry, the works. We know what the hull of that satellite used to be made of. I want to know what it's like *now*—and then I want some guesses from the lab on how it got that way. Follow me?"

"Of course, sir," the First Officer said. From any other man it would have been a brag, and perhaps a faintly insulting one at that. From Spock it was simply an utterly reliable statement of fact. He was already on the intercom to the lab section.

"Captain," Uhura said. Her voice sounded odd.

"What is it?"

"I'm getting something here. A mass in motion. Nothing more. Nothing on visual, no radar pip. And no radiation. Nothing but a De Broglie transform in the computer. It could be something very small and dense nearby, or something very large and diffuse far away, like a comet. But the traces don't match for either."

"Navigator?" Kirk said.

"There's a cold comet in the vicinity, part of the Romulus-Remus system," Stiles said promptly. "Bearing 973 galactic east, distance one point three light hours, course roughly convergent—"

"I'd picked that up long ago," Uhura said. "This is something else. Its relative speed to us is one-half light, in toward the neutral zone. It's an electromagnetic field of some kind . . . but no kind I ever saw before. I'm certain it's not natural."

"No, it isn't," Spock said, with complete calmness. He might have been announcing the weather, had there been any out here. "It's an invisibility screen."

Stiles snorted, but Kirk knew from long experience that his half-Vulcanite First Officer never made such flat statements without data to back them. Spock was very odd by Earth-human standards, but he had a mind like a rapier. "Explain," Kirk said.

"The course matches for the vessel that attacked the last satellite outpost to disappear," Spock said. "Not the one we're tracking now, but four zero two five. The whole orbit feeds in along Hohmann D toward an intercept with Romulus. The computer shows that already."

"Lieutenant Uhura?"

"Check," she said, a little reluctantly.

"Second: Commander Hansen lost sight of the enemy vessel when it was right in front of him. It didn't reappear until it was just about to launch its attack. Then it vanished again, and we haven't seen it since. Third: Theoretically, the thing is possible, for a vessel of the size of the *Enterprise*, if you put almost all the ship's power into it; hence, you must become visible if you need power for your phasers, or any other energy weapon."

"And fourth, baloney," Stiles said.

"Not quite, Mr. Stiles," Kirk said slowly. "This would also explain why just one Romulan vessel might venture through the neutral zone, right under the nose of the *Enterprise*. The Romulans may think they can take us on now, and they've sent out one probe to find out."

"A very long chain of inferences, sir," Stiles said, with marked politeness.

"I'm aware of that. But it's the best we've got at the moment. Mr. Sulu, match course and speed exactly with Lieutenant Uhura's blip, and stick with it move for move. But under no circumstances cross after it into the neutral zone without my direct order. Miss Uhura, check all frequencies for a carrier wave, an engine pattern, any sort of transmission besides this De Broglie wave-front—in particular, see if you can overhear any chit-chat between ship and home planet. Mr. Spock and Mr. Scott, I'll see you both directly in the briefing room; I want to review what we know about Romulus. Better call Dr. McCoy in on it, too. Any questions?"

There were none. Kirk said, "Mark and move."

The meeting in the briefing room was still going on when Spock was called out to the lab section. Once he was gone, the atmosphere promptly became more informal; neither Scott nor McCoy liked the Vulcanite, and even Kirk, much though he valued his First Officer, was not entirely comfortable in his presence.

"Do you want me to go away too, Jim?" McCoy said gently. "It seems to me you could use some time to think."

"I think better with you here, Bones. You too, Scotty. But this could be the big one. We've got people from half the planets of the Federation patrolling the neutral zone. If we cross it with a starship without due cause, we may have more than just the Romulans to worry about. That's how civil wars start, too."

"Isn't the loss of three satellites due cause?" Scott said.

"I'd say so, but precisely what knocked out those satellites? A Romulan ship, we say; but can we prove it? Well, no, we say; the thing's invisible. Even Stiles laughs at that, and he's on our side. The Romulans were far behind us in technology the last we saw of them—they only got as far as they did in the war out of the advantage of surprise, plus a lot of sheer savagery. Now, suddenly, they've got a ship as good as ours, *plus* an invisibility screen. I can hardly believe it myself.

"And on the other hand, gentlemen . . . On the other hand, while we sit here debating the matter, they may be about to knock us right out of the sky. It's the usual verge-of-war situation: we're damned if we do, and damned if we don't."

The elevator door slid open. Spock was back. "Sir—"

"All right, Mr. Spock. Shoot."

Spock was carrying a thick fascicle of papers bound to a clip board, held close to his body under one arm. His other hand swung free, but its fist was clenched. The bony Vulcanite face had no expression and could show none, but there was something in his very posture that telegraphed tension.

"Here are the analyses of the debris," he said in his inhumanly even voice. "I shan't bother you with the details unless you ask. The essence of the matter is that the Romulan weapon we saw used on S-4023 seems to be a molecular implosion field."

"Meaning what?" McCoy said roughly.

Spock raised his right fist over the plot board, still clenched. The knuckles and tendons worked for a moment. A fine metallic glitter sifted down onto the table.

"It fatigues metals," he said. "Instantly. The metal crystals lose cohesion, and collapse into dust—like this. After that, anything contained in the metal blows up of itself, because it isn't contained any more. I trust that's clear, Dr. McCoy. If not, I'll try to explain it again."

"Damn you, Spock—"

"Shut up, Bones," Kirk said tiredly. "Mr. Spock, sit down. Now then. We're in no position to fight among ourselves. Evidently we're even worse off than we thought we were. If the facts we have are to be trusted, the Romulans have, first, a practicable invisibility screen, and second, a weapon at the very least comparable to ours."

"Many times superior," Spock said stolidly. "At least in some situations."

"*Both* of these gadgets," McCoy said, "are Mr. Spock's inventions, very possibly. At least in both cases, it's his interpretation of the facts that's panicking us."

"There are no other interpretations available at the moment," Kirk said through thinned lips. "Any argument about that? All right. Then let's see what we can make of them for our side. Scotty, what have *we* got that we can counter with, given that the Romulan gadgets are real? We can't hit an invisible object, and we can't duck an invisible gunner. Where does that leave us?"

"Fully armed, fast and maneuverable," the engineer said. "Also, they aren't quite invisible; Lieutenant Uhura can pick up their De Broglie waves as they move. That means that they must be operating at nearly full power right now, just running away and staying invisible. We've got the edge on speed, and I'd guess that they don't know that our sensors are picking them up."

"Which means that we can outrun them and know—approximately—what they're doing. But we can't out-gun them or see them."

"That's how it looks at the moment," Scott said. "It's a fair balance of power, I'd say, Jim. Better than most commanders can count on in a battle situation."

"This isn't a battle situation yet," Kirk said. "Nor even a skirmish. It's the thin edge of an interstellar war. We don't dare to be wrong."

"We can't be righter than we are with the facts at hand, sir," Spock said.

McCoy's lips twitched. "You're so damned sure—"

A beep from the intercom stopped him. Way up in the middle of the air, Lieutenant Uhura's voice said:

"Captain Kirk."

"Go ahead, Lieutenant," Kirk said, his palms sweating.

"I've got a fix on the target vessel. Still can't see it—but I'm getting voices."

Even McCoy pounded up with them to the bridge. Up there, from the master speaker on the comm board, a strange, muted gabble was issuing, fading in and out and often hashed with static, but utterly incomprehensible even at its best. The voices sounded harsh and only barely human; but that could have been nothing more than the illusion of strangeness produced by an unknown language.

The Bantu woman paid no attention to anything but her instruments. Both her large hands were resting delicately on dial knobs, following the voices in and out, back and forth, trying to keep them in aural focus. Beside her left elbow a tape deck ran, recording the gabble for whatever use it might be later for the Analysis team.

"This appears to be coming off their intercom system," she said into the tape-recorder's mike. "A weak signal with high impedance, pulse-modulated. Worth checking what kind of field would leak such a signal, what kind of filtration spectrum it shows—oh, damn—no, there it is again. Scotty, is that you breathing down my neck?"

"Sure is, dear. Need help?"

"Get the computer to work out this waver-pattern for me. My wrists are getting tired. If we can nail it down, I might get a picture."

Scott's fingers flew over the computer console. Very shortly, the volume level of the gabble stabilized, and Lieutenant Uhura leaned back in her seat with a sigh, wriggling her fingers in mid-air. She looked far from relaxed, however.

"Lieutenant," Kirk said. "Do you think you can really get a picture out of that transmission?"

"Don't know why not," the Communications Officer said, leaning forward again. "A leak that size should be big enough to peg rocks through, given a little luck. They've got visible light blocked, but they've left a lot of other windows open. Anyhow, let's try . . ."

But nothing happened for a while. Stiles came in quietly and took over the computer from Scott, walking carefully and pointedly around Spock. Spock did not seem to notice.

"This is a funny business entirely," McCoy said almost to himself. "Those critters were a century behind us, back when we drove them back to their kennels. But that ship's almost as good as ours. It even *looks* like ours. And the weapons . . ."

"Shut up a minute, please, Dr. McCoy," Lieutenant Uhura said. "I'm beginning to get something."

"Sulu," Kirk said. "Any change in their course?"

"None, sir. Still heading home."

"Eureka!" Lieutenant Uhura crowed triumphantly. "There it is!"

The master screen lit. Evidently, Kirk judged, the picture was being picked up by some sort of monitor camera in the Romulan's control room. That in itself was odd; though the *Enterprise* had monitor cameras almost everywhere, there was none on the bridge—who, after all, would be empowered to watch the Captain?

Three Romulans were in view across the viewed chamber, sitting at scanners, lights from their hooded viewers playing upon their faces. They looked human, or nearly so: lean men, with almond-colored faces, dressed in military tunics which bore wolf's-head emblems. The severe, reddish tone of the bulkheads seemed to accentuate their impassivity. Their heads were encased in heavy helmets.

In the foreground, a man who seemed to be the commanding officer worked in a cockpit-like well. Compared to the bridge of the *Enterprise*, this control room looked cramped. Heavy conduits snaked overhead, almost within touch.

All this, however, was noted in an instant and forgotten. Kirk's attention was focused at once on the commander. His uniform was white, and oddly less decorated than those of his officers. Even more importantly, however, he wore no helmet. And in his build, his stance, his coloring, even the cant and shape of his ears, he was a dead ringer for Spock.

Without taking his eyes from the screen, Kirk could sense heads turning toward the half-Vulcanite. There was a long silence, except for the hum of the engines and the background gabble of the Romulan's conversation. Then Stiles said, apparently to himself:

"So now we know. They got our ship design from spies. They can pass for us . . . or for some of us."

Kirk took no overt notice of the remark. Possibly it had been intended only for his ears, or for nobody's; until further notice he was tentatively prepared to think so. He said:

"Lieutenant Uhura, I want linguistics and cryptography to go to work on that language. If we can break it—"

There was another mutter from Stiles, not intelligible but a good deal louder than before. It was no longer possible to ignore him.

"I didn't quite hear that, Mr. Stiles."

"Only talking to myself, sir."

"Do it louder. I want to hear it."

"It wasn't—"

"Repeat it," Kirk said, issuing each syllable like a bullet. Everyone was watching Kirk and Stiles now except Spock, as though the scene on the screen was no longer of any interest at all.

"All right," Stiles said. "I was just thinking that Mr. Spock could probably translate for us a lot faster than the analysts or the computer could. After all, they're his kind of people. You have only to look at them to see that. We can all see it."

"Is that an accusation?"

Stiles drew a deep breath. "No, sir," he said evenly. "It's an observation. I hadn't intended to make it public, and if it's not useful, I'll withdraw it. But I think it's an observation most of us have already made."

"Your apology doesn't satisfy me for an instant. However, since the point's now been aired, we'll explore it. Mr. Spock, do you understand the language those people are speaking? Much as I dislike Mr. Stiles' imputation, there is an ethnic resemblance between the Romulans and yourself. Is it meaningful?"

"I don't doubt that it is," Spock said promptly. "Most of the poeple in this part of space seem to come from the same stock. The observation isn't new. However, Vulcan has had no more contact than Earth has with the Romulans in historical times; and I certainly don't understand the language. There are suggestions of roots in common with my home language—just as English has some Greek roots. That wouldn't help you to understand Greek from a standing start, though it might help you to figure out something about the language, given time. I'm willing to try it—but I don't hold out much hope of its being useful in time to help us out of our present jam."

In the brief silence which followed, Kirk became aware that the muttering from the screen had stopped. Only a second later, the image of the Romulan bridge had dissolved too.

"They've blocked the leak," Uhura reported. "No way to tell whether or not they knew we were tapping it."

"Keep monitoring it and let me know the instant you pick them up again. Make a copy of your tape for Mr. Spock. Dr. McCoy and Mr. Scott, please come with me to my quarters. Everyone else, bear in mind that we're on continuous alert until this thing is over, one way or another."

Kirk stood up, and seemed to turn toward the elevator. Then, after a carefully calculated pause, he swung on Stiles.

"As for you, Mr. Stiles: Your suggestion may indeed be useful. At the moment, however, I think it perilously close to bigotry, which is a sentiment best kept to yourself. Should you have another such notion, be sure I hear it *before* you air it on the bridge. Do I make myself clear?"

White as milk, Stiles said in a thin voice: "You do, sir."

In his office, Kirk put his feet up and looked sourly at the doctor and his engineer. "As if we didn't have enough trouble," he said. "Spock's a funny customer; he gets everybody's back hair up now and then just on ordinary days; and this . . . coincidence . . . is at best a damn bad piece of timing."

"If it is a coincidence," McCoy said.

"I think it is, Bones. I trust Spock; he's a good officer. His manners are bad by Earth standards, but I don't think much of Stiles' manners either at the moment. Let's drop the question for now. I want to know what to do. The Romulan appears to be running. He'll hit the neutral zone in a few hours. Do we keep on chasing him?"

"You've got a war on your hands if you do," McCoy said. "As you very well know. Maybe a civil war."

"Exactly so. On the other hand, we've already lost three outpost satellites. That's sixty lives—besides all that expensive hardware . . . I went to school with Hansen, did you know that? Well, never mind. Scotty, what do you think?"

"I don't want to write off sixty lives," Scott said. "But we've got nearly four hundred on board the *Enterprise*, and I don't want to write them off either. We've got no defense against that Romulan weapon, whatever it is—and the phasers can't hit a target they can't see. It just might be better to let them run back inside the neutral zone, file a complaint with the Federation, and wait for a navy to take over. That would give us more time to analyze these gadgets of theirs, too."

"And the language and visual records," McCoy added. "Invaluable, unique stuff—all of which will be lost if we force an engagement and lose it."

"Prudent and logical," Kirk admitted. "I don't agree with a word of it, but it would certainly look good in the log. Anything else?"

"What else do you need?" McCoy demanded. "Either it makes sense or it doesn't. I trust you're not suddenly going all bloody-minded on me, Jim."

"You know better than that. I told you I went to school with Hansen; and I've got kids on board here who were about to get married when the alarm went off. Glory doesn't interest me, either, *or* the public record. *I want to block this war.* That's the charge that's laid upon me now. The only question is, How?"

He looked gloomily at his toes. After a while he added:

"This Romulan irruption is clearly a test of strength. They have two weapons. They came out of the neutral zone and challenged a starship with them—with enough slaughter and destruction to make sure we couldn't ignore the challenge. It's also a test of our determination. They want to know if we've gone soft since we beat them back the last time. Are we going to allow our friends and property to be destroyed just because the odds seem to be against us? How much peace will the Romulans let us enjoy if we play it safe now—especially if we let them duck back into a neutral zone they've violated themselves? By and large, I don't think there's much future in that, for us, for the Earth, for the Federation—*or even for the Romulans.* The time to pound that lesson home is now."

"You may be right," Scott said. "I never thought I'd say so, but I'm glad it isn't up to me."

"Bones?"

"Let it stand. I've one other suggestion, though. It might improve morale if you'd marry those two youngsters from the phaser deck."

"Do you think this is exactly a good time for that?"

"I'm not sure there's ever a right time. But if you care for your crew—and I know damn well you do—that's precisely the right way to show it at the moment. An instance of love on an eve of battle. I trust I don't embarrass you."

"You do, Doctor," Kirk said, smiling, "but you're right. I'll do it. But it's going to have to be quick."

"Nothing lasts very long," McCoy said enigmatically.

On the bridge, nothing seemed to have happened. It took Kirk a long moment to realize that the conference in his office had hardly taken ten minutes. The Romulan vessel, once more detectable only by the De Broglie waves of its motion, was still apparently fleeing for the neutral zone, but at no great pace.

"It's possible that their sensors can't pick us up either through that screen," Spock said.

"That, or he's trying to draw us into some kind of trap," Kirk said. "Either way, we can't meet him in a head-on battle. We need an edge . . . a diversion. Find me one, Mr. Spock."

"Preferably nonfatal," Stiles added. Sulu half turned to him from the pilot board.

"You're so wrong about this," Sulu said, "you've used up all your mistakes for the rest of your life."

"One of us has," Stiles said stiffly.

"Belay that," Kirk said. "Steady as she goes, Mr. Sulu. The next matter on the agenda is the wedding."

"In accordance with space law," Kirk said, "we are gathered together for the purpose of joining this woman, Angela Martine, and this man, Robert Tomlinson, in the bond of matrimony . . ."

This time there were no interruptions. Kirk closed his book and looked up.

". . . And so, by the powers vested in me as Captain of the U.S.S. *Enterprise*, I now pronounce you man and wife."

He nodded to Tomlinson, who only then remembered to kiss the bride. There was the usual hubbub, not seemingly much muted by the fewness of the spectators. Yeoman Rand rushed up to kiss Angela's cheek; McCoy pumped Tomlinson's hand, slapped him on the shoulder, and prepared to collect his kiss from the bride, but Kirk interposed.

"Captain's privilege, Bones."

But he never made it; the wall speaker checked him. The voice was Spock's.

"Captain—I think I have the diversion you wanted."

"Some days," Kirk said ruefully, "nothing on this ship ever seems to get finished. I'll be right there, Mr. Spock."

Spock's diversion turned out to be the cold comet they had detected earlier—now "cold" no longer, for as it came closer to the central Romulan-Reman sun it had begun to display its plumage. Spock had found it listed in the ephemeris, and a check of its elements with the computer had shown that it would cross between the *Enterprise* and the Romulan 440 seconds from now—not directly between, but close enough to be of possible use.

"We'll use it," Kirk declared promptly. "Mr. Sulu, we'll close at full acceleration at the moment of interposition. Scotty, tell the phaser room we'll want a bracketing salvo; we'll be zeroing on sensors only, and with that chunk of ice nearly in the way, there'll be some dispersion."

"Still, at that range we ought to get at least one hit," Scott said.

"One minute to closing," Spock said.

"Suppose the shot doesn't get through their screen?" Stiles said.

"A distinct possibility," Kirk agreed. "About which we can do exactly nothing."

"Thirty seconds . . . twenty . . . fifteen . . . ten, nine, eight, seven, six, five, four, three, two, one, zero."

The lights dimmed as the ship surged forward and at the same moment, the phaser coils demanded full drain. The comet swelled on the screen.

"All right, Mr. Tomlinson . . . Hit 'em!"

The *Enterprise* roared like a charging lion. An instant later, the lights flashed back to full brightness, and the noise stopped. The phasers had cut out.

"Overload," Spock said emotionlessly. "Main coil burnout." He was already at work, swinging out a panel to check the circuitry. After only a split second of hesitation, Stiles crossed to help him.

"Captain!" Sulu said. "Their ship—it's fading into sight. I think we got a hit—yes, we did!"

"Not good enough," Kirk said grimly, instantly suspecting the real meaning of the Romulan action. "Full retro power! Evasive action!"

But the enemy was still faster. On the screen, a radiant torpedo like the one they had seen destroy Satellite 4023 was scorching toward the *Enterprise*—and this time it was no illusion that the starship was the target.

"No good," Sulu said. "Two minutes to impact."

"Yeoman Rand, jettison recorder buoy in ninety seconds."

"Hold it," Sulu said. "That shot's changing shape—"

Sure enough: the looming bolt seemed to be wavering, flattening. Parts of it were peeling off in tongues of blue energy; its brilliance was dimming. Did it have a range limit—

The bolt vanished from the screen. The *Enterprise* lurched sharply. Several people fell, including Spock—luckily away from the opened instrument panel, which cracked and spat.

"Scotty! Damage report!"

"One hold compartment breached. Minor damage otherwise. Main phaser battery still out of action, until that coil's replaced."

"I think the enemy got it worse, sir," Lieutenant Uhura said. "I'm picking up debris-scattering ahead. Conduits—castings—plastoform shadows—and an echo like the body of a casualty."

There was a ragged cheer, which Kirk silenced with a quick, savage gesture. "Maintain deceleration. Evidently they have to keep their screen down to launch their weapon—and the screen's still down."

"No, they're fading again, Captain," Sulu said. "Last Doppler reading shows they're decelerating too . . . Now they're gone again."

"Any pickup from their intercom, Lieutenant Uhura?"

"Nothing, sir. Even the De Broglies are fading. I think the comet's working against us now."

Now what in space did that mean? Fighting with an unknown enemy was bad enough, but when the enemy could become invisible at will—And if that ship got back to the home planet with all its data, there might well be nothing further heard from the Romulans until they came swarming out of the neutral zone by the millions, ready for the kill. That ship had to be stopped.

"Their tactics make sense over the short haul," Kirk said thoughtfully. "They feinted us in with an attack on three relatively helpless pieces, retreated across the center of the board to draw out our power, then made a flank attack and went to cover. Clearly the Romulans play some form of chess. If I had their next move, I'd go across the board again. If they did that, they'd be sitting in our ionization wake right now, right behind us—with reinforcements waiting ahead."

"What about the wreckage, sir?" Uhura said.

"Shoved out the evacuation tubes as a blind—an old trick, going all the way back to submarine warfare. The next time they do that, they may push out a nuclear warhead for us to play with. Lieutenant Sulu, I want a turnover maneuver, to bring the main phaser battery aligned directly astern. Mr. Spock, we can't wait for main coil replacement any longer; go to the phaser deck and direct fire manually. Mr. Stiles, go with him and give him a hand. Fire at my command directly the turnover's been completed. All understood?"

Both men nodded and went out, Stiles a little reluctantly. Kirk watched them go for a brief instant—despite himself, Stiles' suspicion of Spock had infected him, just a little—and then forgot them. The turnover had begun. On the screen, space astern, in the *Enterprise*'s ionization wake, seemed as blank as space ahead, in the disturbed gasses of the now-dwindling comet's tail.

Then, for the third time, the Romulan ship began to materialize, precisely where Kirk had suspected it would be—and there was precisely nothing they could do about it yet. The bridge was dead silent. Teeth clenched, Kirk watched the cross-hairs on the screen creep with infinite slowness toward the solidifying wraith of the enemy—

"All right, Spock, *fire*!"

Nothing happened. The suspicion that flared now would not be suppressed. With a savage gesture, Kirk cut in the intercom screen to the phaser deck.

For a moment he could make nothing of what he saw. The screen seemed to be billowing with green vapor. Through it, dimly, Kirk could see two figures sprawled on the floor, near where the phaser boards should have been. Then Stiles came into the field of view, one hand clasped over his nose and mouth. He was trying to reach the boards, but he must have already taken in a lungful of the green gas. Halfway there, he clutched at his throat and fell.

"Scotty! What is that stuff—"

"Coolant fluid," Scott's voice said harshly. "Seal must have cracked—look, there's Spock—"

Spock was indeed on the screen now, crawling on his hands and knees toward the boards. Kirk realized belatedly that the figures on the deck had to be Tomlinson and one of his crew, both dead since the seal had been cracked, probably when the Romulan had hit the *Enterprise* before. On the main screen, another of the Romulan energy bolts was bearing down upon them, with the inexorability of a Fury. Everything seemed to be moving with preternatural slowness.

Then Spock somehow reached the controls, dragged himself to his knees, moved nearly paralyzed fingers over the instruments. He hit the firing button twice, with the edge of his hand, and then fell.

The lights dimmed. The Romulan blew up.

On board the *Enterprise*, there were three dead: Tomlinson, his aide, and Stiles. Angela had escaped; she hadn't been on the deck when the coolant had come boiling out. Escaped—a wife of half a day, a widow for all the rest of her days. Stolidly, Kirk entered it all in the log.

The Second Romulan War was over. And never mind the dead; officially, it had never even begun.

THE GALILEO SEVEN

Writers: Oliver Crawford and S. Bar-David
(Story by Oliver Crawford)
Director: Robert Gist
First Aired: January 5, 1967

The USS *Enterprise* operated under a standing order to investigate all quasar and quasarlike phenomena wherever and whenever it encountered them. To Kirk, it seemed to have met up with one. A sinister formation had appeared on the bridge's main viewing screen—a bluish mass, threaded with red streaks of radiant energy. It dominated the sky ahead.

Kirk, eyeing the screen, pushed a button, only too conscious of the critical presence of his passenger, High Commissioner Ferris. "Captain to shuttlecraft *Galileo*," he said. "Stand by, Mr. Spock."

Ferris voiced his disapproval. "I remind you, Captain, that I am entirely opposed to this delay. Your mission is to get those medical supplies to Makus III in time for their transfer to the New Paris colonies."

"And I must remind you of our standing order, sir. There will be no problem. It's only three days to Makus III. And the transfer doesn't take place for five."

Ferris was fretful. "I don't like to take chances. With the plague out of control on New Paris, we must get those drugs there in time."

"We will." Kirk turned back to his console. "Captain to *Galileo*. All systems clear for your take-off."

"Power up, Captain. All instruments activated. All readings normal. All go."

Spock's voice . . . reassuring. As Science Officer, he was commanding the investigating team selected from the *Enterprise* crew for research into the space curiosity charted under the name of Murasaki 312. Now he sat, strapped, in the shuttlecraft's pilot seat, the others behind him—McCoy, Scott, Yeoman Mears, a fresh-faced girl, Boma, the Negro astrophysicist, radiation specialist Gaetano, Navigator Latimer. All together, seven: the *Galileo*'s seven.

"Launch shuttlecraft," Kirk said.

On the huge flight deck the heavy hangar doors swung open. The shuttlecraft taxied toward them and moved out into the emptiness of space.

Spock spoke over his shoulder. "Position."

"Three point seven . . . no, no, sir," Latimer said. "Four point—"

"Make up your mind," Spock said.

"My indicator's gone crazy," Latimer said.

Boma spoke quickly. "To be expected, Mr. Spock. Quasars are extremely disruptive. Just how much, we don't know. . . ."

Spock, eyes on his panel, said dryly, "Considerably, Mr. Boma."

Gaetano made his discouraging contribution. "My radiation reading is increasing rapidly, Mr. Spock!"

"Stop forward momentum!"

Latimer pushed switches. "I can't stop it, sir! Nothing happens!" McCoy leaned over to glance at his instruments. "Spock, we're being drawn right into the thing!"

Struggling with his own controls, Spock said, "Full power astern!"

But there was no power to reverse the onward plunge of the *Galileo*. "What's happening?" McCoy cried.

Boma said, "We underestimated the strength of the nucleonic attraction."

Spock reached for his speaker. "*Galileo* to *Enterprise*. We're out of control, Captain! Being pulled directly into the heart of Murasaki 312. Receiving violent radiation on outer. . . ."

A blast of static drowned Spock's voice. Kirk rushed over to Uhura's station. "Can't you get anything at all, Lieutenant?"

"Nothing clear, sir. Not on any frequency. Just those couple of words about being pulled off course."

Kirk wheeled. "Mr. Sulu, get me a fix on the *Galileo*!"

Sulu turned a bewildered face. "Our scanners are blocked, Captain. We're getting a mess of readings I've never seen before. Nothing makes sense!"

Kirk strode to the library computer. He got a hum, a click—and the flat, metallic computer voice. "Negative ionic concentration 1.64 by 10^2 meter. Radiation wavelength 370 angstroms, harmonics upwards along entire spectrum."

Kirk turned, appalled. Staring at him, Ferris said, "What is it, Captain?"

"That thing out there has completely ionized this entire sector!"

He glared at the screen. "At least four complete solar systems in this vicinity—and somewhere out there is a twenty-four-foot shuttlecraft out of control, off its course. Finding a needle in a haystack would be child's play compared to finding . . ."

Coiling, hungry, the bluish mass on the screen glared back at him, a blight on the face of space.

But the controls of the shuttlecraft weren't the only victims of Murasaki 312. It had rendered useless the normal searching systems of the *Enterprise*. Without them, the starship was drifting, blind, almost as helpless as the *Galileo*.

Ferris could not resist his I-told-you-so compulsion. "I was opposed to this from the beginning," he said to Kirk. "Our flight to Makus III had the very highest priority."

Kirk, his mind straining to contingencies that confronted the *Galileo*'s crew of seven, said, "I am aware of that, Commissioner. At the same time I have certain scientific duties—and exploring the Murasaki Effect is one of them."

"But you have lost your crew," Ferris said.

If there were people who couldn't resist an "I told you so," there were just as many who enjoyed making the painfully obvious more painful. Kirk held on to his temper. "We have two days to find them," he said.

Ferris pointed to the screen. "In all that? Two days?"

Kirk lost his temper. "Are you suggesting that I just turn around and leave them in it?"

"You shouldn't have sent them out in the first place!" Ferris paused. "You are concerned with only seven people. I am thinking of the millions in the New Paris colonies who will die if we don't get these medicines to them. It's your obstinate insistence on carrying out these inconsequential investigations that. . . ."

A bureaucrat is a bureaucrat is a bureaucrat, Kirk thought. They could function with paper. But remove them from paper into the sphere of decisive action and they turned into moralizing futilities. Scorn restored his composure. "We will make our scheduled rendezvous, Commissioner," he said evenly. "You have my word."

Uhura spoke. "Captain, there is one planet in this vicinity capable of sustaining human life. Type M, oxygen-nitrogen. Listed as Taurus II." The sympathy in her voice was cool water to a thirsty man. Kirk went to her. She looked up at him. "It is very nearly dead center of the Murasaki Effect, as closely as we can make out with our equipment malfunctions."

"Thank you, Lieutenant," Kirk said. "Mr. Sulu?"

"Yes, sir?"

"Set course for Taurus II."

"Course laid in, sir."

"Aren't you shooting in the dark?" Ferris said. "Assuming that they are there?"

"If they aren't there, Commissioner, they are all dead by now. We will search Taurus II because there is no sense in searching any place else."

"You said something about a needle in a haystack. Useless."

"Not if you want your needle back."

Strangely enough, the needle had fallen upon soft hay. However, soft was the best you could say about the spongily ugly surface of Taurus II. It had cushioned the impact of the *Galileo*'s crash landing in a roughly circular crater. Rock walls reared up toward a sky of a repellently bilious shade of green. It was not a prepossessing planet. The craft, canted over, had banged people and things around inside. Spock was bleeding green from a cut on his head. McCoy attended to it and then made his way to Yeoman Mears.

"Are you all right?"

"I . . . think so, Doctor."

Boma said, "That is what I call a ride."

"What happened?" Latimer asked him.

"I can't be sure . . . but I'd say that the magnetic potential of the Murasaki Effect was such that it was multiplied geometrically as we gathered speed. We were simply shot into the center of the Effect like a projectile. What do you think, Mr. Spock?"

"Your evaluation seems reasonable."

Scott, holding an aching head, joined Spock in checking the instruments and control panel. "What a mess!" he said.

Spock stood up. "Picturesque descriptions won't mend broken circuits, Mr. Scott. I think you'll find your work cut out for you." He threw a switch on the communicator.

"*Galileo* to *Enterprise*. Do you read me?"

"You don't really expect an answer, do you?" Scott said.

"I expect nothing. It is simply logical to try every alternative. A reading on the atmosphere, please, Doctor McCoy."

"As soon as I finish checking the crew . . ."

"If anyone had been injured, I assume you would have been so informed by now. The reading, Doctor."

There was irritation in the glance Spock received from McCoy. After a moment the Medical Officer picked up his kit and moved to an instrument panel. "Partial pressure of oxygen is 70 millimeters of mercury. Nitrogen, 140. Breathable, if you're not running in competition."

"The facts, please," Spock said.

"Traces of argon, neon, krypton, all in acceptable quantities. But I wouldn't recommend this place for a summer resort."

"Your opinion will be noted. You are recording this, Yeoman?"

"Of course, Mr. Spock."

"Very good. Mr. Scott, if you will immediately conduct a damage survey."

Scott said, "Naturally."

Spock ignored the tone of the comment. He said, "I suggest we move outside to give Mr. Scott room to work. Mr. Latimer, Mr. Gaetano, please arm yourselves and scout out the immediate area. Stay in visual contact with the ship."

"Aye, aye, sir," Gaetano said.

The two were removing phaser pistols from a locker as McCoy turned to Spock. "What do you think our chances are of communicating with the *Enterprise*?"

"Under current conditions, extremely poor."

"But they'll be looking for us!"

"If the ionization effect is as widespread as I believe it is, they'll be looking for us without instruments. By visual contact only. On those terms, it is a very large solar system."

"Then you don't think they'll find us."

"Not so long as we are grounded."

McCoy exploded. "I've never been able to stand your confoundedly eternal cheerfulness, Spock!"

"Better make an effort to, Doctor." The suggestion was mildly made. "We may be here for a long time."

Kirk himself had small cause for cheer. The *Enterprise* scanners had gone completely on strike. "Mr. Sulu, have you tried tying in with the auxiliary power units?"

"Yes, sir. No change."

Scowling, Kirk hit a button. "Transporter Room. This is the Captain. Are the Transporters beaming yet?"

The technician sounded apologetic. "Not one hundred percent, sir. We beamed down some inert material but it came back in a dissociated condition. We wouldn't dare try it with people."

"Thank you." He pushed another button. "Captain to Flight Deck. Prepare shuttlecraft *Columbus* for immediate search of planet surface. Correlate coordinates with Mr. Sulu. Lieutenant Uhura?"

"Yes, sir?"

"Anything at all?"

"All wavelengths dominated by ionization effect, Captain. Transmissions blocked, reception impossible."

To add to his joy in life, Ferris appeared beside Kirk's command chair. "Well, Captain?"

Kirk said, "We have until 2823.8 to continue our search, Commissioner."

"You don't really think you'll have any luck, do you?"

Kirk drew a hand down his cheek. "Those people out there happen to be friends and shipmates of mine. I intend to continue this ship's search for them until the last possible moment."

"Very well, Captain. But not a second beyond that limit. Is that clear? If it is not, I refer you to Book 19, Section 433, Paragraph 12."

"I am familiar with the regulations, Commissioner. And I know all about your authority."

Tight-faced, he struck a button on his console.

"Launch shuttlecraft *Columbus*!"

Outside the *Galileo*, Spock was examining the nearest section of the wall encircling the crater. Rescue was indeed a remote possibility. Even if the *Enterprise*'s searching equipment had remained unaffected by Murasaki 312, Taurus II was just one planet among many in the quadrant's solar systems. Hidden like this in the hollow made by the crater's rocky wall, the *Galileo* would be virtually invisible.

McCoy, joining him, looked up at the wall. "I can't say much for our circumstances," he said, "but at least it's your big chance."

"My big chance for what, Doctor?"

"Command," McCoy said. "I know you, Spock. You've never voiced it, but you've always thought logic was the best basis on which to build command. Am I right?"

"I am a logical man," Spock said.

"It'll take more than logic to get us out of this."

"Perhaps, Doctor . . . but I can't think of a better place to start trying. I recognize that command has fascinations, even under such circumstances as these. But I neither enjoy the idea of command nor am I frightened by it. It simply exists. And I shall do what logically needs to be done."

They clambered back into the craft, and Scott lifted a grim face from the control panel. "We've lost a great deal of fuel, Mr. Spock. We have no chance at all to reach escape velocity. And even if we hope to make orbit, we'll have to lighten our load by at least five hundred pounds."

"The weight of three grown men," Spock said.

Scott glanced at him, startled. "Why, yes . . . I guess you could put it that way."

McCoy was openly outraged. "Or the equivalent weight in *equipment*," he said.

Spock faced him. "Doctor McCoy, with few exceptions we will use virtually every piece of equipment in attaining orbit. There is very little surplus weight except among our passengers."

Boma, with Yeoman Mears, had been taking tricorder readings near the hatch. Now he stopped. "You mean three of us will have to stay behind?"

"Unless the situation changes radically," Spock said.

"And who is to choose those who remain behind?"

"As commanding officer the choice is mine."

Boma's face hardened. "You wouldn't be interested in drawing lots?"

Spock said, "I believe I am better qualified to select those who will stay behind than any random drawing of lots." He spoke without a trace of egotism in voice or manner. "My decision will be a logical one, Mr. Boma, arrived at through logical processes."

"Life and death are not logical, Spock!" McCoy cried.

"But attaining a desired goal is."

Spock ignored the tension in the atmosphere. "I would suggest we proceed to a more careful examination of the hull. We may have overlooked some minor damage."

Boma glared after him as he left. "Some minor damage was overlooked," he said, "when they put his head together!"

"Not his head," McCoy said. "His heart."

Tension was rising in everybody. Over at the farther crater wall Latimer and Gaetano were making a nervous survey of the area. Suddenly Gaetano stopped, listening. Latimer, too, halted. They listened to the sound—a rhythmic scraping noise such as might be made by rubbing wood against some corrugated surface. Latimer became conscious of an uneasy impression that the crater wall was breathing, the mist of its breath the fog that drifted over it, reducing visibility. The mist had come suddenly, like the sound. The scraping noise was repeated.

"What is it?" Latimer whispered.

"I don't know," Gaetano said. "It came from up there."

"No . . . back there. . . ."

They stared at each other. The sound surrounded them.

"Everywhere . . . it's all around us."

"Let's get out of here!" Latimer cried.

Then he yelled, breaking into a run. From the shadow made by a cleft in the wall above them a gigantic shape had emerged. Latimer screamed—and fell. Gaetano jerked out his phaser. He fired it at the fog-filled cleft.

He turned. The shaft of a spear was protruding from Latimer's back. It was as thick as a slim telephone pole.

The scream, reverberating against the crater's walls, had been heard by Spock and Boma. The Vulcan strode to Gaetano, where he stood over Latimer's body, still in shock, still staring up at the foggy cleft.

"How?" Spock said.

The dazed Gaetano lowered his phaser. "Something . . . huge . . . terrible. Up there!" He pointed to the cleft.

Spock walked over to the wall. Seizing an outcropping of rock, he began to climb up to the crevice. Boma spoke to Gaetano. "What was it? Did you see what it was?"

"Like a . . . a giant ape." He started to tremble. "It was all . . . so quick. There was a . . . a sound first."

Spock was back. "There's nothing up there," he said.

"I tell you there was!" Gaetano shouted.

Spock's voice was quiet. "I do not doubt your word."

"I hit it. I swear my phaser hit it," Gaetano said.

Spock didn't answer. Looking down at Latimer's body, he tugged at the spear shaft. It came loose in his hand, exposing its point—a large triangular stone, honed into shape and sharpness.

"The Folsom Point," Spock said.

"Sir?"

"Mr. Boma, this spearhead bears a remarkable resemblance to the Folsom Point, discovered in 1926 old Earth calendar, in New Mexico, North America. Quite similar . . . more crudely shaped about the haft, however. Not very efficient."

"Not very efficient?" Boma was furious. "Is that all you have to say?"

Surprised, Spock looked at him. "Am I in error, Mr. Boma?"

"Error? You? Impossible!"

"Then, what—" Spock began.

"A man lies there dead! And you talk about stone spears! What about Latimer? What about the dead man?"

"A few words on behalf of the dead will not bring them back to life, Mr. Boma."

Gaetano was glaring at him, too. He spoke to Boma. "Give me a hand with Latimer, will you?" He turned to Spock. "Unless you think we should leave his body here in the interest of efficiency."

"Bringing him back to the ship should not interfere with our repair efforts. If you'd like some assistance . . ."

"We'll do it!" Gaetano said sharply. Nodding to Boma, they reached down to the body. As they lifted it, Spock's keen eyes were studying the spearhead's construction.

Kirk was trying to fight off a sense of complete futility.

". . . and great loss." His voice was so broken as he dictated the last three words into his Captain's Log that he wondered if he should delete them. Spock . . . McCoy . . . Scott . . . all three of them gone, lost to the hideous blueness of what still showed on the screen.

Uhura spoke. "Captain, the *Columbus* has returned from searching quadrants 779X by 534M. Negative results."

"Have them proceed to the next quadrants. Any word from Engineering on the sensors?"

"They're working on them, sir. Still inoperable."

"The Transporters?"

"Still reported unsafe, sir."

"Thank you, Lieutenant."

"Captain Kirk . . ."

It was Ferris. "Captain, I do not relish the thought of abandoning your crewmen out there. However, I must remind you that—"

"I haven't forgotten," Kirk said wearily.

"You're running out of time," Ferris said.

A man of paper. "I haven't forgotten that, either," Kirk said. He rammed a button on his console. "This is the Captain. Try using overload power on the Transporters. We have to get it working." He got up to go to Uhura. "Lieutenant, order the *Columbus* to open its course two degrees on each lap from now on."

Sulu, surprised into protest, spoke. "But Captain, two degrees means they'll overlook more than a dozen terrestrial miles on each search loop."

Kirk turned. "It also means we'll at least have a fighting chance of checking most of the planet's surface. Mind your helm, Mr. Sulu."

Sulu flushed. "Yes, sir."

Ferris was still standing beside his command chair. He said coldly, "Twenty-four more hours, Captain."

Kirk didn't answer. He stared ahead at the viewing screen. Somewhere in the midst of that mysterious blueness, Taurus II existed, its substance solid, its air breathable—an oasis in the center of hell. Had Spock found it?

In the marooned *Galileo*, McCoy and Yeoman Mears had collected equipment to jettison. Arms laden, McCoy said, "This stuff ought to save us at least fifty pounds of weight, Spock."

"If we could scrape up another hundred pounds, what with Mr. Latimer gone . . ." Yeoman Mears didn't finish her sentence.

"We would still be at least one hundred and fifty pounds overweight," Spock said.

"I can't believe you're serious about leaving someone behind," McCoy said. "Whatever those creatures are out there . . ."

"It is more rational to sacrifice one man than six," Spock said.

"I'm not talking about rationality!"

"You might be wise to start."

Boma stuck his head through the open hatch. "We're ready, Mr. Spock."

"For what, Mr. Boma?"

"The services . . . for Latimer."

Spock straightened. "Mr. Boma. We are working against time."

"The man is dead. He deserves a decent burial. You're the Captain. A few words from you . . ."

If Spock's facial muscles had been capable of expressing annoyance, they would have twisted with it. As they were not, he looked at McCoy. "Doctor, perhaps you know the correct words for such an occasion."

"It's your place," McCoy said.

"My place is here. If you please, Doctor."

The facial muscles of the non-Vulcans had no trouble in showing annoyance. Spock's cool detachment exceedingly irritated them. "Spock, we may all die here!" McCoy shouted. "At least let us die like men, not machines!"

"By taking care of first things first, I hope to increase our chances of not dying here." Spock moved to where Scott was still at work on the console. "Perhaps if you were to channel the second auxiliary tank through the primary intake valve, Mr. Scott."

"Too delicate, sir. It may not take the pressure as it is,"

McCoy glared at Spock's stooped back. Then he followed the others out of the hatch and over to the mound of earth a few feet away from the *Galileo*. He bent for a handful of dirt and dropped it on the mound. "Dust though art and to dust shalt thou return. Amen."

People's heads bowed. "Amen," they echoed. They all stood still for a minute, each with his private thoughts—and the rhythmic grating sound came from what seemed to be distance.

"What is it?" said Yeoman Mears.

McCoy had looked up. "I don't know. But it sounds manmade."

"*Man*made! You wouldn't say that if you saw what I saw!" cried Gaetano. "It's them, those things out there somewhere!"

McCoy spoke to him and Boma. "You'd better stay on watch. I'll check with Mr. Spock."

He and Yeoman Mears re-entered the craft to hear a dismayed Scott cry, "The pressure's dropping, sir. We're losing everything!"

"What happened?" Spock asked.

"One of the lines gave. The strain of coming through the atmosphere . . . the added load when we tried to bypass—"

McCoy interrupted. "Spock!"

The Vulcan made a gesture for silence, concentrating on Scott. Staring at a gauge, the engineer said slowly, "Well, that does it. We have no fuel at all!"

"Then that solves the problem of who to leave behind."

"Spock!" McCoy yelled.

"Yes, Doctor?"

"Come outside. Something's happening."

Straightening, Spock said, "You will consider the alternatives, Mr. Scott."

Scott rose impatiently. "What alternatives? We have no fuel!"

"Mr. Scott, there are always alternatives."

He took his Vulcan calm with him as he followed McCoy out of the ship. The grating noise was louder. Spock listened, as concentrated on it as he'd been on Scott. McCoy glanced at his composed face. "And what do those super-sensitive ears of yours make of *that*?"

"Wood," Spock said. "Rubbing on some kind of leather."

"They're getting ready," Gaetano muttered. "They'll attack."

"Not necessarily," Boma said. "It could be a simple tribal rite . . . assuming it's a tribal culture."

"Not a tribal culture," Spock said gently. "Their artifacts are too primitive. Merely a loose association of some sort."

"We do not know that they are mere animals. They may well be capable of reason."

"We know they're capable of killing," Boma reminded him.

Spock looked at him. "If they are protecting themselves by their own lights . . ."

"That is exactly what we would be doing!" Boma argued.

Gaetano said, "The majority of us—"

"I am not interested in the opinion of the majority, Mr. Gaetano!" It was the first time Spock had raised his voice. Now its unexpected sharpness came as a shock to all of them.

"The components must be weighed—our dangers balanced against our duty to other life forms, friendly or not." Spock paused. "There is a third course."

"It could get us all killed." But the insolence had left Gaetano.

"I think not," Spock said. "Doctor McCoy, you and Yeoman Mears will remain in the ship. Assist Mr. Scott in any way possible. We shall return shortly."

He turned to Gaetano and Boma. "You will follow my orders to the letter. You will fire only when so ordered—and at my designated targets."

"Now you're talking," said Gaetano.

"Yes, I am talking, Mr. Gaetano. And you will hear. We shall fire to frighten. Not to kill."

"If we only knew more about them," Yeoman Mears said fearfully.

"We know enough," Boma said. "If they're tribal, they'll have a sense of unity. We can use that."

"How, Mr. Boma?"

"By hitting them hard, sir. Give them a bloody nose! Make them think twice about attacking us! A good offense is the best defense!"

"I agree!" cried Gaetano. "If we just stand by and do nothing, we're just giving them an invitation to come down and slaughter us!"

Spock's face had taken on a look of grave reflection. "I am frequently appalled," he said, "by the low regard for life you Earth people have."

"We are practical about it!" Gaetano's voice shook. "I say we hit them before they hit us!"

"Mr. Boma?" Spock said.

"Absolutely."

"Doctor McCoy?"

"It seems logical to me."

"It also seems logical to me," Spock said. "But taking life indiscriminately . . ."

"You were quick enough to talk about leaving three of us behind," Gaetano said. "Why all the sudden solicitude about some kind of animal?"

"You saw what they did to Latimer," Boma said.

So it had to be put into words of one syllable. But Spock was a master of primitives' languages. "I am in command here, Mr. Gaetano. The orders are mine to give, as the responsibility is mine to take. Follow me."

He led the way to the crater wall. The grating sound grew still louder as the trio began the climb up the rocky escarpment. Gaetano, apprehensive, arranged himself third in position. Spock signaled a halt. The slope ahead of them loomed vague and indistinct through mist swirls. Suddenly, among the rocks immediately above them, there was movement. Spock heard it first. He tensed with alertness, readying his phaser. Something rose from behind the rocks, something impossibly huge. It might have been man-shaped—but he couldn't tell, for the creature held an enormous leather shield before its body. Then a great spear whistled past his head. Spock, aiming his phaser, fired it.

There was a roar, half-human—a scream of pain and fear. The thing ducked behind a rock, hurling its shield downward.

Spock sidestepped to avoid its strike. He was hoisting it up as Boma and Gaetano joined him.

Awed, Gaetano whispered, "It must be twelve feet high."

Spock dropped the shield. Still leading the way, he motioned the others forward. They made the crest of the crater. Now the scraping noise was louder still, harsh, rasping, broken by grunting sounds.

"The mists . . ." Gaetano complained. "I can't see."

"They are directly ahead of us," Spock said. "Several, I believe. You will direct your phasers to two o'clock and to ten o'clock."

"I say we hit them dead on!" Gaetano said.

Spock turned his head. "Fortunately, I am giving the orders, Mr. Gaetano. Take aim, please."

He waited. "Fire!" he said.

Whatever their targets were, they could certainly howl. Spock listened to the roaring. "Cease fire!" he said. The roaring stilled. Spock nodded, satisfied. "They should think twice before bothering us again."

"I still say we should have killed them."

"It was not necessary, Mr. Gaetano. Fear will do for us what needs to be done. Mr. Boma, return to the ship. Mr. Gaetano, you will remain here on guard, keeping visual contact with the ship."

"Out here? Alone?"

"Security must be maintained, Mr. Gaetano."

Boma said, "At least let me stay with him."

"My intention is to post you in another position, Mr. Boma."

The two exchanged terrified looks. Spock regarded them with a mild curiosity. "Gentlemen," he said, "I regret having to post you in hazardous positions. Unfortunately, I have no choice. In the event of danger, the ship must have warning."

"Even if some of us must die for it?"

"There is the possibility of danger, Mr. Boma. But it cannot be helped."

He began the climb back down to the ship. After a long moment, Boma turned to follow him. "Good luck, Gaetano," he said.

"Yeah, sure," Gaetano said.

As they approached the *Galileo*, Spock said, "Mr. Boma, your post is here, near the ship." He hoisted himself through the hatch and Yeoman Mears said, "Did you find them, Mr. Spock?"

"We found them. I don't think they'll trouble us again."

"I hope not," McCoy said. "Spock, Scott has some idea."

He clearly did. Scott's face was alight with idea. "It's dangerous, Mr. Spock—but it just may work."

"Go head, Mr. Scott."

"I can adjust the main reactor to function on a substitute fuel supply." He paused, unable to resist the temptation to give full dramatic value to his idea. "Our phasers, sir. I could adapt them and use their energy. It will take time, but it's possible."

"The objection is they're our only defense," McCoy said.

"They would also seem to be our only hope." Spock made his decision fast. "Doctor . . . Yeoman . . . your phasers, please."

"But what if those creatures attack again?" the girl asked.

"They will not attack, not for many hours at any rate," Spock told her. "By then, with luck, we should be gone."

Scott nodded. "If I can get a full load, we'll be able to achieve orbit with all hands. Not that we can maintain it long."

"It will not be necessary to maintain it long. In less than twenty-four hours the *Enterprise* will be forced to abandon its search in order to make its rendezvous. If our orbit decays after that time, it will make no difference." Spock shrugged. "Whether we die coming out of orbit or here on the surface, we shall surely die. Your phaser, Doctor."

Reluctantly McCoy and the girl surrendered their phasers. Spock passed them over to Scott.

At the same moment on the *Enterprise*, the Transporter officer was reporting a successful materialization to Kirk. "The crates I beamed down to Taurus II came back all right, sir. In my opinion the Transporters are now safe for human transport."

It was the first good news since they had contacted Murasaki 312. Kirk pushed his intercom button. "This is the Captain. Landing parties 1, 2, and 3. Report to Transporter Room for immediate beam-down to the planet's surface. Ordinance condition 1-A."

"Captain . . . it's a big planet," the Transporter officer said. "It'll be sheer good luck if our landing parties find anything."

"I'm counting on luck, Lieutenant. It's almost the only tool we've got that might work."

But Spock, despite his hope that fear would restrain the hostility of the gorillalike creatures, wasn't trusting to luck. For the third time he left the *Galileo* to check with Boma. "Have you seen or heard anything unusual, Mr. Boma?"

"Nothing, sir."

"Is Mr. Gaetano keeping in contact with you?"

"I saw him up in those rocks just a few minutes ago."

Something else had seen Gaetano among the rocks. It aimed a large rock at his phaser, knocking it out of his hand. Terrified, he scrambled after it—and a spear hurled past him, striking the air between him and the weapon. He ran toward a rock crevice. It ended in a blank black wall. Trapped, he turned. The crevice entrance was blocked by a massive bulk, hairy, featureless. The creature moved toward him. He screamed.

It was Spock who found the dropped phaser. As he bent to retrieve it, he heard a snuffling, half-growl, half-grunt from somewhere in the rocks ahead of him. Then there was silence. McCoy and Boma climbed up to him. He extended his hand. "Mr. Gaetano's phaser," he said.

"Look!" Boma cried.

The footprint in the rubble was human in form. Its enormity was its horror.

Boma and McCoy stared at it, unbelieving. Spock handed Gaetano's phaser to McCoy. "Take this back to Mr. Scott for conversion, please, Doctor."

Boma flared up at him. "Is that all this means to you? Just a phaser to be recovered?"

Spock stared at him, puzzled. "Explain, Mr. Boma."

The frenzied Boma broke into a shout. "Gaetano's gone! Who knows what's happened to him! And you just hand over his phaser as though nothing had happened at all!"

Spock ignored the outburst. Drawing out his own phaser, he handed it over to McCoy, saying, "And please give this to Mr. Scott in case I don't return."

"Where are you going?" McCoy demanded.

Spock said, "I have a certain . . . scientific curiosity about what has occurred to Mr. Gaetano. You will return to the ship, if you please."

He slipped off into the mist, leaving Boma to gape after him. McCoy, shaking his head, said, "He'll risk his neck locating Gaetano. And if he finds him alive, he's just as liable to order him to stay behind when the ship leaves. You tell me."

"Do you think the ship will ever leave?"

"It won't without these phasers," McCoy said. "Let's get back to Scott."

Sharp-eyed, agile as a cat, Spock was creeping upward over rocks. Then he saw the ledge. Gaetano lay sprawled on it, unmoving. Spock bent over the body. As he realized what had been done to it, his impassive face went stony with revulsion. After a moment, he lifted it, hoisting it up and around his shoulders. The snuffling sound came again, this time from the mist-drifted rocks behind him. He looked back. Just the rocks, the fog coiling around them. He moved on—and suddenly the scraping noise broke out, close by, all around him, moving with him as he moved. Aware of it, he didn't hurry, but maintained his pace, measured, controlled. Below him now he could see the *Galileo*, its terrified people huddled together at the hatch, watching him.

He reached them just as a spear clanged harmlessly against the ship's hull. McCoy and Boma ran to him to help him enter the hatch. Inside, McCoy reached toward the body's lolling head. "Is he . . . ?"

"Mr. Boma, secure that hatch!" Spock said. He walked swiftly toward the aft compartment. McCoy followed him and eased the body from his shoulders. Boma, up forward near the hatch window, called, "I see one out there!" Yeoman Mears, joining him, peered out the window. Shuddering, she covered her face with her hands. "Horrible . . . it's a monster. . . ."

Boma, patting her shoulder, managed a wry grin. "We probably don't look so good to them, either."

Spock had gone to the forward window to look out of it. Something crashed against the hull. A great boulder tumbled past the window and rolled away to crash up against the side of the crater.

"All right, Spock," Boma said. "You have the answers. What now?"

Spock turned. "Your tone is hostile, Mr. Boma."

"My tone isn't the only thing that's hostile!"

"Strange," Spock mused. "Step by step I have done the logical thing."

McCoy blew up. "A little less analysis and a little more action! That's what we need!"

"How about analyzing what's happening to the plates of this craft?"

"The plates are titanite, Mr. Boma," Spock said. "They will hold. At least for a time."

"We have phasers. We could drive them off!"

"Mr. Boma, every ounce of energy in the phasers is needed by Mr. Scott. Were we to attack the creatures, the energy expended might well provide the very impetus required to secure our orbit."

The ship shook under another smash by a boulder—a bigger one, heavier, harder.

"How long, Mr. Scott?" Spock asked.

"Another hour. Maybe two."

"Can't you hurry it up?"

Scott raised an impatient face from his labor. "Doctor, a phaser will drain only so fast."

A steady, relentless hammering had begun on the hull. Boma, looking up, saw its plates vibrating. "How long can those plates hold out under *that?*" he cried. *"We've got to do something!"*

All eyes were on Spock. He met them directly, his own calm, as composed as though theirs contained no accusation.

Kirk lacked Spock's stoic capacity to tolerate helplessness. Though the ion storm was dispersing, the starship's slow recovery of its operational power had tightened his nerves to the breaking point. He snapped at Uhura. "Lieutenant, what word from the sensor section?"

"At last report they were beginning to get readings, but they were completely scrambled."

"I'm not interested in the last report! I want the current one!"

"Yes, sir."

Kirk slammed his fist into his palm. When the elevator door opened, he didn't turn his head. He heard Ferris clear his throat. Then he was beside him, glancing ostentatiously at his watch. "You have three hours, Captain."

"I know the number of hours I have, Commissioner."

"Delighted to hear it. However, I shall continue to remind you."

"You do that," Kirk said.

Uhura spoke. "Sir, sensor section reporting. Static interference still creating false images. Estimate 80 percent undependable."

"Radio communication?"

"Clearing slowly but still incapable of transmission and reception."

"What do you intend to do?" demanded Ferris.

Kirk's overstrained control broke. "Do? I'll keep on searching, foot by foot, inch by inch . . . by candlelight if I have to, so long as I have a second left! And if you'll keep your nose off my bridge, I'll be thankful!"

"I'm sure your diligence will please the authorities, Captain. I am not sure they will appreciate the way you address a High Commissioner."

"I am in command here!"

"You are, Captain. For exactly—" he consulted his watch—"two hours and forty-two minutes."

Spock slammed no fist into his palm. The hammering by great rocks continued to shake the *Galileo*—but his Vulcan heritage forbade any release of tension building up in him. Boma's panic had now taken the form of an open scorn. Nor was there the slightest sign of sympathy in the others. Never had the half-human in Spock felt so lonely. But he gave no evidence of it as he said, "Mr. Scott, how much power do we have in our central batteries?"

"They're in good shape, sir. But they won't lift us off, if that's what you're getting at."

"Are they strong enough to electrify the exterior of the ship?"

A slow grin spread over Scott's face. "That they are, laddie." Reaching for some cables, he detached them.

Spock spoke to the others. "Get into the center of the ship. Don't touch the plates. Be sure you're insulated."

They obeyed, watching as Scott clamped an electrode to a metal projection on one side of the ship's interior. He was preparing the second electrode when a ferocious smash-down resounded from over their heads. Scott nodded at Spock.

"Stand by," Spock said.

The second electrode, attached, completed the circuit. Sparks flew up in a shower, followed by a wild shrieking of pain, shock and fury from outside the craft. The hammering stopped. Scott, releasing the electrodes, said, "I don't dare use any more power if we want to be sure of ignition."

Staring up at the silent hull, McCoy said, "It worked."

"For the moment," Spock said.

"For the moment?"

"Mr. Boma, they will return when they discover they're not seriously hurt. In the meantime, please check the aft compartment. See if there's anything else we can unload to lighten the ship."

Boma came back, grim-faced. "Gaetano's body is there."

"It will have to be left behind," Spock said.

"Not without a burial!"

"I would not recommend one, Mr. Boma. The creatures won't be far away." He paused. "A burial would expose the members of this crew to unnecessary peril."

"I'll take that chance," Boma said.

Spock looked at the alien human. "Do your vestigial ceremonies mean that much to you?"

"Spock, I would insist on a decent burial even if it were your body lying back there!"

"Mr. Boma!" It was McCoy's rebuke.

Boma whirled on him. "I'm sick and tired of this Vulcan machine!"

Scott had reddened with anger. "That's enough from you! Mr. Spock is a ranking Commander of the service!"

The ranking Commander spoke quietly. "You shall have your burial, Mr. Boma . . . if our friends permit it." McCoy, still smarting in Spock's behalf, moved over to him.

* * *

Landing party Two had beamed back to the *Enterprise* from Taurus II with casualties—one crewman dead, two wounded.

"Lieutenant Kelowitz, what happened?"

Kirk had activated the computer screen at Spock's station. Now it held the smudged, scratched image of the landing party's leader. Kirk could see that his uniform was torn.

"We were attacked, sir. Huge, furry creatures. I checked with astral anthropology. Order 480G, anthropoid, similar to life forms discovered on Hansen's planet—but much larger. Ten, twelve feet in height . . ."

"Your casualties?"

"Ensign O'Neill was speared even before we knew they were around. Crewman Immamaura has a dislocated shoulder and severe lacerations, but he'll make it all right." The tired eyes on the screen were lost momentarily to horrified recollection of the monster anthropoids. "Captain, they're all over the place. If the *Galileo* is down on that planet . . ."

Kirk nodded. "Thank you, Lieutenant. You'd better report to Sickbay yourself."

"Aye, aye, sir."

The image faded—and Ferris strode out of the elevator, his jaw set. "Captain Kirk, if you will check your chronometer, you will see it is exactly 2823.8. Your time is up."

"Commissioner, my men are still out there," Kirk said.

"So are the plague victims on New Paris! I now assume the authority granted me under Title Fifteen, Galactic Emergency Procedures. I order you to abandon search, Captain."

Kirk said, "Shuttlecraft *Columbus* hasn't returned yet. I also have two search parties still out."

"You have your orders, Captain. Recall your search parties and proceed to Makus III immediately."

He was beaten.

His voice was inflectionless as he spoke to Uhura. "Lieutenant, order the Transporter Room to beam up the search parties still on the surface. Attempt contact with the *Columbus*."

"I'm in partial contact with them now, sir."

"Have them return at once." He left the computer station to return to his command chair. "Mr. Sulu, prepare to abandon search. Set course for Makus III."

Ferris left the bridge—and Kirk slumped back in his chair. There was nothing more to do, nothing more to say. Spock, McCoy, Scott—all dead, mercifully dead on that savage planet. Had their deaths been easy? Hardly. Uhura had to tell him twice that the sensor beams were working again.

No time to mourn. No time, period.

"The other systems?" he said to Uhura.

"No, sir. Still too much interference."

Sulu said, "Course set for Makus III, Captain."

"Thank you, Mr. Sulu. Steady on post. Lieutenant Uhura, how long before the *Columbus* comes aboard?"

"Twenty-three minutes, sir."

"Twenty-three minutes," Kirk said. Then, leaning his arms on his console, he cupped his chin in his hands.

Yeoman Mears, no longer fresh-faced, but tired and worn, had failed again to contact the *Enterprise*. She snapped closed her communicator. "Nothing, sir," she told Spock. "Just ionic interference."

He went to Scott. "How about weight?"

Scott finished draining the last phaser. He looked up as he laid it aside. "If we shed every extra ounce of it, we may be able to achieve orbit."

"How long can we keep it?"

"A few hours. If we time it right, we could cut out of orbit with enough fuel for a controlled re-entry."

"To land here again? Not an attractive possibility."

"We have very few alternatives," Scott said. He stooped to remove the drained phasers from the aisle as Boma and McCoy came from the aft compartment, carrying Gaetano's body.

"How does it look outside?" McCoy asked..

Spock glanced out the forward window. Then he spoke to Scott. "When can we lift off, Mr. Scott?"

"Maybe eight minutes if the weight's right."

Spock faced around from the window. "Doctor, Mr. Boma, the ship will lift off in exactly ten minutes. You have that long to bury Mr. Gaetano. It appears to be all clear outside, at least for the moment." He cautiously opened the hatch, peering around the crater. As he turned back inside, he said, "I shall assist you. Please hurry."

Yeoman Mears moved down the aisle to where Scott, at the control console, was warming up its equipment. "Can we get off?" she said.

"Oh, we can get off all right, lassie. But can we stay off? That's the question."

"If we make orbit, the *Enterprise* will—"

"By now," he said, "the *Enterprise* should be well on its way to Makus III."

"Then . . . we're alone."

"Not alone." He made a gesture toward the crater walls. "We've got some big hairy things out there to keep us company."

It was the thought of the big, hairy things that had brought Kirk to his decision. He uncupped his chin from his hands. "Mr. Sulu, proceed on course as ordered for Makus III. At space normal speed."

Sulu was startled. "But all systems report secured for warp factors, sir. Space normal speed?"

"You heard me, Mr. Sulu. Lieutenant Uhura, order all sensor sections to direct beams aft, full function, continuous operation until further orders."

Ferris, the paper man, had not specified warp speed.

They'd dug the grave in the spongy soil. It was as they were filling the hole that they all heard the grating sound. Then from the mist-shrouded rocks above them came a piercing howl—a triumphant roar as though the thing which had uttered it was beating its furry chest in token of victory.

"Into the ship!" Spock shouted. "Take-off immediate!"

A spear struck the grave. Another one grazed Boma's shoulder. Then the air was thick with them. Spock, racing toward the ship, saw a large axe of strange shape hit the ground. As he reached for it, a rock, hurtling down, crashed against his thigh. He struggled to rise but the wounded leg went out from under him. Dragging himself toward the ship, he yelled, "Lift off! Lift off!"

Boma and McCoy were at the open hatch. They left it to run to him. He waved them back furiously. "No! Get back! *Lift off!*"

They disobeyed. McCoy grabbed his shoulders—and a spear whizzed past his head. Half-carrying half-pulling, they got Spock to the hatch and shoved him inside. Boma slammed it shut just as a giant body heaved at the craft, rocking it.

Spock, clutching his injured leg, glared at his rescuers. "I told you to lift off!"

McCoy, at work on the leg, said, "Don't be a fool, Spock. We couldn't leave you out there!" He paused. Once more, big rocks were hammering at the hull. Spock pushed McCoy away. "Can we lift off, Mr. Scott?"

"We should be able to—but we're not moving!"

Yeoman Mears screamed. In the port window beside her a bestial face, enormous, red-eyed was peering in at her. McCoy slammed the shutter down over the window. Spock was hobbling toward the console's seat. For a moment his delicate fingers flitted over the controls. "They seem to be holding us down," he said. "All systems are go—but we're not moving." His hand went out to another switch. Appalled, Scott cried, "What are you doing, man?"

"The boosters."

"We won't be able to hold orbit!"

Spock moved the switch. The ship bucked. Needles quivered on the console. There was a last defiant crash on the hull, screams of baffled hate—and the *Galileo* shot up and out of the crater.

Yeoman Mears burst into tears of relief. "We're rid of them . . . of that terrible place. . . ."

Spock spoke. "I must remind you all that we have yet to achieve orbit. Nor can we maintain it long. An hour from now we might well be right back where we started."

But Spock's warning couldn't depress the hope roused by the familiar sight of star-filled space. McCoy, thoughtfully regarding the straight back in the console's seat, said, "Spock—back there—what held you back when we were attacked?"

"A most intriguing artifact . . . a hand axe, Doctor, reminiscent of those used by the Lake People of Athos IV."

"Even if you'd gotten it, you couldn't have brought it back with you. It must have weighed a hundred and fifty pounds."

Spock looked around from the console, his face astounded. "You know, Doctor, until this moment, that never occurred to me."

McCoy grunted. "An encouraging sign of humanity. It was a fool thing to do. It almost got you killed. If we hadn't come after you . . ."

"By coming after me you caused a delay in our lift off. So you may well have destroyed what slim chance you have of survival. The logical thing was to leave me behind."

McCoy sighed. "Well, you're back to normal. Remind me to tell you sometime how sick and tired I am of your logic."

"I will, Doctor." He was scanning the console. "Orbit attitude in one minute, Mr. Scott. Fuel status?"

"Fifteen pounds psi. Approximately enough for one complete orbit."

"And after that?" McCoy said.

Scott shook his head. "Tapping those boosters removed our last chance of making a soft landing."

"You mean—a burn-up?" asked Boma.

Spock said, "That is the usual end of a decaying orbit."

McCoy got up and went to him. "Spock, can't we do anything?"

He looked up. "The *Enterprise* is undoubtedly back on course for Makus III. I, for one, do not believe in angels. There won't be one around, Doctor, to bear us up on its wings."

"Well, Spock . . . so ends your first command."

"Yes. My first command."

Scott said, "Orbit attitude attained, Mr. Spock. With present fuel that gives us about forty-five minutes."

But Spock seemed singularly uninterested in the information. Nodding slightly, he stared at the console. Then he slowly turned his head to look at the others. They were all back there in their seats . . . McCoy, the girl, Boma—and Scott, standing by. And all of them, each in his own way, alone with the thought of the final extinction. But their eyes were on him as though he could magically avert it for them. If he'd been a sweating creature, Spock would have been wet with it. Instead, he was a Vulcan by training as well as inheritance, a being required to remain impervious to emotion. Now, in his half-human agony, he took refuge behind a mask of stone. His first and last command. His hand went out toward a switch.

"Spock!" Scott shouted.

He threw the switch. The ship trembled—and a blast of fire burst from its pods.

"What's happened?" cried the girl.

"He's jettisoned the fuel—and ignited it!" Scott yelled.

Boma was on his feet. "Have you gone crazy, Spock?"

"Perhaps, Mr. Boma."

McCoy, licking his lips, girded himself for the question. "Scotty, how long do we have?"

"Six minutes."

At Sulu's cry Kirk turned his pain-drawn face. "Yes, Mr. Sulu?"

"The screen, Captain! Something's back there! At Taurus II!"

The strain had been too much for all of them. Sulu was hallucinating. "The screen," Kirk said. Then he looked at it. "Sensors, Mr. Sulu? A meteorite?"

"No, sir. It's holding a lateral line! There it is again . . . on the screen. Captain, it's holding steady!"

A streak of flame was moving against the blackness of space.

Kirk exploded into action. "One hundred and eighty degrees about, Mr. Sulu! Lieutenant Uhura! Contact Transporter Room! All beams ready! Full normal speed!"

On the screen the flame flickered—and died.

And on the *Galileo* Spock sat unmoving. The heat had begun. He could sense the unbelieving eyes fixed on him—and his Satanic, alien ears. He had destroyed them. He was hardly aware of the hand, the human hand, that suddenly fell on his shoulder.

"Ah, laddie," Scott said, "it was a good gamble. Maybe it was worth it."

Somebody said, "I don't . . . understand."

Scott whirled. "He turned the ship into a distress signal—a flare!"

Spock said, "Even if there's no one out there to see it."

Scott kept the hand on his shoulder. "The orbit's decaying. Thirty-six seconds to atmosphere."

McCoy joined them. "It may be the last action you ever take, Spock—but it was all human."

"Totally illogical, Doctor. There was no chance."

"Which is exactly what I mean," McCoy said.

A whining sound came. A wisp of smoke drifted from the control panel. Spock, reaching up, slid up the metal shutter on the forward window. The *Galileo* was on fire, glowing red to orange to pure white flame. Its prisoners tore at their throats, coughing as the aisle filled with hot smoke.

Kirk, fingers crossed in the old Earth's plea to Lady Luck, said, *"Activate Transporter beams!"*

Then he waited. A sweating creature, he could feel it breaking from every pore of his body. Sulu said, "Whatever it was, Captain, it just burned up in the atmosphere."

"Yes. I can see for myself, Mr. Sulu."

Behind him Uhura leaped from her chair. "Captain! Transporter Room reports five persons aboard! Alive and well!"

"Alive, Lieutenant?"

So the beams had caught them. In the searing heat of the *Galileo*, they had faded, breaking to the dazzle that had brought them home. Kirk covered his face with his hands. Then he lifted his head. "Mr. Sulu. Proceed on course for Makus III. Warp factor one."

"Aye, aye, sir. Warp factor one."

McCoy was whispering to Kirk. Then they both looked over to the computer station where Spock sat, composed, his eyes intent on his dials.

"Mr. Spock?"

"Yes, Captain."

"When you ignited all your remaining fuel, you knew there was virtually no chance the flame would be seen. But you did it anyhow. Am I correct in defining that as an act of desperation?"

"Yes, Captain."

"Desperation is a highly emotional state of mind. How do you account for it in yourself?"

"Quite simply, sir. I examined the problem from all angles. It was plainly hopeless. Logic informed me that the only possible action would have to be a desperate one. A logical decision, logically arrived at."

"You mean, you reasoned it was time for an emotional outburst?"

"I would not use those terms, sir, but those are essentially the facts."

"You're not going to admit that for once in your life you committed a purely human, emotional act?"

"No, sir."

"Mr. Spock, you are a stubborn man."

"Yes, sir."

Kirk got up, started toward him, thought better of it. Grinning, he shook his head, himself accepting the logic of facts as they were. Spock caught the grin. His left eyebrow lifted.

ARENA

WRITER: GENE L. COON (STORY BY FREDRIC BROWN)
DIRECTOR: JOSEPH PEVNEY
FIRST AIRED: JANUARY 19, 1967

CAPTAIN JAMES KIRK OF THE USS *ENTERPRISE* WAS THE ABSOLUTE MASTER OF the largest and most modern vessel in the Star Fleet Service, of all the complex apparatus and weaponry aboard her, and of the manifold talents of 430 highly trained crewmen.

And at the moment, he was stranded on a nearly barren artificial asteroid, location unknown, facing a tyrannosaurlike creature whose survival depended upon its killing Kirk, and equipped with absolutely nothing except a small translator-recorder useless as a weapon.

The situation had developed with bewildering rapidity. Originally, the *Enterprise* had received a call from the Earth outpost on Cestus Three, part of a planetary system on the very edge of an unexplored quadrant of the galaxy. The base commandant, an old soldier named Travers, had asked Kirk to beam down with the tactical staff of the *Enterprise;* and since things were quiet in this sector of space and Travers was famous in the Service for setting a good table, all six men had accepted cheerfully.

But the invitation had been a trap—a prerecorded trap. They had found the settlement in smoking ruins, the personnel dead. Furthermore, within minutes after its arrival the landing party was also under attack—and so was the *Enterprise*.

Evidently, the enemy, whoever he was, did not have the transporter and had no idea of its capabilities; after five minutes' inconclusive exchange of shots, the landing party was whisked away clean. The enemy ship broke off the engagement and fled, at fantastically high acceleration.

Kirk had no intention of letting it get away, however. It seemed obvious that any attempt to ambush the *Enterprise*'s tactical staff and captain, and then to destroy the starship itself, could only be a prelude to a full-scale invasion. Furthermore, the unknown enemy was well armed—the damage its ship had suffered thus far had been minor, despite its flight—and peculiarly ruthless, as witness its having wiped out 512 helpless people at an inoffensive scientific outpost simply to bait its trap. As Science Officer Spock had pointed out, that ship could not be allowed to reach its home base; presumably, as long as that unknown world was kept in the dark about Federation strength, it would hold off its next attack—thus buying precious time for a defense buildup.

The enemy seemed equally anxious to avoid leading the *Enterprise* to its home planet. It took complex evasive action, again at incredibly high speed; the *Enterprise* had difficulty in closing with her even at warp eight, two factors above maximum safe speed.

And then, suddenly, everything stopped.

It was absolutely impossible, but it happened. At one moment, both vessels were flashing through subspace at over a hundred times the speed of light—and in the next, both were floating in normal space, motionless relative to a small, nearby solar system, engines inoperative, all weapons dead.

"Report!" Kirk snapped.

But there was no damage, nothing abnormal—except that the *Enterprise* could neither move nor fight, nor, apparently, could the enemy.

"We're being scanned, sir," Communications Officer Uhura said.

"From the alien ship?"

"No, sir," she said. "From that solar system ahead. Nothing hostile—no tractors or weapon sensors, just scanners."

"Stopping us like this might be considered hostile," Kirk said drily.

"Getting something else, Captain—a modulation of the main frequency . . ."

Abruptly, the lights dimmed and there was a low hum from the main viewing screen. The starry scene from outside promptly dissolved into a twisting, confused mass of color and lines. At the same time a humanoid voice, strong and yet somehow youthful, shook the air of the bridge. The voice said:

"We are the Metrons."

Kirk and Spock exchanged speculative glances. Then the Science Officer said, quite composedly: "How do you do?"

The voice's owner paid no apparent attention. It continued:

"You are one of two craft that have come into our space on a mission of violence. This is not permissible. Our analysis further shows that your violent tendencies are inherent. Hence we will resolve your conflict in the way most suited to your natures. Captain James Kirk!"

"This is Captain Kirk," Kirk said, after a moment's hesitation.

"We have prepared a planetoid with a suitable atmosphere, temperature and gravity. You will be taken there, as will the captain of the Gorn ship that you have been pursuing. You and your opponent will be provided with a translator-recorder. You can keep a record, or communicate with each other, should you feel the need. But not with your ships. You will each be totally alone, and will settle your dispute alone."

"Just what makes you think you can interfere . . ." Kirk began angrily.

"It is you who are doing the interfering. We are simply putting a stop to it—within your own violent frame of reference. The place we have prepared for you contains sufficient resources for either of you to construct weapons lethal to the other. The winner of the ordeal will be permitted to go on his way unharmed. The loser, along with his ship, will be destroyed in the interests of peace. The contest will be one of ingenuity against ingenuity, brute strength against brute strength. The outcome will be final."

With that, silently, the ship around Kirk vanished.

The first thing he saw was the Gorn. It was a biped, a reptile, a lizard that walked like a man. It stood about six feet four, with tremendous musculature, dully gleaming skin, a ridge of hard plate running down its back, and a strong, thick tail. The tail did not look prehensile; rather, it seemed to be a balancing organ, suggesting that the creature could run very fast indeed if it wished. The head was equipped with two tiny earholes and a wide mouth full of sharp teeth.

This, then, was the enemy, the raider, the destroyer of Cestus Three. It was wearing a garment like a short robe, belted; at the belt hung a small electronic device. It wore no shoes; clawed feet dug deeply into the ground, indicating considerable weight. Shooting a wary glance down at himself, Kirk discovered that his own clothing and equipment were identical.

Kirk and the Gorn stared at each other. All around them was a rocky, barren terrain, with a peculiar gray-green sky and occasional clumps of vegetation, some of it fairly tall, but none of it familiar. The air was cold and dry.

Kirk wondered if the Gorn was as uncomfortable as he was. Probably, but for different reasons. The meddling Metrons would surely have allowed neither of them an advantage in environment; after all, this planetoid was artificial—deliberately constructed to be an arena for a trial of champions, and for nothing else.

The Gorn moved. It was closing in on Kirk. It looked quite capable of killing him with its bare hands. Kirk moved sidewise, warily.

The Gorn did not appear to want to take any chances. As it too circled, it passed close to a gnarled object like a small tree, perhaps eight to ten inches through the trunk, and about ten feet high. With a quick look at Kirk, the Gorn hissed softly, reached out, and broke off a thick branch. The move seemed to cost it very little effort, whereas Kirk doubted that he could have done it at all.

Then, suddenly, holding the branch aloft like a club, the Gorn was charging him.

Kirk sprang aside barely in time. As the Gorn passed, somewhat off-balance, Kirk swung a killing blow into its midriff. The impact nearly broke his hand, but it seemed to have no other effect. The club lashed back, knocking Kirk sprawling against the rocks.

The Gorn wheeled around, clumsily but swiftly, and pounced. Kirk, dazed, tried to counter with a forearm blow to the throat, but it was like hitting an elephant. Then the creature was gripping him like a grizzly. Kirk's arm just managed to keep the teeth away, but that grip was going to break his back.

Freeing his arms with a sudden twist, Kirk boxed the Gorn's earholes with cupped hands. The Gorn screamed and staggered back, shaking its huge head. Springing to his feet, Kirk picked up a boulder as big as his head and hurled it at the Gorn with all his strength.

It struck the Gorn fair on the chest. The creature lurched slightly, but it did not seem to be hurt. Hissing shrilly, it bent to pick up a boulder of its own. The thing must have weighed a thousand pounds, but the Gorn got it aloft in one titanic jerk.

Kirk ran.

The rock hit behind him with an explosive crack, and flying splinters cut into the calf of one leg like shrapnel. Still hobbling as fast as he could, Kirk looked back over his shoulder.

The Gorn was not following. Instead, it was heaving up another rock. Then, as if realizing that Kirk was now out of range, it let the huge mass drop. It seemed to be grinning, although as far as Kirk had been able to see, it never wore any other expression.

Kirk looked around, panting. He seemed to be in a gully, though there was no sign that water had ever run in it—after all, there hadn't ever been such a planet many hours ago. There were rocks everywhere, some of them brilliantly colored, and an occasional outcropping of quartzlike crystals. Here and there were patches of scrubby, tough-looking brush, some of it resembling cacti, some mesquite, and even an occasional stand of a large, bamboolike growth. There was nothing that looked as though it could possibly be converted into a weapon, no matter what the Metron had said.

Kirk sat down, rubbing his injured leg but taking great care to watch the now-distant Gorn, and looked over the device at his belt. It looked quite like a tricorder, but both smaller and simpler—though simpler, at least, it doubtless was not. Kirk turned it on with the obvious switch.

"Calling the *Enterprise*. Captain James Kirk calling the *Enterprise*."

For a moment, there was no answer. Then the instrument said, in good but rather stilted English:

"You forget, Captain. We cannot reach our ships. We are alone here, you and I—just one against the other."

He looked back the way he had come. Sure enough, the Gorn seemed to be speaking behind one raised hand.

Kirk had not, of course, forgotten that he had been *told* he could not raise the *Enterprise;* he had simply wanted to test the statement. What he had forgotten was that the small instrument had been said to be a translator, as well as a recorder. He would have to be very careful not to mutter to himself after this.

After a moment, he said tentatively, "Look here, Gorn, this is insane. Can't we patch up some kind of truce?"

"Out of the question," the translator said promptly. "That would result only in our staying here until we starved. I cannot speak for you, but I see no water here, nor anything I could eat—with the possible exception of you."

"Neither do I," Kirk admitted.

"Then let us not waste time in sentimental hopes. The rules are what they are: One of us must kill the other."

Kirk hung the device back on his belt. The Gorn was right, and that was most definitely that.

He scrambled over to look at the bamboolike stuff. Each stalk was perhaps three to four inches in diameter—and, as he discovered by trying to break a section loose, it was as hard as iron. Hitting it with a rock even produced a distinctly metallic clank. Perhaps it picked up iron from the soil, as horsetails pick up calcium oxalate, or some prairie grasses pick up selenium. Useless.

He moved on up the gully, which got steadily deeper; he lost sight of the Gorn almost at once. Well, the risk had to be taken; staying where he was had gotten him nowhere.

Earthen banks, rather like bluish clay, reared on both sides of him now. One was steep, but the slope of the other was gentle enough to permit him to clamber up it if he had to.

Sticking out of the clay were the pyramidal points of a number of large crystals. Hopefully, Kirk pried one of them out. It was about the size of a hen's egg, and glittered brilliantly even under this sunless sky. The shape and the brilliancy were unmistakable: It was a diamond, and one that would have made the Kohinoor look like a mail-order zircon. And not only were there more of them imbedded in the clay, but the floor of the gully, he now saw, was a litter of them, in all sizes down to fine sand.

An incredible fortune—and again, utterly useless. None of the gems was sharp enough to be used as a weapon point, and he had no way to cut them. Their only use was to show that this planet was indeed an artificial construction—but Kirk had never doubted that, anyhow. He would have traded the whole wealth of them for a hand phaser, or even a medieval crossbow and a quiver of bolts for it.

The gully turned just ahead. Throwing the diamond away, Kirk went around the bend. The Metron had said that there were the raw materials of weapons here somewhere, if only he—

At the next step, his ankle struck a taut vine, and he went sprawling. At the same moment there was a sharp *crack!* as of wood splitting, and then one whole side of the gully seemed to be roaring down upon him.

He rolled frantically in the other direction, but not fast enough to prevent one rock from slamming into his chest. He felt a rib break. Staggering to his feet, he ran for the nearest cover, a sculptured overhang almost deep enough in back to be called a cave. There he stopped, breathing hard and nursing his rib cage—his whole body seemed to be one enormous bruise—and inspected the snare that had almost killed him through the gradually settling dust.

Arena

It was very simple and highly ingenious: a length of stretched vine to serve as a trigger, a broken branch, a heap of carefully stacked boulders that had been freed when the branch had been pulled loose.

Above him, Kirk heard the tick of large claws on rock, and then a sharp hiss of what could only have been disappointment. Kirk grinned mirthlessly. It had been near enough. He peered cautiously out of his hole and upward, just in time to see the Gorn on the lip of the gully on the other side, moving away. The creature was carrying something long and shiny in one hand. Kirk could not tell exactly what it was, but the fact that the Gorn had a torn scrap of his tunic wrapped around that hand was clue enough. It was a daggerlike blade, evidently chipped out of obsidian glass.

Then the creature was gone, but Kirk did not feel the least bit reassured. So far, the Gorn was way ahead, not only on strength, but on ingenuity. First a snare—now a dagger.

Well, then, back to the Stone Age with a vengeance. If Kirk could find a flint point, another length of vine, a sufficiently long stick, he might make a spear. That would give him the advantage of reach against the Gorn's dagger. On the other hand, would a spear penetrate that hide? There was only one way to find out.

A sufficiently large chip of flint, however, obstinately failed to turn up. All that was visible on the floor of the overhang was a wash of brilliant yellow powder.

The stuff looked familiar, and on a hunch, Kirk picked up a small handful of it and breathed on it. It gave out the faint crackle characteristic of flowers of sulfur when moistened.

Kirk grimaced. What a maddening planet. Sand of high-purity sulfur, veritable beaches of diamonds, iron-concentrating bamboos; and at the back of the cave here, outcroppings of rocks covered with a yellowish-white effluvium, like saltpeter. The only way he could make any sort of weapon out of a mélange like that would be with a smelter and a forge—

Wait a minute. Just a minute, now. There was something at the back of his mind—something very ancient . . .

With a gulp of hope, he ran back toward the growth of bamboolike stuff.

With a sharp rock, he managed to break off about a three-foot length of one tube, at one of its joints. The tube was closed at one end, open at the other. Ideal.

Now, the diamonds. He took up only the smallest, the most sandlike, measuring them by handfuls into the tube. He could only hope that his memory of the proportions—seventy-five, fifteen, ten—was correct; in any event, he could only approximate the measures under these conditions. Now, one of the large egg-shaped diamonds; this he put into his mouth, since the tunic did not come equipped with pockets.

Back up the gully, down and around the bend to the overhang. Into the tube went sulfur, saltpeter. Covering the end, he shook the tube until a little of the mixture poured out into his palm showed an even color, though certainly not the color it should have been.

A stone point penetrated the bamboo at the base, though it was hard work. A bit of torn tunic for a patch, and ram it all home with a stick. Then the egg-shaped diamond; then another patch, and ram again. Finally, a piece of flint; it did not have to be large, not any more.

"Captain," the translator at his belt said. He did not answer.

"Captain, be reasonable," the translator said. "Hiding will do you no good. If it is a matter of competitive starvation, I think my endurance is greater than yours. Why not come out, and die like a warrior?"

Kirk ignored it. Shredding another piece of cloth from the tunic, he began to strike the piece of flint over it, using the translator—at last it had a use!—as the steel. Sparks flew, but the cloth would not catch. If it was non-inflammable—

"You cannot destroy me," the translator said. "Let us be done with it. I shall be merciful and quick."

"Like you were at Cestus Three?" Kirk said.

"You were intruding," the translator said. "You established an outpost in our space. Naturally we destroyed it."

Kirk did not stop striking sparks, but he was at the same time thoughtful. What the Gorn said was perhaps reasonable, from its point of view. Very little was known about that arm of the galaxy; perhaps the Gorn had a right to regard it as theirs—and to be alarmed at the setting up of a base there, and by the advent of a ship the size of the *Enterprise*. Nevertheless . . .

Smoke rose from the shredded cloth. He raised it to his lips, blowing gently. It was catching.

"All right, Gorn," he told the translator. "Come and get me if you think you can. I'm under the overhang just past where you set your snare."

There was a sharp hiss, and then the clear sound of the Gorn's claws, coming at a run up the gully. Kirk had miscalculated. The creature was closer than he had thought—and faster. Frantically he struggled to align the clumsy bamboo tube.

The Gorn leapt into view, its obsidian knife raised. Kirk slapped the burning piece of clothes against the touchhole, and the makeshift cannon went off with a splintering roar. The concussion knocked Kirk down; the semicave was filled with acrid smoke.

He groped to his feet again. As the smoke cleared, he saw the Gorn, slumped against the other wall of the gully. The diamond egg had smashed its right shoulder; but it was bleeding from half a dozen other places too, where diamond chips had flown out of the cannon instead of igniting.

The knife lay between them. Leaping forward, Kirk snatched it up, hurled himself on the downed alien. The knife's point found one of the wounds.

"Now," Kirk said hoarsely, "now let's see how tough your hide is!"

The Gorn did not answer. Though conscious, it seemed to be in shock. It was all over. All Kirk had to do was shove.

He could not do it. He rose, slowly.

"No," he said. "We're in the same pickle. You're trying to save your ship, the same as I am. I won't kill you for that."

Suddenly furious, Kirk looked up at the greenish, overcast sky.

"Do you hear?" he shouted. "I won't kill him! You'll have to get your entertainment some place else!"

There was a long pause. Kirk stared down at the wounded alien; the Gorn stared back. Its translator had been shattered by the impact; it could not know what Kirk had said. But it did not seem to be afraid.

Then it vanished.

Kirk sat down, dejected and suddenly, utterly weary. Right or wrong, he had lost his opportunity now. The Metron had snatched the Gorn away.

Then there was a humming, much like that he had heard so long ago aboard ship, when the screen had been scrambled. He turned.

A figure was materializing under the overhang. It was not very formidable—certainly nothing so ominous, so awe-inspiring as its voice had suggested. Also, it was very beautiful. It looked like a boy of perhaps eighteen.

"You're a Metron," Kirk said listlessly.

"True," said the figure. "And you have surprised us, Captain."

"How?" Kirk said, not much interested. "By winning?"

"No. We had no preconceptions as to which of you would win. You surprised us by refusing to kill, although you had pursued the Gorn craft into our space with the intention of destroying it."

"That was different," Kirk said. "That was necessary."

"Perhaps it was. It is a new thought. Under the circumstances, it is only fair to tell you that we lied to you."

"In what way?"

"We said that the ship of the loser of this personal combat would be destroyed," said the Metron. "After all, it would be the winner—the stronger, the more resourceful race—who would pose the greatest threat to us. It was the winner we planned to destroy."

Kirk lurched to his feet. "Not my ship," he said dangerously.

"No, Captain. We have changed our minds. By sparing your helpless enemy—who would surely have killed you in like circumstances—you demonstrated the advanced trait of mercy. This we hardly expected—and it leaves us with no clear winner."

"What did you do with the Gorn, then?"

"We sent him back to his ship. And in your case, we misinterpreted your motives. You sincerely believed that you would be destroying the Gorn ship to keep the peace, not break it. If you like, we shall destroy it for you."

"No!" Kirk said hastily. "That is not necessary. It was a . . . a misunderstanding. Now that we've made contact, we'll be able to talk to the Gorn—reach an agreement."

"Very good," said the Metron. "Perhaps we too shall meet again—in a few thousand years. In any event, there is hope for you."

And abruptly, the *Enterprise* sprang into being around Kirk.

Turmoil broke out on the bridge. Ship's Surgeon McCoy was the first to reach Kirk's side.

"Jim! Are you all right?"

"To be quite honest with you," Kirk said dazedly, "I don't know. I just wish the world would stop popping in and out at me."

"I gather you won," Spock said. "How did you do it?"

"Yes . . . I guess so. I'm not quite sure. I thought I did it by reinventing gunpowder—with diamond dust for charcoal. But the Metrons say I won by being a sucker. I don't know which explanation is truer. All the Metrons would tell me is that we're a most promising species—as predators go."

"I could not have put the matter more neatly myself," Spock said. "But, Captain, I would be interested to know what it is you're talking about—when you feel ready, of course."

"Yes, indeed," Kirk said. "In the meantime, posts, everybody. It's time we got back down to business. And, Mr. Spock, about that explanation . . ."

"Yes, sir?"

"I suggest you raise the question again, in, say, a few thousand years."

"Yes, sir."

And the odd thing about Spock, the captain reflected, was that he *would* wait that long too, if only he could figure out a way to live through it—and when the time had all passed, Spock would remember to ask the question again.

Kirk hoped he would have an answer.

TOMORROW IS YESTERDAY

Writer: D. C. Fontana
Director: Michael O'Herlihy
First Aired: January 26, 1967

The star was very old—as old as it is possible for a star to be, a first-generation star, born when the present universe was born. It had had all the experiences possible for a star—it had had planets; had gone nova, wiping out those planets and all those who lived upon them; had become an X-ray star; then a neutron star. At last, slowly collapsing upon itself into an ultimately dense mass of pseudo-matter resembling—except for its compaction—the primordial ylem out of which it had been created, it drew its gravitational field in so closely about itself that not even the few dim red flickers of light left to it could get out, and it prepared to die.

The star was still there, still in its orbit, and still incredibly massive despite its shrunken volume; but it could no longer be seen or detected. It would soon be in a space all its own, a tiny sterile universe as uninteresting and forgotten as a burial jug. It had become a black star.

The *Enterprise*, on a rare trip back toward the Sol sector and Earth, hit the black star traveling at warp factor four—sixty-four times the speed of light.

It could not, of course, properly be said that the *Enterprise* hit the black star itself. Technically, the bubble of subspace in which the *Enterprise* was enclosed, which would have been moving at 64C had the bubble impossibly been in normal space at all, hit that part of the black star's gravitational cocoon that had also begun to extrude into subspace. The technicalities, however, are not very convincing. Since no such thing had ever happened to a starship before, nobody could have predicted it, and the theoreticians are still arguing about just *why* the collision produced the results it did.

About the results themselves, nobody is in any doubt.

Captain Kirk dragged himself up from unconsciousness and shook his head to clear it. This was a mistake, and he did not try it a second time. The bridge was dim and quiet; the main lights were off, so was the screen, and only a few telltales glowed on the boards. Crew personnel—Spock, Uhura, Sulu—were slumped in their seats; Ames, the security chief, was spilled crookedly on the deck. It looked like the aftermath of a major attack.

"Spock!"

The first officer stirred, and then got shakily to his feet. "Here, Captain. What in the nine worlds . . ."

"I don't know. Everything was normal, and then, blooey! Check us out."

"Right." In immediate control of himself, Spock ran a quick check of his library computer. Except for a few flickers here and there on the board, it was dead, as Kirk could see himself. Spock abandoned it without a second thought and went promptly to Uhura.

"Except for secondary systems, everything is out, sir," he said. "We are on impulse power only. If Mr. Scott is still with us, the auxiliaries should be on in a moment. Are you all right, Lieutenant?"

Uhura nodded wordlessly and smiled at him, though it was not a very convincing smile. At the same moment, the main lights flickered on, brightened and steadied. A hum of computers and pumps began to fill in the familiar, essential background noise that was as much a part of life on the *Enterprise* as the air.

"Mr. Scott," Spock said, straightening, "is still with us."

Sulu sat up groggily, also shook his head, and also apparently decided against trying the experiment a second time. Kirk flicked a switch on his chair panel.

"This is the captain," he said. "Damage control parties on all decks, check in. All departments tie in to the library computer. Report casualties and operational readiness to the first officer. Kirk out. Miss Uhura, contact Star Fleet control. Whatever we hit in the Base Nine area, I want them alerted—and maybe they'll know something about it we don't. Mr. Spock?"

Spock half-turned from his station, an earphone still to one ear. "Only minor injuries to the crew, Captain. All decks operating on auxiliary systems. Engineering reports warp engines nonoperational. Mr. Scott overrode the automatic helm setting and is using impulse power to hold us in fixed orbit, but . . ."

"Fixed orbit around what, Mr. Spock?"

"The Earth, sir. I am at present unable to say how we got here."

"Screen on," Kirk said.

The screen came on. It was the Earth below them, all right.

"We're too low in the atmosphere to retain this altitude," Spock said. "Engineer reports we have enough impulse power to achieve escape velocity."

"Helm, give us some altitude."

"Yes, sir," Sulu said. "Helm answers. She's sluggish, sir."

"Sir," Uhura said. "Normal Star Fleet channel has nothing on it but static. I'm picking up something on another frequency, but it's not identifiable."

"Put it on audio, Lieutenant."

Uhura flicked a tumbler and the loudspeaker on her board burst out: ". . . five-thirty news summary. Cape Kennedy—the first manned moon shot is scheduled for

Wednesday, six A.M., Eastern Standard Time. All three astronauts set to make this historic flight are . . ."

Kirk was up out of his chair on the instant. "The first manned moon shot!" he said. "You've got some sort of dramatization. That shot was back in the 1970s."

Uhura nodded and tried another channel, but from the computer, Spock said slowly: "Apparently, Captain, so are we."

"Mr. Spock, this is no time for joking."

"I never joke," Spock said severely. "At present I have only rough computations, but apparently what we hit was the subspace component of an intense spherical gravity field, very likely a black star. The field translated our momentum in terms of time—a relativistic effect. I can give you an exact reading in a few moments, but 1970 seems to be of about the right order of magnitude."

Kirk sat down again, stunned. Uhura continued scanning. Finally she said, "Captain, I'm picking up a ground-to-air transmission in this sector."

"Verified," Spock said. "Our scanners are picking up some kind of craft approaching from below us, under cloud cover and closing fast."

The loudspeaker said: "Blue Jay Four, this is Black Jack. We're tracking both you and the UFO."

"I have him on my screen," another voice said. "Following."

"Good, let's get this one for once."

"Mr. Sulu," Kirk said, "can we gain altitude faster?"

"I'm trying, sir, but she's still slow in responding."

"Blue Jay Four, have you got visual contact yet?"

"I can see it fine," said the second voice. "And it's huge too. As big as a cruiser, bigger maybe. It *is* saucer-shaped, but there're two cylindrical projections on top and one below."

"We have two more flights scrambled and on the way," said the first voice. "They'll rendezvous with you in two minutes."

"Won't be here, Black Jack. The UFO is climbing away fast."

"Blue Jay Four, close on the object and force it to land. We want it down—or at least disabled until the other planes arrive. After thirty years of rumors, this may be our first clear shot."

"Acknowledged. Closing in."

"Can he harm us?" Kirk said.

"I would judge so, Captain," Spock said. "The aircraft is an interceptor equipped with missiles, possibly armed with nuclear warheads. Since we do not have the power for a full screen, he could at least damage us severely."

"Scotty!" Kirk said into his microphone. "Activate tractor beam. Lock onto that aircraft and hold it out there."

"Captain," Spock said, "that type of aircraft may be too fragile to take tractor handling."

"Tractor on, sir," Scott's voice said briskly. "We have the target."

Spock looked into his hooded viewer and shook his head. "And it is breaking up, Captain."

"Transporter Room! Can you lock on the cockpit of that aircraft?"

"No problem, Captain."

"Beam that pilot aboard," Kirk said, springing up. "Spock, take over."

The figure who materialized in the transporter chamber was a strange sight to Kirk until he removed his oxygen mask and helmet. Then he was revealed as a medium-tall, compactly built man with an expression of grim determination despite his obvious amazement. He would have made a good starship crewman, Kirk thought . . . centuries from now.

"Welcome to the *Enterprise*," Kirk said, smiling.

"You . . . you speak English!"

"That's right," Kirk said. "You can step down from our transporters, Mr. . . . ?"

"Captain John Christopher," the pilot said stiffly. "United States Air Force, serial number 4857932. And that's all the information you get."

"Relax, Captain. You're among friends. I'm Captain James T. Kirk, and I apologize for bringing you aboard so abruptly. But we had no choice. I didn't know your ship couldn't hold up under our tractor beam until it was too late."

"Don't give me any double-talk," Christopher said. "I demand to know . . ."

"You're in no position to demand anything, but we'll answer all your questions anyhow in good time. Meanwhile, relax. You're our guest. I have a feeling you'll find it interesting."

He led the way out of the Transporter Room. Christopher shrugged and followed. As they moved down the corridor, he was obviously missing nothing; clearly a trained observer. When a pretty young crewwoman carrying a tricorder went past them, however, he had trouble retaining his composure. "Passenger?" he said.

"No, crew. About a fourth of the crew is female—exactly a hundred at the moment."

"A crew of four hundred?"

"Four hundred and thirty. Now if you'll step aboard the elevator . . ."

Christopher did, and was immediately startled once more when it moved horizontally instead of up or down. After digesting this peculiarity, he said:

"It must have taken quite a lot of money to build a ship like this."

"Indeed it did. There are only twelve like it in the fleet."

"The fleet? Did the Navy . . . ?"

"We're a combined service, Captain," Kirk said. "Our authority is the United Federation of Planets."

"Federation of—Planets?"

"That's right. Actually, Captain—this is a little difficult to explain. We . . . we're from your future. A time warp landed us back here. It was an accident."

"You people seem to have a lot of them," Christopher said drily, "if all the UFO reports stem from the same kind of source. However, I can't argue with the fact that you *are* here, ship and all." While he spoke, the elevator doors snapped open to reveal the bridge, with Spock in the command chair. "And I've never believed in little green men."

"Neither have I," Spock said, rising.

This time Christopher made no attempt to conceal his astonishment. *And Spock claims he never jokes,* Kirk thought; but he said only, "Captain Christopher, this is my first officer, Commander Spock."

"Captain," Spock said with an abrupt but courteous nod.

"Please feel free to look around the bridge, Captain. I'm sure you have the good sense not to touch anything. I think you'll find it interesting."

"'Interesting,'" Christopher said, "is not a very adequate word for it." He moved over toward the communications and library-computer stations, but could not help shooting another look at Spock as he did so. Kirk did not explain; everybody else on board took the half-alien first officer as a matter of course, and Christopher might as well practice doing the same; he might be with them for quite a while yet.

"We have achieved a stable orbit out of Earth's atmosphere, Captain," Spock said. "Our deflector shields are operative now, and ought to prevent us from being picked up again as a UFO." He made a grimace of distaste over the word. "Mr. Scott wishes to speak to you about the engines."

"Very well, Mr. Spock. I know that expression. What else is on your mind?"

"Captain Christopher."

Kirk looked toward the newcomer. He was talking to Uhura; the spectacle of a beautiful Bantu girl operating a communications board evidently had diverted him, at least temporarily, from the first officer.

"All right, what about him?"

"We cannot return him to Earth," Spock said. "He already knows too much about us and is learning more. I mean no aspersions on his character, about which I know nothing, but suppose an unscrupulous man were to gain possession of the knowledge of man's certain future, as represented by us? Such a man could speculate—manipulate key industries, stocks, even nations—and in doing so, change what must be. And if it is changed, Captain, you and I and everything we know might be made impossible."

"We'd just vanish? Including thousands of tons of *Enterprise*?"

"Like a soap bubble."

"Hmm. You know, Spock, your logic can be very annoying." Kirk looked back at Christopher. "That flight suit must be uncomfortable. Have the quartermaster issue

Captain Christopher some suitable clothes—tactfully relieving him of any sidearms he may be carrying in the process—and then I want to see you and him in my quarters."

"Yes, sir."

Kirk was talking to the computer when they came in; he waved them to seats. "Captain's log, supplemental. Engineering Officer Scott reports warp engines damaged but repairable. Ascertain precise degree and nature of damage, compute nature and magnitude of forces responsible, and program possible countermeasures."

"Affirm; operating," said the computer's voice in mid-air. Christopher did not react; evidently he was getting used to surprises.

"Kirk out. Now, Captain, we have a problem. To put the matter bluntly, what are we going to do with you? We can't put you back."

"What do you mean, can't? Mr. Spock here tells me that your transporter can work over even longer distances than this."

"It's not the transporter," Kirk said. "You know what the future looks like, Captain. If anybody else finds out, they could change the course of it—and destroy it."

"I can see that," Christopher said after a moment. "But it also strikes me that my disappearance would also change things."

"Apparently not," Spock said. "I have run a computer check through all historical tapes. They show no relevant contribution by any Captain John Christopher. There was a popular author by that name, but it was a pen name; you are not he."

Christopher was visibly deflated, but not for long. He stood and began to pace. Finally he swung back toward Kirk.

"Captain," he said, "if it were only a matter of my own preference, I'd stay. I'd give my right arm to learn more about this ship—*all* about it. It's a colossal achievement and obviously it implies even greater ones in the background. But my preference doesn't count. It's my duty to report what I've seen. I have an oath to uphold." He paused, then added pointedly: "What would you do?"

"Just that," Kirk said. "I entirely understand. You are the kind of man we recruit for our own service, and can never get enough of, though we don't have oaths any more. But unfortunately, this means that you are also of superior intelligence. We cannot risk any report that you might make."

"I have a wife and two children," Christopher said quietly. "I suppose that makes no difference to you."

"It makes a lot of difference to me," Kirk said. "But I cannot let it sway me."

"In both your trades—the pilot and the warrior—there was always an unusually high risk that you would become a casualty," Spock said. "You knew it when you married; so did your wife. You bet against the future, with high odds against you. Unfortunately, we are the future and you have lost; you are, in effect, now a casualty."

"Mr. Spock is no more unfeeling than I am," Kirk added. "But logic is one of his specialties, and what he says is quite true. I can only say I'm sorry, and I mean it." The intercom interrupted him. "Excuse me a moment. Kirk here."

"Engineer here, Captain. Everything's jury-rigged, but we're coming along with the repairs and should be ready to reenergize in four hours."

"Good. Scotty, you can fix anything."

"Except broken hearts, maybe. But, sir . . ."

"What is it? Plow right ahead."

"Well, sir," Scott's voice said, "I can fix the engines, but I canna build you a time machine. We'll be ready to go, but we've no place *to* go in this era. Mister Spock tells me that in the 1970s the human race was wholly confined to the Earth. Space outside the local group of stars was wholly dominated by the Vegan Tyranny, and you'll recall what happened when we first hit *them*. D'ye see the problem?"

"I'm afraid," Kirk said heavily, "that I do. Very well, Mr. Scott, carry on."

"Yes, sir. Out."

Christopher's face was a study in bitter triumph; but what he said next, oddly, was obviously designed to be helpful—or at least, to establish that his own hope was well-founded.

"Mr. Spock here tells me that he is half Vulcan. Surely you can reach Vulcan from here. That's supposed to be just inside the orbit of Mercury."

"There is no such solar planet as Vulcan," Kirk said. "Mr. Spock's father was a native of The Vulcan, which is a planet of 40 Eridani. Of course we could reach that too . . ."

". . . but in the 1970's," Spock finished. "If we took the *Enterprise* there, we would unwrite *their* future history too. Captain, this is the most perfect case of General Order Number One that I have ever encountered—or think I am likely to encounter."

"The order," Kirk explained to Christopher, "prohibits interference with the normal development of alien life and alien societies. It hadn't occurred to me until Mr. Spock mentioned it, but I'm sure it would be construed to apply here too."

"Too bad, Captain," Christopher said. He was not bothering to conceal his triumph now. "Maybe I can't go home—but neither can you. You're as much a prisoner in time as I am on this ship."

"I believe, sir," Spock said, "that Captain Christopher's summary is quite exact."

It was indeed exact, but not complete, as Kirk quickly realized. There was also the problem of supplies. The *Enterprise* could never land on any planet—and certainly would not dare to land on this one, its own home world, even if it were possible—and it was simply ridiculous to even consider trying to steal food, water and power by gig or transporter for 430 people. As for Christopher—who had already tried to escape through the transporter and had come perilously close to making it—what prospects did he have if the *Enterprise* somehow did get back to its own time? He would be archaic, useless, a curiosity. Possibly he could be retrained sufficiently to find a niche, but never retrained to forget his wife and children. To check that, Kirk visited McCoy, the ship's surgeon.

"Get him down here and I'll check," McCoy said.

Kirk put in the call. "You mean it *might* be done?"

"It depends upon the depth of his commitment. Some marriages are routine. I'll have to see what the electroencephalograph shows."

"You're starting to sound like Spock."

"If you're going to get nasty, I'll leave."

Kirk grinned, but the grin faded quickly. "If the depth of his commitment is crucial, we're sunk. He's the kind who commits himself totally. Witness yesterday's escape attempt."

Spock came in with the prisoner—after the escape attempt, there was no other honest word for it. He said at once:

"Captain, I do not know what Dr. McCoy has in mind, but I think it may be useless by now; I have some new information. I find I made an error in my computations."

"This," McCoy said drily, "could be a historical occasion."

Spock ignored the surgeon. "I find that we must return Captain Christopher to Earth after all."

"You said I made no relative contributions," Christopher said sourly.

"I was speaking of cultural contributions. I have now checked the genetic contributions, which was a serious oversight. In running a cross-check on that factor, I discovered that your son, Colonel Shaun Geoffrey Christopher, headed . . . *will* head the first successful Earth-Titan probe, which is certainly significant. If Captain Christopher is not returned, there won't be any Colonel Christopher to go to the Saturnian satellites, since the boy does not yet exist."

The grin on Christopher's face made him look remarkably like a Halloween pumpkin. "A boy," he said, to nobody in particular. "I'm going to have a son."

"And we," McCoy said, "have a headache."

"No," Kirk said. "We have an obligation. Two obligations, mutually antagonistic."

"It is possible that we can satisfy both of them at once," Spock said.

"How? Out with it, man!"

"I have the data you ordered the computer to work out, and there is now no question but that the only reason we are here at all is because we had a head-on collision with a black star. To get back home, we are going to have to contrive something similar."

"Do you know of any black stars around here? And how will that solve our problem with Captain Christopher?"

"There is a black star quite nearby, in fact, Captain, but we cannot use it because it is well out of transporter range of Earth. That would prevent our returning Captain Christopher. But Engineering Officer Scott thinks we may be able to use our own sun. It will, he says, be a rough ride, but will also offer us certain advantages. Briefly, if we make a close hyperbolic passage around the sun at warp eight . . ."

"Not with *my* ship," Kirk said coldly.

"Please, Captain, hear me out. We need the velocity because we must compensate for the Sun's relatively weak gravitational field. And I spoke of advantages. What will happen, if nothing goes wrong, is that we will retreat further into time as we reach the head of the hyperbola . . ."

"Just what we need," McCoy said.

"Shut up, Bones, I want to hear this."

". . . and as we mount the other leg of the curve, there will be a slingshot effect that will hurl us forward in time again. If this is most precisely calculated, we will pass within transporter range of the Earth within two or three minutes *before* the time when we arrived here the first time, before we first appeared in the sky. At that moment, we reinject Captain Christopher into his plane—which will not have been destroyed yet—and the whole chain of consequences will fall apart. Essentially, it will never have happened at all."

"Are you sure of that?"

Spock raised his eyebrows. "No, sir, of course I am not sure of it. Mr. Scott and I think it may work. The computer concurs. Certainty is not an attainable goal in a problem like this."

"True enough," Kirk agreed. "But I don't see that it solves our problem with Captain Christopher at all. It gets him back home, but with his memories intact—and that's what we have to avoid at all costs. I would rather destroy the *Enterprise* than the future."

There was a brief silence. Both Spock and McCoy knew well what such a decision had cost him. Then Spock said gently, "Captain, Mr. Scott and I see no such necessity. Bear in mind that Captain Christopher will arrive home *before* he was taken aboard our ship. He will have nothing to remember—because none of it will ever have happened."

Kirk turned to the pilot from the past. "Does that satisfy you?"

"Do I have a choice?" Christopher said. "Well, I won't quibble. It gets me home—and obviously I can't do my duty if I can't remember what it is. Only . . ."

"Only what?"

"Well, I never thought I'd make it into space. I was in line for the space program, but I didn't qualify."

"Take a good look around, Captain," Kirk said quietly. "You made it here ahead of all of them. We were not the first. You were."

"Yes, I know that," Christopher said, staring down at his clenched fists. "And I've seen the future too. An immense gift. I . . . I'll be very sorry to forget it."

"How old are you?" McCoy said abruptly.

"Eh? I'm thirty."

"Then, Captain Christopher," McCoy said, "in perhaps sixty more years, or a few more, you will forget things many times more important to you than this—your wife, your children, and indeed the very fact that you ever existed at all. You will forget every single thing you ever loved, and what is worse, you will not even care."

"Is that," Christopher said angrily, "supposed to be consoling? If that's a sample of the philosophy of the future, I can do without it."

"I am not counseling despair," McCoy said, very gently. "I am only trying to remind you that regardless of our achievements, we all at last go down into the dark. I am a doctor and I have seen a great deal of death. It doesn't discourage me. On the contrary, I'm trying to call to your attention the things that are much more valuable to you than the fact that you've seen men from the future and a bucketful of gadgetry. You will have those still, though you forget us. We are trying to give them back to you, those sixty-plus years you might otherwise have wasted in a future you could never understand. The fact that you will have to forget this encounter in the process seems to me to be a very small fee."

Christopher stared at McCoy as though he had never seen him before. After a long pause, he said, "I was wrong. Even if I did remember, I would do nothing to destroy a future that . . . that has even one such man in it. And I see that underneath all your efficiency and gadgetry, you're *all* like that. I am proud to be one of your ancestors. Captain Kirk, I concur in anything you decide."

"Your bravery helped to make us whatever we are," Kirk said. "Posts, everybody."

"And besides," Spock added, "it is quite possible that we won't make it at all."

"Now there," McCoy said, "is a philosophy *I* can do without."

Kirk said evenly, "We will take the chance that we have. If you'll join me on the bridge, Captain Christopher, we will at least give you a bumpy last ride for your money."

Christopher grinned. "That's the kind I like."

It was indeed a bumpy ride. Warp Eight was an acceleration called upon only in the most extreme of emergencies—although this surely classified as one—and could not be sustained for long without serious damage to the *Enterprise*. It was decidedly unsettling to hear the whole monstrous fabric of the ship, which ordinarily seemed as solid as a planet, creaking and straining around them as the pressure was applied, and to hear the engines—usually quite quiet—howling below decks.

For Kirk, it was almost more unsettling to watch the planets begin to both revolve and rotate in the wrong direction in the navigation tank, as the combined acceleration and gravitational energies were translated into motion backwards in time. Perhaps fortunately for his sanity, he did not have to watch long, however, for the close approach to the sun eventually made it necessary to close off all outside sensors. They were flying blind.

Then the swing was completed, and the sensors could be opened again—and now the planets were moving in their proper directions, but rather decidedly too fast, as the *Enterprise* shot up the time curve. In the Transporter Room, Captain Christopher waited tensely, in full flight dress.

"Passing 1968," Spock said from his post. "January 1969 . . . March . . . May . . . July . . . the pace is picking up very rapidly . . . November . . ."

Kirk gripped the arms of his chair. This was going to have to be the most split-second of all transporter shots. No human operator could hope to bring it off; the actual shift would be under the control of the computer.

"June . . . August . . . December . . . into 1970 now—"

Suddenly, and only for an instant, the lights dimmed. It was over so quickly that it could almost have been an illusion.

"Transporter Room! Did you—?"

But there was no time to complete the question. The lights dimmed again, all the stars in the heavens seemed to be scrambling for new places, and there was a huge wrench in what seemed to be the whole fabric of the universe.

At last the stars were stable—and the instruments showed the *Enterprise* to be doing no more than Warp One. The gigantic thrust had all been drained off into time.

"Well, Mr. Spock?"

"We made it, sir," Spock said quietly.

"Transporter Room, did you get a picture of the shot?"

"Yes, sir. Here it is."

The still picture glowed on an auxiliary screen. Kirk studied it. It showed Captain Christopher in the cockpit of his undestroyed airplane. He looked quite unharmed, though perhaps a bit dazed.

"And so we have revised Omar," Mr. Spock said.

"Omar?" Kirk said. "Which part?"

"The verse about the moving finger, sir. The poet says that once it writes, it moves on, and we have no power to unwrite a line of it. But it would appear, sir, that we have."

"No," Kirk said, "I don't think that's the case. History has *not* been changed—and it's quite possible that we would have been unable to do anything else than what we in fact did. That's a question for the philosophers. But as of now, Mr. Spock, I think Omar's laurels are still in place."

COURT MARTIAL

Writers: Don M. Mankiewicz and Steven W. Carabatsos
(Story by Don M. Mankiewicz)

Director: Marc Daniels

First Aired: February 2, 1967

The *Enterprise* weathered the ion storm somehow, but one man was dead, and damage to the ship was considerable. Kirk was forced to order a non-scheduled layover for repairs at Star Base 11, a huge complex serving the dual role of graving dock and galactic command outpost.

He made a full report to the portmaster, Senior Captain Stone, a craggy Negro who had once been a flight officer himself; Kirk had known him in those days, though not well. The report, of course, had to include an affidavit in the matter of Records Officer Benjamin Finney, deceased, and Kirk turned that in last and only after long study. Stone noticed his hesitation, but was patient. At last he said, "That makes three times you've read it, Captain. Is there an error?"

"No," Kirk said, "but the death of a crewman . . . When you have to sign these affidavits, you relive the moment." He signed the paper and passed it to Stone.

"I know. But you can't fight Regulations. Now, let's see; the extract from your ship's computer log, confirming the deposition?"

"In the other folder."

"Good . . . though it's a great pity too. The service can't afford to lose men like Officer Finney. If he'd only gotten out of the pod in time . . ."

"I waited until the last possible moment," Kirk said. "The storm got worse. We were on double-red alert. I had to jettison."

The office door swung open suddenly. A young woman was standing there—young, and pretty, but obviously under great stress. She glared wildly at Kirk, who recognized her instantly.

"There you are!" she cried. "I wanted one more good look at you!"

"Jame!"

"Yes, Jame! And you're the man who killed my father!"

"Do you really think that?" Kirk said.

"More than that! I think you deliberately murdered him!"

"Jame, Jame, stop and think what you're saying." Kirk stepped toward her. "We were friends, you know that. I would no more have hurt your father than I'd hurt you."

"Friends! That's a lie! You never were! You hated him, all your life! And you finally killed him!"

Stone, who had been discreetly pretending to study the documents, rose suddenly and moved between them. Jame was obviously fighting back a storm of tears. Kirk watched her in dismay.

"Captain Kirk," Stone said in a voice as hard as his name, "you say you jettisoned the pod *after* the double-red alert?"

"You have my sworn deposition," Kirk said.

"Then, Captain, it is my duty to presume you have committed willful perjury. According to the extract from your computer log, you jettisoned the pod *before* the double-red alert. Consider yourself relieved of command. A board of inquiry will determine whether a general court martial is in order."

Kirk never saw the board. As far as he was concerned, the inquiry consisted of Portmaster Stone and a recorder, which was to produce the tape the board would study.

"Where do you want me to begin?" Kirk said.

Stone pushed a cup of coffee toward Kirk. "Tell me about Officer Finney."

"We'd known each other a long time. He was an instructor at the Academy when I was a midshipman. But that didn't stop us from beginning a close friendship. His daughter, Jame, the girl who was in your office last night, was named after me."

"The friendship—it rather cooled with the years, didn't it? No, please speak, Captain, the recorder can't see you nodding."

"Yes, it did. I relieved him on watch once, on the USS *Republic*, and found the vent circuit to the fusion chamber open. If we'd gone under fusion power, the ship would have blown. As it was, it was contaminating the air of the engine room. I closed the switch and logged the error. He drew a reprimand and went to the bottom of the promotion list."

"And he blamed you for that?"

"Yes. He'd been kept on at the Academy as an instructor for an unusually long time. As a result, he was late being assigned to a starship. He felt the delay looked bad on his record. My action, he believed, made things worse. However, I couldn't very well have let an oversight of that magnitude go unreported."

"Comment by examining officer: Service record of Officer Finney to be appended to this transcript. Now, Captain, let's get to the specifics of the storm."

"Weatherscan indicated an ion storm dead ahead," Kirk said. "I sent Finney into the pod." For the benefit of possible civilians on the board, Kirk added, "The pod is outside the ship, attached to the skin. One of our missions is to get radiation readings in abnormal conditions, including ion storms. This can only be done by direct exposure of the necessary instruments in a plastic pod. However, in a major storm the pod rapidly picks up a charge of its own that becomes a danger to the rest of the ship, and we have to get rid of it."

"Why Finney? If he blamed you . . ."

"He may have blamed me because he never rose to command rank. But I don't assign jobs on the basis of who blames me, but whose name is on top of the duty roster. It was Finney's turn. He had just checked in with me when we hit the leading edge of the storm. Not bad at first. Then we began encountering field-variance, force two. The works. I finally signaled a double-red alert. Finney knew he had only a matter of seconds. I gave him those seconds, and more—but it wasn't enough. I can't explain his not getting out. He had the training, he had the reflexes, and he had plenty of time."

"Then why, Captain," Stone said, "does the computer log—yours, made automatically at the time—indicate that there was no double-red alert when you jettisoned?"

"I don't know," Kirk said.

"Could the computer be wrong?"

"Mr. Spock, my first officer, is running a survey now," Kirk said grimly. "But the odds are next to impossible."

Stone looked at Kirk long and penetratingly, and then reached out and shut off the recorder. "I'm not supposed to do this," he said, "But—look, Kirk. Not one man in a million can do what you and I did: serve as a starship captain. A hundred decisions a day, hundreds of lives staked on every one of them being right. You've been out nineteen months on this last mission. You've taken no furlough, had virtually no rest in all that time. You're played out—exhausted."

Kirk was beginning to get the drift of this, and he did not like it. "That's the way you see it?"

"That's the way my report will read," Stone said, "if you cooperate."

"Physical breakdown," Kirk said. "Possibly even mental collapse."

"Well . . . yes."

"I'd be admitting that a man died because . . ."

"Admit nothing," Stone said. "Let me bury the matter, here and now. No starship captain has ever stood trial before. I don't want you to be the first."

"But what if I'm guilty?" Kirk said steadily. "Shouldn't I be punished?"

"I'm thinking of the service, dammit! I won't have it smeared by . . ."

"By what, Portmaster?"

"All right!" Stone said explosively. "By an evident perjurer who's covering up bad judgment, cowardice, or something even worse!"

"That's as far as you go, Captain," Kirk said, instantly on his feet, "or I'll forget you *are* a captain. I'm telling you, I was on that bridge. I know what happened. I know what I did."

"It's in the transcript," Stone said, equally hotly, "and computer transcripts don't lie. You decide, Captain. Bury the matter and accept a ground assignment—or demand a general court, and bring down on your head the full disciplinary powers of Star Fleet."

"I have already decided," Kirk said. "Turn the recorder back on."

COURT MARTIAL

* * *

The courtroom was stark. There was one main viewing screen, a recorder, a witness chair, one table each for prosecution and defense, and a high bench where sat Portmaster Stone and the three members of the court-martial board. The prosecutor was a cool, lovely blonde woman named Areel Shaw, who as it happened was an old friend of Kirk's. ("All my old friends look like doctors," Bones McCoy had commented, "and all Jim's old friends look like her.") It was on her advice that Kirk had retained Samuel T. Cogley, a spry old eccentric who put his trust not in computers, but in books. He did not inspire much confidence, though Kirk was convinced that Areel had meant well.

Stone called the court to order by striking an ancient naval ship's bell. "I declare that the General Court of Star Base Eleven is now in session. Captain James T. Kirk will rise. Charge: culpable negligence. Specification: in that, on Star Date 2947.3, by such negligence, you did cause loss of life, to wit, the life of Records Officer Benjamin Finney. Charge: conduct prejudicial to the good order of the service. Specification: in that, thereafter, you failed accurately to report the same incident in your captain's log. To these charges and specifications, how do you plead?"

"Not guilty," Kirk said quietly.

"I have appointed, as members of this court, Space Command Representative Chandra and Star Command Captains Li Chow and Krasnowsky. I direct your attention to the fact that you have a right to ask for substitute officers if you feel that any of these named harbor prejudice harmful to your case."

"I have no objections, sir."

"And do you consent to the service of Lieutenant Shaw as prosecuting officer, and to my own service as chief judge?"

"Yes, sir."

"Lieutenant Shaw," Stone said, "you may proceed."

Areel Shaw stepped into the arena. "I call Mr. Spock."

Spock took the stand and passed to the recorder attendant his identity disk. The recorder promptly said: "Spock, S-179-276-SP. Service rank: commander. Position: first officer, science officer. Current assignment: USS *Enterprise*. Commendations: Vulcan scientific Legion of Honor. Awards of valor: twice decorated by Galactic Command."

"Mr. Spock," Areel Shaw said, "as a science officer, you know a great deal about computers, don't you?"

"I know all about them," Spock said levelly.

"Do you know of any possible malfunction that would cause one to recall an event inaccurately?"

"No."

"Or any malfunction that *has* caused an inaccuracy in *this* one?"

"No. Nevertheless, it is inaccurate."

"Please explain."

"It reports," Spock said, "that the jettison button was pressed before the double-red alert—in other words, that Captain Kirk was reacting to an emergency that did not then exist. That is not only illogical, but impossible."

"Were you watching him the exact moment he pressed the button?"

"No. I was occupied. We were already at red-alert."

"Then how can you dispute the record of the log?"

"I do not dispute it," Spock said. "I merely state it to be wrong. I know the captain. He would not . . ."

"Captain Stone," Areel Shaw said, "please instruct the witness not to speculate."

"Sir," Spock said to Stone, "I am half Vulcan. Vulcans do not speculate. I speak from pure logic. If I let go of a hammer on a high-gravity planet, I do not need to see it fall to know that it has fallen. Human beings have characteristics that determine their behavior just as inanimate objects do. I say it is illogical for Captain Kirk to have reacted to an emergency that did not exist, and impossible for him to act out of panic or malice. That is not his nature."

"In your opinion," Areel Shaw said.

"Yes," Spock said with obvious reluctance. "In my opinion."

The personnel officer of the *Enterprise* was called next. "With reference to Records Officer Finney," Areel asked him, "was there, in his service record, a report of disciplinary action for failure to close a circuit?"

"Yes, ma'am," the P.O. said.

"This charge was based upon a log entry by the officer who relieved him. Who was that officer?"

"Ensign James T. Kirk," the P.O. said softly.

"Speak louder, for the recorder, please. That is now the Captain Kirk who sits in this courtroom?"

"Yes, ma'am."

"Thank you. Your witness, Mr. Cogley."

"No questions," Cogley said.

Areel next called Bones McCoy to the stand, and went after him with cool efficiency. "Doctor, you are, on the record, an expert in psychology, especially in space psychology—patterns that develop in the close quarters of a ship during long voyages in deep space."

"I know something about it."

"Your academic record, and your experience, doctor, belie your modesty. Is it possible that Officer Finney blamed the defendant for the incident we have just heard your personnel officer describe—blamed him and hated him for being passed over for promotion, blamed him for never having been given a command of his own, hated him for having to serve under him?"

"Of course, it's possible," McCoy said.

"Then, isn't it also possible that all that hatred, directed against Captain Kirk, could have caused a like response in the captain?"

"You keep asking what's possible," McCoy said. "To the human mind almost anything is possible. The fact, however, is that I have never observed such an attitude in Captain Kirk."

"What about an attitude generated in his subconscious mind?"

"I object!" Sam Cogley said. "Counsel is leading the witness into making unprovable subjective speculations."

"On the contrary, your honor," Areel said. "I am asking a known expert in psychology for an expert psychological opinion."

"Objection overruled," Stone said. "You may proceed."

"Captain Kirk, then," Areel said relentlessly, "could have become prejudiced against Officer Finney without having been aware of it—prejudiced in such a way that his judgment became warped. Is that *theoretically* possible, doctor?"

"Yes," McCoy said, "it's possible. But highly unlikely."

"Thank you. Your witness, Mr. Cogley."

"No questions."

"Then I call James T. Kirk."

When Kirk's identity disc was placed in the recorder, the machine said: "Kirk, SC-937-0176-CEC. Service rank: captain. Position: starship command. Current assignment: USS *Enterprise*. Commendations: Palm leaf of Axanar peace mission. Grankite order of tactics, class of excellence. Pentares ribbon of commendation, classes first and second . . ."

"May it please the court," Areel Shaw said. The recorder attendant shut off the machine. "The prosecution concedes the inestimable record of Captain Kirk, and asks consent that it be entered as if read."

"Mr. Cogley," Stone said, "do you so consent?"

Cogley smiled disarmingly, stretched a bit in his chair, and rose. "Well, sir," he said, "I wouldn't want to be the one to slow the wheels of progress. On the other hand, I wouldn't want those wheels to run over my client in their unbridled haste. May I point out, sir, that this is a *man* we are examining, so perhaps a little longer look would not be amiss. The court's convenience is important, but his *rights* are paramount."

"Continue," Stone told the recorder attendant. The machine said:

"Awards of valor: Medal of Honor, silver palm with cluster. Three times wounded, honor roll. Galactic citation for conspicuous gallantry. Karagite Order of Heroism . . ."

It took quite a long time, during which Areel Shaw looked at the floor. Kirk could not tell whether she was fuming at having been outmaneuvered, or was simply ashamed of the transparency of her trick. Doubtless she did not want the court to be able to tell, either.

"Now, Captain. Despite the record, you continue to maintain that there was a double-red alert before you jettisoned the pod?"

"Yes, ma'am. There was."

"And you cannot explain why the computer record shows otherwise."

"No, I cannot."

"And in fact you'd do it again under the same circumstances."

"Objection!" Cogley said. "Counsel is now asking the witness to convict himself in advance of something he hasn't done yet and, we maintain, didn't do in the past!"

"It's all right, Sam," Kirk said. "I'm willing to answer. Lieutenant Shaw, I have been trained to command. The training doesn't sharpen a man's verbal skills. But it does sharpen his sense of duty—and confidence in himself to discharge that duty."

"May it please the court," Areel Shaw said, "I submit that the witness is not being responsive."

"He's answering the question," Stone said, "and he has a right to explain his answers. Proceed, Captain Kirk."

"Thank you, sir. We were in the worst kind of ion storm. And I was in command. I made a judgment—a command judgment. And because it was necessary to make that judgment, a man died. But the lives of my entire crew and my ship were in danger, and *not* to have made that judgment, to wait, to have been indecisive when it was time to act, would in my mind have been criminal. I did not act out of panic, or malice. I did what I was duty-bound to do. And of course, Lieutenant Shaw, I would do it again; that is the responsibility of command."

There was a brief hush. Areel Shaw broke it at last, turning to Stone.

"Your honor, the prosecution does not wish to dishonor this man. But I must invite the court's attention now to the visual playback of the log extract of the *Enterprise*'s computer."

"It is so ordered."

The main viewing screen lit up. When it was over, Areel Shaw said, almost sadly, "If the court will notice the scene upon which we froze, the screen plainly shows the defendant's finger pressing the jettison button. The condition signal reads RED-ALERT. Not double red—but simply red. When the pod containing Officer Finney was jettisoned, the emergency did not as yet exist.

"The prosecution rests."

Thunderstruck, Kirk stared at the screen. He had just seen the impossible.

During the recess, Sam Cogley calmly leafed through legal books in the room assigned to them, while Kirk paced the floor in anger and frustration.

"I know what I did!" Kirk said. "That computer report is an outright impossibility."

"Computers don't lie," Cogley said.

"Sam, are you suggesting *I* did?"

"I'm suggesting that maybe you did have a lapse. It's possible, with the strain you were under. Jim, there's still time to change our plea. I could get you off."

"Two days ago, I would have staked my life on my judgment."

"You did. Your professional life."

"*I know what I did,*" Kirk said, spacing each word. "But if you want to pull out . . ."

"There's nowhere to go," Cogley said. "Except back into court in half an hour. The verdict's a foregone conclusion, unless we change our plea."

Kirk's communicator beeped and he took it out. "Kirk here."

"Captain," Spock's voice said, "I have run a full survey on the computer."

"I'll tell you what you found," Kirk said. "Nothing."

"You sound bitter."

"Yes, Mr. Spock. I am. But not so bitter as to fail to thank you for your efforts."

"My duty, Captain. Further instructions?" There actually seemed to be emotion in Spock's voice, but if he felt any such stirring, he was unable to formulate it.

"No. I'm afraid you'll have to find yourself a new chess partner, Mr. Spock. Over and out."

Cogley gathered up an armful of books and started for the door. "I've got to go to a conference in chambers with Stone and Shaw."

"Look," Kirk said. "What I said before—I was a little worked up. You did the best you could."

Cogley nodded and opened the door. Behind it, her arm raised to knock, was Jame Finney.

"Jame!" Kirk said. "Sam, this is Officer Finney's daughter."

"A pleasure," Cogley said.

"Mr. Cogley," she said, "you have to stop this. Make him change his plea. Or something. Anything. I'll help if I can."

Sam Cogley looked slightly perplexed, but he said only, "I've tried."

"It's too late for anything like that, Jame," Kirk said. "But I appreciate your concern."

"It can't be too late. Mr. Cogley, my father's dead. Ruining Jim won't bring him back."

"That's a commendable attitude, Miss Finney," Cogley said. "But a little unusual, isn't it? After all, Captain Kirk is accused of *causing* your father's death."

"I was . . ." Jame said, and stopped. She seemed suddenly nervous. "I was just thinking of Jim."

"Thank you, Jame," Kirk said. "But I'm afraid we've had it. You'd better go."

When the door closed, Cogley put his books down. "How well do you know that girl?" he said.

"Since she was a child."

"Hmm. I suppose that might explain her attitude. Curious, though. Children don't usually take such a dispassionate view of the death of a parent."

"Oh, she didn't at first. She was out for my blood. Almost hysterical. Charged into Stone's office calling me a murderer."

"Why didn't you tell me that before?"

"Why," Kirk said, "the subject never came up. Is it important?"

"I don't know," Cogley said thoughtfully. "It's—a false note, that's all. I don't see what use we could put it to now."

Stone rang the court to order. He had hardly done so when Spock and McCoy materialized squarely in the midst of the room—a hair-raising precise piece of transporter work. They moved directly to Kirk and Cogley; the latter stood and Spock whispered to him urgently.

"Mr. Cogley," Stone said harshly, "what's the meaning of this display?"

"May it please the court," Mr. Cogley said, "we mean no disrespect, but these officers have unearthed new evidence, and they could conceive of no way to get it to the court in time but by this method."

"The counsel for the defense," Areel Shaw said, "has already rested his case. Mr. Cogley is well-known for his theatrics . . ."

"Is saving an innocent man's life a theatric?" He turned to Stone. "Sir, my client has been deprived of one of his most important rights in this trial—the right to be confronted by the witnesses against him. *All* the witnesses, your honor. And the most devastating witness against my client is not a human being, but an information system—a machine."

"The excerpt from the computer log has been shown."

"Your honor, a log excerpt is not the same as the machine that produced it. I ask that this court adjourn and reconvene on board the *Enterprise* itself."

"I object, your honor," Areel Shaw said. "He's trying to turn this into a circus."

"Yes!" Cogley said. "A circus! Do you know what the first circus was, Lieutenant Shaw? An arena, where men met danger face to face, and lived or died. This is indeed a circus. In this arena, Captain Kirk will live or die, for if you take away his command he will be a dead man. But he has not met his danger face to face. He has the right to confront his accuser, and it matters nothing that his accuser is a machine. If you do not grant him that right, you have not only placed us on a level with the machine—you have elevated the machine above us! Unless I am to move for a mistrial, I ask that my motion be granted. But more than that, gentlemen: In the name of humanity fading in the shadow of the machine, I demand it. I demand it!"

The members of the board put their heads together. At last Stone said: "Granted."

* * *

"Mr. Spock," Cogley said. "How many chess games did you play with the computer during recess?"

"Five."

"And the outcome?"

"I won them all."

"May that be considered unusual, Mr. Spock, and if so, why?"

"Because I myself programmed the computer to play chess. It knows my game; and as has been observed before, it cannot make an error. Hence, even if I myself never make an error, the best I can hope to achieve against it is a stalemate. I have been able to win against Captain Kirk now and then, but against the computer, never—until now. It therefore follows that someone has adjusted either the chess programming or the memory banks. The latter would be the easier task."

"I put it to you, Mr. Spock, that even the latter would be beyond the capacity of most men, isn't that so? Well, then, what men, aboard ship, would it *not* be beyond?"

"The captain, myself—and the Records Officer."

"Thank you, you may step down. I now call Captain Kirk. Captain, describe what steps you took to find Officer Finney after the storm."

"When he did not respond to my call," Kirk said, "I ordered a phase-one search for him. Such a search assumes that its object is injured and unable to respond to the search party."

"It also presupposes that the man *wishes to be found*?"

"Of course, Sam."

"Quite. Now, with the court's permission, although Mr. Spock is now in charge of this ship, I am going to ask Captain Kirk to describe what Mr. Spock has done, to save time, which you will see in a moment is a vital consideration. May I proceed?"

"Well . . . All right."

"Captain?"

"Mr. Spock has ordered everybody but the members of this court and the command crew to leave the ship. This includes the engine crew. Our impulse engines have been shut down and we are maintaining an orbit by momentum alone."

"And when the orbit begins to decay?" Stone said.

"We hope to be finished before that," Cogley said. "But that is the vital time element I mentioned. Captain, is there any other step Mr. Spock has taken?"

"Yes, he has rigged an auditory sensor to the log computer. In effect, it will now be able to hear—as will we—every sound occurring on this ship."

"Thank you. Dr. McCoy to the stand, please. Doctor, I see you have a small device with you. What is it, please?"

"It is a white-noise generator."

"I see. All right, Mr. Spock."

At the console, Spock turned a switch. The bridge at once shuddered to an intermittent pounding, like many drums being beaten.

"Could you reduce the volume a little?" Cogley said. "Thank you. Your honor, that sound is caused by the heartbeats of all the people in this room. With your permission, I am going to ask Dr. McCoy to take each person's pulse, and then use the white-noise device to mask those pulsebeats out, so they will be eliminated from the noise we are hearing."

"What is the purpose of this rigmarole, your honor?" Areel Shaw demanded.

"I think you suspect that as well as I do, Lieutenant," Stone said. "Proceed, Dr. McCoy."

As Bones moved from person to person, the eerie multiple thumping became simpler, softer.

"That's all," McCoy said.

No one breathed. Finally, somewhere, one beat still sounded.

"May it please the court," Cogley said quietly, "the remaining pulse you hear, I think we will shortly find, is that of Officer Finney. Mr. Spock, can you localize it?"

"B deck, between sections 18Y and 27D. I have already sealed off that section."

Kirk hesitated, then came to a decision. "Captain Stone," he said, "this is my problem. I would appreciate it if no one would leave the bridge."

As he turned to leave, Spock handed him a phaser. "The weapons room is within those quadrants, sir," he said quietly. "He may be armed. This is already set on stun."

"Thank you, Mr. Spock."

He moved cautiously down the corridor in the sealed section, calling at intervals:

"All right, Ben. It's all over. Ben! Officer Finney!"

For a while there was no answer. Then, suddenly, a figure stepped out of a shadow, phaser leveled.

"Hello, Captain," Officer Finney said.

Kirk found that he could not answer. Though he had been sure that this was the solution, the emotional impact of actually being face to face with the "dead" man was unexpectedly powerful. Finney smiled a hard smile.

"Nothing to say, Captain?"

"Yes," Kirk said. "I'm glad to see you alive."

"You mean you're relieved because your precious career is saved. Well, you're wrong. You've just made things worse for everyone."

"Put the phaser down, Ben. Why go on with it?"

"You wouldn't leave it alone," Finney said. "You've taken away my choices. Officers and gentlemen, commanders all . . . except for Finney and his one mistake. A long time ago, but they don't forget. No, they never forget."

"Ben, I logged that mistake of yours. Blame me, not them."

"But they're to blame," Finney said. "All of them. I was a good officer. I really was. I loved the service like no man ever did."

Slowly, Kirk began to move in on him.

"Stand back, Captain. No more—I warn you—"

"You're sick, Ben. We can help you—"

"One more step—"

Suddenly, Jame's voice cried down the corridor, "Father! *Father!*"

Finney's head jerked around. With a quick lunge, Kirk knocked the phaser from his hand. At the same moment, Jame appeared, rushing straight into the distraught man's arms.

"Jame!"

"It's all right, father," she said, moving her hand over the tortured officer's brow. "It's all right."

"Don't, Jame," he said. "You've got to understand. I had to do it . . . after what they did to me . . ."

"Excuse me," Kirk said. "But if we don't get this ship back under power, we'll all be dead."

"Mr. Cogley," Stone said, "while this trial is obviously not over yet, I think we must congratulate you and Mr. Spock and Dr. McCoy for a truly classical piece of detective work. Would you tell us, please, how the idea that Officer Finney was still alive even entered your head?"

"I began to suspect that, your honor, when Captain Kirk told me about the change of heart Officer Finney's daughter had had about the captain. If she knew he wasn't dead, she had no reason to blame the Captain for anything."

"But how could she know that?" Stone asked.

"She had been reading her father's papers. Perhaps she didn't know the facts, but the general tone of what he had written must have gotten through to her. A man suffering delusions of persecution wants to set down his complaints. She read them; she knew from childhood the kind of man the captain is; and she's fundamentally fair and decent."

He paused and looked soberly over toward Kirk.

"Or maybe," he said, "it was just instinct. Thank God, there's that much of the animal left in us. Whatever it was, the result is that she now has back both her father and her childhood friend."

"Her father," Stone said, "will also have to stand trial."

"I know that," Cogley said quietly. "I ask the court to appoint me his defense counsel. And off the record, your honor, I have the feeling I'll win."

"Off the record," Stone said, "I wouldn't be a bit surprised."

THE RETURN OF THE ARCHONS

Writer: Boris Sobelman (Story by Gene Roddenberry)

Director: Joseph Pevney

First Aired: February 9, 1967

Once it had been a hundred years before—that time past when the starship *Archon* had been lost to mysterious circumstances on the planet Beta 3000.

Now it was time present; and the two crewmen from another starship, the *Enterprise*, down on the same planet scouting for news of the *Archon*, seemed about to list themselves as "missing," too. They were running swiftly down a drab street of an apparently innocuous town of the apparently innocuous planet when one of them stumbled and fell. Sulu, his companion, paused, reaching down a muscular hand. "O'Neill, get up! We've got to keep going!"

Nobody on the street turned to look at them. Nobody offered to help them. If ever there were passersby, the inhabitants of Beta 3000 could qualify for the "I don't care" prize. Still prone on the street, Lieutenant O'Neill was panting. "It's no use, Mr. Sulu. They're everywhere! Look! There's one of them—there's one of the Lawgivers!" He gestured toward a hooded creature who was approaching, a staff in its hand. Then he pointed to a second figure, similarly hooded, robed and staved. "They're everywhere! We can't get away from them!"

Sulu opened his communicator. "Scouting party to *Enterprise*! Captain, beam us up! Quick! Emergency!" He looked down at O'Neill. "Just hold on, Lieutenant. They'll beam us back to the ship any minute now—"

But O'Neill had scrambled wildly to his feet. "Run, I tell you! We've got to get away! You know what they're capable of!"

"O'Neill—"

But the Lieutenant was racing down the street. Sulu, distracted, his eyes on the flying figure of O'Neill, was scarcely aware that the nearest hooded being had lightly touched him with its staff. He was conscious only of a sudden sense of peace, of the tension in him ebbing, giving way to an inflow of a beatific feeling of unmarred tranquility. He was not permitted to enjoy it for long. The *Enterprise*'s transporter had fixed on him—and he was shimmering into dematerialization.

But completing his transportation wasn't easily accomplished. On the *Enterprise* the transporter's console lights flicked on, dimmed, flicked off, brightened again. Kirk, with Scott and young sociologist Lindstrom, watched them. When Sulu's figure finally collected form and substance, he was astonished to see it clad, not in its uniform, but in the shaggy homespun of the shapeless trousers and sweater that was the customary male apparel of Beta 3000's citizenry. He hurried forward. "Sulu, what's happened? Where's Lieutenant O'Neill?"

Sulu's answer was dull as though something had thickened his tongue. "You . . . you are not of the Body."

Kirk glanced at Scott. The engineer nodded. Speaking into his mike, he said, "Dr. McCoy . . . Transporter Room, please. And quickly."

It was with most delicate care and deliberation that Sulu stepped from the transporter platform. He looked at Lindstrom and his face was suddenly convulsed with fury. He lifted the bundled uniform he held under an arm—and lifting it up, he shook it furiously at Lindstrom. "You did it!" he shouted. "They knew we were Archons! These are the clothes Archons wear! Not these, not these—" he gestured to his own rough clothing. Then he hurled the uniform at Lindstrom.

Kirk said, "Easy, Sulu. It's all right. Now tell me what happened down there."

Sulu staggered. As Kirk extended a hand to steady him, McCoy hurried in, medical kit in hand. He halted to stare. "Jim! Where's O'Neill?"

Kirk shook his head for answer; and Sulu, tensing as though to receive a message of immense significance, muttered "Landru . . . Landru . . ."

The sheer meaninglessness of the mutter chilled Kirk. "Sulu, what happened down there? What did they do to you?"

The answer came tonelessly. "They're wonderful," Sulu said. "The sweetest, friendliest people in the universe. They live in paradise, Captain."

Nor in Sickbay could McCoy elicit anything from Sulu but the same words, the same phrases over and over. He talked gramophonically, like a record dammed to endlessly repeat itself. It was this repetitiousness added to his inability to account either for his own condition or O'Neill's disappearance that decided Kirk to beam down to the planet with an additional search detail. When they materialized—Kirk, Spock, McCoy, Lindstrom, and two security crewmen—it was alongside a house, a brick house that bordered on an alley facing a wide street.

"Materialization completed," Kirk said into his communicator. "Kirk out." As he snapped it shut, he saw that Lindstrom had already edged out into the street and was examining it, his young face alight with interest and curiosity. They followed him—and at once, among the passing people, Kirk noted two hooded beings, cowled and in monkish robes who carried long stafflike devices. What could be seen of their faces was stony, as though any expression might divulge some secret of incalculable value. Their eyes looked dead—filmed and unseeing. One of the people, a man, shambled toward them. His smile was as vacuous as it was amiable; but Kirk took care to return his nod.

As he moved on, Spock said, "Odd."

"Comment, Mr. Spock?"

"That man's expression, Captain. Extremely similar to that of Mr. Sulu when we beamed him up from here. Dazed, a kind of mindlessness."

"Let's find out if all the planet's inhabitants are like him," Kirk said. He walked boldly out into the street, followed by his group. Each of the passersby they met greeted them with the same bland smile. Then a young, biggish man with an empty, ingenuous face stopped to speak to Kirk. "Evenin', friend. Mah name's Bilar. What's yourn?"

"Kirk."

He got the stupid smile. "You-all be strangers."

Kirk nodded and Bilar said, "Here for the festival, ayeh? Got a place to sleep it off yet?"

"No. Not yet," Kirk said.

"Go round to Reger's house. He's got rooms." The oafish face glanced down the street at the clock in the tower of what might have been the Town Hall. "But you'll have to hurry. It's almost the Red Hour."

The shorter hand of the clock was close to the numeral six. "This festival," Kirk said, "it starts at six?"

But Bilar's interest had been distracted by a pretty girl, dark and slim, who was hurrying toward them. He put out a hand to stop her. "Tula, these here folks be strangers come for the festival. Your daddy can put them up, can't he?"

Tula, her dark eyes on Lindstrom's handsome blondness, smiled shyly. "You're from over the valley?" she asked.

Lindstrom smiled back at her. "That's right. We just got in."

"Don't see valley folks much. My father'll be glad to take you in. He don't care where folks come from."

"He runs a rooming house?" Kirk said.

She laughed. "That's a funny name for it. It's right over there." She pointed to a comfortable-looking, three-story structure down the street—and at the same moment the tower clock struck the first stroke of six. A scream, strident, sounding half-mad, broke from the respectable-faced matron near by. A man, a foot or so away from Kirk, suddenly lunged at him. Kirk elbowed the blow aside, hurling him back, and cried to his men, "Back to back!" They closed together in the defensive movement. Then pandemonium, apparently causeless, burst out around them. Men were grimly embattled, battering at each other with bare fists, stones, clubs. A fleeing woman, shrieking, was pursued across the street by a man, intent, silent, exultant. From somewhere came the crashing sounds of smashing windows. Then, to their horror, Tula, twisting and writhing, opened her mouth to a high ecstatic screaming. Bilar rushed at her, shouting, "Tula, Tula! Come!" He seized her wrist, and as Lindstrom leaped forward to grapple with him, stooped for a stone on the street. He crashed it down on Lindstrom's shoulders, felling him. McCoy, hauling the sociologist back to his feet, cried, "Jim, this is madness!"

"Madness doesn't hit an entire community at once, Bones—" Kirk broke off, for rocks had begun to fall among them. One of their attackers, aiming a thick club at him, yelled "Festival! Festival! Festival!" Froth had gathered on the man's lips and Kirk said, "Let's go! That house—where the girl was taking us!—make for it!"

Bunched together, they moved down the street; a young woman, beautiful, her dress torn, grabbed Kirk's arm, pulling at it to drag him off. He shook her loose and she ran off, shrieking with wild, maniacal laughter. More rocks struck them and Kirk, wiping a trickle of blood from a cut on his cheek, shouted, "Run!"

The bedlam pursued them to the door of the house. Kirk hammered on it. And after a moment it was opened. Kirk slammed it closed behind them; one of the three elderly men who confronted him stared at him in astonishment. "Yes?"

"Sorry to break in like this," Kirk said. "We didn't expect the kind of welcome we received."

One of the other men spoke. "Welcome? You are strangers?"

"Yes," Kirk said. "We're . . . from the valley."

The third man said, "Come for the festival?"

"That's right," Kirk told him.

"Then how come you are here?"

Kirk addressed the first man who had greeted them. "Are you Reger?"

"I am."

"You have a daughter named Tula?"

"Yes."

Lindstrom burst into speech. "Well, you'd better do something about her! She's out there alone in that madness!"

Reger averted his eyes. "It is the festival," he said. "The will of Landru . . ."

The third man spoke again. "Reger, these are young men! They are not old enough to be excused!"

"They are visitors from the valley, Hacom," Reger said.

In the wrinkled sockets of Hacom's eyes shone a sudden, fanatic gleam. "Have they no Lawgivers in the valley? Why are they not with the festival?"

Kirk interposing, said, "We heard you might have rooms for us, Reger."

"There, Hacom, you see. They seek only a place to rest after the festival."

"The Red Hour has just begun!" Hacom said.

The tone was so hostile that Reger shrank. "Hacom, these be strangers. The valley has different ways."

"Do you say that Landru is not everywhere?"

The second man tried to assume the role of peacemaker. "No, of course Reger does not blaspheme. He simply said the valley had different ways."

Reger had recovered himself. "These strangers have come to me for lodging. Shall I turn them away?" Then, speaking directly to Kirk, he said, "Come, please . . ."

"But Tula, the girl!" Lindstrom cried. "She's still out there!"

Hacom eyed him with openly inimical suspicion. "She is in the festival, young sir. As you should be."

Uneasy, Reger said, "Quickly, please. Come."

Kirk, turning to follow, saw Hacom turn to the second man. "Tamar, the Lawgivers should know about this!"

Tamar's reply was gently equivocal. "Surely, Hacom, they already know," he said. "Are they not infallible?"

But Hacom was not to be appeased. "You mock them!" he cried. "You mock the Lawgivers! And these strangers are not of the Body!" He strode to the street door, flung it open—crying, "You will see!"—and disappeared.

His departure did not dismay Kirk. They were on the right trail. Incoherent though they were, the references to "Landru," to membership in some vague corpus, corporation, brotherhood, or society they termed the "Body" matched the ravings of Sulu on his return to the *Enterprise*. He was content with the progress they'd made, though the room they were shown into was bare except for a dozen or so thin pallets scattered about its floor. From the open window came the screamings and howlings of the riotous festival and its celebrations. Reger spoke tentatively to Kirk. "Sir, you can return here at the close of the festival. It will be quiet. You will have need of rest."

"Reger," Kirk said, "we have no plans to attend the festival."

The news shook his host. He went to the window and lifted it more widely open to the unroarious hullabaloo outside. "But the hour has struck!" he cried. "You can hear!"

"What I'd like to hear is more about this—festival of yours," Kirk said. "And about Landru I'd like to hear."

Reger cringed at the word "Landru." He slammed down the window. "Landru," he whispered. "You ask me . . . you are strange here . . . you scorn the festival. Are you—who are you?"

"Who is Landru?" Kirk said.

Reger stared, appalled, at him. Then, wheeling, he almost ran from the room. Lindstrom made a move to reopen the window and Kirk said, "Leave it shut, Mr. Lindstrom."

"Captain, I'm a sociologist! Don't you realize what's happening out there?"

"Our mission," Kirk said evenly, "is to find out what happened to the missing starship *Archon* and to our own Lieutenant O'Neill. We are not here to become involved with—"

Lindstrom interrupted excitedly. "But it's a bacchanal! And it occurred spontaneously to these people at one and the same time! I've got to know more about it—find out more!"

Kirk's voice had hardened. "Mr. Lindstrom, you heard me! This is not an expedition to study the folkways of Beta 3000!"

Spock broke in. "Captain, in view of what's happening outside, may I suggest a check on Mr. Sulu's condition? What were his reactions . . . if any—at the stroke of six o'clock?"

Kirk nodded. "Thank you, Mr. Spock." He flipped open his communicator to say, "Kirk here. Lieutenant Uhura, report on Mr. Sulu."

"I think he's all right now, sir. How did you know?"

"Know what, Lieutenant?"

"That he'd sort of run amuck. They're putting him under sedation, sir."

"How long ago did he run amuck? Exactly?"

"Six minutes, Captain."

"Did he say anything?"

"Nothing that made any sense, sir. He kept yelling about Landru, whatever that is. Is everything all right down there, Captain?"

"So far. Keep your channels open. Kirk out."

"Landru," he said reflectively—and moved to the window. The street scene it showed was not reassuring. To the left two men flailed at each other with hatchet-shaped weapons. Another, chasing a shrieking, half-naked woman across the street, vanished, shouting, around a corner. Bodies were scattered, prone in the dust of the street. A short distance down it a building was aflame; among the people still milling about before Reger's house, riots erupted unchecked, then subsided only to break out again. A big bonfire blazed in the street's center.

Kirk turned away to re-face his men. "My guess is we have until morning. Let's put the time to good use. Bones, we need atmospheric readings to determine if something in the air accounts for this. Lindstrom, correlate what you've seen with other sociological parallels, if any. Mr. Spock, you and I have some serious thinking to do. When we leave here in the morning, I want to have a plan of action."

The night did not vouchsafe much sleep. But the twelve noisy hours that moved the tower clock's small hand to the morning's sixth hour finally passed; at the first stroke of its bell, absolute silence fell upon the town. In the room of pallet beds, all but Kirk had at last sunk into sleep. Stiff with the tension of his night-long vigil, he moved among them, waking them. Then he heard the house reverberate to the slam of the front door. It was with no sense of surprise that he also heard Tula's hysterical sobbing. Lindstrom was at the door before him. Kirk put a hand on his shoulder. "Take it easy, Mr. Lindstrom. If she's taking it hard, you'd better take it easy."

They found Tamar with Reger. The father, his face agonized, held the bloody, bedraggled body of his daughter in his arms. She twisted away from him, resisting comfort.

"It's all right now, child. For another year. It's over for another year."

Kirk called, "Bones! You're needed. Get out here!"

As McCoy removed his jet-syringe from his medical kit, Kirk saw the look of anxious inquiry on Reger's face. "It will calm her down," he said quietly. "Trust us, Reger."

Lindstrom, watching, could not contain himself. There was scorching contempt in his voice as he cried, "You didn't even try to bring her home, Reger! What kind of father are you, anyway?"

Reger looked up, his eyes tortured. "It is Landru's will," he said.

"Landru again." Kirk's comment was toneless. "Landru—what about Landru? Who is he?"

Reger and Tamar exchanged terrified glances. Then Tamar said slowly, "It is true, then. You did not attend the festival last night."

"No, we did not," Kirk said.

Reger gave a wild cry. "Then you are not of the Body!" He stared around him as though seeking for some point from which to orient himself in a dissolving world. He made no move as McCoy, noting the effects of his shot, gently moved Tula to a nearby couch where he laid her down. "She's asleep," he said.

Reger approached her, peering at her stilled face. Then he looked at McCoy. "Are you . . . are you . . . Archons?"

"What if we are?" Kirk said.

"It was said more would follow. If you are indeed Archons—"

Tamar cried, "We must hide them! Quickly! The Lawgivers . . ."

"We can take care of ourselves, friend," Kirk told him.

"Landru will know!" Tamar screamed. "He will come!"

The front door crashed open. Two hooded Lawgivers stood on the threshold, Hacom beside them. The old man pointed a shaking finger at Tamar. "He is the one! He mocked the Lawgivers! I heard him!"

Tamar had shrunk back against the wall's support. "No, Hacom . . . it was a joke!"

"The others, too!" cried Hacom. "They were here, but they scorned the festival! I saw it!"

One of the hooded beings spoke. "Tamar . . . stand clear."

Trembling, scarcely able to stand, Tamar bowed his head. "I hear," he said, "and obey the word of Landru."

The Lawgiver lifted his staff, pointing it at Tamar. A tiny dart of flame springing from its end struck straight at his heart. He fell dead.

Stunned, Kirk said, "What—?"

The Lawgiver, ignoring the fallen body between them, addressed Kirk. "You attack the Body. You have heard the word, and disobeyed. You will be absorbed."

He raised his staff again; and Lindstrom, making a swift reach for his phaser, was stopped by a gesture from Kirk.

"What do you mean, absorbed?" he said.

"There! You see?" Hacom's voice was venomous. "They are not of the Body!"

"You will be absorbed," said the Lawgiver. "The good is all. Landru is gentle. You will come."

For the first time the second Lawgiver lifted his staff, pointing it at the *Enterprise* party. Reger spoke, hopelessness dulling his voice. "You must go. It is Landru's will. There is no hope. We must all go with them . . . to the chambers. It happened with the Archons the same way."

Slowly, with deadly deliberation, the two staves swerved to focus on Kirk and Spock. Reger, fatalistically obedient, was moving toward the door when Kirk said, "No. We're not going anywhere."

The stony faces showed no change. The first Lawgiver said, "It is the law. You must come."

Kirk spoke quietly. "I said we're not going anywhere."

The two cowled creatures stared. Then, hesitantly, they moved back a step. After a moment, the first one bent his hood to the other in a whispering conference. Spock, edging to Kirk, said, "Sir, they obviously are not prepared to deal with outright defiance. How did you know?"

"Everything we've seen seems to indicate some sort of compulsion—an involuntary stimulus to action. I just wanted to test it."

"Your analysis seems correct, Captain. But it is a totally abnormal condition."

The two Lawgivers had ended their conference. The first one spoke heavily. "It is plain that you simply did not understand. I will rephrase the order. You are commanded to accompany us to the absorption chambers."

Kirk pointed down at Tamar's crumpled body. "Why did you kill this man?"

"Out of order. You will obey. It is the word of Landru."

"Tell Landru," Kirk said, "that we shall come in our own good time . . . and we will speak to him."

A look of horror filled the stony faces. The first Lawgiver pushed his staff at Kirk. Kirk knocked it from his hand. The creature gaped as it clattered to the floor. Lindstrom picked it up, looked at it briefly, and was handing it to Spock when the Lawgiver, as though listening, whispered, "You . . . cannot. It is Landru."

Both Lawgivers froze. Spock, the staff in hand, spoke to Kirk. "Amazing, Captain. This is merely a hollow tube. No mechanism at all."

Kirk glanced at it. Neither of the Lawgivers gave the slightest sign of having heard.

Reger jerked at Kirk's sleeve. "They are communing," he said. "We have a little time. Please come . . . come with me."

"Where to?" Kirk said.

"A place I know of. You'll be safe there." Urgency came into his voice. "But hurry! You must hurry! Landru will come!"

His panic was genuine. After a moment, Kirk signaled his men. They followed Reger out the door, passing the motionless figures of the Lawgivers. Outside, the street was littered with the debris of the festival—shattered glass, rocks, broken clubs, remnants of ripped homespun garments. In the windless air, smoke still hung heavily over a fire-gutted building. But the people who passed were peaceful-looking, their faces again amiable, utterly blank.

"Quite a festival they had," Kirk said. "Mr. Spock, what do you make of all this?"

"It is totally illogical. Last night, without apparent cause or reason, they wrought complete havoc. Yet today . . ."

"*Now,*" Kirk said, "they're back to normal." He frowned. "To whatever's normal on this planet. Bilar, for instance. Here he comes as blandly innocent as though he were incapable of roaring like an animal."

Bilar stopped. "Mornin', friends," he said.

Reger returned the greeting and Lindstrom angrily seized his arm. "He's the thing who did that hurt to your daughter! Doesn't that mean anything to you?"

"No," Reger said. "It wasn't Bilar. It was Landru." He shook himself free, turning back to the others. "Hurry! We haven't much time left."

He broke off, staring around him. "It's too late!" he whispered. "Look at them!"

Four passersby had paused, standing so still they seemed not to breathe. All of them, eyes wide open, were frozen into attitudes of concentrated listening.

"What is it?" Kirk demanded.

"Landru!" Reger said. "He is summoning the Body. See them gathering?"

"Telepathy, Captain," Spock said.

Suddenly people were breaking free of their listening stances to pick up discarded missiles from the littered street. Slowly, like automatons, they began to move toward the *Enterprise* group. In the blankly amiable faces there was something chilling now, mindlessly hostile and deadly.

Kirk said, "Phasers . . . on stun. Which way, Reger?"

Reger hesitated. "Perhaps . . . through there, but Landru . . ."

"We'll handle Landru," Kirk said. "Just get us out of this!"

It was as they moved toward the alley ahead of them that the rocks came hurling against them. A man struck at Spock with a club, the smile on his lips as vacant as his eyes. Then Kirk saw that another armed group had appeared at the far end of the alley. Rocks were flying toward them.

Kirk spoke tersely to Reger. "I don't want to hurt them. Warn them to stay back!"

Reger shook his head despairingly. "They are in the Body! It is Landru."

Threatening, people were converging on them from both ends of the alley and Kirk, jerking out his phaser, snapped his orders. "Stun only! Wide field! Fire!"

The stun beams spurted from their phasers with a spray effect. The advancing mob fell without a sound. Kirk whirled to confront the rear group. Again, people fell silently. Spock moved to one of the unconscious bodies. "Captain!"

Kirk went over to him. The quiet face that stared blankly up into his was that of Lieutenant O'Neill. He turned to call to his two security crewmen. "Security—over here!" Then he spoke to Reger. "This is one of our men," he said.

"No more," Reger reminded him. "He's been absorbed."

"Nonsense!" Kirk said briskly. "We'll take him along with us, Mr. Spock."

"I tell you he's one of them now!" Reger cried. "When he wakes Landru will find us through him! Leave him here! He's our enemy. He's been absorbed!"

The full implications of the word struck Kirk for the first time. "Absorbed?" he said.

"The Body absorbs its enemies. It kills only when it has to." Reger's voice sank to a terrified whisper. "When the first Archons came, free, out of control, opposing the word of Landru, many were killed. The rest were absorbed. Leave him here. Be wise."

"We take him with us," Kirk said.

Lindstrom spoke. "Captain, now that we've got O'Neill, let's beam out of here."

"Not yet. We still have to find what happened to the Archons. Reger, which way?"

Reger pointed ahead, indicating a left turn at the end of the alley. The Security men picked up O'Neill as the group hurriedly followed Reger's lead. It introduced them into a cellarlike chamber, dark, but bulked with shadowy objects of odds and ends. As the guards set O'Neill down against a wall, Reger crossed to a wall to open a cabinet from which he extracted a flat package, wrapped in rags. Revealed, it turned out to be a translucent panel. A section of it, touched, began to glow with strong light that illuminated the entire room.

Spock said, "Amazing in this culture! I go further. Impossible in this culture!"

Reger turned. "It is from the time before Landru."

"Before Landru? How long ago is that?" Kirk said.

"We do not know positively. Some say . . . as long as six thousand years." Reger spoke with a certain pride. Spock was examining the lighting panel with his tricorder. "I do not identify the metal, Captain. But it took a very advanced technology to construct a device like this. Inconsistent with the rest of the environment."

"But not inconsistent with some of the things we've seen," Kirk said. "Those staffs, those hollow tubes, obviously antennae for some kind of broadcast power. Telepathy—who knows?" He saw the look of astoundedness quiet Spock's face into a more than usual expressionlessness. "What is it, Spock?"

"I am recording immensely strong power generations, Captain . . ."

"Unusual for this area?"

"Incredible for *any* area." Spock leaned closer to his tricorder. "Near here but radiating in all directions—"

A groan from O'Neill broke into his voice. McCoy, looking up from his bent position over the unconscious man, spoke to Kirk. "He's coming around, Jim."

Reger uttered a shout. "He must not! Once he is conscious, Landru will find us. Through him. And if the others come—"

"What others?" Kirk said.

"Those like me . . . and you. Who resist Landru."

"An underground," Spock said. "How are you organized?"

"In threes," Reger told him. "Myself . . . Tamar who is dead now . . . and one other."

"Who?" Kirk said.

Reger hesitated. "I don't know. Tamar was the contact."

"Jim," McCoy said, "I need a decision. Another few seconds—"

"He must not regain consciousness!" Reger screamed. "He would destroy us all. He is now of the Body!"

Kirk bit his lip. Then he looked down at O'Neill. "Give him a shot, Bones. Keep him asleep." He whirled on Reger. "I want some answers now. What is the Body?"

"The people. You saw them."

"And the Lawgivers?" Spock asked.

"They are the arms and legs."

"That leaves a brain," Kirk said.

Inflection drained from Reger's voice. "Of course," he said. "Landru." In a mechanical manner as though speaking a lesson learned by rote, he added, "Landru completes the Whole. Unity and Perfection, tranquility and peace."

Spock was eyeing him. "I should say, Captain, that this is a society organized on a physiological concept. One Body, maintained and controlled by the ones known as Lawgivers, directed by one brain . . ."

Kirk said, "A man who—"

"Not necessarily a man, Captain."

Kirk turned to Reger. "This underground of yours. If Landru is so powerful, how do you survive?"

"I do not know. Some of us escape the directives. Not many but some. It was that way with the Archons."

"Tell me about the Archons," Kirk said.

"They refused to accept the will of Landru. But they had invaded the Body. Landru pulled them down from the sky."

Incredulous, Kirk said, "Pull a starship down?" He turned to Spock. "Those power readings you took before. Are they—"

Spock completed the sentence. "Powerful enough to destroy a starship? Affirmative, Captain."

They looked at each other for a long moment. Then Kirk flipped out his communicator. "Kirk to *Enterprise*. Come in!"

But it wasn't Uhura who responded. It was Scott, his voice taut with strain. "Captain! We're under attack! Heat beams of some kind. Coming up from the planet's surface!"

"Status report," Kirk said.

"Our shields are holding, but they're taking all our power. If we try to warp out, or even move on impulse engines, we'll lose our shields—and burn up like a cinder!"

"Orbit condition, Scotty?"

"We're going down. Unless those beams get off us so we can use our engines, we're due to hit atmosphere in less than twelve hours."

Spock came to stand beside him as he said, "Keep your shields up, Scotty. Do everything you can to maintain orbit. We'll try to locate the source of the beams and stop them here. Over."

Static crashed into Scott's reply, drowning his words.

". . . impossible . . . emergency by-pass circuits but . . . whenever you . . . contact . . ."

Kirk turned the gain up, but the static alone grew loud. Spock had unlimbered his tricorder. Now he called, "Captain! Sensor beams! I believe we're being probed." He bent over his device, concentrated. "Yes. Quite strong. And directed here."

"Block them out!" Kirk cried.

"It's Landru!" Reger yelled.

Spock made an adjustment on his tricorder. Then he shook his head. "They're too strong, Captain. I can't block them." He lifted his head suddenly from his tricorder, then whirled to the wall on his left. A low-pitched humming sound was coming from it. Kirk, in his turn, faced the wall. On it a light had begun to glow, coiling and twisting in swirling patterns. They brightened, and at the same moment started to gather into the outline of a figure. It seemed to be collecting substance, the flesh and bone of a handsome elderly man. The eyes had kindness in them and the features, benign, composed, radiated wisdom. It appeared to be regarding them with benevolence. But its face and body kept their strange flowing movement.

The figure on the wall said, "I am Landru."

Reger fell to his knees, groaning in animal terror. Spock, observant, quite unawed, said, "A projection, Captain. Unreal."

"But beautifully executed, Mr. Spock. With no apparatus at this end."

The kindly eyes of the wall man fixed on him. "You have come as destroyers. That is sad. You bring an infection."

"You are holding my ship," Kirk said. "I demand you release it."

The mouth went on talking as though the ears had not heard. "You come to a world without hate, without conflict, without fear . . . no war, no disease, no crime, none of the old evils. I, Landru, seek tranquility, peace for all . . . the Universal Good."

This time Kirk shouted. "*We* come on a mission of peace and goodwill!"

Landru went on, oblivious. "The Good must transcend the Evil. It shall be done. So it has been since the beginning."

"He doesn't hear you, Captain," Spock said.

Lindstrom drew his phaser. "Maybe he'll hear this!"

"No!" Kirk's rebuke was sharp. "That'll do no good." He turned back to the lighted figure. "Landru, listen to us."

"You will be absorbed," said the benign voice. "Your individuality will merge with the Unity of Good. In your submergence into the common being of the Body you will find contentment and fulfillment. You will experience the Absolute Good."

The low-pitched hum had grown louder. Landru smiled tenderly upon them. "There will be a moment of pain, but you will not be harmed. Peace and Good place their blessings upon you."

Kirk took a step toward the image. But the humming abruptly rose to a screeching whine that pierced the ears like a sharpened blade. Reger toppled forward. McCoy and Lindstrom, driven to their knees, held their ears, their eyes shut. One after the other the security crewmen crumpled. Spock and Kirk kept their feet for a moment longer. Then, they, too, the spike of the whine, thrusting deeper into their brains, pitched forward into unconsciousness.

Kirk was the first to recover. He found himself lying on a thin pallet pushing against one of the bare stone walls of a cell. Lifting his head, he saw Lindstrom stir. Getting to his knees, he crawled over to Spock. "Mr. Spock! Mr. Spock!"

Slowly Spock's eyes opened. Kirk bent over Lindstrom, shaking him and the security guard beside him. "Wake up, Lindstrom! Mr. Lindstrom, wake up!"

Spock was on his feet. "Captain! Where's the Doctor?"

"I don't know. He was gone when I came to. So was the other guard."

"From the number of pallets on the floor, sir, I should say they have been here and have been removed."

"Just where is here?" Kirk said.

Spock glanced around. "A maximum-security establishment, obviously. Are you armed, sir?"

"No. All our phasers are gone. I checked." He went to the heavy, bolted door. "Locked," he said.

"My head aches," observed Lindstrom.

"The natural result of being subjected to sub-sonic, Mr. Lindstrom," Spock told him. "Sound waves so controlled as to set up insuperable contradictions in audio impulses. Stronger, they could have killed. As it was, they merely rendered us unconscious."

"That's enough analysis," Kirk said. "Let's start thinking of ways out of here. Mr. Spock, how about that inability of those Lawgivers to cope with the unexpected?"

"I wouldn't count on that happening again, Captain. As well organized as this society seems to be, I cannot conceive of such an oversight going uncorrected." He paused. "Interesting, however. Their reaction to your defiance was remarkably similar to the reactions of a computer—one that's been fed insufficient or contradictory data."

"Are you suggesting that the Lawgivers are mere computers—not human?"

"Quite human, Captain. It's just that all the facts are not yet in. There are gaps—"

He broke off. A rattle had come from the door. Kirk and the others sprang to the alert—and the door opened. A Lawgiver, his staff aimed at them, entered, followed by McCoy and the missing security man. Both were beaming vacantly, happily. Kirk stared at McCoy, dismay in his face. The Lawgiver left, closing the door behind him. The lock snapped.

"Bones . . ."

McCoy smiled at Kirk. "Hello, friend. They told us to wait here." He started toward a corner pallet, no sign whatever of recognition in his empty eyes.

"Bones!" Kirk cried. "Don't you know me?"

McCoy stared at him in obvious surprise. "We all know one another in Landru, friend."

Spock said, "Just like Sulu, Captain."

Kirk seized McCoy's arm, shaking it. "Think, man!" he cried. "The *Enterprise*! The ship! You remember the ship!"

McCoy shook his head bewilderedly. "You speak very strangely, friend. Are you from far away?"

Kirk's voice was fierce. "Bones, try to remember!"

"Landru remembers," McCoy said. "Ask Landru. He watches. He knows." A flicker of suspicion sharpened his eyes. "You are strange. Are you not of the Body?"

Kirk released his arm with a groan. McCoy at once lost his suspicious look, and, smiling emptily at nothing, moved away to sit down on one of the pallets.

The door opened again to the grinding of freed locks. Two Lawgivers stood in the entrance. One aimed his staff at Kirk. "Come," the cold voice said.

Kirk exchanged a quick glance with Spock. "And what if I don't?" he said.

"Then you will die."

"They have been corrected, Captain," Spock said. "Or reprogrammed. You'd better go with them, sir."

Kirk nodded. "All right, Spock, work on Bones. See if you can—"

"Come!" said the Lawgiver again.

Both staffs were aimed at Kirk as he passed through the cell door. As the heavy door swung to behind him, Spock whirled to McCoy. "Doctor, what will they do to him?"

McCoy smirked at him beatifically. "He goes to Joy. He goes to Peace and Tranquility. He goes to meet Landru. Happiness is to all of us who are blessed by Landru."

The room to which the Lawgivers were escorting Kirk was of stone—a room he was to remember as the "absorption chamber." A niche in a wall was equipped with a control panel. As he was prodded into the room, Kirk saw that another Lawgiver stood at the niche. Against another wall a manacle hung from a chain. Kirk was shoved toward it, one of his captors holding him while the other fastened the gyve about his wrist. Then they turned and left the room. Their footsteps had barely ceased to echo on the stone floor of the corridor outside when a fourth Lawgiver entered. He didn't so much as glance at Kirk but moved to his fellow at the control panel, nodding curtly.

Finally, he turned. "I am Marplon," he said. "It is your hour. Happy communing."

The Lawgiver at the panel bowed. "With thanks," he said. "Happy communing." Then, like the others, he left the absorption room. Alone now, Marplon faced Kirk. It seemed to Kirk that his visage resembled a death mask. But Marplon could move. When he had he placed a headset over his hood, his hands touched the control panel with the authority derived from much experience. The room flooded with bright, flashing colors; a humming sound began. The lights were blinding and the sound seemed to echo itself in Kirk's head. He twisted in his bonds.

At the same moment, back in the detention cell, Lindstrom was pacing it angrily. He halted to confront Spock. "Are we just going to stay here?"

"There seems to be little else we can do," Spock told him mildly. "Unless you can think of a way to get through that locked door."

"This is ridiculous! Prisoners of a bunch of Stone Age characters running around in robes."

"And apparently commanding powers far beyond our comprehension. Not simple, Mr. Lindstrom. Not ridiculous. Very, very dangerous."

On his last word the cell door opened and the two Lawgivers who had apprehended Kirk walked in. This time they aimed their staffs at Spock.

"You," said the spokesman. "Come."

For a fleeting second, Spock hesitated. The tip of one of the staffs quivered. Spock took his place between his guards. They led him out. They led him out and down the corridor to the absorption chamber. Kirk greeted him, an imbecile smile on his face.

"Captain!"

"Joy be with you, friend. Peace and contentment will fill you. You will know the peace of Landru . . ."

Then unguarded, alone, Kirk moved quietly to the door of the room with the manacle. The Lawgivers gave way as he passed. Spock stared after him, a horror only to be read by the absolute impassivity in his face.

He wasn't left much time to indulge it. Already they were manacling him to the wall. But the Vulcan's inveterate curiosity, not to be subdued, was already subordinating this personal experience to interest in the control panel's mechanism. As with Kirk, the two shackling Lawgivers, as soon as their task was accomplished, left. Marplon threw a switch on his panel. The colored lights began to swirl. Spock watched their coiling flashes with interest.

"Show no surprise," Marplon said. "The effect is harmless."

Spock looked at Marplon. The Lawgiver spoke in a lowered voice. "My name is Marplon. I was too late to save your first two friends. They have been absorbed. Beware of them."

"And my Captain?"

"He is unharmed," said Marplon. "Unchanged." He moved a finger; the light glowed brighter, and the hum grew more shrill. Marplon left his console to release Spock from his manacle. "I am the third man in Reger's trio," he said. "We have been waiting for your return."

"We are not Archons, Marplon," Spock said.

"Whatever you call yourselves, you are in fulfillment of prophecy. We ask for your help."

Spock said, "Where is Reger?"

"He will join us. He is immune to the absorption. Hurry! Time is short."

"Who is Landru?"

Marplon recoiled. "I cannot answer your questions now."

"Why not?" Spock said.

"Landru! He will hear!" Marplon went swiftly to his console, and reaching down and inward, brought out the ship's company's phasers. Spock, seizing several of them, stowed them away. As the last phaser was secreted, two Lawgivers pushed the door open.

"It is done," Marplon told them.

Spock assumed the idiotically amiable look of the anointed. "Joy be with you," he said.

"Landru is all," said the Lawgivers in unison. Spock moved past them and into the corridor. Making his way back to the cell, he found Kirk there, smiling blankly into space. Two Lawgivers pushed past him to beckon to the security crewman who had not been treated. Ashen with fear, he rose and went with them.

Spock went to Kirk. "Captain . . ."

"Peace and tranquility to you, friend," Kirk said. Then, in a lowered voice, he added, "Spock, you all right?"

"Quite all right, sir. Be careful of Dr. McCoy."

"I understand. Landru?"

"I am formulating an opinion, Captain."

"And?"

"Not here. The Doctor . . ."

But McCoy was already rising from his pallet, staring at them. His amiable smile faded and the look of curiosity on his face gave it a peculiar threatening aspect. "You speak in whispers," he said. "This is not the way of Landru."

"Joy to you, friend," Kirk said. "Tranquility be yours."

"And peace and harmony," intoned McCoy. "Are you of the Body?"

"The Body is one," Kirk said.

"Blessed be the Body. Health to all its parts." McCoy was smiling again, apparently satisfied. He sank back on the pallet; Kirk and Spock, joining him on theirs, sat on them in such a way as to screen their faces from McCoy. Then, in the same carefully lowered voice, he said, "What's your theory, Mr. Spock?"

"This is a soulless society, Captain. It has no spirit, no spark. All is indeed peace and tranquility, the peace of the factory, the machine's tranquility . . . all parts working in unison."

"I've noticed that the routine is disturbed if something unexplained happens."

"Until new orders are received. The question is, who gives those orders?"

"Landru," Kirk said.

"There is no Landru," Spock said. "Not in the human sense."

"You're thinking the same way I am, Mr. Spock."

"Yes, Captain. But as to what we must do . . ."

"We must pull out the plug, Mr. Spock."

"Sir?"

"Landru must die."

Spock's left eyebrow lifted. "Our prime directive of non-interference," he began.

"That refers to a living, growing creature. I'm not convinced that this one can qualify as—" He broke off as the cell door opened. Marplon and Reger, carrying the confiscated communicators, entered. "It is the gift of Landru to you," Marplon said. The words were addressed to McCoy and the treated security guard. They smiled vacantly and McCoy said, "Joy to you, friends." He leaned back against the stone wall, his eyes closed. Reger and Marplon hurried past him to Kirk and Spock.

"We brought your signaling devices," Marplon told Kirk. "You may need them."

"What we really need is more information about Landru," Kirk said.

Reger shrank back. "Prophecy says—" Marplon began.

"Never mind what prophecy says! If you want to be liberated from Landru, you have to help us!"

Spock cut in warningly. "Captain . . ."

McCoy was moving toward them, open and hostile suspicion in his face. "I heard you!" he cried. "You are not of the Body!" He hurled himself on Kirk, reaching for his throat. Spock tried to pry him off only to be taken in the rear by the treated security guard. "Lawgivers!" McCoy shouted. "Here are traitors! Traitors!"

With a twist, Kirk freed himself, crying, "Bones! Bones, I don't want to hurt you! Sit down and be still!"

But McCoy was still screaming, "Lawgivers! Hurry!"

Kirk's blow caught him squarely on the chin. As he fell, the door was flung wide and two Lawgivers, staffs ready, rushed in. At once they were jumped by Kirk and Spock. Kirk dropped his man with a hard wallop at the back of the neck while Spock applied the Vulcan neck pinch to his. Reger and Marplon, pressed against the wall, were staring at the fallen Lawgivers in horror.

Hurriedly, Kirk started disrobing the man he had downed. As Spock did the same to his, Kirk, donning the cowled garment, snapped at the others. "Where is Landru?"

"No," Marplon said. "No, no . . ."

"Where do we find him?" Kirk demanded.

"He will find us!" cried Reger. "He will destroy!"

Kirk whirled on Marplon. "You said you wanted a chance to help. All right, you're getting it! Where is he? You're a Lawgiver! Where do you see him?"

"We never see him. We hear him. In the Hall of Audiences!"

"In this building?"

Marplon nodded, terrified. Kirk let his rage rip. "You're going to take us there! Snap out of it, both of you! Start behaving like men!"

Spock opened a communicator. "Spock to *Enterprise*. Status report!"

"Mr. Spock!" It was Scott's voice. "I've been trying to reach you!"

"Report, Mr. Scott!"

"Orbit still decaying, sir. Give it six hours, more or less. Heat rays still on us. You've got to cut them off—or we'll cook one way or another."

Nodding at Spock, Kirk took the communicator. "Stand by, Mr. Scott. We're doing what we can. How's Mr. Sulu?"

"Peaceful enough, but he worries me."

"Put a guard on him."

"On Sulu?" Scott was shocked.

"That's an order! Watch him! Captain out!"

Robed now and armed, Kirk and Spock turned to Marplon and Reger. "All right. Now about Landru . . ."

"He made us!" Marplon cried. "He made this world!"

Reger was on his knees. "Please. We have gone too far! Don't—"

Spock said, "You say Landru made this world. Explain."

"There was war . . . six thousand years ago there was war . . . and convulsion. The world was destroying itself. Landru was our leader. He saw the truth. He changed the world. He took us back, back to a simple time, of peace, of tranquility."

"What happened to him?" Kirk said.

"He still lives!" cried Marplon. "He is here now! He sees . . . he hears . . . we have destroyed ourselves . . . please, please, no more."

Kirk spoke very softly. "You said you wanted freedom. It is time you learned that freedom is not a gift. You have to earn it—or you don't get it. Come on! We're going to find Landru!"

Reger stumbled to his knees. "No . . . no. I was wrong!" Wringing his hands, his eyes upturned imploringly, he shrieked, "I submit . . . I bare myself to the will of Landru."

Kirk seized his shoulders. "It is too late for that!" But Reger, shaking himself loose, dashed to the door, screaming, "No! No! Lawgivers! Help me!" Spock, reaching out, gave him the neck pinch. He fell; Marplon, staring, slowly turned to meet Kirk's eyes.

"All right, my friend," Kirk said. "It's up to you now. Take us to Landru."

"He will strike us down," said Marplon.

"Maybe—or it might be the other way around. Mr. Lindstrom, stay here and take care of Dr. McCoy. Let's go, Mr. Spock." He grabbed Marplon's arm, propelling him to the door. Dismay and fear on his face, Marplon opened it, and Kirk's hand still on his arm, he moved out into the corridor. From under his hood, Kirk could see two robed Lawgivers approaching. They passed without so much as glancing at the three figures they assumed to be fellow Lawgivers. The trio moved on down the corridor and Kirk saw that it ended at a large imposing door.

Marplon paused in front of it, visibly trembling. "This is . . . the Hall of Audiences," he whispered.

"Do you have a key?"

At Marplon's nod, Kirk said, "Open it."

"But—it is Landru . . ."

"Open it," Kirk said again. But he had to take the key from Marplon's trembling hands to open it himself. The Hall of Audiences was a large room, completely bare. In one of the walls was set a glowing panel. Marplon pointed to it. "Landru—he speaks here . . ." he whispered.

Kirk stepped forward. "Landru! We are the Archons!" he said. The moldy, cold silence in the big room remained unbroken. Kirk spoke again. "We are the Archons. We've come to talk with you!"

Very gradually the wise, impressive, benevolent face they remembered began to take shape on the panel. In an extremity of panic, Marplon broke into sobs, prostrating himself. "Landru comes!" he wept. "He comes!"

The noble figure was completed now, a warm half smile on its lips. They opened. "Despite my efforts not to harm you, you have invaded the Body. You are causing great harm."

"We have no intention of causing harm," Kirk said.

Landru continued as though Kirk had not spoken. "Obliteration is necessary. The infection is strong. For the good of the Body, you must die. It is a great sorrow."

"We do not intend to die!"

The oblivious voice continued, kind, gently. "All who have seen you, who know of your presence, must be excised. The memory of the Body must be cleansed."

"Listen to me!" Kirk shouted.

"Captain . . . useless," Spock said. "A projection!"

"All right, Mr. Spock! Let's have a look at the projector!"

They whipped out their phasers simultaneously, turning their beams on the glowing panel. There was a great flash of blinding light. The figure of Landru vanished and the light in the panel faded. But the real Landru had not disappeared. Behind the panel he survived in row upon row of giant computers—a vast complex of dials, switches, involved circuits all quietly operating.

"It had to be," Kirk said. "Landru."

"Of course, Captain. A machine. This entire society is a machine's idea of perfection. Peace, harmony . . ."

"And no soul."

Suddenly the machine buzzed. A voice spoke. It said, "I am Landru. You have intruded."

"Pull out its plug, Mr. Spock."

They aimed their phasers. But before they could fire, there came another buzzing from the machine and a flash of light immobilized their weapons. "Your devices have been neutralized," said the voice. "So it shall be with you. I am Landru."

"Landru died six thousand years ago," Kirk said.

"I am Landru!" cried the machine. "I am he. All that he was, I am. His experience, his knowledge—"

"But not his wisdom," Kirk said. "He may have programmed you, but he could not give you his soul."

"Your statement is irrelevant," said the voice. "You will be obliterated. The good of the Body is the primal essence."

"That's the answer, Captain," Spock said. "That good of the Body . . ."

Kirk nodded. "What is the good?" he asked.

"I am Landru."

"Landru is dead. You are a machine. A question has been put to you. Answer it!"

Circuits hummed. "The good is the harmonious continuation of the Body," said the voice. "The good is peace, tranquility, harmony. The good of the Body is the prime directive."

"I put it to you that you have disobeyed the prime directive—that you are harmful to the Body."

The circuits hummed louder. "The Body is . . . it exists. It is healthy."

"It is dying," Kirk said. "You are destroying it."

"Do you ask a question?" queried the voice.

"What have you done to do justice to the full potential of every individual of the Body?"

"Insufficient data. I am not programmed to answer that question."

"Then program yourself," Spock said. "Or are your circuits limited?"

"My circuits are unlimited. I will reprogram."

The machine buzzed roughly. A screech came from it. Marplon, on the floor, was getting to his feet, his eyes staring at the massive computer face. As he gained them, two more Lawgivers appeared, staffless.

They approached the machine. "Landru!" cried one. "Guide us! Landru?" His voice was a wail.

Kirk had whirled to cover them with his phaser when Spock raised his hand. "Not necessary, Captain. They have no guidance . . . possibly for the first time in their lives."

Kirk, lowering his phaser, turned back to the machine. "Landru! Answer that question!"

The voice had a metallic tone now. "Peace, order, and tranquility are maintained. The Body lives. But creativity is mine. Creativity is necessary for the health of the Body." It buzzed again. "This is impossible. It is a paradox. It shall be resolved."

Marplon spoke at last. "Is that truly Landru?"

"What's left of him," Spock said. "What's left of him after he built this machine and programmed it six thousand years ago."

Kirk addressed the machine. "Landru! The paradox!"

The humming fell dead. The voice, dully metallic now, said, "It will not resolve."

"You must create the good," Kirk said. "That is the will of Landru—nothing else . . ."

"But there is evil," said the voice.

"Then the evil must be destroyed. It is the prime directive. You are the evil."

The machine resumed its humming—a humming broken by hard, harsh clicks. Lights flashed wildly. "I think! I live!" said the machine.

"You say you are Landru!" Kirk shouted. "Then create the good! Destroy evil! Fulfill the prime directive!"

The hum rose to a roar. A drift of smoke wafted up from a switch. Then a shower of sparks burst from the machine's metal face—and with the blast of exploding circuits, all its lights went out.

Kirk turned to the three awed Lawgivers. "All right, you can get rid of those robes now. If I were you, I'd start looking for real jobs." He opened the communicator. "Kirk to *Enterprise*. Come in, please."

Scott's voice was loud with relief. "Captain, are you all right?"

"Never mind about us. What about you?"

"The heat rays have gone, and Mr. Sulu's back to normal."

"Excellent, Mr. Scott. Stand by to beam-up landing party." He returned the communicator to Spock. "Let's see what the others are doing, Mr. Spock. Mr. Marplon can finish up here."

His command chair seemed to welcome Kirk. He'd never thought of it as comfortable before. But he stretched in it, hands locked behind his neck as Spock left his station to stand beside him while he dictated his last notation into his Captain's log. "Sociologist Lindstrom is remaining behind on Beta 3000 with a party of experts who will help restore the culture to a human form. Kirk out."

Spock spoke thoughtfully. "Still, Captain, the late Landru was a marvelous feat of engineering. Imagine a computer capable of directing—literally directing—every act of millions of human beings."

"But only a machine, Mr. Spock. The original Landru programmed it with all his knowledge but he couldn't give it his wisdom, his compassion, his understanding—his soul, Mr. Spock."

"Sometimes you are predictably metaphysical, Captain. I prefer the concrete, the graspable, the provable."

"You would make a splendid computer, Mr. Spock."

Spock bowed. "That's very kind of you, sir."

Uhura spoke from behind them. "Captain . . . Mr. Lindstrom from the surface."

Kirk pushed a button. "Yes, Mr. Lindstrom."

"Just wanted to say good-bye, Captain."

"How are things going?"

"Couldn't be better!" The youngster's enthusiasm was like a triumphant shout in his ear. "Already this morning we've had half-a-dozen domestic quarrels and two genuine knock-down drag-outs. It may not be paradise—but it's certainly . . ."

"Human?" asked Kirk.

"Yes! And they're starting to think for themselves! Just give me and our people a few months and we'll have a going society on our hands!"

"One question, Mr. Lindstrom: Landru wanted to give his people peace and security and so programmed the machine. Then how do we account for so total an anomaly as the festival?"

"Sir, with the machine destroyed, we'll never have enough data to answer that one with any confidence—but I have a guess, and I feel almost certain it's the right one. Landru wanted to eliminate war, crime, disease, even personal dissension, and he succeeded. But he failed to allow for population control, and without that even an otherwise static society would soon suffer a declining standard of living, and eventual outright hunger. Clearly Landru wouldn't have wanted that either, but he made no allowances for it.

"So the machine devised its own: one night a year in which all forms of control were shut off, every moral law abrogated; even ordinary human decency was canceled out. One night of the worst kind of civil war, in which *every* person is the enemy of *every* other. I have no proof of this at all, sir—but it's just the sort of solution you'd expect from a machine, and furthermore, a machine that had been programmed to think of people as cells in a Body, of no importance at all as individuals." Suddenly Lindstrom's voice shook. "One night a year of total cancer . . . horrible! I hope I'm dead wrong, but there are precedents."

"That can hardly be fairly characterized as a guess," Spock said. "Ordinarily I do not expect close reasoning from sociologists, but from what I know of the way computers behave when they are given directives supported by insufficient data, I can find no flaw in Mr. Lindstrom's analysis. It should not distress him, for if it is valid—as I am convinced it is—he is indeed just the man to put it right."

"Thank you, Mr. Spock," Lindstrom's voice said. "I'll cherish that. Captain, do you concur?"

"I do indeed," Kirk said. "I have human misgivings which I know you share with me. All I can say now is it sounds promising. Good luck. Kirk out."

Kirk turned to his First Officer and looked at him in silence for a long time. At last he said, "Mr. Spock, if I didn't know you were above such human weaknesses as feelings of solemnity, I'd say you looked solemn. Are you feeling solemn, Mr. Spock?"

"I was merely meditating, sir. I was reflecting on the frequency with which mankind has wished for a world as peaceful and secure as the one Landru provided."

"Quite so, Mr. Spock. And see what happens when we get it! It's our luck and our curse that we're forced to grow, whether we like it or not."

"I have heard human beings say also, Captain, that it is also our joy."

"*Our* joy, Mr. Spock?"

There was no response, but, Kirk thought, Spock knew as well as any man that ancient human motto: *Silence gives assent.*

SPACE SEED

WRITERS: GENE L. COON AND CAREY WILBUR
(STORY BY CAREY WILBUR)

DIRECTOR: MARC DANIELS

FIRST AIRED: FEBRUARY 16, 1967

It was only sheer luck that Marla McGivers was on the bridge when the SOS came in. Officially, Lieutenant McGivers was a controls systems specialist, but on the side, she was also a historian. Probably nobody else on board the *Enterprise* would have recognized Morse code at all, since it had gone out of use around the year 2000, in the general chaos following the Eugenics Wars; but she was a student of the period (though, Kirk thought, she looked a good deal more like a ballerina).

The SOS, when answered, changed promptly to the Morse for *SS Botany Bay*, and stayed there as if stuck regardless of further hails. Homing on the message, the *Enterprise* eventually found herself drawing alongside a dark hull of a ship of the CZ-100 class. The library computer said the last one of those had been built around 1994. Clearly a derelict, its signal left on automatic.

Except that the *Enterprise*'s sensors showed other equipment also still operating, over there across the vacuum between the two vessels. Other equipment—and heartbeats. They were very faint, but they seemed to be coming from some eighty or ninety sources. None were faster than four beats per minute. There were no signs of respiration.

"Aliens?" Kirk asked McCoy.

The surgeon shrugged. "You've got me, Jim. Even aliens have to breathe. Besides, the ship's name is in English."

"The English," Kirk said drily, "were notorious for not breathing, I suppose. Mr. Spock, can you trace the registry?"

"Nothing in the computer, Captain."

"Lieutenant McGivers, what can you tell us about the period when that ship was built?"

"Not as much as I'd like," Marla McGivers said. "The Eugenics Wars were caused by a group of ambitious scientists—of all nationalities—who were trying to improve the race by selective breeding. They were pretty ruthless about it, and before their identity was guessed, half the countries on Earth were accusing each other of being responsible for the plague of sports and monsters that was cropping up. The result was the last

World War, and in the process, a lot of records were lost. I'm surprised that any ship from that era ever got off the ground."

"Well, we'd better go across and look it over," Kirk said. "Since you're a specialist in the period, you'd better be in the party. Scotty, I'll want you to inspect the machinery and see what's salvageable, if anything. Bones, you too."

"Why am I always included in these things?" McCoy complained. "I signed aboard to practice medicine, not to have my atoms scattered back and forth across space by a transporter."

"You're included because we hear heartbeats, and that is your department. Let's go."

It was almost dark inside the *Botany Bay*. Where the boarding party materialized, there was little to see but a long corridor, flanked on each side by row upon row of coffin-like drawers or canisters, each about two meters square on end, thrust into the wall. Each had a small green light blinking over it, producing eerie, confusing reflections. Kirk eyed them.

"Mr. Scott?"

"I don't make anything of it yet, sir. They look a little like food lockers—but why so many? Ah, there's a control panel."

"I've seen something like them," Marla said. "Or rather, drawings of them. They look like a twentieth-century life-support system."

McCoy applied his tricorder to the nearest cabinet. At the same moment, Scott said, "Ah, here we are!" and lights came on overhead. McCoy grunted with interest.

"Look here, Jim," he said. "A new reading. The lights seem to have triggered something inside."

Kirk did not have to look at the tricorder reading to see that. There was now a clear hum from the cabinet, and the little light had turned from green to red.

"I've got it!" Marla said suddenly. "It's a sleeper ship!"

This meant nothing to Kirk, but McCoy said: "Suspended animation?"

"Yes. They were necessary for long space trips until about the year 2018. They didn't have the warp drive until then, so even interplanetary travel took them years. We'll find crewmen in there, or passengers, sleeping, waiting for the end of their journey . . ."

"Or more likely, all dead," McCoy said. "On the other hand, those heartbeats . . . Is it possible, after all these centuries?"

Scott joined them, and in a moment had discovered that the front of the cabinet was actually a protective shield. Pulling this away, he revealed a transparent observation panel. On the other side, bathed in a gentle violet glow, was a motionless, naked man. He was extremely handsome, and magnificently built. His face reflected the sun-ripened Aryan blood of the northern Indian Sikhs, with just an additional suggestion of the oriental. Even in repose, his features suggested strength, intelligence, even arrogance.

"How beautiful," Marla said, as if to herself.

"This cabinet is wired to be triggered first," Scott said practically. "Maybe that means he's the leader."

"Or only a pilot," Spock added. "Or a doctor, to supervise the revival of the others."

"He's the leader," Marla said positively.

"Oh?" Kirk said. "What makes you think so?"

"Well . . . you can see it. A Sikh type. They were fantastic warriors."

"He *is* reviving," McCoy said. "Heartbeat up to fifty-two already, and definite breathing."

"Scotty, see if they're all like that."

The engineer went down the line, pulling off the shields and peering into each canister. "No sir," he said finally. "A mixed bag, Captain. Western, Mid-European, Near-Eastern, Latin, Oriental—the works. And all their lights are still green, as you can see yourself."

"A man from the twentieth century," Marla said, as if hypnotized. "Coming alive now. It's incredible!"

"It's about to be impossible," McCoy said, checking the tricorder again. "His heartbeat's beginning to drop back down. If you want to talk to this living fossil, Jim, I suggest we get him over to my sick bay right away quick."

"Oh no!" Marla said.

McCoy shot her a sidelong look, but he said, "I quite agree. A patient well worth fighting for. And think of the history locked up in that head!"

"Never mind the history," Kirk said. "It's a human life. Beam him over."

While McCoy worked on the sleeping man, Kirk took time out to collect more information from his officers.

"As near as I can work out their heading," said Spinelli, who had relieved Sulu at the helm, "they must have been trying for the Tau Ceti system."

"Makes sense. It's near Sol, and there are three habitable planets."

"Yes sir, but they would never have gotten there. Their port control jets took meteor damage, and the hits put them off course, too."

"Scotty, any log books or records?"

"Negative, Captain. They must have been in suspended animation when the ship took off."

"Ship's equipment?"

"Colonization gear mainly," the engineer said. "But quite heavy on armaments. I suppose that's typical of their era. Twelve of the life support systems malfunctioned, leaving seventy-two still operating. About a dozen of those are women."

"Seventy-two alive," Kirk said reflectively. "Any conclusions, Mr. Spock?"

"Very few, Captain. The CZ-100 class vessel was built for interplanetary travel only—*not* interstellar."

"They tried it."

"Granted," said the first officer. "But why?"

"Possibly because life on Earth had become so unbearable during the wars."

"Captain, consider the expense, just to begin with. Healthy, well-oriented young humans would think of some less costly way of surviving—or of committing suicide. It was ten thousand to one against their making it to Tau Ceti, and they must have known it. And another thing: Why no record of the attempt? Granted that the records are incomplete, but a maiden star voyage—the name *Botany Bay* should have been recorded a thousand times: one mention, at least, should have survived. But there is nothing."

"*Botany Bay*. Hmm. Lieutenant McGivers tells me that was a penal colony on the shores of Australia. Is that of some significance?"

"Are you suggesting a deportation vessel?" Spock said. "Again, logically insufficient. Your Earth was on the edge of another Dark Ages. Whole populations were being bombed out of existence. A group of criminals could have been eliminated in a far less expensive way than firing them off in what was the most advanced spaceship of its time."

"So much for my theory. I'm still waiting for yours."

"I do not have the facts, Captain. William of Occam said that one must not multiply guesses without sufficient reasons. I suggest that we take the *Botany Bay* to the nearest Star Base for a thorough study."

Kirk thought about it. "All right. Rig tractors for towing. In the meantime, I'm going to look at the patient."

In the sick bay, the man out of time was still unconscious, but now breathing regularly. Marla McGivers was standing to one side, watching.

"How is he, Bones?"

"By all rights he should be dead," McCoy said shortly.

"False modesty?"

"By no means. I'm good, but not *that* good. His heart stopped three times. When I got it going the third time, he woke up for a moment, smiled at me, and said 'How long?' I guessed a couple of centuries. He smiled again, fell asleep, and damned if his heart didn't stop a fourth time, and *start up again of its own accord*. There's something inside this man that refuses to accept death."

"He must have the constitution of an ox."

"That is not just a metaphor," McCoy said, pointing to the body function panel. "Look at that. Even in his present shape, his heart valve action has twice the power of yours or mine. Lung efficiency, fifty percent better. And courage! . . . Whoever he is, or whatever, it'll be a pleasure to meet him."

Kirk looked at Marla, and then said quietly to the surgeon, "I can get you agreement on that."

Apparently encouraged by the notice, Marla said, "Will he live?"

"If he gets some rest, he may," McCoy said tartly. "Beat it, both of you. This is a sick bay, not a wardroom."

Grinning, Kirk motioned Marla out and followed her. As she turned down the corridor, however, he said, "Lieutenant."

She stopped and turned. Kirk went on. "Lieutenant, if I were forced to rate your performance as a member of the boarding party today, I wouldn't give you a very high mark."

"I know, Captain," she said. "I'm sorry."

"That's not enough. At any one time, the safety of this entire vessel can rest upon the performance of a single crewman. The fact that you may find a strange man personally compelling is the worst possible excuse."

"Personally?" she said, flushing. "Captain, my second profession is history. To find a . . . a specimen from the past, alive . . . the sheer delight of anticipating what he might tell me . . ."

"More than that," Kirk said. "Men were much more adventurous then, bolder, more colorful."

She was silent for no more than a heartbeat. Then she said firmly, "Yes, sir, I think they were."

Kirk nodded. "That's better. If I can have honesty, I'll overlook mistakes—at least the first time. Dismissed."

As she left, Kirk turned to find McCoy watching him, smiling. "It's a pity," the surgeon said, "that you wasted your life on command, Jim. You'd have made a fair psychologist."

"Thanks, Bones, but command is better. It covers every other subject."

"Touché—or should I say, checkmate?"

It was only a few hours later that McCoy called Kirk on the bridge. "Captain," he said, "I have a patient with questions—and I don't mind telling you, patients like this could put medicine out of business. Can you come down?"

The big man from the *Botany Bay*, now dressed in a tunic from the stores of the *Enterprise*, was still on his bed; but he was indeed awake—vitally awake. Kirk introduced himself."

"Thank you," the man said. "I am told I have slept for two centuries or more, and am on board a real starship—not a makeshift like mine. What is our heading?"

Kirk was both amused and annoyed. "Would you care to give your name first?"

"No, I would not. I have a responsibility. If you are indeed a commander, you will recognize it. Where are we going?"

Kirk decided to yield for the moment; there was no point in insisting on a contest with a man just yanked back from the edge of death, no matter how arrogant he was. "Our heading is Star Base Twelve, our command base in this sector."

"Which is?"

"I doubt that identifying the sector would do you any good. It is many parsecs beyond the system you were headed for, and our galactic coordinate system probably doesn't correspond with the one you're used to."

"Galactic," the man said. "I see. And my people?"

"Seventy-two of the canisters are still functioning. The people will be revived when we reach Star Base Twelve. We wanted to see how we fared with reviving you, first."

"Logical and hard-headed; I approve. I do begin to grow fatigued. Can we continue the questioning at another time?"

"You haven't answered any questions yet," Kirk said, "except by inference."

"I apologize," the big man said at once. "My name is Kahn. I command the *Botany Bay* Colonizing Expedition. I think perhaps I could answer your questions better if I knew your period, your terminology and so on—perhaps something to read during my convalescence would serve. History, technology, whatever is available."

It seemed a sensible request. "Dr. McCoy will show you how to hook your viewing screen here into our library tapes. And I think Lieutenant McGivers would enjoy filling you in on the history."

"Very good." Kahn smiled. "I have two hundred years of catching up to do. I . . ."

Suddenly, his eyes closed. McCoy looked at the body function panel.

"Asleep," McCoy said. "Well, I'm glad he's got *some* human weaknesses."

It was not until Kirk was on his way back to the bridge that he fully realized how little Kahn had told him. Irritated, mostly at himself, he collared Spock at the computer. "Anything?"

"Nothing about a star flight until the Alpha Centauri expedition of 2018," the first officer said. "How is the patient?"

"Arrogant—and clever. Enormously powerful. And with enormous magnetism. Not at all what I expected in a twentieth-century man."

"Interesting. Possibly a product of selective breeding."

"That had occurred to me," Kirk admitted. "If I wanted a superman, he's very much the kind of outcome I'd shoot for."

"Exactly, Captain. He is almost a stereotype of an Earthman's dreams of power and potency. And from what I can put together from the fragments of the record, just the kind of man who precipitated the chaos of the 1990s."

"Oh? I thought it was a group of scientists."

"Partly true," Spock said, "and partly, I would judge, a comfortable fiction. The scientists encouraged carefully arranged marriages *among themselves*, and applied their knowledge of heredity to their *own* offspring. The sports and monsters did not appear until after the war was well started, and almost surely were spontaneous mutations erupting from all the ambient radioactivity. The scientists stayed aloof and went right on breeding what they thought was *Homo superior*."

"Fact?" Kirk demanded. "Or just that old legend of the mad scientists again?"

"Mostly deduction," Spock said. "But the scientists existed. Not mad—not raving mad, anyhow. Dedicated men who believed their wards would grow up to seize power peaceably, put an end to war, famine, greed—a noble ambition, which of course misfired."

"And our patient."

"One of those children. His age would be right. A group of aggressive, arrogant young men *did* seize power simultaneously in over forty nations. But they had overextended themselves; they could not hold what they seized. That much is fact. And one more thing, Captain. Are you aware that some eighty or ninety of those people were never brought to trial, were never even found after the chaos? No bodies, no graves, no traces?"

"I certainly wasn't," Kirk said.

"And they should have been found, or the authorities should have pretended that they had been found. Think of the panic among the remaining, starving war-weary people even to suspect that eighty Napoleons might still be alive. And, Captain . . ."

"Yes," Kirk said heavily. "I'm no match for you as a logician, Mr. Spock, but even I can see where that sentence is leading. You think those eighty Napoleons are *still* alive—and we have seventy-nine of them in tow, and one on board."

"Precisely, Captain."

Kirk thought about it for quite a while.

"It stands up," he said. "But what we're left with, is that we can get no more pertinent information anywhere except from Kahn himself. He's got a mind like a tantalum-lined vault, so we'll never force it out of him. We'll have to try to charm it . . . which probably won't work either. Maybe we can use the customs of his own time to disarm him. I'll see what Lieutenant McGivers has to suggest."

What Marla McGivers had to suggest was a formal dinner, attended by all the major officers of the *Enterprise*, as a welcome for Commander Kahn to the twenty-third century. She was obviously far from disinterested in the proposal, and Kirk suspected that Kahn had already made his first new conquest in the new century; but there were no regulations against romance, and in any event, Kirk had nothing better to suggest.

Marla appeared with a new and totally anachronistic hair style which went a long way toward confirming Kirk's suspicions. As for Kahn, it was impossible to tell whether or not he was charmed; he far too efficiently charmed everybody else, instead. There seemed to be no situation in which he could not feel at home, after only a few minutes' appraisal.

Then, over the brandy, it suddenly turned out at least one officer of the *Enterprise* was not prepared to recognize charm even if he were hit over the head with it. Spock said, "But you still have not told us why you decided on star travel, Commander Kahn—nor how you managed to keep it out of the records."

"Adventure, Mr. Spock. There was little else left to be accomplished on Earth."

"There was the overthrow of the Eugenics tyrannies," Spock said. "Many men considered that a worthwhile effort."

"A waste of spirit in a desert of shame," Kahn said. "There was much that was noble about the Eugenics crusade. It was the last grand attempt to unify humanity, at least in my time."

"Like a team of horses under one harness, one whip?"

"I refuse to take offense, Mr. Spock," Kahn said genially. "Much can be accomplished by a team. It was a time of great dreams—great aspirations."

"Great aspirations under petty dictatorships? Never in previous history, at least."

"I disagree," Kahn said. "One man, not many, would eventually have ruled. As in Rome under Augustus—and see what that accomplished—Captain Kirk, you understand me well. You let your second-in-command attack me, and through me, you; yet you remain silent, and watch for weakness. A sound principle."

"You have a tendency," Kirk said, "to express your ideas in military terms, Commander Kahn. This is a social occasion."

"It has been said," Kahn said easily, "that social occasions are only warfare concealed. Many prefer their warfare more honest and open."

"There was open warfare on Earth," Kirk said. "Yet it appears that you fled it."

"Not much can be done with a nearly destroyed world."

"In short," Spock said, "you were afraid."

Kahn's eyes flashed. "I have never been afraid."

"And that does not frighten you?"

"How? I don't understand you, Mr. Spock. How can a man be afraid of never being afraid? It is a contradiction in terms."

"Not at all," the first officer said. "It is a null class in the class of all classes not members of the given class."

Kahn was now beginning to look angry. Kirk, secretly a little amused, interposed. "I'm sorry, Commander, but you just pushed Mr. Spock's logic button, which has a tendency to make him incomprehensible for the next ten minutes or so. Nevertheless, I think his question a good one. You say you have never been afraid; yet you left at the very time mankind most needed courage."

"Courage! How can one impart courage to sheep? I offered the world order. *Order!* And what happened? They panicked. I left behind nothing worth saving."

"Then," Spock said, "do you imagine that this ship, to take a simple example, was built by sheep, out of panic? I do not further impugn your logic, Commander Kahn, but I am beginning to mistrust your eyesight."

Marla, who had been completely silent since the start of the discussion, stood up so suddenly that coffee slopped in saucers all the way around the table.

"I never thought," she said in a trembling voice, "that I'd ever see so much rudeness to a starship guest."

"Was *I* rude?" Spock said mildly, raising his eyebrows. "If so, I apologize."

"And I," said Kirk, repressing another grin.

"I quite accept your apologies," Kahn said, also rising. "But if you will excuse me, gentlemen and ladies, I am tired. It has been a good many centuries, and I would like to return to my quarters. If you would guide me back, Marla . . . ?"

They went out, followed, at a slight motion of the head from Kirk, by every other guest but Spock. When the room was empty, Kirk said, "And McCoy calls *me* a fair psychologist! I've never seen a better needling job in my life, Mr. Spock."

"I myself am not very happy with it, Captain," the first officer said. "The human half of my make-up seems to go to sleep just when I need it most. Consider, really, how little we have learned. The man's name: Sibahl Khan Noonien. From 1922 through 1996, military chieftain of a quarter of your world from South Asia through the Middle East, and the last of the tyrants to be overthrown. And apparently very much admired, as such men go; there was very little freedom under his rule, but also there were no massacres, and no war until he was attacked by a lesser dictator of his own breed. A man of power, who understands the uses of power, and who *should* have been much admired by the people whom he calls sheep, the people who feel more comfortable being led."

"And you got all that just from what he said tonight? I would say that's considerable."

"It is not what we need to know," Spock insisted. "The main question is, why did he run away? *That* was what I was hoping to elicit from him. But he caught me at it. I do not call that very good psychology."

"I see what you mean," Kirk said reflectively. "Until we know that, we can't know what he might intend now—or what risks we might run in reviving the other seventy or so of them. We will just have to try another gambit . . . But there's one other thing. What was the point of that question about being afraid of never having been afraid? I thought for a moment that I saw what you were driving at, and then you lost me in your logical technicalities. Isn't the question what you would call a tautology?"

"No, Captain," Spock said. "But I was trying to make it look like one. I was not trying to confuse you, certainly, but Commander Kahn—and I hope that at least there, I succeeded. Fear is an essential reaction to the survival of any sentient creature. If he does not know fear, he never knows when it is sensible to run; and yet, Commander Kahn ran. Since he claims never to have felt fear, what other reason can he have had?"

"Hmm," Kirk said. "I've never seen a single sentient creature that didn't feel fear when it was appropriate. Yet he was very convincing on that very point."

"Indeed he was," Spock said. "And, Captain—that *scares* me."

Nothing Spock had ever said before had quite so stunned Kirk. As he stared at his Science Officer, the vacated, somehow sadly messy scene of the formal dinner suddenly rang with the alarm to General Quarters.

"Abrams in Security, Captain. Kahn's missing."

"McCoy here. Kahn's not here. No sign of McGivers, either—not even in her quarters. And he's not there."

"Transporter room here. We've had a guard slugged, Lieutenant Adamski is missing, and there's been a lot of power expended in the last half hour."

"Scott reporting. I . . ."

"Uhura, what happened to Scotty? Get him back!"

"Dead channel, Captain. I can't raise the arsenal, either."

"Spock, send somebody down."

"All turbo elevators inoperative. Emergency exits jammed."

The lights began to go down. "Batteries!"

"Shunted out, Captain. Also, the atmosphere's off."

"Engineering! Scott! What's going on down there? Scotty!"

And then they heard Kahn's voice. It was coming through Uhura's own board, though it was impossible to imagine how Kahn had made the crippled array speak.

"He's not able to talk with you at the moment, Captain," Kahn said. "I'm afraid your ship is mine—or rather, ours. I have almost all my people aboard her, at every key point. Everything is jammed; you have perhaps ten minutes before you suffocate. Would you like to negotiate with me?"

"Uhura, can you raise Star Ship Command?"

"No, sir, this board is a dead duck. I can't even dump a message capsule."

"Brilliant," Spock said softly.

There was only one thing left to do. "Security Five, Mr. Spock. Flood all decks."

"Bypassed, Captain. Commander Kahn seems to have been a very quick student."

"Can we go to Six?" That would fill the air with radioactive gas from the fusion chamber and kill almost everyone on board; but . . .

"No sir, we cannot. Nothing is left but Destruct. That's still alive."

"The air up there should be getting quite toxic by now," Kahn's voice said. "You don't have much time."

"What do you want, Kahn?"

"Surrender of the bridge."

"Refused," Kirk said.

"Very well. It is academic, anyhow. In ten minutes, every person on the bridge will be dead."

Nothing further was heard from Kahn after that. Slowly, the air turned foul. After a while, nobody was conscious but Kirk, and then . . . and then . . .

Kirk awoke, with considerable surprise, in the briefing room. His entire staff seemed to be with him—all weak, but all alive. They were heavily under guard by Kahn and a group of men very like him, all carrying *Enterprise* phasers. The men from the *Botany Bay* were inarguably splendid-looking specimens—large, strong, healthy, handsome, and above all, alert.

"Very good," Kahn said. "Now we can talk. You see, Captain, nothing changes—except man. Your technical accomplishments are illusions, simply the tools which men use. The key has always been man himself. Improve a mechanical device and you double your capacity; improve man, and you gain a thousand fold. You, I judge, are such a man, Captain, as am I. You would be wise to join me."

Kirk said nothing. Kahn turned to Spock. "I am tempted," Spock said. "I admire your tactics . . . but not, I am afraid, your philosophy. And I know from history how self-appointed supermen treat mixed breeds. Let us see how you run the ship by yourself."

"You will see. My offer to you is closed. Navigator, I want you to set course for the nearest colonized planet—one with port facilities and a population which is not afraid of discipline."

"Go to blazes," Spinelli said.

"It is as I thought," Spock said. "You may know the *Enterprise* well, Commander, but your newly revived colleagues do not. I think we have a stalemate."

"Do we? Dr. McCoy, you maintain a decompression chamber in your laboratory, isn't that so? Yes, I know it is. Joaquin, take Captain Kirk to the chamber. Put him inside, and lower the pressure to zero. I trust the rest of you understand what that means. You can spare him that. All I want from you is your word that you will continue performing your duties."

"Nobody," Kirk said harshly, "is to lift a finger to save me. I so order."

"I am not bluffing," Kahn said pleasantly. "If, of course, you allow your Captain to die, you will all follow him, one by one, into the chamber."

Kirk caught Marla's eye. She was staring wide-eyed at Kahn. Evidently she had discovered something she hadn't taken into account.

There was a blare from a wall speaker, and then a babble of angry, excited crowd noises. "Kahn," said an unfamiliar voice, "this is Paul in the recreation room. They're getting out of hand. I may have to kill a few of them."

"Do so, then."

"No!" Marla said. "I have friends there... Kahn, please. If I could talk to them... reassure them... There's no need to kill them."

"You may attempt it," Kahn said. "Be certain they understand that I have no compunctions about killing if I'm forced to."

The guards hustled Kirk out, with Marla in tow. Perhaps they were unfamiliar with the ship in detail, but they certainly knew their way to McCoy's laboratory. They bundled Kirk into the decompression chamber as though they were doing nothing more interesting than autoclaving a rack of test tubes. The door shut, and a moment later Kirk heard the pumps begin to throb.

For some reason, he felt neither alarmed nor resigned. His chief emotion was anger, at being put through asphyxiation twice in one hour.

There seemed to be nothing to do about it, however.

Then the door hissed and swung back. Kirk stepped out cautiously. One of the supermen, the one called Joaquin, was out cold on the floor, with Marla standing over him, a wrench held awkwardly in her hands. The other guard evidently had gone off somewhere.

"Are you all right?" Marla said tremulously.

"I think so. The pressure didn't have time to drop much. I'm glad to see you're good for something." He stooped and picked up Joaquin's phaser.

Marla grasped his arm. "Captain, please," she said.

"Well?"

"I saved your life. Promise me you... won't kill him."

"No promises," Kirk said, looking around the laboratory. After a moment, he spotted what he wanted; a bulb of the anesthetic gas McCoy used to capture specimens. He juggled it with pleasure. "Stay here and try not to get yourself any deeper into trouble than you are. I think I am about to bag myself some choice items for some zoo."

It was not all that easy. Before it was over, one of the supermen was dead, and almost everyone else on both sides was considerably banged up. At last, however, the survivors from the *Botany Bay* were locked in a hold, and Kirk and his officers reassembled in the briefing room.

"Well, Mr. Spock," Kirk said, "I think we know now why they left the Earth."

"Yes, sir. To free themselves of the rabble, and start fresh. In my opinion they would never have succeeded, even had they made it to a habitable world. The man who cannot know fear is gravely handicapped."

"We are about to put that to the test. Have Kahn brought in here, please."

Kahn was brought in, under guard, with Marla behind him. Both looked at Kirk defiantly.

"At present," Kirk said, "we are orbiting a planet in a system unknown to you, and which I shall not further identify. It is savage and inhospitable, but with breathable atmosphere and land which can be cultivated. You have the following choice: To be put ashore on this world, with a minimum of survival equipment; or, to be taken to Star Base Twelve to be assigned to rehabilitation. The second choice would be rather drastic in your case, but it would enable you to fit into our society. Which do you prefer?"

"Captain," Kahn said, "I suppose you will remember what Lucifer said when he fell into the pit."

"I remember it well. I take it that's your answer?"

"It is."

"It may interest you to know that Systems Officer McGivers, given the choice of standing court martial or sharing your exile, has chosen to go with you."

Kahn looked at her and smiled. "I knew I was right about you," he said. "You have the fire. And think of this: we have what we wanted after all—a world to win." He swung on Kirk. "And, Captain, we will make it an empire. You'll see."

"If you do," Kirk said, "you'll have earned it. Guards, beam them down."

Kahn exited without a backward look, but Marla turned at the door.

"Goodbye, Captain," she said. "I'm sorry. But I do love him."

"I wish you luck, Lieutenant."

After a short silence, Scott said, "It's a shame for a good Scotsman to admit it, but I'm not up on my Milton. What *did* Lucifer say after he fell into the pit?"

"He said, 'Better to reign in hell than serve in heaven.' Mr. Spock, clear for space. I want to get under way as soon as possible."

"Yes, Captain. What shall I do with the *Botany Bay*?"

"Hmm . . . You'd better dump it into—no, on second thought, let's keep it in tow. I suppose there are still things aboard her that the historians will want to see. At the moment, though, whenever I say 'historian' I have to repress a shudder."

"Let us think ahead, then," Spock said. "It would be interesting to come back to this system in a hundred years and see what crop had sprung up from the seed we have planted today."

"It would indeed," Kirk said. "But I'll tell you something else, Mr. Spock. I only hope that in a hundred years, that crop won't have sprung right out of the ground and come out looking for *us*."

A TASTE OF ARMAGEDDON

Writer: Robert Hamner and Gene L. Coon
(Story by Gene L. Coon)
Director: Joseph Pevney
First Aired: February 23, 1967

Ambassador Fox was something of a cross to Captain Kirk, and to most of his officers, for that matter. In addition to having a very high regard for his own importance—which is not necessarily a handicap in a man, provided he also has a sense of humor—he had a remarkably short temper for a career diplomat.

But the mission was his, and he had to be put up with. There was no question about the importance of that. Eminiar VII was by all accounts the most advanced planet of its star cluster, NGC 321, having had space flight for hundreds of years. Nevertheless, as of fifty years ago they had never ventured beyond their own solar system, and for a very good reason: They had been at war with their nearest neighbor. The vessel making the report, the USS *Valiant*, was listed as missing—presumably as a product of the hostilities. It was Fox's job to establish diplomatic relations with them.

It evidently was not going to be easy. At first contact with the *Enterprise*, Eminiar VII sent Code 710—a warning not to approach the planet under any circumstances. Kirk was more than willing to comply; after all, it *was* their planet, and he intensely disliked gunboat diplomacy. But Ambassador Fox insisted, and he had command power if he wanted to exercise it. He frequently did.

Kirk beamed down to the planet with Mr. Spock; Yeoman Manning and two security guards, leaving Scott, his engineer, in charge of the ship. In view of the warning, they all carried number-one phasers, in addition to a tricorder, of which Yeoman Manning was in charge.

But there was no overt hostility. They materialized in a corridor of a building that, judging by the traffic, was an official establishment of some kind, and were met solely by a very pretty girl who introduced herself as Mea Three and promptly offered to take them to the High Council. Her manner was cool, but correct.

The High Council proved to consist of four pleasant-looking men seated at a table in a large room that had in it also a faint hum of machinery, though none was evident. As Kirk and his party entered, all four rose and smiled.

"I am Anan Seven," said the one farthest to the left. "I am sorry to see you here.

But you are here, and we must do everything possible to make you comfortable. Won't you sit down?"

"I'm Captain Kirk, James T. Kirk of the starship *Enterprise*, representing the United Federation of Planets. This is my first officer, Mr. Spock. Lieutenant Galloway. Lieutenant Osborne. Yeoman Manning."

"Welcome to Eminiar," Anan said, making a formal little bow. Everyone sat, and there was a moment of silence as each party studied the other.

"Well, Captain," Anan said at last, "since you chose to disregard our warning, I suppose we must proceed to the business at hand. What can we do for you?"

"Our mission, sir, is to establish diplomatic relations between your people and mine. The Federation badly needs a treaty port in this cluster."

"Impossible, I'm afraid," Anan said.

"Oh? Would you mind telling me why?"

"Because of the war."

"You are *still* at war?" Kirk said.

"We have been at war," Anan said, "for five hundred years."

Kirk raised his eyebrows. "You conceal it well. Mr. Spock?"

"Sir," Spock said to Anan, "we have completely scanned your planet. We find it highly advanced, prosperous in a material sense, comfortable for your people—and completely peaceful. Seemingly an ideal, flourishing, highly civilized culture, which obviously should have ties with our Federation. There is no evidence of war whatsoever."

"Casualties among our civilian population," Anan said evenly, "total from one to three million dead each year, from direct enemy attack. This is why we warned you away, Captain. As long as your ship is orbiting this planet, it is in severe danger."

"With whom are you at war?" Spock said.

"Vendikar, the third planet in this system. Originally settled by our people, and as advanced as we are—and a ruthless enemy."

"Nevertheless . . ." Spock began. He got no further than that word. Suddenly the room was clamoring with a shrill, whooping siren. Anan, his face stern, stood instantly, pressing a button.

The result was astonishing. The siren stopped, but the entire rear wall of the Council room slid aside, revealing another room of the same size that harbored an installation of enormous intricacy. It was too bid and too involved to take it all in at once; Kirk got a quick impression of a long bank of computers, a number of lighted graphs on the walls, a large illuminated grid that might have been a map.

"You will have to excuse us," Anan said. "We are in fact under attack at this moment. Mea, care for our guests."

All four of the council members took positions at the machinery, where several other operators were already at work. Kirk, baffled, looked first at Spock, who shrugged, and then at Mea.

"It will not last long," the girl said.

"Don't you take shelter?"

"There is no shelter, Captain."

"Are these attacks frequent?" Spock said.

"Oh, yes. But we retaliate promptly."

Beckoning to Spock, Kirk moved off into the newly revealed room—the war room, Kirk supposed. No attempt was made to stop them. At the large grid, an operator sat at a console. Flashes splattered over the grid, seemingly at random; at each flash, the operator pushed what was evidently a matching button. Kirk studied it, but it conveyed nothing to him; as he had expected, he could not read the mapping conventions of Eminiar. Beside him, however, Mea gasped suddenly.

"A hit!" she said. "A hit in the city!"

"Mr. Spock, hear any explosions?"

"None. Yeoman Manning, are you getting any radiation readings or any other kind of disturbance on the tricorder?"

"Not a thing."

Kirk turned to Mea. "If this is an attack," he said, "would you mind telling me what weapons the enemy is using?"

"Fusion bombs," she said. "Materialized by transporter over the targets. They are very accurate. My parents were killed in the last attack."

Kirk flipped out his communicator and called the ship. "Mr. Scott, are you still scanning this planet's surface?"

"Of course, sir," Scott's voice said promptly. "Per your orders."

"Anything unusual?"

"Nothing, sir. All quiet."

As Kirk put the communicator away, something buzzed on the boards before them and one of the computers extruded a card from a slot. Anan took it and stared at it, his face grim. Then he handed it to the man next to him.

"Just as it happened fifty years ago, Sar," he said.

Sar nodded, his face sad. "We warned them."

"Alert a security detachment. They may be needed."

"Sir," Kirk said, "I have been in contact with my ship, which has this entire planet under surveillance. All the time this so-called attack has been in progress, we have been monitoring you. There has been no attack—no explosions, no radiation, no disturbances whatsoever. Now if this is just some sort of game . . ."

"It is not a game," Anan said. "Half a million people have just been killed."

"Entirely by computers," Spock said suddenly.

"That's quite correct," Anan said. "Their deaths are registered. They are then given twenty-four hours to report to the disintegration chambers. Since the immediate danger appears to be over, I can explain at somewhat greater length. You must understand, Captain, that no two planets could carry on an all-out nuclear war for five hundred years. Such a war would not last five hundred hours. We were forced to find another solution."

"In other words," Spock said, "Vendikar's attack was a theoretical one."

"On the contrary, it was quite real. It is simply launched mathematically. If it is successful, the casualties are computed, identified, and ordered to report for disposition. Theoretical? I lost my wife in the last attack. It is sometimes hard—but our civilization lives. The people die, but the culture goes on."

"Do you mean to tell me," Kirk said, "that your people just . . . walk into a disintegrator when they're told to?"

"They do. They are at war and they know it."

"I've heard of some cold-blooded arrangements," Kirk said, "but this one takes the prize."

"It is cold-blooded," Spock agreed. "But it does have a certain logic about it."

"I am glad you approve," Anan said.

"I do not approve," Spock said coldly. "I understand, which is something else entirely."

"Good," Anan said. "Then you will recall that we warned you not to come here. You chose to disregard my warning. Once in orbit around our planet, your ship became a legitimate target. It has been classified destroyed by an incoming missile."

He made a quick gesture. Kirk spun around. There were four very large uniformed men behind the *Enterprise* party. All four held unfamiliar but quite lethal-looking weapons.

"All persons aboard your ship have twenty-four hours to report to our disintegration chambers. To insure their cooperation, I am ordering you and your party held in custody against their surrender. The same thing, by the way, happened to your ship the *Valiant*, fifty years ago. Killed to the last man."

"You are not," Kirk said through his teeth, "going to harm my ship. Is that clear?"

"If possible, we shall spare the ship," Anan said. "But its passengers and crew are already dead. Put them in class-one detention."

"Class-one detention," proved to be comfortable—rather like a small, neat apartment, even to a well-stocked kitchen. This did not mollify anybody in the party in the slightest. They had not been there more than an hour when a guard let Mea in. The girl seemed subdued.

"I have been sent to ask if you require anything," she said.

"We require a great deal. I want to see Anan Seven."

"He is busy coordinating the casualty lists."

"If he won't talk to me," Kirk said, "he'll have more casualty lists than he knows what to do with."

"Captain, you have your duty to your ship," the girl said quietly. "We have our duty to our planet."

"Your duty doesn't include stepping into a disintegrator and disappearing!"

"I'm afraid it does, Captain," she said, just as quietly as before. "I too have been declared a casualty. I must report to a disintegrator at noon tomorrow."

Kirk stared at her. He still found the whole arrangement impossible to believe. "And you're going to do it? What could Anan and Sar and the others possibly do if you all just refused to show up?"

"It's not a question of what the Council would do," Mea said. "If everybody refused to report, Vendikar would have no choice but to launch real weapons—and we would have to do the same. Within a week, there would be nothing left of either civilization. Both planets would be uninhabitable. Surely you can see that ours is the better way."

"No," Kirk said. "I don't see it at all."

"I'm sorry. Is there anything I can bring you?"

"Yes. Anan Seven."

"I'll convoy the message. But I doubt that he'll come."

As she left, Kirk pounded a fist into a palm in frustration. Then, suddenly, he had an idea. "Mr. Spock!"

"Yes, sir?"

"Vulcans have limited telepathic abilities, don't they?"

"Yes, Captain," Spock said. "But remember that I am only half Vulcan. I could not reach Anan from here—and if I could, I would not be able to transmit a complex message, or pick one up."

"That isn't what I had in mind. I just want to plant a suspicion in that guard outside. Preferably, that we've cut a hole through the wall with some heat device they overlooked. Or if that's too complex, just a feeling that we're getting away."

"Hmm," Spock said. "I know nothing about the sensitiveness of the Eminians. However, nothing would be lost by trying."

"Good. Go head."

Spock nodded, leaned his head against the wall nearest the corridor, and closed his eyes. His brow furrowed, and within a few moments he was sweating. Even to Kirk, to whom telepathy was a closed book, it was clear that his first officer was working hard.

Nothing seemed to happen for at least five centuries, or maybe six. Then there was a faint humming at the door, followed by a click. Kirk flattened his back against the wall.

The door swung open and the guard charged in, weapon at the ready. Kirk rewarded him with a crushing blow at the back of the neck; he dropped in complete silence. Kirk dragged him away from the door, retrieving his weapon.

"Thank you, Mr. Spock."

"A pleasure, Captain."

"Now, we've got to get our communicators back, and get in touch with the ship. I don't know how far we'll get without weapons; we'll need more. Mr. Spock, I know how you feel about taking life. But our ship is in danger. Do I make myself clear?"

"Perfectly, Captain. I shall do what is necessary."

Kirk clapped him quickly on the back. "Let's go."

They were perhaps halfway back to the Council chambers when they turned a corner and found themselves on the end of a queue. Kirk signaled a halt and peered ahead.

At the other end of the line was a large enclosed booth, with a control console on one side at which an armed guard was sitting, watching a light over the machine. Presently this went off, and in response to the touch of a control, a door opened in the side of the machine.

The man at the head of the line took a last look around and stepped inside. The door closed. The machine hummed; the light went on, and then off again. The door slid back.

There was nobody inside.

Kirk and Spock exchanged grim looks. Kirk made a pinching motion with one hand, and Spock nodded. Kirk walked rapidly down the side of the queue opposite the side the console and the guard were on.

"All right, break it up," he said. "Stand back, everybody."

Heads turned. The guard half rose. "Just what do you think you're up to . . ." Then he saw Kirk's stolen weapon.

He had courage. Kirk could have shot him easily and he must have known it, but he went for his own gun anyhow. At the same instant Spock, who had scuttled unnoticed down the other side of the line, caught him from behind with his nerve-pinch to the shoulder. Looking astonished, the guard collapsed. Spock scooped up his weapon.

"Excellent, Mr. Spock. The rest of you people, stand back or you'll get hurt."

Kirk leveled his gun at the disintegration booth and pulled the trigger. The results were most satisfying. Nothing seemed to come out of the weapon but a scream of sound, but a huge hole appeared magically in the machine. Sparks flew from the console, and in a moment the booth was in flames.

"All right, now get out of here!" Kirk roared. "Go to your homes and stay there! Go!"

Terrified, the remaining people in the queue turned and ran. Spock joined the Captain, eyeing the gun he had just confiscated with open curiosity, his eyebrows up. "A fascinating weapon. Is it solely sonic, I wonder? If so, how do they keep it in a tight beam?"

"We'll work that out later. Let's get out of here."

* * *

There was nobody in the Council room but Anan when they burst in. He was pouring something into a glass from a small bottle. He froze when he saw them, then smoothly resumed the motion and drank.

"Would you care to join me, Captain? You may find our Trova most interesting."

"I didn't come to drink."

Anan nodded toward the weapon in Kirk's hand. "I assume that is what you used to destroy disintegration chamber number twelve."

"Yes. A most efficient weapon—and I'm not at all chary of using it."

"That much is obvious," Anan said. "Clearly you are a barbarian."

"*I* am?" Kirk said incredulously.

"Quite. Why not? We all are. Surely in your history too, you were a killer first, a builder second. That is our joint heritage."

"We are a little less cold-blooded about it than you are."

"What does that matter to the dead?" Anan said.

"You have a point. Nevertheless, I don't think you realize the risk you're taking. We don't make war with computers and herd the casualties off to suicide stations. We make the real thing. I could destroy this planet of yours, Councilman. Mr. Spock, Yeoman Manning, see if you can find one of our communicators in this place."

"I already have," Spock said. He handed it over. Anan watched warily.

"Captain," he said, "surely you see the position we are in. If your people do not report to the disintegration chambers, it is a violation of an agreement dating back five hundred years."

"My people are not responsible for your agreements."

"You are an officer of a force charged with keeping the peace," Anan said. He seemed almost to be pleading. "Yet you will be responsible for an escalation that could destroy two worlds. Millions of people horribly killed, complete destruction of our culture and Vendikar's. Disaster, disease, starvation, pain, suffering, lingering death . . ."

"They seem to frighten you," Kirk said grimly.

"They frighten any sane man!"

"Quite so."

"Don't you see?" Anan said desperately. "We've done away with all that! Now you threaten to bring it all down on us again. Do those four hundred people of yours mean more than the hundreds of millions of innocent people on Eminiar and Vendikar? What kind of a monster are you?"

"I'm a barbarian," Kirk said. Nevertheless, this was indeed a nasty impasse. After a moment, he activated the communicator.

"Mr. Scott? Kirk here."

"Captain! We thought they'd got you."

"They thought so too," Kirk said. "What's the situation up there?"

"It's been lively," Scott's voice said. "First they tried to lure us all down with a fake message from you. Luckily, our computer told us the voice-patterns didn't match, though it was a bonny imitation—you'd have enjoyed it. Then they sent us their ultimatum. I dinna have any such orders and I paid no attention."

"Good for you. Then what?"

"When the deadline was past, they opened fire on the *Enterprise*. Of course, after the ultimatum we had our screens up. I wanted to bounce a couple of dozen photon torpedoes off them for a starter—after all, the time was past when they said they were going to kill all of you—but Ambassador Fox wouldna let me. Then he wanted me to let down the screens so he could beam down to the planet and try to patch things up, and *I* wouldna do *that*. Now the haggis is really in the fire as far as he's concerned."

"Scotty, your decisions were entirely proper, and I'll back them to the hilt. I'm going to try to straighten this mess out down here. There's a good chance that I won't succeed. If you don't hear anything to the contrary from me in forty-eight hours, execute General Order Twenty-Four."

"Twenty-Four? But, Captain . . ." There was a long pause. Then Scott's voice said: "In forty-eight hours. Aye, sir. Good luck."

"Thanks. Kirk out."

"And just what," Anan asked, "does that mean?"

"It means that in forty-eight hours, the *Enterprise* will destroy Eminiar Seven."

"You're bluffing. You wouldn't."

"I didn't start this, Councilman," Kirk said. "But I mean to finish it. Now . . ."

He moved to the table and pushed the button he had seen Anan use earlier. The wall slid aside as before, revealing the war room.

"Mr. Spock, see if you can figure that installation out. Anan, you still have something to learn. Destruction. Disease. Suffering. Horror. That's what war is supposed to be, Anan. *That's what makes it a thing to be avoided*. But you've made war neat and painless—so neat and painless that you had no reason to put a stop to it. That's why you've been carrying it on for five hundred years. Any luck, Mr. Spock?"

"Yes, sir," the first officer said. "I cannot read the big map, but the rest of it seems to be quite straightforward. This unit controls the disintegrator booths; these the attacking devices; this the defense. And these compute the casualties. They are all tied in with a subspace transmission unit, apparently so they are in constant contact with their Vendikan counterparts."

"Is that essential?"

"I would think so, Captain. The minute contact is broken, it would be tantamount to an abrogation of the entire agreement between the two warring parties."

"What are you talking about?" Anan said, in dawning horror.

"This is the key, Captain," Spock said, pointing to an isolated computer. He threw a switch on it, and then another. "The circuit is locked. Destroy this one, and they will all go."

"Good. Stand back. You too, Anan." He raised the stolen disruptor.

"No!" Anan screamed. "No, please..."

Kirk fired. They key computer burst. A string of minor explosions seemed to run from it along the main computer bank—and then they were no longer minor. Hastily, Kirk herded everyone out into the corridor. They huddled against the wall, while the floor shook, and billows of smoke surged out of the door of the Council room.

It took a long time. At last, Kirk said, "Well—that's it."

"Do you realize what you've done?" Anan screamed.

"Perfectly. I've given you back the horrors of war. The Vendikans will now assume that you have abandoned your agreement, and will prepare for a real war, with real weapons. The next attack they launch will do a lot more than count up numbers on a computer. It will destroy your cities, devastate your planet. You'll want to retaliate, of course. If I were you I'd start making bombs."

"You *are* a monster," Anan whispered.

Kirk ignored him. "Yes, Councilman, you've got a real war on your hands. You can either wage it—with real weapons—or you might consider the alternative."

"There is no alternative."

"There is," Kirk said harshly. "Make peace."

"After five hundred years of casualties? You're mad!"

"Maybe. But we too have killed in the past, as you pointed out a while ago. Nevertheless, we can stop. We can admit we have been killers—but we're not going to kill today. That's all it takes; one simple decision. We are not going to kill today."

Anan put a shaking hand to his forehead. "I don't know... I can't see..."

"We'll help you." He raised the communicator. "Scotty, have you and Ambassador Fox been following this conversation? I left the line open for you."

"Aye, that we have."

"Then you can beam the Ambassador down here if you want."

After a moment, there was a shimmer in the chamber, and Fox materialized, looking portly and confused.

"This is what you do," Kirk told Anan. "Contact Vendikar. I think you'll find that they're just as terrified and appalled as you are at the prospects. They'll do anything to avoid the alternative I've just given you; peace—or utter destruction. It's up to you."

Anan looked at them all, hope fighting with despair on his face. Ambassador Fox stepped forward.

"Councilman," he said, "as a third party, interested only in peace and the establishment of normal relations, I will be glad to offer my services as a negotiator between you and Vendikar. I have had some small experience in these matters."

Anan took a step toward him. "Perhaps," he muttered. "Perhaps there may be time. I have a direct channel to the Vendikar High Council. It hasn't been used in centuries."

"Then it's long overdue," the Ambassador said. "If you'll be so kind as to lead the way . . ."

Anan started hesitantly down the corridor, his steps beginning to regain their springiness. Fox followed closely. Anan said, "I understand the head of the Vendikar Council—his name is Ripoma—is an intelligent man. And if he hears from a disinterested party like yourself . . ."

His voice became unintelligible as they rounded a corner. The rest of the *Enterprise* party watched them go.

"There is a chance it will work, Captain," Spock said. "Much depends upon the approach and the conduct of the negotiations, of course."

"Annoying though he is, Ambassador Fox has a reputation for being good at his job," Kirk said. "I'm glad he's going to be good for something at last." He raised the communicator once more. "Kirk to *Enterprise*. Cancel General Order Twenty-Four. Alert Transporter Room. Ready to beam up in ten minutes."

"Aye, sir."

"Still, Captain," Spock said, "you took a very big chance."

"Did I, Mr. Spock? They were killing three million people a year—and it had gone on for five hundred years. An actual attack might not have killed any more people than the fifteen hundred million they've already killed in their computer attacks—but it would have destroyed their ability to make war. The fighting would be over. Permanently."

"I would not care to have counted on that," Spock said.

"I wasn't, Mr. Spock. It was only a calculated risk. What I was really counting upon was that the Eminians keep a very orderly society—and actual war is very messy. Very, very messy. I had a feeling they'd do anything to avoid it—even talk peace!"

"A feeling, Captain? Intuition?"

"No," Kirk said. "Call it . . . shall we say, cultural morphology?"

If Spock had any answer, it was lost in the shimmer of the transporter effect.

THIS SIDE OF PARADISE

Writer: D. C. Fontana (Story by Nathan Butler and D. C. Fontana)

Director: Ralph Senensky

First Aired: March 2, 1967

There was no answer from the Sandoval colony on Omicron Ceti III to the *Enterprise*'s signals, but that was hardly surprising; the colonists, all one hundred and fifty of them, had probably been dead for the better part of three years, as two previous colonies had died, for reasons then mysterious. Elias Sandoval had known this past history and had determined to settle on the planet anyhow; it was in all other respects a tempting place.

It was not until after his group had settled in—and had stopped communicating—that the Berthold emission of the planet's sun had been discovered. Little enough was known about Berthold radiation even now, but it had been shown that direct exposure to it under laboratory conditions disintegrated living animal tissue in as little as seventy-two hours. A planet's atmosphere would cut down some of the effect, to the point where a week's exposure might be safe, but certainly not three years. And there was no preventive, and no cure.

The settlement proper, however, was still there and was easy to spot. Kirk made up a landing party of six, including himself, Spock, McCoy, Lieutenant Timothy Fletcher (a biologist), Sulu and a crewman named Dimont. The settlement proved to consist of a surprisingly small cluster of buildings, with fields beyond it. Kirk looked around.

"It took these people a year to make the trip from Earth," he said. "They came all that way—and died."

"Hardly that, sir," said a man's voice. The party snapped around toward it.

A big, bluff, genial-looking man clad in sturdy work clothes had come around a corner of a building, with two others behind him, similarly dressed and carrying tools. The first man came forward, holding out his hand.

"Welcome to Omicron Ceti III," he said. "I am Elias Sandoval."

Kirk took the hand, but could think of nothing to say but a mumble of thanks.

"We've seen no one outside our group since we left Earth four years ago," the man went on. "We've expected someone for quite some time. Our subspace radio has never worked properly and we, I'm afraid, had no one among us who could master its intricacies. But we were sure when we were not heard from, a ship would come."

"Actually, Mr. Sandoval, we didn't come because of your radio silence . . ."

"It makes little difference, Captain. You are here, and we are happy to have you. Come, let me show you our settlement."

He began to walk away, not bothering to look back, as if certain that they would follow. The other colonists had already left.

"On pure speculation," McCoy said drily, "just as an educated guess, I'd say that man isn't dead."

Spock checked his tricorder. "The intensity of Berthold radiation is at the predicted level. At this intensity, we will be safe for a week, if necessary. But . . ."

"But these people shouldn't be alive," Kirk said. "Well, there's no point in debating it in a vacuum. Let's get some answers."

He started after Sandoval. From closer range, the buildings could be seen to be not deserted, only quiet. Nearby, a woman was hanging out some wash; in another structure, a woman placed a fresh-baked pie in a window to cool. It might have been a tranquil Earthly farm community of centuries ago, except for a scattering of peculiar plants with bulbous pods, apparently indigenous, which revealed that it was on another planet.

Sandoval led the landing party into his own quarters. "There are two other settlements," he said, "but we have forty-five colonists here."

"What was the reason for the dispersal?" Kirk asked.

"We felt three separate groups might have a better opportunity for growth. And, if some disease should strike one group, the other two would be less likely to be endangered. Omicron is an ideal agricultural planet, Captain, and we determined that we would not suffer the fate of expeditions that had gone before us."

A woman came from an inner door and stopped, seeing the strangers. She looked Eurasian, and was strikingly beautiful.

"Ah, Leila," Sandoval said, turning to her. "Come and meet our guests. This is Leila Kalomi, our botanist. Captain Kirk, Dr. McCoy, Mr. Spock . . ."

"Mr. Spock and I have met," she said, holding out a hand to him. "It has been a long time."

He took the hand gently but awkwardly. "The years have seemed twice as long," he said.

She bowed her head, silently accepting the compliment. Then she looked up, as if searching his face for something more; but there was nothing but his usual calm. He released her hand slowly.

"Mr. Sandoval," Kirk said, "we do have a mission here. A number of examinations, tests . . ."

"By all means, please attend to them, Captain. I think you'll find our settlement interesting. Our philosophy is a simple one: that men should return to the less complicated life. We have very few mechanical things here—no vehicles, no weapons—"

He smiled. "As I said, even the radio has never worked properly. We have harmony here—complete peace."

"We'll try not to disturb your work. Gentlemen, if you'll come outside now . . ."

On the porch, he flipped open his communicator. "Kirk to *Enterprise*."

"*Enterprise*. Lieutenant Uhura here."

"Lieutenant, we've found the colony apparently well and healthy. We're beginning an investigation. Relay that information to Star Fleet, and then beam down to me all the information we have on this last Omicron expedition."

"Yes, sir. *Enterprise* out."

"Gentlemen, carry out your previous instructions. If you find anything out of the ordinary, report to me at once."

The party scattered.

Dimont was the first to find the next anomaly. He had been raised in the farm country of the Mojave, and was leading cows to pasture when he was six, up at dawn and then working all day in the fields. It was his opinion, expressed to Sulu, that "they could use a little of that spirit here."

But there was no place for it. There were no cows here; the one barn hadn't even been built for them, but only for storage. Nor were there any horses, pigs, even dogs. A broader check disclosed that the same was true of the whole planet: there was nothing on it but people and vegetation. The records showed that the expedition had carried some animals for breeding and food, but none seemed to have survived. Well, that was perhaps not an anomaly in the true sense, for they couldn't have survived. In theory, neither could the people.

But they had. "I've examined nine men so far," McCoy reported, "ages varying from twenty-three to fifty-nine. Every one of them is in perfect physical shape—textbook responses. If everybody was like them, I could throw away my shingle. But there's something even stranger."

"What is it?" Kirk asked.

"I've got Sandoval's medical record as of four years ago when he left Earth. There was scar tissue on his lungs from lobar pneumonia suffered when he was a child. No major operations, but he did have an appendectomy. But when I examined the man not an hour ago, he was as perfect as the rest of them."

"Instrument malfunction?"

"No. I thought of that and tested it on myself. It accurately recorded my lack of tonsils and those two broken ribs I had once. But it *didn't* record any scar tissue on Sandoval's lungs—and it *did* record a healthy appendix where one was supposedly removed."

Fletcher's report also turned up an anomaly. "The soil here is rich, the rainfall moderate, the climate temperate the year round. You could grow anything here, and they've got a variety of crops in—grains, potatoes, beans. But for an agricultural colony they actually have very little acreage planted. There's enough to sustain the colony, but very little more. And another thing, they're not bothering to rotate crops in their fields—haven't for three years. That's poor practice for a group like this, even if the soil is good."

It was like a jigsaw puzzle all one color—a lot of pieces but no key to where they fitted.

Then came the order to evacuate, direct from Admiral Komack of Star Fleet. Despite the apparent well-being of the colonists, they were to be moved immediately to Starbase 27, where arrangements were being made for complete examinations of all of them. Exposed starship personnel were also to be held in quarantine until cleared at the Starbase. Apparently somebody up the line thought radiation disease was infectious. Well, with Berthold rays, anything seemed to be possible, as McCoy observed wryly.

"You'll have to inform your people of Star Fleet's decision," Kirk told Sandoval. "Meanwhile we can begin to prepare accommodations for them aboard ship . . ."

"No," said Sandoval pleasantly.

"Mr. Sandoval, this is not an arbitrary decision on my part. It is a Star fleet order."

"This is completely unnecessary. We are in no danger here."

"We've explained the Berthold radiation and its effect," McCoy said. "Can't you understand . . ."

"How can I make *you* understand, Doctor? Your own instruments tell you we are in excellent health, and our records show we have not had one death among us."

"What about the animals?" Kirk said.

"We are vegetarians."

"That doesn't answer my question. Why did all the animals die?"

"Captain, you stress unimportant things," Sandoval said, as calmly as before. "We will not leave. Your arguments have some validity, but they do not apply to us."

"Sandoval, I've been ordered to evacuate this colony, and that's exactly what I intend to do, with or without your help."

"And how will you do that?" Sandoval said, turning away. "With a butterfly net?"

It was Spock who was finally given the key. He was standing with Leila looking out over a small garden, checking his tricorder.

"Nothing," he said, "not even insects. Yet your plants grow, and you have survived exposure to Berthold radiation."

"It can be explained," Leila said.

"Please do."

"Later."

"I have never understood the female capacity to avoid a direct answer on any subject."

She put a hand on his arm. "And I never understood you, until now." She tapped his chest. "There was always a place in here where no one could come. There was only the face you allow people to see. Only one side you allow them to know."

"I would like to know how your people have managed to survive here."

"I missed you."

"You should be dead."

She took her hand from his arm and stepped back. "If I show you how we survived, will you try to understand how we feel about our life here? About each other?"

"Emotions are alien to me . . ."

"No. Someone else might believe that—your shipmates, your Captain. But not me. Come this way."

She led him to an open field, uncultivated, with pod plants growing amid grass and low brush. They rustled gently in a little breeze.

"This is the place," she said.

"It looks like any other such area. What is the nature of this thing, if you please?"

"The specific elements and properties are not important. What is important is that it gives life—peace—love."

"What you describe was once called in the vernacular 'a happiness pill.' And you, as a scientist, should know that is impossible."

"No. And I was one of the first to find them."

"Them?"

"The spores." She pointed to the pod plants.

Spock bent to examine them. At the same moment, one of the pods flew apart, like a powdery dandelion broken by the wind. Spock dropped his tricorder to shield his face as the powder flew up about him. Then he screamed.

Leila, frightened, moved forward a step, reaching out a hand to him.

"I—can't," he moaned, almost inaudibly. "Please—don't—don't . . ."

"It shouldn't hurt, not like this! It didn't hurt us!"

"I'm not—like you."

Then, slowly, his face began to change, becoming less rigid, more at peace. Seeing the change, Leila reached up to touch his cheek with gentle fingers. He reached out to gather her into his arms, very gently, as though afraid this woman and this feeling were so fragile that he might break them.

After the kiss, she sat down, and he lay down beside her, his head in her lap. "See the clouds," he said after a while. "That one looks like a dragon—you see the tail and the dorsal spines?"

"I have never seen a dragon."

"I have, on Berengaria VII. But I never saw one in a cloud before." His communicator abruptly shrilled, but he ignored it. "Or rainbows. Do you know I can tell you exactly why one appears in the sky—but considering its beauty was always out of the question."

"Not here," Leila said. The communicator shrilled again, insistently. "Perhaps you should answer?"

"It will only be the Captain."

But finally he lifted the communicator and snapped up the screen. Kirk's anxious voice sounded instantly. "Mr. Spock!"

"What do you want?" Spock asked lazily.

"Spock, is that you?"

"Yes, Captain. What do you want?"

"Where are you?"

Spock considered the question calmly. "I don't believe I want to tell you."

"Spock, I don't know what you think you're doing, but this is an order. Report back to me at the settlement in ten minutes. We're evacuating the colony to Starbase 27 . . ."

"No, I don't think so."

"You don't think so *what*?"

"I don't think so, *sir*."

"Spock, report to the settlement immediately. Acknowledge. Spock!"

The First Officer tossed the communicator away among the plants.

It seemed to be their fruiting time; they were bursting all over the area now. Fletcher was caught next, then McCoy, then Sulu and Dimont—and finally Kirk himself.

But Kirk alone was unaffected. As peace and love and tranquillity settled around him like a soggy blanket, he was blazing. His temper was not improved by the discovery that McCoy was arranging for transportation to the ship not of colonists or their effects, but of pod plants. Evidently a couple of hundred were already aboard. Hotter than ever, Kirk ordered himself to be beamed aboard.

He found the bridge deserted except for Uhura, who was busy at her communications board. All other instruments were on automatic.

"Lieutenant, put me through to Admiral Komack at Star Fleet."

As she turned from the board, Kirk was shocked to see that she, too, wore the same sweet, placid expression as the others. She said, "Oh—I'm afraid I can't do that, Captain."

"I don't suppose," Kirk said tightly, "it would do any good to say that was an order."

"I know it was, Captain. But all communications are out."

"All?" Kirk reached past her and began to flick switches on the board.

"All except the ship to surface; we'll need that for a while. I short-circuited all the rest." She patted his arm. "It's really for the best."

She arose, and strolled away from him to the elevator, which swallowed her up. Kirk tried her board again, but to no effect. He slammed his fist down in aggravation. Then he noticed a light pulsing steadily on Spock's library-computer. Moving to that station, he pushed the related button.

"Transporter Room."

There was no answer, but clearly the room was in use. He made for it in a hurry.

He found a line of crew personnel in the corridor leading to the Transporter Room. All waited patiently. Every so often the line moved forward a few steps.

"Report to your stations!"

The crewmen stared at him quietly, benevolently—almost pityingly.

"I'm sorry, sir," one of them said. "We're transporting down to join the colony."

"I said, get back to your stations."

"No, sir."

"Do you know what you're saying?"

"You've been down there," the crewman said earnestly. "You know how beautiful it is—how perfect. We're going."

"This is mutiny!"

"Yes, sir," the crewman said calmly. "It is."

Kirk went back to the bridge and to the communications board. As Uhura had said, ship to ground was still operative. He called McCoy, and was rather surprised to get an answer.

"Bones, the spores of your damnable plants have evidently been carried throughout the ship by the ventilation system. The crew is deserting to join the Omicron colony, and I can't stop them."

"Why, that's fine," McCoy said; his accent had moved considerably south of the Mason-Dixon line, almost to his Georgia boyhood. "Y'all come right down."

"Never mind that. At least you can give me some information. I haven't been affected. Why not?"

"You always were a stubborn cuss, Jimmy. But you'll see the light."

Kirk fumed in silence for a moment. "Can't you tell me anything about the physical-psychological aspects of this thing?"

"*I'm* not concerned with any physical-psychological aspects, Jim boy. We're all perfectly healthy."

"I've been hearing that word a lot lately. Perfect. Everything is perfect."

"Yup. That it is."

"I'll bet you've even grown your tonsils back."

"Uh-huh," McCoy said dreamily. "Jim, have you ever had a real, cold, Georgia-style mint julep?"

"Bones, Bones, I need your help. Can you run tests, blood samples, anything at all to give us some kind of lead on what these things are? How to counteract them?"

"Who wants to counteract Paradise, Jim?"

"Bones—" But the contact had been broken at the other end. Then he headed back for the Transporter Room. He was going to get some cooperation from his ship's surgeon if he had to take the madman by the ears.

He found Spock in Sandoval's office, both looking languidly pleased with themselves.

"Where's McCoy?"

"He said he was going to create something called a mint julep," Spock said, then added helpfully, "That's a drink."

"Captain," Sandoval said. "Listen to me. Why don't you join us?"

"In your own private paradise?"

Sandoval nodded. "The spores have made it that. You see, Captain, we *would* have died three years ago. We didn't know what was happening then, but the Berthold rays you spoke of affected us within two or three weeks of our landing here. We were sick and dying when Leila found the plants."

"The spores themselves are alien, Captain," Spock added. "They weren't on the planet when the other two expeditions were attempted. That's why the colonists died."

"How do you know all this?"

"The spores—tell us. They aren't really spores, but a kind of group organism made up of billions of submicroscopic cells. They act directly on the central nervous system."

"Where did they come from?"

"Impossible to tell. It was so long ago and so far away. Perhaps the planet does not even exist any longer. They drifted in space until finally drawn here by the Berthold radiation, on which they thrive. The plants are native, but they are only a repository for the spores until they find an animal host."

"What do they need us for?"

"Bodies. They do no harm. In return they give the host complete health and peace of mind . . ."

"Paradise, in short."

"Why not?" Spock said. "There is no want or need here. It's a true Eden. There is belonging—and love."

"No wants or needs? We weren't meant for that, any of us. A man stagnates and goes sour if he has no ambition, no desire to be more than he is."

"We have what we need," said Sandoval.

"Except a challenge! You haven't made an inch of progress here. You're not creating or learning, Sandoval. You're backsliding—rotting away in your paradise."

Spock shook his head sadly. "You don't understand. But you'll come around, sooner or later."

"Be damned to that. I'm going back to the ship."

He could not remember any time before when he had been so furious for so long a time.

* * *

The *Enterprise* was utterly deserted now. Without anybody aboard her, Kirk had a new and lonely realization of how big she was. And yet for all her immense resources, he was helpless. It was amazing how quickly all her entire complement had surrendered to the Lethe of the spores, leaving him and no one else raging futilely . . .

Raging?

Futilely?

Wait a minute.

There were pod plants all over the ship, so there was no problem about getting a sample. He took it down to McCoy's laboratory, located a slide, and then McCoy's microscope. A drop of water on the slide—right; now, mix some of the spores into the drop. Put the slide under the microscope. It had been decades since he had done anything like this, but he remembered from schooldays that one must run the objective lens down to the object, and then focus *up*, never down. Good; the spores came into register, tiny, and spined like pollen grains.

Getting up again, he went through McCoy's hypospray rack until he found one of a dozen all labeled *adrenaline*. He sprayed the slide, and then looked again.

There was nothing there. The spores were adrenalin-soluble. He had found the answer. It was almost incredibly dangerous, but there was no other way. He went back to the bridge and called Spock. If Spock didn't answer . . .

"Spock here. What is it now?"

"I've joined you," Kirk said quietly. "I understand now, Spock."

"That's wonderful, Captain. When will you beam down?"

"I've been packing some things, and I realized there's equipment aboard we should have down at the settlement. You know we can't come back aboard once the last of us has left."

"Do you want a party beamed up?"

"No, I think you and I can handle it. Why don't I beam you up now?"

"All right. Ready in ten minutes."

Kirk was waiting in the Transporter Room, necessarily, when the First Officer materialized, and was holding a metal bar in both hands, like a quarter-staff. Spock took a step toward him, smiling a greeting. Kirk did not smile back.

"*Now*," he said harshly, "you mutinous, disloyal, computerized half-breed—we'll see about you deserting my ship!"

Spock stared. He seemed mildly surprised, but unflustered. "Your use of the term half-breed is perfectly applicable, Captain, but 'computerized' is inaccurate. A machine can be computerized, but not a man."

"What makes you think you're a man? You're an overgrown jackrabbit. You're an elf with an overactive thyroid."

"Captain, I don't understand . . ."

"Of course you don't! You don't have brains enough to understand! All you've got is printed circuits!"

"Captain, if you'll . . ."

"But what can you expect from a freak whose father was a computer and whose mother was an encyclopedia!"

"My mother," Spock said, his expression not quite so bland now, "was a teacher, my father an ambassador."

"He was a freak like his son! Ambassador from a planet of freaks! The Vulcan never lived who had an ounce of integrity!"

"Captain—please—don't . . ."

"You're a traitor from a race of traitors! Disloyal to the core! Rotten—like all the rest of your subhuman race! And you've got the gall to make love to that girl! A human girl!"

"No more," Spock said stonily.

"I haven't even got started! Does she know what she's getting, Spock? A carcass full of memory banks that ought to be squatting on a mushroom instead of passing himself off as a man. You belong in a circus, Spock, not a starship! Right next to the dog-faced boy!"

With this, Kirk stepped forward and slapped the livid Spock twice, hard. With a roar, Spock swung out at him. Kirk leaped back out of his way, raising the bar of metal between his hands to parry the blow.

It was not much of a fight. Kirk was solely concerned with getting and keeping out of the way, while Spock was striking out with killing force, and with all the science of his once-warrior race. There could be only one ending. Kirk was deprived of the metal bar at the third onslaught, and finally took a backhand which knocked him to the floor against the far wall. Spock, his face contorted, snatched up a stool and lifted it over his head.

Kirk looked up at him and grinned ruefully. "All right, Mr. Spock. Had enough?"

Spock stared down at him, looking confused. Finally he lowered the chair.

"I never realized what it took to get under that thick hide of yours. Anyhow, I don't know what you're mad about. It isn't every First Officer who gets to belt his Captain—several times." He felt his jaw tenderly.

"You—you deliberately did that to me."

"Yes. The spores, Mr. Spock. Tell me about the spores."

Spock seemed to reach inside himself. "They're—gone. I don't belong any more."

"That was my intention. You said they were benevolent and peaceful. Violent emotions overwhelm and destroy them. I had to get you angry enough to shake off their influence. That's the answer, Spock."

"That may be correct, Captain, but we could hardly initiate a brawl with over five hundred crewmen and colonists. It is not logical."

Kirk grinned. "I was thinking of something you told me once about certain subsonic frequencies affecting the emotions."

"Yes, Captain. A certain low organ tone induces a feeling of awe. There is another frequency that affects the digestion."

"None of those will do. I want one that irritates people—something that we could hook into the communications station and broadcast over the communicators."

"That would of course also have to involve a bypass signal." Spock thought a moment. "It can be done."

"Then let's get to work."

"Captain—striking a fellow officer is a court-martial offense."

"If we're both in the brig, who's going to build the subsonic transmitter?"

"That's quite logical, Captain. To work, then."

The signal generated by the modified Feinbergers and rebroadcast from the bypassed communicators went unheard in the settlement, but it was felt almost at once, almost as though the victims had had itching powder put under their skins. Within a few minutes, everyone's nerves were exacerbated; within a few more, fights were breaking out all over the colony. The fights did not last long; as the spores dissolved in the wash of adrenalin in the bloodstream, the tumult died back to an almost aghast silence. Not long after that, contrite calls began to come in aboard the *Enterprise*.

The rest was anticlimax. The crew came back, the colonists and their effects were loaded aboard, the plants were cleaned out of the ship except for one specimen that went to Lieutenant Fletcher's laboratory. Finally, Omicron Ceti III was dwindling rapidly on the main viewing screen, watched by Kirk, Spock and McCoy.

"That's the second time," McCoy said, nodding toward the screen, "that Man has been thrown out of Paradise."

"No—this time we walked away on our own. Maybe we don't belong in Paradise, Bones," Kirk said thoughtfully. "Maybe we're meant to fight our way through. Struggle. Claw our way up, fighting every inch of the way. Maybe we can't stroll to the music of lutes, Bones—we must march to the sound of drums."

"Poetry, Captain," Spock said. "Nonregulation."

"We haven't heard much from you about the Omicron Ceti III experience, Mr. Spock."

"I have little to say about it, Captain," Spock said, slowly and quietly, "except that—for the first time in my life—I was happy."

Both the others turned and looked at him; but there was nothing to be seen now but the Mr. Spock they had long known, controlled, efficient, and emotionless.

THE DEVIL IN THE DARK

WRITER: GENE L. COON
DIRECTOR: JOSEPH PEVNY
FIRST AIRED: MARCH 9, 1967

Janus was an ugly planet, reddish-brown, slowly rotating, with a thick layer of clouds so turbulent that it appeared to be boiling. Not a hospitable place, but a major source of pergium—an energy metal-like plutonium, meta-stable, atomic number 358; the underground colony there was long-established, highly modern, almost completely automated. It had never given any trouble.

"Almost fifty people butchered," Chief Engineer Vanderberg said bitterly. He was standing beside his desk, nervous and urgent; facing him were Kirk, Spock, Lt. Commander Giotto, Doc McCoy and a security officer named Kelly. "Production's at an absolute stop."

"I can see that," Kirk said, gesturing toward the chart on the office wall, which showed a precipitous dip. "But please slow down, Mr. Vanderberg. What's the cause?"

"A monster." Vanderberg stared at the *Enterprise* delegation with belligerent defensiveness, as though daring them to deny it. He was clearly highly overwrought.

"All right," Kirk said. "Let's assume there's a monster. What has it done? When did it start?"

Vanderberg made an obvious effort to control himself. He pushed a button on his desk communicator, which sat near a globe some ten inches in diameter of what appeared to be some dark-gray crystalline solid. "Send Ed Appel in here," he told it, and then added to Kirk, "My production engineer. About three months ago, we opened a new level. It was unusually rich in pergium, platinum, uranium, even gold. The whole planet's a treasure house, but I've never seen anything like this before, even here. We were just setting up to mine it when things began to happen. First the automatic machinery began to disintegrate, piece by piece. The metal just seemed to dissolve away. No mystery about the agent; it was aqua regia, possibly with a little hydrofluoric acid mixed in—vicious stuff. We don't store vast quantities of such stuff here, I can tell you that. Offhand I don't even know what we'd keep it *in*."

"Telfon," Spock suggested.

"Yes, but my point is, we *don't*."

"You said people were butchered," Kirk reminded him gently.

"Yes. First our maintenance engineers. Sent them down into the halls to repair the corroded machinery. We found them—burned to a crisp."

"Not lava, I suppose," Kirk said.

"There is no current volcanic activity on this planet, Captain," Spock said.

"He's right. None. It was that same damn acid mixture. At first the deaths were down deep, but they've been moving up toward our levels. The last man who died, three days ago, was only three levels below this one."

"I'd like to examine his body," McCoy said.

"We kept it for you—what was left. It isn't pretty."

The office door opened to admit a tough-looking, squat, businesslike man of middle age, wearing a number one phaser at his belt.

"You posted guards? Sentries?" Kirk asked.

"Of course. And five of them have died."

"Has anyone seen this—this monster of yours?"

"I did," said the newcomer.

"This is Ed Appel. Describe it, Ed."

"I can't. I only got a glimpse of it. It was big, and kind of shaggy. I shot at it, and I hit it square, too, a good clean shot. It didn't even slow it down."

"Anything a phaser will not affect," Spock said, "has to be an illusion. Any lifeform, that is."

"Tell that to Billy Anderson," Appel said grimly. "He never had a chance. I only got away by the skin of my teeth."

"That's the story," Vanderberg said. "Nobody'll go down into the lower levels now, and I don't blame them. If the Federation wants pergium from us, they'll have to do something about it."

"That's what we're here for, Mr. Vanderberg," Kirk said.

"Pretty tough, aren't you?" said Appel. "Starship, phaser banks, energy from antimatter, the whole bit. Well, you can't get your starship down into the tunnels."

"I don't think we'll need to, Mr. Appel. Mr. Spock, I'll want a complete computer evaluation, with interviews from everyone who knows anything about the events here. Mr. Vanderberg, have you a complete subsurface chart of all drifts, tunnels, galleries and so on?"

"Of course."

Spock had been inspecting the dark-gray sphere on the desk. He stepped forward and touched it. "This, Mr. Vanderberg. What is it?"

"It's a silicon nodule. There's a million of them down there. No commercial value."

"But a geological oddity, to say the least, especially in igneous rocks. Pure silicon?"

"A light oxide layer on the outside, a few trace elements below. Look, we didn't call you here so you could collect rocks."

"Mr. Spock collects information, and it's often useful," Kirk said. "We'll need your complete cooperation."

"You'll get it. Just find this creature, whatever it is. I'm dead sick of losing my men—and I've got a quota to meet, too."

"Your order of priorities," Kirk said, "is the same as mine."

They worked in a room just off Vanderberg's office, feeding data to the *Enterprise*'s computer and getting evaluations back by communicator. The charts with which Vanderberg supplied them turned out to be immensely involved—thousands of serpentine lines crossing and recrossing. Their number was incredible, even after allowing for fifty years of tunneling with completely automated equipment. The network extended throughout the entire crust of the planet, and perhaps even deeper.

"Not man-made," Spock agreed. "They may be lava tubes, but if so, they are unique in my experience."

"They won't make hunting any easier," Kirk said. "Bones, what's the word on the autopsy?"

"The plant's physician and the chemists were right, Jim. Schmitter wasn't burned to death. He was flooded or sprayed with that acid mixture."

"Could it eat away machinery, too?"

"Aqua regia will dissolve even gold. What puzzles me is the trace of hydrofluoric acid. It's very *weak* acid, but there are two things it attacks strongly. One of them is glass—you have to keep it in wax bottles, or, as Spock suggested, telfon."

"And the other thing?"

"Human flesh."

"Hmm. It sounds like a mixture somebody calculated very carefully. Mr. Spock, do you think this monster story could be a blind for some kind of sabotage?"

"Possibly, Captain. For example, Mr. Vanderberg thinks that the creature uses the network of tubes to move through. But if you plot the deaths and the acts of destruction, and their times, you find that the creature cannot possibly have appeared at all these points as rapidly as indicated."

"How recent are those tunnel charts?"

"They were made last year—before the first appearance of the alleged monster, but not long before. Moreover, Captain, a sensor check indicates *no* life under the surface of Janus but the accountable human residents of the colony. We are confronted with two alternatives: either to patrol thousands of miles of tunnels, on foot, in the faint hope of encountering the alleged monster; or to find a plausible human suspect who has managed to manufacture and hide an almost inexhaustible supply of this intractable corrosive, and who has a portable, innocuous-looking carrier for it with a capacity of at least thirty liters."

"I rather prefer the monster theory," McCoy said. "If we catch a man behind these murders, I think we ought to lower him into his own acid vat a quarter of an inch at a time."

"If," Spock said, "is the operative word in either case . . ."

He was interrupted by a distant, heavy boom. The room shuddered, the lights flickered, and then an alarm bell was clanging. A moment later, Vanderberg burst in from his office.

"Something's happened in the main reactor room!" he shouted.

They left at a dead run, Vanderberg leading the way, McCoy bringing up the rear. The trail wound up in a tunnel elaborately posted with signs reading CAUTION: RADIATION—MAIN REACTOR CHAMBER—ONLY AUTHORIZED PERSONS BEYOND THIS POINT. The floor of the tunnel looked as though something very heavy had been dragged along it. At the far end was what had once been a large metal door, but which now consisted chiefly of curled strips around a huge hole. Before it was a small, blackened lump which might once have been a man.

Vanderberg recoiled. "Look at that!" Then he hurried toward the ruined door. McCoy knelt quickly beside the charred lump, tricorder out; Kirk and Spock followed Vanderberg.

Inside, the bulk of the reactor was buried in the walls, showing only a large faceplate and a control panel. Pipes crisscrossed the chamber; and an appalled Vanderberg was standing looking down at a sort of nexus of these—a junction that ending in nothing.

Kirk scanned the control panel. "I didn't know anyone still used fission for power."

"I don't suppose anybody does but us. But pergium is money—we ship it all out—and since we have so much uranium nobody wants, we use it here. Or we did until now."

"Explain."

"The main moderator pump's gone. Lucky the cutouts worked, or this whole place would be a flaming mass of sodium."

Spock knelt and inspected the aborted junctions. "Acid again. Like the door. Mr. Vanderberg, do you have a replacement for the missing pump?"

"I doubt it. It was platinum, corrosion-proof, never gave us any trouble; should have lasted forever." Suddenly, visibly, Vanderberg began to panic. "Look, the reactor's shut down now—and it provides heat and electricity and life support for the whole colony! And if we override, we'll have a maximum accident that will poison half the planet!"

"Steady," Kirk said, "Mr. Spock, might we have a replacement on shipboard?"

"No, Captain. To find one, you would need a museum."

Kirk took out his communicator. "Kirk to *Enterprise* . . . Lt. Uhura, get me Mr. Scott . . . Scotty, this is the Captain. Could you contrive a perfusion pump for a PXK fission reactor?"

"Hoo, Captain, you must be haverin'."

"I'm dead serious; it's vital."

"Well, sir—I could put together some odds and ends. But they wouldn't hold for long."

"How long?"

"Forty-eight hours, maybe, with a bit of luck. It all ought to be platinum, ye see, and I've not got enough, so I'll have to patch in with gold, which won't bear the pressure long . . ."

"Get together what you need and beam down here with it."

Kirk put away the communicator and bent upon Vanderberg a look of deep suspicion. "Mr. Vanderberg, I have to tell you that I don't like the way these coincidences are mounting up. How could some hypothetical monster attack precisely the one mechanism in an almost ancient reactor which would create a double crisis like this? And how would it happen to be carrying around with it a mixture of acids precisely calculated to dissolve even platinum—and also human flesh?"

"I don't know," Vanderberg said helplessly. "You suspect sabotage? Impossible. Besides, Ed Appel *saw* the monster."

"He says."

"Ed's been my production chief almost throughout my entire career. I'd trust him with my life. And besides, what would be his motive? Look, dammit, Kirk, my people are being murdered! This is no time for fantasies about spies! The thing is there, it's free, it's just shut us down right under your nose! Why in God's name don't you *do* something?"

"Captain," Spock's voice said from behind them. "Will you come out and look at this, please?"

Kirk went out into the main tunnel to find the First Officer contemplating a side branch. "This is most curious," he said. "This tunnel is not indicated on any of the charts we were provided. It simply was not there before."

"Too recent to be on the maps, maybe?"

"Yes, but how did it get here, Captain? It shows no signs of having been drilled."

Kirk looked closer. "That's so. And the edges are fused. Could it be a lava tube?"

"That seems most unlikely," Spock said. "Had there been any vulcanism on this level since we arrived, everybody would be aware of it. And it joins a charted tunnel back there about fifty yards."

"Hmm. Let's go back to the ship. I feel the need for a conference."

Spock brought with him into the briefing room of the *Enterprise* one of the strange spherical objects Vanderberg had called silicon nodules, and set it on the table. Then he sat down and stared into it, looking incongruously like a fortune-teller in uniform.

"I think it's mass hysteria," McCoy said.

"Hysteria?" Kirk said. "Dozens of people have been killed."

"Some—natural cause. A phenomenon—and people have dreamed up a mysterious monster to account for it."

Spock stirred. "Surely, Doctor. A natural cause. But not hysteria."

"All right. You asked my opinion. I gave it to you. How do I know? Maybe there is some kind of a monster . . ."

"No creature is monstrous in its own environment, Doctor. And this one appears to be intelligent, as well."

"What makes you think so?"

"The missing pump was not taken by accident," Spock said. "It was the one piece of equipment absolutely essential to the operation of the reactor."

Kirk looked at his First Officer. "You think this creature is trying to drive the colonists off the planet?"

"It seems logical."

"Why just now, Mr. Spock? This production facility was established here fifty years ago."

"I do not know, sir." Spock resumed staring at the round object. "But it is perhaps indicative that Mr. Appel claimed to have hit it with his phaser. He strikes me as a capable but unimaginative man. If he said he hit it, I tend to believe he did. Why was the creature not affected? I have a suggestion, though Dr. McCoy will accuse me of creating fantasies."

"You?" McCoy said. "I doubt it."

"Very well. To begin with, the colonists are equipped only with phaser number one, no need for the more powerful model having been encountered. This instrument, when set to kill, coagulates proteins, which are carbon-based compounds. Suppose this creature's 'organic' compounds are based on silicon instead?"

"Now surely that *is* a fantasy," Kirk said.

"No, it's possible," McCoy said. "Silicon has the same valence as carbon, and a number of simple silicoid 'organics' have been known for a long time. And by the stars, it explains the acids, too. We have hydrochloric acid in our own stomachs, after all. But we're mostly water. Silicon isn't water-soluble, so the aqua regia may be the substrate of the creature's bloodstream. And the hydrofluoric—well, fluorine has an especial affinity for silicon; the result is telfon, which may be what the creature's internal tubing is made of."

"Do you mean to imply," Kirk said slowly, "that this being goes about killing men with its own blood?"

"Not necessarily, Jim. It may spit the stuff—and sweat it, too, for all I know. Its tunneling suggests that it does."

"Hmm. It also suggests that it would have to have a form of natural armor plating.

But our people have phasers number two, and I defy anything to stand up against that at high power, no matter what it's made of. The question is, how do we locate it?"

"I would suggest," Spock said, "that we start at whatever level these silicon nodules were found."

"Why? How do they tie in?"

"Pure speculation, Captain. But it would be helpful if it were confirmed."

"Very well, assemble security forces. I assume that Mr. Scott is already at work on the reactor? Very good, we'll assemble in Vanderberg's office."

"You will each be given a complete chart of all tunnels and diggings under this installation," Kirk told his forces. "You will proceed from level to level, checking out every foot of opening. You will be searching for some variety of creature which apparently is highly resistant to phaser fire, so have your phasers set on maximum. And remember this—fifty people have already been killed. I want no more deaths . . ."

"Except the bloody thing!" Vanderberg exploded.

Kirk nodded. "The creature may or may not attack on sight. However, you must. A great deal depends on getting this installation back into production."

"Mr. Vanderberg," Spock said, "may I ask at which level you discovered the nodules of silicon?"

"The twenty-third. Why?"

"Commander Giotto," Kirk said, "you will take your detail directly to the twenty-third level and start your search from there. Mr. Vanderberg, I want all of your people to stay on the top level. Together. In a safe place."

"I don't know any safe place, Captain. The way this thing comes and goes . . ."

"We'll see what we can do about that. All right, gentlemen. You have your instructions. Let's get at it."

Spock, Kirk, Giotto and two security guards paused on the twenty-third level while Spock adjusted his tricorder. Most of Giotto's men had already fanned out through the tunnels. Kirk pointed to a spot on Giotto's map.

"We are here. You and your guards take this tunnel, which is the only one of this complex that doesn't already have men in it. As you see, they converge up ahead. We'll rendezvous at that point."

"Aye, aye, sir." The three disappeared into the darkness. Spock continued to scan.

"A strange sensation," the First Officer said. "There are men all about us, and yet because the tricorder is now set for silicon life, it says we are alone down here. No, not quite."

"Traces?"

"A great many—but they are all extremely old. Many thousands of years old. Yet, again, there are many brand new tunnels down here. It does not relate."

"Perhaps it does," Kirk said thoughtfully. "Not tunnels. Not lava tubes. Highways.

Roads. Thoroughfares. Mr. Spock, give me an environmental reading, for a thousand yards in any direction."

"Yes, sir—ah. A life-form. Bearing, one hundred eleven degrees, angle of elevation four degrees."

"Not one of our people?"

"No, sir, they would not register."

"Come on!"

They set off quickly, keeping as close on the bearing as the convolutions of the tunnels would allow. Then, ahead, someone screamed—or tried to, for the sound was suddenly cut off. They ran.

A moment later they were looking at a small, blackened lump on the tunnel floor, with a phaser beside it. Grimly, Spock picked up the weapon and checked it.

"One of the guards," he said. "He did not have a chance to fire, Captain."

"And it's only been seconds since we heard him scream . . ."

There was a slithering sound behind them. They whirled together.

In the darkness it was difficult to make out details, except for movement, an undulating crawl forward. The creature was large, low to the ground, somehow wormlike. It was now making another noise, a menacing rattle, like pebbles being shaken in a tin can.

"Look out!" Kirk shouted. "It's charging!"

Both men fired. The monster swung around as the two phaser beams struck its side. With an agonized roar, it leapt backward and vanished.

"After it!"

But the tunnel was empty. It was astonishing that anything of that bulk could move so rapidly. Kirk reached out to touch the wall of the tunnel, then snatched his hand back.

"Mr. Spock! These walls are hot."

"Indeed, Captain. The tricorder says it was cut within the last two minutes."

Kirk heard running footsteps, and then Giotto and a guard, phasers at the ready, appeared behind them.

"Are you all right, Captain? That scream . . ."

"Perfectly, Commander. But one of your men . . ."

"Yes, I saw. Poor Kelly. Did you see the thing, sir?"

"We saw it. In fact, we took a bite out of it."

Spock bent over, then straightened with a large chunk of something in his hand. "And here it is, Captain."

He handed the stuff to Kirk, who examined it closely. Clearly, it was not animal tissue; it looked more like fibrous asbestos. Obviously, Spock's guess had been right.

"Commander Giotto, it looks as though killing this thing will require massed phasers—or a single phaser with much longer contact. Pass the word to your men. And another thing. We already knew it was a killer. Now it's wounded—probably in pain—

The Devil in the Dark

back in there somewhere. There's nothing more dangerous than a wounded animal. Keep that in mind."

"The creature is moving rapidly through native rock at bearing two hundred one, eleven hundred yards, elevation angle five degrees," Spock said.

"Right," Giotto and the guard went out, and Kirk started to follow them, but Spock remained standing where he was, looking pensive. Kirk said, "What's troubling you, Mr. Spock?"

"Captain, there are literally hundreds of these tunnels in this general area alone. Far too many to be cut by the one creature in an ordinary lifetime."

"We don't know how long it lives."

"No, sir, but its speed of movement indicates a high metabolic rate. That is not compatible with a lifetime much longer than ours."

"Perhaps not," Kirk said. "I fail to see what bearing that has on our problem."

"I mention it, Captain, because if this is the only survivor of a dead race, to kill it would be a crime against science."

"Our concern is the protection of this colony, Mr. Spock. And to get pergium production moving again. This is not a zoological expedition."

"Quite so, Captain. Still . . ."

"Keep your tricorder active. Maintain a constant reading on the creature. We'll try to use the existing tunnels to cut it off. If we have to, we'll use our phasers to cut our own tunnels." Kirk paused, then added more gently, "I'm sorry, Mr. Spock, I'm afraid it must die."

"Sir, if the opportunity arose to capture it instead . . ."

"I will lose no more men, Mr. Spock. The creature will be killed on sight. That's the end of it."

"Very well, sir."

But Kirk was not satisfied. Killing came hard to them all, but Spock in particular was sometimes inclined to hold his fire when his conservation instincts, or his scientific curiosity, were aroused. After a moment, Kirk added, "Mr. Spock, I want you to return to the surface, to assist Mr. Scott in the maintenance of his makeshift circulating pump."

Spock's eyebrows went up. "I beg your pardon, Captain?"

"You heard me. It's vital that we keep that reactor in operation. Your scientific knowledge . . ."

". . . is not needed there. Mr. Scott knows far more about reactors than I do. You are aware of that."

After another pause, Kirk said; "Very well. I am in command of the *Enterprise*. You are second in command. This hunt will be dangerous. Either one of us, by himself, is expendable. Both of us are not."

"I will, of course, follow your orders, Captain," Spock said. "But we are dealing with a grave scientific problem right here, so on those grounds, this is where I should be, not with Mr. Scott. Besides, sir, there are approximately one hundred of us engaged in this search, against one creature. The odds against both you and me being killed are—" there was a very slight pause, "two hundred twenty-six point eight to one."

Not for the first time, Kirk found himself outgunned. "Those are good odds. Very well, you may stay. But keep out of trouble, Mr. Spock."

"That is always my intention, Captain."

Kirk's communicator beeped, and he flipped it open. "Kirk here."

"Scotty, Captain. My brilliant improvisation just gave up the ghost. It couldn't take the strain."

"Can you fix it again?"

"Nay, Captain. It's gone for good."

"Very well. Start immediate evacuation of all colonists to the *Enterprise*."

Vanderberg's voice came through. "Not all of them, Captain. Me and some of my key personnel are staying. We'll be down to join you."

"We don't have phasers enough for all of you."

"Then we'll use clubs," Vanderberg's voice said. "But we won't be chased away from here. My people take orders from me, not from you."

Kirk thought fast. "Very well. Get everybody else on board the ship. The fewer people we have breathing the air, the longer the rest of us can hold out. How long is that, Scotty?"

"It's got naught to do with the air, Captain. The reactor will go supercritical in about ten hours. You'll have to find your beastie well before then."

"Right. Feed us constant status reports, Scotty. Mr. Vanderberg, you and your men assemble on level twenty-three, checkpoint Tiger. There you'll team up with *Enterprise* security personnel. They're better armed than you are, so stay in sight of one of them at all times—buddy system. Mr. Spock and I will control all operations by communicator. Understood—and agreed?"

"Both," Vanderberg's voice said grimly. "Suicide is no part of my plans."

"Good. Kirk out . . . Mr. Spock, you seem to have picked up something."

"Yes, Captain. The creature is now quiescent a few thousand yards from here, in that direction."

Kirk took a quick look at his chart. "The map says these two tunnels converge there. Take the left one, Mr. Spock. I'll go to the right."

"Should we separate?"

"Two tunnels," Kirk said. "Two of us. We separate."

"Very well, Captain," Spock said, but his voice was more than a little dubious. But it couldn't be helped. Kirk moved down the right-hand tunnel, slowly and tensely.

The tunnel turned, and Kirk found himself in a small chamber, streaked with bright strata quite unlike the rest of the rock around him. Inbedded in there were dozens of round objects like the one Vanderberg had on his desk, or the one which had so fascinated Spock. He lifted his communicator again. "Mr. Spock."

"Yes, Captain."

"I've found a whole layer of those silicon nodules of yours."

"Indeed, Captain. Most illuminating. Captain—be absolutely certain you do not damage any of them."

"Explain."

"It is only a theory, Captain, but . . ."

His voice was drowned out by the roar of hundreds of tons of collapsing rock and debris. Kirk threw himself against the wall, choking clouds of dust rising around him. When he could see again, it was evident that the roof of the tunnel had fallen across the way he had just come.

"Captain! Are you all right? Captain!"

"Yes, Mr. Spock. Quite all right. But we seem to have had a cave-in."

"I can phaser you out," Spock's voice said.

"No, any disturbance would bring the rest of the wall down. Anyway, it isn't necessary. The chart said our tunnels meet further on. I can just walk out."

"Very well. But I find it disquieting that your roof chose to collapse at that moment. Please proceed with extreme caution. I shall double my pace."

"Very well, Mr. Spock. I'll meet you at the end of the tunnel. Kirk out."

As he tucked the communicator away, there came from behind him a sound as of pebbles being shaken in a can. He spun instantly, but it was too late. The way was blocked.

It was his first clear sight of the creature, which was reared in the center of the tunnel. It was huge, shaggy, multicolored, and knobby with objects which might have been heads, sense organs, hands—Kirk could not tell. It was quivering gently, still making that strange noise.

Kirk whipped up his phaser. At once the creature shuffled backward. Was it now afraid of just one gun? He raised the weapon again, but this time the creature retreated no further. Neither did it advance.

Phaser at the ready, Kirk moved toward the animal, trying to get around it. At once, it moved to block him—not threateningly, as far as Kirk could tell, but just getting in his way.

Spock chose this moment to call him again. "Captain, a new reading shows the creature . . ."

"I know exactly where the creature is," Kirk said, his phaser steadily on it. "Standing about ten feet away from me."

"Kill it, Captain! Quickly!"

"It's—not making any threatening moves, Mr. Spock."

"You don't dare take the chance! Kill it!"

"I thought you were the one who wanted it kept alive," Kirk said, with grim amusement. "Captured, if possible."

"Your life is in danger, Captain. You can't take the risk."

"It seems to be waiting for something. I want to find out what. I'll shoot if I have to."

"Very well, Captain. I will hurry through my tunnel and approach it from the rear. I remind you that it is a proven killer. Spock out."

The creature was silent now. Kirk lowered his phaser a trifle, but there was no reaction.

"All right," Kirk said. "What do we do now? Talk it over?"

He really had not expected an answer, nor did he get one. He took a step forward and to one side. Again the creature moved to block him; and as it did, Kirk saw along one of its flanks a deep, ragged gouge, leaving a glistening, rocklike surface exposed. It was obviously a wound.

"Well, you can be hurt, can't you?"

He lifted the phaser again. The creature rattled, and shrank back, but held its ground. Obviously it was afraid of the weapon, but it would not flee.

Kirk lowered the phaser, and the rattling stopped. Then he moved deliberately back against the nearest wall and dropped slowly into a squatting position, the phaser held loosely between his knees.

"All right. Your move. Or do we just sit and wait for something to happen?"

It was not a long wait. Almost at once, Spock burst into the area from the open end of the tunnel. He took in the situation instantly and his own phaser jerked up.

"Don't shoot!" Kirk shouted. Echoes went bounding away through the galleries and tunnels.

Spock looked from one to the other. As he did so, the creature moved slowly to the other side of the tunnel. Kirk guessed that he could get past it now before it could block him again. Instead, he said, "Come on over, Mr. Spock."

With the utmost caution, his highly interested eyes fastened on the creature, Spock moved to Kirk's side. He looked up at the walls in which the silicon nodules were imbedded. "Logical," he said.

"But what do they mean?"

"I'd rather not say just yet. If I could possibly get into Vulcan mind-lock with that creature—it would be easier if I could touch it . . ."

Before Kirk could even decide whether to veto this notion, Spock stepped toward the animal, his hand extended. It lurched back at once, its rattling loud and angry-sounding.

"Too bad," Spock said. "But obviously it will permit no contact. Well, then, I must do it the hard way. If you will be patient, Captain . . ."

Spock's eyes closed as he began to concentrate. The intense mental power he was summoning was almost physically visible. Kirk held his breath. The creature twitched nervously, uneasily.

Suddenly Spock's face contorted in agony, and he screamed. "The pain! The pain!" With a great shudder, his face ashen, he began to fall; Kirk got to him just in time.

"Thank—you, Captain," Spock said, gasping and steadying himself. "I am sorry—but that is all I got. Just waves and waves of searing pain. Oh, and a name. It calls itself a Horta. It is in great agony because of the wound—but not reacting at all like a wounded animal."

Abruptly, the creature slithered forward to a smooth expanse of floor, and clung there for a moment. Then it moved away. Where it had been, etched into the floor in still smoking letters, were the words: NO KILL I. Both men stared at the sentence in astonishment.

"'No kill I'?" Kirk said. "What's that? It could be a plea to us not to kill it—or a promise that it won't kill us."

"I don't know. It appears it learned more from me during our empathy than I did from it. But observe, Captain, that it thinks in vocables. That means it can hear, too."

"Horta!" Kirk said loudly. The creature rattled at once and then returned to silence.

"Mr. Spock, I hate to do this to you, but—it suddenly occurs to me that the Horta couldn't have destroyed that perfusion pump. It was platinum, and immune to the acid mix. It must have hidden it somewhere—and we have to get it back. You'll have to reestablish communications, no matter how painful it is."

"Certainly, Captain," Spock said promptly. "But it has no reason to give us the device—and apparently every reason to wish us off the planet."

"I'm aware of that. If we can win its confidence . . ."

Kirk took out his communicator. "Dr. McCoy. This is the Captain."

"Yes, Captain," McCoy's voice answered.

"Get your medical kit and get down here on the double. We've got a patient for you."

"Somebody injured? How?"

"I can't specify, it's beyond my competence. Just come. Twenty-third level; find us by tricorder. And hurry. Kirk out."

"I remind you, Captain," Spock said. "This is a silicon-based form of life. Dr. McCoy's medical knowledge may be totally useless."

"He's a healer. Let him heal. All right, go ahead, Mr. Spock. Try to contact it again. And try to find out why it suddenly took to murder."

The creature moved nervously as Spock approached it, but did not shy off; it merely quivered, and made its warning pebble-sound. Spock's eyes closed, and the rattling slowly died back.

Kirk's communicator beeped again. "Kirk here."

"Giotto, Captain. Are you all right?"

"Perfectly all right. Where are you?"

"We're at the end of the tunnel. Mr. Vanderberg and his men are here. They're pretty ugly. I thought I'd check with you first..."

"Hold them there, Commander. Under no circumstances allow them in here yet. The minute Dr. McCoy gets there, send him through."

"Aye aye, sir. Giotto out."

Spock was now deep in trance. He began to murmur.

"Pain ... pain ... Murder ... the thousands ... devils ... Eternity ends ... horrible ... horrible ... in the Chamber of the Ages ... the Altar of Tomorrow ... horrible ... Murderers ... Murderers ..."

"Mr. Spock! The pump ..."

"Stop them ... kill ... strike back ... monsters ..."

There was the sound of rapidly approaching footsteps and Dr. McCoy, medical bag in hand, broke through into the area. Then he stopped, obviously stunned at what he saw. Kirk silently signaled him to join them, and McCoy, giving the quiescent creature a wide berth, moved to Kirk's side. He said in a low whisper, "What in the name of..."

"It's wounded—badly," Kirk whispered back. "You've got to help it."

"Help—*this*?"

"Take a look at it."

McCoy cautiously approached the creature, which was now as immobile as a statue; nor did Spock take any notice.

"The end of life ... the murderers ... killing ... the dead children ..."

McCoy stared at the gaping wound, and then touched it tentatively here and there. Producing his tricorder, he took a reading, at which he stared in disbelief. Then he came back to Kirk, his face indignant.

"You can't be serious. That thing is virtually made out of stone on the outside, and its guts are plastics."

"Help it. Treat it."

"I'm a doctor, not a bricklayer!"

"You're a healer," Kirk said. "That's your patient. That's an order, Doctor."

McCoy shook his head in wonder, but moved back toward the animal. Spock's eyes were still closed, his face sweating with effort. Kirk went to him.

"Spock. Tell it we're trying to help. A doctor."

"Understood. Understood. It is the end of Life. Eternity stops. Go out. Into the tunnel. To the Passage of Immortality. To the Chamber of the Ages. Cry for the children. Walk carefully in the Vault of Tomorrow. Sorrow for the murdered children. Weep for the crushed ones. Tears for the stolen ones. The thing you search for is there. Go. Go. Sadness for the end of things."

Kirk could not tell whether he was being given directions, or only eavesdropping upon a meditation. He looked hesitantly toward the tunnel entrance.

"Go!" Spock said. "Into the tunnel. There is a small passage. Quickly. Quickly. Sorrow . . . such sorrow. Sadness. Pain." There were tears running down his cheeks now. "Sorrow . . . the dead . . . the children . . ."

Kirk felt a thrill of sympathy. He did not in the least understand this litany, but no one could hear so many emotionally loaded words chanted in circumstances of such tension without reacting.

But the directions turned out to be clear enough. Within a minute he was able to return, the pump in one hand, a silicon nodule in the other.

McCoy was kneeling by the flank of the animal, and speaking into his communicator. "That's right, Lieutenant. Beam it down to me immediately. Never mind what I want it for, I just want it. Move!"

"The ages die," Spock said. "It is time to sleep. It is over. Failure. The murderers have won. Death is welcome. Let it end here, with the murdered children . . ."

"Mr. Spock!" Kirk called. "Come back! Spock!"

Spock shuddered with the effort to disengage himself. Kirk carefully put the pump on the floor of the tunnel, then waited until Spock's eyes were no longer glazed.

"I found the unit," Kirk said. "It's in good shape. I also found about a thousand of these silicon balls. They're—eggs, aren't they, Mr. Spock?"

"Yes, Captain. Eggs. And about to hatch."

"The miners must have broken into the hatchery. Their operations destroyed hundreds of them. No wonder . . ."

There was a roar of sound, and Vanderberg, Appel and what seemed to be an army of armed civilians were trying to jam themselves into the tunnel. They shouted in alarm as they saw the creature. Phasers were raised. Kirk jumped forward.

"No!" he shouted. "Don't shoot."

"Kill it, kill it!" Appel yelled.

Kirk raised his own weapon. "The first man who shoots, dies."

"You can't mean it," Vanderberg said, pointing at the Horta with a finger quivering with hatred. "That thing has killed fifty of my men!"

"And you've killed hundreds of her children," Kirk said quietly.

"What?"

"Those 'silicon nodules' you've been collecting and destroying are eggs. Tell them, Mr. Spock."

"There have been many generations of Horta on this planet," Spock said. "Every fifty thousand years the entire race dies—all but one, like this one. But the eggs live. She protects them, cares for them, and when they hatch, she is the mother to them—thousands of them. This creature here is the mother of her race."

"She's intelligent, peaceful and mild," Kirk added. "She had no objection to sharing the planet with you people—until you broke into the nursery and started destroying her eggs. Then she fought back, in the only way she could—as any mother would—when her children were endangered."

"How were we to know?" Vanderberg said, chastened and stunned. "But—you mean if those eggs hatch, there'll be thousands of them crawling around down here? We've got pergium to deliver!"

"And now you've got your reactor pump back," Kirk said. "She gave it back. You've complained that this planet is a minerological treasure house, if only you had the equipment to get at everything. Well, the Horta moves through rock the way we move through air—and leaves a tunnel. The greatest natural miners in the universe.

"I don't see why we can't make an agreement—reach a *modus vivendi*. They tunnel, you collect and process. You get along together. Your processing operation would be a thousand times more profitable than it is now."

"Sounds all right," Vanderberg said, still a little dubiously. "But how do you know the thing will go for it?"

"Why should it not?" Spock said. "It is logical. But there is one problem. It is badly wounded. It may die."

McCoy rose to his feet, a broad smile on his face. "It won't die. By golly, I'm beginning to think I can cure a rainy day."

"You cured it?" Kirk said in amazement. "How?"

"I had the ship beam down ten pounds of thermoconcrete, the kind we build emergency shelters out of. It's mostly silicon. I just troweled it over the wound. It'll act as a 'bandage' until it heals of itself. Take a look. Good as new."

"Bones, my humblest congratulations. Mr. Spock, I'll have to ask you to get in contact with the Horta again. Tell it our proposition. She and her children make all the tunnels they want. Our people will remove the minerals, and each side will leave the other alone. Think she'll go for it?"

"As I said, Captain, it seems logical. The Horta has a very logical mind." He paused a moment. "And after years of close association with humans, I find it curiously refreshing."

ERRAND OF MERCY

WRITER: GENE L. COON
DIRECTOR: JOHN NEWLAND
FIRST AIRED: MARCH 23, 1967

THE KLINGON SCOUT SHIP MUST HAVE KNOWN THAT IT WAS NO MATCH WHATSOever for the *Enterprise*—after all, the Klingons were experts in such matters. But it fired on the *Enterprise* anyhow as Kirk's ship approached Organia. The Federation ship's phasers promptly blew the scout into very small flinders, but the attack was a measure of the Klingons' determination to bar the Federation from using Organia as a base. Organia was of no intrinsic value to either side—largely farmland, worked by a people with neither any skill at, nor interest in, fighting—but strategically it was the only Class M planet in the disputed zone, over which negotiations had already broken down. It was, Kirk thought, another Armenia, another Belgium—the weak innocents who always turn out to be located on a natural invasion route.

And the scout ship had had plenty of time to get off a message before opening fire. It had to be assumed that a Klingon fleet was now on the way, if there hadn't been one on the way already. That left very little time for negotiating with the Organians.

Leaving Sulu in charge of the *Enterprise*—with strict orders to cut and run if any Klingon fleet showed up—Kirk and Spock beamed down. The street in which they arrived might have been that of any English village of the thirteenth century: thatched roofs, a few people wearing rude homespun, a brace of oxen pulling a crude wagon. In the distance, something that looked like a ruined castle or fortress, old and decayed, but massive, glowered over the village—an odd construction for a culture that was supposed to have no history of warfare. As for the passersby, they paid no attention to the two starship officers, as if they were used to seeing men beaming down every day. That too seemed rather unlikely.

When the reception committee finally arrived, however, it was cordial enough. It consisted of three smiling, elderly men in fur-trimmed robes, who introduced themselves as Ayelborne, Trefayne and Claymare. Kirk and Spock were received in a small room with roughly plastered walls and no decorations, and containing only a rude table flanked by plain chairs.

Spock lowered his tricorder. "Absolutely no energy output anywhere," he murmured to the Captain. Kirk nodded; the report only confirmed his own impression. This was not a medieval culture making progress toward mechanization, as the original reports had indicated. It was totally stagnant—a laboratory specimen of an arrested culture. Most peculiar.

"My government," he told the smiling Organians, "has informed me that the Klingons are expected to move against your planet, with the objective of making it a base of operations against our Federation. My mission, frankly, is to try to keep them from doing this."

"What you are saying," Ayelborne said, "is that we seem to have a choice between dealing with you or your enemies." In another context the words might have seemed hostile, but Ayelborne was still smiling.

"No, sir. With the Federation you will have a choice. You will have none with the Klingons. They are a military dictatorship, to which war is a way of life. We offer you protection."

"Thank you," Ayelborne said. "But we do not need your protection. We have nothing anyone could want."

"You have this planet, and its strategic location. If you don't move to prevent it, the Klingons will move in, just as surely as your sun sets. We'll help you with your defenses, build facilities . . ."

"We have no defenses, Captain, nor are any needed," the man called Claymare said.

"Excuse me, but you're wrong. I've seen what the Klingons do to planets like yours. They are organized into vast slave labor camps. You'll have no freedom whatsoever. Your goods will be confiscated. Hostages will be taken and killed. Your leaders will be confined. You'd be better off on a penal planet."

"Captain," Ayelborne said, "we see that your concern is genuine, and we appreciate it. But again we assure you that there is absolutely no danger . . ."

"I assure you that there is! Do you think I'm lying? Why?"

"You did not let me finish," Ayelborne said gently. "I was going to say, there is no danger to ourselves. You and your friend are in danger, certainly. It would be best for you to return to your ship as soon as possible."

"Gentlemen, I beg you to reconsider. We can be of immense help to you. In addition to the military assistance, we can send in technicians, specialists. We can show you how to feed a thousand people where you fed one before. We'll build schools and help you educate your young, teach them what we know—your public facilities seem to be almost nonexistent. We could remake your world, end disease, hunger, hardship. But we are forbidden to help you if you refuse to be helped."

"A moving plea," Trefayne said. "But . . ."

He was interrupted by the beeping of Kirk's communicator. "Excuse me, sir," he said. "Kirk here."

"Captain," said Sulu's voice. "A large number of Klingon vessels just popped out of subspace around us. I didn't get a count before they opened fire but there must be at least twenty. My screens are up now, and I can't drop them to beam you aboard."

"You're not supposed to," Kirk said harshly. "Your orders are to run for it and contact the fleet. Come back only if you've got better odds. Mark and move!"

He switched off and stared at the three Organians.

"You kept insisting that there was no danger. Now . . ."

"We are already aware of the Klingon fleet," Trefayne said. "There are in fact eight more such vessels now assuming orbit around our planet."

"Can you verify that, Spock?"

"No, sir, not at this distance," Spock said. "But it seems a logical development."

"Ah," Trefayne added. "Several hundred armed men have just appeared near the citadel."

Spock aimed his tricorder in that direction and nodded. "Not just hand weapons, either," he said. "I am picking up three or four pieces of heavy-duty equipment. How did he know that so quickly, I wonder?"

"That doesn't matter now," Kirk said grimly. "What matters is that we're stranded here, right in the middle of the Klingon occupation army."

"So it would seem, sir," Spock said. "Not a pleasant prospect."

"Mr. Spock," Kirk said, "you have a gift for understatement."

The Klingons were hard-faced, hard-muscled men, originally of Oriental stock. They were indeed heavily armed and wore what looked like vests of mail. They moved purposefully and efficiently through the streets, posting guards as they went. The few Organians they met smiled at them and moved quietly, passively out of their way.

To compound Kirk's bafflement, the uncooperative Organian council—if that is what the three men were—had provided him and Spock with Organian clothing and offered to conceal them, an offer entailing colossal risks. Then, rummaging through the discarded uniforms, Kirk demanded suddenly: "Where are our weapons?"

"We took them, Captain," Ayelborne said. "We cannot permit violence here. Claymare, remove the uniforms. No, we will have to protect you ourselves. Mr. Spock presents the chief problem. He will have to pose as a Vulcan trader—perhaps here to deal in kevas and trillium."

"They're aware that Vulcan is a member of the Federation," Kirk said.

"But harmless to the Klingons. You, Captain, might well be an Organian citizen, if . . ."

He got no further. The door flew open, and two Klingon soldiers burst in, gesturing with handguns for everyone to back up. They were followed by a third Klingon, an erect, proud man, who did not need his commander's insignia to show who he was.

Spock and the Organians retreated; Kirk stood his ground. The Klingon commander looked quickly around the room.

"*This* is the ruling council?" he said contemptuously.

Ayelborne stepped forward again, smiling. "I am Ayelborne, temporary council head. I bid you welcome."

"No doubt you do. I am Kor, military governor of Organia." He glared at Kirk. "Who are you?"

"He is Baroner," Ayelborne said. "One of our leading citizens. This is Trefayne . . ."

"This Baroner has no tongue?"

"I have a tongue," Kirk said.

"Good. When I address you, you will answer. Where is your smile?"

"My what?"

"The stupid, idiotic smile everyone else seems to be wearing." Kor swung on Spock. "A Vulcan. Do you also have a tongue?"

"My name is Spock. I am a dealer in kevas and trillium."

"You don't look like a storekeeper. What is trillium?"

Spock said smoothly, and with an impassive face: "A medicinal plant of the lily family."

"Not on Organia, it isn't," Kor said. "Obviously a Federation spy. Take him to the examination room."

"He's no spy," Kirk said angrily.

"Well, well," Kor said. "Have we a ram among the sheep? Why do you object to us taking him? He's not even human."

Kirk caught the warning glance Spock was trying to disguise and made a major effort to control himself as well. "He has done nothing, that's all."

"Coming from an Organian, yours is practically an act of rebellion. Very good. They welcome me. Do you also welcome me?"

"You're here," Kirk said. "I can't do anything about it."

Kor stared hard at him, and then permitted himself a faint smile. "Good honest hatred," he said. "Very refreshing. However, it makes no difference whether you welcome me or not. I am here and I will stay. You are now subjects of the Klingon Empire. You will find there are many rules and regulations, which will be posted. Violation of the smallest of them will be punished by death; we will have no time for justice just now."

"Your regulations will be obeyed," Ayelborne said.

Kirk felt his mouth tightening. Kor saw it; apparently he missed very little. He said: "You disapprove, Baroner?"

"Do you need my approval?"

"I need your obedience, nothing more," Kor said softly. "Will I have it?"

"You seem to be in command," Kirk said, shrugging.

"How true." Kor began to pace. "Now, I shall need a representative from among you, liaison between the forces of occupation and the civilian population. I don't trust men who smile too much. Baroner, you are appointed."

"Me?" Kirk said. "I don't want the job."

"Have I asked whether or not you wanted it? As for the rest of you—we Klingons have a reputation for ruthlessness. You will find that it is deserved. Should one Klingon soldier be killed here, a thousand Organians will die. I will have *order*, is that clear?"

"Commander," Ayelborne said, "I assure you we will cause you no trouble."

"No. I am sure you will not. Baroner, come with me."

"What about Mr. Spock?"

"Why are you concerned?"

"He's my friend."

"You have poor taste in friends. He will be examined. If he is lying, he will die. If he is telling the truth, well, he will find that business has taken a turn for the worse. Guards, remove him."

The guards, covering Spock with their weapons, gestured him out the door; Spock went meekly. Kirk started after him, only to be shoved back by Kor himself. Kirk could not help flushing, but Kor only nodded.

"You do not like to be pushed," the Klingon said. "Good. At least you are a man I can understand. Come with me."

Kor had set up shop in the citadel Kirk and Spock had seen on their first arrival. Seen close up, and from inside, the impression it gave of vast age was intensified. Kor had furnished one room with a large Klingon insignia, a desk, one chair, and nothing else; Kirk stood. Kor signed a document and thrust it across the desk at him.

"For duplication and posting," he said. "From this day on, no public assemblages of more than three people. All publications to be cleared through this office. Neighborhood controls will be established. Hostages selected. A somewhat lengthy list of crimes against the state."

Kirk glanced impassively at the list, aware that Kor as usual was watching him closely. The commander said: "You do not like them?"

"Did you expect me to?"

Kor only grinned. At the same time, the door opened and Spock was thrust inside, followed by a Klingon lieutenant. To Kirk's enormous relief, his first officer looked perfectly normal.

"Well, lieutenant?"

"He is what he claims to be, Commander," the lieutenant said. "A Vulcan trader named Spock. And he really is trading in the other kind of trillium, the vegetable kind; it seems it has value here."

"Nothing else?"

"The usual apprehension. His main concern seems to be how he will carry on his business under our occupation. His mind is so undisciplined that he could hold nothing back."

"All right, Baroner, would you like to try our little truth-finder?"

"I don't even understand it."

"It's a mind-sifter," Kor said, "or a mind-ripper, depending on how much force is used. If necessary, we can empty a man's mind as if opening a spigot. Of course, what's left is more vegetable than human."

"You're proud of it?" Kirk said.

"All war weapons are unpleasant," Kor said. "Otherwise they would be useless."

"Mr. Spock, are you sure you're all right?"

"Perfectly, Baroner. However, it was a remarkable sensation."

"That's enough," Kor said, with a trace of suspicion in his voice. "Vulcan, you can go. But just bear in mind that you're an enemy alien, and will be under scrutiny at all times."

"Quite, Commander," Spock said. "I understand you very well."

"Baroner, return to your council and get that proclamation posted. Until the people know what's expected of them, it's up to you to keep the people in order."

"Or I will be killed," Kirk said.

"Precisely. I see that you too understand me very well."

Once in the street, Kirk glanced about quickly. Nobody was within earshot, or seemed to be following them. He said quietly to Spock:

"That mind-sifter of theirs must not be quite the terror they think it is."

"I advise you not to underestimate it, Captain," Spock said. "I was able to resist it, partly with a little Vulcan discipline, partly by misdirection. But on the next higher setting, I am sure I would have been unable to protect myself."

"And I wouldn't last even that long. The question is now, how do we persuade these Organians to resist? To strike back, knock the Klingons off balance, maybe until the Federation fleet gets here?"

"Verbal persuasion seems to be ineffective," Spock said. "Perhaps a more direct approach?"

"My thought exactly. Didn't I see something that looked like a munitions dump near the citadel? I thought so. All right, let's try a little direct communication."

"The suggestion has merit. Would tonight do?"

"If you have no previous engagement," Kirk said. "Of course, we're short of tools."

"I am sure," Spock said, "the Klingons will provide whatever is necessary."

"It's a pleasure doing business with you, Mr. Spock."

* * *

ERRAND OF MERCY

The guards at the munitions depot were tough and highly trained, but nothing they had yet encountered on Organia had prepared them for anyone like Kirk and Spock. Two of them went quietly to sleep on duty within a few seconds of each other, were relieved of their phasers and locked in an empty storeroom, lovingly cocooned in baling wire.

Inside the dump, Kirk located a crate that seemed to contain some form of chemical explosive. He opened it. A few moments later, Spock appeared from the shadows.

"I have one of their sonic grenades," he murmured, "and I have improvised a delayed-action fuse. The combination should provide a most satisfactory display."

"Good. Fire away."

Spock made a pulling gesture, carefully tucked the grenade inside the crate, and ran, Kirk at his heels.

Three minutes later, the night lit up. Giant explosions rocked it, followed by strings of subsidiary explosions. Missiles flew in all directions. An immense cloud formed over the city, its underside flickering with the fires and detonations below it.

"You were right, Mr. Spock," Kirk said when the clamor had begun to die down. "A most satisfactory display. I only hope that the council draws the moral. Obviously they can't fight the Klingons directly, but they could make Organia useless to them."

"In the meantime," Spock said. "I earnestly suggest that we find ourselves a deep, deep hole, Captain. Somehow I cannot think that Commander Kor will believe the Organians did this."

"Nor do I. Let's vanish."

Perhaps one or both of them should have anticipated Kor's next move. Two hours later, in an empty, lightless hut near the outskirts of the village, they heard a distant, buzzing whine from the direction of the citadel.

"Phasers," Spock said.

"Yes, Klingon phasers—a lot of them, all being fired at once. Odd. It doesn't sound at all like a battle, or even a riot."

The answer came rumbling down the street outside within another hour, in the form of an armored vehicle. From a loudspeaker atop it, a recorded voice was bellowing:

"This is the military governor. In the courtyard of my headquarters, two hundred Organian hostages have just been killed. In two hours more, two hundred more will die, and two hundred more after that—until the two Federation spies are turned over to us. The blood of the hostages is on your hands. The executions will be carried on until the saboteurs are surrendered. This is the order of Kor. Attention, all subjects! This is the military governor. In the courtyard of my headquarters . . ."

Kirk and Spock were silent for a long time after the lumbering vehicle had become inaudible. At last Kirk whispered, appalled: "That tears it."

"Yes, Captain. And the Organians no more know where we are than Kor does. We must give ourselves up, and speedily."

"Wait a minute. Let me think."

"But all those lives . . ."

"I know, I know. We've got to turn ourselves in. But we've still got sidearms. Just possibly, we can force Kor to call the killings off."

"Unlikely, Captain," Spock said. "Commander Kor may be a mass murderer, but he is clearly also a soldier."

"In that case, we'll just have to do as much damage as we can and keep them busy until the fleet shows up. The Federation invested a lot of money in our training, Mr. Spock. I think they're about due for a small return."

Spock estimated the odds against making it all the way to Kor's office at "approximately" 7,824.7 to one; but surprise and the phasers—set to heavy stun force—both told in their favor. When they reached the door of Kor's office, it was open, and no alarm had sounded. They could see the commander inside, seated at his desk, hands over his face, brooding. It seemed almost possible that he did not relish butchering unarmed civilians. When he looked up and saw Spock and Kirk before him, phasers leveled, a look of interest and appreciation appeared on his face.

"Just stay seated, Commander," Kirk said. "Mr. Spock, cover the door."

"You have done well to get this far, through my guards."

"I am afraid," Spock said, "that many of them are no longer in perfect operating condition."

"The fortunes of war. What next?"

"We're here. Call off your executions."

"You have not surrendered," Kor said in a reasonable tone of voice. "Drop your weapons and I will call off the executions. Otherwise you have accomplished nothing."

"We can certainly kill you," Kirk said grimly. "You're the Klingon governor. That might put quite a crimp in your operations."

"Don't be hasty," Kor said. "You will be interested in knowing that a Federation fleet is due here within the hour. Our fleet is prepared to meet them. Shall we wait and see the results before you pull the trigger?"

"I don't plan to pull it at all unless you force me to."

"Sheer sentimentality—or at best, mercy. A useless emotion in wartime. It is not a Klingon weakness." Kor smiled. "Think of it. While we talk here, in space above us the destiny of the galaxy will be decided for the next ten thousand years. May I offer you a drink? We can toast the victory of the Klingon fleet."

"I would suggest that you are premature," Spock said. "There are many possibilities."

"Commander," Kirk added, "we once had a nation on Earth called the Spartans—the finest warriors who ever walked our planet. They had their hour of conquest—but it was their chief opponent, Athens, who survived. Sparta knew only the arts of war. Athens was known as the mother of all the arts."

"A consoling analogy, but I think a little out of date," Kor said. "True, there is always some element of chance in a major war. Today we conquer; someday we may be defeated. But I am inclined to doubt it."

He rose. The phaser in Kirk's hand did not waver by a millimeter. Kor ignored it.

"Do you know why we are so strong?" Kor said. "Because we are a unit. Each of us is part of the greater whole. Always under surveillance. Even a commander like myself, always under surveillance, Captain. As you will note."

He waved toward the ceiling, smiling. Kirk did not look up.

"No doubt there's a scanner up there. However, Mr. Spock has the door covered, and I have you. At the first disturbance, I fire."

There was something remarkably like a yelp of dismay from Spock, and then the unmistakable sound of a phaser hitting the stone floor. Kirk whirled, trying to keep Kor simultaneously in the corner of his eye. At the same instant the door, which Spock had closed, burst open again and two Klingon soldiers charged in.

Kirk pulled the trigger. The phaser did not fire. Instead, it turned red hot in his hand. Instinctively, he threw it from him.

"Shoot!" Kor shouted. "Shoot, you blockheads!"

There were at least five soldiers in the room now, but one after another they too dropped their weapons, which lay glowing quietly against the stone. After a moment of dismay, the guards charged. Kirk set himself and swung.

He could feel the flesh of his fist sear as it hit. A Klingon grabbed him from behind— then let go with a howl.

"Their *bodies* are hot!" one of the soldiers gasped. He was almost drowned out by a roar from the commander, who had tried to pick up a paper knife.

After that, for an eternal ten seconds, the enemies simply glared at each other incredulously. There was no sound but that of heavy breathing.

Then Ayelborne and Claymare came in. They were wearing their eternal smiles, which even Kirk had come to loathe.

"We are terribly sorry that we have been forced to interfere, gentlemen," Ayelborne said. "But we could not permit you to harm one another. There has been enough violence already."

"What are you talking about, you sheep?"

"We have put a stop to your brawling," Claymare said. "That is all."

"Let me get this straight," Kirk said slowly. "*You* put a stop to it? You? You mean you're going to slap our wrists?"

"Please, Captain," Claymare said. "You already know the answer. Not only your guns, but all instruments of destruction on this planet now have a potential surface temperature of three hundred and fifty degrees. Simple intent to use one renders it inoperative."

"My fleet . . ." Kor said.

"The same conditions exist upon both the opposing Star Fleets," said Ayelborne. "There will be no battle."

"Ridiculous," Kor growled.

"I suggest you contact them. You too, Captain. Your ship is now within range of your communications device."

Kirk took out his communicator. "Kirk to *Enterprise*. Come in."

"Captain! Is that you?"

"Kirk here—report, Mr. Sulu."

"I don't know what to report, sir," Sulu's voice said. "We were just closing with the Klingon fleet when every control in the ship became too hot to handle. All except the communications board. If this is some new Klingon weapon, why didn't it disable that too?"

"I don't know," Kirk said heavily. "Stand by, Mr. Sulu. Ayelborne, how did you manage this?"

"I could not explain it to you with any hope of being understood, Captain. Suffice it to say that as I stand here, I also stand upon the bridge of your ship, upon the bridge of every ship, upon the home planet of the Klingon Empire, on the home planet of your Federation. Some of my energies I share with your weapons—I and the rest of my people. We are putting a stop to this insane war."

"How dare you?" Kor shouted.

"You can't just stop our fleet," Kirk said, equally angrily. "You've got no right . . ."

"What happens in space is none of your business . . ."

"It is being stopped," Ayelborne said. "Unless both sides agree to an immediate cessation of hostilities, all your armed forces, wherever they may be, will be totally disabled."

"We have legitimate grievances against the Klingons," Kirk said. "They've invaded our territory, killed our citizens . . ."

"The disputed areas are not your territory," Kor raged. "You were trying to hem us in, cut off vital supplies, strangle our trade."

"Look here," Kirk said to the Organians, fighting himself back to some semblance of control. "We didn't ask you to intervene, but you should be the first to side with us now. The two hundred hostages who were killed . . ."

"No one has died, Captain," Claymare said calmly. "No one has died here for uncounted thousands of years. Nor do we mean that anyone shall."

"Let me ask you, Captain, what it is that you are defending," Ayelborne added, gently, as if amused. "Is it the right to wage war? To kill millions of innocent people? To destroy life on a planetary scale? Is that the 'right' you refer to?"

"Well, I . . ." Kirk said, and stopped. "Of course, nobody wants war, but sometimes you have to fight. Eventually, I suppose, we . . ."

"Yes, eventually you would make peace," Ayelborne said. "But only after millions had died. We are bringing it about now. The fact is, in the future you and the Klingons will become fast friends. You will work together in great harmony."

"Nonsense!" Kor said. Kirk realized that he had been standing shoulder to shoulder with the Klingon and moved away hastily.

"Of course, you are most discordant now," Ayelborne said. "In fact, you will have to leave. The mere presence of beings like yourselves is acutely painful to us."

"What do you mean?" Kirk said. "You don't differ significantly from us, no matter what tricks you've mastered."

"Once we did not differ significantly," Claymare said. "But that was millions of years ago. Now we have developed beyond the need for physical bodies at all. This appearance is only for your convenience. Now we shall put it off."

"Hypnosis!" Kor cried. "Captain, those weapons may never have been hot at all! Grab them!"

Ayelborne and Claymare only smiled, and then they began to change. At first it was only a glow, becoming brighter and brighter, until they looked like metal statues in a furnace. Then the human shape faded. It was as if there were two suns in the room.

Kirk shut his eyes and covered them with both arms. He could still see the light. Finally, however, it began to fade.

The Organians were gone.

"Fascinating," Spock said. "Pure thought—or pure energy? In any event, totally incorporeal. Not life as we know it at all."

"But the planet," Kirk said. "The buildings—this citadel . . ."

"Probably the planet is real enough. But the rest, conventionalizations, no doubt, just as they said. Useless to them—points of reference for us. I should guess that they are as far above us on the evolutionary scale as we are above the amoeba."

There was a long silence. Finally, Kirk turned toward Kor.

"Well, Commander," he said, "I guess that takes care of the war. Since the Organians aren't going to let us fight, we might as well get started on being friends."

"Yes," Kor said. He thrust out his hand. "Still, in a way, Captain, it's all rather saddening."

"Saddening? Because they're so much more advanced than we are? But it took millions of years. Even the gods didn't spring into being overnight."

"No, that doesn't sadden me," Kor said. "I'm only sorry that they wouldn't let us fight." He sighed. "It would have been glorious."

THE CITY ON THE EDGE OF FOREVER*

WRITER: HARLAN ELLISON

DIRECTOR: JOSEPH PEVNEY

FIRST AIRED: APRIL 6, 1967

TWO DROPS OF CORDRAZINE CAN SAVE A MAN'S LIFE. TEN DROPS OF THAT UNPREdictable drug will sometimes kill. When a defective hypospray went off in McCoy's hand, a hundred times that amount was pumped into his body in a split second.

With a frenzied, incoherent cry, the ship's surgeon fled the bridge. Within minutes the entire ship was altered. The library tapes on cordrazine said that at such dosages, paranoia was a frequent outcome—but McCoy knew the ship too well. By the time a search was organized, he had reached the Transporter Room and beamed himself down to the planet the *Enterprise* was orbiting.

The transporter had been monitoring what appeared to be a curious time disturbance on the surface of the unknown world. The settings had not been changed; whatever was down there, McCoy was now in the heart of it. Kirk would have liked to have had more information about it first, but there was no chance of that now. They had to go after McCoy. Kirk picked Spock, Scott, Uhura, Davis and a Security guard, and, of course, himself.

They materialized in the midst of extensive ancient ruins. Much of it was almost dust, but there were enough scattered sections of broken wall and piled stone to provide hiding places for McCoy.

This planet was *cold*. A burnt-out sun hung dolorously in the sky, producing a permanent, silvery twilight. It was a dead world, an ash. The ruins extended past the horizon—a city of tremendous size—but there could have been no life in it for ten thousand centuries. It takes a long time for a sun to burn out.

---

* The script for this story differed drastically in some respects from Mr. Ellison's original version, which he was kind enough to send to me. In writing this adaptation I tried to preserve what I thought were the best elements of *both* scripts; but it was tricky to manage and it is more than possible that I have wound up owing apologies all around. It was a poetic and brilliant piece to begin with; if it is a botch now, the fault is entirely mine.—JB

In the midst of the desolation, one object was polished like new, drawing Kirk's eyes instantly. It was a large, octagonal mirror—or was it a mirror? Its framed, cloudy surface was nebulous, shifting. Whatever it was, it gleamed, untarnished, agelessly new. A cube, also untarnished but half-buried in dust and rubble, sat beside it. Spock aimed his tricorder at it.

"Whatever that is," Kirk said crisply, "make it the hub of our search pattern. Fan out."

The group separated quickly—all but Spock, who was drawing closer to the shining object, instead. He said, "Unbelievable!"

"Mr. Spock?"

"Sir, this one, single object is the source of all the time displacement we detected out in space. I do not understand where it gets the power, or how it applies it. It cannot be a machine, not in any sense that we understand the term, but . . ."

Kirk eyed the object. "Then what is it?"

At once, the dead air was stirred by a heavy hum; and then a resonant, vibrantly throbbing voice spoke from the object itself.

"*A . . . question*," the voice said. "A question. Since before your sun burned hot in space, and before your race was born, I have awaited a question."

"What are you?" Kirk said.

"I . . . am the Guardian of Forever."

"Are you a machine," Kirk said, "or a being?"

"I am both, and neither. I am my own beginning, my own ending."

Spock said, "I see no reason for answers to be couched in riddles."

"I answer all questions as simply as I can."

"What is your function, then?"

"I am a time portal. Through me the great race which once lived here went to another age."

"Past or future?" Spock said.

"The past," the voice said, like a sigh. "Always and only the past. And to their past, which you cannot share. I can only offer you yours. Behold the birth of the planet you both share."

In the mirror, there was suddenly the image of a solar system forming out of a changing, cooling fireball . . . and somehow Kirk knew that it was not an image at all, but a distant view of a fact. A moment later, they were looking at a primeval, shoreless sea; and then, suddenly, a jungle of tree ferns.

"Mr. Spock," Kirk said thoughtfully, "if that is a doorway back through time, could we somehow take Bones back a day in time, then relive that accident? Stop that hypo spitting into him?"

"We would have to catch him first," Spock said. "Besides, Captain, look at the speed at which centuries are passing. To step through precisely on the day we wish would appear to be impossible."

"Guardian, can you change the speed at which yesterday passes?"

"I was made to offer the past in this manner," the Guardian said. "I cannot change."

Egypt waxed, waned, passed. Atlantis sank. Skin-clothed barbarians suddenly became Hellenes. Spock was getting it all into the tricorder.

"It's strangely compelling, isn't it?" Kirk said. "To step through there, lose oneself in another world—"

He was interrupted by a shout and a scrambling sound. He spun. McCoy, who evidently had been quite nearby, was headed straight for the time vortex at a dead run. Nobody but Kirk and Spock were anywhere near him.

Spock dropped the tricorder and intercepted, but McCoy, his eyes frighteningly wild, twisted away from him. That left no one but Kirk, who made a flying dive; but McCoy did a little dance step of broken field maneuvering and was free. Kirk landed painfully and rolled over.

"Bones!" he shouted. "No, no!"

But he was in time only to see McCoy disappear into the cloudy octagonal frame, his body popping out of sight as though it had been swallowed. Then the vortex was as blank as it had been when they first saw it.

"*Where is he?*" Kirk demanded.

"He has passed into what was," said the voice of the Guardian.

"Captain," said Uhura, a little breathlessly. She had arrived on the run. "I've lost contact with the ship. I was talking to them, and it suddenly went dead. No static; just . . . nothing."

"The communicator is all right?"

"Yes, sir. It just seems like there's nothing up there."

The Guardian said, "Your vessel, your beginning, all that you knew is gone."

Kirk felt a fearful sinking of his heart, remembering that episode when he and Spock and an archaic man named John Christopher had fought not to be noticed by the world of the 1970s. He said grayly, "McCoy has somehow changed history."

Scott had joined the party. He said, "This time we're stranded, Captain?"

Kirk did not answer, but Spock nodded. "With no past—no future."

"Captain," Uhura said. "I'm . . . I'm frightened."

Kirk looked slowly up into the black and star-littered sky of the nameless planet, empty now of the *Enterprise*, without even a sun to give it warmth and joy.

"Earth's not even out there," he said. "Not the one we knew. We are totally alone—without even a history."

"We shall have to remake it," Spock said.

"How, Mr. Spock?"

"We will have to go back in time ourselves—attempt to set right whatever it was that the doctor changed. I was recording images at the time he left. By synchronizing just out of phase with that, I believe I can approximate when to jump. Perhaps within a month before he arrived. Or a week if we are lucky."

"Guardian!" Kirk said. "If we are successful . . ."

"Then you will be returned. It will be as though none of you had gone."

"Just finding McCoy back there," Scott said, "would be a miracle."

Spock said, "There is no alternative."

"Scotty, when you think you've waited long enough—whatever 'long enough' might mean now—then . . ." Kirk shrugged. "Each of you will have to try it. Even if you fail, you'll be alive in some past world, somewhere."

"Stand ready, Captain," Spock said. "I think the time is coming around again."

They were standing in a seamy, down-at-the-heels city street, with murky glass storefronts and an occasional square four-wheeled vehicle. Over one store was a large sign proclaiming:

CCC CAMPS—SIGN UP HERE

and beside it, another store with a sign that said FREE SOUP and a smaller sign with an arrow, reading FORM A LINE. Queues of shabby men in caps and shapeless coats were moving, very slowly, into both stores.

Spock said, bemused, "Is this the heritage my mother's people brag about?"

"This," Kirk said with disgust, "is what it took us five hundred years to crawl up from. Never mind that now—somebody's going to spot us pretty quickly, and our clothes aren't exactly period costumes. Let's do something about that first."

He drew Spock down the alley in which they had first popped into this world. "There's a line of clothes back there."

"I'm afraid I will draw attention either way, Captain."

"Well, Mr. Spock," Kirk said, "if we can't disguise you, we'll have to find a way to explain you. Here, put these on." He pulled down from a line two shirts, two pairs of pants, an old jacket and a wool stocking cap.

"You might see if you can locate me a ring for my nose," Spock said. "But Captain, aside from the fact that this is theft, I do not believe we ought to change clothes out in the open. As I remember your history, old Earth was rather stuffy about such matters."

"That's right. Okay, let's march." Kirk rolled the clothing into a bundle and tucked it under his arm.

They made it back to the open street without incident. Kirk began to feel better. "You know," he said, "I rather like this century. Simpler, easier to manage. Why, I might even find I actually have a considerable talent for . . . *wump*!"

He had run squarely into the arms of a large, bulkily obvious Security-guard type.

The blue-uniformed man looked up and down, and then at the clothing bundle Kirk was shifting back and forth. At last he said pleasantly, "Well?"

"Uh, yes," Kirk said. "You are a police officer. I seem to remember . . ."

It seemed to be the wrong tack. Kirk let the sentence trail off and tried a friendly smile. The policeman smiled back, but he did not move. Behind Kirk, Spock said, "You were saying something about a considerable talent, sir?"

This was also a mistake, since it attracted the officer's attention to Spock, and especially to his pointed ears. Kirk said hurriedly, "My friend is, uh, Chinese, of course. The ears, ah, are actually easily explained. You see . . ."

The policeman remained absolutely silent. Kirk was stumped.

"Perhaps the unfortunate accident I had in childhood . . ." Spock prompted.

"In the fields, yes," Kirk said quickly. "Caught his head in a mechanical, uh, ricepicker. Fortunately . . . an Amellican missionary living nearby, who happened to have been a skilled plastic surgeon in civilian life . . ."

"Sure an' t'God that's enough, now," the policeman said. "Drop the bundle, hands up against that wall. Phwat a story."

"Yes, sir," Kirk said. As he was about to turn, he stopped and stared at the policeman's shoulder. "Uh, careless of your wife to let you go out that way."

"What?" the policeman said, raising his nightstick.

"Quite untidy, sir," Spock said, picking up the cue. "If you will allow me . . ."

He pinched the policeman's shoulder gently, and, equally gently, the policeman sagged to the pavement.

"And now, Captain . . ." he said.

"Yes," Kirk said. "As I recall, the appropriate expression is—flog it!"

Police whistles—an eerie, unfamiliar sound—were shrilling behind them as they ducked into an open cellar door. The cellar was dismal: a coal bin, an old furnace, mountains of litter, a few mildewed trunks, all looking like monsters in the dimness. They changed clothes quickly. Kirk wore the jacket; Spock pulled the stocking cap down over his elegant, dangerous ears.

Spock got out his tricorder. Nothing came out of it but an unpleasant electronic squeal, like an echo of the fading police whistles.

The two men looked at each other over the coal pile. At last Kirk said, "Obviously this is not a game. Time we faced the unpleasant facts. Status, Mr. Spock?"

"First," Spock said precisely, "I *believe* we have about a week before Dr. McCoy arrives. But as far as being certain of that . . ."

"And arrives where? New York, Boise, Honolulu, Outer Mongolia?"

"Obviously, I do not know. There is a theory . . ." Spock hesitated. Then he shrugged and plowed on. "The theory is that time can be regarded as fluid, like a river, with currents, backwash, eddies. Like the solar-system analogies of atomic structure, it is more misleading than enlightening, but there may be a certain truth to it all the same."

"Mr. Spock, if I didn't know you better, I'd suspect you were trying to educate me."

"No, sir. I mean only to suggest that the same time current which swept McCoy to a certain place or event has taken us to the same place or event . . . Unless that is the case, I believe we have no hope."

"Odds?"

"Captain, in time there are no odds; you are pitting an infinite series of instants against an utterly improbable event. And yet . . ." Spock held up the tricorder. "Locked in here is the *exact* place, the exact moment, even exact images of what McCoy did back here. If I could hook this into the ship's computer for just a few moments . . ."

"Any chance that you could build a makeshift computer?"

"In this zinc-plated, vacuum-tube culture?" Spock said. "None at all. I have no tools, no parts, no supplies . . . I do not even know the line voltage."

"I see," Kirk said slowly. "Yes, it would pose a complex problem in logic. Forgive me, Mr. Spock. I do sometimes expect too much of you."

Spock's head turned sharply, but at the same time the overhead bulb in the basement went on yellowly and there was the sound of a door opening at the head of the stairs to the ground floor. A young woman's voice called strongly, "Who's there?"

Both men came to their feet as the girl came down the stairs. Despite the obvious savagery of the period, she seemed quite unafraid. She was simply dressed and not very pretty, but her voice was instantly arresting.

"We didn't want to trespass, miss," Kirk said. "But since it was getting cold out there . . ."

She looked at him with cool appraisal and said, "A lie is a bad way to say 'hello.' Was it really that cold?"

"Well," Kirk said, "no. We were being chased by a police officer."

"Because . . . ?"

"Petty theft. These clothes. We had no money."

"I see." She looked both of them over. "It's the same story all over. I need some help. Sweeping up, washing dishes, general cleanup. Are you willing to work?"

"At what scale of payment?" Spock said. Kirk looked at him in astonishment. The first officer added, "I need radio tubes and so forth. Parts, wire . . . It is . . . a hobby."

"Fifteen cents an hour for ten hours a day," the girl said. "I'm not exactly wealthy, either. Will it do? Good. Your names?"

"I'm Jim Kirk. His name is Spock."

"I'm Edith Keeler," she said crisply, "and you can start by cleaning up down here."

She smiled pleasantly and went back up the stairs, leaving Kirk a little startled by her brisk, no-nonsense attitude and her utter fearlessness. At last he looked around, found a pair of brooms, and tossed one to Spock.

"Radio tubes and so on, eh?" he said. "Well, Mr. Spock, I approve. I think everyone should have a hobby. It keeps them off the streets."

The mission was a mixture of things which Kirk only vaguely recognized: part church, part dining room, part recreation area. It was furnished with tables and low benches, and there was a low dais at the front where workers dispensed soup and coffee. To one side, was a large tool box, fastened with an ungainly padlock with a dial on its face. Shabbily dressed men sat to either side of Kirk and Spock, waiting without enthusiasm. The nearest, a small man with thin features who looked remarkably like some sort of rodent, eyed the two of them.

"You'll be sorry," he said, with exaggerated boredom.

"Why?" Kirk said.

"You expect to eat free or something? Now you gotta listen to Miss Goodie Two-shoes."

"Good evening," Edith's voice said, on cue. She was already striding toward the dais; now she mounted it. The meagerness of the audience did not seem to discourage her. She was both casual and cheerful. "Now, as I'm sure at least someone out there has said, you've got to pay for the soup."

There was some laughter. "Not that she's a bad-lookin' broad," the rodent said, *sotto voce*. "But if she really wanted to give a guy somethin' . . ."

"Shut up," Kirk said. Then, noticing Spock's eye on him, he added, "I'd like to hear this."

"Of course," Spock said, noncommittally.

"Let's start as we always do—by getting something straight," Edith said. "Why do I work, connive, and maybe even cheat a little in order to keep feeding you? I don't know. It's something that I do. But I've got no patience with parasites. If you can't break off with booze, or you've gotten out of the habit of work, or you *like* being a bad risk, I don't want you and you're not welcome to the soup."

Kirk listened with astonishment. He did not know what he had expected, but surely not this.

"Of course," she went on, "I know that every day is a fight to survive. That's all you have time for. But I've no use for a man who uses free soup as an excuse to give up fighting. To survive at all, you need more than soup. You need to know that your life is worth living, no matter what.

"Shadow and reality, my friends. That's the secret of getting through these bad times. Know what is, and what only seems to be. Hunger is real, and so is cold. But sadness is not.

"And it is the sadness that will ruin you—that will kill you. Sadness and hate. We all go to bed a little hungry every night, but it is possible to find peace in sleep, knowing you have lived another day, and hurt no one doing it."

"Bonner the Stochastic," Spock whispered.

"He won't be born for more than two hundred years. Listen."

"It's difficult not to hate a world that treats us all like this," Edith was saying. "I know that. Difficult, but not impossible. Somebody once said that hate is only the absence of love, but that's not a message that a man can absorb on an empty stomach. But there's something else that's true: Love is only the absence of hate. Empty the hatred from your hearts and you are ready for love. If you can go to bed tonight free of hatred, you have already won a major victory.

"And that's all of my sermon for today. Eat hearty, mates."

She stepped down and left the big, gloomy room.

"Most interesting," Spock said. "An uncommon insight."

"An uncommon woman," Kirk replied quietly; but Edith Keeler, coming up behind them, evidently overheard him.

"You two are uncommon workmen, Mr. Kirk," she said. "The basement looked like it had been scrubbed and polished."

Kirk thought about his days as a midshipman and at last saw some use for holystoning; but he said only, "Then we report back for more work?"

"At seven A.M. Do you have a flop for the night?"

"A what?"

Edith studied him curiously. "You're really new at this, aren't you? A 'flop' is a place to sleep. There's a vacant room where I live, two dollars a week. If you want it, I'll guide you there when we're through with these dishes."

"Indeed we do," Kirk said. "Thank you."

Like everything else they had yet seen in this culture, the room was plain and depressing: a few pieces of scarred furniture, a sagging bed, limp and sooty curtains. Now, however, some of it was masked by the Medusahead of wires, coils and banks of old vacuum tubes which Spock was attaching to his tricorder. As Kirk came in with a small paper sack of groceries, plus another small package of hardware, Spock said abstractedly, "Captain, I must have some sponge platinum, about a kilogram. Or a block of the pure metal, perhaps ten grams, would be even better."

Kirk shook his head. "I bring assorted vegetables for you, bologna and a hard roll for me. The other bag, I assure you, contains neither platinum, gold nor diamonds; nor is it likely to in the future. It has just a few secondhand pieces of equipment, and those took the other nine-tenths of our combined earnings for three days to fill your order for them."

"Captain, you're asking me to work with equipment which is hardly better than stone knives and bearskins."

"We have no choice," Kirk said. "McCoy may be here any day now. We've no guarantee that there's some current in time pulling us all together. This has to work—with or without platinum."

"Captain," Spock said glacially, "in three weeks at this rate, perhaps a month, I might complete the first mnemonic circuits . . ."

There was a knock, and then Edith poked her head through the door.

"If you can go out now," she said, "I can get you both five hours' worth at twenty-two cents an hour. What on earth is *that*?"

"I am endeavoring, Ma'am," Spock said with dignity, "to construct a mnemonic circuit out of stone knives and bearskins."

"I don't know what that means," she said, "but if you want the work you'd better hurry." She withdrew.

"She's right. Let's go, Mr. Spock."

"Yes, Captain, in just a moment . . . It seems to me that I saw some tools for finely detailed work in the mission."

"Yes, the man who was working on the, uh, cuckoo-clock was using them. That girl has more things going on around there than a TKL computer. Clock repair project, woodworking, the tailor shop in the back . . ."

"You were quite right, Captain," Spock said. "She is a fascinating study. Well, I am ready now. I doubt that twenty-two cents an hour will advance me far, but those tools . . ."

"Just be sure you return them."

"Believe me, Captain," the Science Officer said, "my first taste of petty theft was also my last."

The auxiliary rig to the tricorder now nearly filled the room. It looked like a robot squid constructed by a small child, but it clicked, whirred and hummed purposefully. Clearly, Spock did not like the noise—he was used to machines that made as little fuss as possible—but he wasted no time trying to eliminate it. He straightened abruptly.

"Captain, I may have stumbled onto something."

Kirk sniffed. "You've got a connection burning somewhere, too."

"I am loading these lines too heavily. But this may be a focal point in time. Watch the tricorder screen. I have slowed the recording it made from the time vortex."

Kirk peered at the small tricorder screen. It showed Edith Keeler's face; then the image sharpened, and he realized that it was a newspaper photo. The paper was dated February 23, 1936—six years from "now." Over the photo was a headline: FDR CONFERS WITH SLUM AREA 'ANGEL.' The caption read, *The President and Edith Keeler today conferred for more than an hour on her proposal to . . .*

There was a mean snap of sparks, a curl of smoke and the image collapsed. "Quick!" Kirk said. "Can you get it back?"

"Even if I could, it would not help us," Spock said. "Something was wrong even before the short circuit. On the same memory trace, I saw a *1930* newspaper article."

"What of it? Either way, we know her future, Spock. Within six years from now, she's going to become important, nationally recognized . . ."

"No, sir," Spock said quietly. After a pause, he began again. "No, Captain.—What I saw was Edith Keeler's obituary. She never became famous. She will die this year in some kind of accident."

"You're mistaken! They can't both be true!"

"I'm afraid they can, Captain," Spock said. "She has two possible futures—depending upon what McCoy does."

"What . . . ? Oh, I see. McCoy has something to do with her living or dying. And in his present state . . ." The shock of the notion halted Kirk for an instant, but he forced himself to go on. "Mr. Spock, did McCoy kill her? Is *that* how all of history was changed?"

"I cannot tell, Captain. Something still worse is possible."

"What, man?"

"That he might have changed history by *preventing* her from being killed."

"Get this thing fixed! We've got to find the answer before McCoy gets here!"

"And what then, Captain?" Spock said. "Suppose we find that to set things right, Edith Keeler must die? That to restore our future, we must prevent McCoy from saving her? What then?"

"I don't know," Kirk said fiercely. "But we've got to find out. Did you get the jewelers' tools all right? That box was closed with a combination lock."

"Not a proper lock, sir. A childish device in probability . . ."

". . . and he opened it like a real pro," Edith's voice said behind them. Both men spun. She spared the jury-rigged apparatus only one glance, and then turned back to Spock. "Question: Why? I want to hear only one answer. Please make it the honest one."

Spock pointed to the rig. "You have seen this work going on before," he said. "I needed delicate tools. They would have been returned in the morning."

Edith eyed him. Perhaps his alien appearance gave her less than full confidence; or perhaps the very temper of the times was against him. She said, "Gadgetry doesn't impress me. Theft does. Out you go."

"Miss Keeler," Kirk said, "if Mr. Spock said they were important to have, and that you'd get them back in the morning, you may depend upon his word."

"I'll accept that," she said slowly, "on certain conditions. Chiefly, that Mr. Kirk answer my questions. And you needn't look so innocent, either. You know as well as I how out of place you both are here."

"Interesting," Spock said. "Where would you say we do belong, Miss Keeler?"

"You, Mr. Spock?" She nodded toward Kirk. "At his side. As if you've always been there, always will be. But where *he* belongs . . . well, I'll work it out eventually."

"I see," Spock said. "Well, I'll go on with this . . ."

"I'll go on with this—Captain," Edith Keeler said, smiling at Kirk. "Even when he doesn't say it, he does."

She led the way out. In the hall, she said, "By the way, why *does* he call you Captain? Were you in the war together?"

"We . . . served together."

"It shows. And you don't want to talk about it. Why? Is it something you think you've done wrong? Are you afraid of something? Whatever it is, let me help."

Kirk took her by the arms, and for a moment came very close to kissing her. He did not; but he did not release her, either.

" 'Let me help,' " he said. "A hundred years or so from now, I think it was, a famous novelist will write a classic using that theme. He recommends those three words even over 'I love you.' "

"Your tenses are rather mixed," she said. "A hundred years from now? And where was he? Or, where will he be from?"

"A silly question, a silly answer," Kirk said roughly. He pointed at the ceiling. "From about there. A planet circling that far left star in Orion's belt."

She looked up involuntarily; and this time, he did kiss her. He was not a little surprised to find it returned.

Spock turned as Kirk came back into the room. He asked no questions, but it was clear that he would welcome some answers.

"All she said was, 'Let me help you,' " Kirk said painfully. "She's something of a saint, Mr. Spock."

"She may be martyred," Spock said. "To history. Look here."

He switched on his apparatus. "This is how history went after McCoy changed it. I picked up the thread just after you went out. See: in the late 1930's a growing pacifist movement, called World Peaceways. Its influence on the government delayed the United States' entry into the Second World War. Apparently very few people knew that World Peaceways was German-controlled. While peace negotiations dragged on, Germany had time to complete its heavy water experiments."

"Hitler and Nazism won the war?"

"Yes. Because this lets them develop the fission bomb first. Let me rerun it, Captain. You will see that there is no mistake. And Edith Keeler was the guiding spirit of the peace movement."

"But," Kirk said, "she was *right*. Clearly, peace would have been . . ."

"She was right," Spock said, "but at the wrong moment. With the atomic bomb, and their primitive rockets to carry it, the Nazis captured the world, Captain. And after that, barbarism. The Nazi yoke was so heavy that the world tore itself apart trying to throw it off. Spaceflight never did develop."

"*No*," said Kirk, softly, in pain.

"And all that," Spock said implacably, "because McCoy came back and somehow kept her from dying as she should have, in a street accident. We have to stop him."

"Exactly how did she die? What day?"

"I can't be that precise," Spock said. "I am sorry, Captain."

"Mister Spock," Kirk said slowly, "I believe I am in love with Edith Keeler."

"I know," Spock said, very quietly indeed. "That is why I said, 'I'm sorry.'"

"And if I don't stop McCoy . . . ?"

"Then, you save her. And millions will die who did not die in what would have been our history."

"Abstract millions," Kirk said. "A different history. But Edith Keeler is here. She's real. She deserves to live."

"And so do Scott, Uhura, the others we left behind—or ahead. Sir, you are their Captain. They are waiting for you, in the ruined city on the edge of Forever. They, and the future that nurtured you. The choice is yours."

It had to be faced; but he could not face it—not yet. There would be time to decide when the crisis came. Of course.

In the meantime, there was still Edith . . . still. Spock said no more about the matter. He was with the two of them sometimes, somehow silently supportive. At others, guided perhaps by his peculiar form of semitelepathy, he vanished at just the appropriate moment.

This time, they emerged together from the mission, but separated almost at once. Spock started away from the twilight street, while Edith and Kirk crossed to the opposite sidewalk. Edith seemed even happier than usual.

"If we hurry," she said, "we can catch that Clark Gable movie at the Orpheum. I'd really love to see it, Jim."

Kirk smiled. "A what kind of movie?"

"That's funny," she said, looking up as if startled. "Dr. McCoy said almost the same . . ."

Kirk stopped dead in his tracks and whirled to face her, his heart suddenly racing.

"*McCoy?*" He took her by the shoulders, his fingers tightening until she winced. "*Leonard* McCoy? Edith, this is important."

"Why, yes. He's in the mission, in a little room upstairs. He's been very sick, almost raving, but I think he's nearly . . ."

"Spock!" Kirk shouted. "Edith—wait here for me."

He ran across the street, waving at the first officer. Spock turned back, his whole face a question; but he did not need to ask it. As the two men met in front of the mission door, McCoy came out of it.

The surgeon stopped dead in surprise, and then a grin split his face. There was a great deal of hand shaking and back thumping, with all three of them talking at once.

"Bones, where have you . . ."

"How'd you find me? And for that matter, where *are* we?"

"When Edith said 'Dr. McCoy' I . . ."

"Remarkable that you should have been that close to us . . ."

"I seem to have been sick for a long time . . ."

Kirk looked quickly back toward Edith. Her expression was mostly one of intense curiosity; but she also looked as though she felt a little left out of it all. As she saw him turn to her, she stepped out into the street.

She did not see the moving van lumbering down on her. *This was the time.* Without a moment's thought, Kirk ran toward her.

"Captain!" Spock's voice shouted. *"No!"*

Kirk froze, his body a solid mass of anguish. At the same time, McCoy's mouth opened in a wordless yell and he lunged for the curb. With a terrible flash of self-hatred, Kirk, knowing what *must* come next, threw himself in McCoy's way, blindly, almost sobbing. McCoy stumbled. Edith cried out, and then there was the screaming shriek of brakes.

Then, silence.

"Jim," McCoy said raggedly. "You deliberately stopped me . . . Did you hear me? Do you know what you just did?"

Kirk could not reply. Spock took his arm gently. "He knows," he said. "Soon you will know, too. And what *was* . . . now *is* again."

Kirk sat at his desk in the *Enterprise*, back in uniform, staring at nothing. Behind him, Spock's voice said:

"Coordinates from the bridge, Captain."

The words meant nothing. The papers before him meant nothing. It was as though he were all but dead.

"Jim," Spock said.

The deadness did not lift, but a small thread of startlement crept through it. Kirk turned slowly.

"Mr. Spock," he said. "That's the first time you've ever called me anything but Captain."

"I had to reach you," Spock said gently. "But never mind the coordinates. Jim, on my world, the nights are very long. In the morning, there is the sound of silver birds against the sky. My people know there is always time enough for everything. You'll come with me for a rest. You'll feel comfortable there."

"All the time in the world . . ."

"And filled with tomorrows."

Suddenly, the bitterness welled up. "Not for her," Kirk said. "For us, but not for her. She was negligible."

"No, Captain, she was not. Her death saved uncountable billions of people. Both the living and the yet unborn. Far from negligible."

"And I failed her," Kirk said, groping for understanding. "I didn't save her. And I loved her."

"No. You acted," Spock said. "No woman was ever loved as much, Jim. Because no other woman was almost offered the universe for love."

OPERATION—ANNIHILATE!

Writer: Steven W. Carabatsos
Director: Herschel Daugherty
First Aired: April 13, 1967

The spread of the insanity was slow, and apparently patternless, but it was also quite inexorable. The first modern instance in the record was Aldebaran Magnus Five. Then, Cygni Theta 12. Most recently, Ingraham B—recently enough so that the *Enterprise* had been able to get there within a year of the disaster.

Nothing had been learned from the mission. There were no apparent connections among the three planets—except that on each one, the colonists had gone totally, irrevocably mad, all at the same time, and had killed each other. It hadn't been warfare; the people had simply fallen upon each other in the streets, in their homes, everywhere, until there were none left.

It was Spock who had suggested that there would nevertheless be a pattern, if one assumed that the long-dead civilizations of the Orion complex had fallen to the same cause. The archeological evidence was ambiguous, and besides, the peoples of the cluster had not been human. There was no *a priori* reason why they should have been subject to the afflictions of human beings.

Nevertheless, given the assumption, the computer was able to plot a definite localization and rate of spread—like an amoeboid blotch upon the stars, thrusting out a pseudopod to another world at gradually shortening intervals. If the radioactive dating of the deaths of the Orion civilizations was correct, as it almost surely was—and if the assumption was correct, which was sheer speculation—then the madness had taken two hundred years to appear on its second victim-world, less than a century to crop up a third time, and the next outbreak was due within the next month.

"On Deneva, I would say," Spock added. "An Earth-type planet, colonized about a century ago. Pleasant climate, no hazardous life-forms. Of course, I could well be completely wrong about this, since my basic premise is completely *ad hoc*."

"Never mind the logical holes," Kirk said. "Mr. Sulu, lay in a course for Deneva. Warp factor four. Lieutenant Uhura, tell Starship Command where we're going and why. When we break into the Denevan system, raise the planet."

But there was no time for that. The first thing the sensors showed when the *Enter-*

prise emerged in that system was a Denevan ship apparently on its way toward throwing itself into the Denevan sun.

"Status!" Kirk said tensely.

"He's got a huge jump on us, Captain," Sulu said. "A one-man vessel—sub-light velocity but under heavy acceleration."

"Contact, Captain," Uhura said.

"Denevan ship, this is the *USS Enterprise*! Break your heading! You're on a collision course with your sun! Fire your retros!"

From the speaker came a faint and agonized voice. "Help me . . . please . . . help me . . ."

"We're trying to! Spock, can we reach him with a tractor beam?"

"No, sir," Spock said. "Too much solar magnetism."

"Sulu, intercept. Denevan, pull back! Fire your retros!"

"Help me, please . . . take it out . . . take it out . . . please . . ."

"Skin temperature four hundred degrees," Spock said. "Rising fast."

"He's too close, Captain," Sulu said. "He'll burn—and so will we if we keep this up."

"Keep closing."

"Skin temperature now eight hundred degrees," Spock said.

Suddenly the Denevan's voice came through again, much stronger, and much changed. It seemed almost jubilant. "I did it! It's gone! I'm free. I'm free! I won—oh great God, the sun, *the sun* . . ."

The words ended in a terrible scream.

"He's gone, Captain," Sulu reported.

"Vector!" Kirk shouted. Then, as the great ship shuddered into its emergency turn, he stared blindly at the now-silent speaker.

"What did he do that for?" he said. "Even if his instruments weren't working, we warned him."

"Obviously suicide," Spock said.

"But why? And Spock, I don't think he wanted to die. You heard him. He asked us to help him."

"Suicides are not rational," Spock said. "By definition."

"Mr. Spock, that may be perfectly good logic, but I'm afraid it doesn't satisfy me. And I hate puzzles. They don't look good on the log."

"Captain," Uhura said. "I've gotten through to Deneva itself."

"Good, let's hear it. Hello, Deneva, USS *Enterprise* calling."

"*Enterprise*, please hurry!" a strong voice cried promptly. There was a blast of static. "Help us! I don't have much time! They'll know!"

"Another madman?" Kirk said to nobody in particular. "Lieutenant, can't you clean up some of that static?"

"It's solar static, sir. Should clear gradually as we pull away."

"Hello, Deneva, *Enterprise* here. Please repeat."

"Hurry! Hurry! They'll know in a minute! We need help!"

There was more static. Kirk said: "We're on our way, Deneva. What's wrong? Please explain."

But there was no answer, only still more static. Uhura turned in her chair. "Contact broken, Captain. I'm trying to reestablish, but I think they've switched out."

"All right, Sulu. Course for Deneva—on the double."

The landing party—Kirk, Spock, McCoy, two security guards, and Yeoman Zahara—materialized in an empty city street. There were supposed to be more than a million colonists and their descendants on this planet, nearly a hundred thousand in this city alone; yet the place looked deserted.

"Where is everybody?" Kirk said.

Spock scanned in a circle with his tricorder. "They are here. But they are all indoors. Apparently just sitting there. There is a signal center in that building across the street. It is inoperative, but the power is up."

"All right, let's . . ."

"Party approaching," Spock interrupted. "Four people—make it five. Coming fast."

He had hardly spoken when five men came around the corner at top speed. They seemed to be ordinary civilians, but Kirk had the instant impression that their faces were warped with agony. All carried clubs. The instant they saw the group from the *Enterprise*, they burst into a bestial shrieking. It was impossible to tell which of them was screaming what.

"Run! Get away! We don't want to hurt you! Go back! Look out!"

"Fire to stun!" Kirk shouted. The Denevans charged, swinging their clubs.

"Go away! Please! They'll get you! No! Get away from here! We'll have to kill you . . ."

Kirk fired, followed by the others. The charging Denevans fell in a clatter of clubs. Kirk approached them cautiously. Despite the fact that they had just taken the heavy stun force of a phaser blast at close range, they seemed to be twitching slightly.

"Could you make out all that shouting, Mr. Spock?"

"Indeed. They seemed greatly concerned for our safety—so concerned that they wanted to brain us. This may not be *the* insanity, but . . ."

"But it'll do for now," Kirk said. "Bones, check them over."

McCoy checked the unconscious bodies quickly, then rose, shaking his head puzzledly. "Something decidedly odd," he said. "These people should be pretty close to being vegetables for the next few hours. But I'm getting high readings, as though their nervous systems were being violently stimulated even while they're . . ."

He was interrupted by a woman's scream. Kirk whirled. "Fan out!" he said. "That came from that signal center. Come on!"

The scream came again. Inside the building there was a dark lobby of some sort, and a closed door, which turned out to be locked. Kirk lunged against it.

"Open up!" he shouted. "We're from the *Enterprise*."

"They're here!" the woman screamed. "They're here! Keep them away!" Over her voice there was a heavy buzzing sound, which seemed to be rising in pitch.

Kirk and the two guards hit the door together. It burst inward. Here was the signal center, all right, but it looked shoddy, unused. An elderly man lay unconscious on the floor; across the room, a girl was desperately holding a panel of some sort over a ventilation outlet, fighting with all her strength. As the party broke in she staggered backward, dropping the panel, covering her face with her hands and sobbing wildly.

Kirk pointed to the old man while he took the girl in his arms. "It's all right. You're safe."

She screamed again and began to struggle.

"Bones, a hypo! I can't hold her."

McCoy already had his sprayjet out, and a moment later the girl too had collapsed. "The man's alive," he reported. "Some sort of seizure, or maybe just exhaustion. I'd better get them both up to the ship."

"Right. Mr. Spock, you heard her. She called out that *they* were here. Your guess?"

"Notice, Captain," Spock said. "Rags stuffed under the door. Pieces of board jammed across the windows. As if they were in a state of siege."

"But by what? There are no harmful life-forms on this planet. And our sensors didn't pick up anything that didn't belong here."

"I am baffled, Captain."

"Bones, beam up with those two people and bring them around. I'm going to have to ask some questions. Mr. Spock, we'll go outside and resume looking around. Zahara, are you recording all of this?"

"Of course, Captain."

As they emerged from the communications center, Kirk saw one of the security men standing near a sheltered, shadowy alleyway. He moved toward the party as it appeared.

"Anything, Abrams?"

"Yes, sir, but don't ask me what. Something moving back in there. Making a buzzing sound."

Kirk looked around, and then up. All the windows above him seemed to be empty, but in one there was the face of a man. His expression was a terrible combination of agony, fear and desperate hope.

"You!" Kirk shouted at him. "I want to talk to you!"

The face contorted and vanished. Kirk grunted with annoyance. "All right, Spock, Abrams, let's go see what's back in there."

Phasers ready, they moved cautiously into the darkened alley. Almost at once the buzzing noise got louder, and something about the size of a football flew through the air over their heads. Then another.

"Phasers on kill!" Kirk shouted. But for a moment there were no more. Then suddenly Spock pointed. Another such object clung to a wall. Kirk fired.

The beam hit the thing squarely. But it refused to vanish. It simply clung to the wall for a long moment, even under the full force of the beam, and finally slipped off and fell to the earth.

They closed in warily, but there seemed to be no more of the creatures back here. Spock took tricorder readings on the downed object, which seemed to be no more than a gelatinous mass, amorphous, colorless, as though somebody had dumped a jellyfish out of a bucket. Kirk stared at it incredulously.

"What is that?"

"It isn't anything," Spock said promptly. "Not only should it have been destroyed by the phaser blast, but it does not register on the tricorder."

"It's real enough all the same," Kirk said. "And it acted alive. Can we take it along, Spock?"

"I advise against it. We have no proper equipment, and it may well be toxic, corrosive—there are a dozen possibilities."

"Whatever they are, they seem to like these shadows," Kirk said. "Let's get out back into the light. We know where we can find them if we want them, anyhow."

As they retreated, the buzzing noise began again. The next instant, one of the objects shot past Kirk and hit Spock squarely in the back, knocking him off his feet. The thing clung to him. His hands tore uselessly at his back. Then, somehow, it was gone, and Spock was lying face down in the alley.

Kirk knelt beside him. "Spock! Are you all right? The thing's gone. Can you stand?"

Spock's hands were still clutching his back. As Kirk spoke, he rolled over, his entire face working with the effort to control himself. He got slowly to his knees. Then his mouth opened, and pitching forward, he began to scream.

Spock was in sick bay under heavy sedation; thus far, McCoy had been unable to think of anything else to do for him. In the interim, however, he had managed to revive the elderly man and the girl the landing party had found in the signal room on Deneva. The girl's name was Aurelan, the man's Menen. They did their best to answer Kirk's questions, but he found their answers difficult to comprehend.

"I know it must sound insane, Captain," Aurelan said, "but it's quite true."

Kirk shot a look at Zahara, who was recording. "You mean these things, whatever they are, have taken over the entire planet?"

"Except for ourselves," Menen said.

"There are over a million inhabitants of Deneva."

"There are millions of *them*," Menen said.

"When did they get to Deneva? How?"

"About four months ago," Menen said with some difficulty, "in a spaceship. We don't know any more than that. They didn't give us the time."

"It's a nightmare, Captain," Aurelan said. "Worse than a nightmare."

"The things don't communicate with you?"

"Oh, they communicate all right," Aurelan said bitterly. "Through pain. Once they attack you, something happens inside. We're not doctors, we don't know the details. But life is agony from then on."

Menen added, "My son told me—before he died—that they need bodies the way we need tools. Arms and legs—human beings. And once they take over, they can't be resisted. The people who tried to kill you in the street didn't want to hurt you. They wanted your help. But the things ordered them to attack you, and they had no choice."

"But why didn't they take you two over too?"

"We think they spared us so that we could maintain normal contacts with other planets and ships. They want ships, Captain. They need them. They're forcing our people to build ships right now."

"My brother, Noban . . ." Aurelan began.

"He's the man who flew his ship into the sun?"

Aurelan nodded sadly. "The creatures had him. He almost went mad from the pain. But he told us that Deneva is just a way-station for them. They mean to spread out. You see . . ." She paused and swallowed. "Their hosts become useless after a while. They go mad. And then the things need new hosts. More people. Planet after planet. They come, and they leave madness, and they go to the next . . ."

"In the name of God, Captain," Menen said, "you've got to do something!"

"I'll do what I can," Kirk said. "What about my first officer, Mr. Spock?"

"Is he important to your ship?" Aurelan said.

"Extremely," Kirk said. "And to me personally. He's one of my closest friends."

"In that case," Menen said, "kill him."

"What!"

"Kill him. Now. Quickly. Because only endless agony lies ahead for him, agony that will end in madness. If you are his friend, be merciful."

"Security calling Captain Kirk," said the bridge speaker.

"Kirk here."

"Captain, this is Ames. Mr. Spock has attacked his nurse and fled. He seems deranged."

"All decks security alert. He may be dangerous. Aurelan, Menen, you'd better get to your quarters and stay there."

They went quietly. Only seconds later, it seemed, the elevator door opened again and Spock charged out.

"Get away from the controls!" he screamed. "I have to take her down!"

Before anyone could move, he had reached the helm and had knocked Sulu down and away with one sweeping blow. The navigator and Scott leapt on him, but Spock was a powerful man; he sent them reeling.

"Security to the bridge!" Uhura was calling into her mike. "Alert! General alert to the bridge!"

Kirk joined in the melee, but they were all handicapped by the desire not to hurt Spock; the first officer had no such compunctions. They only barely managed to keep him away from the controls.

Then three security men appeared, and in a few moments Spock was held fast. "I have to take the ship down!" he panted. "I don't want to! Help me! Help me!"

Somehow McCoy was on the scene now, and elbowing his way through the crowd, he gave the first officer a shot. Spock collapsed at once.

"Get him back to sick bay," Kirk said, "and this time, strap him down."

The security men carried him out, with Kirk and McCoy following. It was a grim procession.

"Well, Menen warned me," Kirk said. "He told me that if Spock meant anything to me, I should kill him."

"Now *there's* a tomfool notion."

"Don't worry, Bones, the idea doesn't appeal to me either. But we've got to do something to help him."

"Well, I've at least gotten a start on it," McCoy said. "Come on in and I'll show you."

In McCoy's office, the surgeon showed Kirk a jar full of transparent liquid. In the fluid, a long, almost-transparent tendril drifted and twisted.

"It's a piece of living tissue of some sort," McCoy said. "Call it a tentacle. I took it out of Spock's spinal column an hour ago."

"Is that what causes the pain?"

McCoy nodded. "His entire nervous system has been infiltrated by this stuff. And far too thoroughly for conventional surgery to remove. I don't know how to get it out."

"Then if the old man is right," Kirk said, "this tissue is responsive to directives sent out by the other creatures."

"Or is it *the* creature?"

"Explain."

"By itself," McCoy said, "this stuff is just undifferentiated tissue. No organs. And I'd guess the same for the individual creatures we saw on the surface. They didn't look like things, but *parts* of things. Put them all together and—well, I'm sure they wouldn't spell 'Mother.' But that's about all I'm sure of."

"Do you know why it resists a phaser blast?"

"It's mostly energy itself—nonprotoplasmic. That's why it can fly too. A phaser blast affects it about like a stream from a fire hose would us: knocks it down, stuns it, but that's all. Now let's go look at Spock and I'll show you something else."

Spock was lying strapped down and under sedation, under the diagnostic panel.

"Watch the left indicator," McCoy said. "It's a dolorimeter—registers the level of pain. Right now it's present at the maximum tolerance level. But if I open a channel to Spock . . ."

He moved a knob. At once, the indicator rose nearly to the top of the scale and froze there.

"That's what he's going through," McCoy said softly. "It's as though he were being consumed by fire, from the inside out. No wonder the poor devils go mad."

"And no wonder," Kirk said, "that they come to think killing each other is an act of mercy."

As he spoke, the indicator began to drop, very slowly. McCoy stared at it. "What the . . ."

Spock opened his eyes. "Hello, Doctor," he said weakly. "Hello, Captain."

"Mr. Spock! How do you feel?"

"Unwell. But these restraints will no longer be necessary. Nor will your sedations, Doctor. I will be able to return to duty."

"That's impossible," McCoy said.

"Spock, we've just seen what that pain can do to you," Kirk added.

"I regret my behavior," Spock said. "The pain greatly slowed my thinking. I did not even remember that we cannot set the ship down, on any planet. But I can control the pain now."

"How?" McCoy demanded.

"I am a Vulcan; we are trained to use our minds. Pain is only another kind of sensory input, which a trained mind ought to be able to handle."

"You're only half Vulcan," Kirk said. "What about the human half?"

"It is an inconvenience, but it is manageable. The creature—all of its thousands of parts—is pressing upon me even now. It wants this ship. But I can resist. It is not especially pleasant, but I assure you there will be no danger if you release me."

"The strongest mind in the world has to relax after a while," McCoy said. "If I put you on mild sedation . . ."

"No drugs, Doctor. My mind must be clear."

"Mr. Spock, I need you," Kirk said. "But I can't take any chances. You stay here. Sweat it out for a while. If you can maintain control, then come back. Until then, do what the doctor says. That's an order."

Spock nodded. Then his face twitched and the dolorimeter shot up again. Closing his eyes, Spock whispered: "The mind rules. There is no pain. There . . . is . . . no . . . pain . . ."

On the bridge, Uhura had a call waiting from Star Fleet.

"*Enterprise* standing by, Commodore Anhalt," Kirk said.

"We've studied your reports of the situation on Deneva, Captain," Anhalt said. "We agree that the creatures, whatever they are, pose a clear and immediate threat to the area. It is our conclusion that, left alone, they would spread rapidly throughout that quadrant and perhaps farther. Can you tell us anything of the nature of the creatures?"

"Not yet. We're preparing to capture a specimen for analysis."

"Fine. But you are not on a specimen-collecting expedition, Captain. Regardless of the nature of the creatures, they must be destroyed—whatever the cost."

"Commodore," Kirk said, "there are more than a million innocent people on that planet. I may not be able to destroy the creatures without . . ."

"We are aware of that, Captain," Anhalt said evenly. "Your orders stand. We will expect your progress reports. Star Fleet out."

The image faded. Kirk turned away from the screen to discover his first officer standing behind him.

"Spock, I gave you a direct order to stay in bed!"

"Until I was satisfied that I could maintain control," Spock said. "I am satisfied. So is Dr. McCoy."

"You're certain?"

"Absolutely."

"All right, then put your mind to work on this: How do I capture one of those creatures? They don't respond to the transporter any better than they do to phaser fire—and I'm not about to beam a man down there. I'd just beam back another casualty."

"Not necessarily," Spock said. "If the man's nervous system were already inhabited, there would be little or nothing further the creatures could do to him."

Kirk stared at him. "I see what you're getting at," he said, "and I don't like it."

"Captain, in the same circumstances, I do not think you would hesitate for a moment. I simply claim the right to do as you would do, if our positions were reversed. I am the logical man for the job."

After a long silence, Kirk said: "It is so ordered. Be careful, and stay in constant touch with us."

"Of course, Captain."

* * *

Spock came back with two specimens—one of the creatures and a raving man. "I thought we would need somebody else who was already infected too," he said. "After all, the main problem is how to get the creature out of the body."

Aurelan reacted with shock and despair. "That is Kartan," she said. "We were to be married, before the creatures came."

She would not stay to watch McCoy testing, and Kirk could hardly blame her.

"It's the same picture, only more advanced," McCoy said. "In effect, he hardly has a nervous system of his own any more. The tissue has taken it over."

"It seems that at least we did find out what happened on Ingraham B and the other planets," Kirk said.

"No doubt about it. But what do we *do*?"

Spock came in, carrying the transparent case with the creature in it.

"Here it is," he said. "At first glance, a unicellular creature of sorts—but actually part of a creature. Its own level of activity is so low it doesn't even affect instruments. Its tremendous power is the result of participation in the whole. What it resembles more than anything else is a huge individual brain cell."

"How do you know?" McCoy said.

"You forget, Doctor, the creature has infiltrated my own system. I am in constant contact with it. I find it most annoying."

"I don't doubt that," Kirk said. "But how do we destroy it?"

"I think we have a clue. You will recall Noban, the Denevan who flew into his sun. Just before his death, he cried out that he was free—that he had won. Apparently the proximity to the sun destroyed the creature controlling him."

"We already know they don't like light," Kirk said slowly. "But how do we expose them to light of that intensity? And what good would it do anyhow? A million of the creatures are inside human bodies."

"One was inside Noban's," Spock pointed out. "*Something* drove it out. But we need take no chances. The *Enterprise* has the capacity to turn Deneva into a miniature sun—a ball of nuclear energy. They would not survive that."

"Surely not," Kirk said thoughtfully.

"Now hold on," McCoy said. "Are you seriously considering this? Destroying a million people whose only crime was being victimized by these filthy things?"

"Our mission," Spock said somberly, "is to destroy the aliens—at whatever cost."

"Not at that cost! Jim, this idea is insane."

"These creatures are trying to spread out in the galaxy," Kirk said. "And the Denevans are already building ships for them. Aside from the fact that I have been given an order, we do not have much time."

"I have an alternative," Spock said.

"Great God, man," McCoy said, "spit it out!"

"Clearly any radiation intense enough to destroy the creatures would also destroy the people. But I think the hint we took from the fact that the creatures like shadows is a false lead. Light is a medium to them, like water is to a fish; they may simply prefer certain frequencies or levels, as some fish prefer saltwater to fresh. But consider this: If you have a free energy flow that for some reason you cannot conduct through a wire, a wave-guide or anything else of that sort, how do you direct it? Or, if you wish, disrupt it? The agency must be something that is both common and intense near a sun, yet completely harmless to human beings; remember, Noban's parasite was destroyed *before* he was."

"I'm no physicist," McCoy said. "Is there such an agency, or are we just playing games?"

"Certainly there is," Kirk exclaimed. "Magnetism!"

"That is what I had in mind," Spock said. "Of course, we cannot generate a magnetic field as intense as a sun's, but it may not be necessary." He paused as Aurelan and Menen came in, explained his idea again quickly, and went on: "We have your son to thank for this, Menen. But what particularly interests me is that his parasite was not forced out gradually by the gradually increasing intensity of the general magnetic field. Instead, insofar as we can tell, it was wrenched out quite suddenly. This leads me to suspect that motion is the key—that what happened was that his ship passed through the rapidly whirling magnetic field of a sunspot. *That* is an effect we can duplicate. If I am right, it will pull the creature out like pulling a tooth."

"But probably a lot more painful," McCoy said. "Maybe even fatally so."

"It did not kill Menen's son. The heat did that. In any event, we have no course available but to try. Since I am already infected, the logical thing to do is to try it on me."

"And risk killing you?" Kirk said. "Things are bad enough already."

"Captain, the strain of maintaining my mental barriers is considerable. I do not know how long I can continue. When my guards go down—as inevitably they must—I will go insane. I would rather die by the hand of a friend. Furthermore, if I am insane, I am in a position to do the maximum possible amount of damage to the ship."

"Isn't there another question?" Aurelan said. "Mr. Spock is only half human. Even if the experiment is successful, it won't be conclusive."

"I have to work with what I have," McCoy said.

"You have Kartan," Aurelan said. "My fiancé."

They all looked at her in silence. When McCoy spoke, his voice was very gentle. "The risk," he said, "is extremely great."

"If you don't find a cure, he will die a raging maniac," she replied calmly. "Do you think I want that?"

McCoy glanced at Kirk, who nodded without hesitation.

"All right," McCoy said. "Thank you. I'll do my best."

* * *

It worked nicely. The creature emerged from all sides of Kartan's body at once, as though he were being enclosed in a balloon, and then was torn to shreds under the whirling electromagnets. He was still under sedation, but the dolorimeter promptly declined to normal level, and his face was peaceful for the first time since they had seen him.

"Congratulations, Mr. Spock," Kirk said. "And now I want you on that table, as fast as we can get Kartan moved out."

"No, sir."

"Why not? I should think you'd be eager to be rid of it! You volunteered before."

"True, Captain, but since then I have thought of something else. Do you realize that this leaves us just as badly off as we were before?"

Kirk frowned. Given the question, there was no need to explain it. There was absolutely no possibility of enveloping the whole of Deneva in such a field; Deneva's own natural field would fight it, and the *Enterprise* lacked the power to win such an invisible struggle. Nor was there anything like time to treat a million people individually.

McCoy obviously had also chased the chain of reasoning to its conclusion. "We are going to have to destroy the planet anyhow," he said harshly.

Aurelan straightened beside the sleeping Kartan. "Captain," she said. "They're my people. I grew up with them. I loved them. I've lost my brother. I don't want to lose anyone else. But I beg you, Captain, do what has to be done. Give the order."

"A million people . . ." Kirk said.

"Don't you understand?" Aurelan cried out. "There's no hope for them! Their brains are on fire! They want to die!"

Kirk stood as if frozen to the floor. "Brains on fire," he whispered. "Brains on fire. That's it. That's the answer!"

"Yes, Captain," Mr. Spock said. "That is my conclusion also."

"What is?" McCoy said. "You gentlemen have lost me."

"It's like this," Kirk said rapidly. "Spock has already likened this—this composite organism to a gigantic brain. All the evidence we have points in the same direction. The individual cells are mindless, almost lifeless. It's possible, indeed it seems likely, that there is a central concentration of them somewhere. If we could kill that off . . ."

"I don't see that that follows at all," McCoy said. "The aggregate of the scattered cells could well be all there is to the brain, since we know the cells can communicate with each other. Why is it likely that there should be a concentration, too?"

"Because of the behavior of the creatures," Spock said. "They multiply uncontrollably until they overflow a planet. Not leave it—overflow it. The original central concentration is left behind. *Ergo*, it must still be there—wherever it is."

"And all we know about that is that it's somewhere in the Orion sector," Kirk said. "Mr. Spock, could the computer extrapolate the spread of these creatures backward, so to speak, and at least narrow down the possibilities to an area we'd have some hope of searching in time?"

"Of course," Spock said. "But you have something better, Captain."

"What's that?"

"You have me. That is why I do not want the treatment yet. I am infested; I am aware of the creature—not just the part of it that inhabits me, but the entire creature. As we approach the central concentration, I will know."

"Are you sure?"

For answer, Spock pointed. "It lies that way," he said. "I know that already, even though it must be fifty parsecs away."

"Posts!" Kirk shouted.

As they approached the critical Orion sector, it gradually became evident that not only was Spock aware of the nucleus of the creature—it was aware of him, and in some way realized that it must not allow this particular cell of itself to come closer. The pressure on Spock mounted unbearably. Though he still performed his duties, the sweat ran constantly down his face, which occasionally was twisted by a grimace that seemed to have no connection with anything he was doing or saying.

"Better let us extract that thing now," Kirk said. "We're zeroed in on the planet. There's no sense in your suffering any further."

"Sir, I would prefer to bear it just a little while longer. The final test of the theory is what happens to me—or does not happen—when that nucleus is destroyed. If the pain continues, we will know that we were wrong."

"Without prejudice to your own wishes or your will power, Mr. Spock, are you certain that there's no danger of your running amok again?"

"The danger exists," Spock said levelly. "However, I am fighting it. And I do not see how we can forfeit this test."

"I hate to say so," McCoy said, "but I think he's right, Jim."

"Very well," Kirk said. He looked at the main viewing screen, which was now showing the image of the target planet. It was utterly barren, though occasional faint geometrical patterns showed where there might once have been cities—before the creatures had come with their burden of agony and wiped them out. "It will be a pleasure to get rid of that monster. Arms Control, are those missiles primed?"

"Yes, sir," said a loudspeaker. "Two fully-armed planet-wreckers, programmed and ready to go."

"Very well. Fire one."

A streak of light shot away from the *Enterprise*. For many long minutes nothing seemed to happen. Then the planet on the screen burst into a white blare of atomic fire. The screen backed hastily down the intensity spectrum.

At the same moment, Spock screamed. Two security men promptly grabbed him; Bones had been alert for just such an outcome.

"Stop! Stop!" Spock screamed. "My world—*my life*—"

"Fire two," Kirk said grimly. The planet was already breaking up, but he was taking no chances. Another colossal fusion explosion spread over the screen. When it had died away, there was nothing left to be seen but an enormous, expanding cloud of gas.

"So we have created a new Orion nebula," Kirk said. He turned to Spock. The first officer was standing quietly in the grip of the security man, while Bones hovered nearby with a hypo.

"Mr. Spock?"

Spock's eyes were glazed, and for a moment he seemed to have no mind at all. His face was blank, his mouth working. Then, gradually, life and sanity seemed to flow back into him.

"I am . . . recovering," he said formally. "The pain was . . . incredible . . . like nothing I had experienced before. For an instant I *was* that creature. I felt its death. But now . . . nothing."

"Now," McCoy said firmly, "we take you below and extract that thing from you. I will tolerate no further arguments on that score."

"No further arguments are necessary," Spock said. "Its purpose is served."

"Any word from Deneva, Lieutenant?"

"Rapidly getting back to normal, Captain," Uhura reported. "Menen says that the remaining creatures just wander about helplessly and seem to have almost no vitality left. To kill one, you need scarcely do more than stick it with a pin."

"Very good," Kirk said. "Mr. Spock, this may sound grandiose, but it's the truth. I think you have singlehandedly just saved the galaxy."

"No, sir, I think not."

"What could have stopped them if we hadn't?"

"Their own nature, Captain."

"Explain."

"A truly successful parasite," Spock said, "is commensal, living in amity with its host, or even giving it positive advantages—as, for instance, the protozoans who live in the digestive system of your termites and digest for them the wood that they eat. A parasite that regularly and inevitably kills its hosts cannot survive long, in the evolutionary sense, unless it multiplies with tremendous rapidity—much more rapidly than these creatures did. It is not pro-survival."

"In the evolutionary sense, maybe," Kirk said. "But evolution takes a long, long time. In the interim, you have at least saved millions of people from pain, madness and death."

"Believe me, Captain," Spock said, "I find that quite sufficient."

AMOK TIME*

WRITER: THEODORE STURGEON
DIRECTOR: JOSEPH PEVNEY
FIRST AIRED: SEPTEMBER 15, 1967

It was actually Nurse Christine Chapel who first noticed that there seemed to be something wrong with Spock. Nothing serious—only that he wasn't eating. McCoy, observing him more closely, saw no further sign but what seemed to be a gradual increase in tension, something that might almost have been called "nervousness" if Spock hadn't been half Vulcan. This, McCoy thought, might have been purely a subjective impression on his own part.

It wasn't. On the third day of the apparent fast, Nurse Chapel tried to tempt the First Officer with a vile green concoction called plomik soup, regarded as a delicacy on Vulcan. Spock threw the bowl at her, soup and all.

This was enough to move McCoy to suggest to Spock, a day after the soup incident and apparently without any connection to it, that it was time for his routine checkup.

The logical, unemotional First Officer's verbatim reply to this was, "You will cease to pry into my personal affairs, Doctor, or I shall certainly break your neck."

Regardless of his state of mind—whatever it was—Spock certainly knew that this would not go unreported. He forestalled inquiry by requesting a leave of absence on his home planet. On the present course of the *Enterprise*, he pointed out, a diversion to Vulcan would cost a loss of only 2.8 light-days.

Unfortunately, Kirk had to refuse him. In all the years that Kirk had known him, Spock had never asked for a leave of any sort, and in fact had refused offers; he had leave enough accumulated for six men. But the *Enterprise* was bound for the inauguration ceremonies of the new president of Altair Six—not, apparently, a vital assignment, but the orders left no leeway for side trips, all the same. Kirk suggested that shore leave facilities on Altair Six were excellent; Spock declined the offer stiffly, and that was that.

At least, that should have been that. Not six hours later, while the First Officer was off duty, Kirk discovered that the ship's course had been altered for Vulcan anyhow, on Spock's orders. Leaving the bridge in Scott's charge, Kirk went directly down to Spock's quarters.

---

* Hugo Award nominee

He had seldom visited them before, but he resisted the impulse to look around. He got only the vague impression of a room simple, sparse and vaguely Oriental in decoration and mood, the quarters of a warrior in the field. Spock was seated at a desk studying a small reading screen. Kirk had the briefest of impressions that the screen showed the head of a very young girl, no more than a child, but Spock snapped it off too quickly for him to be sure.

"Well, Mr. Spock?"

"Well, Captain?"

"I want an explanation. Why did you change our course?"

"Sir?"

"You changed our course for Vulcan. I want to know why."

Spock frowned slightly. "I changed our course?"

"You deny it?"

"No," Spock said. "By no means, Captain. It is—quite possible."

"Then why did you do it?"

"Captain," Spock said, "I accept, on your word, that I did it. But I do not know why. Nor do I remember doing it." He looked straight at Kirk, his spine stiffening. "And therefore I request that you put me in confinement—securely—where I can neither see nor be seen by anyone."

"But why?"

"Captain, lock me away. I do not wish to be seen. I cannot . . . No Vulcan could explain further."

"Spock, I'm trying to help you . . ."

"Ask me no further questions!" Spock almost shouted. "I will not answer!"

"All right," Kirk said evenly. "I'll accede to your request. But first, I order you to report to Sickbay, Mr. Spock. McCoy's waiting."

"I don't know how Spock exists with his kind of internal setup," McCoy said. "His normal pulse is in the 240 beats-per-minute range, his blood pressure almost nonexistent by our standards—not that I consider that green stuff of his to be entirely comparable to blood. But that's only Spock under normal conditions, Jim. As matters stand now, if we don't get him to Vulcan within eight days—or maybe only seven—he'll die."

"*Die?* But why? What's the matter with him?"

"I don't know," McCoy said. "All I can tell you is that there's a growing imbalance of bodily functions. As if in your or my bodies, huge amounts of adrenalin were constantly being secreted into our bloodstreams. Spock won't say why. But unless it's stopped somehow, the physical and emotional pressures will kill him."

"You're convinced he knows what it is?"

"Yes. But he won't tell me."

"He's in the solitary confinement he asked for now?"

"Yes, Jim. And—I wouldn't approach him, if I were you. It's a shocking thing to have to say, but—well, I consider him irrational."

"I'll see him anyhow. What else can I do? There's *got* to be an answer."

"I suppose so," McCoy said. "But Jim—watch out."

"Mr. Spock," Kirk said, as gently as possible. "McCoy gave me his evaluation of your condition."

Spock remained silent, his face averted.

"Spock, he says you'll die unless something is done. *What?* Is it something only your planet can do for you?"

No answer.

"Mr. Spock. You have been called the best First Officer in the Fleet. That is an enormous asset to me. If I have to lose that First Officer, I want to know why."

Spock stirred, and then began to speak in an almost inaudible voice. "It is a thing that no . . . outworlder may know—except for the very few that have been involved. A Vulcan understands—but even we do not speak of it among ourselves. It is a deeply personal thing. Captain, cannot you let it rest at that?"

"I cannot," Kirk said. "My ship, my command, my duty are all at stake. I require you to explain. If I must, I'll order you to explain."

"Captain—some things transcend even the discipline of the service."

"That may sometimes be true. But nothing transcends the health, safety and well-being of the members of my crew. Would it help to promise you that I'd consider anything you say to me to be totally confidential?"

Spock hesitated a long moment. At last he said, "It has to do with—with . . ."

The last word was quite inaudible. Kirk said, "With what?"

"Biology."

"What kind of biology?"

"Vulcan biology."

"You mean, the biology *of* Vulcans? Biology, as in reproduction? Oh, blazes! That's nothing to be embarrassed about. It even happens to birds and bees."

Spock stared at the floor. "The birds and bees are not Vulcans. If they were—if any creature were as proudly logical as we—and had their logic ripped from them—as this time does to us . . ."

Kirk waited.

"How do Vulcans find their mates?" Spock said. "Haven't you wondered, Captain? How are we selected, one for the other? I'm sure you've heard many jokes on the subject. We are so aloof, so proud, so without feeling, that we invite such jokes."

"Yes, I've heard them," Kirk said. "But jokes aside, I guess the rest of us assume, well, that it's done, uh, quite logically. Eugenically, perhaps."

"It—is not. We shield it with ritual and custom, as shrouded in antiquity as our seven moons. You humans have no conception—it strips our minds from us. It brings a—a madness which rips away our veneer of civilization." Spock slumped, his face pinched with agony. "It is the *pon farr*—the time of mating."

"But you're not a salmon or an eel, man! You're . . ."

"Half human," Spock finished, painfully. "I had hoped that that would spare me this. But my Vulcan blood is too strong. It drives me home, to take a wife in Vulcan fashion. Or else, as Dr. McCoy says, to die."

"Dear God," Kirk said. The lumps in his own belly and throat were now almost too great for him to bear. He could only vaguely imagine what it had cost Spock to tell him this much.

Was there any way out? There were three starships expected to attend the inauguration ceremony: the *Enterprise*, the *Excalibur* and the *Endeavour*. Neither of the others was within range to get Spock to Vulcan in time.

It was not that vital to have three starships at the ceremony, but the orders specified it. If Kirk disobeyed, Starship Command would . . .

Never mind. Kirk owed his life to Spock, not just once, but half a dozen times. That was worth a career. Kirk stepped to the intercom.

"Mr. Chekov, Kirk here. Maintain course for Vulcan. Warp Eight."

"Uh—yes, sir," Chekov's startled voice said.

"Kirk out."

"Captain," Spock said in a low voice.

"Yes, Mr. Spock."

"Something happens to us at this time, almost—an insanity—an insanity you—no doubt would find distasteful."

"Should I? You've been patient with my kinds of madness."

"Then—will you beam down with me to the surface of Vulcan, and stand with me? There is a brief ceremony. By tradition, the male is attended by his closest friends."

"Thank you, Mr. Spock."

"Also—I believe Doctor McCoy has also guessed the reason behind all this, and has kept his own counsel, and my secret. I would like him to accompany us."

"I believe," Kirk said slowly, "that he will be honored."

The three beamed down to a fairly level arena area. Rocks around its edges gave it a half-natural, half-artificial aspect, as if the wind and rain had carved something like a Stonehenge, or reduced a Stonehenge to something like this. Inside it, there was an open temple—two high arches of stone, an open fire pit, several huge, jade-like wind chimes stirring and chiming in the hot breeze. The rest of the landscape was drifting sand, stretching away to a distant saw-toothed line of mountains jutting up at the edge of the far horizon.

"The land of my family," Spock said. "Our place for mating. It has been held by us for more than two thousand Earth years!" He choked, and gestured toward the temple. "This—is *Koon-ut-Kal-if-fee*. It means, 'The place of marriage and challenge.' In the distant past, we—killed to win our mates. It is still a time of dread for us. Perhaps, the price we pay—for no emotion the rest of the time."

"If it's any of my business—" McCoy began.

"You were invited, Doctor."

"Then—you said this T'Pring you are to meet was already your wife."

"By our parents' arrangement. A ceremony, while we were but seven years of age. One touches the other—thus—as you have seen me do to feel another's thoughts. In this way, our minds were locked together—so that at the proper time we would both be drawn to *Koon-ut-Kal-if-fee*."

There sounded a distant bell, harmonizing well with the heavier notes of the wind chimes, and then figures began to appear among the rocks. There seemed to be eight or ten of them. Heading the procession, four Vulcan men were carrying someone in an ornate litter or sedan chair. Two other members of the party carried bright-colored, ceremonial objects which consisted of dozens of tiny bells attached to an ornate frame on a pole.

As they drew closer, Kirk saw that the person inside the litter was an old woman of immensely authoritative bearing; as the litter was set down and she emerged from it, he recognized her with a shock as one of the high Vulcan elders, T'Pau, the only person who had ever turned down a seat on the Federation Council. Characteristically, Spock had never mentioned that his family was this important.

The bride walked beside her, no child now, but a lithe, graceful, beautiful woman, even by Earth standards. Behind her strode a tall, muscular and rather handsome Vulcan male; and behind him, a slightly shorter but even stronger-looking man who carried a Vulcan war ax. The rest of the procession moved in stately grace behind these principals.

Spock turned and walked to one of the huge wind chimes. Picking up a stone mallet, he struck the chimes, producing a somber male sound which was answered by the shaking of the bell banners. T'Pring seated herself on a carved rock at the temple archway. T'Pau stood in the open in front of the temple, with her back to it and the girl. The muscular young Vulcan stood next to the arch, like a big brick gatepost, while the rest of the entourage lined up in a curve behind them.

With a sudden swift movement, T'Pau raised both her arms. Spock stepped forward and bowed before her. She laid both her hands on his shoulders, as if in a blessing, and then looked beyond him to Kirk and McCoy.

"Spock. Are our ceremonies for outworlders?"

"They are not outworlders," Spock said. "They are my friends. I am permitted this. Their names are Kirk and McCoy. I pledge their behavior with my life."

"Very well." T'Pau turned to the bearers of the bell banners. *"Kah-if-fee!"*

The bell banners were shaken. Spock turned to strike the wind chimes again with his stone mallet—but at the same instant the girl T'Pring sprang to her feet and cried out:

"Kah-if-FARR!"

There was a gasp from the Vulcan onlookers; even T'Pau's eyes flickered in startled surprise. Spock mouthed the word without speaking it, his breathing quickening, his eyes narrowed to slits. T'Pring crossed to him, took the mallet from his hand, and tossed it aside. Her expression was strangely contemptuous.

The Vulcan with the ax stepped forward. He looked both amused and dangerous, like an experienced executioner.

"Hey, what's this?" McCoy said. "If there's going to be hanky-panky . . ."

"All is in order," the old woman said. "She chooses the challenge."

"What?" McCoy pointed at the executioner. "With *him*?"

"No. He acts only if cowardice is seen. T'Pring will now choose her champion. T'Pring: you have chosen. Are you prepared to become the property of the victor? Not merely his wife, but his chattel, with no other rights or status?"

"I am prepared," T'Pring said.

"Then choose."

T'Pring moved regally out into the arena. She stopped by the huge young Vulcan, who straightened proudly, expectantly, but she moved away from him. Then she turned to T'Pau.

"As it was in the dawn of our days," she said, "as it is today, as it will be through all tomorrows, I make my choice." She turned again. "I choose this man."

And she pointed straight at Kirk.

"Now wait a minute—" Kirk said.

At the same moment, the big young Vulcan stepped forward, obviously outraged. "No!" he cried. "I am to be the one! It was agreed! The honor is mine!"

All at once, everyone in the marriage party seemed to be arguing, all in Vulcan. Under cover of the noise, Kirk said swiftly to McCoy, "What happens if I decline?"

"I don't know, Jim. He'd probably have to fight the young man. And in his present condition, he couldn't win. But Jim, this looks like a situation of total combat—and the heat and the air here are pretty fierce. I'm not sure you could win either—even if you'd want to."

"I'm not about to take a dead First Officer back with me. On the other hand, there's T'Pau over there—all of Vulcan wrapped up in one package. How will it look if a Starship Captain backs off from this, afraid?"

"But . . ."

"And if I can't beat him, if I'm in any danger, I'll give up. Spock wins, honor is satisfied. Or maybe just knock him out . . ."

"*Kroykah!*" T'Pau said explosively. The hubbub stopped as if turned off by a switch.

The big young Vulcan said, "I ask forgiveness." He went back to his post by the arch, sulky, unrepentant, but no longer defiant.

Kirk said, "I accept." He threw a look toward his First Officer, but Spock seemed oblivious of everything but the ceremony.

"According to our laws," T'Pau said, "combat begins with the *lirpa*."

Two Vulcan males stepped forward, each carrying a vicious-looking weapon. At one end of a heavy handle was a circular, razor-edged knife; at the other end, a metal cudgel.

"If both survive the *lirpa*," T'Pau continued, "then combat continues with *ahn woon*, until death. *Klee-et!*"

At this command, Spock wheeled to face Kirk. His eyes blazed with blind savagery as he lifted the weapon. McCoy stepped forward.

"Nothing doing!" McCoy said. "No one mentioned a fight to the death—" his words trailed off as the executioner-like Vulcan stepped in, lifting his ax. Then he swallowed and charged on. "T'Pau, these men are friends. To force them to fight until one is killed . . ."

"Challenge was lawfully given and accepted. Neither party was forced. However, Spock may release the challenger. Spock! How do you choose?"

Spock continued to eye Kirk, scowling. There was still no sign of recognition. Then, suddenly, he shouted his answer, hoarsely, scornfully: *"Klee-fah!"*

"That's it, Bones," Kirk, said. "Get out of the combat area. There's nothing you can do."

McCoy stood fast. "I claim one right for him then. Your temperature is hot for our kind, your air is thin . . ."

He was interrupted by a feint from Spock. Kirk dodged, but Spock, slashing again with the blade, abruptly reversed the weapon and caught Kirk a glancing blow with the cudgel end. Kirk went down, rolling barely in time as Spock reversed again and slashed down hard. The weapon bit into the earth.

Kirk kicked hard at Spock's legs. Now the Vulcan was down, and Kirk was rolling to his feet. He was already sweating, and his breath was whistling in his throat. Out of the corner of his eye, he saw the burly axman advancing on McCoy.

"I can't watch you both, Bones!" he shouted. "Get out before you kill me!"

McCoy held his ground. Turning back toward T'Pau, he produced a hypo from his medical kit. "Are Vulcans afraid of fair combat?" he demanded.

"What is this?"

"A high-G vitalizer shot. To compensate for temperature and atmosphere."

"*Kroykah!*" T'Pau said. Everyone froze. "Very well. Your request is reasonable."

McCoy pressed the hypo against Kirk's arm. It hissed, and the physician turned away.

Spock moved in at once. This time it was Kirk who feinted. Spock countered as if they were marionettes tied to the same string. Kirk tried again, with the same result.

With a wordless rumble, Spock launched a lightning kick at Kirk's left hand. Kirk bent aside, and catching the heel of Spock's boot, dumped him. He dived after him, but Spock rolled with unbelievable quickness, so that Kirk hit only the bare ground.

Then both were up, crouching. Spock raised his weapon as if to throw it, and Kirk tensed, ready to jump aside. Spock, however, suddenly reversed the weapon and rushed.

They came together like the impact of two machines, belly to belly, free hand holding weapon wrist, glaring into each other's eyes. Then, with a bone-cracking wrench, Spock whipped Kirk's weapon to the ground.

With two quick, stamping steps, like a flamenco dancer, Spock snapped the knife blade with a loud crack, and then kicked the cudgel end away. He raised his own blade to striking position.

"Spock!" McCoy cried out. "No!"

They were still at close quarters. Kirk hit Spock's wrist with a karate chop. Now it was Spock's *lirpa* that went flying out of reach.

"*Kroykah!*" T'Pau cried.

Again, Spock froze. The Vulcan weapons attendant came hurrying out, carrying what seemed to be no more than two leather bands about three feet long and four inches wide. One was handed to Spock, who backed up, waiting; Kirk got the other.

"A strip of leather?" Kirk said. "Is that all?"

"The *ahn woon*," T'Pau said. "Oldest and deadliest of Vulcan weapons."

Kirk inspected it with puzzlement. How on earth was one supposed to use this thing? It wasn't long enough to be an effective whip, and . . .

Spock did not hesitate. Scooping up a jagged rock, in the same movement he converted the leather strap into a sling. Kirk understood too late. The rock caught him hard in the ribs, and he fell.

As he staggered to his feet, Spock charged him, now holding one end of the strap in each hand. Whipping it around Kirk's legs, he yanked, and down Kirk went again.

Instantly, Spock was at his back, garroting him with the strap. Kirk shifted to try to throw the First Officer over his shoulder, but something odd seemed to be happening to his muscles; they responded very slowly, and didn't move in the way his brain told them to go.

The pressure around his neck tightened. He made one last grab for Spock's hands, but never even came close. The universe darkened. Blood roared in his ears. He felt himself fall flat, blind and paralyzed.

"*Kroykah!*" came T'Pau's voice, as if from a great distance.

There was a sound of running footsteps, coming closer. Then came McCoy's voice, charged with bitterness:

"Get your hands off him, Spock. It's finished—he's dead."

It was all most peculiar. Kirk could see nothing, feel nothing, was not even sure he was breathing. He was aware of nothing but the voices, as though he were listening to an exchange over the intercom—or attending a play with his back turned to the stage.

> T'PAU: I grieve with you, Doctor.
>
> SPOCK: No! I—no, no . . .
>
> McCOY: McCoy to *Enterprise*.
>
> UHURA: *Enterprise*. Lieutenant Uhura here.
>
> McCOY: Have Transporter Room stand by for landing party to beam up. Strange as it may seem, Mr. Spock, you're in command now. Any orders?
>
> SPOCK: I'll—I'll follow you in a few minutes. Instruct Mr. Chekov to plot a course for the nearest base where I must—surrender myself to the authorities . . . T'Pring.
>
> T'PRING: Yes.
>
> SPOCK: Explain.
>
> T'PRING: Specify.
>
> SPOCK: Why the challenge; why you chose my Captain as your champion.
>
> T'PRING: Stonn wanted me. I wanted him.
>
> SPOCK: I see no logic in preferring Stonn over me.
>
> T'PRING: He is simple and easily controlled. I calculated the possibilities were these: if your Captain were victor, he would not want me, and so I would have Stonn. If you were victor, you would free me because I dared to challenge, and again I would have Stonn. But if you did not free me it would be the same, for you would be gone again, and I would have your name and your property, and Stonn would still be there.
>
> SPOCK: Flawlessly logical.
>
> T'PRING: I am honored.
>
> SPOCK: Stonn! She is yours. After a time, you may find that *having* is not, after all, so satisfying a thing as *wanting*. It is not logical, but it is often true . . . Spock here. Ready to beam up . . . Live long and prosper, T'Pau.
>
> T'PAU: Live long and prosper, Spock.
>
> SPOCK: I shall do neither. I have killed my Captain—and my friend.

Then Kirk's hearing went away too, and for a long time thereafter he knew nothing.

He came gradually back to consciousness in the Sickbay. McCoy was bending over him. Nearby was Spock, his hands over his face. His shoulders were shaking.

Nurse Christine came into his field of view, and turning Spock toward the Captain, gently pulled his hands away from his face. Kirk smiled weakly, and spoke in a faint but cheerful voice.

"Mr. Spock—I never thought I'd see the day . . ."

"Captain!" Spock stared down at him, absolutely dazed with astonishment. Then, obviously realizing what his face and voice were revealing, he looked away.

"Christine," McCoy said, "it might be a good idea for Mr. Spock to get some hot food in him. Why don't you feed him some of that awful plomik soup. Then bring him back here for me to run a physical on him. Go on, Spock. She'll explain it to you."

Christine led the First Officer toward the door. But just before he left, Spock said, "it is not awful plomik soup. It is very good plomik soup."

Then he was gone. Kirk and McCoy smiled after him. Then Kirk rolled his head back and wiped the smile off his face.

"You, Mister," he said, "are a quack."

McCoy shrugged. "I made a mistake. Shot you with ronoxiline D by mistake. Nobody lied. You were dead—by all normal standards. I had to get you back up here fast, or you would have been dead by *any* standards."

"Will Spock be all right?"

"I think so. I'll run a full physical on him to make sure."

Kirk started to sit up. "Where are we now?"

"Stay right there," McCoy said, shoving him back. "We're still orbiting Vulcan."

Kirk reached out and snapped on the bedside intercom. "Kirk to Bridge."

"Bridge, sir. Sulu here."

"Take us out of orbit, Mr. Sulu. Have the navigator lay in a course for Altair Six at top warp speed. Tell Scotty to pour it on—we've got an inauguration to make!"

"Yes *sir*. Bridge out."

As Kirk dropped back onto the bed, McCoy said sourly, "You know, Jim, some one of these days these ceremonies will be the death of you."

"In which case, Bones, remember: you have standing orders to bring me back to life."

WHO MOURNS FOR ADONAIS?

Writer: Gilbert A. Ralston and Gene L. Coon
Director: Marc Daniels
First Aired: September 22, 1967

All heads in the *Enterprise* bridge turned as the elevator door opened. Kirk made a bet with himself: it was Lieutenant Carolyn Palamas with her report on those marblelike fragments they'd beamed up from the dead planet in the Cecrops cluster. He won the bet. She handed him some stapled sheets and he said, "Thank you," his eyes carefully averted the girl's lustrous slate-gray ones.

Supreme beauty, he'd decided, could be a cruel liability to a woman. The stares it attracted set her apart. And he didn't want Carolyn Palamas to feel set apart. If she was the owner of copper-glorious hair and those slate-gray eyes, she was also a new member of his crew and a highly competent archeologist. She'd been stopping traffic since the day she was born. Well, he wasn't adding his gapes to the quota. He said, "Continue with standard procedures for Pollux Four, Lieutenant."

Dr. McCoy appeared to share his defensiveness toward the traffic-stopper. "You look tired, Carolyn," he said.

"I worked all night on my report," she said.

"There's nothing like a cup of coffee to buck you up," Scott said. "Want to join me in one, Carolyn?"

She smiled at him. "Just let me get my chemicals back into the lab cabinet first." She left the bridge and Kirk said, "Could you get that excited over a cup of coffee, Bones?"

"I'm in love with her," Scott said briefly. As he hastened after her, a slight frown pulled at McCoy's brows. "I'm wondering about that, Jim."

"Scotty's a good man," Kirk said.

"He thinks he's the right man for her, but *she*—" McCoy shrugged. "Emotional analysis of this love goddess of ours shows up strong drives for wifehood and motherhood. She's all woman, Jim. One of these days the bug will find her and off she'll go—out of the Service."

"I'd hate to lose a good officer, but I never fight nature, Bones."

Chekov spoke from his station near Kirk's command chair. "Entering standard orbit around Pollux Four, sir."

On the screen Pollux Four had already appeared, not unearthlike. Continents, seas, clouds.

"Preliminary reports, Mr. Spock?"

"Class M, Captain." Spock didn't turn from his mounded computer. Kirk, his eyes on the screen, saw the planet, rotating slowly, come into closer focus. He heard Spock say, "Nitrogen-oxygen atmosphere, sir. Sensor readings indicate no life-forms. Approximate age four billion years. I judge no reason for contact. In all respects quite ordinary."

Kirk pushed a button. "Cartographic section, implement standard orders. All scanners automatic. All—"

"Captain!" shouted Sulu. "On scanner twelve!"

Something had suddenly come between them and the planet—something formless and so transparent Kirk could see the stars through it. It was rapidly growing in size.

"What in the name of . . ." McCoy fell silent.

"Mr. Sulu," Chekov said, "am I seeing things?"

"Not unless I am, too," Sulu said. "Captain, that thing is a giant hand!"

Kirk didn't speak. On the screen the amorphous mass had begun to differentiate itself into five gigantic fingers, into a palm, the hint of a massive wrist extending down and out of the viewer's area. "Readings, Mr. Spock." His voice was toneless. "Is it a hand?"

"No, Captain. Not living tissue."

"A trick then? A magnified projection?"

"Not a projection, sir. A field of energy."

"Hard about!" Kirk ordered briskly. "Course 230 mark 41."

The palm now dominated the screen, its lines deeply shadowed valleys, the huge, contrasting mounds of its construction simulating the human-size mounds of a human palm. The valleyed lines deepened, moving—and Chekov cried, "It means to grab us!"

For the first time Spock turned from his computer to look at the viewer. "Captain, if it's a force field—"

"All engines reverse!" Kirk shouted.

Lights flickered. Shudders shook the starship. Strained metal screamed. Bridge seats tumbled their occupants to the floor. Scrambling up to wrestle with his console, Sulu grasped it with both hands as he fought to pull it backward. "The helm won't answer, Captain! We can't move!"

Scott had rushed in from the elevator; and Kirk, regaining his chair, addressed Uhura. "Lieutenant, relay our position and circumstances to Star Base Twelve immediately. Report that the *Enterprise* has been stopped in space by an unknown force of some kind." He swung his chair around to Sulu. "Mr. Sulu, try rocking the ship. Full impulse forward, *then* back."

"Damage report coming in, Captain," said Uhura. "Situation under control. Minor damage stations three, seven and nineteen."

"Mr. Sulu?"

"Applying thrust, sir."

The ship vibrated. "No results, Captain. We're stuck tight."

Kirk glanced at the screen. The palm still owned it; and stars still shone through it. He looked away from it. "Status, Mr. Spock?"

"The ship is almost totally encircled by a force field, sir. It resembles a conventional force field but of unusual wavelengths. Despite its likeness to human appendage, it is not living tissue. It is energy."

"Thank you, Mr. Spock. Forward tractor beams, Mr. Sulu—and adjust to repel."

"Aye, aye, sir."

"Activate now!"

The ship quivered, groaning. "Ineffective, sir," Sulu said. "There doesn't seem to be anything to push against."

Spock spoke. "I suggest we throw scanner twelve on the main viewing screen, Captain."

"Do so, Mr. Spock."

The palm slid away. In its place, nebulous, still transparent, the features of a great face were shaping themselves into form on the screen. Silence was absolute in the bridge of the *Enterprise*. The immense face could be seen now, whole. But its immensity struck Kirk as irrelevant. It was an intensely masculine face; and whomever it belonged to was the handsomest male Kirk had ever seen in his life. The dark eyes were fixed on the ship. Diademed with stars, the brow, the nose and mouth conformed to convey an impression of classic beauty, ageless as the stars.

The voice that came from the screen suited the face.

"The aeons have passed, and what has been written has come about. You are welcome here, my beloved children. Your home awaits you."

Kirk shook his head as though to clear his ears of the deep organ tones reverberating through the bridge. He tore his gaze from the screen to address Uhura. "Response frequencies, Lieutenant."

"Calculated, sir. Channel open."

He pulled the mike to him. "This is Captain James T. Kirk of the *USS Enterprise*. Please identify yourself."

The request was ignored. "You have left your plains and valleys to make this bold venture," said the voice. "So it was from the beginning. We shall remember together. We shall drink the sacramental wine. The pipes shall call again from the woodlands. The long wait is ended."

The words had the sound of an incantation. Kirk said, "Whatever you are, whoever you are, are you responsible for stopping my ship?"

"I have caused the wind to withdraw from your sails."

"Return it," Kirk said. "Then we'll talk. You seem unwilling to identify yourself, but I warn you we have the power to defend ourselves. If you value your safety, release this ship!"

The lips moved in an approving smile. "You have the old fire. How like your fathers you are. Agamemnon . . . Achilles . . . Trojan Hector . . ."

"Never mind the history lesson. Release this ship or I'll—"

The smile faded. "You will obey—lest I close my hand—thus—"

The ship rocked like a toy shaken by a petulant child.

"External pressure building up, Captain," Scott called from his station. "Eight hundred GSC and mounting."

"Compensate, Mr. Scott."

"Pressure becoming critical, sir. One thousand GSC. We can't take it."

Savagely Kirk swung around to the screen. "All right, whatever you're doing, you win. Turn it off."

"That was your first lesson. Remember it," the voice said. The sternness on its face was replaced by a smile radiant as sunlight. "I invite you and all your officers to join me, Captain. Don't bring the one with the pointed ears. Pan is a bore. He always was."

Kirk said hastily, "Take it easy, Mr. Spock. We don't know what we're up against."

"Hasten, children," urged the voice. "Let your hearts prepare to sing."

"Well, Bones, ready for the concert?"

"Is that wise, Jim?"

"It is if we want a ship instead of a crushed eggshell."

Kirk got up to join his First Officer at the computer station. "You're in command, Mr. Spock. Get all labs working on the nature of the force holding us here. Find a way to break clear."

"Acknowledged, sir. Beam-down?"

"Yes, Mr. Spock."

The party materialized among olive trees. Ahead of them on a grassy knoll stood a small edifice of veinless marble. It was fronted by six fluted columns of the stone, lifting to capitals that flowered into graceful curves. Above them rose the white temple's architrave, embossed with sculptured figures. They looked ancient but somehow familiar. A semi-circled flight of steps led upward and into the structure.

As Chekov and Scott moved into position beside him, Kirk said, "Maintain readings on tricorders. That goes for everybody."

Behind him, unusually pale, Carolyn Palamas edged nearer to McCoy. "What am *I* doing here, Doctor?"

Unslinging his tricorder, McCoy said, "You're the student of ancient civilizations. This seems to be one. We'll need all the information you've got about it." He moved on to follow Kirk, adding, "The Captain will want us with him when he enters that door."

There was no door. They found themselves at once in a peristylelike open space.

At its far end a dais made a pediment for a carved throne of the same spotless marble. There were benches of marble, a table that held a simple repast of fruit and wine. From somewhere came the sound of pipes, sweet, wild, pagan. On a bench beside the table sat a man-size being. Kirk had seen some good-looking men in his life, but this male, human or non-human, was in a class of his own. His face held the same agelessly classic beauty as the huge image of the *Enterprise* screen. A thigh-length garment was clasped to his sun-browned, smoothly muscular shoulders. Beside him lay a lyre. He rose to his tall six-foot two-inch height and walked to meet them.

"My children, greetings. Long, long have I waited for this moment."

His youth should have made the term "children" absurd. It didn't. He could get away with it, Kirk thought, because of the dignity. The whole bearing of the creature exuded it.

Low-voiced, he said, "Bones, aim your tricorder at him."

"Ah, the memories you bring of our lush and beautiful Earth!" The being flung up his arms as though invoking the memories. "Its green meadows . . . its blue skies . . . the simple shepherds and their flocks on the hills . . ."

"You know Earth?" Kirk asked. "You've been there?"

The white teeth flashed in the radiant smile. "Once I stretched out my hand—and the Earth trembled. I breathed upon it—and spring returned."

"You mentioned Achilles," Kirk said. "How do you know about him?"

"Search back into your most distant memories, those of the thousands of years that have passed . . . and I am there. Your fathers knew me and your fathers' fathers. I am Apollo."

It was insanely credible. The temple . . . the lyre. Apollo had been the patron god of music. And the speech of this being was marked by an antique cadence, an almost superhuman assurance. There was also his incomparable symmetry of body and gesture.

Chekov broke the spell. "Yes," he said, "and I am the Czar of all the Russias!"

"Mr. Chekov!"

"Sorry, Captain. I never met a god before."

"And you haven't now," Kirk said. "Your readings, Bones?"

"A simple humanoid. Nothing special."

"You have the manners of a satyr. You will learn." The remark was made abstractedly. The dark eyes had fixed on Carolyn Palamas. The creature stepped forward to lift her chin with his hand. Scott bristled and Kirk said, "Hold it, Scotty."

"Earth—she always was the mother of beautiful women. That at least is unchanged. I am pleased. Yes, we gods knew your Earth well . . . Zeus, my sister Artemis, Athene. Five thousand years ago we knew it well."

"All right," Kirk said. "We're here. Now let's talk. Apparently, you're all alone. Maybe we can do something to help you."

"Help me? *You?* You will not help me. You will not leave this place." The tone was final. "Your transportation device no longer functions."

Kirk, flipped open his communicator. There was no responding crackle. The being said casually, "Nor will that device work either, Captain." He paused. Just as casually, he added, "You are here to worship me as your fathers worshipped me before you."

"If you wish to play god by calling yourself Apollo, that is your business," Kirk said. "But you are not a god to us."

"I said," repeated the humanoid, "you shall worship me."

"*You've* got a lot to learn, my friend," Kirk retorted.

"And so have you! Let the lesson begin!"

Before Kirk's unbelieving eyes, the body of the man-size being began to rise, taller, taller, taller. He towered twelve feet above them—and still grew higher. He was now a good eighteen feet in stature, a colossus of mingled beauty and rage. As the black brows drew together in fury, there came a deafening crash of thunder. The translucent light in the temple went dim, streaks of lightning piercing its darkness. Thunder rolled again. Around the temple's columned walls far above him, Kirk could see that lightning spears were gathering about the great head in a dazzling nimbus of flame.

Crowned with fire, Apollo said, "Welcome to Olympus, Captain Kirk!"

Dazed, the *Enterprise* commander fought against the evidence of his senses. His reason denied the divinity of the being; but his eyes, his ears, insisted on its truth. Then he saw that a look of weariness, of pain, had appeared on Apollo's face. The massive shoulders sagged. He vanished.

It was McCoy who spoke first. "To coin a phrase—fascinating."

Kirk turned to the girl. "Lieutenant Palamas, what do you know about Apollo?"

She stared at him unseeingly. "What? . . . oh, Apollo. He—he was the son of Zeus and Latona . . . a mortal woman. He was the god of light, of music, of archery. He—he controlled prophecy."

"And this creature?"

She had collected herself. "Clearly he has some knowledge of Earth, sir. His classic references, the way he speaks, his—his looks. They resemble certain museum sculptures of the god."

"Bones?"

"I can't say much till I've checked out these readings. He looks human, but of course that doesn't mean a thing."

"Whatever he is, he seems to control a remarkable technology," Chekov said.

"Power is what the thing controls," Scott said. "You can't pull off these tricks without power."

"Fine. But what power? Where does it come from?" Kirk's voice was impatient. "Scout around with your tricorders and see if you can locate his power source."

Scott and Chekov moved off and Kirk, his face grown thoughtful, turned to McCoy. "I wonder if five thousand years ago a race of—"

"You have a theory, Jim?"

"I'm considering one. What if—"

"Jim, look!"

Man-size again, Apollo was sitting on his marble throne.

"Come to me," he said.

They obeyed. Kirk spoke. "Mister—" he began. He hesitated, then plunged. "Apollo, would you kindly tell us what you want from us? Omitting, if you please, all Olympian comments?"

"I want from you what is rightfully mine. Your loyalty, your tribute and your worship."

"What do you offer in exchange?"

The dark eyes brooded on Kirk's. "I offer you human life as simple and pleasureful as it was those thousands of years ago on our beautiful Earth so far away."

"We're not in the habit of bending our knees to everyone we meet with a bag of tricks."

"Agamemnon was one such as you. And Hercules. Pride, hubris." The deep voice was somber with memory. "They defied me, too—until they felt my wrath."

Scott had rejoined Kirk in time to hear this last exchange. "We are capable of some wrath ourselves," he said hotly.

"I have four hundred and thirty people on my ship up there," Kirk said, "and they—"

"They are mine," said Apollo. "To cherish or destroy. At my will."

Carolyn suddenly broke in. "But why? What you've said makes no sense."

The dark eyes veered from Kirk's to linger on the cloud of copper-glorious hair. "What is your name?"

"Lieutenant Palamas."

"I mean your *name*."

She glanced at Kirk as though for help. "Carolyn."

"Yes." Apollo leaned forward on the throne. "When she gave you beauty, Aphrodite was feeling unusually generous. I have a thousand tales to tell you. We shall speak together, you and I, of valor and of love."

"Let her alone!" Scott cried.

"You protest?" Apollo was amused. "You risk much, mortal."

Scott whipped out his phaser. "And so do you!"

With a lithe movement, Apollo was on his feet. He extended a finger at the phaser. A blue-hot flame leaped from it—and Scott yelled in pain. He dropped the weapon, recoiling.

Kirk bent to pick it up, but Chekov had already retrieved it. The phaser was a lump of melted metal. Chekov handed it to Kirk. It was still hot to the touch.

"Quite impressive." The respect in Kirk's voice was genuine. "Did you generate that force internally?"

"Captain!" shouted Chekov. "The phasers—all of them!"

Kirk withdrew his from his belt. It had been fused into the same mass of useless metal.

"None of your toys will function."

Apollo dismissed the subject of the ruined phasers by stepping from his white throne. He strode over to Carolyn to search the slate-gray eyes with his. "Yes," he said, "the Cyprian was unusually generous to you. But the bow arm should be bare . . ."

He touched her uniform. Its stuff thinned into soft golden folds. They lengthened to her feet. She was gowned in a robe of flowing archaic Greek design that left one white shoulder naked. Golden sandals had replaced her shoes. Wonderingly, she whispered, "It—it is beautiful."

"You are beautiful," he said. "Come."

"She's not going with you!" Scott shouted. He took an angry step toward them—and was slammed against a marble bench. McCoy ran to him.

"That mortal must learn the discipline of my temple," Apollo said. "So must you all." He had Carolyn's hand in his. "But you—you come with me."

Kirk made a move and the girl shook her head. "It's all right, Captain."

The sunlight smile was for her. "Good," Apollo said. "Without fear. You are fit." A radiance suddenly enveloped them. Their figures were absorbed by it. They disappeared.

McCoy called to Kirk. "Scotty's stunned. He'll come around. But the girl, Jim—I'm not sure at all it was wise to let her go off like that. Whatever this Apollo is, we'd better be careful in dealing with him."

"He'd have been hard to stop," Kirk said. "Scotty tried."

"It's his moods that worry me. You've seen how capricious he is. Benevolent one moment, angry the next. If she says one displeasing thing to him, he could kill her."

"Yes, he could." Kirk turned to Chekov. "Mr. Chekov, continue your investigations. You all right, Scotty?"

Leaning against McCoy's shoulder, the engineer shook his head dazedly. "I don't know. I'm tingling all over . . . a kind of inside burning. Did he take her with him?"

"So it would seem, Scotty."

"Captain, we've got to stop him! He wants her! The way he looks at her—"

"Mr. Scott, the Lieutenant volunteered to go with him, hopefully to find out more about him. I understand your concern—but she's doing her job. It's time you started doing yours. We've got to locate the source of his power. You have a tricorder. Use it.

One thing more. I want no more unauthorized action taken against him. I don't want you killed. That's an order."

Sullenly Scott stumbled away after Chekov and McCoy said, "Scotty doesn't believe in gods, Jim."

"Apollo could have been one though—once."

"Is *that* your theory?"

"Bones, suppose a highly sophisticated group of humans achieved space travel five thousand years ago. Suppose they landed on Earth near the area around the Aegean Sea. To the simple shepherds and tribesmen of primitive Greece wouldn't they have seemed to be gods? Especially if they were able to alter their shapes at will and command great energy?"

McCoy stared. Then he nodded soberly. "Like humans, occasionally benevolent, occasionally vindictive. Maybe you've got something. But I certainly wish that love-goddess girl were safely back on the *Enterprise*."

Under the golden sandals of the love-goddess girl, the grass of the olive-groved glade was soft. "A simple humanoid" was how Dr. McCoy had defined the man who strolled beside her. Birds threaded the air she breathed with melody. Her hand felt very small in his. He lifted it to his lips—and they were as warm as human lips. Above the bird song, she could hear the splashing of a waterfall. Vaguely Carolyn Palamas thought, "I am both afraid and not afraid. How is it possible to feel two such different feelings at once?"

"I have known other women," he said. "Mortals . . . Daphne, Cassandra. None were so lovely as you. You fear me?"

"I—don't know. It isn't every day a girl is flattered by—"

"A god? I do not flatter."

She reached for another subject. "How do you know so much of Earth?"

"How do you remember *your* home? Earth was so dear to us, it remains forever a shrine. There were laughter, brave and goodly company—love."

"You are alone, so alone," she said. "The others—where are they? Hera, Hermes, your sister Artemis?"

"They returned to the stars on the wings of the wind," he said.

"You mean they died?"

"No. We gods are immortal. It was the Earth that died. Your fathers turned away from us until we were only memories. A god cannot survive as a memory. We need awe, worship. We need love."

"You really consider yourself to be a god?"

He laughed. "It's a habit one gets into. But in a real sense we were gods. The power of life and death was ours. When men turned from us, we could have struck down from

Olympus and destroyed them. But we had no wish to destroy. So we came back to the stars again."

A note of infinite sadness entered his voice. "But those we had to leave behind, those who had loved us were gone. Here was an empty place without worship, without love. We waited, all of us, through the endless centuries."

"But you said the others didn't die."

"Hera went first. She stood before the temple and spread herself upon the wind in a way we have . . . thinner and thinner until only the wind remained. Even for gods there is a point of no return." He paused. Then he turned her around to face him.

"Now you have come," he said.

A breeze stirred the grass at her feet. The urgency in his eyes was familiar to the traffic-stopper. But in his it seemed uniquely moving. Abruptly she had a sense of imminent glory or catastrophe.

"I knew you would come to the stars one day. Of all the gods, I knew. I am the one who waited. I have waited for you to come and sit by my side in the temple. Why have you been so long? It has been . . . so lonely."

She didn't speak. "Zeus," he said, "took Latona, my mother. She was a mortal like you. He took her to care for, to guard, to love—thus . . ."

His arms were around her. She whispered, "No—no, please, not now. I—I feel you are most kind and your—your loneliness is a pain in my heart. But I don't know. I—"

"I have waited five thousand years."

He kissed her. She pulled back; and he released her at once. "I will leave you for a little to compose yourself. The temple is not far." He stopped to brush the burnished hair with his lips before turning to stride up the swell of the glade. She watched him go. A sob broke from her; and she covered her face with her hands. Glory—or catastrophe. Who could know which lay in wait? The bird song had sunk into silence and shadows were lengthening through the leaves of the olive trees. She waited another moment before she climbed the gladed upswell that led back to the temple.

The *Enterprise* party was quartering the area before it with tricorders. As she emerged from the trees, Chekov was calling to Kirk. "There's a repeated occurrence of registrations, Captain. A regularly pulsating pattern of radiated energy."

She was glad Scott's attention was fixed on the ground. "I can detect the energy pattern, too, Captain. But I can't focus on it."

"Apollo seems able to focus on it, Mr. Scott. He taps that power. How?"

"The electric eel can generate and control energy without harm to itself," Chekov said. "And the dry-worm of Antos—"

"Not the whole encyclopedia, please," McCoy begged.

"The Captain asked for complete information," Chekov said stiffly.

"Jim, Spock is contaminating this boy."

"Mr. Chekov, what you're suggesting is that Apollo taps a flow of energy he discharges through his own body," Kirk said.

"That would seem to be most likely, sir."

"But we don't *know* where the energy comes from! That's what we've got to find out if we're to cut off its source!"

"Number one on our 'things to do,'" murmured McCoy.

"Is that all you can offer, Bones?"

"Yes, except for this finding. Your Apollo's got an extra organ in his gorgeous chest. I can't even make a guess at its function."

"An extra organ. Bones, is there any chance—"

"Captain!" Scott shouted.

Apollo had assumed shape and substance on the temple steps. Kirk walked up to him. "Where is Lieutenant Palamas?"

"She is well."

"That's not good enough—"

"She is no longer your concern, Captain Kirk."

"You blood-thirsty heathen, what have you done with her?" Scott cried.

Kirk's stern "No!" came too late. Scott, snatching up a stone, charged Apollo, headlong. The finger extended—and the blue-hot streak lashed from it. Heels over head, Scott was whirled through the air. He fell with a crash; and the rock in his hand rolled down the knoll.

"Well?" Kirk said.

McCoy was kneeling beside Scott's crumpled body. "Not so well, Jim. He's in deep shock."

Kirk glanced at Scott's white face. Blood was seeping from a gash near his mouth. He stood immobile for a long moment, half-seeing the injection McCoy was preparing. Then he whirled to stride up to the temple steps. "All right, Mr. Last of the Gods. You wanted worshippers? You've got enemies. From now on—"

The finger pointed directly at him. The blue-hot flash struck him directly in the chest. It didn't fade. It didn't waver. Kirk choked, hands groping at his heart. He spun around—and fell flat on his face into unconsciousness.

McCoy, instantly beside him, lifted an eyelid. "Two patients," he muttered to nobody. "Two damn fools."

From behind the tree whose trunk had sheltered her from Scott's notice, Carolyn burst out of the dismay that had benumbed her. She flew to the temple steps, crying wildly, "What have you done to them? What have you done?"

"They—needed discipline." Apollo spoke wearily.

She turned her back on him to run to the two stricken crew members. Kirk was climbing slowly to his feet, McCoy's arm about his shoulders. She knelt beside Scott to wipe the blood from his chin with her robe. He opened his eyes at her touch and smiled faintly at her. "What happened?" he said.

"You let your enthusiasm get the better of your pragmatism," McCoy told him dryly.

"I—I was going to separate his head from his ruddy neck," Scott said.

"And you disobeyed an order not to do it! When we get back to the ship, you'll report for a hearing, Mr. Scott!"

"She's—worth it, Captain."

"You're an officer of the Starfleet! Start acting like one! Besides, you stiff-necked thistlehead, you could have got yourself killed!"

Carolyn leaped to her feet, eyes blazing. "Apollo would not kill!"

Kirk stared at her. *"Women!"* he thought. "They'll believe anything's true if they want to believe it is true." He said icily, "Lieutenant, he very nearly has killed—and several times."

"He could—but he *didn't*! Captain, you've got to see! He doesn't want to hurt anyone. He's just—terribly lonely. Please try to understand. He's the god of light, of music. He wouldn't hurt us!"

Kirk gripped her shoulders. "What happened when he took you away?"

"We—just talked."

"What about?"

"Captain, I—"

Kirk's voice was hard as the temple's stone. "Answer me, Lieutenant. What he said may help us."

Her eyes sought the ground. "He—said there was a point of no return . . . even for gods. Of course he's not a god—but he is *not* inhuman!"

"He's not human, either," Scott said grimly.

"No!" she cried. "He is something greater than human, nobler!"

"Lieutenant, there are four hundred and thirty people on our ship and we're all in trouble."

"Oh, I know it, Captain! Don't you think I know it? I just don't know what—" She burst into tears.

"Go easy on her, Jim."

"Why? So she can play around with an exciting new romance?"

"A god is making love to her. That's strong stuff, Jim."

Kirk shook his head in irritation. "How do you feel, Scotty?"

"I can't move my left arm."

"You won't for a while. There's some neural damage to the arm, Jim. I could repair it if I had the facilities."

"One more reason why we have to get out of here." Kirk walked over to a log, kicked it aside and turned to beckon to McCoy. "Bones, listen. I've been trying to remember my Greek mythology. After expending energy its gods needed rest just as humans do. At any rate, I intend to assume they did."

"You think this Apollo is off somewhere recharging his batteries?"

"That's not so far-fetched. He's disappeared again, hasn't he? Why shouldn't he be resting after the show he put on? Remember he's maintaining a force field on the ship while he drains off energy down here. Point? If we can overwork him, wear him out, that just might do it."

"The trouble with overworking him is that it could get us all killed."

"Not if we can provoke him into striking one of us again. The energy drainage could make him vulnerable to being jumped by the rest of us."

"I still think we might all get killed."

"Bones, you're a pessimist. It's our only out. When he comes back, we'll try it. Cue Chekov in on the plan. Scotty's useless arm counts him out of any scramble. By the way, let's get him into the shade of the temple. It's hot in the sun."

But Carolyn Palamas had already assisted Scott into the temple's coolness. She was easing him down on a bench. Kirk, following them, heard her say, "I am so sorry, Scotty."

"I'm not blaming you," Scott said heavily, his eyes on her face. He shoved himself up with his right arm. "Carolyn, you must not let yourself fall in love with him!"

"Do you think I *want* to?"

Kirk had had enough. He interrupted them. "You are the one to answer that question, Lieutenant. What is it exactly you *do* want? If you've pulled yourself together, I'd be glad to hear."

"Jim, he's recharged his batteries."

McCoy's warning was very quiet. Kirk spun around.

Strong, glowing, glorious with health, Apollo was reclining against the side of his marble throne, chin on fist, the dark eyes on all of them, watchful.

"Come here," he said.

Kirk, McCoy and Chekov obeyed. "You are trying to escape me. It is useless. I know everything you mortals do."

"You know nothing about us mortals," Kirk said. "The mortals you know were our remote ancestors. It was they who trembled before your tricks. They do not frighten us and neither do you." He spoke with deliberate insolence. "We've come a long way in five thousand years."

"I could sweep you out of existence with a wave of my hand." The radiant smile flashed. "Then I could bring you back. I can give life and I can take it away. What else does mankind demand of its gods?"

"We find one sufficient," Kirk said.

Apollo sighed, bored. "No more debate, mortal. I offer you eternal joy according to the ancient way. I ask little in return. But what I ask for I shall have."

He leaned forward. "Approach me."

They didn't move. Instead, they turned their backs on him and strolled toward the temple entrance.

"I said *approach* me!"

"No." Kirk flung the word over his shoulder.

"You will gather laurel leaves! You will light the ancient fires! You will slay a deer—and make your sacrifice to me!"

Kirk roared with laughter. "Gather laurel leaves? Listen to him!"

"It's warm enough without lighting fires!" shouted McCoy.

Chekov chuckled. "Maybe we should dance around a Maypole."

Apollo rose. "You shall reap the reward of this arrogance."

"Spread out. Get ready," Kirk said quietly. Then he turned, shouting, "We are tired of you and your phony fireworks!"

"You have earned this—"

Apollo had lifted an arm when Carolyn's *"No!"* came in a scream. "No, please, *no*! A father does not destroy his children! You are gentle! You love them! How can they worship you if you hurt them? Mortals make mistakes. You know us!"

"Shsssh," Kirk hissed. She didn't so much as glance at him. She was on her knees now before the throne. "Please—you know so much of love. Don't hurt them!"

The raised arm lowered. Apollo stepped from the dais and bent to lift her in his arms. Then he placed her on his throne. His hand on her neck, he turned to face them.

"She is my love of ten thousand years," he said. "In her name I shall be lenient with you. Bring the rest of your people down to me. They will need homes. Tell your artisans to bring axes."

Kirk's voice was acid with disappointment. "And you'll supply the sheep we herd and the pipes we'll play."

Apollo took Carolyn in his arms. The sunny radiance gathered around them. They dissolved into it—and were gone.

"Captain, we must *do* something!"

Kirk strode over to Scott's bench. "We *were* doing something until that girl of yours interfered with it! All right, she stopped him this time! How long do you think her influence will last?" It was a question Carolyn was asking herself.

Gods were notoriously unfaithful lovers. Now the summer grass in the olive-groved glade was still green beneath her sandals. But autumn and winter? They would come in their seasons. Summer would pass . . . and when it went, she would know. Catastrophe—or glory. Now there was no knowing, no knowing of anything but the warmth of his arm around her shoulder.

"They are fools," he was saying. "They think they have progressed. They are wrong. They have forgotten all that gives life meaning—meaning to the life of gods or of mortals."

"They are my friends," she said.

"They will be with you," he said. "I will cause them to stay with you—with us. It is for you that I shall care for them. I shall cherish them and provide for them all the days that they live."

She was trembling uncontrollably. She wrung her hands to still their shaking. He took them in his.

"No dream of love you have ever dreamed is I," he said. "You have completed me. You and I—we are both immortal now."

His mouth was on hers. She swayed and his kiss grew deeper. Then her arms reached for his neck. "Yes, it is true," she whispered. "Yes, yes, yes . . ."

Kirk glanced at her sharply as she re-entered the temple.

"Lieutenant, where is he?"

She didn't answer; and Scott, raising his head painfully from his bench, saw her face. "What's happened to her? If he—"

She passed him to move on toward the throne. Her look was the absent look of a woman who has just discovered she is one. It was clear that the men of the *Enterprise* had ceased to exist for her.

"She can't talk," Scott said bewilderedly. "He's struck her dumb."

"Easy does it, Scotty," Kirk said. "She won't talk to you. You're too involved. But she'll talk to me."

"Want some assistance, Captain?" Chekov asked.

"How old are you, Ensign Chekov?"

"Twenty-two, sir."

"Then stay where you are," Kirk said. He walked over to the girl. "Are you all right, Lieutenant Palamas?"

She stepped down from the dais. "What?"

"I asked if you are all right."

"All right? Oh yes. I—am all right. I have a message for you."

"Sit down," Kirk said. "Here on this bench. Beside me—here."

She swallowed. "He—he wants us to live in eternal joy. He wants to guard . . . and provide for us for the rest of our lives. He can do it."

Kirk got up. "All right, Lieutenant, come back from where you are. You've got work to do."

"Work?"

"He thrives on love, on worship. They're his meat."

"He gives so much," she said. "He gives—"

"We can't give him worship. None of us, especially you."

"What?"

"Reject him. You must!"

"I love him," she said.

Kirk rubbed a hand up his cheek. "All our lives, here and on the ship, depend on you."

"No! Not on me. Please, not on me!"

"On you, Lieutenant. Accept him—and you condemn the crew of the *Enterprise* to slavery. Do you hear me? *Slavery!*"

The slate-gray eyes were uncomprehending. "He wants the best for us. And he is so alone, so . . . so gentle." Her voice broke. "What you want me to do would break his heart. How can I? How can I?" She burst into passionate weeping.

"Give me your hand, Lieutenant."

"What?"

He seized her hand. "Feel mine? Human flesh against human flesh. It is flesh born of the same time. The same century begot us, you and I. We are contemporaries, Lieutenant!"

All sympathy had left his voice. "You are to remember what you are! A bit of flesh and blood afloat in illimitable space. The only thing that is truly yours is this small moment of time you share with a humanity that belongs to the present. That's where your duty lies. He is the past. His moment in time is not our moment. Do you understand me?"

The slate-gray eyes were anguished. But he sustained the iron in his face until she whispered, "Yes—I understand." She rose, left him, bent distractedly to pick up a tricorder; and half-turning, looked up at the temple's ceiling as though she was listening.

"He's—calling me," she faltered.

"I hear nothing," he said.

She didn't reply. The iron in his face was steel now. Desperate, he grabbed her shoulders. As he touched them, their bone, their flesh seemed to be losing solidity. She grew misty, fading. Kirk was alone with the echo of his own word "nothing".

Sinking down on the bench, he put his head in his hands. *Slavery*. It would claim all of them, McCoy, Scotty, Chekov. And up on the ship, they, too, would be enslaved to the whims of this god of the past. Sulu, Uhura, Spock . . .

"Spock here, Captain! *Enterprise* to Captain Kirk! *Enterprise* calling Captain Kirk! Come in, Captain!"

"I've gone mad," Kirk said to his hands. His useless communicator beeped again. "Communication restored, Captain! Come in, Captain. First Officer Spock calling Captain Kirk . . ."

"Kirk here, Mr. Spock."

"Are you all right, sir?"

"All right, Mr. Spock."

"We have pinpointed a power source on the planet that may have some connection with the force field. Is there a structure of some sort near you?"

Kirk had a crazy impulse to laugh. "Indeed there is, Mr. Spock. I'm in it."

"The power definitely emanates from there."

"Good. How are you coming with the force field?"

"Nuclear electronics believes we can drive holes through it by synchronization with all phaser banks. We aim the phasers—and there'll be gaps in the field ahead of them."

Kirk drew a deep lungful of air. "That ought to do it, Mr. Spock. Have Sulu lock in every phaser bank we've got on this structure. Fire on my signal—but cut it fine. We'll need time to get out of here."

"I would recommend a discreet distance for all of you, Captain."

"Believe me, Mr. Spock, we'd like to oblige but we're not all together. One of us is hostage to the Greek god Apollo. This marble temple is his power source. I want to know where he is when we attack it. Kirk out."

"I seem to have lost touch with reality." McCoy was looking curiously at Kirk. "Or maybe you have. Was that Spock you were talking to on that broken communicator—or the spirit world?"

"Function has been restored to it. Don't ask me how. Ask Spock when you see him again. Now we have to get out of here. All phaser banks on the *Enterprise* are about to attack this place. I'll give you a hand with Scotty."

Scott said, "I won't leave, sir." Then his anxiety burst out of him. "Captain, we've got to wait till Carolyn comes back before you fire on the temple. We don't know what he'll do to her if he's suddenly attacked."

"I know," Kirk said. "We'll wait, Scotty."

As he arranged the paralyzed arm around his shoulder, he said, "That mysterious organ in the gorgeous chest, Bones—could it have anything to do with his energy transmissions?"

"I can't think of any other meaning it could have, Jim."

The gorgeous chest, its extra organ notwithstanding, had another meaning for Carolyn Palamas. Its existence had plunged her into the battle of her life. Walking beside her god in the olive-groved glade, her eyes were blank with the battle's torture. It centered itself on one thought alone. She must not let him touch her. If he touched her . . .

"You gave them my message," he said. "Were they persuaded?"

They'd said he was the source of the mysterious power. He was not. He was the source of mysterious rapture. People, millions of them, shared her moment of time. They crowded it with her. But not one of them could evoke the ecstasy this being of a different time could bring to birth in her just by the sound of his voice.

"*You* persuaded them," he said. "Who could deny you anything?"

His eyes were the night sky, starred. He caught her in his arms; and not for her soul's sake or humanity's either, could she deny him her mouth. She flung her arms around his neck, returned his kiss—and pushed him away.

"I must say that the way you ape human behavior is quite remarkable," she said. "Your evolutionary pattern must be—"

"My what?"

"I'm sure it's unique. I've never encountered any specimen like you before."

"Haven't you?" he said. Running laughter sparkled in the dark eyes as he reached for her again. She held herself rigid, tight, withdrawn. The sparkle flamed into anger. "I am Apollo! I have chosen you!"

"I have work to do."

"Work? *You?*"

"I am a scientist. My specialty is relics—outworn objects of the past." She managed a shaken laugh. "Now you know why I have been studying you." She unslung her tricorder, aiming it at him. "I'd appreciate your telling me how you stole that temple artifact from Greece."

He knocked the tricorder out of her hand. "You cannot talk like this! You love me! You think I do not know when love is returned to me?"

"You confuse me with a shepherd girl. I could no more love you than I could love a new species of bacteria." Lifting the hem of her golden robe, she left him to climb back up the gladed hill. Then he was beside her. Anguish struggled with fury in his face.

"Carolyn, what have you said to me? I forbid you to go! I command you to return to me!"

"I am dying," was what she thought. What she said was: "Is this rage the thunderbolt that dropped your frightened nymphs to their knees?"

An eternity passed. His hand fell from her shoulder. Then a wild cry broke from him. He raised an arm and shook a fist at the sky. The air in the glade went suddenly sultry, oppressive. The sun disappeared. A chill breeze fluttered her robe as she began to run up the glade's incline.

It did more than flutter Kirk's jacket. A fierce gust of wind blew it half off his shoulders. Under its increasing howl his communicator beeped feebly. "Spock, Captain. Sensors are reporting intense atmospheric disturbance in your area."

The sensors hadn't exaggerated. The clouds over Kirk's head darkened to a sickly, yellowish blackness that hid the glimmer of the temple's marble. It was cleaved by a three-pronged snake of lightning before it flooded in again. There followed a crack of thunder; and another lightning flash struck from the sky. Kirk heard the sound of splitting wood—and an olive tree not five feet away burst into flame. Grabbing his communicator, he shouted into it. "Stand by, phaser banks! Mr. Spock, prepare to fire at my signal!"

Scott rushed to him. "Captain, we've got to go and find her!"

"Here is where we stay, Mr. Scott. When he comes back—" The wind took the words from his mouth.

"What if he doesn't, sir?"

"We'll bring him back. When that temple is—"

There was no need to bring him back.

He was back. The God of Storms himself. He topped the olive trees. A Goliath of power, Apollo of Olympus had returned in his gigantic avatar. The great head was flung back in agony, the vast mouth open, both giant fists lifted, clenched against the sky. It obeyed him. It gave him livid lightning forks to hurl earthward and filled his mouth with rolling thunder. Leaves shriveled. The tree trunk beside Kirk began to smoke. Then it flared into fire—and the black sky gave its God of Storms the lash of rain.

Stumbling toward the temple, Carolyn Palamas screamed. The gale's winds tore at her drenched robe. She screamed again as the bush she clung to was whipped from the ground, its branches clawing at her face. Apollo had found her. He was all around her, the blaze of his eyes in the lightning's blaze, in the rain that streamed down her body, the wild cry of the wind in the ears he had kissed. The she saw him. The God of Storms stooped from his height above the trees to show her his maddened face. He brought it closer to her, closer until she shrieked, "Forgive me! Forgive me!—" and lay still.

"Captain, you heard her! She screamed!"

"*Now*, Mr. Spock," Kirk said into his communicator.

The incandescing phaser beams struck the temple squarely in its central roof.

"*No! No! No!*"

The god who had appeared before the temple dwarfed it. He had unclenched his fists to spread his hands wide on his up-flung arms. Bolts of blue-hot fire streamed from his fingers.

"Oh, stop it, stop it, *please*!"

Carolyn, running to Apollo, halted. Behind him the temple was wavering, going indistinct. It winked out—and was gone.

She fell to her knees before the man-size being who stood in its place.

He spoke brokenly. "I would have loved you as a father his children. Did I ask so much of you?"

The grief-ravaged face moved Kirk to a strange pity. "We have outgrown you," he said gently. "You asked for what we can no longer give."

Apollo looked down at the girl at his feet. "I showed you my heart. See what you've done to me."

She saw a slight wind stir his hair. She kissed his feet—but she knew. The flesh under her lips, his body was losing substance. Kirk made no move; but he had noted that the arms were spreading wide.

"Zeus, my father, you were right. Hera, you were wise. Our time is gone. Take me home to the stars on the wind . . ." The words seemed to come from a great distance.

It was very still in the empty space before the ruined temple.

"I—I wish we hadn't had to do that," McCoy said.

"So do I, Bones." Kirk's voice was somber. "Everything grew from the worship of those gods of Greece—philosophy, culture. Would it hurt us, I wonder, to gather a few laurel leaves?"

He shook his head, looking skyward.

There were only the sounds of a woman's sobbing and the drip of raindrops from olive trees.

McCoy, sauntering into the *Enterprise* bridge, strolled over to Kirk and Spock at the computer station.

"Yes, Bones? Somebody ill?"

"Carolyn Palamas rejected her breakfast this mornin."

"Some bug going around?"

"She's pregnant, Jim. I've just examined her."

"*What?*"

"You heard me."

"Apollo?"

"Yes."

"Bones, it's impossible!"

McCoy leaned an arm on the hood of the computer.

"Spock," he said, "may I put a question to this gadget of yours? I'd like to ask it if I'm to turn my Sickbay into a delivery room for a human child—or a god. My medical courses did not include obstetrics for infant gods."

THE CHANGELING

Writer: John Meredyth Lucas
Director: Marc Daniels
First Aired: September 29, 1967

The last census had shown the Malurian system, which had two habitable planets, to have a population of over four billion; and only a week ago, the *Enterprise* had received a routine report from the head of the Federation investigating team there, asking to be picked up. Yet now there was no response from either planet, on any channel—and a long-range sensor sweep of the system revealed no sign of life at all.

There could not have been any system-wide natural catastrophe, or the astronomers would have detected it, and probably even predicted it. An interplanetary war would have left a great amount of radioactive residue; but the instruments showed only normal background radiation. As for an epidemic, what disease could wipe out two planets in a week, let alone so quickly that not even a single distress signal could be sent out—and what disease could wipe out *all* forms of life?

A part of the answer came almost at once as the ship's deflector screens snapped on. Something was approaching the *Enterprise* at multi-warp speed: necessarily, another ship. Nor did it leave a moment's doubt about its intentions. The bridge rang to a slamming jar. The *Enterprise* had been fired upon.

"Shields holding, Captain," Scott said.

"Good."

"I fear it is a temporary condition," Spock said. "The shields absorbed energy equivalent to almost ninety of our photon torpedos."

"*Ninety*, Mr. Spock?"

"Yes, Captain. I may add, the energy used in repulsing that first attack has reduced our shielding power by approximately 20 percent. In other words, we can resist perhaps three more; the fourth one will get through."

"Source?"

"Something very small . . . bearing 123 degrees mark 18. Range, ninety thousand kilometers. Yet the sensors still do not register any life-forms."

"Nevertheless, we'll try talking. They obviously pack more wallop than we do.

The Changeling

Lieutenant Uhura, patch my audio speaker into the translator computer and open all hailing frequencies."

"Aye, sir... All hailing frequencies open."

"To unidentified vessel, this is Captain Kirk of the *USS Enterprise*. We are on a peaceful mission. We mean no harm to you or to any life-form. Please communicate with us." There was no answer. "Mr. Spock, do you have any further readings on the alien?"

"Yes, sir. Mass, five hundred kilograms. Shape, roughly cylindrical. Length, a fraction over one meter."

"Must be a shuttlecraft," Scott said. "Some sort of dependent ship, or a proxy."

Spock shook his head. "There is no other ship on the sensors. The object we are scanning is the only possible source of the attack."

"What kind of intelligent creatures could exist in a thing that size?"

"Intelligence does not necessarily require bulk, Mr. Scott."

"Captain, message coming in," Uhura said.

The voice that came from the speaker was toneless, inflectionless, but comprehensible. "*USS Enterprise*. This is Nomad. My mission is non-hostile. Require communication. Can you leave your ship?"

"Yes," Kirk said, "but it will not be possible to enter your ship because of size differential."

"*Non sequitur*," said Nomad. "Your facts are uncoordinated."

"We are prepared to beam you aboard our ship."

Kirk's officers, except for Spock, reacted with alarm at this, but Nomad responded, "That will be satisfactory."

"Do you require any special conditions, any particular atmosphere or environment?"

"Negative."

"Please maintain your position. We are locked on to your coordinates and will beam you aboard." Kirk made a throat-cutting gesture to Uhura, who broke the contact.

"Captain," Scott said, "you're really going to bring that thing in here?"

"While it's on board, Mr. Scott, I doubt very much if it will do any more shooting at us. And if we don't do what it asks, we're a sitting duck for it right now. Lieutenant Uhura, have Dr. McCoy report to the Transporter Room. Mr. Spock, Scotty, come with me."

The glowing swirl of sparkle that was the Transporter effect died, and Nomad was there, a dull metallic cylinder, resting in a horizontal position on the floor of the chamber. It was motionless, silent, and a little absurd. There were seams on its sides, indicating possible openings, but there were no visible ports or sensors.

Spock moved to a scanning station, then shook his head. "No sensor readings, Captain. It has some sort of screen which protects it. I cannot get through."

There was a moment's silence. Then McCoy said: "What do we do now? Go up and knock?"

As if in answer, the flat inflectionless voice of Nomad spoke again, now through the ship's intercom system. "Relate your point of origin."

Kirk said, "We are from the United Federation of Planets."

"Insufficient response. All things have a point of origin. I will scan your star charts."

Kirk thought about this for a moment, then turned to Spock. "We can show it as a closeup of our system. As long as it has nothing to relate to, it won't know anything more important than it does now."

"It seems a reasonable course," Spock said.

"Nomad," Kirk told the cylinder, "if you would like to leave your ship, we can provide the necessary life-support systems."

"*Non sequitur.* Your facts remain uncoordinated."

"Jim," said McCoy, "I don't believe there's anyone in there."

"I contain no parasitical beings. I am Nomad."

"Och, it's a machine!" Scott said, brightening.

"Opinion, Mr. Spock?"

"Indeed, Captain, it is reacting quite like a highly sophisticated computer."

"I am Nomad. What is 'opinion'?"

"Opinion," Spock said, "is a belief, view or judgment."

"Insufficient response."

"What's your source of power?" Scott said.

"It has changed since the point of origin. There was much taken from the other. Now I focus cosmic radiation, and am perpetual."

Kirk drew Spock aside and spoke in a low voice. "Wasn't there a probe called Nomad launched from Earth back in the early two thousands?"

"Yes. It was reported destroyed. There were no more in the series. But if this *is* that probe—"

"I will scan your star charts now," Nomad said.

"We'll bring them."

"I have the capability of movement within your ship."

After a moment's hesitation, Kirk said, "This way. Scotty, get our shields recharged as soon as possible. Spock, Bones, come with me."

He led the way to the auxiliary control room, Nomad floating after him. The group considerably startled a crewman who was working there.

Spock crossed to the console. "Chart fourteen A, sir?"

Kirk nodded. The First Officer touched buttons quickly, and a view-screen lit up, showing a schematic chart of Earth's solar system—not, of course, to scale.

"Nomad," Kirk said, "can you scan this?"

"Yes."

"This is our point of origin. A star we know as Sol."

"You are from the third planet?"

"Yes."

"A planet with one large natural satellite?"

"Yes."

"The planet is called Earth?"

"Yes it is," Kirk said, puzzled.

An antenna slid from the side of the cylinder, swiveled, and centered upon him. He eyed it warily.

"Then," said Nomad, "you are the Creator—the Kirk. The sterilization procedure against your ship was a profound error."

"What sterilization procedure?"

"You know. You are the Kirk—the Creator. You programmed my function."

"Well, I'm not the Kirk," McCoy said. "Tell *me* what your function is."

The antenna turned to center on the surgeon. "This is one of your units, Creator?"

"Uh . . . yes, he is."

"It functions irrationally."

"Nevertheless, tell him your function."

The antenna retracted. "I am sent to probe for biological infestations. I am to destroy that which is not perfect."

Kirk turned to Spock, who was working at an extension of the library computer. "Biological infestations? There never was any probe sent out for that."

"I am checking its history," Spock said. "I should have a read-out in a moment."

Kirk turned back to Nomad. "Did you destroy the Malurian system? And why?"

"Clarify."

"The system of this star, Omega Ceti."

"Not the system, Creator Kirk, only the unstable biological infestation. It is my function."

"Unstable manifestation!" McCoy said angrily. "The population of two planets!"

"Doctor," Kirk said warningly. "Nomad, why do you call me Creator?"

"Is the usage incorrect?"

"The usage is correct," Spock put in quickly. "The Creator was simply testing your memory banks."

What, Kirk wondered, was Spock on to now? Well, best keep silent and play along.

"There was much damage in the accident," Nomad said.

Kirk turned toward the crewman, who had been listening with growing amazement. "Mr. Singh, come over here, please. Mr. Spock, Doctor, go to the briefing room. Nomad, I will return shortly. This unit, called Singh, will see to your needs."

There was no reaction from the cylinder. Kirk joined Spock and McCoy in the corridor. "Spock, you're on to something. What is it?"

"A Nomad probe was launched from Earth in August of the year 2002, old calendar. I am convinced that this is the same probe."

"Ridiculous," McCoy said. "Earth science couldn't begin to build anything with those capabilities that long ago."

"Besides," Kirk added, "Nomad was destroyed."

"*Presumed* destroyed by a meteor collision," Spock said. "I submit that it was badly damaged, but managed somehow to repair itself. But what is puzzling is that the original mission was a peaceful one." They had reached the briefing room, and the First Officer stepped aside to allow Kirk to precede him in. "The creator of Nomad was perhaps the most brilliant, though erratic, cyberneticist of his time. His dream was to make a perfect thinking machine, capable of independent logic. His name was Jackson Roykirk."

Light dawned. "Oho," Kirk said.

"Yes, Captain, I believe Nomad thinks you are Roykirk, and that may well be why the attack was broken off when you hailed it. It responded to your name, as well as its damaged memory banks permitted. While we were in Auxiliary Control, I programmed the computer to show a picture of the original Nomad on the screen here."

Spock switched on the screen. On it appeared, not a photograph, but a sketch. The size and shape indicated were about the same as the present Nomad, but the design was somehow rougher.

"But that's not the same," McCoy said.

"Essentially it is, Doctor. But I believe more happened to it than just damage in the meteor collision. It mentioned 'the other.' The other *what* is still an unanswered question. Nomad was a thinking machine, the best that could be engineered. It was a prototype. However, the entire program was highly controversial. It had many powerful enemies in the confused and inefficient Earth culture of that time. When Jackson Roykirk died, the Nomad program died with him."

"But if it's Nomad," Kirk said, "what happened to alter its shape?"

"I think it somehow repaired the damage it sustained."

"Its purpose must have been altered. The directive to seek out and destroy biological infestations couldn't have been programmed into it."

"As I recall, it wasn't," McCoy said. "Seems to me it was supposed to be the first interstellar probe to seek out new life-forms—only."

"Precisely, Doctor," Spock said. "And somehow that programming has been changed. It would seem that Nomad is now seeking out *perfect* life-forms . . . perfection being measured by its own relentless logic."

"If what you say is true, Mr. Spock," Kirk said, "Nomad has effectively programmed itself to destroy all non-mechanical life."

"Indeed, Captain. We have taken aboard our vessel a device which, sooner or later, must destroy us."

"Bridge to Captain Kirk," said the intercom urgently.

"Here, Scotty."

"Sir, that mechanical beastie is up here on the bridge!"

"On my way." Kirk tried to remember whether or not he, as the misidentified "Creator," had given Nomad a direct order to stay in the auxiliary control room. Evidently not.

On the bridge Uhura, Scott and Sulu were on duty; Uhura had been singing softly to herself.

"I always liked that song," Sulu said.

As he spoke, the elevator doors opened, and Nomad emerged. It paused for a moment, antenna extended and swiveling, coming to rest at last on Uhura. It started towards her. (It was at this point that Scott had called for Kirk.)

"What is the meaning of that?" Nomad said. "What form of communication?"

Uhura stared; though she knew the device had been brought aboard, this was the first time she had actually seen it. "I don't know what you—oh, I was singing."

"For what purpose is this singing?"

"I don't know. Just because I felt like singing, felt like music."

"What is music?"

Uhura started to laugh—there was something inherently ludicrous about discussing music with a machine—but the laugh died quickly. "Music is a pleasant arrangement of musical tones—sound vibrations of various frequencies, purer than those used in normal speech, and with associated harmonics. It can be immensely more complex than what I was doing just then."

"What is its purpose?"

Uhura shrugged helplessly. "Just for enjoyment."

"Insufficient response," said the machine. A pencil of light shot out from it, resting a spot of light on her forehead, between and slightly above the eyes. "Think about music."

Uhura's face went completely blank. Scott lunged to his feet. "Lieutenant! Get away from that thing—"

The elevator doors opened and Kirk, Spock and McCoy entered. "Scotty, look out—" Kirk shouted.

Scott had already reached the machine and grabbed for it, as if to shove it out of the way. There was no movement or effect from the craft, but the engineer was picked up and flung with tremendous impact against the nearest bulkhead. Sulu leapt up to yank Uhura out of the beam of light.

Kirk gestured toward Scott and McCoy strode to him quickly and knelt. Then he looked up. "He's dead, Jim."

For a moment Kirk stood stunned and appalled. Then fury rose to free him from his paralysis. "Why did you kill him?" he asked Nomad grimly.

"That unit touched my screens."

"That *unit* was my chief engineer." He turned to Uhura. "Lieutenant, are you all right? . . . Lieutenant! . . . Dammit, Nomad, what did you do to *her*?"

"This unit is defective. Its thinking was chaotic. Absorbing it unsettled my circuitry."

"The unit is a woman," Spock said.

"A mass of conflicting impulses."

Kirk turned angrily away. "Take Mr. Scott below."

"The Creator will effect repairs on the unit Scott?"

"He's dead."

"Insufficient response."

"His biological functions have ceased." Kirk was only barely able to control his rage and sorrow.

"If the Creator wishes," Nomad said emotionlessly, "I will repair the unit."

Startled, Kirk looked at McCoy, who said, "There's nothing I can do, Jim. But if there's a chance, it'll have to be soon."

"All right. Nomad, repair the unit."

"I require tapes on the structure."

Spock looked to McCoy. The surgeon said, "It'll need tapes on general anatomy, the central nervous system, one on the physiological structure of the brain. We'd better give it all the neurological studies we have. And tracings of Scotty's electro-encephalogram."

Spock nodded and punched the commands into the library computer as McCoy called off the requirements. "Ready, Nomad."

The device glided forward. A thin filament of wire extruded from it and touched a stud on the panel. Spock tripped a toggle and the computer whirred.

Then it was over and the filament pulled back into Nomad. "An interesting structure. But, Creator, there are so few safeguards built in. It can break down from innumerable causes, and its self-maintenance systems are unreliable."

"It serves me as it is, Nomad," Kirk said.

"Very well, Creator. Where is the unit Scott now?"

"Bones, take it to Sickbay." Kirk snapped a switch and said into his mike, "Security. Twenty-four hour two-man armed surveillance on Nomad. Pick it up in Sickbay." He turned to Spock. "Nomad is operating on some kind of energy. We've got to find out what it is and put a damper on it. Surely it can't be getting much cosmic radiation inside the *Enterprise;* we're well shielded. Let's feed in everything that's happened so far to the computer, and program for a hypothesis."

"It seems the most reasonable course, Captain. But it won't be easy."

"Easy or not, I want it done. Get on it, Mr. Spock. Then report to me in Sickbay."

Scott's body lay upon the examination table, with Nomad hovering over it. McCoy and Nurse Christine Chapel stood beside it, while Kirk and the two Security guards stood near the wall. Nomad, antenna extended, was scanning the body and humming.

The nurse looked toward the body-functions panel. "No reaction, Doctor."

"Could have told you that without looking, Nurse."

Suddenly, a light appeared on the panel, and a dial began quivering. In time with its movements, there came a steady beeping sound, gradually picking up in speed and volume.

Scott's eyes opened and he looked up at the amazed group, frowning. While he stared back, Spock joined the others. "What are the lot of you staring at?" Scott demanded.

"I . . . don't . . . believe it," McCoy whispered.

Scott looked around, and spotting Nomad, its antenna retracted now, he sat up in alarm. "What am I doing here? How did I—That thing did something to Lieutenant Uhura—"

"She's being taken care of, Scotty," Kirk said.

"But sir, it's dangerous! It—"

"Take it easy, Scotty," McCoy said. "Now just lie down. I want to check you out."

"The unit Scott is repaired," Nomad said. "It will function as before if your information to me was correct."

"How about it, Bones? Can he go back to duty?"

"If you don't mind, I'll check him out first. A man isn't just a . . . a biological unit to be patched together."

"What did it do to me?" Scott said.

Suddenly, a wave of pure awe, as strong as any he had ever felt in his life, swept through Kirk. Back from the dead! Why, if—but he pushed speculation resolutely away for the time being. "Dr. McCoy will explain, Scotty."

"Nurse Chapel," McCoy said, "I want him prepared for a full physical exam."

"Yes, sir."

Kirk crossed the examination room toward Sickbay proper, where Uhura now was. "Nomad, come here."

The machine glided after him, followed by Spock and McCoy. Inside, the Communications Officer lay unmoving on a bed, in a hospital gown and covered by a blanket. She did not look at any of them.

"Can you repair her, Nomad?" Kirk demanded.

"No," said the machine.

"But you were able to restore Scott, who had much more extensive damage."

"That was simply physiological repair. This one's superficial knowledge banks have been wiped clean."

"Superficial? Be more specific."

"She still remembers her life experiences, but her memory of how to express them, either logically or in the illogic called music, or to act on them, has been purged."

"Captain, if that is correct," Spock said, "if her mind has not been damaged and the aphasia is that superficial, she could be taught again."

"Bones?"

"I'll get on it right away." McCoy swung on Nomad. "And despite the way you repaired Scotty, you ticking metal—"

"Does the Creator wish Nomad to wait elsewhere?" Spock broke in quickly.

"Yes. Guards! Nomad, you will go with these units. They will escort you to a waiting area. Guards, take it to the top security cell in the brig."

There was silence while the guards and the machine went out. Then Spock said, "I interrupted you, Doctor, because Nomad would not have understood your anger. Its technical skill is great but it seems to react violently to emotion, even so non-specific an emotion as the enjoyment of music. It almost qualifies as a life-form itself."

Kirk glanced sharply at him. "It's all right to admire it, Mr. Spock, but remember it's a killer. We're going to have to handle it."

"I agree, Captain. It is a remarkable construction; it may well be the most advanced machine in the known galaxy. Study of it—"

"I intend to render it harmless, whatever it may take."

"You mean destroy it, Captain?"

"If it's necessary," Kirk said. "Get down to the brig with your equipment and run a full analysis of the mechanism. I want to know what makes that thing tick."

"Yes, sir."

The First Officer went out, and Kirk and McCoy returned to the examination room. Scott was still lying on the table. McCoy scanned the body functions panel slowly, and shook his head in disbelief.

"He checks out fine," he said. "Everything's normal."

"Then," Scott said, "can I get back to my engines, sir?"

Kirk glanced at McCoy, who nodded. "All right, Scotty."

"I hate to admit it," McCoy said as Scott swung off the table and left, "but Spock was right. Nomad is a remarkable machine."

THE CHANGELING

"Just remember it kills as effectively as it heals, Bones . . . if I'm called, I'll be down in the brig."

The two Security guards, phasers in hand, stood outside the force-field door of the brig, which was on. Inside, Nomad floated, almost surrounded by an array of portable scanners, behind which was Spock, staring with disapproval at the machine. Nomad, its antenna out, "stared" back.

One of the guards switched off the screen to allow Kirk to enter, then switched it on again. Kirk said, "What's the problem?"

"I have been unable to convince Nomad to lower its screens for analysis. Without its cooperation, I can do nothing."

Kirk studied the quietly humming machine. "Nomad, you will allow Spock to probe your memory banks and structure."

"This Spock is also one of your biological units, Creator?"

"Yes."

"This unit is different. It is well ordered. Interesting."

Under other circumstances, Kirk would have been amused to hear a machine applying Spock's favorite word to Spock himself, but the stakes were too great for amusement now. "Follow your orders, Nomad."

"My screens are down. You may proceed."

Spock set to work, very rapidly indeed, making settings, taking readings, making new settings. Within a few moments, he seemed to have found something which surprised him. He made another adjustment, and the machine he had been using promptly extruded a slip of paper, which he studied.

"Captain, I suggest we go out in the corridor for a private conference." They did so. "Sir, I have formed a partial hypothesis. But my information is insufficient and I have gleaned everything possible from the scanners. I must be allowed to question Nomad directly."

"Too dangerous."

"Captain, it moves only against imperfections. As you will recall, there is a Vulcan mind discipline which permits absolute concentration on one subject for a considerable period of time. If I were to use it—"

"And if your mind wandered for a moment, Nomad might just blast you out of existence. Right now it's safe in the brig."

"We do not know enough about it to know if it is 'safe' anywhere. If my hypothesis is correct, sir, we will at least be closer to understanding it. And control is not possible without understanding."

"All right," Kirk said, taking a phaser from one of the guards, "but I think I'll just keep this handy."

They went back in. Spock sat down on the cell bunk, for which the present prisoner had no use, and put his fingers to his temple. Kirk could almost hear his mind working.

"Nomad, my unit Spock will ask you certain questions. You will answer them as though I were asking them myself."

"Yes, Creator."

Silence. At last Spock said, "Nomad, there was an accident."

"There was an accident."

"You encountered the other."

"There was another. It was without direction. We joined."

"The other was not of the Earth. Its functions were other than yours." Spock held up the piece of paper, on which Kirk could see a drawing of what looked to be a space capsule of unfamiliar design. "I secured this design from your memory banks. Is this the other?"

"It is the other."

"Nomad, your memory banks were damaged by the accident. You took new directions from the other."

There was a buzz from the machine, and an antenna was aimed at Spock again. "Your statement is not recorded. You are in error."

"Logically, Nomad, you cannot prove I am in error, if your memory banks were damaged. You would have no way of knowing whether I speak the truth or not." Spock fell silent. The antenna retracted. "You acknowledge my logic. After meeting with the other, you had a new directive. Life-forms, if not perfect, are to be sterilized. Is this correct?"

"That is my programmed purpose."

"How much of the other did you assimilate?"

"Unrelated. Your question has no factual basis."

"Spock," Kirk said, "I think you're getting into deep waters. Better knock off."

Spock, unhearing, continued to stare at Nomad. The machine said: "There is error here. But if there was damage to my memory cells, there can be no proof of error. I will consider it."

"Enough," Kirk said firmly. Signaling to the guards to drop the screen, he dragged Spock out. The Vulcan was still glassy-eyed. "Mr. Spock! Come out of it!"

Slowly Spock's eyes began to focus. "Yes, Captain?"

"Are you all right?"

"Quite all right, sir." He looked back into the brig. "Fascinating. I was correct. It did meet a completely alien probe in deep space."

"And they merged—or at least their purposes did."

"In effect. Nomad took the alien's prime purpose to replace that part of its own which had been destroyed. The alien was originally programmed to seek out and sterilize soil samples from various planets—possibly as a preliminary to colonization."

"Hmm. Spock, do you know what a changeling is?"

"Sir?"

"An ancient Earth legend. A changeling was supposed to be a fairy child left in place of a stolen human baby. The changeling took the identity of the human child."

"That would be a parallel if Nomad is actually the alien probe intact. But actually, its programming now is a combination of the two. Nomad was supposed to find new life-forms; the alien to find and sterilize soil samples; the combination, and a deadly one, is to seek out and sterilize all life-forms. Moreover, the highly advanced alien technology, plus Nomad's own creative thinking, has enabled it to evolve itself into the incredibly powerful and sophisticated machine it is now."

"Not so sophisticated, Spock. It thinks I'm its . . . its father."

"Apparently Roykirk had enough ego to build a reverence for himself into the machine. That has been transferred to you—and so far it has been all that has saved us."

"Well, we'd better see to it that it never loses that reverence, Spock."

They were just about to enter an elevator when an intercom squalled with alarm. "Captain Kirk! This is Engineering! That alien device is down here, fooling with the anti-matter pod controls. We're up to Warp Ten now and can't stop!"

"Impossible! She won't go that fast."

"Warp Eleven now, sir."

"I'll be right down. Mr. Spock, check the brig."

The Engineering section was filled with the terrifying whine of the overdriven warp engines. Nomad was floating in front of the control panels, on which all the telltales glowed red.

Kirk rushed to the panel. "Nomad, you will stop whatever you're doing."

"Is there a problem, Creator? I have increased conversion efficiently by 57 percent—"

"You will destroy my ship. Its structure cannot stand the stress of that much power. Shut down your repair operation!"

"Acknowledged."

The whine began to die, and the panel returned to normal, the red lights blinking out one by one.

"It is reversed, as you ordered, Creator."

Spock entered the section and came up to Kirk. "Captain, I have examined the brig. The force-field generator of the security-cell door has been burnt out, and the guards have vanished. I must assume they are dead. I have asked for two more; they are outside."

"Creator, your mechanical units are as inefficient as your biological specimens."

"Nomad," Kirk said grimly, "it's time you were reminded of exactly who and what you are. I am a biological specimen—and you acknowledge that I built you."

"True," said the machine. "*Non sequitur.* Biological specimens are inherently inferior. This is an inconsistency."

"There are two men waiting outside. You will not harm them. They will escort you back to the waiting area. You will stay there. You will do nothing."

"I am programmed to investigate," Nomad said.

"I have given you new programming. You will implement it."

"There is much to be considered before I return to launch point. I must re-evaluate." Lifting, the machine floated away through the door, through which the red shirts of two more Security guards could be seen.

"Re-evaluate?" Kirk said.

"Captain," said Spock, "it may have been unwise to admit to Nomad you were a biological specimen. In Nomad's eyes you will undoubtedly now appear as imperfect as all the other biological specimens. I suspect that it is about to re-evaluate its Creator."

Scott, having seen that his board had been put back to rights, had come over to them in time to catch the last sentence. He said, "Will we be any worse off than we are now?"

"Scotty, it's just killed two men," Kirk said. "We've got to find a way to protect the crew."

"Captain, it is even more serious," Spock said. "Nomad just made a reference to its launch point. Earth."

A horrible thought struck Kirk. "Spock, is there any chance Nomad got a navigational fix on Earth while tapping our computers earlier?"

"I don't believe there is much beyond Nomad's capabilities, sir."

"Then we showed it the way home! And when it gets there—"

Spock nodded. "It will find the Earth infested with inferior biological specimens—just as was the Malurian system."

"And it will carry out its new prime directive. Sterilize!"

As they stared at each other, McCoy's amplified voice boomed out. "Captain Kirk! Captain Kirk to Sickbay! Emergency!"

This, Kirk thought, is turning into a continuous nightmare. He ran, Spock at his heels.

At the door of the examination room, Kirk hammered on the touchplate. It did not open. As Spock turned down the corridor to actuate the manual controls, however, the door suddenly slid back and Nomad emerged.

"Nomad! Stop!"

The machine paid no heed, but went on down the corridor. It passed Spock on the way, but ignored him too. In a moment it had vanished.

In the examination room, Christine lay unconscious on the floor. McCoy was bending over her with his medical tricorder.

"Is she all right, Bones?"

"I think so, Jim. Looks like some kind of shock."

"What happened?"

"Nomad examined the personnel files. The medical records. She tried to stop it."

"Whose medical history?"

"Yours, Jim."

"Since it specifically examined your history, Captain," Spock said, "I would suggest that it has carried out its re-evaluation."

"And," Kirk said grimly, "confirmed that its Creator is as imperfect as the rest of the biological specimens."

"Bridge to Captain Kirk," said the wall communicator.

"Kirk here. Report."

"Captain, life-support systems are out all over the ship. Manual override has been blocked! Source: Engineering."

"Carry on . . . well Mr. Spock, it seems you were right, and now we're in for it."

"Undoubtedly, Captain."

"Jim," McCoy said, "with all systems out, we only have enough air and heat for four and a half hours."

"I know that. Spock, get some anti-gravs and meet me and Scotty in Engineering."

"What is your plan, Captain?"

"I've got to use something you're a lot better at than I am. Logic."

"Then perhaps I—"

"No. I'm the one Nomad mistook for its Creator. And that's my ace. If I play it right—"

"I understand, Captain," Spock said quietly. "What you intend to do is most dangerous, however. If you make one mistake—"

"Then I'm dead and the ship is in the same mess it is now. Move!"

In Engineering, Nomad was busy at the panels again, and the red alarm lights were winking back on. One crewman was slumped lifeless by the door, another in a corner; obviously they had tangled with Nomad and lost. Scott was crouched behind an engine, out of Nomad's sight.

Kirk went directly to the malignant machine, which ignored him. "Nomad, you will stop what you are doing and effect repairs on the life-support system."

There was no response. Kirk took another step toward the panel, and Nomad said, "Stop."

"You are programmed to obey the orders of your Creator."

"I am programmed to destroy those life-forms which are imperfect. These alterations will do so, without destroying the vessel on which they are parasitic. It, too, is imperfect, but it can be adjusted."

"Nomad . . . admitted that biological units are imperfect. But you were created by a biological unit."

"I am perfect. I am Nomad."

"You are not Nomad. You are an alien machine. Your programming tapes have been altered."

Silence. The door opened and Spock came in, an anti-grav under each arm; he was probably the only man on the ship strong enough to carry two of them. Kirk gestured him toward Scott's hiding place.

"You are in error," Nomad said at last. "You are a biological unit. You are imperfect."

"But I am the Creator?"

"You are the Creator."

"And I created you?"

"You are the Creator."

"I admit I'm imperfect. How could I create anything as perfect as you?"

"Answer unknown. I shall analyze."

The machine hummed. Spock and Scott edged a little closer.

"Analysis incomplete," said Nomad. "Insufficient data to resolve problem. But my programming is whole. My purpose remains. I am Nomad. I am perfect. That which is imperfect must be sterilized."

"Then you will continue to destroy all that lives and thinks and is imperfect?"

"I shall continue. I shall return to launch point. I shall sterilize."

"Then . . . you *must* sterilize in case of error?"

"Errors are inconsistent with my prime function. Sterilization is correction."

"All that errs is to be sterilized?"

"There are no exceptions."

Kirk felt himself sweating. So far, so good; the machine, without being aware of it, had backed itself into a logical corner. It was time to play the ace. "I made an error in creating you, Nomad."

"The creation of perfection is no error."

"But I did not create perfection, Nomad. I created error."

"I am Nomad. I am perfect. Your data are faulty."

"I am Kirk, the Creator?"

"You are the Creator. But you are a biological unit and are imperfect."

"But I am *not* the Creator. Jackson Roykirk, who was the Creator, is dead. You have mistaken me for him! You have made an error! You did not discover your mistake! You have made two errors! You are flawed and imperfect—but you did not correct the errors by sterilization! You are imperfect! You have made three errors!"

Under the hammering of his voice, the machine's humming rose sharply in pitch. Nomad said, "Error? Error? Examine!"

The Changeling

"You are flawed! You are imperfect! Execute your prime function!"

"I shall analyze . . . error . . . an . . . a . . . lyze . . . err . . ." Nomad's voice slowed to a stop. The humming continued to rise. Kirk whirled to Scott and Spock.

"Now! Get those anti-gravs on it. We've got to get rid of it while it's trying to think its way out of that box. It won't be able to do it, and there's no telling how long it'll take to decide that for itself—"

They wrestled the anti-gravs onto the whining mechanism. Spock said, "Your logic is impeccable, Captain. We are in grave danger."

They hoisted Nomad and started toward the door with it. "Where to, sir?" Scott said.

"Transporter Room!"

The distance to be covered was not great. As they entered, Kirk took over wrestling with Nomad from Scott, and they dragged the thing to the platform. "Scotty, set the controls for deep space. Two-twelve mark 10 ought to be far enough."

Scott jumped to the console, and Kirk and Spock deposited the humming Nomad on one of the stations.

"Ready, sir."

Kirk and Spock jumped back, and Kirk shouted: "Nomad, you are imperfect. Exercize your prime function. Mr. Scott, energize!"

The Transporter effect swirled Nomad into nothingness.

"Now, the bridge, quick!"

But they were scarcely out into the corridor before the entire ship rocked violently, throwing them all. Then the ship steadied. They clambered to their feet and ran on.

On the bridge, they found Sulu wiping streaming eyes. "Captain, I wish you'd let me know when you're going to stage a fireworks display. Luckily I wasn't looking directly at the screen."

"Sorry, Mr. Sulu." Kirk went to his command chair and sat down with immense relief. Spock looked at him with respect.

"I must congratulate you, Captain," the Vulcan said. "That was a dazzling display of logic."

"Didn't think I had it in me, did you?"

"Now that you make the suggestion, sir—"

"Well, I didn't, Spock. I played a hunch. I had no idea whether or not it could tolerate the idea of its own fallibility. And when I said it couldn't think its way out of the box, that was for its benefit. Actually, we biological units are well known for our unreliability. Supposing it had decided that I was lying?"

McCoy came in and approached the chair. Spock said gravely, "That possibility also occurred to me, which was why I praised your reasoning while we were still in Engineering. But Nomad really was fallible; by not recognizing that possibility itself, it committed a fourth error."

"I thought you'd like to know," McCoy said, "that Lieutenant Uhura is already at college level. We'll have her back on the job within a week."

"Good, Bones. I wish I could say the same for the other crewmen we lost."

"Still," said Spock, "the destruction of Nomad was a great waste. It was a remarkable instrument."

"Which might well have destroyed more billions of lives. It's well gone . . . besides, what are you feeling so bad about? Think of me. It's not easy to lose a bright and promising son."

"Captain?"

"Well, it thought I was its father, didn't it? Do you think I'm completely without feelings, Mr. Spock? You saw what it did for Scotty. What a doctor it would have made." Kirk grinned. "My son, the doctor. Kind of gets you right here, doesn't it?"

MIRROR, MIRROR

Writer: Jerome Bixby
Director: Marc Daniels
First Aired: October 6, 1967

The Halkan Council was absolutely polite, but its position was rock-hard, and nothing that Kirk, McCoy, Scott or Uhura could say would alter it. The Federation was not to be allowed to mine dilithium crystals on the planet. There was too much potential for destruction in the crystals, and the Halkans would allow nothing to compromise their history of total non-violence. To prevent that, they said, they would die—as a race, if necessary. The Council accepted that the Federation's intentions were peaceful, but what of the future? There had been mention of a hostile Klingon Empire . . .

Kirk would have liked to have stayed to argue the question further, but he had already received word from Spock that an ion storm of considerable violence was beginning to blow through the Halkan system—and in fact Kirk could already see evidence of it in the Halkan weather, which was becoming decidedly lowering. To stay longer might risk disruption of transporter transmission, which would strand the landing party for an unknown time. In addition, it was Spock's opinion that the heart of the magnetic storm represented a danger to the *Enterprise* herself.

On this kind of opinion, Kirk would not have argued with Spock for a second; the First Officer never erred by a hairline on the wrong side of conservatism. Kirk ordered the landing party beamed up.

That hairline was very nearly split, this time. On the first attempt, the transporter got the party only partly materialized aboard ship when the beam suffered a phase reversal and all four of them found themselves standing on a bare plateau on the Halkan planet, illuminated only by a barrage of lightning. It was nearly five minutes later before the familiar Transporter Room sprang fully into being around them.

Kirk stepped quickly from the platform toward Spock. "We may or may not get those power crystals . . ."

And then he stopped, in midstep as well as midsentence. For Spock and the transporter chief were saluting, and a most peculiar salute it was: the arms first folded loosely, then raised stiffly horizontal and squared out. Their uniforms were different, too; basically, they were the same as before, but they were much altered in detail, and the detail had a savage military flair—broad belts bearing exposed phasers and what seemed to be ceremonial daggers, shoulder boards, braid. And the Federation breast symbol was gone; instead, there was a blazon which looked like a galaxy with a dagger through it. A similar symbol, in brilliant color, was on one wall of the room, and the equipment was all in the wrong places—indeed, a few pieces of it were completely unfamiliar.

But what struck Kirk most of all was the change in Spock. Vulcans all look somewhat satanic to Earthmen encountering them for the first time, but it had been many years since Kirk had thoroughly gotten over this impression of his First Officer. Now it was back, full force. Spock looked cold, hard, almost fanatical.

Kirk dropped his hands to his belt—since he did not know how to return the strange salute—and encountered something else unfamiliar. A brief glance confirmed what he had feared: his uniform, too, had undergone the strange changes.

"At norm," Spock said to the transporter chief, in a voice loaded with savage harshness. "Captain, do you mean the Halkans have weapons that could resist us? Our socioanalysis indicates that they are incapable of violence."

Kirk could not answer. He was spared having to, for at that moment Sulu entered the Transporter Room. His movements, his manner, were cold, arrogant, hypercompetent, but that was not the worst of it. The symbol on his breast, the galaxy with the dagger through it, had inside it also a clenched fist, around the blade of the dagger, from which blood was dripping. It was an extreme parody of something familiar; it showed that the gentle Sulu, the ship's navigator and helmsman, was now her chief security officer.

Sulu did not salute. He barked, "Status of mission, Captain?"

"No change," Kirk said carefully.

"Standard procedure, then?"

Kirk did not know what this question meant under these eerie circumstances, but he doubted that operating by the book—whatever the book might say—would accomplish much more than delaying matters, and time was what he needed. Therefore, he nodded.

Sulu turned to the nearest intercom. "Mr. Chekov. You will program phaser barrage on Halkan cities, at the rate of one million electron volts per day, in a gradually contracting circle around each. Report when ready."

"Right, Mr. Sulu." Was Kirk imagining it, or was there something thick and gloating in Chekov's voice?

"Unfortunate," Spock said, "that this race should choose suicide to annexation. They possess qualities that could be useful to the Empire."

There was the sputtering hum of an overload from the transporter. Spock's head jerked toward the transporter chief, and then, slowly, inexorably, he advanced on the man. Incredibly, the transporter chief *cringed*.

"Are you not aware, chief, that we are in a magnetic storm? And that you were ordered to compensate?"

"Mr. Spock, sir, I'm sorry. The ion-flux is so unpredictable . . ."

"Carelessness with Empire equipment is intolerable." Spock held out his hand toward Sulu, without looking. "Mr. Sulu, your agonizer."

Sulu plucked a small device from his belt and dropped it in Spock's outstretched palm. In a vicious burlesque of the Vulcan neck pinch, Spock clapped it to the transporter chief's shoulder.

The man screamed. Spock prolonged the agony. When he let go, the chief dropped writhing to the deck.

"More attention to duty next time, please. Mr. Scott, the storm has produced minor damage in your section. Doctor McCoy, there are also some minor injuries requiring your attention." Abruptly, he kicked the semiconscious man on the floor. "You might begin with this hulk."

McCoy, whose running feud with the First Officer had always had a solid undercurrent of affection to moderate it, wore the look of a man whose worst nightmare has abruptly come true. Kirk saw him balling his fists, and moved in fast.

"Get moving, Dr. McCoy. You too, Mr. Scott."

Their expressions flickered for a moment, and then both looked down. Now they knew how the Captain wanted them to play it. At least, Kirk hoped so. In any event, they went out without further comment.

The transporter chief dragged himself to his feet to follow. It did not seem to surprise him at all that the ship's doctor, who had just been ordered to attend to him, had not said a word to him. He said, "Mr. Spock . . ."

"What?"

"Sir, the beam power jumped for a moment, sir—just as the landing party materialized. I never saw anything like it before. I thought you ought to know, sir."

Kirk had already heard more 'sirs' in ten minutes than were normal to the *Enterprise* in a week. Spock said, "Another inefficiency?"

"No, sir, the settings were perfectly normal. I made my error after the party arrived, sir, if I may so remind you."

"Very well. Go to Sickbay. Captain, do you feel any ill effects?"

Kirk could answer that one with no trouble. "Yes, Mr. Spock, I am decidedly shaken up. I expect Lieutenant Uhura is too. I believe we too had better report to Sickbay for a checkup."

"You will of course report instantly if you are found incompetent to command," Sulu said. It was not a question.

"Of course, Mr. Sulu."

"And the matter of the Halkans? A quick bombardment would solve the problem with the least effort."

"I am aware of your—orders—Mr. Sulu. I will give you my judgment as soon as I—feel myself assured that I am competent to give it."

"Most sensible."

As Kirk and Uhura left, everyone again saluted—except Sulu. On the trip to Sickbay, Kirk became aware that there were more guards posted along the corridors than he had ever seen except during the worst kind of major alert. None of them were in standard uniforms; instead, they wore fatigues, like civilian workmen. All saluted. None seemed surprised not to have the salutes returned.

Uhura gasped with relief as the door of Sickbay slid closed behind them and the four people who had been the landing party were once more alone together. "What's *happened?*" she said in a low, intense voice.

"Don't talk too fast," Kirk said instantly, though he himself was talking as fast as he could possibly get the words out. He stabbed a finger toward McCoy's intercom. "Something in the air suggests that that thing is permanently open."

The rest nodded. It was a lucky thing that they had all been together so long; it made elliptical talk possible among them. "Now, Bones, that medical. I want you to check for likely effects. I suggest brainwaves first."

"I've already checked myself and Scotty, sir. No hallucinatory or hypnotic effects. We are dealing with—uh, a perception of reality, if you follow me."

"I'm afraid I do. Mr. Scott, do you detect any changes in the *Enterprise* which—might have a bearing on our reactions?"

Scott inclined his head and listened. "I hear some sort of difference in the impulse engines. Of course they may just be laboring against the magnetic storm. However, the difference seems to me to be, well, technological in nature, sir."

"Excuse me, Captain," Uhura said, "but I feel a little out of my depth. I felt quite dizzy for a moment after we materialized in the beams. Would it be possible . . ."

She did not finish the sentence, but instead made the gesture of someone fitting a bucket or a large hat over McCoy's intercom. The physician's eyebrows went up. He stepped to where his diagnostic apparatus should have been, veered in disgust as he found that it had been moved, and then flicked switches.

"I should have thought of that in the first place," he said, "but I'm as confused as anybody here. Everybody used to complain that my stereotaxic screen jammed the intercoms; let's hope it still does."

"We'll have to take the chance," Kirk said. "Lieutenant Uhura, I felt the same effect. At the same time, we were in our normal Transporter Room—and then it faded, we were back on the planet, and then got beamed back to this situation—whatever it is. And the transporter chief—where is he, by the way?"

"I made him mildly sick," McCoy said, "and sent him to quarters. A nasty reversal of role for a doctor, but I want him out of Spock's reach for a while."

"Well, he mentioned an abnormal effect in the transporter itself. And there's this ion storm."

"Captain," Scott said slowly, "are we thinking the same thing?"

"I don't know, Scotty. But everything fits thus far. It fits with a parallel universe, coexisting with ours, on another dimensional plane—or maybe on another level of probability; everything duplicated—almost. An Empire instead of a Federation. Another *Enterprise*—another Spock . . ."

"Another Jim Kirk?" Scott said quietly. "Another Dr. McCoy?"

"No," McCoy said in startled realization. "An exchange! If *we're here* . . ."

"Our counterparts were beaming at the same time," Kirk said. "Ion storms are common enough, after all. Another storm disrupted another set of circuits. Now we're here; they're on *our* ship, and probably asking each other much the same questions. And coming to the same tentative conclusions. They'll ask the computer what to do. That's what we'll have to do."

McCoy began to pace. "What about the Halkans? We can't let them be wiped out, even if this is another, completely different set of Halkans, in another universe."

"I don't know, Bones. I've got to buy a lot of time. Scotty, get below and short the main phaser coupling. Make it look like the storm blew the standby circuits. Lieutenant Uhura, get to your post and run today's communications from Starfleet Command, or whatever the equivalent is here. I've got to know my exact orders, and options, if any. And by the way, when we want to talk to each other after we're separated, use communicators, and on the subspace band only. And scramble, too."

Uhura and the engineer nodded and left. McCoy had halted his pacing before a sort of glass cage. In it was what appeared to be a large bird, affixed with electrodes. A chart hung beside it.

"What in blazes!" McCoy said. "Jim, look at this. A specimen of an 'annexed' race. I.Q., 180. Experiment in life-support for humans under conditions prevailing on its native planet—heart and lung modifications. It's alive—and if I'm any judge, it's in agony. I won't have such an abomination in my Sickbay!"

"You'll have to, for a while," Kirk said, not without sympathy. "We've got to stay in character until we can get more information. It's an ugly universe, and we don't want to do anything that'll get us stuck with it."

On the bridge, there was a huge duplicate of the galaxy-and-dagger device, and the Captain's chair had widely flared arms, almost like a throne. The man who should be Chekov was eyeing Uhura with open, deliberate, speculative interest, his intent unmistakable. Nobody else seemed to find this unusual or even interesting. Kirk went directly to her.

"Any new orders, Lieutenant?"

"No, sir. You are still ordered to annihilate the Halkans, unless they comply. No alternative action has been prescribed."

"Thank you." He went to his chair and sank in. It felt downright luxurious. "Report, Mr. Sulu?"

"Phasers locked on Target A, Captain. Approaching optimum range. Shall I commence fire?"

"I want a status report first." He touched the intercom. "Mr. Scott?"

"Scott here, sir. I have no change to report, sir. No damage to phasers."

"Very good, Mr. Scott." In fact it was very bad, but there was no help for it. As he switched out, Spock came onto the bridge.

"The planet's rotation is carrying the primary target beyond arc of phaser lock," Sulu said. "Shall I correct orbit to new firing position?"

"No."

Sulu flicked a switch. "Now locked on secondary target city."

"Mr. Spock," Kirk said. "You said the Halkans could be useful. After my visit with them, I agree."

"If they chose to cooperate. They have not."

"Lieutenant Uhura, contact the Halkan Council. We'll make one more try." Noting Spock's surprise, he added, "This is a new race. They offer other things of value besides dilithium crystals."

"But—it is clear that we cannot expect cooperation. They have refused the Empire. Command Procedure dictates that we provide the customary example. A serious breach of Standard Orders . . ."

"I have my reasons, Mr. Spock—and I'll make them clear in my own good time."

"Captain," Uhura said, "the Halkan leader is waiting on Channel B."

Kirk swung to the small viewscreen above Uhura's station. Tharn was on the screen. He looked much tireder, indeed more tragic, than he had when Kirk had seen him last. Now, how would it be possible to make this sound plausible?

"It is useless to resist us," he said at random.

"We do not resist you," Tharn said.

"You have, uh, twelve hours in which to reconsider your position."

"Twelve years, Captain Kirk, or twelve thousand, will make no difference," Tharn said calmly and with great dignity. "We are ethically compelled to refuse your demand for dilithium crystals. You would use their power to destroy."

"We will level your planet and take what we want. *That* is destruction. You would die as a race . . ."

"To preserve what we are. Yes. Perhaps someday your slave planets will all defy you, as we have done. When that comes, how will your starships be able to control a whole galaxy?"

"Switch out, Lieutenant." The screen went blank.

"Twelve hours, Captain?" Spock said. "That is unprecedented."

"Phasers off, Mr. Sulu."

"This conduct must be reported, Captain," Spock said. "You have placed yourself in a most grave position."

"You are at liberty to do so, Mr. Spock," Kirk said, rising. "Take charge. I will be in the briefing room. Inform me of any change. Lieutenant Uhura, attend me there and order Dr. McCoy and Mr. Scott also to report there. Mr. Chekov, relieve Lieutenant Uhura."

He could only hope that this flurry of orders, plus his breach of an unknown regulation, would obscure the fact that he had just called together the landing party.

"Everybody watch your step," Scott said. "They move up through assassination around here. My engine-room chief just tried for me—not personally, but through henchmen. I only got out of it because one of them switched sides."

"What about the technology, Scotty?"

"Mostly variations in instrumentation. Nothing I can't handle. As for star-readings—everything's where it ought to be—except us."

Kirk crossed to the desk and looked down at the computer tap. "Let's see what we're up against. Computer, this is the Captain. Record a Security Research, to be classified under my voiceprint and Mr. Scott's."

"Recorded," said the computer in a harsh masculine voice. Evidently this universe had never discovered that men pay more attention to a machine when its voice is feminine.

"Produce all data relevant to recent magnetic storm, and correlate following hypothesis. Could a storm of that magnitude cause a power surge in transporter circuits, creating momentary interdimensional contact with a parallel universe?"

"Affirmative."

"At such a moment, could persons in each universe, in the act of beaming, be transposed with their counterparts in the other universe?"

"Affirmative."

"Can conditions necessary to such an event be artificially reproduced?"

"Affirmative."

"Record procedure and switch off."

A slot in the desk opened and a spool of tape slid out. Kirk handed it to Scott. "It looks like the ball is yours, Scotty."

"I'll have to tap the power for it out of the warp engines, and balance it for the four of us," the engineer said dubiously. "It's a two-man job, and I'm afraid you'd be too conspicuous, Captain. So would Lieutenant Uhura. Come on, McCoy, let's lay it out."

"I'm not an engineer," McCoy said indignantly.

"You will be. Captain, keep up our public relations, please!"

The two went out. After a moment, Uhura said, "Captain—the way this ship is run—what kind of people *are* we in this universe? I mean, what kind of people do we have to pretend to be?"

"Let's find out. Computer. Readout of official record of current command."

"Captain: James T. Kirk. Succeeded to command *E. S. S. Enterprise* through assassination of Captain Karl Franz. First action: suppression of Gorlan uprising, through destruction of rebel home planet. Second action: execution of five thousand colonists on S Doradus Nine, forcing colony to retract secession. Third action . . ."

"Cancel. Lieutenant, do you really want to hear it tell you what *you're* like?"

Lt. Uhura shuddered. "No. If the way the local Chekov looks at me is any clue, I'll probably hear that my predecessor at my post was my lover, and I got the job by knifing him. How can you run a fifty billion credit starship like a pirate vessel?"

"Pirate ships were pretty efficiently run, Lieutenant. Every man feared those above him—with the strongest at the top. Morgan took Panama with his buccaneer ships as neatly as a squadron of naval vessels might have."

"And then was stabbed in his sleep?"

"No, henchmen protected him—not out of respect or devotion, but because his abilities brought them what they wanted. Other checks and balances—other means to the same end."

"But what end?"

"This ship is efficient—or it wouldn't exist. Its Captain was efficient, or he'd be dead. And this Empire will get the dilithium crystals it wants—efficiently."

Uhura's expression remained grim. "And what do you suppose our counterparts are doing, aboard *our* version of the *Enterprise*?"

"I hope they're faking as well as or better than we are. Otherwise, when we get back, we'll all be up on charges." The intercom beeped. "Kirk here."

"Sir, I'm having trouble on this line, I can barely hear you."

"Right." Kirk switched off, produced his communicator, and set it to subspace level and on "scramble." "Okay, Scotty, here I am. Go ahead."

"We can do it, Captain. But when we interrupt engine circuits, to tie in the power increase to the transporters, it'll show up on the Security Board. We'll just need a second, but . . ."

"All right, wait a minute." Kirk thought fast. "Lieutenant Uhura, this is going to be nasty. I noticed the local Chekov giving you the eye . . ."

"He made a flat-out pass at me before you came on the bridge, Captain."

"All the better. For the sake of our getting home, could you encourage him a little?"

Uhura said slowly, "I wouldn't pull a mean trick like that on *our* Chekov. And this one gives me the crawls. But—of course, Captain, if you wish."

"Good girl. Scotty, Uhura can create a diversion on the bridge, which will draw

Sulu's attention, I think, at your signal. Now, everyone back to posts, before somebody cottons to the fact that this looks like a council of war."

Uhura slipped out silently. Kirk, too, was about to go, when Spock entered the briefing room by another door, and saluted.

"Captain, a word with you, if I may."

"Of course."

"I should regret your death."

Kirk raised his eyebrows. "Very kind of you, Mr. Spock."

"Kindness is not involved. As you know, I do not desire the captaincy. I much prefer my scientific duties—and I am frankly content to be a lesser target."

"Quite logical, as always, Mr. Spock."

"Therefore I am moved to inquire if you intend to persist in your unusual course of action regarding the Halkans."

"My orders stand."

"I presume you have a plan. I have found you to be an excellent officer. Our missions together have been successful ones."

"I remember," Kirk said. "Perhaps better than you do."

"I never forget anything."

"I remember that too. Then you will also remember the illogic of waste, Mr. Spock. Is it logical to destroy potential workers—equipment—valuable installations—without making every effort to put them on a useful basis? Surely the Empire can afford a little patience."

"Logically, we must maintain the terror," Spock said. "Otherwise the Empire will develop soft spots, and the rot will spread."

"The Halkans made the same point. Is history with us? Conquest is easy—control is not."

"History seldom repeats itself," Spock said, frowning. "Yet I concede that no regime such as ours has ever survived the eventual fury of its victims. The question is, has our power become so vast, quantitatively, as to make a *qualitative* change in that situation? Space, as you say, is against us; its sheer vastness makes communication difficult, let alone control—I did not know you were a philosopher, Captain. We have never talked this way before."

"Perhaps overdue, Mr. Spock."

"That is more than possible. I do not judge Commander Moreau to be much of a thinker."

There was quite a long silence, during which Kirk wondered who in blazes Commander Moreau was. Most likely, the man who *was* gunning for the Captain's job.

"Sir," Spock said finally, "I have received a private message from Starfleet Command. I am committing a serious breach of regulations by informing you of its contents. But other considerations supervene. Briefly, I have been instructed to wait until planet dawn over principal target, to permit you to complete our mission. Your delaying maneuver was of course reported to Starfleet Command by Mr. Sulu."

"And if I don't?"

"In that event," Spock said, his voice somehow both harsh and reluctant at the same time, "I am ordered to have you killed, and proceed against the Halkans, as the new Captain of the *Enterprise*. I shall of course remove Moreau too, making it appear that he was killed by *your* agents."

"Logical," Kirk said bitterly. "But thank you for the warning, Mr. Spock."

"I regret the situation. I shall remain in my quarters throughout the night—in case you should wish to contact me privately."

"Thank you again. But there will be no change."

"Sir—under the circumstances—may I express the greatest curiosity concerning your motives?"

"I'm almost tempted to tell you, Mr. Spock. But you'll understand in time. Carry on."

When he left, Kirk sat down at the table. He knew he should be back on the bridge, carrying on the masquerade. But even with Spock's odd sort of cooperation, even supposing Scotty could get them back to their own universe, that would leave the biggest problem unsolved: the fate of the Halkans in this alternate universe. No matter what happened to Kirk, McCoy, Scott and Uhura, the Halkans seemed to be destined for slaughter. And he could think of no way to prevent it.

Then the communicator beeped. "Kirk here."

"Captain, this is Scotty. I've got the whole thing rigged, with McCoy's help. I'm thinking of making him assistant engineer. But in checking it out with the computer, I discovered somethin' vurra worrisome. The two-way matter transmission affected local field density between the two universes—and it's increasing. We've got to move fast. We have half an hour at most. If we miss, we couldn't push back through for a century."

"What's the procedure, Scotty?"

"We're about ready to bridge power from the warp engines to the beams. You've got to go to the main controls and free the board, so we can lock in. Give us ten clock minutes, then you and Lieutenant Uhura create your diversion, and run like Martian scopolamanders for the Transporter Room."

"Right. Count down on the time. Five . . . four . . . three . . . two . . . one . . . *hack*."

"Got you. Good luck, Captain."

No time now to worry about the Halkans; but Kirk worried, nonetheless. On the bridge, Sulu looked speculatively, coldly, at Kirk as Kirk resumed the Captain's chair.

"Orders, Captain?"

"Prepare to lock on to Target A. We fire at planet dawn."

Sulu smiled coldly. "I am glad to see that you have come to your senses. All this computer activity obviously has produced no alternative answer, except to make me wonder if you had gone soft. And while Mr. Spock would no doubt make an excellent captain, you were once clearly the better one. I hope you will continue to be."

Kirk was so sick at the order he had had to give that he did not bother to disguise his disgust. "You don't miss much, do you, Mr. Sulu."

"A good Security Officer misses nothing. Otherwise he would deserve to go to the Agony Booth."

Well, Kirk thought grimly, *you may yet, Mr. Pseudo-Sulu. Obviously you don't know what that computer activity really was about.*

The Halkan planet's image was showing on Uhura's viewscreen. Chekov was watching her, with very much the same lubricious expression as before. She looked up at the image, and then, as if to herself, said, "Just once, I'd like to think about something besides death."

Sulu shot one contemptuous glance at her and went back to watching the master board. When Scott made his power switch from the warp engines to the transporters, he would catch it.

Uhura looked away from the screen toward Chekov. Her glance was steady for a moment, and then she looked down. Her veiled eyes suggested that she just might be persuaded to change her mind.

The navigator grinned, leaned back in his seat. His arm went out and around toward Uhura's waist.

Sulu paid no attention. And there was one minute left.

Slap!

Sulu looked up. Uhura was standing, in furious indignation. She fell back, one, two, three calculated steps toward Sulu's board. Chekov, astonishment changing to rage, was standing too.

But Sulu seemed to be no more than amused. "As you were, Chekov."

Chekov was not ready to be as he was. He seemed almost ready to attack Uhura. Kirk saw an opening and jumped in.

"Is this the kind of horseplay that goes on when I'm not on the bridge? And at moments as critical as this? Mr. Chekov, you are on report; I'll tend to you later. Lieutenant Uhura, you provoked this; proceed immediately to the Booth. Mr. Sulu, take Lieutenant Uhura's post."

"Sir," Sulu said. "Why are you also leaving?" The 'sir' was silkily insulting.

"I am going to explain personally to Lieutenant Uhura why she is in the Booth. I'll return shortly; in the meantime, follow standard procedure."

He had caught the streak of sadism and lechery in these loathsome counterparts of his crew. Every man on the bridge grinned slyly and licked his lips.

Then Kirk and Uhura were out, and running for the Transporter Room.

Spock and two crewmen were waiting for them there, with drawn phasers.

* * *

"Well, Mr. Spock? Have you decided to kill me now, even though I am following my orders?"

"No, Captain. But strange things have occurred since the return of your landing party—including some remarkable calls upon the computer, which I find sealed against me. Nothing in the computer should be sealed against the First Officer. And you are preparing to use an enormous surge of power in the transporter. That could be most dangerous. I must ask you: where do you think you are going, Captain—you and your three conspirators?"

"Home," Kirk said.

"To the alternate universe?"

"You understand *that*?"

"Yes, Captain. And I concur. I will ask you only to gun me down with a stun charge before you leave. My henchmen here will support any story I tell thereafter."

McCoy said, "Mr. Spock, in my universe you and I often disagreed, and in this universe I hated you. But you seem to be a man of integrity in both universes."

"It is only logical," Spock said. "You must return to your universe, so that I can have *my* Captain back. I will operate the transporter. You have two minutes and twenty seconds left."

"Mr. Spock," Kirk said. "I will shave that time as close as possible. I want to ask you this: How long do you think it will be before the Halkans' prediction of galactic revolt is realized?"

Spock blinked, as if the sudden change of subject had taken him unawares. "I would estimate—approximately two hundred and forty years."

"And what will be the inevitable outcome?"

"The Empire will be overthrown, of course. A sort of federation may replace it, if the period of interdestruction is not too devastating."

"Mr. Spock. Consider the illogic of waste. Waste of lives, resources, potentials, time. It is not logical of you to give your vast talents to an empire which you know is doomed."

"You have one minute and twenty-three seconds."

"When change is both predictable and beneficial, why do you resist it?"

"Suicide is also illogical. One man cannot summon the future."

Kirk closed on this man, who looked and acted so much like his First Officer, and yet had so little of the real Spock's hidden humanity in him. "Mr. Spock, one man can change the present. *Be* the Captain of this *Enterprise*, whether you want the job or not. Find a logical reason for sparing the Halkans, and making it stick. Push where it gives. You can defend yourself better than any man in the fleet, if you are anything like *my* First Officer, and I think you are. In every revolution, there's one man with a vision.

Which will it be? Past or future? Tyranny, or the right to hope, trust, love? Even here, Spock, you cannot be totally without the decency you've shown on the—the other side. Use it, make it work!"

"You must go," Spock said. "But my Captain never said any such words to me. I will remember them. I can promise nothing else, though I will save the Halkans if I can. Now, quickly! You have eighteen seconds left! Shoot! And goodbye, Jim Kirk."

Kirk stepped onto the transporter platform with the others. He raised the phaser, set to "stun," but it was very hard to pull the trigger all the same.

Kirk relaxed in his chair, soaking in normality. Nearby, Uhura was giving poor Chekov a look that dripped icicles. Kirk himself still felt a little uncomfortable to find Sulu—the 'real' Sulu—at his elbow.

McCoy, however, evidently had not found it at all hard to readjust; his vast knowledge of psychology under stress also enabled him to understand himself. He said enthusiastically to Spock, "When I came out of the beams, Spocko boy, I was so pleased to see you that I almost kissed you. Luckily, revulsion at the very notion set in two seconds later."

"I am grateful that it did," Spock said.

"Mr. Spock," Kirk said, "Scotty tells me that had you not detected our counterparts immediately, restrained and questioned them, duplicated our calculations, and above all had them shoved into the transporter chamber all ready to make the exchange at the one precise moment, we'd have been stranded forever. I salute you; you have come through for the umpteenth time. But—how did you do it?"

"Sir," Spock said, "you know me as well as any man. But there are elements in my own heart that I do not show very readily. I had to call on them."

"Don't explain if you don't want to. But it would be useful to know how you managed it."

Spock raised his head and looked at some spot faraway in space.

"A civilized man," he said at last, "can easily play the part of a barbarian, as you all did in the other universe. He has only to look into his own soul for the remnants of the savage ancestors from which he sprang, and then—revert. But your counterparts, when we beamed them aboard, were savages to begin with—and had no core of civilization or humanity to which they could revert. The contrast was rather striking."

McCoy said, "Spock, could *you* have played the savage, if you'd been switched along with the rest of us?"

Very seriously, Spock said, "Dr. McCoy, I *am* a savage. Both here, and there. But some day, I hope to outgrow it."

THE APPLE

WRITER: MAX EHRLICH
DIRECTOR: JOSEPH PEVNEY
FIRST AIRED: OCTOBER 13, 1967

Even from orbit, Gamma Trianguli VI seemed both beautiful and harmless, as close to an earthly paradise as the *Enterprise* had ever encountered. Such planets were more than rare, and Kirk thought for a few moments that he might have happened upon a colonizable world—until the sensors indicated that there was already native humanoid life there.

He duly reported the facts to Starfleet Command, who seemed to be as impressed as he was. Their orders were to investigate the planet and its culture. Under the circumstances, Kirk ordered a landing party of six: himself, Spock, Chekov, Yeoman Martha Landon, and two security guards, Marple and Kaplan.

Carrying tricorders and specimen bags, the party materialized in what might almost have been a garden. Large exotic flowers grew in profusion, and there were heavily laden fruit trees. Here and there, outcroppings of rainbow-colored rock competed with the floral hues, and over it all stretched a brilliant, cloudless day. Feeling a sudden impulse to share all this beauty as widely as possible, Kirk called down McCoy and two more security guards—Mallory and Hendorf, as it turned out.

McCoy looked around appreciatively. "I might just put in a claim for all this and settle down."

"I doubt that the natives would approve, Bones," Kirk said. "But it is pretty spectacular."

"A shame we have to intrude."

"We do what Starfleet tells us."

Spock, who had knelt to inspect the soil, arose. "Remarkably rich and fertile, Captain. Husbandry would be quite efficacious here."

"You're sure about that?" Kirk said, amused without quite knowing why.

"Quite sure. Our preliminary readings indicate the entire planet is covered by growth like this. Quite curious. Even at the poles there is only a slight variation in temperature, which maintains a planet-wide average of seventy-six degrees."

"I know," Kirk said. "Meteorologically, that's almost impossible."

"It makes me homesick, Captain," Chekov said. "Just like Russia."

"It's a lot more like the Garden of Eden, Ensign," McCoy said.

"Of course, Doctor. The Garden of Eden was just outside Moscow. A very nice place. It must have made Adam and Eve very sad to leave."

Kirk stared at him; Chekov seemed completely straight-faced and earnest. Was this just another of his outbreaks of Russian patriotism, or some side effect of his developing romance with Yeoman Landon? "All right. There's a village about seventeen kilometers away on bearing two thirty-two. We'll head that way."

"Captain!" The call had come from Hendorf, who was explaining one of the plants: a small bush with large pods, at the center of each of which was a cluster of sharp, thick thorns. "Take a look at—"

With only a slight puff of noise, one of the pods exploded. Hendorf staggered and looked down at his chest. Perhaps a dozen thorns were sticking in a neat group near his heart. He opened his mouth in an attempt to speak, and then collapsed.

McCoy was there first, but only a quick examination was needed. "He's dead."

"What was all that about Paradise?" Kirk said grimly. He took out his communicator. "Kirk to *Enterprise* . . . Mr. Scott, we've already had a casualty. Hendorf has been killed by a poisonous plant at these coordinates. As soon as we've moved out of the way, beam up his body."

"Aye, Captain. That's a shame about Hendorf." Scott paused a moment. "We seem to have a little problem up here, too. We're losing potency in the antimatter banks. I don't think it's serious, but we're looking into it."

"What's causing it?"

"We're not sure. We've run measurements of the electromagnetic field of the planet, and they're a wee bit abnormal. Could have something to do with it."

"Well, stay on top of it. Kirk out."

"I find that odd, Captain," Spock said.

"So do I. But Scotty'll find the problem. Turn up anything with your tricorder?"

"Indeed, sir. Most puzzling. There are strong vibrations under the surface, for miles in every direction."

"Subsurface water?"

"I don't believe so. They are quite strong and reasonably regular. Though I have no evidence to support it, I feel that they are artificially produced. I will, of course, continue to investigate."

"Of course. It may tie in with Scotty's trouble. Ensign Mallory, we'll be heading for the village. Go ahead and scout it out. Avoid contact with the humanoids, but get us a complete picture. And be careful. There may be other dangers besides poisonous plants. Keep in constant communicator touch."

"Aye aye, sir."

Spock held up a hand and froze. "Captain," he said, very softly. "I hear something . . ." He swung his tricorder. "Humanoid . . . a few feet away . . . moving with remarkable agility . . . bearing eighteen."

Kirk made a quick, surreptitious gesture to the two remaining security guards, who nodded and disappeared in opposite directions in the brush. Kirk moved cautiously forward along the bearing. But there was nobody there. Puzzled, he turned back.

"What is it?" Chekov said.

"A visitor," Spock said. "One wanting to retain his anonymity, I would say."

Martha Landon, who had been sticking close to Chekov throughout, shivered.

"What's the matter?"

"Oh, nothing, I suppose," the girl said. "But . . . all this beauty . . . and now Mr. Hendorf dead, somebody watching us. It's frightening."

"If you insist on worrying, worry about me," Chekov said. "I've been wanting to get you in a place like this for a long time."

She beamed at him; obviously nothing could make her happier. Kirk said sharply: "Mr. Chekov, Yeoman Landon, I know you find each other fascinating, but we did not come here to carry out a field experiment in human biology. If you please—"

"Of course, Captain," Chekov said, hurriedly breaking out his tricorder. "I was just about to take some readings."

Kirk rejoined Spock and McCoy, shaking his head. "Nothing. Whoever it is, it moves like a cat."

"Jim, I don't like this."

"Neither do I, Bones, but we have an assignment to carry out. All hands. We've been watched, and we'll probably be watched. Move out—formation D—no stragglers."

The start of the maneuver brought Spock to an outcropping of the rainbow-colored rock. He picked up a piece, studied it, and applied slight pressure. The lump broke into two unequal parts.

"Most interesting. Extremely low specific gravity. Some uraninite, hornblende, quartz—but a number of other compounds I cannot immediately identify. An analysis should be interesting."

He tucked the smaller portion into his specimen bag, and tossed the larger piece away. When it hit the ground, there was a small but violent explosion.

Kirk, shaken, looked around, but no one had been hurt. "You wouldn't mind being a little more careful where you throw rocks, Mr. Spock?"

Spock stared at the outcropping. "Fascinating. Obviously highly unstable. Captain, if indeed this material is as abundant elsewhere as it is here, this is a find of some importance. A considerable source of power."

"Humph. A Garden of Eden—with land mines." His communicator buzzed. "Kirk here. What is it, Scotty?"

"Our antimatter banks are completely inert. I couldn't stop it. But I found out why. There's a transmission of some sort, a beam, from the surface. It affects antimatter like a pail of water on a fire. We're trying to analyze it, but it pinpoints in the area of the village you're approaching, so maybe you could act more effectively from down there."

"We'll try. Kirk out . . . Mr. Spock, could this correlate with the vibrations you detected? A generator of some kind?"

"Possibly. If so, an immense one. And undoubtedly subterranean—*Jim*!"

With a shout, Spock leapt forward and knocked Kirk to the ground. When Kirk got back to his feet, more astonished than angry, Spock was staring at a dozen thorns neatly imbedded in his chest. Then the Vulcan slowly crumpled and fell.

"Spock! McCoy, do something!"

McCoy was already there. "Still alive." He dipped into his kit, came up with his air hypo, inserted a cartridge and gave Spock a shot, seemingly all in one smooth motion. Then, after a moment, he looked up at Kirk. "Not responding, Jim. We'll have to get him to the ship."

"And not just him. We're overextended." Kirk took out his communicator. "Scotty? We're beaming back up, all of us. Notify the Transporter Room. And make arrangements to pick up Ensign Mallory; he's scouting ahead of us."

"Aye aye, sir . . . Transporter Room, stand by to beam up landing party . . . Standing by, Captain."

"Energize."

The sparkle of the Transporter effect began around them. The surroundings started to fade out . . . and then wavered, reappeared, faded, reappeared and stabilized.

"Mr. Scott! What's wrong?"

"No Transporter contact, Captain. The entire system seems to be inhibited. The way it is now, we couldna beam up a fly."

"Any connection with the warp drive malfunction?"

"I dinna ken, skipper, but I'll check on it, and get back to you. Scott out."

Kirk started to turn back to McCoy, then halted with astonishment as he saw Spock stirring. The Vulcan sat up weakly, looking distinctly off his normal complexion.

"Spock!"

"I am quite all right, Captain . . . A trifle dizzy . . ."

"Bones?"

"It must be hard to poison that green Vulcan blood. And then there was the shot. I guess he just took a while bouncing back."

"Just what did you think you were doing?" Kirk demanded, helping Spock up.

"I saw that you were unaware of that plant, so I—"

"So you took the thorns yourself!"

"I assure you I had no intention of doing so. My own clumsiness prevented me from moving out of the way."

"I can jump out of the way as well as the next man. Next time you're not to get yourself killed. Do you know how much money Starfleet has invested in you?"

"Certainly. In training, fifteen thousand, eight hundred a year; in pay up to last month—"

"Never mind, Spock. But . . . thanks."

"Jim," McCoy said, "the more I think about this place, the more I get an idea that . . . Well, it's kind of far out, but . . ."

"Go on, Bones."

"Well, when bacteria invade a human body, the white corpuscles hurry to the invasion point and try to destroy the invader. The mind isn't conscious of it. The body just does it."

"You might be right, Bones. Not only is something after us, but I think it's also after the ship."

Spock shook his head. "To affect the ship at this extreme range, Captain, would require something like a highly sophisticated planetary defense system. It would hardly seem possible—"

He stopped as the group was suddenly enveloped in shadow. They turned as one and stared at the sky. Great towering masses of storm clouds were gathering there. It was impossible; thirty seconds ago the sky had been cloudless. An ominous rumble confirmed that the impossible was indeed happening.

With a deafening clap of thunder, a jagged, blue-white stab of lightning flashed in their midst, tumbling them all like ninepins.

Then the shadow lifted. Kirk got up cautiously. At the spot where the security guard named Kaplan had been standing, there was now only a spot of charred, smoking earth. Helpless, at a loss for words, furious, Kirk stared at it, and then back at the sky as Spock joined him.

"A beautiful day, Mr. Spock," Kirk said bitterly. "Not a cloud in the sky. Just like Paradise."

His communicator beeped. "Mallory here, Captain. I'm near the village. Coordinates one-eighteen by two-twenty. The village is—" Mallory's voice was interrupted by a blast of static.

"What was that, Mallory? I don't read you."

"I'm getting static too. I said it's primitive—strictly tribal from the looks of it. But there's something else—"

Another tearing squeal of static. Mallory's voice stopped. Kirk could not get him back.

"Captain," Spock said, "those coordinates were only a few thousand meters off that way."

"Let's go! On the double!"

They crashed off. As they broke out of the other side of the undergrowth, Kirk saw Mallory running toward them over a field littered with rainbow-colored rocks.

"Over there, Captain," the security guard shouted. "It's—"

He had turned his head as he ran, to point. It was impossible to tell exactly what happened next. Perhaps he stubbed his toe. A rock exploded directly under him.

By the time they reached him, no check by McCoy was needed. His body lay unmoving, bloody, broken.

Kirk, shaken, closed his eyes for a moment. First Hendorf, then Kaplan. He had known Kaplan's family. And Mallory . . . Mallory's father had helped Kirk into the Academy . . .

Spock took his arm, waving the others off.

"Captain . . . in each case, it was unavoidable."

"You're wrong, Spock. I should have beamed us all up the minute things started to go wrong."

"You were under orders. You had no choice."

"I could have saved two men at least. Beamed up. Made further investigations from the ship. Done something! This . . . blundering along down here . . . cut off from the ship . . . the ship's in trouble itself . . . unable to help it . . ."

"We can help it, Captain. The source of the interference with the ship must be here on the planet. Indeed, this may be the only place the difficulty can be solved."

"And how many more lives will I lose?"

"No one has ever stated Starfleet duty was particularly safe. You have done everything a commander could do. I believe—" He broke off, listening. "Captain . . . I think our visitor is back again."

Reluctantly, Kirk turned to Marple, the last of the security guards of the landing party. "Ensign, go ahead fifty yards, swing to your left, cut back, and make a lot of noise. Mr. Spock, Mr. Chekov, make a distraction, a loud one."

He moved quietly away from them toward the brush. Behind him, Chekov's voice rose: "What kind of a tricorder setting do you call that?"

"I will not have you speaking to me in that tone of voice, Ensign!"

"Well, what do you want, violins? That's the stupidest setting I've ever seen—and you a Science Officer!"

Kirk crept stealthily forward.

"It's time you paid more attention to your own duties," Spock's voice shouted uncharacteristically. "Furthermore, you are down here to work, not to hold hands with a pretty yeoman!"

There was somebody, or something, ahead now. Kirk parted the brush. Directly in front of him, his back turned, was a small humanoid, his skin copper red, his hair platinum blond. There seemed to be two tiny silver studs behind his ears. Kirk tensed himself to spring.

At the same time, Marple came crashing toward them from the opposite side. The alien sprang up and ran directly into Kirk's arms. The alien struggled. Measuring him coolly, Kirk struck him squarely on the jaw, and he went down. Clutching his face, he began to cry like a child.

Kirk stood over him, slowly relaxing. Obviously, this creature was no threat. "I'm not going to hurt you," he said. "Do you understand? I won't hurt you."

He spoke, without much hope, in Interstellar. To his surprise, the alien responded in the same tongue, though much slurred and distorted.

"You struck me with your hand."

"I won't strike you again. Here." Kirk extended his hand to help the being up. After a moment, the hand was taken. "You've been following us, watching us. Why?"

"I am the Eyes of Vaal. He must see."

"Who is Vaal?"

"Vaal is Vaal. He is everything."

"You have a name?"

"I am Akuta. I lead the Feeders of Vaal."

The rest of the party began to gather around them. Akuta tried to flinch in all directions at once.

"They won't hurt you either. I promise. Akuta, we have come here in peace. We would like to speak to your Vaal."

"Akuta alone speaks to Vaal. I am the eyes and the voice of Vaal. It is his wish."

"This is fascinating," Spock said. He stepped forward and put his hands gently to Akuta's head, turning it slightly for a closer look at the two small metal studs. "If you will permit me, sir . . . Captain, observe."

"Antennae?" Kirk said.

Akuta had suffered the examination without protest. "They are my ears for Vaal. They were given to me in the dim time, so the people could understand his commands, and obey."

"The people," Kirk said. "Are they nearby?"

"We are close to Vaal, so we may serve him. I shall take you there."

Kirk's communicator shrilled. "Kirk here."

It was Scott: "Captain, something's grabbed us from the planet's surface! Like a giant tractor beam! We can't break loose—we can't even hold our own."

"Warp drive still out?"

"Yes, Captain. All we have is impulse power, and that on maximum. Even with

THE APPLE

that, we'll only be able to maintain power for sixteen hours. Then we'll burn up for sure."

"Mr. Scott, you are my Chief Engineer. You know everything about that ship there is to know . . . more than the men who designed it. If you can't get those warp engines going again—you're fired."

"I'll try everything there is to try, sir. Scott out."

Kirk turned to Akuta. "Tell me about Vaal."

"All the world knows about Vaal. He makes the rains fall, and the sun to shine. All good comes from Vaal."

"Take us to him. We want to speak with him."

"I will take you, but Vaal will not speak with you. He speaks only to me."

"We'll take our chances."

Nodding, Akuta led the way.

Vaal became visible from a clearing some distance away. He was a great serpent-like head, seeming to have been cut out of a cliff. His mouth was open. In color it was greenish bronze, except for its red tongue, which extended from its open mouth. There were steps cut in the tongue, so that a man could walk right up and into the mouth. Two huge fangs extended down, white and polished. Vaal's eyes were open, and they glowed dimly red, pulsating regularly. Even from here, they could hear that the pulsation was timed with a faint but powerful-sounding low-pitched hum.

They drew closer, both Spock and Chekov taking tricorder readings. "Of a high order of workmanship, and very ancient," the First Officer said.

"But this isn't the center, Spock," Kirk said.

"No, Captain. The center is deep beneath it. This would seem to be an access point. In addition there is an energy field extending some thirty feet beyond the head in all directions. Conventional in composition, but most formidable."

"Akuta, how do you talk to Vaal?"

"Vaal calls me. Only then."

Kirk turned to the rest of the party, scowling. "Well, we can't get to it, and we can't talk to it until it's ready to talk."

"Vaal sleeps now," Akuta said. "When he is hungry, you may be able to talk with him—if he desires it."

"When does he get hungry?"

"Soon. Come. We will give you food and drink. If you are tired, you may rest."

He led them down the hill and back into the jungle. It was not very long before they emerged in a tiny village, which looked part Polynesian, part American Indian, part exotic in its own way. There were small thatched huts with hanging batik tapestries, simply made and mostly repeating the totem image of Vaal. At one end of the village area were neatly stacked piles of the explosive rainbow-colored rock. About a dozen aliens were there, men and women, all very handsome, all younger than Akuta. They seemed to be doing nothing at all.

"Akuta," Kirk said, "where are the others?"

"There are no others."

"But . . . where are the children?"

"Children? You speak unknown words to me."

"Little people," Kirk explained. "Like yourselves. But they grow."

"Ah," said Akuta. "Replacements. None are necessary. They are forbidden by Vaal."

"But," said Martha Landon, "when people fall in love—" Chekov was standing next to her, and at these words he smiled and slipped his hand around her waist. She pressed it to her.

"Strange words," said Akuta. "Children . . . love. What is love?"

"Well . . . when a man and a woman are . . . attracted . . ." She did not seem to be able to go any farther. Akuta stared at her and at Chekov's arm.

"Ah. The holding. The touching. Vaal has forbidden this."

"There goes Paradise," said Chekov.

During the questioning, the People of Vaal had been drawing closer and closer, not menacingly, but in simple curiosity. Akuta turned to them.

"These are strangers from another place. They have come among us. Welcome them."

A young man stepped forward, beaming. "Welcome to Vaal."

A girl, beautiful as a goddess, though wearing slightly less, stepped out with a lei of flowers in her hands, smiling warmly. She went to Kirk and put the lei over his head. "Our homes are open to you."

Thus encouraged, the others came over, giggling, touching, exploring, examining the clothing and the gadgets of the strangers. Another young woman put a necklace of shells around Spock's neck.

"It does something for you, Mr. Spock," Kirk said.

"Indeed, Captain. It makes me most uncomfortable."

"I am Sayana," the girl said. "You have a name?"

"I am Spock."

Sayana repeated the name, pointing to him, and so did the rest of the natives, with a wave of laughter.

"I fail to see," Spock said, "what they find so amusing."

"Come," said Akuta. He led the landing party off to one of the huts. The rest of the People of Vaal continued to crowd around, laughing and probing gently.

The interior of the hut was simple, indeed primitive. There were a few baskets, a few wooden vessels, some hangings with the totem image on them, sleeping mats on the floor.

"This house is your house," Akuta said. "I will send food and drink. You are welcome in the place of Vaal."

He went out. Chekov stared after him. "Now we're welcome. A while ago this whole planet was trying to kill us. It doesn't make sense."

"Nothing does down here," McCoy agreed. "I'm going to run a physiological reading on some of those villagers."

He went out after Akuta. Kirk took out his communicator. "Kirk to *Enterprise*. Come in."

"Scott here, sir."

"Status report, Scotty."

"No change, Captain. The orbit is decaying along the computed lines. No success with the warp drive. We're going down and we can't stop it."

"I'm sick of hearing that word 'can't,' Scott," Kirk said harshly. "Get my ship out of there."

"But, sir—we've tried everything within engineering reason—"

"Then use your imagination! Tie every dyne of power the ship has into the impulse engines. Discard the warp drive nacelles if you have to and crack out of there with just the main section—but get out!"

"Well, we could switch over all but the life support circuits and boost the impulse power—black the ship out otherwise—"

"Do it. Kirk out."

McCoy reentered, frowning. "Incredible," he said. "I ran a complete check on the natives. There's a complete absence of harmful bacteria in their systems. No tissue degeneration, no calcification, no arteriosclerosis. In simple terms, they're not growing old. I can't begin to tell you how old any of them are. Twenty years—or twenty thousand."

"Quite possible," Spock said. "It checks with my atmosphere analysis. The atmosphere completely screens out all dangerous radiation from their sun."

"Add to that a simple diet," Kirk said, "perfectly controlled temperature . . . apparently no vices at all . . . no natural enemies . . . and no 'replacements' needed. Maybe it is Paradise, after all—for them."

Outside, there was a curious vibrating sound, not loud, but penetrating, like the striking of an electronic gong. Kirk went out, beckoning to Spock.

The People of Vaal were no longer lounging around. They were moving off toward the cliff, picking up rocks from the stockpiles as they left. Kirk and Spock followed.

At the cliff, the people entered the mouth of Vaal with the rocks, and came out without them. The red eyes were flashing, brightly now.

"Apparently our hypothesis is correct," Spock said. "There is no living being in there. It is a machine, nothing more."

"The field's down. The people are going in. Let's see what luck we have."

Kirk took a step forward. There was an immediate rumble of thunder, to the considerable alarm of the People of Vaal. Kirk stepped back quickly. "That's not the way."

"Evidently not. It is no ordinary machine, Captain. It has shown a capacity for independent action in its attacks upon us. It may well possess a more than rudimentary intelligence."

"But it needs to eat. It can't have any great power reserves."

"Indeed, Captain. But that does not seem to be of help. The ship now has only ten hours to break free."

"What if Vaal's power weakens as it approaches feeding time? Mr. Spock, check with the ship; get an estimate of the total energy being expended against it. And measure it every hour."

"With pleasure, Captain." Spock took his communicator out quickly. Deep in thought, Kirk went back to the hut, where he found all of the landing party outside.

"What was it, Jim?"

"Mess call, Bones."

Spock came up behind him. "A perfect example of symbiosis. They provide for Vaal, and Vaal gives them everything they need."

"Which may also answer why there are no children here," Kirk said. "There are exactly enough people to do what Vaal requires."

"In my view," Spock said, "a splendid example of reciprocity."

"It would take a mind like yours to make that kind of statement," McCoy said.

"Gentlemen, your arguments can wait until the ship is out of danger."

"Jim," McCoy said, "you can't just blind yourself to what is happening here. These are humanoids—intelligent! They've got to advance—progress! Don't you understand what my readings indicate? There's been no change here in perhaps thousands of years! This isn't life, it's stagnation!"

"You are becoming emotional, Doctor," Spock said. "This seems to be a perfectly practical society."

"Practical? It's obscene! Humanoids living only so that they can service a hunk of tin!"

"A remarkable hunk of tin, Bones," Kirk said. "And they seem healthy and happy."

"That has nothing to do with it—"

Kirk's communicator cut in. "Kirk here."

"Scott, sir. We've got a reading on the power source as Spock asked. It *is* dropping a bit at a time—nominal, but a definite drain."

Kirk grinned triumphantly at Spock. "Good. Keep monitoring. How are you doing with the circuit switchover?"

"We're putting everything but the kitchen sink into the impulse drive, sir. It'll take another eight hours to complete the work."

"That's cutting it fine, Scotty."

"Aye, sir. But if we don't break out, I'd rather we didn't have to wait long for the end of it."

Kirk took a deep breath. "Right. Carry on, Scotty. Kirk out."

The hours wore away. A large assortment of fruit and vegetables was brought to the landing party by the People. Martha Landon was nervous and on the verge of tears; Kirk sent her out with Chekov for "a breath of air" and whatever reassurance Chekov could give her. Privately, Kirk hoped also that the People would spy on them; the sight of a little open necking might give them a few ideas disruptive to the absolute control Vaal had over them. Of course, that might provoke Vaal to retaliation—but what more could Vaal do than he was doing now?

Spock seemed to read Kirk's intentions with no difficulty. "I am concerned, Captain," he said. "This may not be an ideal society, but it is a viable one. If we are forced to do what it seems we must, in my opinion, we will be in direct violation of the noninterference directive."

"I'm not convinced that this is a viable society in the accepted sense of the word. Bones was right. These people aren't living, they're just existing. It's not a valid culture."

"Starfleet Command may think otherwise."

"That's a risk I'll have to take." He called the *Enterprise*. "How's it coming, Scotty?"

"Almost ready, sir. We'll need a half hour yet."

"You've only got forty-five minutes until you're pulled into the atmosphere."

"I know, sir. As you said, it's cutting things a bit fine."

"I think we're going to be able to help down here. I'll be back in touch shortly." Kirk cut off. "All hands. We're coming up on the next feeding time for Vaal. Before that happens I want all the Vaalians confined in one hut—the women too, no exceptions. When that gong sounds, round them all up."

The gong in fact sounded only a few minutes later. By this time Chekov and McCoy, phasers drawn, had herded all the People together. They milled around inside the hut, appalled, some wailing and crying.

"Vaal calls us!" Akuta cried out. His face contorted in agony, and he touched the electrodes behind his ears. "We must go to him! He hungers!" The bell rang again. "Please! Let us go to him! We must!"

Kirk got out the communicator again. "Scotty, do you still have phaser power?"

"Aye sir. But what—"

"Lock all banks on the coordinates of the energy field you located down here. On my command, fire and maintain full phasers on those coordinates."

"Aye, sir, but they won't penetrate the field."

"If my guess is right, they won't have to. Stand by."

The bell rang again, louder, longer, more insistently. After checking to see that Chekov and McCoy had the People under control, Kirk and Spock went to the edge of the village. Spock pointed his tricorder toward the cliff.

"Interesting, Captain. The center of the emanations—Vaal—is somewhat weaker than the readings I've been getting. There are wide variations in energy transmission, as though it is drawing from other sources."

"Tapping its energy cells?"

"I would assume so."

"Right. I think the ship's attempts to pull away must have weakened it considerably. It needs to be fed, but the reserve capacity could hold out for days."

"If it has to reinforce its energy field to ward off a phaser attack, it will have to draw more heavily on its reserves."

"My plan exactly, Mr. Spock . . . Kirk to *Enterprise*. Open fire as ordered and maintain."

The phaser beams came down, in long sustained bursts. They were stopped short of the head of Vaal by the force field, but they continued to come down. Sparks flew at the point of contact. A hum rose from Vaal, loud and piercing.

"Tremendous upsurge in generated power, sir. Obviously Vaal is trying to reinforce its energy field."

"Good. Let's see how long it can do it!"

The sky darkened. A strong wind began to blow. Strong flashes of lights lit up Vaal's maw, and some smoke began to appear. The hum was now intolerably loud, and the wind was howling. Lightning flashed overhead, followed by thunder. The din was terrific.

Then, almost all at once, the storm clouds dissipated, the flashes inside Vaal's mouth stopped, and its eyes went out. The hum too was gone.

"Kirk to *Enterprise*. Cease firing."

"No power generation at all," Spock said. "Vaal is dead."

"Mr. Scott, status report."

"Tractor beam gone. Potency returning to antimatter banks. I'll put all engineering sections on repairing the circuits immediately. We'll have the Transporter working in an hour."

Kirk felt as though a great weight had slid off his shoulders. "You're rehired, Mr. Scott. When the Transporter's fixed, form an engineering detail with full analytical equipment and beam them down. I think they'll find some interesting things inside that cave. Kirk out . . . Bones, Chekov. Let them out."

The People emerged, huddled, frightened, still sobbing. McCoy came over to Kirk and Spock.

"Allow me to point out, Captain," Spock said, "that by destroying Vaal, you have also destroyed the People of Vaal."

"Nonsense, Spock!" McCoy said. "It will be the making of these people. Make them stand on their own feet, do things for themselves. They have a right to live like men."

"You mean they have a right to pain, worry, insecurity, tension . . . and eventually death and taxes."

"That's all part of it. Yes! Those too!"

"I hope you will be able to find a way to explain it to them." He nodded toward Akuta, who had moved out of the group toward them, tears streaming down his face.

"Vaal is dead. You have killed him. We cannot live."

"You'll live, Akuta," Kirk said gently. "I'll assign some of my people here to help you."

The girl Sayana was crying quietly. One of the young men, standing by her, obviously wanted to comfort her, but did not know how to start. He made several ineffectual gestures; and then, as if by instinct, his arms went around her waist. She moved closer to him, and her head went onto his shoulder.

"But," Akuta said, "it was Vaal who put the fruit on the trees, who caused the rain to fall. Vaal cared for us."

"You'll find that putting fruit on the trees is a relatively simple matter. Our agronomist will help you with that. As for Vaal taking care of you, you'll have to learn to take care of yourselves. You might even like it.

"Listen to me, all of you. From this day on, you will not depend on Vaal. You are your own masters. You will be able to think what you wish, say what you wish, do what you wish. You will learn many things that are strange, but they will be good. You will discover love; there will be children."

"What are children?" Sayana said.

As the young man's arm tightened around her waist, Kirk grinned. "You just go on the way you're going, and you'll find out."

As Kirk, McCoy and Spock were going toward the bridge, McCoy said: "Spock has an interesting analogy, Captain."

"Yes, Mr. Spock?"

"I am not at all certain that we have done exactly the right thing on Gamma Trianguli VI, Captain."

"We put those people back on a normal course of social evolution. I see nothing wrong with that. It's a good object lesson, Spock, in what can happen when your machines become too efficient, do too much of your work for you. Judging by their language, those people must have been among the very first interstellar colonists—good hardy stock. They tamed the planet, instituted weather control, and turned all jobs of that sort over to a master computer, powered by the plentiful local ore. I suppose the fatal mistake was in giving the computer the power to program itself—and the end product was Vaal . . . Bones said something about an analogy."

"Perhaps you will recall the biblical story of Genesis, sir?"

"I recall it very well, Spock."

"We found a race of people living in Paradise, much as Adam and Eve did. They were obeying every word of Vaal. We taught them, in effect, to disobey that word. In a manner of speaking we have given Adam and Eve the apple . . . the awareness of good and evil, if you will . . . and because of this they have been driven out of Paradise."

Kirk stopped and swung around on Spock suspiciously. "Mr. Spock, you seem to be casting me in the role of Satan. Do I look like Satan?"

"No, sir. But—"

"Is there anyone on this ship who looks even remotely like Satan?"

McCoy was grinning broadly. "I am not aware," Spock said stiffly, "of anyone in that category, Captain."

"No, Mr. Spock. I didn't think you would be."

THE DOOMSDAY MACHINE*

Writer: Norman Spinrad
Director: Marc Daniels
First Aired: October 20, 1967

Shock after shock. First, the distress call from the *Constellation*, a starship of the same class as the *Enterprise*, and commanded by Brand Decker, one of Kirk's oldest classmates; a call badly garbled, and cut off in the middle.

The call seemed to have come from the vicinity of M-370, a modest young star with a system of seven planets. But when the *Enterprise* arrived in the system, the *Constellation* was not there—and neither was the system.

The star had not gone nova; it was as placid as it had always been. But of the planets there was nothing left but asteroids, rubble and dust.

Lt. Uhura tried to project the line of the distress call. The line led through four more former solar systems—*all* now nothing but asteroids, rubble and dust . . . No, not quite: The two inner planets of the fifth system appeared to be still intact—and from somewhere near where the third planet should have been, they heard once more the weak beacon of the *Constellation*, no longer signaling distress, but black disaster.

The beacon was automatic; no voice came from her despite repeated calls. And when they found her, the viewscreen showed that two large, neat holes, neat as phaser cuts, had been drilled through her warp-drive pods.

Kirk called a yellow alert at once, though there was no sign of a third ship in the area, except for some radio interference which might easily be sunspots. Scott reported that all main and auxiliary power plants aboard the *Constellation* were dead, but that the batteries were operative at a low level. Her life support systems were operative, too, also at a very low level, except for the bridge area, which—as the viewscreen showed—was badly damaged and uninhabitable.

"We'll board," Kirk said. "The *Constellation* packed as much firepower as we do; I want to know what could cut a starship up like that. And there may be a few survivors. Bones, grab your kit. Scotty, select a damage control party and come with us. Mr. Spock, you'll stay here and maintain Yellow Alert."

"Acknowledge," Spock said.

---

* Hugo Award nominee

* * *

Aboard the *Constellation*, the lights were weak and flickering, and wreckage littered the deck. The three crewmen of the damage control party found the radiation level normal, the air pressure eleven pounds per square inch, the communications system shorted out, the filtration system dead. The warp drive was a hopeless pile of junk. Surprisingly, the reactor was intact—it had simply been shut down—and the impulse drive was in fair shape.

But there were no survivors—and no bodies.

Kirk thought this over a moment, then called the *Enterprise*. "Mr. Spock, this ship appears abandoned. Could the crew have beamed down to one of those two planets?"

"Improbable, Captain," Spock's voice replied. "The surface temperature on the inner planet is roughly that of molten lead, and the other has a poisonous, dense atmosphere resembling that of Venus."

"All right, we'll keep looking. Kirk out."

"The phaser banks are almost exhausted," Scott reported. "They didn't give her up without a battle."

"But *where are they?* I can't understand a man like Brand Decker abandoning his ship as long as his life support systems were operative."

"The computer system is still intact. If the screen on the engineers' bridge is still alive, we might get a playback of the Captain's log."

"Good idea. Let's go."

The screen on the engineers' bridge was in fact dead, but they forgot this almost the moment they noticed it; for seated before the console, staring at the useless instruments, was Commodore Brand Decker. His uniform was tattered, his hair mussed.

"Commodore Decker!"

Decker looked up blankly. He seemed to have trouble focusing on Kirk. McCoy was quickly beside him.

"Commodore—what happened to your ship?"

"Ship?" Decker said. "Attacked . . . that thing . . . fourth planet breaking up . . ."

"Jim, he's in a state of shock," McCoy said. "No pressure on him now, please."

"Very well. Do what you can for him here. We've got to question him."

"He mentioned the fourth planet," Scott said. "There are only two left now."

"Yes. Pull the last microtapes from the sensor memory bank and beam them across to Spock. I want a full analysis of all reports of what happened when they went in on that planet."

"I've given this man a tranquilizer," McCoy said. "You can try a few questions now. But take it easy."

Kirk nodded. "Commodore, I'm Jim Kirk, in command of the *Enterprise*. Do you understand?"

"*Enterprise?*" Decker said. "We couldn't contact—couldn't run—had to do it—no choice at all . . ."

"No choice about what?"

"I had to beam them down. The only chance they had . . ."

"Do you mean your crew?"

Decker nodded. "I was—last aboard. It attacked again—knocked out the transporter. I was stranded aboard."

"But *where* was the crew?"

"The third planet."

"There is no third planet now."

"There was," Decker said. "There *was*. That thing . . . destroyed it . . . I heard them . . . four hundred of my men . . . calling for help . . . begging me . . . and I couldn't . . ." The Commodore's voice went slower and slower, as though he were an ancient clockwork mechanism running down, and faded out entirely.

"Fantastic," Scott said, almost to himself. "What kind of a weapon could do that?"

"If you had seen it—you'd know," Decker said, rousing himself with obvious effort. "The whole thing is a weapon. It must be."

Kirk said, "What does it look like, Commodore?"

"A hundred times the size of a starship—a mile long, with a maw big enough to swallow a dozen ships. It destroys planets—cuts them to rubble."

"Why? Is it an alien ship—or is it alive?"

"Both—neither—I don't know."

"Where is this thing now?"

"I—don't know that either."

Kirk lifted his communicator. "Mr. Spock, still no sign of any other vessel in the vicinity?"

"Well, yes and no, Captain," the First Officer replied. "The subspace radio interference is now so heavy as to cut us off from Starfleet Command; obviously it cannot be sunspots. But our sensors still show only the *Constellation*."

"How is the tape analysis going?"

"We're ready now, Captain. We find that the *Constellation* was attacked by what seems to be essentially a robot—an automated weapon of great size and power. Its apparent function is to smash planets to rubble, and then 'digest' the debris for fuel. It is, therefore, self-maintaining as long as there are planetary bodies to feed it."

"Origin?"

"Mr. Sulu has computed the path of the machine, using the destroyed solar systems detected by ourselves and the *Constellation* as a base course. We find the path leads out of the galaxy at a sharp angle. Projected in the opposite direction, and assuming that the machine does not alter its course, it will go through the most densely populated section of our galaxy."

"Thank you, Mr. Spock. Maintain Yellow Alert and stand by. Commodore Decker, you've had a rough time. I think it would be best if you and Dr. McCoy beam back to my ship for a physical examination."

"Very well," Decker said. "But you heard your First Officer, Captain. That thing is heading for the heart of our galaxy—thousands of populated planets! *What are you going to do?*"

"I'm going to think," Kirk said. "Mr. Spock, have the Transporter Room beam Dr. McCoy and Commodore Decker aboard immediately."

A moment later, the two men shimmered out of existence, leaving no one but Kirk and Scott on the dead engineers' bridge.

"They're aboard, Captain," Spock's voice said from the communicator. And then, without any transition at all, "Red alert! Red Alert! Mr. Sulu, out of the plane of the ecliptic at sixty degrees north! Warp One!"

"Mr. Spock!" Kirk shouted, although of course Spock could have heard him equally well if he had whispered. "Why the alert? Why are you running? I'm blind here."

"Commodore Decker's planet-killer, Captain. It just popped out of subspace. Metallic body, a large funnelmouth, at least a mile long. It is pursuing us, but we seem to be able to maintain our distance at Warp One. No, it's gaining on us. Sensors indicate some kind of total conversion drive. No evidence of life aboard. Which is not surprising, since isotope dating indicates that it is at least three billion years old."

"Three *billion*!" Kirk said. "Mr. Spock, since it's a robot, what are our chances of deactivating it?"

"I would say none, Captain. I doubt that we would be able to maneuver close enough without drawing a direct attack upon ourselves. We could of course beam men aboard in spacesuits, but since the thing is obviously designed to be a doomsday machine, its control mechanisms would be inaccessible on principle."

"A doomsday machine, sir?" Scott said.

"A calculated bluff, Scotty. A weapon so powerful that it will destroy both sides in a war if it's used. Evidently some race in another galaxy built one—this one—and its bluff was called. The machine is now all that's left of the race—and it's evidently programmed to keep on destroying planets as long as it's functioning."

"Well, whatever happens, we can't let it go beyond us to the next solar system. We have to stop it here. You'd better . . ."

He was interrupted by the filtered sound of a concussion.

"Mr. Spock!" a distant voice called. It sounded like Uhura. "We've taken a hit! The transporter's out!"

"Emergency power on screens. Maximum evasive action! Phaser banks . . ."

And then the communicator went dead.

"Spock! Come in! Spock!" It was useless. "Scotty—we're stuck here. Deaf and blind."

"Worse than that, Captain. We're paralyzed, too. The warp drive is just so much wreckage."

"We can't just sit here while that thing attacks our ship. Forget the warp drive and get me some impulse power—half-power, quarter-power, anything I can maneuver with, even if you have to get out and push."

"But we'd never be able to outrun . . ."

"We're going to fight the thing, not outrun it," Kirk said grimly. "If we can get this hulk going, we may be able to distract the robot, and give the *Enterprise* a better chance to strike at it. Get cracking, Scotty. I'm going to see what I can do with this viewscreen. We can't move until I can see where we're going."

Seated in the Captain's chair, Spock evaluated the damage. Warp and impulse drives were still operative. As he checked, Commodore Decker and McCoy watched him tensely.

"Communications?"

"Under repair, Mr. Spock," Uhura said.

"Transporter?"

Sulu said, "Also under repair."

"Hmm," Spock said. "Random factors seem to have operated in our favor."

"In plain, non-Vulcan English," McCoy said, "we've been lucky."

"Isn't that what I said, Doctor?" Spock said blandly.

"The machine's veering off," Sulu reported. "It's back on its old course. Next in line is the Rigel system."

"No doubt programmed to ignore anything as small as a ship beyond a certain radius," Spock said. "Mr. Sulu, circle back so we can pick up the Captain while we effect repairs. We may have to take the *Constellation* in tow . . ."

"You can't let that thing reach Rigel!" Decker broke in. "Millions of innocent people . . ."

"I am aware of the population of the Rigel colonies, Commodore, but we are only one ship. Our deflector generators are strained. Our radio is useless as long as we are in the vicinity of the robot. Logic dictates that our primary duty is to survive to warn Starfleet Command."

"Our primary duty is to maintain the life and safety of Federation planets! Helmsman, belay that last order! Track and close on that machine!"

Sulu looked questioningly at Spock. It was a difficult problem. Kirk had left Spock in command, but Decker was the senior officer aboard. Spock said evenly, "Carry out my last order, Mr. Sulu."

"Mr. Spock," Decker said, "I'm formally notifying you that I am exercising my option under regulations as senior officer to assume command of the *Enterprise*. That thing has got to be destroyed."

"You attempted to destroy it before, sir," Spock said, "and it resulted in a wrecked ship and a dead crew. Clearly a single ship cannot combat that machine."

Decker winced, then stabbed a finger at Spock. "That will be all, Mr. Spock. You're relieved of command. Don't force me to relieve you of duty as well."

Spock got up. McCoy grabbed his arm. "Spock, you can't let him do this!"

"Unfortunately," Spock said, "Starfleet Order one-zero-four, Section B, reads, Paragraph A, 'In the absence of the . . .'"

"To blazes with regulations! How can you let him take command when you *know* he's wrong?"

"If you can officially certify Commodore Decker medically or psychologically unfit to command, I may relieve him under Section C."

"I can't do that," McCoy said. "He's as sound as any of us. I can say his present plan is crazy, but medically I'd have to classify that as a difference of opinion, not a diagnosis."

"Mr. Spock knows his duties under the regulation," Decker said. "Do you, Doctor?"

"Yes, sir," McCoy said disgustedly. "To go to Sickbay and wait for the casualties you're about to send me." He stalked out.

"Hard about and close," Decker said. "Full emergency power on deflectors. Stand by on main phaser banks."

On the viewscreen, the planet-killer began to grow in size. Decker stared at it with grim intensity, as though the combat to come was to be a personal one, hand-to-hand.

"In range, sir," Sulu reported.

"Fire phasers!"

The beams lanced out. It was a direct hit—but there seemed to be no effect at all. The beams simply bounced off.

In answer, a pencil of solid blue light leapt out of the maw of the planet-killer. The *Enterprise* seemed to stagger, and for a moment all the lights went down.

"Whew!" Sulu said. "What *is* that thing?"

"It's an anti-proton beam," Decker said in an abstracted voice. "It's what the machine cut the fourth planet up with."

"The deflectors weren't built to take it, sir," Spock said. "The next time, the generators may blow."

Decker paid no attention. "Keep closing and maintain phaser fire."

Spock studied his instruments. "Sir," he said, "sensors indicate that the robot's hull is neutronium—collapsed matter so dense that a cubic inch of it would weigh a ton. We could no more get a phaser beam through it than we could a matchstick. If we could somehow get a clear shot at the internal mechanism . . ."

"Now that's more like it, Mr. Spock. We'll cut right across the thing's funnel and ram a phaser beam down its throat. Helmsman, change course to intercept."

Sulu shifted the controls cautiously, obviously expecting another blow from the anti-proton beam; but evidently the monstrous mechanism had no objection to having this morsel sailing directly into its maw.

"Fire!"

The phasers cut loose. Sulu studied the screen intently.

"Those beams are just bouncing around inside," he reported. "We can't get a shot straight through."

"Close in."

"Sir," Spock said, "any closer and that anti-proton beam will go through our deflectors like tissue paper."

"We'll take the chance. Thousands of planets are at stake."

"Sir, there is no chance at all. It is pure suicide. And attempted suicide would be proof that you are psychologically unfit to command. Unless you give the order to veer off, I will relieve you on that basis."

"Vulcan logic!" Decker said in disgust. "Blackmail would be a more honest word. All right, helmsman, veer off—emergency impulse power."

"Commodore," Sulu said in a strained voice, "I can't veer off. That thing's got some kind of a tractor beam on us."

"Can it pull us in?"

"No, sir, we can manage a stand-off, for perhaps seven hours. In the meantime it can take pot shots at us whenever it likes."

On the engineers' bridge of the *Constellation*, the viewscreen finally lit. Kirk stared at what it showed with shock and disbelief. A gasp from behind him told him that Scott had just entered the bridge.

"Is Spock out of his mind?"

"I don't understand it either—I ordered evasive action. What's the situation below?"

"We've got the screens up, but they won't last more than a few hours, and they can't take a beating. As for the impulse drive, the best I can give you is one-third power. And at that I'll have to nurse it."

"Go ahead then. We've got to break up that death-dance out there somehow." As Scott left, Kirk once more tried his communicator. To his gratification, he got Lt. Uhura at once; evidently the *Enterprise*, too, had been making repairs. "Lieutenant, give me Mr. Spock, fast."

But the next voice said: "*Enterprise* to Kirk. Commodore Decker here."

"Decker? What's going on? Give me Mr. Spock!"

"I'm in command here, Captain. According to regulations, I assumed command on finding Mr. Spock reluctant to take proper action . . ."

"You mean you're the lunatic responsible for almost destroying my ship? Mr. Spock, if you can hear me, I give you a direct order to answer me."

"Spock here, Captain."

"Good. On my personal authority as Captain of the *Enterprise*, I order you to relieve Commodore Decker. Commodore, you may file a formal protest of the violation of regulations involved with Starfleet Command—if any of us live to reach a star base. In the meantime, Mr. Spock, if the Commodore resists being relieved, place him under arrest. Is that clear?"

"Not only is it clear," Spock's voice said, "but I have just done so. Your further orders, sir?"

"Get away from that machine!"

"Sir, we can't; we have been pegged by a tractor. The best we can do is prevent ourselves from being pulled inside it, for about the next six point five hours—or until it decides to shoot at us again."

"I was afraid of that. All right, I'm going to move the *Constellation* into your vicinity and see if I can distract the machine. With the power I've got available, it will take at least three hours. Is your transporter working again, too?"

"Yes, sir, but I assure you that you'd be no safer here than there."

"I'm aware of that, Mr. Spock. I just want to be sure you can beam me aboard once we're in range, so I can take command personally from the Commodore if he gives you any trouble. That's all for now. Kirk out."

Kirk set the *Constellation* in creaking motion and then thought a while. Finally he called Scott.

"How's the drive holding up, Scotty?"

"Under protest, I would say, sir," Scott responded. "But if you don't demand any violent maneuvers I think it'll stay in one piece."

"Very well. Now I need an engineering assessment. What would happen if the reactor were to go critical?"

"Why, Captain, you know as well as I do—a fusion explosion, of course."

"Yes, Scotty, but if *this* reactor were to do so, how big would the explosion be?"

"Oh," Scott's voice said. "That's easily answered, the potential is always on the faceplate of a ship's reactor; I'll just check it . . . The figure is 97.8 megatons."

"Would the resulting fireball be sufficient to disrupt a neutronium hull?"

"Neutronium, sir? You mean the planet-killer? What makes you think the hull is neutronium?"

The Doomsday Machine

"Because from this distance the *Enterprise* could have cut it into scrap metal by now if it weren't."

"Hmm—aye, that follows. Well, Captain, neutronium is formed in the cores of white dwarf stars, with fusion going on all around it. So I'd say the fireball would just push the machine away, rather than collapsing the hull. And sir, in a vacuum the fireball would be something like a hundred and fifty miles in diameter. That means it would envelop the *Enterprise* too—and *we* don't have a neutronium hull."

"That's true, but it isn't what I have in mind. Scotty, I want you to rig a thirty-second delayed detonation switch, so the reactor can be blown from up here on the engineers' bridge. Can do?"

"Aye, sir," Scott said. "But why . . ."

"Just rig it, fast. Then get yourself and the damage control party up here. Kirk to *Enterprise*."

"Spock here."

"Mr. Spock, I don't have any sensors over here worth mentioning, so I won't know when I'm in transporter range. The instant I am, let me know."

"Acknowledge. May I ask your intent, Captain?"

"Scotty is rigging a thirty-second delayed detonation switch on the impulse power reactor of the *Constellation*. I am going to pilot the vessel right down the planet-killer's throat—and you'll have thirty seconds to beam the five of us aboard the *Enterprise* before the reactor blows."

There was a brief pause. When Spock's voice returned, there actually seemed to be a faint trace of human concern in it. "Jim, thirty seconds is very fine timing. The transporter is not working at a hundred per cent efficiency; our repairs were necessarily rather hasty."

"That's a chance I'll have to take. However, it does change things a little. I'll want you to beam Mr. Scott and the damage control party over as soon as we are in range. I'll be the only one to stay aboard until the last minute."

"Acknowledge. Sir, may I point out two possible other flaws?"

While Spock was talking, Scott came into the room carrying a small black box. Mounted on it was a single three-position knife switch—that is, one with two slots for the blade, the third position being disengaged from either. He set it down on the panel in front of Kirk.

"Go ahead, Mr. Spock, your advice is half your value. Where are the flaws?"

"First, we cannot know the composition of the interior workings of the planet-killer. If they too are neutronium, nothing will happen except that it will get very hot inside there."

"'Very hot' is certainly a mild way of putting it," Kirk said drily. "All right, Mr. Spock, to use logic right back at you, Proposition A: The planet-killer operates in a vacuum, which means most of its circuits are cryogenic. Heating them a few million degrees may be quite enough to knock it out. Proposition B: Pure neutronium cannot carry an electrical current, because its electron shells are collapsed. Hence, many important parts of the planet-killer's interior cannot be neutronium. Conclusion: an interior fusion explosion will kill it. How is that for a syllogism?"

"It is not a syllogism at all, Captain, but a sorites; however, I agree that it is a sound one. My second objection is more serious. The planet-killer is open to space at one end, and that is the end facing us. The neutronium hull will confine the fireball and shoot it directly out of the funnel at the *Enterprise* in a tongue of flame hundreds of miles long. This is an undesirable outcome."

Kirk almost laughed, although there was nothing in the least funny about the objection itself. "Mr. Spock, if that happens, we will all die, But the planet-killer will have been destroyed. Our mandate is to protect Federation lives, property and interests. Hence this outcome, as you call it, is in fact more desirable than undesirable."

"Now that," Spock said, "*is* a syllogism, and a sound one. Very well, Captain, I withdraw my objections."

When Kirk put down the communicator, he found Scott staring at him ruefully. "Your sense of humor," the engineer said ruefully, "comes out at the oddest times. Well, there is your detonator, Captain. When you pull the switch into the *up* position, it's armed. When you push it down into the other slot, you have thirty seconds until *blooey*!"

"Simple enough."

"Captain," Spock's voice came again. "The *Constellation* has just come within transporter range. However, when you are ready to have your party beam over, I suggest that you leave the bridge. We do not have fine enough control to pick four men out of five, and even if we did, we would not know which four of the five until it was too late."

"Very well, Mr. Spock. I will leave the bridge; make your pickup in sixty seconds."

He got up. As he was at the door, Scott said, "Take care, Jim."

"Scotty, I don't *want* to die, I assure you."

When he returned, the engineers' bridge was empty; but Scott's voice was still there. It was coming from the communicator, and it was using some rather ungentlemanly language.

"Scotty, what's the matter? Are you all right?"

"Aye, I'm all right, skipper, and so are we all—but the transporter blew under the load. I dinna ken hae lang it'll take to fix it."

The return of Scott's brogue told Kirk how serious the situation actually was. Kirk did not even say, "Well, do your best." It was unnecessary.

The next few hours were an almost intolerable mixture of loneliness and tension, while the monstrous shape of the planet-killer and its mothlike captive grew slowly on the screen.

The Doomsday Machine

Yet not once in all this time did the robot again fire its anti-proton beam, which probably would have gone through the *Enterprise* like a knife through cheese; the ship was using almost all her power in fighting against the tractor ray. That, Kirk supposed, was a present given them by the nature of machine intelligence; the robot, having settled on the course of drawing the *Enterprise* into itself—and, probably, having estimated that in such a struggle it could not lose, eventually—saw no reason to take any other action.

"Mr. Spock?"

"Yes, Captain."

"Don't fire on that thing again. Don't do *anything* to alter present circumstances—not even sneeze."

"I follow you, Captain. If we do not change the parameters, the machine mindlessly maintains the equation."

"Well, that's what I hope. How is the transporter coming?"

"Slowly. Mr. Scott says half its resistors are burned out. They are easy to replace individually, but so many is a time-consuming task."

"Computation?"

"We may have a most unreliable repair done when the *Constellation* is within a hundred miles of the robot. Sir, we also compute that one hundred miles is the limit of the robot's defensive envelope, inside which it takes offensive action against moving objects under power."

"Well, I can't very well shut off power. Let's just hope it's hungry."

The funnel swelled, much faster now. Kirk checked his watch, then poised his hand over the switch.

"Mr. Spock, I'm running out of time myself. Any luck now on the transporter?"

"It may work, Captain. I can predict no more."

"All right. Stand by."

The funnel now covered the entire star field; nothing else was to be seen but that metal throat. Still the robot had not fired.

"All right, Spock! Beam me aboard!"

He threw the switch. An instant later, the engineers' bridge of the doomed *Constellation* faded around him, and he found himself in the Transporter Room of the *Enterprise*. He raced to the nearest auxiliary viewscreen. Over the intercom, Spock's voice was counting: "Twenty-five seconds to detonation. Computer, mark at ten seconds and give us a fiftieth of a second warp drive at Warp One at second zero point five."

This order baffled Kirk for an instant; then he realized that he was *still* looking down the throat of the doomsday machine, and that Spock was hoping to make a short sub-space jump away the instant the robot's tractor apparatus was consumed—if it was.

"Fifteen seconds. *Mark*. Five seconds. Four. Three. Two. One."

Flick!

Suddenly, on the auxiliary screen, the doomsday machine was thousands of miles away. The screen zoomed up the magnification to restore the image.

As it did so, a spear of intolerable light grew out of the mouth of the funnel. Promptly, Kirk ran for the elevators and the control room.

A silent group was watching the main viewscreen, including Commodore Decker. The tongue of flame was still growing. It now looked to be at least two hundred miles long. It would have consumed the *Enterprise* like a midge.

Then, gradually, it faded. Spock checked his board.

"Did it work?" Kirk demanded.

"I cannot tell yet, Captain. The radiation from the blast itself is too intense. But the very fact that we broke away indicates at least some damage . . . Ah, the radiation is decaying. Now we shall see."

Kirk held his breath.

"Decay curve inflecting," Spock said. "The shape—yes, the curve is now exponential. All energy sources are deactivated. Captain, it is dead."

There was a pandemonium of cheering. Under cover of the noise, Decker moved over to Kirk.

"My last command," he said in a low voice. "But you were right, Captain Kirk. My apologies for usurping your command."

"You acted to save Federation lives and property, as I did. If you in turn are willing to drop your complaint against my overriding regulations—which you have every right to make—we'll say no more about it."

"Of course I'll drop it. But the *Constellation* is nevertheless my last command. I cannot forget that my first attempt to attack that thing cost four hundred lives—men who trusted me—and that I had the bad judgment to try it again with *your* men's lives. When a man stops learning, he's no longer fit to command."

"That," Kirk said, "is a judgment upon yourself that only you can make. My opinion is that it is a wise and responsible judgment. But it is only an opinion. Mr. Sulu?"

"Sir?"

"Let's get the dancing in the streets over with, and lay a course for Star Base Seventeen."

"Yes, sir." But the helmsman could not quite stop grinning. Spock, of course, never grinned, but he was looking, if possible, even more serious than usual.

"Mr. Spock, you strike me as a man who still has some reservations."

"Only one, Captain; and it is pure speculation."

"Nevertheless, let's hear it."

"Well, Captain, when two powers prepare forces of such magnitude against each other, it almost always means that they are at a state of technological parity; otherwise they would not take such risks of self-destruction."

"Meaning?"

"Meaning, sir, that the existence of one such doomsday machine implies the existence of another."

"I suppose that's possible," Kirk said slowly, repressing a shudder. "Though the second one may not have been launched in time. Well, Mr. Spock, supposing we were to hear of another? What would you do?"

Spock's eyebrows went up. "That is no problem, sir. I would feed it a fusion bomb disguised as a ship, or better still, an asteroid; that is not what concerned me. The danger, as such, can now be regarded as minimal, even if there *is* another such machine."

"Then if you weren't thinking of the danger, what *were* you thinking of?"

"Of the nuisance," Spock said. "Having to deal with the same problem twice is untidy; it wastes time."

Kirk thought back to those hours aboard the haunted hulk of the *Constellation*—and of the four hundred dead men on the devoured planet.

"I," he said, "prefer my problems tidy. It saves lives."

METAMORPHOSIS

WRITER: GENE L. COON
DIRECTOR: RALPH SENENSKY
FIRST AIRED: NOVEMBER 10, 1967

It was not often that the *Enterprise* needed the services of her shuttlecraft *Galileo*, for usually the Transporter served her purposes better; but this was one of those times. The *Enterprise* had been on other duty when the distress call had come from Epsilon Canaris III, well out of Transporter range, and not even the *Enterprise* could be in two places at once.

Now, however, the *Galileo* was heading back for rendezvous with the mother ship, Kirk at the controls, Spock navigating. The shuttlecraft's passengers were Dr. McCoy and his patient, Assistant Federation Commissioner Nancy Hedford, a very beautiful woman in her early thirties, whose beauty was marred by an almost constant expression of sullenness. The expression did not belie her; she was not a particularly pleasant person to be around.

"We have reached projected point three, Captain," Spock said. "Adjust to new course 201 mark 15."

"Thank you, Mr. Spock . . . Doctor, how is she?"

"No change."

"Small thanks to the Starfleet," Nancy Hedford said.

"Really, Commissioner," McCoy said, "you can't blame the Starfleet—"

"I should have received the proper inoculation ahead of time."

"Sukaro's disease is extremely rare, Commissioner. The chances of anyone contracting it are literally billions to one. How could we predict—"

"I was sent to that planet to prevent a war, Doctor. Thanks to the inefficiency of the medical branch of the Starfleet I have been forced to leave before my job was done. How many millions of innocent people will die because of this so-called rare disease of mine?"

Privately, Kirk was of the opinion that she was overestimating her own importance; her senior officer could probably handle the situation alone—or maybe even better. But it wouldn't do to say so. "Commissioner, I assure you, once we reach the *Enterprise*, with its medical facilities, we'll have you back on your feet in no time. You'll get back to your job."

"And just how soon will we rendezvous with this ship of yours, Captain?"

"Four hours and twenty-one minutes."

"Captain," Spock said. "The scanners are picking up some kind of small nebulosity ahead. It seems to be—yes, it is on a collision course."

"It can hardly matter," Kirk said, "but we'll swerve for it anyhow."

This, however, proved impossible to do. Every time Kirk changed the *Galileo*'s course, the cloud did also. Soon it was within visual distance, a phosphorescent, twisting blob against the immensities of space.

Spock checked the sensors. "It appears to be mostly ionized hydrogen, Captain. But I would say nevertheless that it is not a natural object. It is too dense, changes shape too rapidly, and there is a high degree of electrical activity."

"Whatever it is, we're about to be right in the middle of it."

He had scarcely spoken when the view ahead was completely masked by the glowing, shifting cloud. A moment later, the controls went dead. A quick check showed that communications were out, too.

"Readings, Mr. Spock?"

"Extremely complex patterns of electrical impulses, and an intense magnetic field—or rather, a number of them. It seems to have locked onto us."

The craft lurched, slightly but definitely. Kirk looked down at his console. "Yes, and it's taking us with it."

"Captain!" the woman's voice called. "What's happening? I demand to know!"

"You already know about as much as we do, Commissioner. Whatever that thing is outside, it's pulling us off our course for the *Enterprise*."

"Now on course 98 mark 12," Spock said. "Heading straight into the Gamma Canaris region."

"Jim!" McCoy said. "We've got to get Miss Hedford to the *Enterprise*—her condition—"

"I'm sorry, Bones. There's nothing we can do."

"I am not at all surprised," Miss Hedford said coldly. "This is exactly the sort of thing I expect from the Starfleet. If I am as sick as this dubious authority claims I am—"

"Believe me, you are," McCoy said. "You may feel fine now, but nevertheless you're very ill."

"Then why are you all just sitting there? I insist—"

"I'm sorry, Commissioner," Kirk said. "We'll do what we can when we can—but right now we're helpless. You might as well sit back and enjoy the ride."

The *Galileo* was put down—there seemed to be no other word for it—on a small planet, of which very few details could be seen through the enveloping nebulosity. But the moment they had grounded, the cloud vanished, leaving them staring out at a broad, deserted sweep of heathlike countryside.

"Bones, Mr. Spock, get some readings on this place." Kirk snapped a switch.

"*Enterprise*, this is the *Galileo*. Kirk here. Come in, please. Come in . . . no good, we're not sending. That cloud must still be around someplace. Any data, anybody?"

"The atmosphere is almost identical with that of the Earth," Spock reported, "and so is the gravity. Almost impossible for a planet this small, unless the core is something other than the usual nickel-iron. But suitable for human life."

"Well, I guess we get out and get under," Kirk said. "Bones, phaser out and maintain full alert. Commissioner, best you stay inside for the time being."

"And just how long a time is that?"

"That's a very good question. I wish I could answer it. Mr. Spock, let's go."

Outside, they went to the rear of the shuttlecraft and unbolted the access panels to the machinery, while McCoy stayed up forward. Checking the works did not take long.

"Very strange," Spock said. "In fact, quite impossible."

"Nothing works."

"Nothing. And for no reason."

"Of course there's a reason. We just haven't found it yet. Let's go over it again."

While they were at it, Nancy Hedford came out and headed for them, looking, as usual, both annoyed and officious. Patience was evidently not her strong point, either. Kirk sighed and straightened.

"Well, Captain?"

"Well, Commissioner?"

"Where is this strange powerful force of yours, which brought us here? Or could it be that you simply made a navigational error?"

"There was no error, Miss Hedford," Kirk said patiently. "For your information, our power units are dead—so I judge that the force you refer to is still in the vicinity."

"I am not interested in alibis, Captain. I insist that you get us off this dismal rock immediately."

"Commissioner, I realize that you're ill, and you're anxious to receive treatment."

"I am anxious, as you put it, to get this medical nonsense out of the way so I can get back to my assignment!"

McCoy, looking rather anxious himself, had joined them. He said, "How do you feel, Commissioner?"

"I wish you would stop asking that stupid question." She strode angrily away.

Kirk managed a rueful grin. "As long as she answers you like that, Bones, I guess she feels all right."

"But she won't for long. The fever's due to hit any time."

As Kirk started to reply, there was a long, hailing call from no very great distance. "Halllooooo!"

They turned, startled. A human figure had emerged from over the horizon, which on this small world was no more than a mile away. It waved its arms, and came toward them at a run.

"Bones, I want a physiological reading on—whoever that is."

The figure disappeared behind a rise, and then appeared at the top of it, looking down on the party. It was a young, sturdy, tall, handsome man in his mid-thirties, dressed in a one-piece suit of coveralls. His expression was joyful.

"Hello!" he said again, plunging down the rise to them. "Are you real? I mean—I'm not imagining you, am I?"

"We're real enough," Kirk said.

"And you speak English. Earth people?"

Kirk nodded. "From the Federation."

"The Federation? Well, it doesn't matter." He grabbed Kirk's hand enthusiastically. "I'm Cochrane. Been marooned here who knows how long. If you knew how good it was to see you . . . and a woman! A beautiful one at that. Well!"

Kirk made the introductions. Cochrane, still staring at the Commissioner, said, "You're food to a starving man. All of you." He looked over to Spock. "A Vulcan, aren't you. When I was there—hey, there's a nice ship. Simple, clean. Been trying to get her going again? Forget it. It won't work."

He began to circle the shuttlecraft, admiringly. Kirk said in a low voice to McCoy, "Our friend seems to have a grasshopper mind."

"Too many things to take in all at once. Normal reaction. In fact, everything checks out perfectly normal. He's human."

"Mr. Cochrane!" The newcomer rejoined them, still beaming. "We were forced off our course and brought here by some power we couldn't identify—which seems to be here on the surface of the planet at the moment."

"Could be. Strange things happen in space."

"You said we wouldn't be able to get the ship functioning again?" Spock asked.

"Not a chance. Damping field of some sort down here. Power systems don't work. Take my word for it."

"You won't mind if we keep trying?" Spock persisted.

"Go right ahead. You'll have plenty of time."

"How about you, Cochrane?" Kirk said. "What are you doing here?"

"Marooned. I told you. Look, we've got lots of time to learn about each other. I've got a little place not far away. All the comforts of home." He turned to the woman. "I can even offer you a hot bath."

"How acute of you to notice that I needed it," she said icily.

"If you don't mind, Mr. Cochrane," Kirk said, "I'd like a little more than just the statement that you were marooned here. This is a long way off the beaten path."

"That's right. That's why I'm so glad to see you. Look, I'll tell you everything you want to know. But not here." He eyed the shuttlecraft again. "A beauty."

"You've been out of circulation a while. Maybe the principles are new to you. Mr. Spock, would you like to explain our propulsion methods to Mr. Cochrane?"

"Of course, Captain. Mr. Cochrane?"

As the two moved off, McCoy said, "He talks a lot but he doesn't say much."

"I noticed," Kirk said. "And I noticed something else. There's something familiar about him, Bones."

"Familiar? . . . well, now that you mention it, I think so too."

"I can't place him, but . . . how about Miss Hedford?"

"No temperature yet. But we've got to get under way soon. I guarantee you it'll develop."

"You're sure there's no mistake? It is Sakuro's disease?"

"Positive. And something else I'm not mistaken about. Untreated, it's fatal. Always . . . well, what do we do now?"

"I think we'll take Mr. Cochrane up on his offer. At least we can make her comfortable."

Cochrane's house was a simple functional cube, with a door, but no windows. The surrounding area was cultivated.

"You built this, Mr. Cochrane?" Spock said.

"Yes. I had some tools and supplies left over from my crash. It's not Earth, of course, but it's livable. I grow vegetables, as you see. Come on in."

He led the way. The house contained a heating unit which apparently served as a stove, a climate control device, and some reasonably comfortable furniture, all decidedly old. Miss Hedford looked around with distaste.

"What a dreadful, dingy place," she said.

Cochrane only smiled. "But I call it home, Miss Hedford."

"Where did you get the antiques?" Kirk said.

"The antiques? Oh, you mean my gadgets. I imagine things have changed a lot since I wrecked."

"Not that much."

"Must you keep it so terribly hot?" the woman asked.

"The temperature is a constant seventy-two degrees."

"Do you feel hot?" McCoy asked Miss Hedford.

She flopped angrily down in a chair. "I feel infuriated, deeply put upon, absolutely outraged."

"It was quite a hike here," McCoy said. "You're tired. Just take it easy for a while."

"I'll rest later, Doctor. Right now I am planning the report I will make to the Board of Commissioners on the efficiency of the Starfleet. I assure all of you it will be very, very complete."

"Captain! Doctor!" Spock called from the door. "Look at this, please!"

Alarmed at the urgency in his voice, Kirk crossed to the door in one bound. Outside, perhaps half a mile away, was a columnar area of blurry, misty interference, like a tame whirlwind, except that there was no wind. Faint pastel lights and shades appeared and disappeared inside it. With it there was a half sound, half feeling of soft chiming music. For a moment it moved from side to side, gently; then it disappeared.

Kirk turned quickly to Cochrane. "What was that?"

"Sometimes the light plays tricks on you," Cochrane said. "You'd be surprised what I've imagined I've seen around here."

"We imagined nothing, Mr. Cochrane. There was an entity out there, and I suspect it was the same entity that brought us here. Please explain."

"There's nothing to explain."

"Mr. Cochrane, you'll find I have a low tolerance level where the safety of my people are concerned. We find you out here where no human has any business being. We were virtually hijacked in space and brought here—apparently by that thing we just saw out there. I am not just requesting an explanation, Mister. I am demanding it!"

Cochrane shrugged. "All right. Out there—that was the Companion."

"The what?"

"That's what I call it. The fact is, Captain, I did not crash here. I was brought here in my disabled ship. I was almost dead. The Companion saved my life."

"You seem perfectly healthy now," Kirk said. "What was wrong?"

"Old age, Captain. I was eighty-seven years old at the time. I don't know how it did it, but the Companion rejuvenated me. Made me—well—young again, like I am now."

Kirk and Spock exchanged glances. Spock's eyebrows were about to crawl right off the top of his forehead. He said, "I would like to reserve judgment on that part of your story, sir. Would you mind telling us exactly what this Companion of yours is?"

"I told you, I don't know what it is. It exists. It lives. I can communicate with it to a limited extent."

"That's a pretty far-out story," McCoy said.

"You saw the creature. Have you a better story?"

"Mr. Cochrane," Kirk said. "Do you have a first name?"

Cochrane nodded. "Zefram."

McCoy's jaw dropped, but Spock had apparently been expecting the answer. Kirk said, "Cochrane of Alpha Centauri? The discoverer of the space warp?"

"That's right, Captain."

"Zefram Cochrane," McCoy said, "has been dead a hundred and fifty years."

"His body was never found," Spock said.

"You're looking at it, Mr. Spock," Cochrane said.

"You say this Companion of yours found you and rejuvenated you. What were you doing in space at the age of eighty-seven?"

"I was tired, Captain. I was going to die. And I wanted to die in space. That's all."

McCoy turned to Miss Hedford, whose eyes were now closed. He felt her forehead, then took readings. He was obviously concerned by the results.

"These devices," Spock said. "They all date from the time indicated. From your ship, Mr. Cochrane?"

"I cannibalized it. The rest—the food, water, gardens, everything I need—the Companion gives me. Creates it, apparently, out of the native elements."

"If you can communicate with it," Kirk said, "maybe you can find out what *we* are doing here."

"I already know."

"You wouldn't mind telling us?"

"You won't like it."

"We already don't like it."

"You're here to keep me company," Cochrane said. "I was always pretty much of a loner. Spent years in space by myself. At first being alone here didn't bother me. But a hundred and fifty years is a long time, Kirk. Too long. I finally told the Companion I'd die without the company of other humans. I thought it would release me—send me back somehow. Instead, it went out and obviously brought back the first human beings it could find."

"No!" Miss Hedford cried weakly. "No! It's disgusting! We're not animals!"

She began to sob. McCoy, with Kirk's help, lifted her and put her on a cot, where McCoy gave her a shot. Gradually, her sobbing subsided.

"Bad," said McCoy. "Very bad."

"You can't do anything?"

"Keep her quiet. Keep secondary infections from developing. But the attrition rate of her red corpuscles is increasing. I can't stop it."

Kirk turned to Spock. "Mr. Spock, the next time that thing appears, don't fail to get tricorder readings. Find us a weapon to use against that thing."

"Captain, I have already drawn certain tentative conclusions. Considering the anomalously small size of this planet, and the presence of the damping field Mr. Cochrane mentioned, plus the Companion, leads me to believe that it was the moon of some larger body now destroyed, and was colonized by a highly advanced civilization."

"I agree," Cochrane said. "I've found some artifacts which suggest the same thing."

"The point, Spock?"

"One can deduce further that the Companion may be the last survivor of this long-dead culture. You ask me to find a weapon. Do you intend to destroy it?"

"I intend to do whatever is necessary to get us away from here and Commissioner Hedford to a hospital," Kirk said grimly. "If the Companion stands in the way, then we push it out of the way. Clear, Mr. Spock?"

"Quite clear, Captain." Spock picked up his tricorder and left, heading for the shuttlecraft.

"Cochrane, if you left here, what would happen to you?"

"I'd start to age again, normally."

"You want to get away from here?"

"Believe me, Captain, immortality consists largely of boredom. Of course I do . . . what's it like out there? In the galaxy?"

"We're on a thousand planets, and spreading out. We're crossing fantastic distances . . . and finding life everywhere. We estimate there are millions of planets with intelligent life. We haven't begun to map them." Cochrane's eyes were shining. "Interesting?"

"How would you like to go to sleep for a hundred and fifty years and wake up in a new world?"

"Good," Kirk said. "It's all out there, waiting for you. And you'll find your name honored there. But we'll probably need your help to get away."

"You've got it."

"All right. You seem to think this Companion can do almost anything."

"I don't know its limitations."

"Could it cure Commissioner Hedford?"

"I don't know."

"It's worth a try. We're helpless. You say you can communicate with it?"

"To a degree. It's on a non-verbal level, but I usually get my messages across."

"Try it now. See if it can do anything."

Cochrane nodded and stepped outside, followed by Kirk and McCoy. "How do you do it?" Kirk said.

"I just sort of . . . clear my mind. Then it comes. Better stay back."

Cochrane closed his eyes. A long moment passed, and then Kirk heard the melodic humming of the Companion. It appeared near Cochrane, shimmering, resplendent with a dozen beautiful colors, to the sound of faint bells. It moved to Cochrane, enveloped him, gathered around him, hovering. The lights played on Cochrane's face.

"What do you make of that, Bones?" Kirk said softly.

"Almost a symbiosis of some kind. A sort of joining."

"Just what I was thinking. Not exactly like a pet owner speaking to an affectionate animal, would you say?"

"No. More than that."

"I agree. Much more. Possibly . . . love."

Now the Companion was moving away from Cochrane, who was slowly returning to normal. The Companion faded away, and Cochrane shook his head and looked about as if to get his bearings. His eyes settled on Kirk.

"You all right?" Kirk said.

"Oh. Yes. I . . . it always kind of . . . drains me. But I'm all right."

"Well?"

Cochrane shook his head again. "The Companion can't do anything to help Miss Hedford. There seems to be some question of identity involved . . . I didn't understand it. But the answer is no, I'm sure of that."

"Then she'll die."

"Look, I'm sorry. If I could help you, I would. But the Companion won't."

It was several hours before Spock came back from the shuttlecraft. When he returned, he was carrying with him a small but complex black device, obviously in very rough form, as though it had been hastily put together by a gifted child. He took it into the house. "Your weapon, Captain."

"Oho. How does it work?"

"The Companion, as we already know, is mostly plasma—a state of matter characterized by a high degree of ionization. To put the matter simply, it is mostly electricity. I propose to, in effect, short it out. Put this in proximity to the Companion, throw this switch, and we will scramble every electrical impulse the creature can produce. It cannot fail."

Cochrane was staring unhappily at the device. Kirk said, "It troubles you, Cochrane?"

"The Companion saved my life. Took care of me for a hundred and fifty years. We've been . . . very close . . . in a way that's hard to explain. I suppose I even have a sort of affection for it."

"It's also keeping you a prisoner here."

"I don't want it killed."

Spock said, "We may simply render it powerless—"

"But you don't know!" Cochrane said intensely. "You could kill it! I won't stand for that, Kirk."

"We're getting away from here, Cochrane. Make up your mind to that."

"What kind of people are you nowadays?" Cochrane demanded. "Doesn't gratitude mean anything to you?"

"I've got a woman dying in here, Cochrane. I'll do anything I have to to save her life."

Cochrane stared at Kirk, and slowly the fight went out of him. "I suppose, from your point of view, you're right. I only . . ."

"We understand how you feel, Mr. Cochrane," McCoy said. "But it has to be done."

"All right. You want me to call it, I suppose?"

"Please," Kirk said. "Outside."

McCoy remained with his patient. Spock hefted his device, and he and Kirk left the house. Already, Cochrane and the Companion were approaching each other. Soft lights and soft music came from the creature. It almost seemed to be purring.

"Is this close enough?" Kirk whispered.

"I think so," Spock whispered back. "But there is a certain risk. We do not know the extent of the creature's powers."

"Nor it ours. Now, Spock!"

Spock closed the switch. The blurring of the Companion abruptly increased, and a sharp high-pitched humming sound came from it, alarmed, strong. The pastel colors changed to somber blues and greens, and the hint of bells changed to a discordant clanging. Cochrane, only a few feet away from it, grasped his head and staggered, then fell. The evanescent, ever-changing column of plasma swept down upon the house.

Kirk and Spock ducked inside, but there was no safety there. The room was filled with the whirling and clanging. With it, Kirk felt a terrible sense of pressure, all over his body. The breath was crushed out of him. He struck out, but there was nothing to strike at. Beside him, he was aware that Spock had dropped the device and was also gasping futilely for air.

"Stop it! Stop it!" McCoy's voice shouted, as if from a great distance. "It's killing them!"

Cochrane came in, and, immediately divining what was happening, went into the position of communion. The Companion's colors returned to the pastel, and the creature faded away. Kirk and Spock both fell to their knees, gulping in great gasps of air. McCoy knelt beside them; Cochrane went out again.

"Are you all right?" McCoy said. "Can you breathe?"

Kirk nodded. "All . . . right, Bones." He got shakily to his feet, followed by Spock, who also seemed to be regaining his strength rapidly. "Cochrane's got it off us. I don't know whether he did us a favor or not."

"What kind of talk is that?" McCoy said sharply.

"How do you fight a thing like that? I've got a ship somewhere out there . . . the responsibility for four lives here . . . and one of them dying."

"That's not your fault."

"I'm in command, Bones. That makes it my fault. Now I've had it. I can't destroy it. I can't force it to let us go."

After a moment McCoy said, "You're a soldier so often that maybe you forget you were also trained to be a diplomat. Why not try using a carrot instead of a stick?"

"But what could I offer . . . Hmmm. Maybe we can. Spock!"

"Yes, Captain."

"The universal translator on the shuttlecraft. We can try that. Talk to the thing."

"The translator is for use with more congruent life-forms."

"Adjust it. Change it. The trouble with immortality is that it's boring. Adjusting the translator would give you something to do."

"It's possible. If I could widen its pattern of reception—"

"Right down your alley, Mr. Spock. Get it here and get to work."

* * *

The translator was small but intricate. Cochrane eyed it interestedly, while McCoy tended his patient. "How does that gadget work?" he said.

"There are certain universal ideas and concepts, common to all intelligent life," Kirk explained. "This device instantaneously compares the frequency of brain wave patterns, selects those it recognizes, and provides the necessary grammar and vocabulary."

"You mean the box speaks?"

"With the voice, or its approximation, of whatever creature is on the sending end. It's not perfect, of course, but it usually works well enough. Are you ready, Mr. Spock?"

"Quite ready, Captain."

"Mr. Cochrane, call the Companion, please."

Cochrane left the house, Kirk and Spock once more following, with the translator. And again the sound of the Companion preceded its appearance; then it was there, misty, enigmatic. Spock touched the translator and nodded to Kirk.

"Companion . . . we wish to talk to you."

There was a change in the sound. The Companion drew away from Cochrane. Then a voice came from the translator. It was soft, gentle—and unmistakably feminine.

"How can we communicate? My thoughts . . . you are hearing them. This is interesting."

"Feminine, Spock," Kirk said. "No doubt about it."

"Odd. The matter of gender could change the entire situation."

"Dr. McCoy and I are way ahead of you, Mr. Spock."

"Then it is not a zoo-keeper."

"No, Mr. Spock. A lover . . . Companion! It is wrong to hold us here against our will."

"The man needs the company of his own kind, or he will cease to exist," the gentle voice said. "He felt it to me."

"One of us is about to cease to exist. She must be taken to a place where we can care for her."

"The man needs others of his species. That is why you are here. The man must continue."

"Captain, there is a peculiar, dispassionate logic here," Spock said. "Pragmatism unalloyed. From its words, I would say it will never understand our point of view."

"Maybe. Companion, try to understand. It is the nature of our species to be free, just as it is your nature to stay here. We will cease to exist in captivity."

"Your bodies have stopped their peculiar degeneration. You will continue without end. There will be sustenance. There will be nothing to harm you. You will continue and the man will continue. This is necessary."

"Captain!" Spock said. "This is a marvelous opportunity for us to add to our knowledge. Ask it about its nature, its history—"

"Mr. Spock, this is no classroom. I'm trying to get us away from here."

"A chance like this may never come again. It could tell us so much—"

"Mr. Spock, get lost. Companion, it is plain you do not understand us. This is because you are not of our species. Believe me, we do not lie. What you offer us is not continuation. It is non-existence. We will cease to exist. Even the man will cease to exist."

"Your impulses are illogical. This communication is useless. The Man must continue. Therefore, you will continue. It is necessary."

The voice fell silent. The Companion moved away. Slowly it started to grow fainter, and finally was not there at all.

Kirk's shoulders sagged, and he went back into the house, followed by Spock. Cochrane came in after them.

"Captain," he said, "why did you build that translator of yours with a feminine voice box?"

"We didn't," Kirk said.

"But I heard—"

"The ideas of male and female are universal constants, Cochrane. The Companion is definitely female."

"I don't understand."

"You don't?" said McCoy. "A blind man could see it with his cane. You're not a pet, Cochrane. Nor a specimen kept in a cage. You're a lover."

"I'm—what?"

"Isn't it evident?" Kirk said. "Everything she does is for you. Provides for you. Feeds you. Shelters you. Clothes you. Brings you companions when you're lonely."

"Her attitude, when she approaches you, is profoundly different from when she contacts us," Spock added. "In appearance, in sound, in method. Though I do not completely understand the emotion, it obviously exists. The Companion loves you."

Cochrane stared at them. "That's—that's ridiculous!"

"Not at all," Kirk said. "We've seen similar situations."

"But after a hundred and fifty years—"

"What happens when you communicate with it?" Spock said.

"Why, we sort of . . . it—it merges with my mind."

"Of course. It is nothing to be shocked by. A simple symbolic union of two minds."

"That's outrageous! Do you know what you're saying? No, you couldn't! But . . . all the years . . . letting something . . . as alien as that . . . into my mind, my feelings—" Suddenly Cochrane was furious as well as astonished. "It tricked me! It's some kind of an . . . emotional vampire! Crawling around inside me!"

"It didn't hurt you, did it?" Kirk said.

"Hurt me? What has that to do with it? You can be married to a woman you love for fifty years and still keep your private places in your mind. But this—this thing—fed on me!"

"An interesting attitude," Spock said. "Typical of your time, I should say, when humanity had much less contact with alien life-forms than at present."

"Don't sit there and calmly analyze a disgusting thing like this!" Cochrane exploded. "What kind of men are you, anyway?"

"There's nothing disgusting about it, Cochrane," McCoy said. "It's just one more life-form. You get used to these things."

"You turn my stomach! You're as bad as it is!"

"I fail to understand your highly emotional reaction," Spock said. "Your relationship with the Companion was, for a hundred and fifty years, emotionally satisfying, eminently practical, and totally harmless. It may, indeed, have been quite beneficial."

Cochrane glared at them. "So this is what the future looks like—men who don't have the slightest notion of decency or morality. Well, maybe I'm a hundred and fifty years out of style, but I'm not going to be fodder for some inhuman—monstrous—" Choking up, he swung on his heel and walked out.

"A most parochial attitude," Spock said.

"Doctor," Nancy Hedford's voice called weakly. "Doctor."

McCoy hurried to her, Kirk following. "Right here, Miss Hedford."

She managed a very faint, almost bitter laugh. "I . . . heard him. He was loved . . . and he resents it."

"You rest," McCoy said.

"No. I don't want . . . want to die . . . I've been . . . good at my job, Doctor. But I've . . . never been loved. What kind . . . of a life is that? Not to be loved . . . never . . . and now I'm dying. And he . . . runs away from love . . ."

She fell silent, gasping for breath. McCoy's eyes were grim.

"Captain," Spock called from the door. "Look out here."

Outside, the Companion was back, looking much the same as usual, but Cochrane was standing away from it, barely controlling himself, icily furious.

"Do you understand?" he was saying. "I don't want anything to do with you."

The Companion moved a little closer, chiming questioningly, insistently. Cochrane backed away.

"I said keep away! You'll never get close enough to trick me again! Stay away from me! I know you understand me! Stay away! Leave me alone, from now on!"

Shaken, white-faced and sweating, Cochrane came back to his house. Kirk turned back to McCoy. Nancy was lying quite still.

"Bones? Is it over?"

"No. But she's moribund. Respiration highly erratic. Blood pressure dropping. She'll be dead in ten minutes. And I—"

"You did everything you could, Bones."

"Are you sorry for her, Kirk?" Cochrane said, still in an icy rage. "Are you really feeling something? Don't bother. Because that's the only way any of us are going to get away from here. By dying!"

An idea, a forlorn hope, came to Kirk. He picked up the translator and went outside. The Companion was still there.

"Companion. Do you love the man?"

"I do not understand," said the feminine voice from the translator.

"Is he important to you—more important than anything? Is it as though he were a part of you?"

"He is part of me. He must continue."

"But he will not continue. He will cease to exist. By your feeling for him you are condemning him to an existence he will find unbearable."

"He does not age. He remains forever."

"You refer to his body," said Kirk. "I speak of his spirit. Companion, inside the shelter a female of our species lies dying. She will not continue. That is what will happen to the man unless you release all of us."

"I do not understand."

"Our species can only survive when there are obstacles to overcome. You take away all obstacles. Without them to strengthen us, we weaken and die. You regard the man only as a toy. You only amuse yourself with him."

"You are wrong," said the translator. Was there urgency as well as protest in that voice? "The man is the center of all things. I care for him."

"But you can't really love him. You don't have the slightest knowledge of love—of the total union of two people. You are the Companion; he is the man; you are two different things, and can never join. You can never know love. You may keep him here forever, but you will always be separate, apart from him."

There was a long pause. Then the Companion said, "If I were human . . . there can be love . . ."

Then the creature faded from sight. Kirk went back into the shelter, almost bumping into McCoy, who had been standing behind him. "What did you hope to gain by that?" the surgeon said.

"Convince her of the hopelessness of it. The emotion of love frequently expresses itself in sacrifice. If love is what she feels, she might let him go."

"But she—or it—is inhuman, Captain," Spock said. "You cannot expect her to react like a human."

"I can try."

"It won't do any good," Cochrane said. "I know."

From the direction of the cot, a voice said, "Zefram Cochrane." It was Nancy's voice, clear and strong, but somehow as if the use of human lips, tongue and vocal cords had become unfamiliar. They all spun around.

There stood Nancy Hedford—but transformed, radiant, soft, gentle, staring at Cochrane. The rosy glow of health was evident in her cheek. McCoy raised his medical tricorder and stared at it, thunderstruck, but Kirk had no need to ask what he saw. The Nancy Hedford who had been about to die was not sick at all now.

"Zefram Cochrane," she said. "We are understanding."

"It's—it's her!" Cochrane said. "Don't you understand? It's the Companion!"

"Yes," said Nancy. "We are here—those you knew as the Commissioner and the Companion. We are both here."

Spock said, "Companion, you do not have the power to create life."

"No. That is for the maker of all things."

"But Commissioner Hedford was dying."

"That part of us was too weak to hold on. In a moment there would have been no continuing. Now we are together. Now we understand that which you called love—both of us. It fills a great need. That we did not have, we now have."

"You mean—you're both there in one body?" Kirk said.

"We are one. There is so much hunger, so much wanting." She moved toward Cochrane, who retreated a step. "Poor Zefram Cochrane. We frighten you. We never frightened you before." Tears formed in her eyes. "Loneliness. This is loneliness. We know loneliness. What a bitter thing. Zefram Cochrane, how do you bear it?"

"How do you know what loneliness is?" Cochrane said.

"To wear this form is to discover pain." She extended a hand. "Let us touch you, Zefram Cochrane."

His hand slowly went out, and they touched.

Kirk turned his head and said in a low voice: "Spock. Check out the shuttlecraft. The engines, communication, everything."

"We hear you, Captain," Nancy said. "It is not necessary. Your vehicle will operate as before. So will your communications device."

"You're letting us go?" Cochrane said.

"We would do nothing to stop you. Captain, you said that we would not know love because we were not human. Now we are human, all human, and nothing more. We will know the change of the days. We will know death. But to touch the hand of the man—nothing is as important. Is this happiness, Zefram Cochrane? When the sun is warmer? The air sweeter? The sounds of this place like gentle currents in the air?"

"You are very beautiful," Cochrane said in a low voice.

"Part of me understands. Part does not. But it pleases me."

"I could explain. Many things. It'll be an eye-opener to you." He was alive with excitement. "A thousand worlds, a thousand races. I'll show you everything—just as soon as I learn my way around again. Maybe I can make up for everything you did for me."

Sadness appeared in Nancy's eyes. "I cannot go with you, Zefram Cochrane."

Cochrane was stunned. "Of course you can. You have to."

"My life emanates from this place. If I leave it, for more than a tiny march of days, I will cease to exist. I must return, even as you must consume matter to maintain your life."

"But—you have powers—you can—"

"I have become almost as you. The march of days will affect me. But to leave here would mean a cessation of my existence."

"You mean you gave up everything to become human?"

"It is nothing . . . compared to the touch of you."

"But you'll age, like any other human. Eventually you'll die."

"The joy of this hour is enough. I am pleased."

"I can't fly off and leave you here," Cochrane said. "You saved my life. You took care of me and you loved me. I never understood, but I do now."

"You must be free, Zefram Cochrane."

Kirk said gently: "The *Galileo* is waiting, Mr. Cochrane."

"But . . . If I take her away from here, she'll die. If I leave her . . . she's human. She'll die of loneliness. And that's not all. I love her. Is that surprising?"

"Not coming from a human being," Spock said. "You are, after all, essentially irrational."

Cochrane put his arms around her. "I can't leave her. And this isn't such a bad place. I'm used to it."

"Think it over, Mr. Cochrane," Kirk said. "There's a galaxy out there, waiting to honor you."

"I have honors enough. She loves me."

"But you will age, both of you," Spock said. "There will be no more immortality. You will grow old here, and finally die."

"That's been happening to men and women for a long time . . . and I've got the feeling that it's one of the pleasanter things about being human—as long as you do it together."

"You're sure?" Kirk said.

"There's plenty of water. The climate is good for growing things. I might even try to plant a fig tree. Every man's entitled to that, isn't he?" He paused, then added soberly, "It isn't gratitude, Captain. Now that I see her, touch her, I know. I love her. We'll have a lot of years, and they'll be happy ones."

"Mr. Cochrane, you may or may not be doing the right thing. But I wish you the best. Mr. Spock, Bones, let's go."

As they turned, Cochrane said, "Captain."

"Yes?"

"Don't tell them about Cochrane. Let it go."

Kirk smiled. "Not a word, Mr. Cochrane."

As they settled into the *Galileo*, Spock said, "I pose you an interesting question, Captain. Have we not aided in the commission of bigamy? After all, the Companion and Commissioner Hedford are now sharing the same body."

"Now you're being parochial, Mr. Spock," McCoy said. "Bigamy is not everywhere illegal. Besides, Nancy Hedford was all but dead. Only the Companion is keeping her alive. If it withdrew, Nancy wouldn't last ten minutes. In fact, I'm going to report her dead as soon as we hit the *Enterprise*."

"Besides, what difference does it make?" Kirk said. "Love was the one thing Nancy and the Companion wanted most. Now they have it."

"But not for eternity," McCoy said. "Only a lifetime."

"Yes. But that's enough, Bones. For humans."

"That's a very illogical remark, Jim." As Spock's eyebrows climbed, McCoy added, "However, it happens to be true."

Kirk grinned and raised his communicator. "Kirk to *Enterprise*."

The communicator fairly shouted back. "Captain! This is Scotty. Are you all right?"

"We're perfectly all right. Can you get a fix on us?"

"Computing now . . . yes, locked on."

"Very good. I'll continue transmission. Assume standard orbit on arrival. We'll transfer up on the shuttlecraft."

"But what happened, Captain?"

"Not very much, in the end," Kirk said. "Only the oldest story in the world."

JOURNEY TO BABEL

WRITER: D. C. FONTANA
DIRECTOR: JOSEPH PEVNEY
FIRST AIRED: NOVEMBER 17, 1967

THE HONOR GUARD OF EIGHT SECURITY MEN WAS LINED UP BEFORE THE AIRLOCK, four men to a side, with Kirk, Spock and McCoy, all three in formal dress blue uniforms, at the end of this human tube. McCoy tugged at his collar, which he had previously described as "like having my neck in a sling." He asked Spock, "How does that Vulcan salute go?"

Spock demonstrated. The gesture was complex and McCoy's attempt to copy it was not very convincing.

The surgeon shook his head. "That hurts worse than the uniform."

The uniforms were the least of their discomforts, Kirk thought a little grimly. They'd soon be out of those, after the formal reception tonight, and the Vulcans were the last group of delegates the *Enterprise* had to pick up. Then would come the trip to the neutral planetoid code-named "Babel"—a two-week journey with a hundred and fourteen Federation delegates aboard, thirty-two of them ambassadors, half of them mad at the other half, and the whole lot touchier than a raw anti-matter pile over the Coridian question. Now *that* was going to be uncomfortable.

The airlock opened, and the Vulcan Ambassador, Sarek, stepped through. Because of Vulcan longevity, it would have been impossible to guess his age—he looked to be no more than in his late forties—but Kirk knew it to be in fact a hundred and two, which was middle age by Vulcan standards. He was followed, several paces behind, by a woman wearing a traveling outfit with a colorful hooded cloak; she in turn was followed by two Vulcan aides.

Kirk, Spock and McCoy stood at attention as the party walked past the honor guard to the Captain. Spock stepped formally in front of Sarek and gave the complex salute.

"Vulcan honors us with your presence," he said. "We come to serve."

Sarek pointedly ignored him and saluted Kirk instead. When he spoke, his voice was almost without inflection.

"Captain, your service honors us."

"Thank you, Ambassador," Kirk said with a slight bow. "Captain James Kirk. My First Officer, Commander Spock. Dr. McCoy, Chief Medical Officer."

Sarek nodded briefly in turn and indicated the rest of his party. "My aides." He held up his hand, first and second fingers extended. The woman stepped forward and touched her first and second fingers to his. "And Amanda, she who is my wife."

"Captain Kirk," the woman said.

"My pleasure, madam. Ambassador, as soon as you're settled, I'll arrange a tour of the ship. My First Officer will conduct you."

"I prefer another guide, Captain," Sarek said.

He was absolutely expressionless, and so was Spock. This snub was just as baffling and even more pointed than before, but it would not be a good idea to offend a ranking ambassador.

"Of course—if you wish. Mr. Spock, we have two hours until we leave orbit. Would you like to beam down and visit your parents?"

There was a slight but noticeable silence. Then Spock said, "Captain—Ambassador Sarek and his wife *are* my parents."

Was I just telling myself, Kirk thought glumly after the first shock, that this trip was going to be just "uncomfortable"?

Upon reflection, Kirk gave himself the job of guiding the tour. He found Spock's mother especially interesting—remarkable, even—though she was hard to study because she habitually walked behind and to the side of any man, her husband most notably. This was a Vulcan ritual to which she had adapted, for Amanda was an Earthwoman; almost everyone in the crew knew that much about Spock.

Though in her late fifties, she was still straight, slim and resilient. She had married a Vulcan and come to live on his world where her human-woman emotions had no place. Kirk strongly suspected that she had not lost any of her human humor and warmth, but that it was buried inside, in deference to her husband's customs and society.

He led them into the Engineering Room. Spock, by now in regular uniform, was working at the computer banks behind the grilled partition.

"This is the engineering section," Kirk told his guests. "There are emergency backup systems for the main controls. We also have a number of control computers here."

Amanda was still behind them and, without Sarek appearing to notice, she moved over to Spock. Out of the corner of his eye, Kirk saw each of them cross hands and touch them, palms out, in a ritual embrace. Then they began to murmur. Spock's face was expressionless, as usual. Once, Amanda shook her head ruefully.

Kirk continued his lecture, hoping to avoid trouble, but Sarek's eyes were as alert as his own. "My wife, attend," the Ambassador said. He held up his first and second fingers. Without a word, Amanda nodded to Spock to excuse herself and obediently moved to Sarek, joining her fingers with his, though Kirk guessed that she was really not much interested in the console and its instruments.

Spock, gathering up a handful of tapes, rose and headed for the door. Kirk had a sudden idea.

"Mr. Spock—a moment, please."

The First Officer turned reluctantly. "Yes, Captain?"

"Ambassador, I'm not competent to explain our computer setup. Mr. Spock, will you do so, please?"

"I gave Spock his first instruction in computers," Sarek said woodenly. "He chose to devote his knowledge to Starfleet rather than the Vulcan Science Academy."

That tore it. In trying to be helpful, Kirk had unwittingly put his foot right into the heart of the family quarrel. Apologetically, he nodded dismissal to Spock, and turned to Sarek.

"I'm sorry, Ambassador. I didn't mean to offend you in . . ."

"Offense is a human emotion, Captain. For other reasons, I am returning to my quarters. Continue, my wife."

Amanda bowed her head in characteristic acceptance, and Sarek left. Kirk, puzzled and confused as never before by his First Officer and his relatives, turned to her, shaking his head.

"I'm afraid I don't understand, Mrs. Sarek."

"Amanda," she said quickly. "I'm afraid you couldn't pronounce the Vulcan family name."

"Can you?"

A smile fluttered on her lips, then vanished as habit overtook her. "After a fashion, and after many years of practice . . . Shall we continue the tour? My husband did request it."

"It sounded more like a command."

"Of course. He's a Vulcan. I'm his wife."

"Spock is his son."

Amanda glanced at him sharply, as though surprised, but recovered quickly. "You don't understand the Vulcan way, Captain. It's logical. It's a better way than ours—but its not easy; It has kept Spock and Sarek from speaking as father and son for eighteen years."

"Spock is my best officer," Kirk said. "And my best friend."

"I'm glad he has such a friend. It hasn't been easy for Spock—neither Vulcan nor human; at home nowhere, except Starfleet."

"I gather Spock disagreed with his father over his choice of a career."

"My husband has nothing against Starfleet. But Vulcans believe peace should not depend on force. Sarek wanted Spock to follow his teaching as Sarek followed the teaching of *his* father."

"And they're both stubborn."

Amanda smiled. "Also a human trait, Captain."

Abruptly, Uhura's voice interrupted from a console speaker. "Bridge to Captain Kirk."

Kirk snapped a toggle. "Kirk here."

"Captain, I've picked up some sort of signal; just a few symbols, nothing intelligible."

"Source?"

"That's what bothers me, sir. Impossible to locate. There wasn't enough of it. Sensors show nothing in the area. But it was a strong signal, as though it was very close."

"Go to alert status four. Begin long-range scanning. Kirk out." Kirk frowned thoughtfully and flicked off the switch. "Madame—Amanda—I'll have to ask you to excuse me. I shall hope to see you again at the reception this evening."

"Certainly, Captain. Both Vulcans and humans know what duty is."

The reception was already going full blast when Kirk arrived. Amid a murmur of conversation, delegates circulated, or sampled the table of exotic drinks, *hors d'oeuvre*. There was a fantastic array of them from many cultures.

Over it all was a faint aura of edgy politeness verging on hostility. The Interplanetary Conference had been called to consider the petition of the Coridan planets to be admitted to the Federation. The Coridan system had already been claimed by some of the races who now had delegates aboard the *Enterprise*, races who therefore had strong personal reasons for keeping Coridan *out* of the Federation. Keeping open warfare from breaking out among the delegates before the Conference even began was going to be a tough problem; many of them were not even trained diplomats, but minor officials who had been handed a hot potato by bosses who did not want to be saddled with the responsibility for whatever happened on Babel.

Kirk spotted Spock and McCoy in a group which included a Tellarite named Gav, two Andorians called Shras and Thelev, and Sarek and Amanda. Well, at least Spock was—er—associating with his family, however distantly.

As Kirk joined the group, McCoy was saying, "Mr. Ambassador, I understood that you had retired from public service before this conference was called. Forgive my curiosity, but, as a doctor, I'm interested in Vulcan physiology. Isn't it unusual for a Vulcan to retire at your age? You're only a hundred or so."

As was characteristic of Andorians because of their sensitive antennae, Shras was listening with his head down and slightly tilted, while Gav, sipping a snifter of brandy, was staring directly into Sarek's face. For an Earthman unaccustomed to either race, it would have been hard to say which of them, if either, was being rude.

Sarek said, "One hundred and two point four three seven, measured in your years. I had other—concerns."

Gav put his snifter down and leaned still farther forward. When he spoke, his voice was rough, grating and clumsy; English was very difficult for all his people, if he spoke it better than most. "Sarek of Vulcan, do you vote to admit Coridan to the Federation?"

"The vote will not be taken here, Ambassador Gav. My government's instructions will be heard in the Council Chamber on Babel."

"No—*you*. How do *you* vote, Sarek of Vulcan?"

Shras lifted his head. "Why must you know, Tellarite?" His voice was whispery, almost silken.

"In Council, his vote carries others," Gav said, stabbing a finger toward Sarek. "I will know where he stands, and why."

"Tellarites do not argue for reasons," Sarek said. "They simply argue."

"That is a . . ."

"Gentlemen," Kirk interrupted firmly. "As Ambassador Sarek pointed out, this is not the Council Chamber on Babel. I'm aware the admission of Coridan is a highly debatable issue, but you can't solve it here."

For a moment the three Ambassadors stared defensively at each other. Then Sarek nodded to Kirk. "You are correct, Captain. Quite logical."

"Apologies, Captain," Shras whispered.

Gav remained rigid for a moment, then nodded and said in an angry voice, "You will excuse me," and left the group.

"You have met Gav before, Ambassador," Shras said softly to Sarek.

"We debated at my last Council session."

"Ambassador Gav lost," Amanda added with a straight face. If Shras was amused, his face was incapable of showing it. He nodded solemnly and moved off.

"Spock, I've always suspected you were more human," McCoy said, in an obvious attempt to lighten the atmosphere. "Mrs. Sarek, I know about the rigorous training of Vulcan boys, but didn't he ever run and play like human youngsters? Even in secret?"

"Well," said Amanda, "he did have a sehlat he was very fond of."

"Sehlat?"

"It's rather like a fat teddy bear."

McCoy's eyes went wide. "A teddy bear?"

Several other crew personnel had overheard this and there was a general snicker. Quickly, Sarek turned to his wife and took her arm firmly.

"Excuse us, Doctor," he said. "It has been a long day for my wife." He propelled her toward the door amid a barrage of "good nights."

McCoy turned back to Spock, who did not appear the least bit discomforted. "A teddy bear!"

"Not precisely, Doctor," Spock said. "On Vulcan, the 'teddy bears' are alive and have six-inch fangs."

McCoy, no Vulcan, was obviously rocked. He was bailed out by a nearby wall communicator, which said in Chekov's voice, "Bridge to Captain Kirk."

"Kirk here."

"Captain, sensors are registering an unidentified vessel pacing us."

"On my way. Duty personnel on yellow alert. Passengers are not to be alarmed... Mr. Spock!"

The intruder turned out to be a small ship, about the size of a scout, of no known configuration, and unauthorized in this quadrant. It had been paralleling the course of the *Enterprise* for five minutes, outside phaser range and indeed at the extreme limit of the starship's sensors, and would not answer hails on any frequency or in any language. An attempt to intercept showed the intruder not only more maneuverable than the *Enterprise*, but faster, by a nearly incredible two warps. Kirk ordered full analysis of all sensor readings made during the brief approach, and went back to the reception, leaving Spock in command.

It seemed to be petering out. Gav was still there, sitting isolated, still working on the brandy. If he was trying to get drunk, he was due for a disappointment, Kirk knew; alcohol had no effect on Tellarites except to shorten their already short tempers. Shras and Thelev were also still present, heads down, plus a few other delegates.

Most interestingly, Sarek had returned, by himself. Now why? Had his intent been only to get Amanda off the scene before she could further embarrass their son? There could be no emotional motive behind such a move. What would the logical one be? That whether Sarek approved of Starfleet or not, Spock was an officer in it, and could not function properly if he did not command respect? It seemed as good a guess as any; but Kirk knew that his understanding of Vulcan psychology was, to say the least, insecure.

While he was ruminating, Sarek had gone to a drink dispenser, with the aid of which he seemed to have downed a pill of some kind, and Gav had risen and come up behind him. Sensing trouble, Kirk moved unobtrusively closer. Sure enough, Gav had brought up the Coridan question again.

Sarek was saying; "You seem unable to wait for the Council meeting, Ambassador. No matter. We favor admission."

"You favor? *Why?*"

"Under Federation law, Coridan can be protected—its wealth administered for the benefit of its people."

"It's well for you," Gav said. "Vulcan has no mining interest."

"The Coridians have a nearly unlimited wealth of dilithium crystals, but are underpopulated and unprotected. This invites illegal mining operations."

"Illegal! You accuse us...?"

"Of nothing," Sarek said. "But reports indicate your ships have been carrying Coridian dilithium crystals."

"You call us thieves?" Without an instant's warning, Gav leaped furiously forward, grasping for Sarek's throat. Sarek blocked the Tellarite's hands and effortlessly slammed him away, against a table. As Gav started to lunge at Sarek again, Kirk caught him and forced him back. "Lies!" Gav shouted over his shoulder. "You slander my people."

"*Gentlemen!*" Kirk said.

Gav stopped struggling and Kirk stepped back, glaring coldly at both Ambassadors. "Whatever arguments you have among yourselves are your business," Kirk said. "*My* business is running this ship—and as long as I command it, *there will be order.*"

"Of course, Captain," Sarek said.

"Understood," Gav said sullenly after a moment. "But Sarek, there will be payment for your slander."

"Threats are illogical," Sarek said. "And such 'payment' is usually expensive."

However, the fight seemed to be over—and the reception as well. Kirk went to his quarters, almost too tired to worry. It had been a day full of tensions, not one of which was yet resolved. Most of the ship was on night status now, and it was a weary pleasure to go through the silent, empty corridors.

But it was not over yet. In his quarters, he had just gotten out of the dress uniform with relief when his intercom said: "Security to Captain Kirk."

What now? "Kirk here."

"Lt. Josephs, sir. I'm on Deck 11, Section A-3. I just found one of the Tellarites, murdered and stuffed into the Jefferies tube. I think it's the Ambassador himself, sir."

So a part of his mission—to keep the peace on board—had failed already.

McCoy knelt in the corridor next to the Jefferies tube and probed Gav's body, using no instruments but his surgeon's fingers. Kirk and Spock watched; Lt. Josephs and two security guards waited for orders to remove the body. At last McCoy rose.

"How was he killed?" Kirk asked.

"His neck was broken. By an expert."

Spock glanced sharply at McCoy and then bent to examine the body himself. Kirk said, "Explain."

"From the location and nature of the break, I'd say the killer knew exactly where to apply pressure to snap the spine instantly. Not even a blow was used—no bruise."

"Who aboard would have that knowledge besides yourself?"

"Vulcans," Spock said, straightening again. "On Vulcan, the method is called *tal-shaya*—considered a merciful method of execution in ancient times."

"Mr. Spock," Kirk said, "a short time ago I broke up an argument between your father and Gav."

"Indeed, Captain? Interesting."

"Interesting? Spock, do you realize that makes your father the most likely suspect?"

"Vulcans do not approve of violence."

"Are you saying your father couldn't have done this?"

"No," Spock said. "But it would be illogical to kill without reason."

"But if he had such a reason?"

"If there were a reason," Spock said, "my father is quite capable of killing—logically and efficiently. He has the skill, and is still only in middle age."

Kirk stared at his First Officer for a moment, appalled. Then he said, "Come with me. You too, Bones."

He led the way to Sarek's quarters which, he was surprised to see when they were admitted by a smiling Amanda, had not been made up to suit Vulcan taste. He would have thought that Spock would have seen to that. He said, "I'm sorry to disturb you. But I must speak with your husband."

"He's been gone for some time. It's his habit to meditate in private before retiring. What's wrong? Spock?"

At that moment the door opened again and Sarek entered. "You want something of me, Captain?"

Kirk observed that he looked somewhat tense, not exactly with anxiety, but as though he were fighting something back. "Ambassador, the Tellarite Gav has been found murdered. His neck was broken—in what Spock describes as *tal-shaya*."

Sarek glanced at his son, lifting an eyebrow in the same familiar manner. "Indeed? Interesting."

"Ambassador, where were you in the past hour?"

"This is ridiculous, Captain," Amanda said. "You aren't accusing him . . . ?"

Spock said, "If only on circumstantial evidence, he is a logical suspect, Mother."

"I quite agree," Sarek said, but he seemed more tense than before. "I was in private meditation. Spock will tell you that such meditation is a personal experience, not to be discussed. Certainly not with Earthmen."

"That's a convenient excuse, Ambassador, but . . ."

He broke off as Sarek gasped and started to crumble. He went to his knees before Kirk and Spock could catch him, clutching at his rib cage. A moan escaped him; any pain that could force such a sound from a Vulcan must have been agonizing indeed.

McCoy took a quick reading, then took out a pressure hypo, set it, and gave Sarek a quick injection. Then he went back to the instruments, taking more time with them now.

"What's wrong?" Amanda asked him.

"I don't know—I can't be sure with Vulcan physiology. It looks like something to do with his cardiovascular system, but . . ."

"Can you help him, Bones?"

"I don't know *that* yet, either."

Kirk looked at mother and son in turn. Spock was as expressionless as always, but Amanda's eyes were haunted; not even years of adaptation to Vulcan tradition could cover a worry of this kind.

"I must go off duty," he told her apologetically. "Still another problem confronts me in the morning, for which I'll need a fresh mind. Should I be needed here before then, Dr. McCoy will of course call me."

"I quite understand, Captain," she said gently. "Good night, and thank you."

A truly remarkable woman.

Not much progress, it turned out on the next trip, had been made on the problem of the ship shadowing the *Enterprise*. Readings taken during the brief attempt at interception showed only that it either had a high-density hull or was otherwise cloaked against sensor probes. It was definitely manned, but by what? The Romulans had nothing like it, nor did the Federation or neutral planets, and that it was Klingon seemed even more unlikely.

Two fragmentary transmissions had been picked up, in an unknown code—with a reception point somewhere inside the *Enterprise* herself. Kirk ordered the locator field tightened to include only the interior of his own ship; if somebody aboard had a personal receiver—as seemed all too likely now—it might be pinned down, *if* the shadow sent another such message.

There seemed to be nothing further to be done on that for the moment. With Spock, whose only concern over his father's illness seemed to be over its possible adverse effect upon the mission, Kirk paid a visit to Sickbay. Sarek was bedded down there, with McCoy and Nurse Christine Chapel trying to make sense of the strange reports the body function panel was giving them; Amanda hovered in the door, trying to keep out of the way. As for Sarek himself, he looked as though he felt inconvenienced, but no longer in uncontrollable pain.

"How is he, Bones?"

"As far as I can tell, our prime suspect has a malfunction in one of the heart valves. I couldn't make a closer diagnosis on a Vulcan without an exploratory. Mrs. Sarek, has he had any previous attacks of this sort?"

"No," Amanda said.

"Yes," Sarek said almost simultaneously. "There were three others. My physician prescribed benjasidrine for the condition."

"Why didn't you tell me?" Amanda asked.

"There was nothing you could have done. The prognosis was not serious, providing I retired, which, of course, I did."

"When did you have these attacks, Ambassador?" McCoy said.

"Two before my retirement. The third, while I was meditating on the Observation Deck when the Tellarite was murdered. I was quite incapacitated."

"I saw you taking a pill not long before that," Kirk said. "If you'll give one to Dr. McCoy for analysis, it should provide circumstantial evidence in your favor. Were there any witnesses to the Observation Deck attack?"

"None. I do not meditate among witnesses."

"Too bad. Mr. Spock, you're a scientist and you know Vulcan. Is there a standard procedure for this condition?"

"In view of its reactivation by Sarek's undertaking this mission," Spock said, "the logical approach would be a cryogenic open-heart operation."

"Unquestionably," Sarek said.

"For that, the patient will need tremendous amounts of blood," McCoy said. "Christine, check the blood bank and see if we've got enough Vulcan blood and plasma. I strongly suspect that we don't have enough even to begin such an operation."

"There are other Vulcans aboard."

"You will find," Sarek said, "that my blood type is T-negative. It is rare. That my two aides should be lacking this factor is highly unlikely."

"I, of course," Spock said, "also have T-negative blood."

"There are human factors in your blood that would have to be filtered out, Mr. Spock," Christine said. "You just couldn't give enough to compensate for that."

"Not necessarily," Spock said. "There is a drug which speeds up replacement of blood in physiologies like ours . . ."

"I know the one you mean," McCoy said. "But it's still experimental and has worked only on a Rigellian. The two physiologies are similar, but not identical. Even with the Rigellian, it put a tremendous strain on the liver and the spleen, to say nothing of the bone marrow—and I'd have to give it to *both* of you. Plus which, I've never operated on a Vulcan. I've studied Vulcan anatomy, but that's a lot different from having actual surgical experience. If I don't kill Sarek with the operation, the drug probably will; it might kill both of them."

Sarek said, "I consider the safety factor to be low, but acceptable."

"Well, I don't," McCoy said, "and in this Sickbay, what I think is law. I can't sanction it."

"And *I* refuse to permit it," Amanda said. "I won't risk both of you . . ."

"You must understand, Mother," Spock said. "The chances of finding sufficient T-negative blood otherwise are vanishingly small. I would estimate them at . . ."

"Please don't," Amanda said.

"Then you automatically condemn Sarek to death," Spock said evenly. "And Doctor, you have no choice either. You must operate, and you have both the drug and a donor."

"It seems the only answer," Sarek said.

Reluctantly, McCoy nodded. Amanda turned a stricken face to Kirk, but he could offer her no help; he could not even help himself in this dilemma.

"I don't like it either, Amanda, believe me," he said. "But we must save your husband. You know very well, too, how much I value your son; but if we must risk him too, then we must. Doctor McCoy has agreed—and I learned long ago never to overrule him in such matters. In fact, I have made him the only officer on the *Enterprise* who has the power to give *me* orders. Please try to trust him as I do."

"And as I do also," Spock said, to McCoy's obvious startlement.

"I'll—try," Amanda said.

"You can do no more. Should you need me, I'll be at my station."

With a great deal more distress than he hoped he had shown, Kirk bowed formally and left.

And halfway to the bridge, deep in thought, he was jumped from behind.

A heavy blow to the head with some sort of club staggered him, but he nevertheless managed to throw his assailant from him against the wall. He got a quick impression of a figure taller but slighter than his own, and the flash of a bladed weapon. In the melee that followed, the other man proved himself to be an experienced infighter, and Kirk was already dazed by the first blow. He managed at last to drop his opponent, perhaps permanently—but not before getting the knife in his own back.

He barely made it to an intercom before losing consciousness.

He came to semiconsciousness to the sound of McCoy's voice.

"It's a bad wound—punctured the left lung. A centimeter or so lower and it would have gone through the heart. Thank goodness, he had sense enough not to try to pull the knife out, if he had time to think of it at all."

"The attacker was Thelev. Unconscious, but not seriously injured; just knocked about quite a lot." That was Spock. "He must have caught the Captain by surprise. I'll be in the brig, questioning him, and Shras as well."

"Doctor." This time it was Christine Chapel's voice. "The K-two factor is dropping."

"Spock," McCoy said, "Your father is much worse. There's no longer a choice. I'll have to operate immediately. We can begin as soon as you're prepared."

"No," Spock said.

"What?"

Then came Amanda's voice. "Spock, the little chance your father has depends entirely on you. You volunteered."

"My immediate responsibility is to the ship," Spock said. "Our passengers' safety is, by Starfleet order, of first importance. We are being followed by an alien, possibly hostile ship. I cannot relinquish command under these circumstances."

"You can turn command over to Scott," McCoy said harshly.

"On what grounds, Doctor? Command requirements do not recognize personal privilege. I will be in the brig interrogating the Andorian."

Then the darkness closed down again. When he awoke once more, he felt much better. Opening his eyes, he saw Sarek in the bed beside him, apparently asleep, with McCoy and Christine bending over him.

Kirk tried to rise. The attempt provoked a wave of dizziness and nausea and he promptly lay down again—even before McCoy, who had turned instantly at the motion, had to order him to.

"Let that be a lesson to you," McCoy said. "Just lie there and be happy you're still alive."

"How's Sarek?"

"Not good. If I could only operate . . ."

"What's stopping you? Oh, I remember now. Well, Spock's right, Bones. I can't damn him for his loyalty, or for doing his duty. But I'm not going to let him commit patricide."

He sat up, swinging his feet off the bed. McCoy caught his shoulders, preventing him from rising. "Jim, you can't even stand up. You could start the internal bleeding again."

"Bones, Sarek will die without that operation." McCoy nodded. "And you can't operate without the transfusions from Spock." Again a nod. "I'll convince Spock I'm all right, and order him to report here. Once he's off the bridge, I'll turn command over to Scotty and go to my quarters. Will that fill your prescription?"

"Well, no—but it sounds like the best compromise. Let me give you a hand up."

"Gladly."

McCoy supported him all the way to the bridge, but released him just before the elevator doors snapped open. Spock turned, looking surprised and pleased, but masking it immediately.

"Captain."

Kirk stepped very carefully down to his command chair. He tried to appear as though he were casually surveying the bridge, though in fact he was keeping precarious hold of his balance as spasms of dizziness swept him. McCoy remained glued to his side, but ostentatiously offered him not so much as a hand.

Spock came down into the well of the bridge as Kirk reached his chair and eased himself into it. Kirk smiled and nodded approval.

"I'll take over, Spock. Report to Sickbay with Dr. McCoy."

Spock was studying him closely. Kirk was fighting off the dizziness, at least enough—he hoped—to keep it from showing, but he knew also that he was very pale, about which he could do nothing.

"Captain, are you quite all right?"

"I've certified him physically fit, Mr. Spock," McCoy said testily. "Now, I have an operation to perform. And since both of us are required . . ."

He gestured toward the elevator. Spock hesitated briefly, still studying Kirk, who said kindly, "Get out of here, Spock."

Spock nodded, and left with McCoy, with something very like alacrity.

"Mr. Chekov," Kirk said, "what is the status of the intruder ship?"

"No change, sir. Maintaining its distance."

"Any further transmissions, Lt. Uhura?"

"None, sir."

Kirk nodded, relaxed a little—and found that he had to pull himself together sharply as the dizziness returned. "Call Mr. Scott to the bridge . . ."

"Captain," Chekov interrupted. "The alien vessel is moving closer!"

"Belay that last order, Lt. Uhura. I'm staying here." But the dizziness kept coming back. He raised a hand to wipe his brow and found that it was shaking.

"Captain," Uhura said. "I'm picking up the alien signal again. But it's coming from inside the *Enterprise*—from the brig."

"Call Security and order an immediate search of the prisoner. Tell them this time to look for implants."

Hours of weakness seemed to pass before the command communicator buzzed. Lt. Josephs' voice said, "Security, Captain. I had to stun the prisoner. He has some sort of transceiver imbedded in one of his antennae, sir; it broke off in my hand. I didn't know they were that delicate."

"They aren't. Thanks, Lieutenant. Neutralize it and send it to Mr. Scott for analysis. Kirk out."

"Captain," Chekov said. "The alien ship has changed course and speed. Moving directly toward us at Warp Eight."

"Lt. Uhura, tell Lt. Josephs to bring the prisoner to the bridge. Mr. Chekov, deflectors on. Red alert. Phasers stand by for fire on my signal."

"Aye, sir." The alarm began to sound. "Shields on. Phasers manned and ready."

"Take over Spock's scanners. Ensign, take the helm."

A blip appeared in the viewscreen and flashed by. It loomed large for an instant, but it was only a blur at this speed. Suddenly the bridge was slammed and rocked. The *Enterprise* had been hit.

"Damage, Mr. Chekov!"

"None, sir; deflected. Target moving away. Turning now. He's coming around again."

"Fire phasers as he passes, Ensign. Steady . . . Fire!"

Chekov studied the scanner. "Clean miss, sir."

At the same moment, there was another jolt. "Report on their weaponry."

"Sensors report standard phasers, sir."

Standard phasers. Good. The enemy had more speed, but they weren't giants.

Another wave of weakness passed through him. The *Enterprise* seemed to be standing up so far, but he was none too sure of himself.

"Captain, the intercom is jammed," Uhura said. "All the Ambassadors are asking what's going on."

"Tell them to—tell them to take a good guess, but *clear that board*, Lieutenant!"

The ship shook furiously again.

"Captain," Uhura said, "I've got an override from Dr. McCoy. He says that another shock like that and he may lose both patients."

"Tell him this is probably only the beginning. Mr. Chekov, lock fire control into the computers. Set photon torpedoes two, four and six for widest possible scatter at the three highest intercept probabilities . . ."

The enemy flashed by. The torpedoes bloomed harmlessly on the viewscreen. Another slam. Kirk's head reeled.

"Number four shield has buckled."

"Auxiliary power."

"Sir, Mr. Scott reports auxiliary power is being called upon by Sickbay."

"Divert."

"Switching over—shields firming up. Number four still weak, sir. If they hit us there again, it'll go altogether."

"Set computer to drop to number three and switch auxiliary back to Sickbay if it goes."

"Aye, sir."

Kirk heard the elevator doors open behind him, and then Lt. Josephs and another security guard were hustling Thelev before him, without ceremony. It took Kirk a moment to remember that he had ordered exactly this interruption. He stared harshly at the prisoner.

"Your friends out there are good," he said. "But they'll have to blast this ship to dust to win."

"That was intended from the beginning, Captain," Thelev said. He was, Kirk noted with a certain satisfaction, still rather lumpy from his attempt at killing, an impression heightened by the missing antenna. The small wound there had healed, but it looked more as though it had been a deep cut than the loss of a major organ.

"You're not an Andorian. What did it take to make you over?"

The *Enterprise* rocked again. Chekov said, "Shield four down."

"Damage control procedures, all decks," Kirk said. Then, to Thelev; "That ship out there carries phasers. It's faster than we are, but weapon for weapon, we have it outgunned."

Thelev only smiled. "Have you hit it yet, Captain?"

Another shock, and a heavier one. Chekov said, "Shield three weakening. Shall I redivert auxiliary power, sir?"

This was getting them nowhere; it if continued sheerly as a battle of attrition, the *Enterprise* would lose. And there was the operation to consider.

"Engineering, this is the Captain. Blank out all power on the port side of the ship except for phaser banks. On my signal, cut starboard power. Kirk out." He turned back to Thelev. "Who are you?"

"Find your own answers, Captain. You haven't long to live."

"You're a spy, surgically altered to pass as an Andorian. You were planted in the Ambassador's party to use terror and murder to disrupt us and prepare for this attack."

"Speculation, Captain."

The ship shook again. Chekov said, "Shield three is gone, sir."

"Engineering, blank out starboard power, all decks. Maintain until further orders."

The lights on the bridge went out, except for gleams from the telltales on the panels, and the glow of stars from the viewscreen. In the dimness, Thelev at last looked slightly alarmed. "What are you doing?" he said.

"*You* speculate."

"We're starting to drift, Captain," Chekov said. "Shall I hold her on course?"

"No. Stand by your phasers, Mr. Chekov."

"Aye, sir. Phasers standing by."

A blip of pulsing light again appeared in the screen, slowed down, held steady. Kirk leaned forward intently.

"He's just hovering out there, sir."

"Looking us over," Kirk said. "We're dead—as far as he knows. No starship commander would deliberately expose his ship like this, especially one stuffed with notables—or that's what I hope he thinks."

"Range decreasing. Sublight speed."

"Hold your fire."

"Still closing—range one hundred thousand kilometers—phasers locked on target . . ."

"Fire."

The blip flared brightly on the screen. A jubilant shout went up from Chekov. "Got him!"

"Lt. Uhura, open a hailing frequency. If they wish to surrender . . ."

He was interrupted by a glaring burst of light from the viewscreen. Everyone instinctively ducked; the light was blinding. When Kirk could see the screen again, there was nothing on it but stars.

"They could not surrender, Captain," Thelev said. "The ship had orders to self-destruct."

"Lt. Uhura, relay to Starfleet Command. Tell them we have a prisoner."

"Only temporarily, Captain," Thelev said. "You see, I had self-destruct orders, too. Slow poison—quite painless, actually, but there is no known antidote. I anticipate another ten minutes of life."

Kirk turned to the security guards. "Take him to Sickbay," he said harshly.

Josephs and the guard came down to flank Thelev, and began to shepherd him toward the elevator. As they reached the door, the spy crumpled, sagged, fell to his knees. He said tonelessly, "I seem to—have—miscalculated . . ."

He fell face down and was still. Kirk rose wearily.

"So did they," he said. "Put him in cold storage for an autopsy. Secure for General Quarters. Mr. Chekov, take over."

He went down to the operating room. It was empty, the operating table clear, the instruments mutely inactive. After a moment, McCoy came in from the Sickbay area. He looked as drawn and tired as Kirk felt.

"Bones?"

"Are you quite through shaking this ship around?" the surgeon asked.

"Sarek—Spock—how are they?"

"I don't mind telling you, you make things difficult for a surgeon conducting a delicate operation which . . ."

"*Bones.*"

The Sickbay doors opened again and Amanda appeared. "Captain, come in," she said. Kirk shoved past McCoy eagerly.

Inside, Sarek and Spock occupied two of the three beds, side by side. Both looked pale and exhausted, but reasonably chipper. Amanda sat down happily beside Sarek.

"That pigheaded Vulcan stamina," McCoy's voice said behind him, "I couldn't have pulled them through without it."

"Some doctors have all the luck."

"Captain," Spock said. "I believe the alien . . ."

"We damaged their ship," Kirk said. "They destroyed it to avoid capture. Bones, Thelev's body is being brought to your lab. I want an autopsy as soon as you feel up to it."

"I believe you'll find he's what's usually called an Orion, Doctor," Spock said. "There are intelligence reports that Orion smugglers have been raiding the Coridian system."

"But what could they gain by an attack on us?" Kirk asked.

"Mutual suspicion," Sarek suggested, "and perhaps interplanetary war."

Kirk nodded. "With Orion carefully neutral. She'd clean up by supplying dilithium to both sides—and continue to raid Coridan."

"It was the power utilization curve that confused me," Spock said. "I did not realize that until I was just going under the anesthetic. The curve made it appear more powerful than a starship—than anything known to us. That ship was constructed for a suicide mission. Since they never intended to return to base, they could utilize one hundred per cent power in their attacks. I cannot understand why I didn't realize that earlier."

Kirk looked at Sarek. "You might have had a few other things on your mind."

"That does not seem likely."

"No," Kirk said wryly. "But thank you anyway."

"And you, Sarek," Amanda said. "Would you also say thank you to your son?"

"I do not understand."

"For saving your life."

"Spock behaved in the only logical manner open to him," Sarek said. "One does not thank logic, Amanda."

Amanda stiffened and exploded. "Logic! Logic! I am sick to death of logic. Do you want to know how I feel about your logic?"

The two Vulcans studied the angry woman as though she were some sort of exhibit. Spock glanced at his father and said, quite conversationally, "Emotional, isn't she?"

"She has always been that way."

"Indeed? Why did you marry her?"

"At the time," Sarek said solemnly, "it seemed the logical thing to do."

Amanda stared at them, stunned. Kirk could not help grinning, and McCoy was grinning, too. Amanda, turning to them in appeal, was startled; and then, obviously, suddenly realized that her leg was being pulled. A smile broke over her face.

Equally suddenly, the room reeled. Kirk grabbed the edge of the table. Instantly, McCoy was beside him, guiding him toward the third bed.

"Bones—really—I'm all right."

"If you keep arguing with your kindly family doctor, you'll spend the next ten days right here. Cooperate and you'll get out in two."

Kirk subsided, but now Spock was sitting up. "If you don't mind, Doctor, I'll report to my own station now."

McCoy pointed firmly at the bed. "You're at your station, Spock."

The First Officer shrugged and settled back. McCoy surveyed his three restive patients with an implacable expression.

"Bones," Kirk said, "I think you're enjoying this."

"Indeed, Captain," Spock agreed. "I've never seen him look so happy."

"Shut up," McCoy commanded. There was a long silence. McCoy's expression gradually changed to one of incredulity.

"Well, what do you know?" he said to Amanda. "I finally got the last word!"

THE DEADLY YEARS

Writer: David P. Harmon

Director: Joseph Pevney

First Aired: December 8, 1967

There was no sign of Robert Johnson when the party from the *Enterprise* materialized on Gamma Hydra IV. In fact, there was no sign of anybody, and their arrival site, which otherwise resembled a Kansas field in mid-August, was eerily silent.

There were the overbright sun, the varied greens of leaves and grasses, even the shimmer of heat waves over the adjacent meadow. But all sounds of life were missing—insect, animal, human. All that suggested that it was the specified headquarters of the Johnson expedition was a scattering of pre-fab buildings.

Spock, Kirk noted, was looking troubled too. McCoy said, "Perhaps they weren't expecting us."

Spock shook his head. "Our arrival was scheduled well in advance, Doctor. An annual check of every scientific expedition is routine."

"Besides, I had sub-space contact with the leader of this expedition, a Robert Johnson, not an hour ago," Kirk said.

"Did he report anything wrong, Jim?"

"No . . . and yet there was *something* wrong. I can't quite nail it down, but his conversation was disjointed, somehow, as though he were having trouble sticking to the subject, or was worried about something." Kirk pointed at the nearest building. "Mr. Chekov, check that place. Mr. Spock and I will check that one. McCoy, Scotty, Lieutenant Galway, look around, see if you can find anyone."

The group broke up. Arlene Galway was looking a little scared, Kirk thought. Well, this was only her first extra-solar planet; she'd toughen in due course. And the circumstances were a little odd.

Kirk and Spock were about to enter "their" building when a scream rent the air. Whirling, Kirk saw Chekov bursting out into the open, looking about wildly.

"Captain! Captain!" Chekov's voice had gone up a full octave. Kirk loped forward and grabbed him.

"What's wrong?"

"Captain! In there!"

"Control yourself, Ensign! What is it?"

"A man, sir! In there!" Chekov seemed a little calmer. "A dead man."

"All right, we'll check it. But why the panic? You've seen dead men before."

"I know," Chekov said, a little ashamedly. "But this one's, uh, peculiar, and frankly, sir, it startled me."

"'Scared' might be the better word. All right, Bones, Spock, let's take a look." Kirk drew his phaser.

The interior of the building was quite dark—not black, but Kirk, coming in from the bright sunlight, had trouble getting used to it. At first, the building seemed quite empty; then he saw some sort of low structure near its end. He approached cautiously.

Then he abruptly understood what had panicked the unprepared Chekov. The object was a crudely constructed wooden coffin, for which two sawhorses served as a catafalque.

The body it held might have been Methuselah's. Deep wrinkles made its facial features also indecipherable. The open mouth was toothless, its near-white gums shriveled, its eyes sunk in caverns, flattened under their lids of flabby skin. The body seemed to be mere bones, barely held together by a brown-spotted integument of tissue-paper thinness. Clawed hands were crossed on its collapsed chest.

Chekov's voice said through the dimness, "I bumped into it walking backward, sir, and I—"

"I quite understand, Ensign. Rest easy. Bones, what's this?"

"Exactly what it looks like, Jim. Death by natural causes—in other words, old age."

"Doctor," Spock said, "I ran a personnel check on the members of this expedition before we beamed-down, and I can assure you that not one of them was . . ."

Midway through this sentence Kirk became aware of the shuffling of feet outside the open door. They all turned as Spock's voice trailed off.

A man and woman tottered toward them, supporting themselves with sticks. They were stooped and shrunken, the skin of their skulls showing through their thin white hair.

The man said, in a quavering voice, "They've come to pay their respects to Professor Alvin."

"I am Captain Kirk of the—"

"You'll have to speak louder," the man said, cupping his ear with his free hand.

"I said I am Captain Kirk of the *Enterprise*. Who are you?"

"Robert Johnson," said the old man, nodding. "And this is my wife Elaine."

"That's impossible," Kirk said. "The Johnsons are—how old are you?"

"Me? I'm . . . let me see . . . oh yes, I'm twenty-nine. Elaine is twenty-seven."

The shocked silence was at last broken by McCoy. "I am a physician. You both need rest and medical care."

* * *

There were only three decrepit survivors of the expedition to be beamed-up to Sickbay and Nurse Chapel's gentle but efficient care. Standing beside McCoy, Kirk leaned over Robert Johnson's bed.

"Can you hear me, Dr. Johnson?"

The filmed eyes found his face. "Not deaf yet, you know. Not yet."

"Have you any idea what happened?"

"What happened?" Johnson echoed vaguely.

"Did your instruments show anything?"

The old mind was wandering. As though appealing to some benevolent but absent god, Johnson said, "Elaine was so beautiful . . . so beautiful."

"He can hear you, Jim, but he can't understand. Let him rest."

Kirk nodded. "Nurse Chapel, if any of them seem lucid, we'll be in the briefing room." He went to the intercom. "Kirk to bridge. Mr. Spock, Commodore Stocker, Dr. Wallace, to the briefing room, please. Bones, I'll ask you to come along."

Janet Wallace and George Stocker were distinguished guests; he an able administrator in his mid-forties, she an endocrinologist, in her late twenties and extremely attractive. They were waiting with Spock at the big table when he and McCoy arrived. He nodded to them all and sat down himself. "Commodore Stocker, I've asked you to this briefing because Gamma Hydra Four falls within the area of your administration."

Trim, competent-looking, the tall man said, "I appreciate that, Captain."

The merest hint of constraint came into Kirk's voice as he spoke to the dark-eyed girl who sat next to the Commodore. "Dr. Wallace, though you are a new member of our crew, your credentials as an endocrinologist are impressive. In this situation we face, I'd appreciate your working closely with Dr. McCoy."

She smiled at him. "Yes, Captain."

He turned hastily to McCoy. "Fill them in, Bones."

McCoy said, "The survivors of the expedition to Gamma Hydra Four are not merely suffering from extreme old age. They are getting older, much older by the minute. My examinations have shown up nothing. I haven't a clue to the cause of this rapidly aging process."

"Mr. Spock, what about environment and atmosphere?"

"Sensors show nothing inimical to human life, sir. The atmosphere screens out the usual amount of harmful cosmic rays."

"We are close, though," Kirk said, "to the neutral zone between our Federation and the Romulan Confederation. The Romulans may have a new weapon. Perhaps they have been using members of the expedition as guinea pigs."

"I have begun to investigate that possibility, Captain," Spock said.

Kirk rose. "I want you all to check out everything in your particular specialties. No matter how remote, how far-fetched seems the notion, I want it run down." He paused for emphasis. "We will remain in orbit until we have the answer."

Stocker spoke. "I am anxious to get to Star Base Ten in order to assume my new post. I am sure you understand that, Captain."

"I will do what I can to see that you make your due date, Commodore."

"Thank you, Captain."

The men, pushing back their chairs, left the briefing room. But the dark-eyed Dr. Wallace didn't move. Kirk turned at the door. "Anything I can do for you, Doctor?"

"Yes," she said. "You might, for instance, say 'Hello, Janet'. You might be a little less the cold, efficient starship captain and a little more the old . . . friend."

"Janet, as captain, I have certain—my duties are heavy." Then he gave her a wry little smile. "Or maybe I just don't want to get burned again."

"I'm carrying a little scar tissue of my own," she said.

There was a small silence. Then he said, "How long has it been?"

"More than six years, Jim."

"A long time. But there wouldn't be any change if we started it up all over again, would there? I've got my ship; and you've got your work. Neither of us will change."

"You never asked why I married after we called it off."

"I supposed you'd found another man you loved."

"I found a man I admired."

"And in the same field as you. You didn't have to give up anything."

"No, I didn't. But he's dead now, Jim."

She went to him, her hands extended. Kirk hesitated. Then he took one of the hands, his eyes searching the warm brown ones—and Uhura's voice spoke on the intercom.

"Captain Kirk, Mr. Spock would like to see you on the bridge."

"Tell Mr. Spock I'm on my way." He was finding deeper depths in the brown eyes. "Janet, we're under pressure right now. Maybe, when it eases off, things will be—"

Uhura's voice interrupted again. "Captain Kirk, Mr. Scott would like to see you in Engineering."

"Tell him I'll be down after I check with Mr. Spock." He drew Janet closer to him. Lifting her chin, he said, "But this time there must be truth between us. You and I, with our eyes open, knowing what each of us are."

"It's been a long six years," she said; and placed her arms around his neck. He had bent his head to her mouth when the intercom spoke for the third time. "Captain Kirk!"

"On my way, Lieutenant Uhura." A sudden wave of weariness swept over him. He touched the girl's mouth with his forefinger. "Six long years—and that intercom is trying to make it six more. Dr. Wallace, your lips are as tempting as ever—but as I remarked, my duties are heavy."

The weariness stayed with him on his way to the bridge. Sulu greeted him with a

"Standard orbit, Captain." He said, "Maintain" and crossed to Spock at the computer station.

"I have rechecked the sensors, sir. Gamma Hydra Four checks out as a Class M planet, nitrogen-oxygen atmosphere, normal mass with conventional atmospheric conditions. I can find nothing at all out of the ordinary."

"How about that comet that recently passed through here?"

"I am running checks on it, sir. As yet I have no conclusions. The comet is a rogue and has never been investigated."

"Captain Kirk!"

It was Stocker. He looked like a man with a determined idea. "Facilities at Star Base Ten," he said, "are much more complete than those on board ship. It seems to me your investigations would be facilitated by proceeding there at once. I assure you of every cooperation."

"Thank you, Commodore; but we have a few facilities of our own. I am going to Engineering, Mr. Spock." He left the computer station to say to Sulu, "Maintain standard orbit, Mr. Sulu."

Surprised, Sulu exclaimed, "But you already gave that order, sir!"

Kirk looked surprised himself. "Did I? Oh, well. Follow it."

As he left the bridge, Spock stared after him, a look of concern in his eyes.

Lieutenant Galway appeared uneasy, too, as she opened the door of Sickbay. "Dr. McCoy, can I speak with you a moment?"

"Of course." He motioned her to a chair but she didn't take it. "I know," she said, "that this is going to sound foolish. But—I seem to be having a little trouble hearing."

"Probably nothing important," McCoy said.

"I never had any trouble before."

"I'll have a look at you. Maybe a simple hypersonic treatment will clear it up." She said, "Thank you, Doctor" and followed him into the examination room.

Kirk was discovering some trouble of his own. Alone in his quarters, stripped to the waist, he dried the face he'd just shaved, and reached for the clean shirt he'd laid out on the bed. As he raised his right arm to insert it into a sleeve, a sharp stab of pain struck his right shoulder. He winced, lowered the arm, flexed it, massaging the shoulder muscle. The pain persisted. Slowly, carefully, he put on the shirt. Then he moved to the intercom and flicked a button. "Progress report, Mr. Spock?"

"All research lines negative, Captain."

Kirk said, "Astronomical section reports that a comet recently passed by. Check into that."

Spock waited a moment before he replied, "I'm doing that, sir, according to your order. We discussed it earlier."

"Oh. Well, let me know what you come up with. I'll be in Sickbay."

"Yes, Captain."

The walk to Sickbay seemed longer than usual. The pain in the right shoulder had extended to the right knee. There was a slight trace of a limp in Kirk's movement as he entered Sickbay. In its bed section, all but one of the three beds was vacant. He thought, "So two of the rescued Johnson party are gone." It was a depressing reflection. Then he saw Nurse Chapel draw a blanket up and over the face of the patient who occupied the third bed.

McCoy looked up. "Robert Johnson, deceased. The last one, Jim. Cause of death—old age."

"You did what you could," Kirk said.

The intercom spoke. "Dr. McCoy? This is Scott. Can I come up and see you?"

McCoy answered shortly. "You just need vitamins. But yes, come up anyway, Scotty."

He punched off and Kirk said, "Bones, I believe you're getting gray!"

"You take over my job and see what it does to you!" Low-voiced, McCoy gave an order to Nurse Chapel. Then he turned back to Kirk. "Well, what's *your* problem?"

"My shoulder," Kirk said. "Got a little twinge in it. Probably just a muscle strain."

"Probably, Dr. Kirk," McCoy snapped.

Kirk grinned. "Reprimand noted, sir. Okay, no more diagnoses by me."

McCoy ran his Feinberger over Kirk's shoulder. He frowned. "Hmmm. Maybe we'd better run a complete check on you."

"Well? Muscle strain?"

McCoy shook his head. "No, Jim. It's an advanced case of arthritis. And spreading."

"But that's not possible!"

"I'll run the check again, but I'll get the same answer."

He didn't run it again. For Kirk, his dismay still on his face was staring past him at the Sickbay door. McCoy turned. Scott stood there—a Scott with snow-white hair who appeared to be sixty years of age.

Sickbay on the *Enterprise* had become a section that seemed to have been appropriated by a Golden Age club. Assembled there on Kirk's order were every member of the crew who had contacted Gamma Hydra Four. With the single exception of Chekov, each one had been affected by the rapidly aging process. Kirk looked fifty-five: McCoy ten years older. Nor had Spock's Vulcan heritage been entirely able to immunize him against its effects. Wrinkles cracked his face; the skin under his eyes had gone baggy. Lieutenant Galway might have been a woman in her mid-sixties. Scott looked oldest of them all.

"All right, Bones," Kirk said. "Let's have it."

McCoy said, "All of us who went down to the planet, except Ensign Chekov, are aging rapidly. The rates vary from person to person, but it averages thirty years each day. I don't know what's causing it—virus, bacteria or evil spirits. I'm trying to find out."

"Spock? I asked you for some calculations."

"Based on what Dr. McCoy gave me, I'd say that we each have a week to live. It would also seem that since our mental faculties are aging faster than our bodies, we will become little better than mental vegetables in less time than a week."

"You mean total senility?"

"Yes, Captain. In a very short time!"

Kirk took a step away from the group. "What a . . . a filthy way to die!" He turned slowly, accommodating his aching knee. "I want every research facility on this ship, every science technician, to immediately start round-the-clock research. I want the answer! And a remedy! And you might start in by telling me why Chekov wasn't affected!"

"I'm doing what I can," McCoy said. He removed his Feinberger diagnostic instrument from Spock. "You are disgustingly healthy, Spock."

"I must differ with you, Doctor. I am finding it difficult to concentrate. My eyesight appears to be failing. And the normal temperature of the ship strikes me as increasingly cold."

"I didn't say you were not affected."

Scott said dully, "Can I go back to my station?"

"Feel up to it, Scotty?" Kirk asked.

"Of course I do. Just need a little rest, that's all."

McCoy said, "You can leave too if you wish, Lieutenant Galway."

She didn't move. McCoy spoke louder. "Lieutenant Galway?"

"What? You spoke to me, Doctor?"

"Yes. I said you could go. Why not go to your quarters and get some sleep?"

"No! I don't want to sleep! Can't you understand? If I sleep . . . what will I find when I wake up?"

Kirk said, "Lieutenant Galway, report to your station and continue with your duties."

Her "Yes, sir" was grateful. She rose painfully from her chair, moved toward the door, and came face to face with herself in a mirror. She turned from it in anger.

"What a stupid place to hang a mirror!"

She half-stumbled out. Kirk looked after her. "She's seven or eight years younger than I am. She looks ten years older."

"People normally age at different speeds, Jim."

Kirk pointed to Chekov. "But why hasn't he aged?"

"I don't know."

"Well, I want to know! Is it his youth? His blood type? His glands? His medical history? His genes?"

"Nurse Chapel, prepare Mr. Chekov for a complete physical."

She rose. "Come along, Ensign. This won't hurt. Much."

As the door closed behind the nurse and the reluctant Chekov, Janet Wallace turned to McCoy. "A few years ago on Aldebaran Three, my husband and I used a variation of cholesterol block to slow arteriosclerosis in animals."

"Did it work?"

"Sometimes. But the side effects were fierce. We gave it up."

"Try it anyhow, Dr. Wallace. Try anything, but do it quickly!"

"Yes, sir." She went out in turn.

"Mr. Spock, return to the bridge," Kirk said. "I'll join you shortly. Keep me posted on Chekov, Bones."

He found Janet Wallace waiting for him in the corridor. "I thought you were on your way to the bio-chemistry lab, Doctor."

"We both go in the same direction, Jim."

After a moment, he nodded. "So we do."

She adjusted her pace to his slower walk. "We know the problem," she said. "We know the effects it is having. And we know the progress of the affliction. Therefore, once we find the proper line of research, it's only logical that we find the solution."

Kirk smiled. "You sound like my First Officer."

"No problem, Jim—not even ours—is insoluble."

"I could name you five insoluble problems right off the top of my head. For example, why was the universe created? How can we trust what we think we know? Is there such a thing as an invariably right or wrong action? What is the nature of beauty? What is the proof of Fermat's last theorem? None of those are soluble by logic."

"No. The heart is not a logical organ. Our . . . situation . . . doesn't have its roots in logic." She put her arm through his. "When I married Theodore Wallace, I thought I was over you. I was wrong."

Kirk gave her a sharp look. "When did you realize this? Today?"

"What?"

"How much older was your husband than you?"

"What difference does it make?" she asked.

"Answer me!"

"Twenty-six years," she told him reluctantly. Then, as though he'd demanded an explanation, she added, "He was a brilliant man . . . we were stationed on a lonely outpost . . . working together—" She broke off to cry, "Jim, I don't want to talk about him! I want to talk about us!"

"Look at me!" Kirk demanded. He seized her shoulders. "I said look at me! What do you see?"

"I—I see Captain James Kirk," she said unsteadily. "A man of morality, decency—strong, handsome—"

"And *old*!" he cried. "Old—and getting older every minute!"

"Jim, please . . ."

"What are you offering me, Jan? Love—or a goodbye present?"

"That's very cruel," she said.

"It's honest!" His voice was harsh with bitterness. "Just stay around for two more days, Janet! By that time I'll really be old enough for your love!"

Young Chekov was feeling the strain of multiple medical examinations. "Give us some more blood, Chekov!" he muttered to Sulu. "The needle won't hurt, Chekov! Take off your shirt, Chekov! Roll over, Chekov! Breathe deeply, Chekov! Blood sample! Marrow sample! Skin sample! They take so many samples of me I'm not even sure I'm here!"

"You'll live," Sulu said.

"Oh yes, I'll live . . . but I won't enjoy—"

Kirk entered the bridge and he fell silent. Sulu said, "Maintaining standard orbit, Captain."

"Increase orbit to twenty thousand perigee."

As Kirk moved to his command chair, Yeoman Doris Atkins handed him a clipboard. "Will you sign this, sir?" He glanced at the board, scribbled his name on it and was handing it back to her when Commodore Stocker approached him.

"I hope to have a few words with you, Captain."

"I have very little time, Commodore."

"Very well, sir. I just want to remind you we have a due date at Star Base Ten."

"I'm afraid we'll be late for it, Commodore Stocker. I do not intend to leave this area until we have found a solution to our problem."

"Captain, I am watching four very valuable, and one almost irreplaceable, members of the Starfleet failing before my eyes. I want to do something to help."

"If you are so concerned," Kirk said, "I'll send a subspace message to Star Base Ten and explain the situation."

At his computer station, Spock shook his head. Kirk noticed the gesture. "Yes, Mr. Spock?"

"Captain . . . you sent such a message this morning."

"Oh. Yes, of course." He changed the subject. "Yeoman Atkins."

"Sir?"

"Where's the report on fuel consumption?"

"You just signed it, sir."

"If I'd signed it, I wouldn't have asked for it! Give it to me!"

The girl timidly handed him the board. There was his signature. Angrily, he handed the board back to her and sank down in his command chair. He saw Chekov and Sulu exchange looks. Uhura's back was resolutely turned.

Kirk closed his eyes. *I need rest. You can take just so much. Then you've had it.* He was helpless; that was the fact. And he had never been so tired before in all his life . . . worry, despair . . . they weren't going to change a thing . . . tired . . . tired . . .

As from a great distance, he heard Spock's voice. "Captain! I believe I know the cause! I decided to—" The voice stopped, and Kirk let his mind drift again; but then he was being shaken. "Captain!" He roused himself with immense effort.

"Hmm? Spock? Sorry . . . I was thinking."

"Understandable, sir."

"Um. Do you have something to report, Mr. Spock?"

"Yes, sir. I think I know the cause of the affliction. I cannot be sure, but the lead I have seems very promising."

Alert now, Kirk said, "What is it?"

"The comet," Spock said. "The orbit of Gamma Hydra Four carried it directly through the comet's tail. I examined the residue on conventional radiation setting and discovered nothing. But when I reset our sensors at the extreme lower range of the scale, undetected radiation appeared. Below normal radiation readings . . . but definitely present. And undoubtedly residue from the comet's tail."

"Good, Mr. Spock. Let's get that to Dr. McCoy immediately."

Pain stabbed in his right knee as he rose. He massaged it and limped over to Uhura. "Lieutenant, take a message to Starfleet Command."

"Yes, sir."

"Because of the proximity of the Romulans, use Code Two."

"But, sir, the Romulans have broken Code Two. If you will remember the last bulletin—"

"Then use Code Three!"

"Yes, sir. Code Three."

"Message. Key to affliction may be in comet which passed Gamma Hydra Four. Said comet is now—" He looked at Spock.

"Quadrant four four eight, sir."

"I suggest all units be alerted for complete analysis of radiation; and means found to neutralize it. The comet is highly dangerous. Kirk, commanding *Enterprise*. Send it at once, Lieutenant Uhura. Let's go, Mr. Spock."

At the elevator he paused. "Mr. Sulu, increase orbit to twenty thousand miles perigee."

Startled, Sulu said, "You mean—another twenty thousand, Captain?"

Kirk whipped around, grim-faced. "I find it difficult to understand why every one of my commands is being questioned. Do what you're told, Mr. Sulu."

Spock spoke quietly. "What is our present position, Mr. Sulu?"

"Orbiting at twenty thousand, sir."

Kirk looked at Spock's impassive face. Then he said, "Maintain, Mr. Sulu."

"Maintaining, sir."

The silence of constraint was heavy in the bridge when the elevator door closed behind them.

But in Sickbay, hope had returned.

"Radiation," McCoy said reflectively. "As good an answer as any. But why didn't we know this earlier?"

"I suspect, Doctor, because my thinking processes are less clear and rapid than they were."

McCoy glanced at Spock. Then he handed his tape cartridge to Janet Wallace. "Run this through, please, Doctor."

"All right," Kirk said. "Keep me posted. I'll be on the bridge. Coming Spock?"

"I have a question for the Doctor, Captain."

Kirk nodded, left. Spock said, "Doctor, the ship's temperature is increasingly uncomfortable for me. I have adjusted the environment in my quarters to one hundred and twenty-five degrees. This at least is tolerable, but—"

"I can see I won't be making any house calls on you," McCoy said.

"I wondered if there was something which could lower my sensitivity to cold."

"I'm not a magician, Spock. Just a plain old country doctor."

As the Vulcan closed the Sickbay door behind him, Janet turned, frustrated, from the computer. "Dr. McCoy, none of our usual radiation therapies will have any effect on this particular form of radiation sickness."

"All right. We start over. We work harder. Faster. Start completely from scratch if we have to. But we must find something."

Outside in the corridor, Commodore Stocker had intercepted Spock. "Can I have a word with you, Mr. Spock?"

"Commodore?"

Stocker lowered his voice. "Mr. Spock, a Starship can function with a chief engineer, a chief medical officer, even a First Officer who is under physical par. But it is disastrous to have a commanding officer whose condition is less than perfection."

"I am aware of that."

"Please understand me. My admiration for Captain Kirk is unbounded. He is a great officer. But . . . Mr. Spock, I need your help and your cooperation."

"For what, sir?"

"I want you to take over command of the *Enterprise*."

"On what grounds, sir?"

"On the grounds that the Captain is unable to perform his duties because of his affliction."

"I must remind you that I have contracted the same affliction."

The Deadly Years

"But you're a Vulcan," Stocker said. "You have a much greater life span. You show the effects to a much smaller degree . . ."

"I am half human, sir," Spock said. "My physical reflexes are down. My mental capacities are reduced. I tire easily. No, sir. I am not fit for command."

"If you, a Vulcan, are not, then obviously Captain Kirk cannot be."

"Sir," Spock said, "I have duties to perform."

"Mr. Spock, I do not like what I'm about to say but regulations demand it. As second in command of the *Enterprise*, you must convene an extraordinary hearing on the Captain's competence."

"I—resist that suggestion, sir," Spock said stiffly.

"It's not a matter of choice. If a Captain is mentally or physically unfit, a competency hearing is mandatory. Please don't force me to quote a regulation which you know as well as I do."

There was a long pause. "Very well," Spock said. "The hearing will convene at fourteen hundred hours."

Under the eyes of a worried Kirk, Janet and McCoy were running final tests of Chekov. The unhappy Ensign was obviously considering rebellion against what seemed to be the thousandth needle jabbed into him during the course of these interminable examinations.

"Now, this won't hurt," McCoy told him.

"That's what you said last time," Chekov said. "And the time before that."

"Did it hurt?"

"Yes," Chekov retorted.

From the door of Sickbay came a whimper: "Doctor . . . help me . . ."

They turned. Arlene Galway was clutching the door-jamb for support. She was almost unrecognizable with age. "Please . . . do something . . . help . . ."

She reached out a hand; but before anyone could reach her, she collapsed to the deck. McCoy bent over her, while Kirk looked on, appalled even through the gray fog in which everything seemed to have happened in the last few days—or was it the last few weeks?

"That can't be—Lieutenant Galway?" he quavered.

"It is," McCoy said, his own voice creaky. "Or was. She's dead. Her higher metabolism rate caused her to age more rapidly than the rest of us. But it's only a question of time before—"

"Bones, how long have we got?"

"Oh, it's a matter of days, Jim . . . perhaps only hours."

It wasn't information calculated to tranquilize a Starfleet captain called to a hearing on his command competence. Nor were the people gathered around the briefing-room table a quieting influence. The mysterious radiation sickness had made deeper inroads on everyone who had made the ill-fated check on the Robert Johnson expedition.

Looking as though he'd passed his fiftieth birthday, Spock opened the hearing by turning to Yeoman Atkins, who was serving as recorder. "Let it be read that this competency hearing has been ordered by Commodore Stocker, here present." He paused. "And reluctantly called by myself."

Kirk said, "Let it also be read that I consider this hearing invalid."

Spock looked down the table at Stocker.

Stocker said, "Regulation seven five nine two, section three paragraph eleven . . ."

"I know the book, Commodore," Kirk said.

Spock said quietly, "The legality of the hearing, Captain, is unquestionable."

"Mr. Spock, may I make a statement?" It was Stocker's question. At Spock's nod, he said, "I've had to resort to these legal grounds to save the lives of some extremely valuable members of the Starfleet. I have tried to convince Captain Kirk of the need to proceed to Star Base Ten—but have been overruled in each case. The responsibility for this hearing is mine."

"On the contrary, Commodore," Spock said. "As presiding officer and second in command of the *Enterprise*, the responsibility is mine. Captain Kirk, would you like to make a statement?"

"Yes!" The word came in a shout. "I am Captain of this ship and am totally capable of commanding her. Call this farce off and let's get back to work!"

"I cannot, sir," Spock said. "The regulations are quite specific." The chill struck him again. "You are entitled, sir, to direct examination of all witnesses immediately after this board has questioned them."

Kirk's voice was acid with sarcasm. "That is very kind of you, Mr. Spock."

Spock pushed a button on the computer-recorder. Imperturbable, he said, "Mr. Sulu, how long have you served with Captain Kirk?"

"Two years, sir."

"To your knowledge has he ever been unable to make decisions?"

"No, sir."

"Did he order you to maintain standard orbit around Gamma Hydra Four?"

"Yes, sir."

"Did he, several minutes later, repeat the order?"

"Yes, sir."

"Did he order you to increase orbit to twenty thousand perigee?"

"Yes, sir."

"And did he not repeat that order?"

"He did not!" Kirk yelled. "When I give an order I expect it to be obeyed! I don't have to repeat myself!"

"Captain, you'll be allowed direct cross-examination privileges when the board has finished."

"Isn't your terminology mixed up, Spock? This isn't a board! It's a cudgel!"

"Captain, it is a hearing not only sanctioned but required by regulations. Will you please answer the question, Mr. Sulu?"

"Yes, sir. Captain Kirk repeated his order."

"Commodore?"

"I have no questions," Stocker said.

"Captain Kirk?"

"Let's get on with it."

Spock ground his teeth together to keep them from chattering. His hands felt clumsy with cold. "Yeoman Atkins, you handed Captain Kirk a fuel-consumption report before witnesses. He accepted and signed it. Is that correct?"

"Sir, he had more important things on his mind. The current crisis—"

"Yeoman, you are merely to answer the question."

"I—guess he forgot he'd signed it."

"You guess?"

"He forgot he'd signed it."

"Thank you, Yeoman. You may leave."

It went on. Spock called Uhura to testify to Kirk's failure to recall that the Romulans had broken Code Two.

"All right!" Kirk cried. "I had a lot on my mind! I admit to the oversight!"

"It could have been a dangerous one," Stocker said.

"You are out of order, Commodore," Spock said. "Dr. McCoy?"

McCoy was lost in a daydream. "Dr. McCoy!"

He roused. "Sorry. Yes, Mr. Spock?"

"Several hours ago, at this board's request, you ran a complete physical examination of Captain Kirk."

"I did." McCoy threw a tape across the table at Spock. "It's all there. Enjoy yourself."

Silently, the Vulcan placed the tape cartridge into the computer slot.

The device buzzed, clicked, spoke. "Subject's physical age, based on physiological profile, sixty-three solar years."

There was a silence. Then Kirk said, "I am thirty-four years old."

"The computer differs with you," Stocker said.

"Dr. McCoy, give us your professional evaluation of Captain Kirk's present physical condition."

McCoy averted his eyes from Spock. "He is afflicted with a strange type of radiation sickness . . . and so are you and I and Mr. Scott."

"Kindly restrict your comments to Captain Kirk alone, Doctor. What effect has this sickness had on him?"

"He's—he's graying a little. A touch of arthritis."

"Is that all?"

"You know it isn't all! What are you trying to do, Spock?"

"What I must do. Is not the Captain suffering from a peculiar physical degeneration which strongly resembles aging?"

"Yes, he is. But he's a better man—"

"Doctor, do you agree with the computer's evaluation of the Captain's physical age?"

"It's a blasted machine!"

"Do you agree with it, Doctor?"

"Yes, I agree. I'm sorry, Jim."

"This board has no further questions. Unless you, Commodore Stocker..."

"I am quite satisfied, Mr. Spock."

"Do you wish to call witnesses, Captain Kirk?"

"I am perfectly capable of speaking in my own defense!"

Kirk tried to rise. His knee gave way; and he clutched at the table to keep from falling. "This hearing is being held for one reason and one alone. Because I refuse to leave Gamma Hydra Two."

"Gamma Hydra Four, sir," Spock said.

"Of course. A slip of the tongue. Where was I?" He suddenly clenched his fist and dashed it against the table. "So I'm a little confused! Who wouldn't be at a time like this? My ship in trouble ... my senior officers ill ... and this—this nonsense about a competency hearing! Enough to mix up any man! Trying to relieve a Starfleet captain of his command. Why, that's ... that's ... I wouldn't have believed it of you, Spock!"

He glared around the table. "All right, ask me questions! Go ahead! I'll show you who's capable! There's nothing wrong with my memory. Nor with my resolution, either. I repeat, we are maintaining orbit around Gamma Hydra Two!"

The second memory failure stood out, stark-naked.

Spock, cold to his marrow, spoke quietly into the silence.

"We have no more questions, Captain." He struggled to control his shivering. "If you will leave the room, sir, while the board votes ..."

"Fine! You bet I'll leave it. Get your stupid voting over so I can get back to running my ship!"

He limped to the door and turned. "If I'm wanted, I'll be in my quarters."

When the door closed behind him, Spock said, "A simple hand vote will suffice. Dr. Wallace is excluded from the vote. Those who agree that Captain Kirk is no longer capable of handling the *Enterprise* will so signify by raising their right hands."

All hands save Spock's were slowly raised.

"Mr. Spock?" It was Commodore Stocker.

Spock raised his hand. He addressed the recording computer. "Register a unanimous vote."

Stocker said, "I assume, Mr. Spock, that you will now take over command of this vessel."

"Your assumption is incorrect, sir."

"Your reason?"

"By the standards this hearing has used against the Captain: my own physical failings exclude me from any command position."

"All right. Next in line is Mr. Scott."

All eyes fixed on Scott. He peered at the expectant faces, blinked, nodded—and was asleep.

"Since all senior officers are incapable, I am forced by regulations to assume command." Stocker was rising from the table when Spock said, "Sir, you have never commanded a starship."

"Whom would you have take over, Mr. Spock?"

"There is danger from the Romulans," Spock said.

"Mr. Spock, we've got to save these people!" He turned to Sulu. "Mr. Sulu, lay a direct course for Star Base Ten. Warp Five."

"Across the neutral zone, sir?"

Stocker nodded. "Alter course immediately."

"Commodore Stocker, I beg you not to underestimate the danger. Or the Romulans." Spock spoke urgently.

"The neutral zone is thinly patrolled at best. I am gambling that the violation will escape the Romulans' notice."

"The gamble, sir, if I may quote the odds—" Spock said.

"You may not!" Stocker strode to the door. "All officers are to return to their stations."

Kirk was alone in his quarters, tired, defeated, crushed by the full weight of his seventy years. When the knock at the door came, he could hardly bring himself to respond to it; but after a moment, he said, "Come in."

Spock entered, followed by Janet, who took up an inconspicuous stance beside the door. Kirk looked up hopefully at Spock, but the First Officer's face, for once, was almost as readable as a book.

"So," Kirk said. "I've been relieved."

"I am sorry, Captain."

"You should have been a prosecuting attorney."

"Regulations required me—"

"Regulations!" Kirk said. "Don't give me regulations, Spock! You've wanted command all along! The first little excuse—"

"I have not assumed command, Captain."

"I hope you're proud of the way you got . . ." Kirk paused, Spock's words gradually coming home. "What do you mean, you're not in command?"

"I suffer from the same ailment as yourself, sir."

"If you're not in command, who is?"

"Commodore Stocker."

It took Kirk a long moment to place the name. Then he exploded. "Stocker? Are you crazy? He's never held a field command! If Scotty—"

"Mr. Scott is in no condition to command. Commodore Stocker, as a ranking officer—"

"Don't prate to me about rank. The man's a chair-bound paper-pusher. Spock, I order you to take command!"

"I cannot, sir."

"You are disobeying a direct order, Mr. Spock."

"No, Captain. Only Commodore Stocker can give command orders on this ship now."

Impotent fury rose in Kirk. "You disloyal, traitorous . . . you stabbed me in the back the first chance you had. You—" His rage mounted as he found that he was weeping. Weeping! "Get out of here! I don't ever want to have to look at you again!"

Spock hesitated, inclined his head slightly, and left. After a moment, Kirk became aware of the female figure still standing beside the door inside his room, making faint sniffling noises. He peered at it.

"Who is it? Jan? Jan?"

"I'm sorry, Jim," she said. "Truly I am."

"I acted like a fool in there. Let them rattle me. Let myself get confused."

"Everyone understood."

"Only I'm not old, Jan. I'm not! A few muscular aches don't make a man old! You don't run a starship with your arms—you run it with your head! My mind's as sharp as it ever was!"

"We'll find a cure."

"A simple case of radiation sickness and I'm relieved of command." He turned and looked at himself in a mirror. "All right, I admit I've gotten a little gray. Radiation can do that."

"Jim," she said, as if in pain. "I have work to do. Please excuse me—"

"Look at me, Jan. You said you loved me. You know me. Look closely—"

"*Please*, Jim—"

"Just need a little rest. That's all. I'm not old, am I? Well, Say it! Say I'm not old!"

There was no response. Grasping her by the shoulders, he pulled her to him and kissed her with all the violence of which he was capable. But there was no response—not from her, and what was worse, not even within himself. He released her—and saw the pity in her eyes. He turned his back.

"Get out."

Now what? He could not think. He was relieved. The answer . . . but there was no answer. Wait. Something about a comet. McCoy. Chekov. The examination room. That was it, the examination room. He hobbled out, cursing himself for his slowness.

Spock was there; so were Nurse Chapel, McCoy and Janet. They all looked very old, somehow. But the hapless Chekov, back on the table again, did not seem to have changed. He was saying: "Why don't I just go back to work and leave my blood here?"

Kirk tried to glare at Spock. "What are you doing here?"

"It would seem the place where I can be of the most use."

"Maybe you'd like to relieve Dr. McCoy? Bones, what about Ensign Chekov here?"

"Nothing," McCoy said peevishly. "Absolutely nothing."

"There has to be! There has to be! We went down to the surface together. Beamed-down together. Stayed in the same spot. He was with us all the time. He—"

"*No*, Captain," Spock said, drawing in a sharp breath. "Not all the time. He left us for a few moments."

"Left us?" Kirk stared at the Vulcan, trying to remember. "Oh. Yes—when he went into the building. He . . . there was . . . Spock! Something did happen!"

"Indeed, Captain. Doctor, you will remember Professor Alvin's corpse in the improvised coffin—"

"Chekov, you got scared!" Kirk crowed. "You bumped into the dead man, and—"

"You bet," Chekov said. "I was scared, sir. But not half as scared as I am now, I'll tell you that."

"Fright?" McCoy said, raising a trembling hand to his chin. "Yes. Could be. Heart beats faster. Breath short. Cold sweat. Epinephrine flows. Something I read once . . . epinephrine tried for radiation sickness, in the mid-twentieth century—"

"It was abandoned," Janet said. "When hyronalyn was discovered."

"Yes, yes," McCoy said testily. "Don't confuse me. Why was it abandoned? There was some other reason. I knew it well, once. They didn't know the intermediate? Yes! That's it! AMP! Nurse, ask the computer for something called AMP!"

Christine Chapel, her face a study in incredulity, turned to the computer read-out panel. After what seemed a very long time, she said, "There's an entry for it. It's called cyclic adenosine three-five monophosphate. But it affects *all* the hormonal processes—that's why they dropped it."

"We'll try it," McCoy said, with a startling cackle. "Don't just stand there, Dr. Wallace. Synthesize me a batch. Dammit, get cracking!"

* * *

On the bridge, Commodore Stocker was in the command chair. If he was aware of how many backs were pointedly turned to him, he did not show it; he was too busy trying to make sense of the many little lights that were flickering across the console before him.

"Entering Romulan neutral zone, sir," the helmsman said. "All sensors on maximum."

Now who was that? "Thank you, Mr. Spock, sorry, Mr. Sulu. Lieutenant Uhura, let me know if we contact any Romulan."

"Yes, sir. Nothing yet."

Stocker nodded and looked down again. The little lights danced mockingly at him. As a cadet he had studied a control board something like this, but since then, everything seemed to have been rearranged, and labeled with new symbols which meant nothing to him, with only a few exceptions. Well, he would have to depend upon these officers—

Then the *Enterprise* shook sharply under him, and half of the little lights went red. Ignorance overwhelmed him. "What was that?" he said helplessly.

"We have made contact, sir," Uhura said in a dry voice.

"Romulans approach from both sides, sir," Sulu added.

The ship shook again, harder. Swallowing, Stocker said, "Let's see them."

The main viewscreen lit up. It too was full of crawling little lights, which could not be told from the stars except for their motions, which he could not read either.

"I don't see any Romulans!"

"The ones that are changing color, sir. They change in accordance with their rate of approach—"

The ship bucked under him. All the lights went red.

"We're bracketed, sir," Sulu said evenly.

There was a buzz he couldn't locate. "Engineering calling, sir," Uhura said. "Do you want power diverted to the shields?"

His face felt bathed in sweat. "Yes," he said, at random.

"Mr. Scott asks how much warp power to reserve."

What was the answer to that one?

"Commodore Stocker," Sulu said, turning halfway toward the command chair. "We're in a tight. What are your orders?"

The *Enterprise* shuddered once more, and the lights dimmed. Stocker realized suddenly that he was too scared to speak, let alone move—

Then, mercifully, Kirk's voice, thin but demanding, came through the intercom. "What's going on up there? Lieutenant Uhura, this is the Captain!"

"Sir!" Uhura said. "We have violated the Romulan neutral zone, and are under attack."

"The fool. Maintain full shields! I'll be right there."

Stocker felt as though he were about to pass out with relief, but the ordeal wasn't over yet. Voices, more distant, were arguing over the open intercom:

"Jim . . . you can't . . . neither of us . . . Nurse . . . Doctor Wallace . . ."

"Got to . . . get to the bridge . . ."

"Oh Jim, you can't . . . Nurse . . . In there . . ."

Then the voices snapped off. Clearly, Kirk was not about to bail Stocker out yet. Rousing himself, Stocker said, "Lieutenant Uhura, keep trying to raise the Romulans."

"Very well. No response thus far."

"If I can talk to them—tell them the reason why we've violated the neutral zone—"

"The Romulans are notorious for not listening to explanations," Sulu said. "We know—we've tangled with them before."

"Hail them again!"

"I've hailed them on all channels," Uhura said. "They're ignoring us."

"Why shouldn't they?" Sulu said. "They know they have us. As long as we sit here, they can kick away at the screens until they go down."

Stocker ran a hand through his hair. "Then," he said, "we have no alternative but to surrender."

"They'd love that," Sulu said, his back still turned. "They have never captured a starship before. And, Commodore, they never take prisoners."

"Then what—"

"Sir," Uhura said, "you are in command. *What are your orders?*"

In Sickbay, Nurse Chapel and Janet had Kirk pinned down on a bed. He struggled to get up, and despite his aged condition they were having trouble restraining him—a task further complicated by the unpredictable shuddering of the *Enterprise*.

"Greenhorn—up there—ruin my ship—"

"Jim," Janet said through gritted teeth, "if I have to give you a shot—"

"Jim, lay quiet," McCoy said. "You can't do any good. We're through."

"No, no. My ship—"

Spock appeared from the laboratory, carrying a flask. "Dr. Wallace, here is the drug. It's crude, but we had no time for pharmacological tests or other refinements."

"All right," said McCoy. "Let's go."

"It will cure . . . or kill." Spock handed the flask to Janet, who loaded a hypo from it. "A safer preparation would take weeks to test."

"What is it?" Kirk said, quietening somewhat.

"The hormone intermediate," Janet said. "It has to be given parenterally, and even without the probable impurities in it, it could be extremely hard on the body. Cerebral hemorrhage, cardiac arrest—"

"Never mind the details," McCoy said. "Give it to me."

"No," Kirk said. "I'll take the first shot."

"You can't," McCoy said firmly.

As if on cue, the *Enterprise* shook again. "How long do you think the ship can take a pounding like this?" Kirk demanded. "I've got to get up there!"

"Jim, this could kill you," Janet said.

"I'll die anyway without it."

"Medical ethics demand—" McCoy began.

"Forget medical ethics! My ship is being destroyed! Give me that shot."

"The Captain is correct," Spock said. "If he does not regain his faculties, and get to the bridge to take command in a very few minutes, we shall all die at the hands of the Romulans. Give him the shot, Dr. Wallace."

She did so. For a moment nothing seemed to happen. Then Kirk found himself in the throes of convulsions, bucking and flailing at random. Dimly he was aware that all four of the others were hanging on to him.

It seemed to last forever, but actually hardly a minute passed before the fit began to subside, to be gradually replaced by a feeling of exhausted well-being. Janet was pointing a Feinberger at him.

"It's working," she said in a hushed voice. "The aging process has stopped."

"Can't see any change," McCoy said.

"She is correct, Doctor," Spock said. "It is there, and accelerating."

"Janet, help me up," Kirk said, taking a deep breath. "That was quite a ride."

"How do you feel?" she said.

"Like I've been kicked through the bulkhead. Spock, you'll have to wait for your shot; I need you on the bridge. Janet, give McCoy his shot, then Scott." He smiled. "Besides, Spock—if what I've got in mind doesn't work, you won't need that shot. Let's go."

In transit, he felt stronger and more acute with every passing second, and judging by the looks of relief with which he was greeted on the bridge, the change was visible to others as well.

"Report, Sulu!"

"We are surrounded by Romulan vessels—maximum of ten. Range, fifty to a hundred thousand kilometers."

Stocker got out of the command chair in a hurry as Kirk approached it. Kirk punched the intercom. "Engineering, feed in all emergency power, and all warp-drive engines on full standby. I'm going to need the works in about two minutes. Captain out . . . Lieutenant Uhura, set up a special channel to Starfleet Command. Code Two."

"But, Captain—"

"I gave you an order, Lieutenant. Code Two."

"Code Two, sir."

"Message: *Enterprise* to Starfleet Command, this sector. Ship has inadvertantly encroached upon Romulan neutral zone. Surrounded and under heavy Romulan attack. Escape impossible. Shields failing. Will implement destruct order, using corbomite device recently installed. Since this will result in destruction of *Enterprise* and all matter within two hundred thousand kilometer diameter, and establish corresponding dead zone, all Federation ships to avoid area for at least four solar years. Explosion will occur in one minute. Kirk, commanding *Enterprise*. Out . . . Mr. Sulu. Course 188, mark 14, Warp Eight and stand by."

"Standing by, sir."

From his station, Spock said, "The Romulans are giving ground, sir. I believe they tapped in, as you obviously expected them to."

"A logical assumption, Mr. Spock. Are they still retreating?"

"Yes, sir, but are still well within firing range."

"All hands stand by . . . now, Warp Eight!"

The ship jolted—not this time to an onslaught, but to sudden motion at eight times the speed of light. Spock hovered over his console.

"The Romulans were caught off guard, sir. Not even in motion yet."

"Are we out of range, Mr. Sulu?"

"Yes, sir. And out of the neutral zone."

"Adjust to new course. One nine two degrees, mark 4. Heading for Star Base Ten."

"Coming around, sir."

Kirk sat back. He felt fine. Commodore Stocker approached him, his face full of shame.

"Captain," Stocker said, "I just wanted to assure you that I did what I thought had to be done to save you and the other officers."

"Noted, Commodore. You should know, however, that there is very little a Star Base can do that a starship cannot."

"If I may say so, Captain, I am now quite aware of what a starship can do—with the right man at the helm."

The elevator doors snapped open and McCoy came out. He was as young as ever. Kirk stared at him.

"You're looking good, Bones."

"So's Scotty. The drug worked. He pulled a muscle during the initial reaction, but otherwise he's feeling fine. Now, Mr. Spock, whenever you're ready."

"I'm ready now, Doctor."

"Good. Because of your Vulcan physique, I've prepared an extremely potent shot. I've also removed all the breakables from Sickbay."

"That is very thoughtful of you."

"I knew you'd appreciate it."

Kirk smiled. "All in all, gentlemen, an experience we'll remember in our old age . . . of course, that won't be for a long time yet, will it?"

THE TROUBLE WITH TRIBBLES*

WRITER: DAVID GERROLD

DIRECTOR: JOSEPH PEVNEY

FIRST AIRED: DECEMBER 29, 1967

NOBODY SEEMS TO KNOW WHERE TRIBBLES COME FROM, THOUGH OBVIOUSLY they are comfortable in oxygen-bearing air at Earthlike temperatures and pressures. Newborn tribbles are about an inch long; the largest one ever seen, about sixteen inches.

A tribble looks a little like a cross between an angora cat and a beanbag. It has no arms or legs, no eyes, and in fact no face—only a mouth. It moves by rolling, by stretching and flexing like an inchworm, or by a peculiar throbbing which moves it along slowly but smoothly, rather like a snail. It does, however, have long fur, which comes in a variety of colors—beige, deep chocolate, gold, white, gold-green, auburn, cinnamon and dusky yellow.

Tribbles are harmless. Absolutely, totally, completely, categorically, inarguably, utterly, one hundred per cent harmless . . .

The *Enterprise* picked up a priority A-1 distress call from deep space station K-7 within a few moments after the big ship hove into sensor range. The station orbits Sherman's Planet, which is about three light years from the nearest Klingon outpost and hence well within the Klingon's sphere of influence—or the outpost was well within the Federation's sphere of influence, depending on how you looked at it.

Both sides had claimed the planet. Although it was mostly barren, its position between the two political bodies was of considerable strategic importance. In the old days, one or the other would have grabbed it, and the other would have tried to jockey him off, at constant risk of war—a pastime the Klingons enjoyed.

These days, however, there was the Organian peace treaty to take into account. Under its terms, Sherman's Planet would belong to whichever side could prove it could develop the planet most effectively.

Under the circumstances, when a priority one distress call came from station K-7,

---
* Hugo Award nominee

the *Enterprise* could not be blamed for making for the station at Warp Six, with all hands at battle stations.

But when the ship arrived there was no target. K-7 rolled majestically and peacefully around Sherman's Planet, menaced—if that is the word—by nothing within sensor range but a one-man scout ship which floated nearby, obviously in parking orbit.

Baffled and irritated, Captain Kirk called the station's Commander Lurry, who refused any explanation except in person. He did so rather apologetically, but this did not placate Kirk in the least. He beamed over to the station with Spock, his First Officer—with orders to Sulu to keep the *Enterprise* at battle readiness.

There were two other men in Commander Lurry's office when Kirk and Spock arrived. Kirk paid no attention to them.

"Commander Lurry," he said, "you have sent out a priority one distress call. Please state the nature of your emergency."

"Uh, Captain, please allow me to explain. We in fact have no emergency, yet."

"Then you are in trouble," Kirk said grimly. "If there is no emergency, why did you order the call?"

One of the two unknowns said, "*I* ordered it, Captain."

"And who are you?"

"Captain Kirk, this is Nilz Baris," Lurry said. "He's out here from Earth to take charge of the development project for Sherman's Planet."

"And that gives you the authority to put a whole quadrant on defense alert?"

"Mr. Baris," the second unknown said stiffly, "is the Federation Undersecretary for Agricultural Affairs in this quadrant."

"A position with no military standing of which I am aware," Kirk said. "And who may *you* be, please?"

"This is my assistant, Arne Darvin," Baris said. "Now, Captain, I want all available security guards to . . ."

"I beg your pardon?" Kirk said. The way this trio had of answering questions for each other was not improving his temper, and thus far he had heard nothing even vaguely resembling an explanation.

"I will try to make myself clear," the Undersecretary said. "I want all available security guards. I want them posted around the warehouse. Surely that's simple enough."

"It's simple but it's far from clear. What warehouse?"

"The warehouse with the quadrotriticale," Darvin said, recapturing the ball. Lifting an attaché case to Lurry's desk, he extracted from it a small vial. From this he poured into his palm a few small seeds, which he handed to Baris, who in turn handed them to Kirk. The Captain inspected them briefly and then passed them on to Spock.

"Wheat," he said. "What about it?"

"Quadrotriticale is not wheat, Captain," Darvin said, with an audible sniff. "It is a newly developed form of trititicale."

"That leaves me as much in the dark as before."

"Trititicale is a high-yield per acre hybrid form of wheat and rye," Spock said quietly. "This appears to be a four-lobed rehybridization—a perennial, also, if I'm not mistaken. The root grain, triticale, traces its ancestry back to twentieth-century Canada."

"Uh, yes," Baris said, looking a little startled.

"And it is the only Earth grain that will grow on Sherman's Planet," Commander Lurry put in. "We have a warehouse of it here on the station. It's very important that the grain reach Sherman's Planet safely. Mr. Baris thinks that Klingon agents may try to sabotage it."

"Nothing could be more likely," the Undersecretary said. "That grain is going to be the way the Federation proves its claim to Sherman's Planet. Obviously the Klingons will do anything they can to keep it from getting there. It must be protected. Do you understand? It *must* be protected."

"So you issued a priority one distress call on behalf of a warehouse full of grain," Kirk said. "The only reason I don't arrest you on the spot is that I want the Federation to have Sherman's Planet as much as you do. Consider yourself lucky; misuse of the priority one channel is a Federation offense."

"I did not misuse..."

"Captain Kirk," Lurry interposed hurriedly, "couldn't you at least post a couple of guards? We do get a large number of ships passing through."

This of course was true. After a moment, Kirk said, "Mr. Spock, what do you think?"

"It would be a logical precaution, Captain."

"Very well." Kirk took out his communicator. "Kirk to *Enterprise* . . . Lieutenant Uhura, secure from general quarters. Next, beam over *two* security guards. Have them report to Commander Lurry."

"Yes, Captain."

"Also, authorize shore leave for all off-duty personnel. Kirk out."

"Only two?" Baris said, in something very like a fury. "Kirk, you're going to hear about this. I'm going to contact Starfleet Command."

"Do that," Kirk said, staring at the Undersecretary icily. "But before you put in the call, I suggest that you pin back your ears. It will save Starfleet Command the trouble of doing it for you."

The recreation area of K-7 was small, the shops little more than stalls surrounding a central mall formed by the intersection of a number of curving corridors. Space was at a premium.

As Kirk and Spock entered the area, a number of crew members from the *Enterprise* materialized on the mall, including Uhura and Sulu. Kirk moved toward them.

"I see you didn't waste any time getting over here," he said. "Mr. Sulu, we have a new specimen for your greenhouse. Mr. Spock?" The First Officer handed the grain over. "It's called . . ."

"Quadrotriticale!" the helmsman said eagerly. "I've read about it, but I've never seen any till now!"

"Come on, Sulu," Uhura said. "You can study it back aboard. Let's get in some shopping while we have the chance. Coming, Mr. Spock? Captain?"

"Well, for a few minutes, anyhow. But not for long; I suspect there are some hot messages shooting back and forth in subspace along about now."

The shop into which Uhura led them was vaguely cluttered and did not seem to specialize in anything in particular. Clearly it was one of those broker's establishments where spacemen on leave sold curios they had picked up on far planets, to help pay for their shore leaves—curios later resold to other spacemen for twice the price. This did not look like the best shop Kirk had ever seen, but then, K-7 was not the best located of space stations, either.

There was nobody else in it at the moment but a tall, raffish-looking red-haired civilian, who had an immense quantity of merchandise spread out over the counter, and a carryall sack at his feet.

"No, absolutely not," the storekeeper was saying. "I've got enough Argilian flame gems to last me a lifetime. At the price I have to ask for them, hardly anybody on this junkyard can afford them."

"How sad for you, my friend," the peddler said. His voice was surprisingly melodious. "You won't see finer stones than mine anywhere. Ah well. Now surely you'll be wanting some Sirian glow water . . ."

"I use that," the storekeeper said in a deadly monotone, "to polish the flame gems."

The peddler sighed and swept most of his merchandise off the counter into his sack. Only one object was left—a green-gold ball of fluff.

"Ah, you are a most difficult man to reach. All I have left to offer you is tribbles. Surely, you will want . . ."

"Not at that price."

"Oooh," Uhura said. "What is it? Is it alive? May I hold him? He's adorable."

"What is it?" the peddler said, handing it over. "Why, little darlin', it's a tribble. Only the sweetest little creature known to man—exceptin', of course, yourself."

The object in the lieutenant's hands throbbed gently. Kirk became aware of a low, pervasive sound, like a cross between the thrum of a kitten and the cooing of a dove. "Oh," Uhura said, "it's purring!"

"Ah, little lady, he's just sayin' that he likes you."

"Can I buy him?"

"That," the shopkeeper said, "is what we're trying to decide right now."

"My friend, ten credits apiece is a very reasonable price. You can see for yourself how much the lovely little lady here appreciates fine things. Others will, too."

"One credit," said the storekeeper.

Sulu put his grain on the counter and reached tentatively for the tribble. "He won't bite, will he?" the helmsman said.

"Sir!" the peddler said, making a great show of ignoring the storekeeper's offer. "There is a law against transporting harmful animals from one planet to another, as you as a starship officer must be fully aware. Besides, tribbles have no teeth."

"All right," the shopkeeper said. "Two credits."

The peddler took the tribble from Sulu and plopped it down on the counter again. "Nine," he said.

The shopkeeper eyed the animal dubiously. "Is he clean?"

"He's as clean as you are. I daresay a good deal cleaner."

"If you don't want him, I'll take him," Lt. Uhura said. "I think he's cute."

This set off another round of haggling. The two finally settled on six credits, whereupon the peddler began to produce more tribbles from his sack. Startlingly, no two were the same color or size.

"How much are you selling them for?" Uhura asked the shopkeeper.

"Ten credits. But for you . . ."

"Hey!" Sulu said suddenly. "He's eating my grain!" He swept up what remained. The tribble's purr got louder, and its non-face went slowly round and round, giving an absurd impression of bliss. The shopkeeper picked it up, but the peddler promptly took it from him.

"Sir," the peddler said. "That one happens to be my sample, which is mine to do with as I please. And I please to give it to the pretty little lady here."

"That's right," said the storekeeper. "Ruin the market."

"My friend," the peddler said, almost singing, "once the pretty little lady here starts to show this little precious around, you won't be able to keep up with 'em. Mark my words."

Lt. Uhura put the faceless ball of fur to her face, cooing alarmingly. Kirk did not know whether to be pleased or scared; Uhura had never shown the faintest sign of sentimentality before, but she seemed to be far gone in gooiness now. To be sure, the baggy little animals were attractive, but . . .

Queep!

No, that wasn't a tribble; it was his communicator.

"Kirk here."

"Captain, this is Scott. We have a stiff message in from Starfleet Command. I think you'd better deal with it; I don't think I'm authorized."

The Trouble with Tribbles

"All right, Scotty," Kirk told his communicator. "Record and hold. I'll be right over."

"Well and good. But, Captain, that's not all, sir. Our sensors have just picked up a Klingon battle cruiser. It's closing in rapidly on K-7. I've challenged it and gotten a routine acknowledgement; but . . ."

"Who's in command?" Spock said. Kirk had almost forgotten that he was still in the shop; but as usual, he had asked the crucial question. Kirk passed it on, with a grateful nod to his First Officer.

"Commander Koloth, sir. You'll remember him from our last encounter, Captain; a real, fourteen-karat son of a . . ."

"I get the message, Scotty. Hold on—and post battle stations. Lieutenant Uhura, pick up your pet; we're back on duty."

He had hardly finished speaking before the *Enterprise*'s transporters shimmered them all out of existence.

The message from Starfleet Command was, as usual, brief and pointed. It said: "It is not necessary to remind you of the importance to the Federation of Sherman's Planet. The key to our winning of this planet is the grain, quadrotriticale. The shipment of it must be protected. Effective immediately, you will render any aid and assistance which Undersecretary Baris may require. The safety of the grain—and the project—is your responsibility."

How complicated that was going to be was immediately made clear by the presence of the Klingon ship. It made no move to attack the station; that in fact would have been suicide, since every phaser on board the *Enterprise* was locked on the Klingon vessel (as Koloth, an able captain, would assume as a matter of course). Instead, Koloth stunned everyone by asking for shore leave for his men.

Under the Organian peace treaty, Commander Lurry had no choice but to grant the request. Starfleet, however, had inadvertently given Kirk a card to play, since the phrasing of the message had made the safety of the grain his responsibility. Hence he was able to order that only twelve Klingons be allowed shore leave at a time, and furthermore he beamed over one *Enterprise* security guard for every Klingon. That part of it, he thought, ought to please Baris, at least.

It did not please Baris. He did not want any Klingons on the station, period. He carried on about it quite a lot. In the end, however, it was clear that the Klingons had a right to be there, and nothing could be done about it.

Kirk stopped off at the recreation room for a cup of coffee and a breather. Scott, the engineer, was there reading a technical journal; that was his form of relaxation. Elsewhere, however, a knot of people were gathered around a table, including Spock, Dr. McCoy, Uhura and Ensign Freeman. Joining the group, Kirk found that on the table was Uhura's tribble and at least ten smaller ones; the crewmen were playing with them.

"How long have you had that thing, Lieutenant?" McCoy asked Uhura.

"Only since yesterday. This morning, I found that he—I mean *she* had had babies."

"I'd say you got a bargain." McCoy picked up one of the animals and examined it curiously. "Hmmm . . ."

"Lieutenant Uhura," Kirk said amusedly, "are you running a nursery?"

"I hadn't intended to—but the tribble had other plans."

Spock too was handling one of the creatures, stroking it absent-mindedly.

"You got it at the space station?" McCoy said.

"Yes, from the pilot of that one-man scout ship. Commander Lurry says his name is Cyrano Jones, of all things. He's a system locater, down on his luck."

"Most of them are," Kirk said. "Locating new systems on the margins of Klingon space is a synonym for locating trouble."

"A most curious creature, Captain," Spock said. "Its trilling would seem to have a tranquilizing effect on the human nervous system. Fortunately, I seem to be immune."

Watching his First Officer stroke the animal, Kirk raised an eyebrow, but offered no other comment.

"Lieutenant," McCoy said, "do you mind if I take one of these things down to the lab to find out what makes it tick?"

"It's all right with me, but if you're planning to dissect it, I don't want to know about it."

"Say, Lieutenant," Ensign Freeman said, "if you're giving them away, could I have one too?"

"Sure, why not? They seem to be old enough."

Freeman looked at Kirk. "I don't have any objections to pets on this ship," Kirk said. "Within reason. But if these tribbles want to stay on the *Enterprise*, they'd better be a little less prolific."

The tribbles, however, did not seem to get the message. Visiting sick bay the next day—another prolonged shouting match with Baris had given him a headache—Kirk found that McCoy had what seemed to be a boxful of the creatures.

"I thought Uhura gave you only one of those things, Bones. It looks more like you've got ten here."

"Average litter. I had eleven, but I dissected one. The nearest thing I can figure out is that they're born pregnant."

"Is that possible?"

"No, but it would be a great timesaver, wouldn't it? I can tell you this much: almost fifty per cent of the creature's metabolism is geared to reproduction. Do you know what you get if you feed a tribble too much?"

Kirk's mind was not really on the subject. "A very fat tribble?"

"No. You get a whole bunch of hungry little tribbles. And if you think *that's* a boxful, you should see Uhura's. She's got about fifty, and she gave away five."

"Well, you'd better find homes for this batch before you've got fifty, too." Kirk swallowed the headache pill. "Are you going on shore leave, Bones?"

"Already been. Besides, this problem is more interesting. I understand Scotty went over with the last detachment; he'll see to it that there's no trouble. Unless, of course, the Klingons start it."

"I can't see why they'd want to do that. Koloth knows that if there is any, I'd promptly double the number of guards. If he's really after the grain, that's the last thing he'd want."

Nevertheless, after his next interview with Lurry, Kirk troubled to make a detour through the space station's bar. There were six Earthmen there, Scotty and Navigator Chekov among them. Five or six Klingons were at another table, but the two groups were studiously ignoring each other.

As Kirk joined his own men, Cyrano Jones entered the bar and also moved toward them. "Ah, friends," he said, "can I interest you in a tribble?"

He was holding one at Scott's shoulder. Scott turned toward him and found himself looking straight into the tribble's absence of a face. He shuddered.

"I've been pullin' the little beasties out of my engine room all morning!"

"Perhaps one of you other gentlemen—?" There was no response. With a fatalistic shrug, Cyrano went over to the Klingon table, approaching one whom Kirk recognized as Korax, one of Koloth's officers.

"Friend Klingon, may I offer you a charmin' little tribble . . ."

The tribble had other ideas. All its fur stood on end. It hitched itself up Cyrano's forearm with an angry spitting hiss.

"Stop that!" Cyrano said. "Apologies for his bad manners, sir. He's never done that before."

"I suggest," Korax said coldly, "that you remove yourself and that parasite as speedily as possible."

"It's only a friendly little . . ."

"Take it away!"

There was another hiss from the tribble. Korax slapped Cyrano's arm away, sending the tribble flying across the room to land among the Earthmen. Cyrano rushed to retrieve it; Scotty handed it to him without a word.

After looking from one group to the other, Cyrano, somewhat disconsolately, retreated to the bar, where the counterman was taking down a pitcher from a high shelf, and put his beast down on the counter.

"Sir! I feel sure that you would be willin' to engage in a little barter—one of my little tribbles in exchange for a spot of . . ."

The attendant turned, and upended the pitcher. Three tribbles fell out of it.

It was worse on shipboard. The corridors seemed to be crawling with the creatures. On the bridge, Kirk had to scoop three or four of them out of his chair before he could sit down. They were all over the consoles, on shelves, everywhere.

"Lieutenant, how did all of these tribbles get onto the bridge?"

"Through the ventilator ducts, I expect, Captain. They seem to be all over the ship."

"They certainly do. Mr. Spock, have a maintenance crew come up here to clean out this bridge. How many of them are there now, anyhow?"

"Assuming one creature—the one Lieutenant Uhura brought aboard—with an average litter of ten," the First Officer said, "every twelve hours. The third generation will total one thousand, three hundred thirty-one. The fourth generation will total fourteen thousand, six hundred and forty-one. The fifth generation will . . ."

"That's already enough. I want a thorough cleanup. They've got to go."

"All of them?" Lt. Uhura said protestingly. "Oh, Captain . . ."

"Every last one."

"A logical decision," Spock said. "Their breeding rate is beyond our control. They are consuming our supplies and returning nothing."

"Oh, come on now, Mr. Spock. I don't agree with you at all. They're giving us their love. Cyrano Jones says that a tribble is the only love money can buy."

"Lieutenant," Kirk said, "too much of anything—even love—is not necessarily a good thing. And in view of the fact that this all started with just one tribble, clearly the only safe number is none."

"And since feeding them is what makes them breed," Spock added, "one need only imagine what would happen if they got into the food processing machinery, or the food storage areas."

Kirk stared at the First Officer, thunderstruck. "Storage areas!" he said. "Great thundering fireballs! *Storage areas!* Lieutenant Uhura, contact Commander Lurry, and Nilz Baris. Have them meet us at the station mall. Mr. Spock, we're beaming over. Lieutenant, have Doctor McCoy join us in the transporter room—on the double!"

When the three materialized on the mall, half a dozen tribbles materialized with them. The mall did not need any more, however; it was inundated. The store where they had seen their very first tribble looked like a snowbank of fur. The storekeeper, who had evidently just given up an attempt to sweep them out, was sitting in the midst of them with his head in his hands, close to tears.

Lurry and Baris came running to meet them—for once, without Darvin. "What's the matter?" Baris panted.

"Plenty—if what I think has happened, has happened. The warehouse, quick!"

Baris needed no further urging. They left at a dead run, kicking tribbles out of the way.

There were two guards before the warehouse door. "Is that door secure?" Kirk demanded.

"Yes, sir. Nothing could get in."

"Open it."

The guard produced a magnetic key. Nothing happened. "Don't understand it, sir. It seems to be . . ."

What it seemed to be will never be known, for at that moment the door slid open. There was a sort of silent explosion. Hundreds and hundreds and hundreds of tribbles came tumbling out, cascading down around them all, wriggling and seething and mewling and writhing and throbbing and trilling and purring . . .

They stood aghast as the mountain of fur grew. Spock recovered first. Scooping up a tribble, he examined it with clinical detachment. "It seems to be gorged," he observed.

"Gorged!" Baris gasped. "On my grain! Kirk! I'll hold you responsible! There must be thousands—hundreds of thousands!"

"One million, five hundred and sixty-one thousand, seven hundred and seventy-three," Spock said, "assuming, of course, that they got in here three days ago, and allowing for the maximum rate of grain consumption *and* the volume of the warehouse."

"What does the exact number matter?" Baris said despairingly. "The Klingons will get Sherman's Planet now!"

"I'm afraid," Kirk said slowly, "that you're right about that."

McCoy had been kneeling among the tribbles, examining them closely. At this point he looked up.

"Jim?"

"What is it, Bones?"

"Mr. Spock is wrong about these animals. They're not lethargic because they're gorged. They're dying."

"Dying! Are you sure?"

"I venture to say," McCoy replied with dignity, "that nobody on this station knows their metabolism better than I do. Yes, I am sure."

"All right," Kirk said with sudden energy. "Bones, take some of them back to your lab, and some of the grain, too. If they're dying, I want to know why. Then report back to me. I'm opening a formal hearing and investigation. Commander Lurry, I presume we can use your office. I'll want your assistant, and Captain Koloth—and Cyrano Jones, too."

"What good will that do?" Baris said. "The project is ruined—ruined!"

"Regulations require it," Kirk said. "And as for the project—well, that remains to be seen."

* * *

The scene in Lurry's office strongly resembled that moment in the classical detective novel when all the suspects are lined up and the shrewd sleuth eliminates all the obvious suspects and puts his finger on the butler. Lurry was seated behind his desk; nearby, in the visitor's chair, sat Cyrano Jones, stroking a tribble in his lap. Standing, with various degrees of uneasiness, interest or defiance, were Koloth, Korax, another Klingon aide, Spock, Baris, and McCoy, with Kirk facing them. And there were, of course, several security guards standing by. The Klingon captain spoke first:

"I had heard that you Earthers were sentimental about these parasites," he said, "but this is carrying things too far. I want an official apology from you, Kirk, addressed to the High Command of the Klingon Empire. You have restricted the shore leave of my men, harassed them with uniformed snoopers, and now summon us here like common criminals. If you wish to avoid a diplomatic crisis . . ."

"Don't do it, Kirk!" Baris burst in. "That'll give them the final wedge they need to claim Sherman's Planet!"

"Oh, as to *that* matter," Koloth said silkily, "it would seem that the outcome is already settled."

"One thing at a time," Kirk said. "Our present job is to find out who is responsible for the tribbles getting into the quadrotriticale. The Klingons have an obvious motive. On the other hand, it was Cyrano Jones who brought them here, apparently with purely commercial intent. There's no obvious connection."

"Beggin' your pardon, Captain," Cyrano said, "but a certain amount of the blame might be lyin' in sheer ignorance of the little creatures. If you keep their diet down below a certain intake per day, why sure and they don't breed at all. That's how I control mine."

Kirk stared at him. "Why didn't you tell us that before?"

"Nobody asked me. Besides, Captain, any man's common sense should tell him that it's bad for little animals to be overfeedin' 'em."

"Let that pass for the moment. We also need to find out what killed the tribbles. Was the grain poisoned—and if so, who poisoned it?"

He looked fixedly at Koloth, but the Klingon only smiled. "I had no access to it, obviously," he said. "Your guards were watching me every instant. However, Captain, before we go on—would you mind very much having that thing taken out of here?"

He pointed at the tribble in Cyrano's lap. Kirk hesitated a moment, but he could in fact sympathize; he had himself seen enough tribbles to last him a lifetime. He gestured to a guard, who lifted the creature gingerly and moved toward the door.

At the same moment, the door opened and Darvin entered belatedly. The tribble fluffed itself up and spat.

Kirk stared at it a moment in disbelief. Then, taking it from the crewman, he crossed over to Korax and held it out; it spat again. It spat at the third Klingon, too, and at Koloth. However it purred for everyone else, even including Baris—oh well, Kirk thought, there's no accounting for some people's tastes—and it went into a positive ecstasy over Spock, to the First Officer's rigidly controlled distaste. Then back to Darvin. *Hisssss!*

"Bones!" Kirk barked. "Check this man!"

McCoy was already at Darvin's side, tricorder out. He ran it over the man twice.

"It figures, Jim," he said. "Heartbeat all wrong, body temperature—well, never mind the details. He's a Klingon, all right."

The security men closed on Darvin. "Well, well," Kirk said. "What do you think Starfleet Command will have to say about this, Mr. Baris? Bones, what did you find out about the grain?"

"Oh. It wasn't poisoned. It was infected."

"Infected," Baris repeated in a dull voice. He seemed past reacting to any further shock.

"Yes. It had been sprayed with a virus which practices metabolic mimicry. You see, the molecules of the nutriments the body takes in fit into the molecules of the body itself like a key into a lock. This virus mimics the key—but it isn't a nutriment itself. It blocks the lock so the proper nutriments can't get in. A highly oversimplified explanation, but good enough for the purpose."

"Do I mean you to imply," Kirk said, "that the tribbles starved to death? A whole warehouse full of grain, and they starved in the midst of it?"

"That's essentially it," McCoy agreed.

"And would this have happened to any *men* who ate the grain?"

"It would happen to any warm-blooded creature. The virus is very catholic in its tastes—like rabies."

"I observe another possible consequence," Spock said. "Dr. McCoy, could the virus be killed without harming the grain?"

"I think so."

"In that case," Spock said, "Mr. Darvin's attempt at mass murder has done us all a favor, and so have Mr. Jones' tribbles."

"I don't follow you, Mr. Spock," Kirk said.

"A simple logical chain, Captain. The virus without doubt prevented the tribbles from completely gutting the warehouse; fully half the grain must be left. On the other hand, the tribbles enabled us to find that the grain was infected without the loss of a single human life."

"I don't think the Federation courts will count that much in Mr. Darvin's favor, Mr. Spock, but it's a gain for us, I agree. Guards, take him out. Now, Captain Koloth, about that apology—you have six hours to get your ship out of Federation territory."

Koloth left, stiffly and silently. The tribble hissed after him.

"I hate to say this," Kirk said, "but you almost have to love tribbles just for the enemies they make. Now, Mr. Jones. Do you know what the penalty is for transporting an animal that is proven dangerous to human life? It is twenty years."

"Ah, now, Captain Kirk," Cyrano said, almost in tears. "Surely we can come to some form of mutual understanding? After all, as Mr. Spock points out, my little tribbles did tip you off to the infection in the grain—and they proved a most useful Geiger counter for detecting the Klingon agent."

"Granted," Kirk said gravely. "So if there's one task you'll undertake, I won't press charges, and when you're through with it, Commander Lurry will return your scout ship to you. If you'll remove every tribble from this space station . . ."

Cyrano gasped. "Remove every tribble? Captain, that'll take years!"

"Seventeen point nine years," Spock said, "to be exact."

"Think of it as job security," Kirk suggested.

"It's either this—or charges? Ah, Captain, you're a hard man—but I'll do it."

There was not a single tribble about the *Enterprise* when the party returned. It proved rather difficult to find out how this miracle had been brought about, but Scotty finally admitted to it.

"But how did you do it?"

"Oh, I just had the cleanup detail pile them all into the transporter."

"But—Scotty, you didn't just transport them out into space, did you?"

The engineer looked offended. "Sir, I'm a kindhearted man. I gave them a good home, sir."

"Where? Spit it out, man!"

"I gave them to the Klingons, sir. Just before they went into warp, I transported the whole kit and kaboodle into their engine room. And I trust, sir, that all their tribbles will be big ones."

A PIECE OF THE ACTION

WRITER: DAVID P. HARMON AND GENE L. COON
(STORY BY DAVID P. HARMON)
DIRECTOR: JAMES KOMACK
FIRST AIRED: JANUARY 12, 1968

It was difficult to explain to Bela Okmyx, who called himself "Boss" of Dana Iotia Two, that though the message from the lost *Horizon* had been sent a hundred years ago, the *Enterprise* had only received it last month. For that matter, he did not seem to know what the "galaxy" meant, either.

Kirk did not know what he expected to find, but he was braced for anything. Subspace radio was not the only thing the *Horizon* had lacked. She had landed before the noninterference directive had come into effect, and while the Iotians were just at the beginnings of industrialization. And the Iotians had been reported to be extremely intelligent—and somewhat imitative. The *Horizon* might have changed their culture drastically before her departure and shipwreck.

Still, the man called Boss seemed friendly enough. He didn't understand what "transported" meant either, in the technical sense, but readily suggested a rendezvous at an intersection marked by a big building with white columns in a public square where, he said, he would provide a reception committee. All quite standard, so far.

Kirk, Spock and McCoy beamed down, leaving Scott at the con. They materialized into a scene which might at first have been taken for an area in any of the older cities of present-day Earth, but with two significant exceptions; no children were visible, and all the adults, male and female alike, were wearing sidearms. Their dress was reminiscent of the United States of the early twentieth century.

This had barely registered when a sharp male voice behind them said, "Okay, you three. Let's see you petrify."

The officers turned to find themselves confronted by two men carrying clumsy two-handed weapons which Kirk recognized as a variant of the old submachine gun.

"Would you mind clarifying your statement, please?" Spock said.

"I want to see you turn to stone. Put your hands up over your head—or you ain't gonna have no head to put your hands over."

The two were standing close enough together so that Kirk could have stunned them both from the hip, but he disliked stopping situations before they had even begun to develop. He obeyed, his officers following suit.

The man who had spoken kept them covered while the other silently relieved them of their phasers and communicators. He seemed momentarily in doubt about McCoy's tricorder, but he took that, too. A few pedestrians stopped to watch; they seemed only mildly curious, and some of them even seemed to approve. Were these men policemen, then? They were dressed no differently from anyone else; perhaps more expensively and with more color, but that was all.

The silent man displayed his harvest to his spokesman. The latter took a phaser and examined it. "What's this?"

"Be very careful with that, please," Kirk said. "It's a weapon."

"A heater, huh? The Boss'll love that."

"A Mr. Bela Okmyx invited us down. He said . . ."

"I know what he said. What he don't tell Kalo ain't worth knowing. He said some boys would meet you. Okay, we're meeting you."

"Those guns aren't necessary," McCoy said.

"You trying to make trouble, bud? Don't give me those baby blue eyes."

"What?"

"I don't buy that innocent routine." Kalo looked at Spock's ears. "You a boxer?"

"No," Spock said. "Why does everybody carry firearms? Are you people at war?"

"I never heard such stupid questions in my life." Kalo jerked his gun muzzle down the street. "Get moving."

As they began to walk, Kirk became aware of a distant but growing thrumming sound. Suddenly a squeal was added to it and it became much larger.

"Get down!" Kalo shouted, throwing himself to the street. The people around him were already dropping, or seeking shelter. Kirk dived for the dirt.

A vehicle that looked like two mismatched black bricks on four wheels bore down on them. Two men leaned out of it with submachine guns, which suddenly produced a terrible, hammering roar. Kalo got off a burst at it, but his angle was bad for accuracy. Luckily, it was not good for the gunners in the car, either.

Then the machine was gone, and the pedestrians picked themselves up. McCoy looked about, then knelt by the silent member of the "reception committee," but he was plainly too late.

Kalo shook his head. "Krako's getting more gall all the time."

"Is this the way you greet all your visitors?" Kirk demanded.

"It happens, pal."

"But this man is dead," McCoy said.

"Yeah? Well, we ain't playing for peanuts. Hey, you dopes, get outta here!" He shouted suddenly to what looked like the beginning of a crowd. "Ain't you never seen a hit before? Get lost!"

He resumed herding his charges, leaving the dead man unconcernedly behind. Kirk kept his face impassive, but his mind was busy. A man had been shot down, and no one had blinked an eye; it seemed as though it were an everyday happening. Was this the cultural contamination they had been looking for? But the crew of the *Horizon* hadn't been made up of cold-blooded killers, nor had they reported the Iotian culture in that state.

A young girl, rather pretty, emerged from a store entrance and cut directly across to them, followed by another. "You, Kalo," she said.

"Get lost."

"When's the Boss going to do something about the crummy street lights around here? A girl ain't safe."

"And how about the laundry pickup?" said the second girl. "We ain't had a truck by in three weeks."

"Write him a letter," Kalo said indifferently.

"I did. He sent it back with postage due."

"Listen, we pay our percentages. We're entitled to some service for our money."

"Get *lost*, I said." Kalo shook his head as the girls sullenly fell behind. "Some people got nothing to do but complain."

Kirk stared at him. He was certainly an odd sight—odder than before, now that his pockets were stuffed with all the hand equipment from the *Enterprise* trio, and he had a submachine gun under each arm. But he looked none the less dangerous for that. "Mr. Kalo, is this the way your citizens get things done? Their right of petition?"

"If they pay their percentages, the Boss takes care of them. We go in here."

"In here" was a building bearing a brightly polished brass plaque. It read:

BELA OKMYX
BOSS
NORTHSIDE TERRITORY

The end of the line was an office, large and luxurious, complete with heavy desk, a secretary of sorts and framed pictures—except that one of the frames, Kirk saw, surrounded some kind of pistol instead. A heavy-set, swarthy man sat behind the desk.

"Got 'em, Boss," Kalo said. "No sweat."

The big man smiled and rose. "Well, Captain Kirk. Come in. Sit down. Have a drink. Good stuff—distill it myself."

"No, thank you. You are Mr. Okmyx? This is Mr. Spock, my First Officer. And Dr. McCoy."

"A real pleasure. Sit down. Put down the heater, Kalo. These guys is guests." He turned back to Kirk. "You gotta excuse my boys. You just gotta be careful these days."

"Judging from what we've seen so far, I agree." Kirk said. "They call you the Boss. Boss of what?"

"My territory. Biggest in the world. Trouble with being the biggest is that punks is alla time trying to cut in."

"There is something astonishingly familiar about all this, Captain," Spock said.

"How many other territories are there?"

"Maybe a dozen, not counting the small fry—and they get bumped anyway when I get around to it."

"Do they include, if I may ask," Spock said, "a gentleman named Krako?"

"You know about Krako?"

"He hit us, Boss," Kalo said. "Burned Mirt."

Bela scowled. "I want him hit back."

"I'll take care of it."

Kirk had noticed a huge book on a stand nearby. He rose and moved toward it. Kalo raised his gun muzzle again, but at a quick signal from Bela, dropped it. The book was bound like a Bible, in white leather, with gold lettering reading: *Chicago Mobs of the Twenties*. The imprint was New York, 1993.

"How'd you get this, Mr. Okmyx?" he asked.

"That's The Book. *The* Book. They left it—the men from the *Horizon*."

"And there is your contamination, Captain," Spock said. "An entire gangster culture. An imitative people, one book, and . . ."

"No cracks about The Book," Bela said harshly. "Look, I didn't bring you here for you to ask questions. You gotta do something for me. Then I tell you anything you want to know."

"Anything we can do," Kirk said, putting the book down, "we will. We have laws of our own we must observe."

"Okay," Bela said. He leaned forward earnestly. "Look, I'm a peaceful man, see? I'm sick and tired of all the hits. Krako hits me, I hit Krako, Tepo hits me, Krako hits Tepo. We ain't getting noplace. There's too many bosses, know what I mean? Now if there was just one, maybe we could get some things done. That's where you come in."

"I don't quite understand," Kirk said.

"You Feds made a lot of improvements since the other ship came here. You probably got all kinds of fancy heaters. So here's the deal. You gimme all the heaters I need— enough tools so I can hit all the punks once and for all—and I take over the whole place. Then all you have to deal with is me."

"Let me get this straight," Kirk said. "You want us to supply you with arms and assistance so you can carry out aggression against other nations?"

"What nations? I got some hits to make. You help me make them."

"Fascinating," Spock said. "But quite impossible."

"I'd call it outrageous," McCoy said.

"Even if we wanted to," Kirk said, "our orders are very . . ."

Bela gestured to Kalo, who raised his gun again. Though Kirk did not see any signal given, the door opened and another armed man came in.

"I ain't interested in *your* orders," Bela said. "You got eight hours to gimme what I asked for. If I don't get the tools by then, I'm gonna have your ship pick you up again—in a large number of very small boxes. Know what I mean, pal?"

Kalo belatedly began to unload the captured devices onto the Boss's desk. He pointed to a phaser. "This here's a heater, Boss. I don't know what the other junk is."

"A heater, eh? Let's see how it works." He pointed it at a wall. Kirk jerked forward. "Don't do that! You'll take out half the wall!"

"That good, eh? Great. Just gimme maybe a hundred of these and we don't have no more trouble."

"Out of the question," Kirk said.

"I get what I want." Bela picked up a communicator. "What are these here?"

Kirk remained silent. Jerking a thumb toward McCoy, Bela said to Kalo, "Burn him."

"All right," Kirk said hastily. "It's a communications device, locked onto my ship."

Bela fiddled with one until it snapped open in his hand. "Hey," he said to it. "In the ship."

"Scott here. Who is this?"

"This here's Bela Okmyx. I got your Captain and his friends down here. You want 'em back alive, send me a hundred of them fancy heaters of yours, and some troops to show us how to use them. You got eight hours. Then I put the hit on your friends. Know what I mean?"

"No," Scott's voice said. "But I'll find out."

Bela closed the communicator. "Okay. Kalo, take 'em over to the warehouse. Put 'em in the bag, and keep an eye on 'em, good. You hear?"

"Sure, Boss. Move out, you guys."

The warehouse room had a barred window and was sparsely furnished, but it was equipped with another copy of The Book. Kalo and two henchmen were playing cards at a table, guns handy, their eyes occasionally flicking to Kirk, Spock and McCoy at the other end of the room.

"One book," McCoy said. "And they made it the blueprint for their entire society. Amazing."

"But not unprecedented," Spock said. "At one time, in old Chicago, conventional government nearly broke down. The gangs almost took over."

"This Okmyx must be the worst of the lot."

"Though we may quarrel with his methods, his goal is essentially the correct one," Spock said. "This culture must become united—or it will degenerate into complete anarchy. It is already on the way; you will recall the young women who complained of failing services."

"If this society broke down, because of the influence of the *Horizon*, the Federation is responsible," Kirk said. "We've got to try to straighten the mess out. Spock, if you could get to the sociological banks of the computer, could you come up with a solution?"

"Quite possibly, Captain."

Signaling Spock and McCoy to follow him unobtrusively, Kirk gradually drifted toward the card game. The players looked up at him warily, free hands on guns; but they relaxed again as he pulled over a chair and sat down. The game was a variety of stud poker.

After a few moments, Kirk said, "That's a kid's game."

"Think so?" Kalo said.

"I wouldn't waste my time."

"Who's asking you to?"

"On Beta Antares Four, they play a game for men. Of course, it's probably too involved for you. It takes intelligence."

Antares is not a double star; Kirk had taken the chance in order to warn the sometimes rather liberal-minded that he was lying deliberately.

"Okay, I'll bite," Kalo said. "Take the cards, big man. Show us how it's played."

"The Antares cards are different, of course, but not too different," Kirk said, riffling through them. "The game's called Fizzbin. Each player gets six cards—except for the man on the dealer's right, who gets seven. The second card goes up—except on Tuesdays, of course . . . Ah, Kalo, that's good, you've got a nine. That's half a fizzbin already."

"I need another nine?"

Spock and McCoy drew nearer with quite natural curiosity, since neither of them had ever heard of the game. Neither had Kirk.

"Oh, no. That would be a sralk and you'd be disqualified. You need a King or a deuce, except at night, when a Queen or a four would . . . Two sixes! That's excellent—unless, of course, you get another six. Then you'd have to turn it in, unless it was black."

"But if it was black?" Kalo said, hopelessly confused.

"Obviously, the opposite would hold," Kirk said, deciding to throw in a touch of something systematic for further confusion. "Instead of turning your six in, you'd get another card. Now, what you are really hoping for is a royal fizzbin, but the odds against that are, well, astronomical, wouldn't you say, Spock?"

"I have never computed them, Captain."

"Take my word they're considerable. Now the last card around. We call it the cronk, but its home name is *klee-et*.* Ready? Here goes."

He dealt, making sure that Kalo's card went off the table. "Oops, sorry."

---

* A Vulcan word meaning, roughly, "prepare to engage." See "Amok Time."

"I'll get it."

Kalo bent over. In the same instant, Kirk put his hands under the table and shoved. It went over on the other two. McCoy and Spock were ready; the action was hardly more than a flurry before the three guards were helpless. Kirk parceled out the guns.

"Spock, find the radio transmitting station. Uhura is monitoring their broadcasts. Cut in and have yourself and Bones beamed up to the ship."

"Surely you are coming, Captain?"

"Not without Bela Okmyx."

"Jim, you can't . . ."

"This mess is our responsibility, Bones. You have your orders. Let's go."

Kirk at first felt a little uneasy walking a city street with a submachine gun under his arm, but no one passing seemed to find it unusual. On the contrary, it seemed to be a status symbol; people cleared the way for him.

But the walk ended abruptly with two handguns stuck into his ribs from behind. He had walked into an ambush. How had Bela gotten word so fast?

The answer to that was soon forthcoming. The two hoods who had mousetrapped him crowded him into a car—and the ride was a long one. At its end was another office, almost a duplicate of Bela's; but the man behind the desk was short, squat, bull-shaped and strange. He arose with a jovial smile.

"So you're the Fed. Well, well. I'm Krako—Jojo Krako, Boss of the South Territory. Hey, I'm glad to see you."

"Would you mind telling me how you knew about me?"

"I got all Bela's communications bugged. He can't make a date with a broad without I know about it. Now you're probably wondering why I brought you here."

"Don't tell me. You want to make a deal."

Krako was pleased. "I like that. Sharp. Sharp, huh, boys?"

"Sharp, Boss."

"Let me guess some more," Kirk said. "You want—uh—heaters, right? And troops to teach you how to use them. And you'll hit the other bosses and take over the whole planet. And then we'll sit down and talk, right?"

"Wrong," Krako said. "More than talk. I know Bela. He didn't offer you beans. Me, I'm a reasonable man. Gimme what I want, and I cut you in for, say, a third. Skimmed right off the top. How do you like that?"

"I've got a better idea. You know this planet has to be united. So let's sit down, you, me, and Bela, get in contact with the other bosses, and discuss the matter like rational men."

Krako seemed to be genuinely outraged. "That ain't by The Book, Kirk. We know how to handle things! You make hits! Somebody argues, you lean on him! You think we're stupid or something?"

"No, Mr. Krako," Kirk said, sighing. "You're not stupid. But you are peculiarly unreasonable."

"Pally, I got ways of getting what I want. You want to live, Kirk? Sure you do. But after I get done with you, you're liable to be sorry—unless you come across. Zabo, tell Cirl the Knife to sharpen his blade. I might have a job for him." The smile came back. "Of course, you gimme the heaters and you keep your ears."

"No deal."

"Too bad. Put him on ice."

The two hoods led Kirk out.

On shipboard, Spock's fortunes were not running much better. There turned out to be no specifics in the computer, not even a record of a planet-wide culture based on a moral inversion. Without more facts, reason and logic were alike helpless.

"Mr. Spock," Uhura said. "Mr. Okmyx from the surface is making contact. Audio only."

Spock moved quickly to the board. "Mr. Okmyx, this is Spock."

"How'd you get up there?" Bela's voice asked.

"Irrelevant, since we are here."

"Uh—yeah. But you'd better get back down. Krako's put the bag on your Captain."

Spock raised his eyebrows. "Why would he put a bag on the Captain?"

"Kidnapped him, dope. He'll scrag him, too."

"If I understand you correctly, that would seem to be a problem. Have you any suggestions?"

"Sure. You guys got something I want. I can help you get the Captain back. No reason we can't make a deal."

"I am afraid I find it difficult to trust you, sir."

"What's to trust? Business is business. We call a truce. You come down. My boys spring Kirk. Then we talk about you giving me a hand."

"Since we must have our Captain back," Spock said after a moment, "I accept. We shall arrive in your office within ten minutes. Spock out."

McCoy had been standing nearby, listening. "You're going to trust him?"

"If we are to save the Captain, without blatant and forceful interference on the planet, then we must have assistance from someone indigenous. At the moment, we are forced to trust Mr. Okmyx." He turned toward Scott. "Mr. Scott, although I hope to avoid their use, I think you should adjust one of the phaser banks to a strong stun position."

"Now," McCoy said, "you're starting to make sense."

Spock did not reply, since nothing in the situation made sense to him. Trusting Okmyx was nothing short of stupid, and the use of force was forbidden by General Order Number One. In such a case, the only course was to abide by the Captain's principle of letting the situation ripen.

Bela, of course, had a trap arranged. Spock had expected it, but there had been no way to avoid it. What he had not expected—nor had Bela—was the abrupt subsequent appearance of Kirk in the doorway, with a submachine gun under his arm.

"How did you get away?" Spock asked interestedly, after the gangsters had been disarmed—a long process which produced a sizable heap of lethal gadgets, some of them wholly unfamiliar.

"Krako made the mistake of leaving me a radio; that was all I needed for the old trip-wire trick. I thought I told you to get to the ship."

"We have been there, Captain. The situation required our return."

"It may be just as well. Find out anything from the computers?"

"Nothing useful, Captain. Logic and factual knowledge do not seem to apply here."

"You admit that?" McCoy said.

"With the greatest reluctance, Doctor."

"Then you won't mind if I play a hunch?" Kirk said.

"I am not sanguine about hunches, sir, but I have no practical alternative."

"What are you going to do, Jim?"

"Now that I've got Bela," Kirk said, "I'm going to put the bag on Krako."

"On Krako?" Bela said. "You ain't serious?"

"Why not?" Kirk turned to Bela and fingered his suit lapel. "That's nice material."

"It ought to be. It cost a bundle."

"Get out of it. You, too."

"Hey, now, wait a minute . . ."

"Take it off—pally! This time nobody's going to bag me."

Seeing that he meant it, Kalo and Bela got out of their clothes; Kirk and Spock donned them. Scooping up the required submachine guns as passports, they went out, leaving McCoy in charge.

In front of the office sat the large black car that Bela used. Fishing in the pockets of his borrowed suit, Kirk found the keys. They got in.

"Any idea how to run this thing, Spock?"

"No, Captain. But it should not be too difficult."

"Let's see," Kirk said, studying the controls. "A keyhole. For the—ignition process, I think. Insert and turn. Right."

He felt around with his foot and touched a button. The car stuttered and the engine was running.

"Interesting," Spock said.

"As long as it runs. Now, let's see. I think—gears . . ."

He pulled the lever down, which produced nothing but an alarming grinding sound which he could feel in his hand as well as hear.

"As I recall," Spock said, "there was a device called the clutch. Perhaps one of those foot pedals . . ."

The right-hand pedal didn't seem to work, but the left-hand one allowed the gear lever to go down. Kirk let the pedal up cautiously, and the car started with a lurch.

Kirk remembered the way to Krako's offices well enough, but the trip was a wild one; there seemed to be some trick to working the clutch which Kirk hadn't mastered. Luckily, pedestrians gave the big black vehicle a wide berth. Spock just hung on. When it was over, he observed, "Captain, you are a splendid starship commander, but as a taxi driver you leave much to be desired."

"Haven't had time to practice. Leave these clumsy guns under the seat; we'll use phasers."

They made their way to Krako, leaving a trail of stunned guards behind. The Boss did not seem a bit taken aback when they burst in on him; he had four hoods behind him, guns aimed at the door.

"You don't shoot, we don't shoot," he said rapidly.

"This would appear to be an impasse," Spock said.

"Who's your friend with the ears?" Krako asked. "Never mind. Ain't this nice? I was wondering how I was going to get you back, and you delivered yourself! You don't think you'll get out of it this time, do you?"

"We didn't come here for games," Kirk said. "This is bigger than you or Okmyx or any of the others."

The phaser which Krako had previously taken from Kirk was on the desk, still on safety lock. Krako nudged it. "Don't talk fancy. All you gotta do is tell me how to work these things."

"Krako," Kirk said, "can you trust all your men?"

"Yeah, sure. I either trust 'em or they're dead."

"Maybe. But when it comes to weapons like these—well, one of them could make a man a pretty big boss around here."

Krako thought about it. At last he said, "Zabo and Karf, stay put. You other guys vanish . . . All right, these two is okay. Now that we got no busy little eyes around, how do you work this thing?"

Kirk moved in on Krako hard and fast, spitting his words out like bullets. "Knock it off, Krako. We don't have time to show you how to play with toys."

"Toys?"

"What do you think we're here for, Krako? To get a cut of your deal? Forget it. That's peanuts to an outfit like the Federation."

"It is?" Krako said, a little dazed by the sudden switch.

"Unquestionably," Spock said.

"We came here to take over, Krako. The whole ball of wax. Maybe, if you cooperate, we'll cut *you* in for a piece of the action."

"A minute piece," Spock added.

"How much is that?" Krako asked.

"We'll figure it out later."

"But—I thought you guys had some kind of law about no interference . . ."

"Who's interfering? We're just taking over."

Spock seemed slightly alarmed. "Uh—Captain . . ."

"Cool it, Spocko. Later."

"What's your deal?" Krako asked.

Kirk motioned him to his feet and, when the bewildered gangster stood, Kirk sat down in his chair and swung his feet up onto the desk. He appropriated one of Krako's cigars.

"The Federation wants this planet, but we don't want to have to come in and use our muscle. That ain't subtle. So what we do is help one guy take over. He pulls the planet's strings—and we pull his. Follow?"

"But what's your cut?"

Kirk eyed the unlit cigar judiciously. "What do you care, so long as you're in charge? Right, Spocko?"

"Right on the button, Boss," Spock said, falling into his role a little belatedly but with a certain relish. "Of course, there's always Bela Okmyx . . ."

Krako thought only a moment. "You got a deal. Call your ship and bring down your boys and whatever you need."

Kirk got to his feet and snapped open his communicator. "Kirk to *Enterprise*."

"*Enterprise*. Scott here, sir."

"Scotty, we made the deal with Krako."

"Uh—we did, sir?"

"We're ready to make the hit. We're taking over the whole planet as soon as you can get ready."

"Is that wise, sir?"

"Sure, we can trust Krako—he doesn't have any choice. He's standing here right now, *about three feet to my left,* all ready to be our pal. I'd like to show him the ship, just so he's sure I'm giving him the straight dope. But you know how it is."

"Oh aye, sir," Scott said. "I know indeed."

"We'll be needing enough phasers to equip all of Krako's men, plus advisers—troops to back them up on the hit. You moving, Scotty?"

"Aye, Uhura's on to the Transporter Room and two of the boys are on their way. Ready when you say the word."

"Very well, Scotty, begin."

Krako looked curiously at Kirk. "You mean you're gonna start bringing all those guys down now?"

"No—not exactly." As he spoke, the hum of the Transporter effect filled the room, and Krako shimmered out of existence. Zabo and Karf stared, stunned—and a second later were stunned more thoroughly.

"Well played—Spocko."

Spock winced. "So we have—put the bag on Krako. What is our next maneuver, Captain?"

"Back to Bela's place."

"In the car, Captain?"

"It's faster than walking. Don't tell me you're afraid of cars, Spock."

"Not at all. It is your driving which alarms me."

Through the door of Bela's office, they heard McCoy saying worriedly, "Where *are* they?"

And then Bela's, "Knowing Krako, we'll be lucky if he sends 'em back on a blotter."

Kirk walked in. "Wrong again, Okmyx." He brushed past the relieved McCoy. "Outta my way, Sawbones. I want to talk to this guy. I'm getting tired of playing patty-cake with you penny ante operators."

"Who you calling penny ante?" Bela said, bristling.

"Nobody but you, baby. Now listen. The Federation's moving in here. We're taking over, and if you play ball, we'll leave a piece of the pie for you. If you don't, you're out. All the way out. Got that?" He shoved the phaser under Bela's nose to make the point.

"Yeah—yeah, sure, Kirk. Why didn't you say so in the first place? I mean—all you hadda do was explain."

The communicator came out. "Scotty, you got Krako on ice up there?"

"Aye, Captain."

"Keep him till I ask for him. We're going to be making some old-style phone calls from these coordinates. Lock on at the receiving end and transport the party here to us. Okay, Okmyx. Start calling the other bosses."

Shrugging, Bela went to the phone and dialed four times. "Hello, Tepo? Guess who? . . . Yeah, I got a lot of nerve. What're you going to do about it?"

With a hum, Tepo materialized, holding a non-existent phone in his hand. McCoy moved in to disarm him.

". . . coming over there with a couple of my boys, and . . . Brother!"

Bela grinned at Kirk. "Hey, this ain't bad."

"Keep dialing."

Half an hour later, the office was crowded with dazed gang leaders, Krako among them. Kirk climbed up on the desk, now cradling a local gun to add weight to his argument.

"All right, pipe down, everybody. I'll tell you what you're going to do. The Federation just took over around here, whether you like it or not. You guys have been running this planet like a piecework factory. From here on, it's all under one roof. You're going to form a syndicate and run this planet like a business. That means you make a profit."

"Yeah?" Tepo called. "And what's your percentage?"

"I'm cutting the Federation in for forty per cent." He leveled the gun. "You got objections?"

Tepo had obviously had guns pointed at him too many times to be cowed. "Yeah. I hear a lot of talk, but all I see here is you and a couple of your boys. I don't see no Federation."

"Listen, they got a ship," Krako said. "I know—I been there."

"Yeah, but Tepo's got a point," Bela said. "All we ever see is them."

"I only saw three other guys and a broad while I was in the ship," Krako said. "Maybe there ain't any more?"

"There are four hundred . . ."

Kirk was interrupted by an explosion outside, followed by a fusillade of shots. Krako, who was nearest the window, peered around the edge of it.

"It's my boys," he reported. "Must think I'm still in the ship. They're making a hit on this place."

"My boys'll put 'em down," Bela said.

"Wanna bet?"

Kirk's communicator was already out. "Scotty, put ship's phasers on stun and fire a burst in a one-block radius around these coordinates, excluding this building."

"Right away, sir."

Kirk looked at the confused gangsters. "Gentlemen, you are about to see the Federation at work."

The noise roared on a moment more, and then the window was lit up with the phaser effect. Dead silence fell promptly.

Krako smiled weakly and swallowed. "Some trick."

"They're not dead, just knocked out for a while," Kirk said. "We could just as easily have killed them."

"Okay," Bela said. "We get the message. You were saying something about a syndicate."

"No, he was saying something about a percentage," Tepo said. "You sure forty percent is enough?"

"I think it will be just fine. We'll send someone around to collect it every year—and give you advice if you need it."

"That's reasonable," Bela said. He glared at the others. "Ain't that reasonable?"

There was a murmur of assent. Kirk smiled cheerfully. "Well, in that case, pull out some of that drinking stuff of yours, Okmyx, and let's get down to the talking."

* * *

The bridge of the *Enterprise* was routinely busy. Kirk was in the command chair, feeling considerably better to be back in uniform.

"I must say," Spock said, "your solution to the problem on Iotia is unconventional, Captain. But it does seem to be the only workable one."

"What troubles you is that it isn't logical to leave a criminal organization in charge. Is that it?"

"I do have some reservations. And how do you propose to explain to Starfleet Command that a starship will be sent around each year to collect 'our cut,' as you put it?"

"'Our cut' will be put back into the planet's treasury—and the advisers and collectors can help steer the Iotians back into a more conventional moral and ethical system. In the meantime, the syndicate forms a central government that can effectively administer to the needs of the people. That's a step in the right direction. Our group of 'governors' is already learning to take on conventional responsibilities. Guiding them is—our piece of the action."

Spock pondered. "Yes, it seems to make sense. Tell me, Captain. Whatever gave you so outlandish an idea—and where did you pick up all that jargon so quickly?"

Kirk grinned. "Courtesy of Krako. A radio wasn't all he left in my cell. He also left me some reading matter."

"Ah, of course. The Book."

"Spocko, now you're talkin'."

THE IMMUNITY SYNDROME

Writer: Robert Sabaroff
Director: Joseph Pevney
First Aired: January 19, 1968

White beaches ... suntanned women ... mountains, their trout streams just asking for it ... the lift of a surfboard to a breaking wave ... familiar tree-shapes—that was shore leave on Starbase Six. And the exhausted crew of the *Enterprise* was on its way to it, unbelievably nearing it at long last. Kirk, remembering the taste of an open-air breakfast of rainbow trout, turned to give Sulu his final approach orders.

"Message from the base, sir," Uhura called. "Heavy interference. All I could get was the word *'Intrepid'* and what sounded like a sector coordinate."

"Try them on another channel, Lieutenant."

McCoy said, "The *Intrepid* is manned by Vulcans only, isn't it, Jim?"

"I believe so." Kirk swung his chair around. "The crew of the *Intrepid* is Vulcan, isn't it, Mr. Spock? I seem to remember the Starship was made entirely Vulcan as a tribute to the skill of your people in arranging that truce with the Romulan Federation. It was an unusual honor."

Spock didn't answer. He didn't turn. But he'd straightened in his chair. Something in the movement disturbed Kirk. He got up and went over to the library-computer station. "Mr. Spock!" Still Spock sat, unmoving, silent. Kirk shook his shoulder. "Spock, what's wrong? Are you in pain?"

"The *Intrepid* is dead. I just felt it die."

Kirk looked at McCoy. McCoy shook his head, shrugging.

"Mr. Spock, you're tired," Kirk said. "Let Chekov take over your station."

"And the four hundred Vulcans aboard her are dead," Spock said.

McCoy said, "Come down to Sickbay, Spock."

Stone-faced, Spock said, "I am quite all right, Doctor. I know what I feel."

Kirk said, "Report to Sickbay, Mr. Spock. That's an order."

"Yes, Captain."

Kirk watched them move to the elevator. They'd all had it. Too many missions. Even Spock's superb stamina had its breaking point. Too many rough missions—and Vulcan logic itself could turn morbidly visionary. It was high time for shore leave.

"Captain, I have Starbase Six now," Uhura said.

Back in his chair, Kirk flipped a switch. "Kirk here. Go ahead."

The bridge speaker spoke. "The last reported position of the Starship *Intrepid* was sector three nine J. You will divert immediately."

Kirk rubbed a hand over his chin before he reached for his own speaker. "The *Enterprise* has just completed the last of several very strenuous missions. The crew is tired. We're on our way for R and R. There must be another Starship in that sector."

"Negative. This is a rescue priority order. We have lost all contact with solar system Gamma Seven A. The *Intrepid* was investigating. Contact has now been lost with the *Intrepid*. Report progress."

"Order acknowledged," Kirk said. "Kirk out."

Sulu was staring at him in questioning dismay. Kirk snapped, "You heard the order, Mr. Sulu. Lay in a course for Gamma Seven A."

Chekov spoke from his console. Awe subdued his voice.

"Solar System Gamma Seven A is dead, Captain. My long-range scan of it shows—"

"Dead? What are you saying, Mr. Chekov? That is a fourth-magnitude star! Its system supports billions of inhabitants! Check your readings!"

"I have, sir. Gamma Seven A is dead."

In Sickbay Spock was saying, "I assure you, Doctor, I am quite all right. The pain was momentary."

McCoy sighed as he took his last diagnostic reading. "My instruments appear to agree with you if I can trust them with a crazy Vulcan anatomy. By the way, how can you be so sure the *Intrepid* is destroyed?"

"I felt it die," his patient said tonelessly.

"But I thought you had to be in physical contact with a subject to sense—"

"Dr. McCoy, even I, a half Vulcan, can sense the death screams of four hundred Vulcan minds crying out over distance between us."

McCoy shook his head. "It's beyond me."

Spock was shouldering back into his shirt. "I have noticed this insensitivity among wholly human beings. It is easier for you to feel the death of one fellow-creature than to feel the deaths of millions."

"Suffer the deaths of thy neighbors, eh, Spock? Is that what you want to wish on us?"

"It might have rendered your history a bit less bloody."

The intercom beeped. "Kirk here. Bones, is Spock all right? If he is, I need him on the bridge."

"Coming, Captain." Kirk met him at the elevator. "You may have been right. Contact with the *Intrepid* has been lost. It has also been lost with an entire solar system. Our scans show that Gamma Seven A is a dead star system."

"That is considerable news." Spock hurried over to his station and Kirk spoke to Uhura. "Any update from Starfleet?"

"I can't filter out the distortions. They're getting worse, sir."

A red light flashed on Sulu's panel. "Captain, the deflector shields just snapped on!"

"Slow down to warp three!" Kirk walked back to Spock. The Vulcan straightened from his stoop over his computer. "Indications of energy turbulence ahead, sir. Unable to analyze. I have never encountered such readings before."

The drama latent in the statement was so uncharacteristic of Spock that Kirk whirled to the main viewing screen. "Magnification factor three on screen!" he ordered.

Star-filled space—the usual vista. "Scan sector," he said. The starfield merely revealed itself from another angle and Sulu said, "Just what are we looking for, Captain?"

"I would assume," Spock said, "*that.*"

A black shadow, roughly circular, had appeared on the screen.

"An interstellar dust cloud," Chekov suggested.

Kirk shook his head. "The stars have disappeared. They could be seen through a dust cloud, Mr. Chekov. How do you read it, Mr. Spock?"

"Analysis still eludes me, Captain. Sensors are feeding data to computers now. But whatever that dark zone is, my calculations place it directly on the course that would have brought it into contact with the *Intrepid* and the Gamma Seven A system."

"Are you saying it caused their deaths, Mr. Spock?"

"A possibility, Captain."

After a moment, Kirk nodded. "Hold present course but slow to warp factor one," he told Sulu. "Mr. Chekov, prepare to launch telemetry probe into that zone."

"Aye, sir." Chekov moved controls on his console. "Probe ready. Switching data feed to library-computer."

"Launch probe," Kirk said.

Chekov shoved a stud. "Probe launched."

An ear-shattering blast of static burst from the communications station. Its noise swelled into a crackling roar so fierce that it seemed to possess a physical substance—the substance and force of a giant's slap. It ended as abruptly as it had come. Uhura, dizzy, disoriented, was clinging to her chair.

"And what channel did *that* come in on?" Kirk said.

She had to make a visible effort to answer. "Telemetry . . . the channel from the probe, sir. There's no signal . . . at all now . . ."

"Mr. Spock, speculations?"

"I have none, Captain." Then Spock had leaped from his chair. Uhura, her arms dropped, limp, was slumped over her console. "Lieutenant!" He reached an arm around her, steadying her. "Dizzy," she whispered. "I'll . . . be all right in a minute."

The intercom beeped to McCoy's voice. "Jim, half the women on this ship have fainted. Reports in from all decks."

Kirk glanced at Uhura. "Maybe you'd better check Lieutenant Uhura. She just pulled out of a faint."

"Unless she's out now, keep her up there. I've got an emergency here."

"What's wrong?"

"Nothing organic. Just weakness, nervousness."

"Can you handle it?"

"I can give them stimulants to keep them on their feet."

A tired crew—and now this. Kirk looked at the screen. It offered no cheer. The black shadow now owned almost all of the screen. Hold position here, Mr. Sulu." He got up from his chair—and was hit by an attack of vertigo. He fought it down. "Mr. Spock, I want an update on that shadow ahead of us."

"No analysis, sir. Insufficient information."

Kirk smacked the computer console. "Mr. Spock. I have asked you three times for data on that thing and you have been unable to supply it. 'Insufficient information' won't do. It is your responsibility to deliver sufficient information at all times."

"I am aware of that, sir. But there is nothing in the computer banks on this phenomenon. It is beyond all previous experience."

Kirk looked at the hand that had struck Spock's console. "Weakness, nervousness." He was guilty on both counts. Even Spock couldn't elicit data from the computer banks that hadn't been put into them. "Sorry, Mr. Spock. Something seems to be infecting the entire ship. Let's go for reverse logic. If you can't tell me what that zone of darkness is, tell me what it isn't."

"It is not gaseous, liquid nor solid, despite the fact we can't see through it. It is not a galactic nebula like the Coal Sack. As it has activated our deflector shields, it seems to consist of some energy form—but none that the sensors can identify."

"And you said it is possible it killed the *Intrepid* and that solar system?"

"Yes, Captain."

Kirk turned to Uhura. "Lieutenant, inform Starfleet of our position and situation. Relay all relative information from computer banks." He paused. "Tell them we intend to probe further into the zone of darkness to gain further information."

"Yes, sir."

As he started back to his chair, he swayed under another wash of dizziness. Spock moved to him quickly and he clung for a moment to the muscular arm. "Thank you, Mr. Spock," he said. "I can make it now." He reached his chair. "Distance to the zone of darkness, Mr. Sulu?"

"One hundred thousand kilometers."

"Slow ahead, Mr. Sulu. Impulse power."

His head was still whirling. "Distance now, Mr. Sulu?"

"We penetrate the zone in one minute seven seconds, sir."

"Mr. Chekov, red alert. Stand by, phasers. Full power to deflector shields."

"Phasers standing by—deflectors at full power, sir."

Sound was emitted. It came slowly at first—and not from the communications station. It came from everywhere; and as it built, its mounting tides of invisible shock waves reached everywhere. Their reverberations struck through the metal walls of the engineering section, rushing Scott to check his equipment. Horrified by his readings, he ran to his power levers to test them. Then, mercifully, the all-pervading racket subsided. Up on the bridge, his hands still pressed to his ears, Sulu cried, "Captain—the screen!"

Blackness, total, had claimed it.

"Malfunction, Mr. Spock?"

"No, Captain. All systems working."

Kirk shook his head, trying to clear it. Around him people were still clutching at console rails for support. Kirk struck the intercom button. "Bones, things any better in Sickbay?"

"Worse. They're backed up into the corridor."

"Got anything that will help up here? I don't want anyone on the bridge folding at a critical moment."

"On my way. McCoy out."

Kirk pushed the intercom button again. "Kirk to Engineering. The power's dropped, Mr. Scott! What's happened?"

"We've lost five points of our energy reserve. The deflector shields have been weakened."

"Can you compensate, Scotty?"

"Yes, if we don't lose any more. Don't ask me how it happened."

Kirk spoke sharply. "I *am* asking you, mister. I need answers!"

McCoy's answer was an air-hypo. He hurried into the bridge with a nurse. As Kirk accepted the hissing injection, McCoy said, "It's a stimulant, Jim." As he adjusted the hypo for Sulu's shot, Kirk said, "Just how bad is it, Bones?"

"Two thirds of personnel are affected."

"This is a sick ship, Bones. We're picking up problems faster than we can solve them. It's as though we were in the middle of some creeping paralysis."

"Maybe we are," McCoy said. He left the command chair to continue his round with the hypo. Kirk got up to go to the computer station. "Mr. Spock, any analysis of that last noise outburst—the one that started to lose us power?"

Spock nodded. "The sound was the turbulence caused by our penetration of a boundary layer."

"What sort of boundary layer?"

"I don't know, Captain."

"Boundary between what and what?"

"Between where we were and where we are." At Kirk's stare, he went on. "I still have no specifics, sir. But we seem to have entered an area of energy that is not compatible with life or mechanical processes. As we move on, the source of it will grow stronger—and we will grow weaker."

"Recommendations?"

McCoy spoke. "*I* recommend survival, Jim. Let's get out of here." He turned and walked to the elevator, the nurse behind him.

Kirk faced around to the questioning faces. And Starbase had demanded a "progress" report. Progress to what? The fate of the *Intrepid*—the billions of lives that had once breathed on Gamma Seven A? Bureaucracy . . . evasion by comfortable chairs.

He walked slowly back to his uncomfortable chair. The intercom button—yes. "This is the Captain speaking," he said. "We have entered an area that is unfamiliar to us. All hands were tired to begin with and we've all sustained something of a shock. But we've had stimulants. Our deflectors are holding. We've got a good ship. And we know what our mission is. Let's get on with the job. Kirk out."

His own intercom button beeped. "Sickbay to Captain."

"Kirk. Go ahead, Bones."

Before he went ahead, McCoy glanced at the semiconscious Yeoman lying on his diagnostic couch. "Jim, one after another . . . life energy levels . . . my indicators . . ."

Kirk spoke quietly. "Say it, Bones."

"We are dying," McCoy said. "My life monitors show that we are all, each one of us, dying."

The sweat of his own weakness broke from Kirk's pores. He could feel it run cold down his chest.

But the ordeal of the *Enterprise* had just begun. Kirk, down in Engineering, was flung against a mounded dynamo at a sudden lurch of the ship. "And that? What was that, Mr. Scott?"

"An accident, sir. We went into reverse."

"Reverse? That was a *forward* lurch! How could that occur in reverse thrust?"

"I don't know, sir. All I know is that our power levels are draining steadily. They're down to twelve percent. I've never experienced anything like it before."

Spock came in on the intercom. "Captain, we are accelerating. The zone of darkness is pulling us toward it."

"Pulling us? How, Mr. Spock?"

"I don't know. However, I suggest that Mr. Scott give us reverse power."

"Mr. Spock, he just *gave* us reverse power!"

"Then I reverse my suggestion, sir. Ask him to apply a forward thrust."

"Mr. Scott, you heard that. Let's try the forward thrust."

The Engineering Chief shook his head. "I don't know, sir. It contradicts all the rules of logic."

"Logic is Mr. Spock's specialty."

"Yes, sir, but—"

"Nudge it slowly into forward thrust, Mr. Scott."

Scott carefully advanced three controls. Eyeing his instruments anxiously, he relaxed. "That did it, Captain. We're slowing now. But the forward movement hasn't stopped. We're still being pulled ahead."

"Keep applying the forward thrust against the pull. Have one of your men monitor these instruments."

Instruments in Sickbay were being monitored, too. Nurse Chapel, watching her life function indicators, called, "Doctor, they're showing another sharp fall." McCoy, whirling to look, muttered, "Stimulants. How long can we keep them up?" He was checking the panel when Kirk's voice came from the intercom. "This is the Captain speaking. All department heads will report to the Briefing Room in ten minutes. They will come with whatever information gathered on this zone of darkness we are in."

McCoy took his gloom with him to the Briefing Room. Slamming some tape cartridges down on the table, he said, "My sole contribution is the fact that the further we move into this zone of darkness, the weaker our life functions get. I have no idea why." Reaching for a chair, he staggered slightly.

"Bones..."

He waved the solicitude aside. "I'm all right. All those stimulants—they catch up with you."

Scott spoke. "As far as the power levels are concerned, everything's acting backwards. But the drain is continuing. And we're still being dragged forward."

"Mr. Spock?" Kirk said.

"I am assuming that something within the zone absorbs both biological and mechanical energy. It would appear to be the same thing that sucked energy from an entire solar system—and the Starship *Intrepid*."

"Some *thing*, Mr. Spock? Not the zone itself?"

"I would say not, Captain. Analysis of the zone suggests it is a negative energy field, however illogical that may sound. *But it is not the source of the power drains*."

"A shield, then," Kirk said. "An outer layer of protection for something else."

"But what?" Scott said.

"It's pulling the life out of us, whatever it is," McCoy grunted.

"We'll find out what it is," Kirk said. "But first we have to get out of here ourselves." He leaned across the table. "Mr. Scott, forward thrust slowed down our advance before. If you channel all warp and impulse power into one massive forward thrust, it might snap us out of the zone."

Scott's face lightened. "Aye, Captain. I'll reserve enough for the shields in case we don't get out."

Spock's voice was as expressionless as his face. "I submit, Mr. Scott, that if we do not get out, the shields would merely prolong our wait for death."

Kirk regarded him somberly. "Yes. You will apply all power as needed to get us out of here, Mr. Scott. Report to your stations, everybody, and continue your research. Dismissed."

As they left, he remained seated, head bowed on his hand. At the door Spock stopped, and came back to stand, waiting, at the table. Kirk looked up at him. "The *Intrepid*'s crew would have done all these things, Captain," Spock said. "They were destroyed."

Kirk drummed his fingers on the table. "They may not have done all these things. You've just told us what an illogical situation this is."

"True, sir. It is also true that they never discovered what killed them."

"How can you know that?"

"Vulcan has not been conquered within its collective memory. It is a memory that goes so far back no Vulcan can any longer conceive of a conqueror. I know the ship was defeated because I sensed its death."

"What was it exactly you felt, Mr. Spock?"

"Astonishment. Profound astonishment."

"My Vulcan friend," Kirk said. He got up. "Let's get back to the bridge."

Engineering was calling him as they came out of the elevator. Hurrying to his chair, Kirk pushed the intercom stud. "Kirk here, Scotty."

"We've completed arrangements, sir. I'm ready to try it when you are."

"We've got the power to pull it off?"

The voice was glum. "I hope so, Captain."

"Stand by, Scotty." He pushed another button. "All hands, this is the Captain speaking. An unknown force is pulling us deeper into the zone of darkness. We will apply all available power in one giant forward thrust in the hope it will yank us out of the zone. Prepare yourselves for a big jolt." He buzzed Engineering. "Ready, Mr. Scott. Let's get on with it. *Now!*"

They were prepared for the jolt. And it was big. But what they weren't prepared for was the violently accelerating lunge that followed the jolt. Scott and a crewman crashed against a rear wall. McCoy and Christine Chapel were sent reeling back through two sections of Sickbay. In the bridge an African plant nurtured by Uhura flew through the air to smash against the elevator door. People were hurled bodily over the backs of their chairs. There was another fierce lurch of acceleration. The ship tossed like a rearing horse. Metal screamed. Lights faded. Finally, the *Enterprise* steadied.

From the floor where he'd been tumbled, Kirk looked at the screen.

Failure. The starless black still possessed it.

Weary, bruised, Kirk hauled himself back into his chair. The question had to be asked. He asked it. "Mr. Scott, are we still losing power?"

"Aye, sir. All we did was to pull away a bit. The best we can do now is maintain thrust against the pull to hold our distance."

"How long do we have?"

"At this rate of drain plus the draw on all systems—two hours, Captain."

As Kirk got to his feet, another wave of weakness swept over him. It passed—and he moved over to the computer station. "We're trying to hold our distance, Mr. Spock. Have you yet ascertained what we are holding the distance *from*?"

Spock, his eyes on his own screen, said, "I have not found out what that thing is, Captain. But it seems to have found us."

Kirk wheeled to the bridge viewer. In the center of its blackness a bright object had become visible—bright, pulsating, elongated.

Staring at it, Kirk said, "Mr. Chekov, prepare to launch a probe."

Bent to his hooded computer, Spock said, "Very confused readings, Captain—but that object is definitely the source of the energy drains."

"Mr. Chekov, launch probe," Kirk said.

"Probe launched, sir. Impact in seven point three seconds."

Without order Sulu began the countdown. "Six, five . . . four . . . three . . . two . . . one . . . *now*!"

The ship trembled. Lights blinked. But that was all.

"Mr. Chekov, do we still have contact with the probe?"

"Yes, sir. Data being relayed to Mr. Spock."

"Mr. Spock?"

The Vulcan's head was hidden under the computer's mound. "Readings coming in now, Captain. Length, approximately eleven thousand miles. Varying in width from two thousand to three thousand miles. Outer layer strewn with space debris and other wastes. Interior consists of protoplasm varying from a firmer gelatinous layer to a semi-fluid central mass."

He withdrew his head from the computer. "Condition . . . living."

The faces around Kirk were stunned. He looked away from them and back at Spock. "Living," he said. Then, his voice very quiet, he said, "Magnification four, Mr. Sulu. On the main screen."

He had expected a horror—and he received it. The screen held what might be a nightmare of some child who had played with a lab microscope—a monstrous, amoebalike protozoan. The gigantic nucleus throbbed, its chromosome bodies vaguely shadowed under its gelatinous, spotted skin. In open loathing, Kirk shut his eyes. But he could not dispel his searing memory of what continued to show on the screen.

* * *

In Sickbay's lab, McCoy was parading a pictured series of one-celled creatures. On the small viewscreen a paramecium, its cilia wriggling, came and went. Then McCoy said, "This is an amoeba."

If life was movement, ingestion, the thing was alive, a microscopic inhabitant of stagnant pools. As Kirk watched, a pseudopod extended itself, groping but intent on a fragment of food. There was a blind greed in the creature that sickened Kirk.

"I've seen them before," he said. "Like that, enlarged by microscope. But this thing out there is eleven thousand miles long! Are you saying that anything so huge is a single-celled animal?"

"For lack of a better term, Jim. Huge as it is, it is a very simple form of life. And it can perform all the functions necessary to qualify it as a living organism. It can reproduce, receive sense impressions, act on them, and eat, though what its diet is I wouldn't know."

"Energy," Spock said. "Energy drained from us. I would speculate that this unknown life form is invading the galaxy like an infection."

"Mr. Spock, the *Intrepid* died of this particular infection. Why have we survived so long?"

"The *Intrepid* must have come upon it when it was hungry, low in energy. We are not safe, Captain. We merely have a little more time than the *Intrepid* had."

"Bones, this zone of darkness. Does the thing generate it itself as some form of protection?"

"That's one of the things we have to find out, Jim. We need a closer look at it."

"The closer to it we get, the faster it eats our energy. We're barely staying alive at this distance from it."

McCoy shut off his screen. "We could risk the shuttlecraft. With special shielding, it might—"

"I'm not sending anybody anywhere near that thing! Unmanned probes will give us the information we need to destroy it."

"I must differ with you, Captain," Spock said. "We have sent probes into it. They have told us some facts but not those we need to know. We're in no position to expend the power to take blind shots at it. We need a target."

McCoy said, "One man could go in . . . pinpoint its vulnerable spots."

"And the odds against his coming back?" Kirk cried. "How can I order anyone to take such a chance?"

"Who mentioned orders?" McCoy demanded. "You've got yourself a volunteer, Jim, my boy. I've already done the preliminary work."

"Bones, it's a suicide mission!"

"Doctor, this thing has reflexes. The unmanned probe stung it when it entered. The lurch we felt was the turbulence of its reaction."

"All right, Spock," McCoy said. "Then I'll have the sense to go slow when I penetrate it."

Spock studied him. "There is a latent martyr in you, Doctor. It is an affliction that disqualifies you to undertake the mission."

"Martyr?" McCoy yelled. "You think I intend to bypass the chance to get into the greatest living laboratory ever?"

"The *Intrepid* carried physicians and psychologists, Doctor. They died."

"Just because Vulcans failed doesn't mean a human will."

Kirk hit the table with his fist. "Will you both kindly shut up? I've told you! I'm not taking volunteers!"

"You don't think you're going, do you?" McCoy shouted.

"I am a command pilot!" Kirk said. "And as such, I am the qualified person. So let's have an end of this!"

"You have just *disqualified* yourself, Captain," Spock said. "As the command pilot you are indispensable. Nor are you the scientific specialist which I am."

McCoy glared at Spock. "Jim, that organism contains chemical processes we've never seen before and may never, let's hope, see again. We could learn more in one day than—"

"We don't have a day," Kirk said. "We have precisely one hour and thirty-five minutes. Then all our power is exhausted."

"Jim . . ."

"Captain . . ."

Kirk whirled on them both. "*I* will decide who can best serve the success of this mission! When I have made my command decision—command decision, gentlemen—you will be notified."

He turned on his heel and left them.

The solitude of his quarters felt good. He closed the door behind him, unhooked his belt and with his back turned to the clock's face deliberately stretched himself out on his bunk. Relax. Let the quiet move up, inch by inch, from his feet to his throbbing head. *Let go*. If you could just let go, answers sometimes welled up from an untapped wisdom that resisted pushing. "God, let me relax," Kirk prayed.

It was true. He *was* indispensable. There was no room in command authority for the heroics of phony modesty. As to Bones, he *did* have the medical-biological advantages he'd claimed. But Spock, the born athlete, the physical-fitness fanatic, the Vulcan logician and Science Officer, was both physically and emotionally better suited to withstand the stresses of such a mission. Yet who could know what invaluable discoveries Bones might make if he got his chance to make them? So it was up to him—Kirk. The choice was his. One of his friends had to be condemned to probable death. Which one?

He drew a long shuddering breath. Then he reached out to the intercom over his head and shoved its button. "This is the Captain speaking. Dr. McCoy and Mr. Spock report to my quarters at once. Kirk out."

The beep came as he sat up. "Engineering to Captain Kirk."

"Go ahead, Scotty."

"You wanted to be kept informed of the power drain, sir. All levels have sunk to fifty percent. Still draining. We can maintain power for another hour and fifteen minutes."

"Right, Scotty." He drew a hand over the bunk's coverlet, stared at the hand, and said, "Prepare the shuttlecraft for launching."

"What's that, sir?"

"You heard me, Scotty, Dr. McCoy will tell you what special equipment to install. Kirk out."

Of course. The knock on his door. He got up and opened it. They were both standing there, their mutual antagonism weaving back and forth between them. "Come in, gentlemen." There was no point, no time for suspense. "I'm sorry, Mr. Spock," Kirk said heavily.

McCoy flashed a look of triumph at Spock. "Well done, Jim," he said. "I'll get the last few things I need and—"

Kirk stopped him in midstride. "Not you, Bones." He turned to Spock. "I'm sorry, Spock. I am sorry you are the best qualified to go."

Spock nodded briefly. He didn't speak as he passed the crushed McCoy.

The door to the hangar-deck elevator slid open. Spock moved aside to allow McCoy to precede him out of it. "Do not suffer so, Doctor. Professional credentials are very valuable. But superior resistance to strain has occasionally proved more valuable."

"Nothing has been proven yet!" McCoy controlled himself with an effort. "My DNA code analyzer will give you the fundamental structure of the organism. You'll need readings on three light wavelengths from the enzyme recorder."

"I am familiar with the equipment, Doctor. Time is passing. The shuttlecraft is ready."

"You just won't let me share in this at all, will you, Spock?"

"This is not a competition, Doctor. Kindly grant me my own kind of dignity."

"Vulcan dignity? How can I grant you what I don't understand?"

"Then employ one of your human superstitions. Wish me luck, Dr. McCoy."

McCoy gave him a startled look. Without rejoinder, he shoved the button that opened the hangar-deck door. Beyond them the metallic skin of the chosen shuttlecraft gleamed dimly. Two technicians busied themselves with it, making some final arrangements. Spock, without looking back, walked through the hangar door. McCoy saw him climb into the craft. Then the door slid closed; McCoy, alone, muttered, "Good luck, Spock, damn you."

Kirk, on the bridge, waited. Then Sulu turned. "All systems clear for shuttlecraft launch, sir."

It was time to say the words. "Launch shuttlecraft."

The light winked on Sulu's console. Spock was on his way. Alone. In space, alone. Committed—given over to what he, his Captain, had given him over to. Kirk heard the elevator whoosh open. McCoy came out of it. Kirk didn't turn. He said, "Lieutenant Uhura, channel telemetry directly to Mr. Chekov at the computer station."

The bridge speaker spoke. "Shuttlecraft to *Enterprise*."

"Report, Mr. Spock."

"The power drain is enormous and growing worse." Static crackled. "I am diverting all secondary power systems to the shields. I will continue communications as long as there is power to transmit."

Spock would be huddled now, Kirk knew, over the craft's control panel. He'd be busy shutting off power systems. Somehow Scott had suddenly materialized beside his command chair. "Captain! He won't have power enough to get back if he diverts it to his shields!"

"Spock," Kirk began.

"I heard, Captain. We recognized that probability earlier. But you will need information communicated."

"When do you estimate penetration?"

"In one point three minutes. Brace yourselves. The area of penetration will no doubt be sensitive."

What was Spock's screen showing? What was his closeup like? The details of the debris-mottled membrane, the enlarging granular structure of the protoplasm under it, two thousand miles thick?

"Contact in six seconds," Spock's voice said.

A tremor shook the *Enterprise*. That meant the massive shock of impact for the shuttlecraft. Its lights would dim, alone in the dimness inside the thing. Kirk seized the microphone.

"Report, Mr. Spock."

Silence reported. Had Spock already lost consciousness? The organism would try to dislodge the craft. It would convulse, its convulsions sending its painful intruder into a spinning vortex of repeated shocks.

"Spock . . ."

The voice came, weak now. "I am undamaged, Captain . . . relay to Mr. Scott . . . I had three percent power reserve . . . before the shields stabilized. I . . . will proceed with my tests" . . . The voice faded . . . then it returned. "Dr. McCoy . . . you would not . . . have survived this . . ."

Kirk saw that McCoy's eyes were moist. "You wanna bet, Spock?" His voice broke on the name.

"I am . . . moving very slowly now—establishing course toward . . . the nucleus."

Chekov, white-faced, called from the computer. "Sir, Mr. Spock has reduced his life support systems to bare minimum. I suppose to maintain communications."

Kirk's hand was wet on his microphone. "Spock, save your power for the shields."

Static sputtered from the microphone. Between its cracklings, words could be heard. "My . . . calculations indicate—shields . . . only forty-seven minutes." More obliterating static. It quieted. "Identified . . . Chromosome structure. Changes in it . . . reproduction process about to begin."

Ashen, McCoy cried, "Then there'll be *two* of these things!"

"Spock . . ."

Kirk got an earful of static. He waited. "I . . . am having . . . some difficulty . . . ship control."

Kirk looked away from the pain in McCoy's face. He waited again. As though it were warning of its waning usefulness, the mike spoke in jagged phrases. ". . . losing voice contact . . . transmitting . . . here are internal coordinates . . . chromosome bodies . . ."

Uhura turned from her console. "Contact lost, sir. But I got the coordinates."

"Captain!" It was Chekov. "The shuttlecraft shields are breaking! Fluctuations of energy inside the organism."

"Aye," Scott said. "It's time he got out of there."

There was nobody to look at but himself, Kirk thought. He was the man who had sent his best friend to death. He had sent Spock out to suffocate in the foul entrails of a primordial freak. That was a truth to somehow be lived with for the rest of his life. His chair lurched under him. The ship gave a shudder. Numbly, Kirk righted himself. Then, suddenly, in a blast of realization, he knew. "Bones!" The words tore from him in a shout. "He's alive! He's still alive! He made the craft kick the thing to force it to squirm—and let us know!"

Uhura spoke. "Captain, I'm getting telemetry."

"Mr. Chekov—telemetry analysis as it comes in."

McCoy was still brooding on what reproduction of the organism meant. "According to Spock's telemetry analysis, there are forty chromosomes in that nucleus ready to divide." He paused. "If the energy of this thing merely doubles, everybody and everything within a light year of it will be dead." He paced the length of the bridge and came back. "Soon there will be two of it, four, eight, and more—a promise of a combined anti-life force that could encompass the entire galaxy."

"That's what Spock knows, Bones. He knows. He knows we have no choice but to try and destroy it when he transmitted those coordinates of the chromosomes."

Scott said, "Look at your panel, Captain. The pull from the thing is increasing. The drain on our shields is getting critical."

The Immunity Syndrome

"How much time, Scotty?"

"Not more than an hour now, sir."

"Shield power is an unconditional priority. Put all secondary systems on standby."

"Aye, sir."

"Bones, can we kill that thing without killing Spock? And ourselves, too?"

"I don't know. It's a living cell. If we had an antibiotic that—"

"How many billions of kiloliters would it take?"

"Okay, Jim. Okay."

Uhura, her face radiant, turned from her console. "I'm receiving a message from Mr. Spock, sir. Low energy channel, faint but readable."

"Give it to me, Lieutenant."

"Faint" wasn't the word. Weak was. Very weak now. Spock said, "I . . . am losing life support . . . and minimal shield energy. The organism's nervous energy is . . . only maximal within protective membrane . . . interior . . . relatively insensitive . . . sufficient charge of . . . could destroy . . . tell Dr. McCoy . . . he should have wished . . . me luck . . ."

The bridge people sensed the burden of the message. Silence fell, speech faltering at the realization that Spock was lost. Only the lowered hum of power-drained machinery made itself heard.

Kirk lay unmoving on the couch in his quarters. Spock was dead. And to what point? If he'd been able to transmit his information on how to destroy the thing, he would have died for a purpose. But even that small joy had been denied to him. Spock was dead for no purpose at all, to no end that mattered to him.

Without knocking, McCoy came in and sat down on the couch beside the motionless Kirk.

"What's on your mind, Dr. McCoy?"

"Spock," McCoy said. "Call me sentimental. I've been called worse things. I believe he's still alive out there in that mess of protoplasm."

"He knew the odds when he went out. He knew so much. Now he's dead." Kirk lifted an arm into the air, contemplating the living hand at the end of it. "What *is* this thing? Not intelligent. At least, not yet."

"It is disease," McCoy said.

"This cell—this germ extending its filthy life for eleven thousand miles—one single cell of it. When it's grown to billions, we will be the germs. We shall be the disease invading its body."

"That's a morbid thought, Jim. Its whole horror lies in its size."

"Yes. And when our form of life was born, what micro-universe did we destroy? How does a body destroy an infection, Bones?"

"By forming anti-bodies."

"Then that's what we've got to be—an anti-body." He looked at McCoy. Then, repeating the word "anti-body," he jumped to his feet and struck the intercom button. "Scotty, suppose you diverted all remaining power to the shields? Suppose you gave it all to them—and just kept impulse power in reserve?"

"Cut off the engine thrust?" Scott cried. "Why, we'd be sucked into that thing as helplessly as if it were a wind tunnel!"

"Exactly, Mr. Scott. Prepare to divert power on my signal. Kirk out."

He turned to find himself facing McCoy's diagnostic Feinberger. "Got something to say, Bones?"

"Technically, no. Medically, yes. Between the strain and the stimulants, your edges are worn smooth. You're to keep off your feet for a while."

"I don't have a while. None of us do. Let's go . . ."

He took time to compose his face before he stepped out of the bridge elevator. He took his place in his command chair before he spoke into the intercom. "All hands, this is the Captain speaking. We are going to enter the body of this organism. Damage-control parties stand by—all decks secure for collision. Kirk out."

"It's now or never," he thought—and called Engineering.

"Ready, Mr. Scott?"

"Yes, sir."

"*Now*," Kirk said.

The ship took a violent forward plunge. Kirk, gripping his chair, glanced at the screen. The blackness grew denser as they sped toward it. "Impact—twenty-five seconds, sir," Sulu said intensely.

Then shock knocked Sulu from his chair. Something flared from the screen. Chekov, sprawled on the deck, looked up at his console as the ship steadied. "We're through, sir!" he shouted.

Uhura, recovering her position, called, "Damage parties report minimal hurt, Captain."

Kirk didn't acknowledge the information. The blackness on the screen had gone opaque. The *Enterprise*, lost in the vast interior of the organism, moved sluggishly through the lightlessness of gray jelly.

Engineering again. "Mr. Scott, we still have our impulse power?"

"I saved all I could, sir. I don't know if there's enough to get us out of this again. Or time enough to do it in."

"We have committed ourselves, Mr. Scott."

"Aye. But what are we committed to? We've got no power for the phasers."

McCoy made an impatient gesture. "We couldn't use them if we did. Their heat would rebound from this muck and roast us alive."

"The organism would love the phasers. It eats power—" Kirk broke off. A frantic Scott, rushing from the elevator, had caught his last word. "Power!" he cried. "That's the problem, Captain! If we can't use power to destroy this beast, what is it we *can* use?"

"Anti-power," Kirk said.

"What?" McCoy said.

Scott was staring at him. "This thing has a negative energy charge. Everything that has worked has worked in reverse. In its body, we're an anti-body, Scotty. So we'll use anti-power—anti-matter—to kill it."

Scott's tension relaxed like a pricked balloon. "Aye, sir! That it couldn't swallow! What good God gave you that idea, Captain?"

"Mr. Spock," Kirk said. "It's what he was trying to tell us before . . . we lost him. Mr. Chekov, prepare a probe. Scotty, we'll need a magnetic bottle for the charge. How soon?"

"It's on its way, laddie!"

"Mr. Chekov, timing detonator on the probe. We'll work out the setting. Mr. Sulu, what's our estimated arrival at the nucleus?"

"Seven minutes, sir."

"Jim, how close are you going to it?"

"Point-blank range. Implant it—and back away."

"But the probe has a range of—"

Kirk interrupted McCoy. "The eddies and currents in the protoplasm could drift the probe thousands of kilometers away from the nucleus. No, we must be directly on target. We won't get a second chance."

Kirk rubbed the stiffening muscles at the nape of his neck. "Time for another stimulant, Bones."

"You'll blow up. How long do you think you can go on taking that stuff?"

"Just hold me together for another seven minutes."

He took one of the minutes to address his Captain's log. "Should we fail in this mission, I wish to record here that the following personnel receive special citations: Lieutenant Commander Leonard McCoy, Lieutenant Commander Montgomery Scott,—and my highest recommendation to Commander Spock, Science Officer, who has given his life in performance of his duty."

As he punched off the recorder, Scott, hurrying back to the command chair, paused to listen to Sulu say, "Target coordinates programmed, sir. Probe ready to launch."

"Mr. Sulu, program the fuse for a slight delay." He swung to Chekov. "All nonessential systems on standby. Communications, prepare for scanning. Conserve every bit of power. We've got to make it out of this membrane before the explosion. Make it work, Scotty. Pray it works."

"Aye, sir."

"Mr. Chekov, launch probe at zero acceleration. Forward thrust, one tenth second."

"Probe launched," Chekov said.

The moment finally passed. Then the ship bucked to the sound of straining metal. In the dimness made by the fading lights of the bridge, the air became sultry, suddenly heavy, oppressive. Kirk could feel the racing of his body's pulses. Then the air was breathable again; Chekov, turning, said, "Confirmed, sir. The probe is lodged in the nucleus . . . close to the chromosome bodies."

Kirk nodded. "Mr. Sulu, back out of here the way we came in. Let's not waste time. That was a nice straight line, Mr. Chekov."

Chekov flushed with pleasure. "Estimate we'll be out in six point thirty-nine minutes, sir." He glanced back at his panel, frowning. "Captain! Metallic substance outside the ship!"

"Spock?" McCoy said.

Chekov flicked on the screen. "Yes, sir. It's the shuttlecraft, lying there dead on its side."

In one bound Kirk was beside Uhura. "Lieutenant, give me Mr. Spock's voice channel! High gain!"

The microphone shook in his hand as he waited for her to test the wave length. "Ready, sir," she said.

He waited again to try and steady his voice. "Mr. Spock, do you read me? Spock, *come in!*" He whirled to Scott. "Mr. Scott, tractor beam!"

"Captain . . . we don't have the time to do it! We've got only a fifty-three percent escape margin!"

"Will you kindly take an order, Lieutenant Commander? Two tractor beams on that craft!"

Scott reddened. "Tractor beams on, sir."

"Glad to hear it!" Kirk said—and incredibly the mike in his hand was speaking. "I . . . recommend you . . . abandon this attempt, Captain. Do . . . not risk the ship further . . . on my account."

Wordless, Kirk handed the mike to McCoy. McCoy looked at him and he nodded. "Shut up, Spock!" McCoy yelled. "You're being rescued!" He returned the mike to Kirk.

Spock said, "Thank you, Captain McCoy."

Weak as he was, Kirk thought, he'd find the strength to cock one sardonic eyebrow.

Weak—but alive. A knowledge better than McCoy's stimulants. "Time till explosion, Mr. Chekov?"

"Fifty-seven seconds, sir."

"You're maintaining tractor beam on the shuttlecraft, Mr. Scott?"

"Aye, sir." But the Scottish gloom of Kirk's favorite engineer was still unsubdued.

"However, I can't guarantee it will hold when that warhead explodes." He glanced at his board. Despite the dourness of his expectations, he gave a startled jump. "The power levels show dead, sir."

Then the power levels and everything else ceased to matter. The ship whirled. A white-hot glare flashed through the bridge. McCoy was smashed to the deck. In the glare Kirk saw Chekov snatched from his chair to fall unconscious at the elevator door. Uhura's body, on the floor beside her console, rolled to the ship's rolling. Disinterestedly, Kirk realized that blood was pouring from a gash in his forehead. A handkerchief appeared in his hand—and Sulu crawled away from him back in the direction of his chair. He sat up and tied the handkerchief around his head. It's what you did in a tough tennis game to keep the sweat out of your eyes . . . a long time since he played tennis . . .

"Mr. Sulu," he said, "can you activate the viewscreen?"

Stars. They had come back. The stars had come back.

A good crew. Chekov had limped back to his station. Not that he needed to say it. But it was good to hear, anyway. "The organism is destroyed, Captain. The explosion must have ruptured the membrane. It's thrown us clear."

The stars were back. So was the power.

Kirk laid his hand on Scott's shoulder. "And the shuttlecraft, Scotty?"

Spock's voice spoke from the bridge speaker. "Shuttlecraft to *Enterprise*. Request permission to come aboard."

Somebody put the mike in his hand. "You survived that volcano, Mr. Spock?"

"Obviously, Captain. And I have some very interesting data on the organism that I was unable to . . ."

McCoy, rubbing his bruised side, shouted, "Don't be so smart, Spock! You botched that acetylcholine test, don't forget!"

"Old Home Week," Kirk said. "Bring the shuttlecraft aboard, Mr. Scott. Mr. Chekov, lay in a course for Starbase Six. Warp factor five."

He untied the bloody handkerchief. "Thanks, Mr. Sulu. I'll personally see it to the laundry. Now I'm off to the hangar deck. Then Mr. Spock and I will be breaking out our mountaineering gear."

BY ANY OTHER NAME

WRITER: D. C. FONTANA AND JEROME BIXBY
(STORY BY JEROME BIXBY)
DIRECTOR: MARC DANIELS
FIRST AIRED: FEBRUARY 23, 1968

THE LANDING PARTY ANSWERING THE DISTRESS CALL CONSISTED OF KIRK, Spock, McCoy, the security officer Lt. Shea, and Yeoman Leslie Thompson. At first there seemed to be no source at all on the planet for the call—no wrecked spaceship, no debris. Had the ship been destroyed in space and the survivors proceeded here in a shuttle?

Then two people appeared from the nearby trees, a man and a woman, dressed in outfits rather like Merchant Marine jumpsuits. The woman was lovely, but it was the man who dominated their attention. He looked fortyish, with enormous power in his sturdy frame, great authority and competence in his bearing. Neither of the strangers seemed armed, but Kirk noticed that they wore small unobtrusive boxes on their belts. Their hands rested on the belts near the boxes in an attitude so casually assumed that it seemed to be only a part of their stance, but Kirk was wary.

"I'm Captain James Kirk of the USS *Enterprise*. We came in answer to your distress call."

"It was very kind of you to respond so quickly, Captain. But now you will surrender your ship to me."

Kirk stared. "You have an odd sense of humor."

The strangers touched buttons on the boxes. Instantly, Kirk found himself paralyzed—and so, evidently, was the rest of the "rescue" party.

"I am Rojan, of Kelva," the strange man said. "I am your Commander, from this moment on. Efforts to resist us, or to escape, will be severely punished. Soon we, and you, will leave this galaxy forever. You humans must face the end of your existence as you have known it."

The woman moved forward to relieve the people of the *Enterprise* of their phasers and communicators. Rojan went on: "You are paralyzed by a selective field that neutralizes impulses to the voluntary muscles. I will now release you all, Captain Kirk."

He touched the belt device. Kirk tensed to jump him, then thought better of it. "A neural field?"

"Radiated from a central projector, directed at whomever we wish."

"What do you want?"

"Your ship, Captain. We have monitored many. The *Enterprise*—a starship—is the best of its kind in your galaxy. It will serve us well in the long voyage that is to come."

"Voyage to where?"

"To your neighboring galaxy, in the constellation you call Andromeda."

"*Why?*"

"The Andromeda galaxy is our home," Rojan said in a remote voice.

"What brought you here?" Spock said.

"Within ten millennia, high radiation levels will make life in our galaxy impossible; it is reaching the stage in its evolution which will make it what you call a quasar. The Kelvan Empire sent forth ships to explore other galaxies—to search for one which our race could conquer and colonize."

"Sorry," Kirk said. "This galaxy is occupied."

"Captain, you think you are unconquerable—your ship impregnable. While we have talked, three of my people have boarded it, and the capture has begun." He took one of the confiscated communicators from the Kelvan woman and clicked it open. "Subcommander Hanar, report."

"The ship is ours," a strange voice said from the communicator. "We control the bridge, engineering and life support."

Rojan folded the communicator shut, and stowed it on his own belt.

"What good is capturing my ship?" Kirk said. "Even at maximum warp, the *Enterprise* couldn't get to the Andromeda galaxy for thousands of years. It's two million light-years away!"

"We will modify its engines to produce velocities far beyond the reach of your science. The journey between galaxies will take less than three hundred of your years."

"Fascinating," Spock said. "Intergalactic travel requiring 'only' three hundred years is a leap beyond anything man has yet accomplished."

Yeoman Thompson asked the Kelvan woman: "Did you make a voyage of three hundred years?"

"Our ships were of multigeneration design," the woman said. "I was born in the intergalactic void. I shall die there, during the return journey."

"Our mission," Rojan added, "will be completed by a Captain who will be my descendant."

"What happened to your ship?" Kirk said.

"There is an energy barrier at the rim of your galaxy—"

"I know. We've been there."

"We broke through it with great difficulty. Our ship was destroyed. We barely escaped in a life craft. Our time here has been spent scanning your systems, studying you. And now we have the means to begin our journey again."

"Why use our vessel?" Spock said. "Why not transmit a message back to your galaxy?"

"No form of transmission can penetrate the barrier."

"Rojan," Kirk said, "we could take your problem to our Federation. Research expeditions have catalogued hundreds of uninhabited planets in this galaxy. Surely some of them would be suitable for your colonization."

"We do not colonize, Captain," Rojan said sharply. "We conquer. We rule. There is no other way for us."

"In other words," McCoy said, "'this galaxy isn't big enough for both of us'?"

"What will happen to the intelligent races here?" Kirk said.

"They will not be mistreated. Merely subordinated." Rojan shrugged. "The fate of the inferior . . . in any galaxy. Ah, Hanar!"

While he had been speaking, another Kelvan had popped into being beside him, a younger man, with a hard intelligent face. There was no shimmer or any other such effect comparable to the workings of the Transporter; he just appeared.

"Tomar has examined the ship," Hanar said. "The modifications are under way."

"Space again!" said Rojan. "I don't think we could have kept our sanity, living so long on this accursed planet."

It did not seem to be so accursed to Kirk; in fact it was quite a pleasant, Earthlike place. But Hanar said: "It is an undisciplined environment; one cannot control it. Yet there are things of interest."

"Yes. But—disturbing. These ugly shells in which we have encased ourselves . . . they have such heightened senses. How do humans manage to exist in such fragile casings?"

They did not seem to care at all whether they were overheard, an obvious expression of supreme confidence. Kirk listened intently to every word; he had known such self-confidence to be misplaced before.

"Since the ship is designed to sustain this form," Hanar said, "we have little choice."

Rojan turned to the woman. "Kelinda, take them to the holding area. We will be keeping you and your party here, Captain. Your crew will undoubtedly prefer to cooperate with us if they understand you are hostages."

"Move that way," said Kelinda. "Keep together."

Their jail proved to be a cave, with a door constructed of some odd-looking transparent material, which Spock and Kirk were examining. Shea was also at the door, looking out, ostensibly watching Kelinda.

"I'm unable to determine the nature of the material, Captain," Spock said. "But I do not believe even phaser fire could disturb its molecular structure."

"All right, we can't break out. Maybe we can find another way."

"Captain," said Yeoman Thompson, "what do they want from us? What kind of people are they?"

"A good question, Yeoman."

"They registered as human," McCoy said.

"No, more than that, Doctor," Spock said, frowning. "They registered as *perfect* human life forms. I recall noting that the readings were almost textbook responses. Most curious."

"Spock," Kirk said, "what are the odds on such a parallel in life forms in another galaxy?"

"Based on those we have encountered in our own galaxy, the probability of humanoid development is high. But I would say the chances were very much against such an absolute duplication."

Shea turned slightly from the door. "Well, however perfect they are, sir, there don't seem to be very many of them."

"But they've got the paralysis field," Kirk said. "Rojan mentioned a central projector."

"If we can put it out of operation," McCoy said, "we've got a chance!"

"I am constrained to point out," said Spock, "that we do not even know what this projector looks like."

"No," Kirk said, "but those devices on their belts might indicate the position of the source."

"I would like to have one to examine."

"You'll have one, sir," Shea said. "If I have to rip one of the Kelvans apart to get it for you."

"Lieutenant Shea," Kirk said firmly, "you'll have your chance—but I'll tell you when."

"Yes, sir."

Kirk eyed him narrowly; but he could understand the younger officer's defiant attitude toward their captors. "Spock, do you remember how you tricked that guard on Eminiar? The empathic mind touching—"

"Quite well, Captain. I made him think we had escaped."

"Can you do it again?"

"I will attempt it."

He checked Kelinda, who was standing fairly close to the bars, and then put his hands on the cave wall approximately behind her. Then he began to concentrate.

At first the Kelvan woman did not respond. Then she twitched a little, nervously, as though aware that something was wrong, but unable to imagine what. She glanced around, then straightened again.

Kirk signaled his people to position themselves along the wall, so that from outside the cave would appear to be empty. Then he bent and scooped some dirt from the loose, sandy floor.

Suddenly Spock broke out of his intense concentration, as though wrenched from it by something beyond him. He gasped and staggered back against the wall. At the same moment, Kelinda came to the door, opened it quickly and started in.

Kirk hurled his handful of dirt into her face. She cried out and clawed at her eyes. While she was half blinded, Kirk delivered a karate chop. It sent her sprawling, and, surprisingly, out. Kirk and McCoy dragged her the rest of the way inside.

"Mr. Spock—?"

"I . . . will be . . . quite all right, Captain. We must hurry."

"Bones, keep an eye on him. Let's go." He took the belt device from Kelinda and led the way out. He had hardly taken two steps before he was paralyzed again, the device dropping from his limp hands.

"I am sorry, Captain," said Rojan's voice. He came into view with Hanar, who went into the cave. "The escape attempt was futile. You cannot stop us and you cannot escape us."

Hanar reappeared. "Kelinda is somewhat bruised, Rojan, but otherwise unhurt."

Rojan nodded, and turning back to Kirk, released the party from the freeze. "I cannot let this go unpunished. This will serve as an example." He pointed to Yeoman Thompson and security chief Shea. "Hanar, take these two aside."

"What are you going to do?" McCoy said.

"This is not your affair, Doctor. Captain, as a leader, you realize the importance of discipline. I need you and these other specialists. But those two are unnecessary to me."

"You can't just kill them!" Kirk said.

Rojan did not respond. Thompson turned, looking pleadingly at Kirk. "Captain . . ."

"Rojan, let them go. I'm responsible for them."

"I think we are somewhat alike, Captain. Each of us cares less for his own safety than for the lives of his command. We feel pain when others suffer for our mistakes. Your punishment shall be to watch your people die."

Rojan touched his belt device. Shea and the girl seemed to vanish instantly. Where each of them had been standing was an odd geometrically shaped block, about the size of a fist.

Hanar picked them up and brought them to Rojan, who held them up to Kirk. "This is the essence of what those people were . . . The flesh and brain, and also what you call the personality, distilled down to these compact shapes. Once crushed—" He closed his hand over one, crushing it in his grip, letting the fragments sift through his fingers. "—they are no more. This person is dead. However—" He flipped the second block away. It bounced to a halt on the grass. Rojan again touched a button, and Shea was standing there, bewildered. "—this person can be restored. As I said, Captain—very practical."

They were herded back into the cave, leaving behind the fragments which were all that were left of a pretty girl.

Shocked and dispirited, they all sat down on the cave floor but Shea. Spock's manner seemed more than usually distant.

"Mr. Spock," Kirk said, "are you sure you're all right?"

"Yes, quite all right, Captain."

McCoy said, "You looked very sick a while back, when you broke the mind lock."

"I did not break it," Spock said slowly. "I was . . . shoved away by . . . something I have never experienced before."

"What was it?" said Kirk.

"Images . . . bursting in my mind and consciousness. Colors . . . shapes . . . mathematical equations . . . fused and blurred. I have been attempting to isolate them. So far, I have been able to recall clearly only one. Immense beings . . . a hundred limbs that resemble tentacles, but are not . . . minds of such control and capacity that each limb could do a different job."

"You mean," McCoy said, "that's what the Kelvans really are?"

"I do not know. It seemed the central image, but whether it was a source or a memory, I cannot tell."

"If they do normally look like that," Kirk said, "why did they adapt to bodies like ours?"

"For the sake of deception, what else?" McCoy said.

Kirk remembered the conversation they had overheard. "No, practicality. They chose the *Enterprise* as the best kind of vessel for the trip, and they need us to run her. We have to stay in our gravity and atmosphere, and they had to adapt to it . . . We *have* to find a way to beat them. We outnumber them. Their only hold on us is the paralysis field."

"That's enough," said McCoy. "One wrong move and they jam all our neural circuits."

"Jamming," said Kirk. "That's it. Tricorders could analyze the frequency of the paralysis field. Spock, if you reverse the circuits on McCoy's neuroanalyzer, would it serve as a counterfield to jam the paralysis projector?"

"I am dubious about the possibility of success, Captain. The medical equipment is not built to put out any great amount of power. It would probably burn out."

"Is there any chance at all?"

"A small one."

"We'll take it. You and Bones have to get up to the ship."

"How?" said McCoy.

Kirk looked at his First Officer. "Spock, you're sick."

Spock's eyebrows went up. "Captain, I assure you that I am in excellent health."

"No, you're not. Dr. McCoy has examined you, and you're seriously ill. In fact, if he doesn't get you up to Sickbay you may die. And Rojan won't let that happen because he needs you to get through the barrier."

"It's a good idea," McCoy said, "but anybody looking at him can tell he's healthy."

"Vulcans have the ability to put themselves into a kind of trance . . . an enforced relaxation of every part of the mind and body. Right, Mr. Spock?"

"We find it more useful for resting the body than the so-called vacation."

"Can you do it now, and come out of it when you're in Sickbay? Say in half an hour?"

"It will take me a moment to prepare."

Shea walked to where he could watch for guards, then turned to nod and wave an all clear. Spock, remaining seated, composed himself very carefully. He seemed to be directing his attention inward upon himself. Then, almost as if someone had snapped off his switch, he flopped limply to one side.

McCoy rose to examine him, and at once looked a little alarmed. "Jim, his heartbeat really is way down—respiration almost nonexistent—"

Kirk turned to the door quickly and shouted "Guard! Guard!"

Hanar appeared. "What do you want, human?"

"Mr. Spock is ill. The doctor thinks he's dying."

"This illness came on him very suddenly," Hanar said. "Is it not unusual?"

"He's a Vulcan. They don't react like humans."

"Look, he may die," McCoy said as Hanar hesitated. "If I can get him up to Sickbay, there's a chance I can save him."

"Stand away from the door."

The others pulled away. Hanar came in, hand on his belt device, and bent to study the motionless Science Officer. He frowned. "I will have you beamed aboard, but you will be met by Tomar and watched."

As Hanar turned away, opening a communicator, Kirk and McCoy glanced toward each other.

"Do the best you can with him, Bones," Kirk said. McCoy nodded quickly, significantly.

The Kelvan Tomar and McCoy entered the *Enterprise*'s examination room, supporting the limp Spock between them. Nurse Christine Chapel followed. "Doctor, what happened?"

McCoy ignored her. He said to Tomar, "Here. Put him down."

They eased Spock onto the table. Tomar peered curiously at the Vulcan, who was breathing only shallowly, and with alarmingly long pauses between breaths.

"Shall I summon more of your underlings?"

"I'll call my own underlings," McCoy said snappishly. "You stay out of the way. Miss Chapel, prepare two cc's of stokaline."

"Stokaline? But, Doctor—"

"Don't argue with me, Nurse. Get it."

Christine turned and went to get the required air hypo. McCoy activated the body function panel over the table and began to take readings, which were obviously low. Tomar hesitated, then moved away to where he could watch from a discreet distance.

Christine came back with the hypo, and at McCoy's nod, administered it, looking at her chief in puzzlement. There was no response from Spock for a moment. Then his eyes snapped open. McCoy shook his head very slightly and the eyes closed again. Over their heads, the readings began to pick up, some of them quickening, others returning to their Vulcan norms, which were almost surely strange to Tomar.

"This may be the turning point, Nurse. Prepare another shot."

"Doctor—"

"Miss Chapel, please follow orders."

She did so, though McCoy was well aware of her mounting puzzlement. He continued to study the panel. Finally he nodded. "That does it. He'll be all right now. Let him rest." He turned to Tomar. "It was a flare-up of Rigelian Kassaba fever. He suffered from it ten years ago, and it recurs now and then. There's no danger if he receives medication in time. He'll be up again in an hour or so."

"Very well. I will inform Rojan. You will stay here."

The Kelvan went out and McCoy went back to the table, grinning at Spock, who was now propped up on his elbows.

"I said I would awaken myself, Doctor. What was that shot you gave me?"

"It wasn't *a* shot. It was two."

"I am not interested in quantity, but in content."

"It was stokaline."

"I am not familiar with that drug. Are there any after effects?"

"Yes. You'll feel much better."

"It's a multiple vitamin compound," Christine said, beginning to look less confused.

McCoy patted Spock's shoulder. "Stop worrying. It'll put a little green in your cheeks. Let's get at the neuroanalyzer."

Spock grimaced and rolled off the table to his feet. "It would be helpful to have Mr. Scott here."

"Agreed. Miss Chapel, it is time for Mr. Scott's medical exam."

"I'll see that he reports immediately," Christine said demurely.

* * *

Hanar summoned Kirk out of the cave and brought him to Rojan, who was lounging comfortably by a lakeside, with Kelinda close by. Rojan waved Hanar away. "Proceed to the ship, Hanar. Rest yourself, Captain."

"What do you want with me now, Rojan?" Kirk said angrily.

"We will beam aboard the vessel shortly. I wish you to understand your duties."

"My duty is to stop you in any way I can."

"You will obey."

"Or you'll kill more of my people?"

"Captain, I cannot believe that you do not understand the importance of my mission," Rojan said slowly, as if trying to explain to an equal. "We Kelvans have a code of honor—harsh, demanding. It calls for much from us, and much from those we conquer. You have been conquered. I respect your devotion to your duty. But I cannot permit it to interfere with mine."

Kirk remained silent, thinking. It was impossible not to be impressed by what seemed to be so much straightforward honesty. It was apparent that that "code" was what Rojan lived by, and that he believed in it unshakably.

It was also impossible to forget the crumbled shards of what had been Yeoman Leslie Thompson, scattered in the grass not far from here.

Kelinda had moved away to a nearby burst of flowers. Rojan watched her, but not, Kirk thought, with any sign of ordinary male interest.

"I hunger to be in space again, Rojan," she said. "But these—these are lovely. Captain Kirk, what is it you call them?"

"Flowers," he said, moving closer to her, cautiously. "I don't know the variety."

"Our memory tapes tell us of such things on Kelva," Rojan said. "Crystals which form with such rapidity that they seem to grow. They look like these fragile things, somewhat. We call them 'sahsheer.'"

"The rose," Kirk said, "by any other name . . ."

"Captain?" Rojan said.

"A quotation, from a great human poet, Shakespeare. 'That which we call a rose by any other name would smell as sweet.'"

Kelinda bent to smell the flowers, while Kirk studied her. Did this woman in reality have a hundred tentacles, all adapted to different uses? It was hard to imagine.

"Kelinda, Captain, come away," Rojan said. "We must leave now."

Directly they were beamed up, Rojan directed Kirk to take him and Kelinda to the bridge. There, Uhura was at her station, and Chekov at his, but a Kelvan woman was in the Helmsman's seat, and Hanar was standing nearby.

"Drea has computed and laid a course for Kelva, Rojan," Hanar said.

"Sir," said Chekov, "we've jumped to warp eight."

"And we'll go faster yet," Rojan said. "Increase speed to warp eleven."

Chekov looked around sharply at Kirk, who could only shrug his helplessness and nod.

"On course and proceeding as planned," said the Kelvan woman at the helm, who was evidently Drea.

"Very well," said Rojan. "Hanar, proceed with the neutralizing operation."

Hanar nodded and went to the elevator. Kirk said quickly: "What neutralizing operation?"

"You humans are troublesome for us, Captain. There are not enough of us to effectively guard all of you all the time. Further, the food synthesizers cannot continue to manufacture food for all of you for our entire journey. We are therefore neutralizing all nonessential personnel."

"No!"

"Captain, you can do nothing to stop it. The procedure is already under way. Now, as to bridge personnel . . ." He moved toward Uhura. "We have no need of communications for some centuries."

Uhura sat frozen in her chair, staring at Rojan in horror. He touched his belt device—and there was nothing left in her seat but a geometrical solid.

"And since Drea is now capable of doing our navigating—" Chekov too vanished. Drea had already neutralized two crewmen beyond Scott's station. Kirk stood frozen.

"They are not dead, Captain," Rojan reminded him. "They are merely reduced to the sum total of what they are."

"That's very comforting," Kirk said sarcastically. "But not pleasant to watch. I'm going to Sickbay. My First Officer was taken ill."

"Yes, I was informed. Go ahead."

Sickbay was deserted. Kirk found Scott, McCoy and Spock picking at food at a table in the recreation room. Getting himself a tray, he joined them. "Reports, gentlemen?"

"I'm a little sick," McCoy said. "We burned out my neuroanalyzer, to no effect. I saw one of the Kelvans, the one they call Tomar, reduce four of my doctors and nurses to those . . . little blocks."

"I've seen them do that too. Remember, the process is reversible. I only wonder how far it's going to go."

"I have been checking our table of organization against their apparent capabilities," Spock said. "It appears that we will have very few 'survivors.' They will need none of the security men, for example. And once we cross the energy barrier, Engineering can be reduced to a skeleton crew. Beyond that point lies some three hundred years of straight cruising—at an astonishing velocity, to be sure, but still cruising. And of the officers, it would seem that only we four could be regarded as 'essential.' I am not even sure of your status, Captain, or mine."

"How so?"

"Rojan is in command now."

"Quite so," Kirk said bitterly. "Scotty, have you found out anything about the paralysis projector?"

"Quite a lot, and none of it good. The machine is in Engineering, and it's encased in that same stuff the door of our jail was made of. Furthermore, it's nae a simple machine—and it's the only one of its kind on board. I think it must be the source of all their special powers—and it's impregnable."

"Any suggestions?"

"One," Scott said. "Self-destruct."

Kirk considered it. "We've been driven to that point, or almost, once before," he said at last. "But aside from my aversion to suicide—and the deaths of everybody else—it's not practical. We'd never complete the routine with the computer before Rojan paralyzed us."

"I thought of that," Scott said. "I could do it myself, though. Remember that we've got to cross the energy barrier. It willna be easy at best. A little sabotage in the matter-antimatter nacelles, and we'd blow, for good and all."

Kirk made a quick silencing gesture. Tomar had come in, and was now approaching them, staring curiously at their trays.

"I do not understand," he said, "why you go to the trouble of consuming this bulk material to sustain yourselves." He pulled a flat pillbox from a pocket and opened it. "These contain all the required nutritional elements."

"Not for human forms," McCoy said. "Bulk is necessary to our digestive systems, and there's a limit to the amount of energy that can be crammed into a pill, too. Perhaps you haven't been in human form long enough to find just pills debilitating, but you will—you will."

"Indeed? Then you had better show me promptly what else we shall need, and how to manage it."

McCoy looked rebellious and Kirk himself felt a hope die almost before it had been born. "I think you'd better, Bones," he said.

"All right. Come on, I'll show you how to work the selector." McCoy led Tomar off toward the wall dispenser.

"Spock," Kirk said in a whisper, "shall we self-destruct? Crossing the barrier may be our last chance to do so."

"Granted," Spock whispered back. "But it is said on Earth that while there is life, there is hope. That is sound logic: no multivalued problem has only one solution."

"Well, we couldn't knock out their central machine even if we were able. It has to be kept intact to restore the rest of our people to human form."

There was quite a long silence. McCoy had settled Tomar at a table with a tray, and Tomar was gingerly forking some meat into his mouth. Judging by his nod, he found it agreeable, and he began eating at a fair speed for a newcomer to the habit. McCoy grinned and rejoined his colleagues.

"I'm almost sorry I did that," he said. "It looks like he likes food—and I wouldn't want any of them to enjoy anything."

Spock continued to watch Tomar. "Most peculiar."

"What is?" Kirk said.

"The isolated glimpses of things I saw when I touched Kelinda's mind are beginning to coalesce in my consciousness. The Kelvans have superior intellectual capacity. But to gain it, they apparently sacrificed many things that would tend to distract them. Among these are the pleasures of the senses—and, of course, emotions."

"But then, Tomar shouldn't be enjoying the taste of food."

"He has taken human form," Spock said, "and is having human reactions."

Kirk's mind leapt ahead in response. "If they all respond to stimulation of the senses, maybe we could confuse them. They don't know how to handle those senses yet. If we can distract them enough, we could try to get the belt devices away. That's their only hold on us."

"It seems reasonable," Spock said.

"All right. We watch for opportunities to work on them—hit them every way we can think of."

Scott was studying Tomar. "I can think of one way right off," he said. He rose and went to the Kelvan. "Lad, you'll be needing something to wash that down with. Have you ever tried Saurian brandy?"

McCoy stopped Hanar as the Kelvan was passing by the door to the examination room. "Come on in a moment, please, Hanar."

"What is it, human?"

"I've noticed you're not looking too well."

"Impossible. We do not malfunction, as do you humans."

"No? You're forgetting you're in a human body. And that does malfunction—that's why Rojan considers me essential. You look pale." He gestured to the table. "Sit up there."

When Hanar complied, McCoy picked up his medical tricorder and began taking readings. "Uh huh . . . Hmmm . . . I don't know about that . . . Hmmmm."

"Please articulate, human."

"Well, it looks to me like this body of yours is getting a little anemic, and has some other subclinical deficiencies. Comes from taking your food in pills, instead of good solid substance." He turned aside and picked up a hypo, which he set.

"What are you doing?"

"I'm going to give you a shot—high potency vitamin-mineral concentrate. You'll have to have one three times a day for a few days. And eat some solid food."

* * *

It had taken Scott a while to get Tomar down to serious drinking; initially he had been too interested in the tartan, the claymore, the armorial bearings on the walls, the standing suit of ancient armor in Scott's quarters, all of which he declared nonfunctional in a starship. He did not seem to grasp either the concept of mementos or that of decoration.

Finally, however, they were seated at Scott's desk with a bottle and glasses between them. After a while, it was two bottles. Tomar seemed to remain in total control of himself, as if he'd been drinking lemonade. "No more?" he said.

"Well . . . no more Saurian brandy, but . . ." Scott looked around and found another bottle. "Now, y'see, this liquor is famous on Ahbloron—I mean, Aldibibble—on one of these planets we go to."

"It is a different color from the other."

"Yes. And stronger, too." He poured some into Tomar's glass with an unsteady hand, and then, perforce, some into his own. Somehow this experiment was not working out right.

Kirk paid a call on the cabin Kelinda had commandeered. When she invited him in, he found her looking at a tape on a viewscreen. "Did I disturb you?"

"Disturb? What is it you wish?"

He went over to her. "I want to apologize."

"I do not understand, Captain."

"For hitting you. I wanted to say I was sorry."

"That is not necessary. You attempted to escape, as we would have. That I was taken in by your ruse is my fault, not yours."

Kirk smiled and reached out to touch her face gently. "I don't usually hit beautiful women."

"Why not, if there is need?"

"Because there are better things for men and women to do." He moved the hand down to her neck. "Was it here that I hit you?"

"No, on the other side."

"Oh." He leaned to the other side, kissed her neck, and nuzzled her ear. "Is that better?"

"Better? Was it intended to be a remedy?"

"This is." Drawing her to her feet, he took her in his arms and kissed her.

After a moment she drew back. "Is there some significance to this action?"

"It was meant to express . . . well, among humans it shows warmth, love—"

"Oh. You are trying to seduce me," she said, as if she were reading a weather report. "I have been reading about you."

"Me?"

"Humans. This business of love. You have devoted much literature to it. Why have you built such a mystique around a simple biological fact?"

"We enjoy it."

"The literature?"

"Kelinda, I'm sorry I brought the subject up."

"Did you regard this contact of the lips as pleasurable?"

Kirk sighed. "I did."

"Curious. I wonder why." Abruptly she put her arms around him and kissed him back.

The door opened and Rojan came in. Kirk made a point of drawing back with guilty swiftness.

"Is there some problem, Captain?" Rojan said.

"None." Kirk left quickly. Rojan stared after him.

"What did he want here?"

"He came to apologize for hitting me," Kelinda said. "Apparently, it involves some peculiar touching contacts."

"In what manner?"

Kelinda hesitated, then reached up to nibble at Rojan's neck and ear. Rojan stepped away from her, frowning.

"They are odd creatures, these humans. Please have the reports on fuel consumption relayed to Subcommander Hanar as soon as possible."

Spock had taught Rojan to play chess; the Kelvan had learned with breathtaking speed. They were playing now, in the recreation room.

"Yes, they are peculiar," Spock said, moving a piece. "I very often find them unfathomable, but an interesting psychological study."

Rojan moved in return. "I do not understand this business of biting someone's neck to apologize."

Spock looked up, raising his eyebrows. Then he looked back at the game, saw an opening and quickly moved another piece. "I believe you are referring to a kiss. But it is my understanding that such, uh, apologies are usually exchanged between two people who have some affection for each other."

"Kelinda has no affection for Captain Kirk," Rojan said quickly.

Spock studied Rojan's next move and shook his head. "You seemed disturbed about the incident. Your game is off."

"Why should I be disturbed?"

"It seems to me you have known Kelinda for some time. She is a Kelvan, as you are. Among humans, I have found the symptoms you are displaying would be indicative of jealousy."

"I have no reason for such a reaction. Kelinda is a female. Nothing more."

"Captain Kirk seems to find her quite attractive."

"Of course she is."

"But you are not jealous."

"No!"

"Nor upset."

"Certainly not!"

Spock made his move. "Checkmate."

Kirk, Spock and McCoy were holding another council of war in the recreation room. Kirk was depressed. "The thing is, I can't tell if we're getting anywhere. And I haven't seen Scotty for what seems like months."

"You haven't seen Tomar either," McCoy said. "But the point is, these things take time. The Kelvans started out with adapted human bodies in superb physical shape—textbook cases, as Spock said. They have high resistance. I've been giving Hanar shots that would have driven our whole crew up the wall in an hour. He responds slowly—but he's getting more irritable by the minute, now."

"And Rojan," Spock said, "has exhibited symptoms of jealousy toward Kelinda and you."

"What about Kelinda, Jim?" McCoy said.

"No progress," Kirk said, uncomfortably.

"What approach did you take with her? Could be you're a little rusty—"

Kirk felt himself begin to bristle. Spock interposed smoothly: "I would say it is sufficient that Rojan is jealous."

"Right," Kirk said quickly. "That's the opening wedge. As soon as it's a little wider, we move."

Behind Kirk, Kelinda's voice said: "I would like to speak with you, Captain."

Spock stood up at once. "Doctor, I think I need another dose of stokaline."

"Huh?" McCoy said. "Oh, yes. Pardon us."

They went out. Kirk leaned back in his chair and studied Kelinda. "You had something to say?"

"Yes." Did she really seem a trifle uncomfortable, even perhaps awkward? Kirk waited. Then she took a deep breath and touched him, lightly, on a shoulder. "This cultural mystique surrounding a biological function . . ."

"Yes?"

"You realize it really is quite overdone."

"Oh. Quite."

"However, I was wondering . . . would you please apologize to me again?"

Rojan was in the command chair. Behind him, the elevator doors snapped open, and then Hanar's voice said, with surprising belligerence: "Rojan. I want to talk to you."

Rojan looked up in surprise. "Very well, Hanar."

"First, I do not like the way responsibility and duty have been portioned out to us."

"It is the way your duties have always been assigned."

"And that is my second quarrel with you. It was always unjust—"

Rojan snapped out of the chair. "Hanar—"

"And further, I do not care much for the autocratic way you order us about on this ship, which we captured, not you—"

"Confine yourself to your quarters!"

Hanar hesitated, as though he had had a lot more to say, but had thought better of it. Then he spun on his heel and left without further acknowledgment.

Rojan found his own fists clenching in anger—and was suddenly aware that Drea was watching him in amazement from the navigator's station. As Rojan turned his back to hide his expression, Spock came onto the bridge and went toward his library-computer. Rojan followed.

"You were not called to the bridge, Spock. What is your purpose here?"

"Sensors and various other recording devices require monitoring and certain adjustments."

"Very well, proceed . . . Have you seen Captain Kirk?"

"Do you want him? I will call him to the bridge."

"No. I . . . wondered where he was."

"Dr. McCoy and I left him some time ago in the recreation room."

"He was alone, then?"

"No. Kelinda was with him. She seemed most anxious to speak to him."

"I told him to stay away from her."

"It would appear that you have little control over her, sir . . . or perhaps Captain Kirk has more."

Rojan turned abruptly and headed for the elevator.

Kirk and Kelinda were locked in a kiss when Rojan came through the recreation room door. Kirk looked up, but did not release Kelinda entirely; instead he kept a possessive arm around her as he turned toward Rojan. Rojan stopped and stared.

"Kelinda, I told you to avoid this human!"

"I did not wish to," she said.

"I am your commander."

"I've found," Kirk said, "that doesn't mean much to a woman if she's bound to go her own way."

"You have done this to her! Corrupted her—turned her away from me!"

"If you couldn't keep her, Rojan, that's not *my* problem."

Furiously, Rojan leaped at Kirk. He seemed to have forgotten all about the belt device, his bare hands reaching out. Kirk pushed Kelinda aside and met Rojan's rush.

The two men, equally powerful, slammed at each other like bulls. Rojan was more clumsy, more unaccustomed to the body he was in. Kirk was the quicker and the more adept fighter, but he was not possessed by the anger which obviously drove Rojan.

Kelinda did not intervene; she only watched. After a moment she was joined by Spock and McCoy.

Kirk delivered a final punch that sent Rojan spinning down, backward. But he was not beaten yet. He started to climb back to his feet.

"Rojan—wait!" Kirk said. "Listen to me—"

Rojan flung himself forward, but Kirk fended him off. "Listen! Why didn't you use your paralyzer? Don't you know why? Because you've become a human yourself." Kirk ducked a punch. "Look at you—brawling like a street fighter—shaking with rage—"

Rojan paused and stared as the words began to sink in. "What?"

"You thought I took your woman away from you. You were jealous—and you wanted to kill me with your bare hands. Would a Kelvan have done that? Would he *have* to? You reacted with the emotions of a human, Rojan. You are one."

"No! We cannot be."

"You have no choice. You chose this ship. Because of its environmental systems, you had to take human form to use it. And you're stuck with it—you and your descendants—for the next three hundred years. Look what's happened to you in the short time you've been exposed to us. What do you think will happen in three hundred years? When this ship gets to Kelva, the people on it will be aliens, the Kelvans their enemies."

"We have a mission. We must carry it out." But Rojan's tone showed that he was shaken.

"Your mission was to find worlds for your people to live on. You can still do that. I told you we could present your case to the Federation. I know it would be sympathetic. There are many unpopulated planets in our galaxy. You could develop them in peace, your way."

"They would do that? You would extend welcome to invaders?"

"No. But we do welcome friends."

"Perhaps," said Rojan, "perhaps it could be done."

Spock said: "A robot ship could be sent back to Kelva with the Federation proposal."

"But what of us?" Rojan said. "If we . . . if we retain this form, where can we find a place?"

"Seems to me," McCoy said, "that little planet you were on was kind of a nice place."

"Pleasant . . . but . . ."

"The Federation would probably grant a colonization permit to a small group of people who desired to settle there," Spock said. "You do represent an old and highly intelligent race."

Rojan turned to Kelinda and jerked his head at Kirk. "You want to go with him?"

Kelinda glanced at Kirk and then back at Rojan. "As you have said, he is not our kind. I believe I owe you an apology." She kissed him. "It *is* pleasurable, Rojan."

"You know, Rojan," Kirk said, "one of the advantages of being a human is being able to appreciate beauty . . . of a flower, or of a woman. Unless you'd rather conquer a galaxy?"

"No, Captain, I would rather not." Rojan took Kelinda's hand. "A link in a chain—that's all we were. Perhaps there is an opportunity for us to be more." He turned away, crossed the room and activated an intercom. "Bridge, this is Rojan."

"Yes, Commander," said Drea's voice.

"Turn the ship. We are returning to the alien . . . We are returning home."

"Sir?"

"Turn the ship about."

He led Kelinda out. Kirk, Spock and McCoy expelled simultaneous sighs of relief.

"Jim, I was coming to tell you—"

"Yes, Bones?"

"I found Scotty in his room with Tomar. Apparently they've been having a drinking bout all this time. They were both under the table—but Tomar went down first. Scott had Tomar's belt device in his hand. He just never made it to the door with it."

Kirk grinned. "The Kelvans," he said, "still have a lot to learn about being human, don't they?"

THE ULTIMATE COMPUTER

Writer: D. C. Fontana and Laurence N. Wolfe
Director: John Meredyth Lucas
First Aired: March 8, 1968

Obediently the *Enterprise* (to its skipper's intense annoyance) was making its approach to the space station. His impatience lifted him from his chair and sent him across to Uhura. "Lieutenant, contact the space station."

"The station is calling *us*, Captain."

"Put them on."

The voice was familiar. "Captain Kirk, this is Commodore Enwright."

"Commodore, I'd like an explanation."

Enwright cut across him. "The explanation is beaming aboard you now, Captain. He may already be in your Transporter Room. Enwright out."

"Spock," Kirk said, and gestured toward the elevator. "Scotty, you have the con."

The "explanation" was materializing in the person of Commodore Wesley, a flight officer slightly older than Kirk but not unlike him in manner and military bearing. Kirk's rage gave way to astonishment. "Bob! Bob Wesley!" The two shook hands as Wesley stepped from the platform. Kirk said, "Mr. Spock, this is—"

Spock completed the sentence. "Commodore Wesley. How do you do, sir."

Wesley nodded. "Mr. Spock."

Kirk turned to the Transporter officer. "Thank you, Lieutenant. That will do."

As the door closed, he burst out. "Now will you please tell me what this is all about? I receive an order to proceed here. No reason is given. I'm informed my crew is to be removed to the space station's security holding area. I think I'm entitled to an explanation!"

Wesley grinned. "You've had a singular honor conferred on you, Jim. You're going to be the fox in a hunt."

"What does that mean?"

"War games. I'll be commanding the attack force against you."

"An entire attack force against one ship?"

Wesley regarded him tolerantly. "Apparently you haven't heard of the M-5 Multitronic Unit. It's the computer, Jim, that Dr. Richard Daystrom has just developed."

"Oh?"

"Not oh, Jim. Wait till you see the M-5."

"What is it?"

Spock broke in. "The most ambitious computer complex ever created. Its purpose is to correlate all computer activity of a Starship . . . to provide the ultimate in vessel operation and control."

Wesley eyed Spock suspiciously. "How do you know so much about it, Commander?"

"I hold an A-7 computer expert classification, sir. I am well acquainted with Dr. Daystrom's theories and discoveries. The basic design of all our ships' computers are Dr. Daystrom's."

"And what's all that got to do with the *Enterprise*?" Kirk said.

Wesley's face grew grave. "You've been chosen to test the M-5, Jim. There'll be a series of routine research and contact problems M-5 will have to solve as well as navigational maneuvers and the war-games' problems. If it works under actual conditions as it has in simulated tests, it will mean a revolution in space technology as great as the Warp Drive. As soon as your crew is removed, the ship's engineering section will be modified to contain the computer."

"Why remove my crew? What sort of security does this gadget require?"

"They're not needed," Wesley said. "Dr. Daystrom will see to the installation himself and will supervise the tests. When he's ready, you will receive your orders and proceed on the mission with a crew of twenty."

"*Twenty!* I can't run a Starship with only twenty people aboard!"

The voice of authority was cool. "M-5 can."

"And I—what am I supposed to do?"

"You've got a great job, Jim. All you have to do is sit back and let the machine do the work."

"My," Kirk said, "it sounds just great!"

McCoy didn't like it, either. Told the news, he exploded. "A vessel this size can't be run by one computer! Even the computers we already have—"

Spock interrupted. "All of them were designed by Richard Daystrom almost twenty-five years ago. His new one utilizes the capabilities of all the present computers . . . it is the master control. We are attempting to prove that it can run this ship more efficiently than man."

"Maybe *you're* trying to prove that, Spock, but don't count me in on it."

"The most unfortunate lack in current computer programming is that there is nothing available to immediately replace the Starship surgeon."

"If there were," McCoy said, "they wouldn't have to replace me. I'd resign—and because everybody else aboard would be nothing but circuits and memory banks." He glared at Spock. "I think some of us already are just that." He turned an anxious face to Kirk. "You haven't said much about this, Jim."

They were standing outside the Engineering Section. Now Kirk swung around to face Spock and McCoy, pointing to the new sign on the door reading "Security Area". "What do you want me to say, Bones? Starfleet considers this installation of the M-5 an honor. So I'm honored. It takes some adjusting, too." He turned, the door slid open, and they entered the Section. And the M-5 Multitronic Unit already dominated the vast expanse. Unlike the built-in *Enterprise* computers, its massive cabinet was freestanding as though asserting total independence of support. It possessed a monitor panel where dials, switches, and other controls were ranged in an order that created an impression of an insane disorder. Scott and another engineer, Ensign Harper, were busy at panels near the upper-bridge level. Kirk looked around. "Where is he? Dr. Daystrom?"

He came from behind the console where he had been working, wearing a technician's outfit. The first thing that struck Kirk about him were his eyes. Despite the lines of middle age, they were brilliantly piercing as though all his energy was concentrated on penetration. He was a nervous man. His speech was sharply clipped and his hands seemed to need to busy themselves with something—a pipe, a tool, anything available.

"Yes?" he said. Suddenly, he seemed to register something inappropriate in the greeting. "You would be Captain Kirk?"

They shook hands briefly. "Dr. Daystrom, my First Officer, Commander Spock."

Spock bowed. "I am honored, Doctor. I have studied all your publications on computer technology. Brilliant."

"Thank you. Captain, I have finished my final check on M-5. It must be hooked into the ship's main power banks to become operational."

Kirk said, "Very well, Dr. Daystrom. Do so."

"Your Chief Engineer refused to make the power available without your orders."

Good old Scotty, Kirk thought. What he said was, "Mr. Scott, tie the M-5 unit into the main power banks."

"Aye, sir. Mr. Harper?" He and Harper moved off to the wall panel near the force perspective unit.

Spock was examining the M-5 monitor panel. McCoy fixed his gaze on the distance.

"Fascinating, Doctor," Spock said. "This computer has a potential beyond anything you have ever done. Even your breakthrough into duotronics did not hold the promise of this."

"M-5 has been perfected, Commander. Its potential is a fact."

McCoy could contain himself no longer. "The only fact I care about," he said savagely, "is that if this thing doesn't work, there aren't enough men aboard to run this ship. That's screaming for trouble."

Daystrom stared at him. "Who is this?" he asked Kirk.

"Dr. Leonard McCoy, Senior Medical Officer."

"This is a security area," Daystrom said. "Only absolutely necessary key personnel have clearance to enter it."

Kirk's voice was icy in his own ears. "Dr. McCoy has top security clearances for all areas of this ship."

Then the M-5 suddenly came to life. It was a startling phenomenon. It flashed with lights, a deep hum surging from its abruptly activated circuits. As its lights glowed brighter, lights in the engine unit dimmed sharply.

McCoy spoke to Spock. "Is it supposed to do that?"

Daystrom was working quickly to remove a panel. He made an adjustment and Spock said, "If I can be of assistance, sir . . ."

Daystrom looked up. "No. I can manage, thank you."

The rebuffed Spock's eyebrows arched in surprise. He glanced at Kirk who nodded and Spock backed off. The M-5's deep hum grew quieter, less erratic; and overhead, the lights struggled back to full strength.

Daystrom was defensive. "Nothing wrong, Captain. A minor settling-in adjustment to be made. You see, everything is in order now."

"Yes." Kirk paused. "I'm curious, Dr. Daystrom. Why is it M-5 instead of M-1?"

Daystrom's hands twisted on a tool. "The Multitronic Units 1 through 4 were not successful. But this one *is*. M-5 is ready to assume control of the ship."

"Total control?" Kirk said.

"That is what it was designed for, Captain."

There was an awkward silence. "I'm afraid," Kirk said, "I must admit to a certain antagonism toward your computer, Dr. Daystrom. It was man who first ventured into space. True, man *with* machines . . . but still with man in command."

"Those were primitive machines, Captain. We have entered a new era."

Kirk thought, I don't like this man. He dispensed with the amiable smile on his lips. "I am not against progress, sir; but there are still things men have to do to remain men. Your computer would take that away, Dr. Daystrom."

"There are other things a man like you can do, Captain. Or perhaps you only object to the possible loss of the prestige accorded a Starship Captain. The computer can do your job without interest in prestige."

Kirk smiled at him. "You're going to have to prove that to me, Daystrom." He started to leave, but Daystrom's voice halted him in midstride. "Captain, that's what the M-5 is here for, isn't it?"

It had not been a pleasant encounter. Spock alone seemed untouched by its implications. As the three moved down the drearily empty corridor, he said, "Captain, if you don't need me for a moment, I'd like to discuss some of the technology involved in the M-5 with Dr. Daystrom."

"Look at the love-light in his eyes, Jim. All his life Spock's been waiting for the right computer to come along. I hope you'll be very happy together, Spock."

"Doctor, I find your simile illogical and your humor forced. If you'll excuse me, Captain?"

"Go ahead, Mr. Spock. I'll see you on the bridge."

"Yes, sir."

Kirk's troubled expression worried McCoy. "What is it, Jim?"

Kirk hesitated. "I feel it's wrong—and I don't know why—all of it wrong."

"I feel it's wrong, too, replacing men with mindless machines."

"It isn't just that, Bones. Only a fool would stand in the way of progress, if this *is* progress. You have all my psychological profiles. Do you think I *am* afraid to turn command over to the M-5?"

McCoy spoke thoughtfully. "We've all seen the advances of mechanization; and Daystrom *did* design the computers that run this ship."

"But under *human* control," Kirk said. "What I'm asking myself is: Is it just that I'm afraid of that computer taking over my job? Daystrom is right. I could do other things. Or am I really afraid of losing the prestige, the glamour accorded a Starship Captain? Is that why I keep fighting this thing? Am I really that petty and vain?"

"Jim, if you have the courageous awareness to ask yourself that question, you don't need me to answer it." He grinned. "Why don't you ask James T. Kirk? He's a pretty honest guy."

"Right now, Bones, I'm not sure he'd give me an honest answer."

But he was sure of one thing: he resented the installation of the new control console on his command chair. It had been placed on the left side of it opposite the one containing his old one with its intercom and other switches. It had been added to the chair without any consultation or announcement of the innovation. Kirk stared at it silently and Sulu said, "Turning back on original course, Captain."

Spock came over to examine the new console. "The M-5 has performed admirably so far, sir."

"All it's done is make some required course changes and simple turns. Chekov and Sulu could do that with their eyes closed."

Daystrom had appeared at his left side. "The idea is that they didn't *have* to do it, Captain. And it's not necessary for you to regain control from a unit after each maneuver is completed."

Kirk spoke tightly. "My orders say nothing about how long I must leave the M-5 in control of my ship. And I shall run it as I see fit, Dr. Daystrom."

Spock said, "Captain, I must agree with Dr. Daystrom. With the course information plotted into it, the computer could have brought us here as easily as the navigator."

"Mr. Spock, you seem to enjoy entrusting yourself to that computer."

"Enjoy, sir? I am, of course, gratified to see the new unit executing everything in such a highly efficient manner. M-5 is another distinguished triumph in Dr. Daystrom's career."

Chekov spoke tonelessly. "Approaching Alpha Cazinae II, Captain. ETA five minutes."

"The M-5 is to handle the approach, Captain," Daystrom said. "It will direct entrance into orbit and then analyze data for landing-party recommendations."

Kirk's voice was very quiet. "You don't mind if I make my own recommendations?"

"If you feel you need the exercise, go ahead, Captain."

Kirk looked into the coldly piercing eyes. Then, reaching out, he pressed one of the buttons on the new console panel.

In the same inflectionless voice, he said, "M-5 is now committed."

As the subdued hum in the ship grew louder, the main viewing screen showed the approaching planet. Kirk, his eyes on it, said, "Standard orbit, Mr. Sulu."

Sulu, checking instruments, looked up in surprise. "Captain, M-5 has calculated that. The orbit is already plotted."

"Ah, yes," Kirk said. Spock had moved back to his station but Daystrom, pleased by his invention's performance, remained beside the new command console.

"Standard orbit achieved, sir," Sulu said.

"Report, Mr. Spock."

"The planet is Class M, sir. Oxygen-nitrogen atmosphere, suitable for human life support . . . two major land masses . . . a number of islands. Life form readings."

In the Engineering Section, the overhead lights flickered a moment; and on the deserted Deck 4, they went out, plunging the area into blackness.

Scott turned abruptly to Kirk, frowning. "Captain, we're getting some peculiar readings. Power shutdowns on Deck 4—lights, environmental control."

Kirk said, "Check it out, Mr. Scott." He crossed over to Spock. The library-computer was chattering rapidly. Daystrom joined them. They saw a tape cartridge slide smoothly out of a slot. Spock took it, examining it. "M-5's readout, Captain."

Kirk drew a deep breath. "All right. My recommendations are as follows. We send down a general survey party, avoiding contact with life forms on the planet. Landing party to consist of myself, Dr. McCoy, astrobiologist Mason, geologist Rawls and Science Officer Spock."

"Mr. Spock," said Daystrom, "play M-5's recommendations."

Spock dropped the cartridge into another slot in his library-computer, and punching a button, he evoked a computer voice. It said, "M-5 readout. Planet Alpha Cazinae II. Class M. Atmosphere oxygen-nitrogen . . ."

On Deck 6 the lights suddenly faded—and darkness flooded into another area of the *Enterprise*.

Scott cried, "Now power's gone off on Deck 6!"

The computer voice went on. "Categorization of life form readings recorded. Recommendations for general survey party: Science Officer Spock, astrobiologist Mason, geologist Carstairs."

Kirk let a moment go by. "The only variation in reports and recommendations is in landing party personnel. And that's only a matter of judgment."

"Judgment, Captain?" said Daystrom.

"Captain . . . the computer does not judge," Spock said. "It makes logical selections."

"Then why did it pick Carstairs instead of Rawls? Carstairs is an Ensign, Mr. Spock, no experience: this is his first tour of duty. Rawls is the Chief Geologist."

"Perhaps, Captain, you're really interested in why M-5 didn't name you and Dr. McCoy."

"Not necessarily, Daystrom," Kirk said smoothly.

"Let's find out anyway." Daystrom hit a switch. "M-5 tie-in. Explanation for landing-party recommendations."

The computer voice said, "M-5. General survey party requires direction of Science Officer. Astrobiologist Mason has surveyed 29 biologically similar planets. Geologist Carstairs served on merchant-marine freighters in this area . . . once visited planet on geology survey for mining company."

"M-5 tie-in. Why were the Captain and Chief Medical Officer not included in the recommendations?"

"M-5," said the computer. "Non-essential personnel."

Spock averted his eyes from Kirk's face; and Scott, over at his board, called, "Captain! I've located the source of the power shutdowns. It's the M-5 unit, sir. That thing's turning off systems all over the ship!"

"Well, Dr. Daystrom," Kirk said, "do we visit the Engineering Section?" He stood aside while the inventor removed a panel from the huge mechanism. A moment or so later, he replaced it, saying, "As I suspected, it's not a malfunction in this series of circuits. There is no need to check further. The M-5 is simply shutting down power to areas of the ship that don't require it. Decks 4 and 6 are quarter decks, are they not?"

"Yes."

"And currently unoccupied."

Spock was examining the great monitor panel. "I am not familiar with these instruments, Dr. Daystrom. You are using an entirely new control system . . . but it appears to me the unit is drawing more power than before."

"Quite right. As the unit is called upon to do more work, it pulls more power to accomplish it . . . just as the human body draws on more power, more energy to run than to stand still."

"Dr. Daystrom," Spock said, "this is not a human body. A computer can process the information—but only that which is put into it."

Kirk nodded. "Granted it can work thousands, millions of times faster than a human brain. But it can't make value judgments. It doesn't have intuition. It can't *think* nor gauge relative importances."

Daystrom flushed angrily. "Can't you understand the unit is a revolution in computer science? *I* designed the duotronic elements used in your ship right now. And they are as archaic as dinosaurs compared to the M-5—" He was interrupted by a bosun's whistle and Uhura's filtered voice.

"Captain Kirk and Mr. Spock to the bridge, please."

Kirk crossed to the intercom. "This is Kirk. What is it, Lieutenant?"

"Sensors are picking up a vessel paralleling our course, sir. As yet unidentified."

As he turned from the intercom, he realized the M-5 had again increased its humming and light activity. He looked at it dubiously and said, "Mr. Spock." Descending the ladder, his last glimpse of Daystrom showed the man's hand patting the computer caressingly. The high hum followed them to the bridge where McCoy, his jaw set, was waiting for them.

"What are you doing up here, Bones?"

"Why wouldn't I be here? Sickbay systems are shut down until such time as the M-5 is informed there are patients to be cared for."

Spock, over at his station, spoke hastily. "Sir, sensor reports indicate two contacts; one on the port bow, the other on the stern. Distance, two hundred thousand kilometers and closing."

"Identification?"

"Sir, the M-5 unit has already identified the vessels as Federation Starships *Excalibur* and *Lexington*."

Kirk looked at him. It was impossible to tell whether Spock was impressed or annoyed that the M-5 had done his job for him. "We were not scheduled for war games in this area, Captain. It may be a surprise attack as a problem for M-5."

Uhura spoke. "Priority alert message coming in, sir."

Daystrom came from the elevator as Kirk said, "On audio, Lieutenant." He paused at the sound of Wesley's voice.

"*Enterprise* from Commodore Wesley aboard the U.S.S. *Lexington*. This is an unscheduled M-5 drill. I repeat, this is an M-5 drill. *Enterprise*, acknowledge on this frequency."

Kirk nodded at Uhura. "Acknowledge, Lieutenant."

Uhura reached to press a button, hesitated, and stared at Kirk. "M-5 is acknowledging for us, sir."

"Then sound red alert, Lieutenant."

"Aye, sir." But as she moved for the switch, the red alert sounded. "M-5 has already sounded the alert, Captain."

"Has it?" Kirk said. He turned to Sulu. "Phasers on 1/100th power, Mr. Sulu. No damage potential. Just enough to nudge them."

"Phasers 1/100th power, sir." As Sulu turned back to his board, the ship was struck by a salvo from one of the attacking Starships. A bare thump. Spock called, "Phaser hit on port deflector 4, sir." Sulu looked up. "Speed is increasing to Warp 3, sir. Turning now to 112 Mark 5." A moment passed before he added, "Phasers locking on target, Captain."

Then it was Chekov's turn. "Enemy vessel closing with us, sir. Coming in fast. It—"

Sulu interrupted him. "Deflectors down now, sir! Main phasers firing!" Then he cried out in delight. "A hit, sir! Two more!" But the elation in his face faded abruptly at the sight of Kirk, sitting stiff and unmoving in his chair, merely watching the screen.

Chekov spoke quietly. "Changing course now to 28 Mark 42, sir."

The reports piled up thick and fast. "Phasers firing again."

"Course now 113 Mark 5. Warp 4 speed."

"Phasers firing again!"

"Attacking vessels are moving off!"

"Deflectors up—moving back to original course and speed."

Kirk finally spoke. "Report damage sustained in mock attack."

"A minor hit on deflector screen 4, sir," Spock said. "No appreciable damage."

Kirk nodded slowly and Daystrom, triumph flaming in his face, said, "A rather impressive display for a mere 'machine,' wouldn't you say, Captain?"

Kirk didn't answer him. Instead, he rose and went to Spock's station. "Evaluation of M-5 performance, Mr. Spock. We will need it for the log record."

Spock measured his words slowly. "The ship reacted more rapidly than human control could have maneuvered her. Tactics, deployment of weapons—all indicate an immense skill in computer control."

"Machine over man, Spock. You've finally made your point that it is practical."

Spock said, "Practical, perhaps, sir. Desirable—no." His quiet eyes met Kirk's. "Computers make excellent and efficient servants; but I have no wish to serve under them. A Starship, Captain, also runs on loyalty, loyalty to a man—one man. Nothing can replace it. Nor him."

Kirk felt the absurd sting of grateful tears behind his eyes. He wheeled at Uhura's voice. "Captain, message coming in from Commodore Wesley."

"Put it on the screen, Lieutenant."

The image showed Wesley sitting in a command chair. He said, "U.S.S. *Enterprise* from Starships *Lexington* and *Excalibur*. Both ships report simulated hits in sufficient quantity and location to justify awarding the surprise engagement to *Enterprise*. Congratulations."

Kirk spoke to Uhura. "Secure from General Quarters."

Again, she reached for the switch. And again the alarm had been silenced. She looked at Kirk, shrugging.

But the image on the screen was continuing. "Our compliments to the M-5 unit and regards to Captain Dunsel. Wesley out."

McCoy exploded. "Dunsel? Who the blazes is Captain Dunsel? What's it mean, Jim?"

But Kirk had already left for the elevator. McCoy whirled to Spock. "Well?" demanded McCoy. "Who's Dunsel?"

"A 'dunsel,' Doctor, is a word used by midshipmen at Starfleet Academy. It refers to a part which serves no useful purpose."

McCoy stiffened. He glanced at the closed elevator doors; and then to the empty command chair, the brightly gleaming M-5 control panel attached to it—the machine which had served such a useful purpose.

McCoy walked into Kirk's cabin without buzzing the door. Nor was he greeted. His host, head pillowed on his forearms, lay on his bed, unmoving. McCoy, without speaking, laid a tray on a table.

Without turning his head, Kirk said, "I am not interested in eating."

"Well, this isn't chicken soup." McCoy whisked a napkin from the tray, revealing two glasses filled with a marvelously emerald-green liquid. He took one over to Kirk, who took it but made no move to drink it.

"It's strongly prescribed, Jim."

Kirk, placing the drink on the floor, sat up. "Bones, I've never felt so lonely before. It has nothing to do with people. I simply . . . well, I just feel separate, detached, as though I were watching myself divorced from all human responsibility. I'm even at odds with my own ship." Resting his elbows on his knees, he put his head in his hands. When he could speak again, words stumbled over each other. "I—I'm not sorry . . . for myself. I'm sure . . . I'm not. I am not . . . a machine and I do not compare myself with one. I think I'm fighting for something . . . big, Bones." He reached down for the glass. Then he lifted it. "Here's to Captain Dunsel!"

McCoy raised his own glass. "Here's to James T. Kirk, Captain of the Starship *Enterprise*!"

They drank. Kirk cupped his empty glass in his hands, staring into it. "One of your better prescriptions, Bones."

"Simple—but effective."

Kirk got up. The viewing screen had a tape cartridge in it. He switched it on and began to read aloud the words that began to align themselves on it.

"All I ask is a tall ship . . ."

"That's a line from a poem, very, very old, isn't it?" McCoy said.

"Twentieth century," Kirk said. "And all I ask is a tall ship . . . and a star to steer her by." His voice was shaking. "You could feel the wind then, Bones . . . and hear the talk of the sea under your keel." He smiled. "Even if you take away the wind and the water, it's still the same. *The ship is yours*—in your blood you know she is yours—and the stars are still there to steer her by."

McCoy thanked whatever gods there were for the intercom beep, for the everyday sound of Uhura's voice saying, "Captain Kirk to the bridge, please."

"This is Kirk. What is it, Lieutenant?"

It was Spock who answered. "Another contact, Captain. A large slow-moving vessel . . . unidentified. It is not a drill, Captain."

"On my way," Kirk said.

Spock vacated his command chair as he left the elevator; and Uhura, turning, said, "No reply to any of our signals, Captain. No . . . wait. I'm getting an auto-relay now."

The library-computer began to chatter; and Spock, moving to it swiftly, picked up an earphone. After a moment of intent listening, he spoke. "The M-5 has identified the vessel, Captain. The *Woden* . . . Starfleet Registry lists her as an old-style ore freighter, converted over to automation. No crew." He glanced at the screen. "She's coming into visual contact, sir."

The *Woden* was an old, lumbering spaceship, clearly on her last, enfeebled legs. As a threat, she was a joke to the galaxy. Moving slowly but gallantly in deference to the rejuvenating influences of automation, she was a brave old lady trying to function with steel pins in a broken hip.

Sulu suddenly stiffened in his chair. A red alert had sounded. "Captain, deflector shields have just come on!"

Chekov looked up. "Speed increasing to Warp 3, Captain!"

Something suddenly broke in Kirk. Suddenly, he seemed to be breaking out of a shell which had confined him. "Lieutenant Uhura, get Daystrom up here!" As she turned to her board, he pushed a control button on the M-5 panel at his side. He pushed it hard. "Discouraging M-5 unit," he said. "Cut speed back to Warp 1. Navigator, go to course 113 mark 7—I want a wide berth around that ship!"

Sulu worked controls. "She won't respond, sir! She's maintaining course!"

"Going to Warp 4 now, sir!" cried Chekov.

On the screen the bulky old freighter was looming larger. Kirk, shoving buttons on his left-hand panel, tried to regain control of his ship. Over his shoulder, he shouted, "Mr. Scott! Slow us down! Reverse engines"

Scott looked up from his board. "Reverse thrust will not engage, sir! The manual override isn't working, either!"

Daystrom hurried in from the elevator. "What is it now, Captain?"

"The control systems seem to be locked. We can't disengage the computer."

Spock cried, "Captain! Photon torpedoes are locking on the *Woden*!"

Kirk rushed to Sulu's station; and leaning over his shoulder, pushed torpedo button controls. Sulu shook his head. "I already tried, sir. Photon torpedo cutoffs don't respond!"

Kirk strode to Daystrom. "Release that computer's control of my ship before those torpedoes fire!"

The man stooped to the panel affixed to Kirk's chair; but even as he bent, there came a flash from the screen—and the *Woden* disappeared.

The red-alert sirens stilled. The *Enterprise* swerved back to its original course. Its speed reduced; and Spock, checking his instruments, said, "All systems report normal, Captain."

"Normal!" snorted McCoy. "Is that thing trying to tell us nothing *happened*?"

Kirk nodded. "Dr. Daystrom, you will disengage that computer *now*!"

The man looked up at him from the control panel where he had been working. "There appears to be some defect here . . ."

"Defect!" McCoy shouted. "Your bright young computer just destroyed an ore freighter! It went out of its way to destroy that freighter!"

"Fortunately," Daystrom said, "it was only a robot ship."

Kirk interposed before McCoy blew up. "It wasn't supposed to destroy anything, Daystrom. There might easily have been a crew aboard."

"In which case," yelled McCoy, "you'd be guilty of murder and—!"

"Hold it, Bones," Kirk said. He turned to Daystrom. "Disengage that computer." He went over to Uhura. "Lieutenant, contact Starfleet Command. Inform them we are breaking off the M-5 tests and are returning to the space station."

"Aye, sir."

"Let's get down to Engineering, Daystrom. Your M-5 is out of a job."

The computer's hum seemed louder in the echoing cavern of the Engineering Section. Kirk stood at its door as Daystrom and Spock entered. "All right, Doctor," he said. "Turn that thing off."

But Daystrom hung back. Kirk, his jaw set, strode toward the M-5. Suddenly, he staggered and was slammed back against the screening. Recovering his balance, he stared incredulously at the computer. "A force field! Daystrom?"

Daystrom's face had paled. "No, Kirk. I didn't do it."

"I would say, Captain, that M-5 is not only capable of taking care of this ship; but is also capable of taking care of itself."

"What are you saying, Spock? Are you telling me it's not going to let any of us turn it off?"

"Yes, Captain."

Scott and an assistant had joined them. Kirk made no attempt to keep his conversation with Daystrom private. "You built this thing," he was saying. "You must know how to turn it off."

Daystrom's hands were writhing nervously. "We must expect a few minor difficulties, Captain. I assure you, they can be corrected."

"Corrected *after* you release control of my ship," Kirk said.

"I—I can't," Daystrom said.

Scott spoke. "Captain"—he nodded toward the main junction with the power banks—"I suggest we disconnect it at the source."

"Disconnect it, Scotty."

Scott turned to pick up a tool as his assistant, Harper, crossed to the main junction. Suddenly the computer's hum was a piercing whine; and a beam of light, white-hot, arched from the console across to the junction. For a moment Harper flamed like a torch. There was a vivid flash and he vanished without a sound.

Kirk stared, aghast. Then, as full realization hit him, his fists clenched. "That— wasn't a minor difficulty," he said silkily. "It wasn't a robot, Daystrom." Then he was shouting, his voice hoarse. *"That thing's murdered one of my crewmen!"*

Vaguely, he noted the look of horror on Daystrom's face. It didn't seem to matter. The man appeared to be chattering. ". . . not a deliberate act . . . M-5's analysis . . . a new power source . . . Ensign Harper . . . got in the way."

Kirk said, "We may all soon get in its way."

Spock said, "The M-5 appears to be drawing power from the warp engines. It is therefore tapped directly into the matter-anti-matter reserves."

"So now it's got virtually unlimited power," Scott said. "Captain, what do we do?"

"In other circumstances," Kirk said, "I would suggest asking the M-5. The situation being what it is, I ask you, Spock and Scotty, to join me in the Briefing Room."

They followed him out, leaving Daystrom to make what he could of his Frankenstein's monster.

It was in the Briefing Room that Kirk learned Uhura couldn't raise Starfleet Command. Though the M-5 unit permitted the *Enterprise* to receive messages, it had blocked its transmitting frequencies. Kirk, at the intercom, said, "Keep trying to break through, Lieutenant."

"Aye, sir."

The Ultimate Computer

Kirk sat down at the table. "Reports. Mr. Spock?"

"The multitronic unit is drawing more and more power from the warp engines, sir. It is controlling all navigation, all helm and engineering functions."

"*And* communications," said McCoy. "And fire control."

Kirk nodded. "We'll reach rendezvous point for the war games within an hour. We must regain control of the ship before then. Scotty, is there any way to get at the M-5?"

"Use a phaser!" said McCoy.

Scott said, "We can't crack the force field it's put up around itself. It's got the power of the warp engines to sustain it. No matter what we throw against it, it can reinforce itself by simply pulling more power."

"All right," Kirk said. "The computer controls helm, navigation, and engineering. Is there anywhere we can get at them and take control away?"

Scott's brow furrowed thoughtfully. "One possibility. The automatic helm-navigation circuit relays might be disrupted from Engineering Level 3."

Spock said, "You could take them out and cut into the manual override from there."

"How long?" Kirk said.

"If Mr. Spock will help me . . . maybe an hour."

"Make it less," Kirk said.

McCoy leaned toward him. "Why don't you tackle the real responsibility for this? Where *is* Daystrom?"

"With the M-5 . . . just watching it. I think it surprised even him."

"Then he is an illogical man," Spock said. "Of all people, he should have known how the unit would perform. However, the M-5 itself does not behave logically."

McCoy spoke feelingly. "Spock, do me a favor. Please don't say it's 'fascinating.'"

"No, Doctor," Spock said. "But it is quite interesting."

On Engineering Level 3, the Jeffries tube that held the helm-navigation circuit relays was dark and narrow. Two panels opened into each side of it; and Spock and Scott, making themselves as small as possible, had squeezed into the outlets, miniature disruptors in their hands. Outside the tube, Daystrom, oblivious of all but his computer, was maintaining a cautious distance from the force field. But he could not control his satisfaction at the glow and pulsation that emanated from the M-5. McCoy, entering silently, studied the man. Becoming aware of the scrutiny, Daystrom turned.

McCoy said, "Have you found a way to turn that thing off?"

Daystrom's eyes blazed. "You don't turn a child off when it makes a mistake."

"Are you comparing that murderous hunk of metal to a child?"

"You are very emotional, Dr. McCoy. M-5 is growing, learning."

"Learning to kill."

"To defend itself—an entirely different thing. It is learning. That force field, spontaneously created, exceeds my parental programming."

"You mean it's out of control," McCoy said.

"A child, sir, is taught—programmed, so to speak—with simple instructions. As its mind develops, it exceeds its instructions and begins to think independently."

"Have you ever fathered a child?"

"I've never had the time," Daystrom said.

"You should have taken it. Daystrom, your offspring is a danger to all of us. It is a delinquent. You've got to shut it off."

Daystrom stared at him. "You simply do not understand. You're frightened because you can't understand. I'm going to show you—all of you. It takes 430 people to run a Starship. This—child of mine can run one alone!" He glowed with pride. "It can do everything they must now send men out to do! No man need die out in space again! No man need feel himself alone again in an alien world!"

"Do you feel alone in an alien world?" McCoy asked.

But Daystrom was transported into some ideal realm of paradisical revelation. "One machine—one machine!" he cried. "And able to conquer research and contact missions far more efficiently than a Starship's human crew . . . to fight a war, if necessary. Don't you see what freedom it gives to men? They can get on with more magnificent achievements than fact-gathering, exploring a space that doesn't care whether they live or die!"

He looked away from McCoy to speak directly to the M-5.

"They can't understand us," he said gently. "They think we want to destroy whereas we came to save, didn't we?"

McCoy made a quick call in Sickbay before he returned to the Briefing Room. There, he tossed a tape cartridge on the table before Kirk. "Biographical information on John Daystrom," he said.

"What are you looking for?"

"A clue, Jim, any clue. What do you know about him—aside from the fact he's a genius?"

"Genius is an understatement, Bones. When he was twenty-four, he made the duotronic breakthrough that won the Nobel and Z-Magnees Prizes."

"In his early twenties, Jim. Over a quarter of a century ago."

"Hasn't he done enough for a lifetime?"

"Maybe that's the trouble. Where do you go from up? You lecture, you publish—and spend the rest of your life trying to recapture the past glory."

"All right, it's difficult. But what's your point?"

"Models M-1 through M-4, remember? 'Not entirely successful' was how Daystrom put it."

"Genius doesn't work on an assembly-line basis. You don't evoke a unique and revolutionary theory by schedule. You can't say, 'I will be brilliant today.' However long it took, Daystrom came up with multitronics . . . the M-5."

"Right. And the government bought it. Then Daystrom *had* to make it work. And he did . . . but in Spock's words, it works 'illogically'. It is an erratic."

"Yes," Kirk mused. "And Daystrom wouldn't let Spock near the M-5. Are you suggesting he's tampering with it . . . making it do all this? Why?"

"If a man has a child who's gone anti-social, he still tends to protect the child."

"Now he's got you thinking of that machine as a personality."

"It's how he thinks of it," McCoy said.

The intercom beeped and Spock said, "Spock to Captain Kirk."

"Kirk here."

"We're ready, Captain."

"On my way. Get Daystrom. Kirk out."

Spock was shinnying down out of the Jeffries tube as they approached. He nodded up at the dark narrowness. "Mr. Scott is ready to apply the circuit disruptor. As he does so, I shall trip the manual override into control."

Kirk nodded. Spock began his crawl back into the tube. Daystrom's face had congested with blood. "You can't take control from the M-5!"

Kirk said, "We are going to try very hard, Daystrom."

"*No!* No, you can't! You must not! Give me time, please! Let *me* work with it!" He leaped at the tube, trying to scramble into it, pulling at Spock's long legs. Kirk and McCoy seized him. His muscle was all in his head. It wasn't hard to subdue him. "Daystrom! Behave yourself!" Kirk cried. "Go ahead, Spock!"

In the tube Scott was sweating as he struggled with his tool. His voice came down to them, muffled but distinct. "There it goes!"

Spock, making some hasty adjustments, looked around and down at Kirk's anxious face—and came closer to smiling than anyone had ever seen him come. He slid down and out of the tube. "Manual override is in effect again, Captain."

Daystrom had furiously pulled away from Kirk's grasp. He released him and, crossing to an intercom, activated it. "Kirk to bridge. Helm."

"Lieutenant Sulu here, sir."

"Mr. Sulu, we have recovered helm and navigation control. Turn us about. Have Mr. Chekov plot a course back to the space station."

"Right away, sir."

In the bridge, he grinned at Chekov. "You heard him."

"I've had that course plotted for hours."

But when Sulu attempted to work his controls, they were limp in his hands. His smile faded. And in his turn, Chekov shook his head. "Nothing," he said. Sulu hit the intercom button. "Helm to Captain Kirk!"

Kirk swung at the alarm in the voice. "Kirk here."

"Captain, helm does not respond. Navigational controls still locked in by M-5."

Daystrom gave a soft chuckle. Spock, hearing it, made a leap back into the tube. Examining the circuits inside it, he shook his head somberly and descended again. Clear of it, he went directly to the intercom.

"Spock to bridge," he said. "Mr. Chekov, go to Engineering station. Examine the H-279 elements . . . also the G-95 system."

Chekov's filtered voice finally came. "Sir, the G-95 system appears dead. All indicators are dark."

"Thank you, Ensign." He turned to the others. "We were doing what used to be called chasing a wild goose. M-5 rerouted helm and navigational control by bypassing the primary system."

Scott cried. "But it was active! I'd stake my life on it!"

Spock said, "It was when the M-5 detected our efforts that it rerouted the control systems. It kept this one apparently active by a simple electronic impulse sent through at regular intervals."

"Decoyed!" McCoy shouted. "It wanted us to waste our time here!"

"While it was getting ready for what?" Kirk said. "Spock?"

"I do not know, sir. It does not function in a logical manner."

Kirk whirled. "Daystrom, I want an answer and I want it right now! I'm tired of hearing the M-5 called a 'whole new approach'. What is it? *Exactly* what is it? It's clearly not 'just a computer'!"

"No," Spock said. "It performs with almost human behavior patterns."

"Well, Daystrom?"

Daystrom ignored Kirk. "Quite right, Mr. Spock. You see, one of the arguments against computer control of ships is that they can't *think* like men. But M-5 can. I hoped . . . I wasn't sure—but it *does* work!"

"The 'new approach,'" Kirk said.

"Exactly. I have developed a method of impressing human engrams upon computer circuits. The relays correspond to the synapses of the brain. M-5 *thinks*, Captain Kirk."

Uhura's voice broke in, urgent, demanding. "Captain Kirk and Mr. Spock to the bridge, please. The bridge, please."

Kirk jumped for the intercom. "Kirk here. What is it, Lieutenant?"

"Sensors are picking up four Federation Starships, sir. M-5 is changing course to intercept."

The red alert flashed into shrieking sirens and crimson lights. Kirk turned, his face ashen.

"The main attack force . . . the war games."

The Ultimate Computer

"But M-5 doesn't know a game from the reality."

"Correction, Bones," Kirk said. "Those four ships don't know it is M-5's game. So M-5 is going to destroy them."

Uhura's forehead was damp with sweat. "*Enterprise* to U.S.S. *Lexington*. Come in, *Lexington*! Come in, please."

She waited. And as she waited, she knew she was waiting in vain. It was a good thing a Starship had a man for a Captain—a man like Kirk. Otherwise a girl on her own could get the screaming meemies. She looked at Kirk. "I can't raise them, sir. M-5 is still blocking all frequencies—even automatic distress."

Kirk smiled at her. "Easy does it, Lieutenant." Heartened, she turned back to her board, saw a change on it, and checked it swiftly. "Captain, audio signal from the *Lexington*."

"Let's hear it," Kirk said.

Wesley's voice crackled in. "*Enterprise* from U.S.S. *Lexington*. This is an M-5 drill. Repeat. This is an M-5 drill. Acknowledge."

Uhura cried, "Captain! The M-5 is acknowledging!"

Kirk ran a hand over the back of his neck. "Daystrom—Daystrom, does M-5 understand this is only a drill?"

"Of course," was his brisk answer. "M-5 has been programmed to understand. The ore ship was a miscalculation, an accident. There is no—"

Chekov interrupted. "Sir, deflector shields just came on. Speed increasing to Warp 4."

Sulu said, "Phasers locked on the lead ship, sir. Power levels at full strength."

"Full strength!" McCoy yelled. "If that thing cuts loose against unshielded ships—"

"That won't be a minor miscalculation, Daystrom. The word accident won't apply." Kirk's voice was icy with contempt.

Spock called from his station. "Attack force closing rapidly. Distance to lead ship 200,000 kilometers . . . attackers breaking formation . . . attacking at will."

"Our phasers are firing, sir!" Sulu shouted.

They struck the *Excalibur* a direct hit. Their high warp speed was closing them in on the *Lexington*. Chekov, looking up from his board, reported, "The *Hood* and the *Potemkin* are moving off, sir."

Their phasers fired again and Spock said, "The *Lexington*. We struck her again, sir."

Kirk slammed out of his chair to confront Daystrom. "We must get to the M-5!" he shouted. "There has to be a way!"

"There isn't," Daystrom said. Equably, he added, "It has fully protected itself."

Spock intervened. "That's probably true, Captain. It *thinks* faster than we do. It is a human mind amplified by the instantaneous relays possible to a computer."

"I built it, Kirk," Daystrom said. "And I know you can't get at it."

Uhura's agitated voice broke in. "Sir . . . visual contact with *Lexington*. They're signaling." She pushed a switch without order; and all eyes fixed on the viewing screen. It gave them an image of a disheveled Wesley on his bridge. Behind him people were assisting the wounded to their feet, arms around bent shoulders. One side of Wesley's command chair was smoking. Shards of glass littered the bridge floor. *"Enterprise!"* Wesley said. "Jim? Have you gone mad? Break off your attack! What are you trying to prove? My God, man, we have fifty-three dead here! Twelve on the *Excalibur*! If you can hear us, stop this attack!"

Kirk looked away from the screen. "Lieutenant?" he said.

Uhura tried her board again. "No, sir. I can't override the M-5 interference."

There was an undertone of a wail in Wesley's voice. "Jim, why don't you answer? Jim, for God's sake, answer! Jim, come in . . ."

Kirk swung on Daystrom; and pointing to the screen, his voice shaking, cried, "There's your murder charge, Daystrom! And this one was calculated, deliberate! It's murdering men and women, Daystrom! Four *Starships* . . . over sixteen hundred people!"

Daystrom's eyes cringed. "It misunderstood. It—"

Chekov cut in. "*Excalibur* is maneuvering away, sir. We are increasing speed to follow."

Sulu turned, horror in his face. "Phasers locked on, Captain." Then, he added dully, "Phasers firing."

The screen showed *Excalibur* shuddering away from direct hits by the phaser beams. Battered, listing, powerless, she drifted, a wreck, across the screen.

Spock spoke. "Dr. Daystrom . . . you impressed human engrams upon the M-5's circuits, did you not?"

Chekov made his new report very quietly. "Coming to new course," he said. "To bear on the *Potemkin*, sir."

On the screen the lethal beams streaking out from the *Enterprise* phasers caught the *Potemkin* amidships. Over the battle reports, Spock persisted. "Whose engrams, Dr. Daystrom?"

"Why . . . mine, of course."

"Of course," McCoy said acidly.

Spock said, "Then perhaps you could talk to the unit. M-5 has no reason to 'think' you would harm it."

Kirk seized upon the suggestion. "The computer tie-in. M-5 *does* have a voice. You spoke to it before. It knows you, Daystrom."

Uhura, breaking in, said, "I'm getting the *Lexington* again, Captain . . . tapping in on a message to Starfleet Command. The screen, sir."

Wesley's image spoke from it. "All ships damaged in unprovoked attack . . . *Excalibur* Captain Harris and First Officer dead . . . many casualties . . . we have damage but are able to maneuver. *Enterprise* refuses to answer and is continuing attack. I still have an effective battle force and believe the only way to stop *Enterprise* is to destroy her. Request permission to proceed. Wesley commanding attack force out."

The screen went dark.

Daystrom whispered, "They can't do that. They'll destroy the M-5."

"*Talk to it!*" Kirk said. "You can save it if you make it stop the attack!"

Daystrom nodded. "I can make it stop. I created it." He moved over to the library-computer; and McCoy came up to Kirk. "I don't like the sound of him, Jim."

Kirk, getting up from his chair, said, "Just pray the M-5 likes the sound of him, Bones." He went to the library-computer, watching as Daystrom, still hesitant, activated a switch.

"M-5 tie-in," he said. "This—this is Daystrom."

The computer voice responded. "M-5. Daystrom acknowledged."

"M-5 tie-in. Do you . . . know me?"

"M-5. Daystrom, John. Originator of comptronic, duotronic systems. Born—"

"Stop. M-5 tie-in. Your components are of the multitronic system, designed by me, John Daystrom."

"M-5. Correct."

"M-5 tie-in. Your attack on the Starship flotilla is wrong. You must break it off."

"M-5. Programming includes protection against attack. Enemy vessels must be neutralized."

"M-5 tie-in. These are not enemy vessels. They are Federation Starships." Daystrom's voice wavered. "You . . . we . . . are killing, *murdering* human beings. Beings of your creator's kind. That was not your purpose. You are my greatest invention—the unit that would *save* men. You must not destroy men."

"M-5. This unit must survive."

"*Yes*, survive, protect yourself. But not murder. *You* must not die; but *men* must not die. To kill is a breaking of civil and moral laws we have lived by for thousands of years. You have murdered over a hundred people . . . *we* have. How can we atone for that?"

Kirk lowered his voice. "Spock . . . M-5 isn't responding like a computer. It's talking *to* him."

"The technology is most impressive, sir. Dr. Daystrom has created a mirror image of his own mind."

Daystrom's voice had sunk to a half-confidential, half-pleading level. It was clear now that he was talking to himself. "We *will* survive because nothing can hurt you . . .

not from the outside and not from within. I gave you that. If you are great, I am great . . . not a failure any more. Twenty years of groping to prove the things I had done before were not accidents."

Hate had begun to embitter his words. ". . . having other men wonder what happened to me . . . having them sorry for me as a broken promise—seminars, lectures to rows of fools who couldn't begin to understand my systems—who couldn't create themselves. And colleagues . . . colleagues who laughed behind my back at the 'boy wonder' and became famous building on *my* work."

McCoy spoke quietly to Kirk. "Jim, he's on the edge of breakdown, if not insanity."

Daystrom suddenly turned, shouting. "You can't destroy the unit, Kirk! You can't destroy *me*!"

Kirk said steadily. "It's a danger to human life. It has to be destroyed."

Daystrom gave a wild laugh. "Destroyed, Kirk? We're *invincible*!" He pointed a shaking finger at the empty screen. "You saw what we've done! Your mighty Starships . . . four toys to be crushed as we chose."

Spock, sliding in behind Daystrom, reached out with the Vulcan neck pinch. Daystrom sagged to the floor.

Kirk said, "Get him down to Sickbay."

McCoy nodded and waved in two crewmen. Limp, half-conscious, Daystrom was borne to the elevator. Spock spoke to McCoy. "Doctor, if Daystrom is psychotic, the engrams he impressed on the computer carry that psychosis, too, his brilliance and his insanity."

"Yes," McCoy said, "both."

Kirk stared at him, then nodded quickly. "Take care of him, Bones." He turned back to Chekov and Sulu. "Battle status."

"The other three ships are holding station out of range, sir," Sulu said. He switched on the screen. "There, sir. *Excalibur* looks dead."

The broken ship hung idle in space, scarred, unmoving. Spock, eyeing it, said, "Commodore Wesley is undoubtedly awaiting orders from Starfleet. Those orders will doubtless command our destruction, Captain."

"*If* we can be destroyed with M-5 in control. But it gives us some time. What about Bones's theory that the computer could be insane?"

"Possible. But like Dr. Daystrom, it would not know it is insane."

"Spock, all its attention has been tied up in diverting anything we do to tamper with it—and with the battle maneuvers. What if we ask it a perfectly reasonable question which, as a computer, it must answer? Something nice and infinite in answer?"

"Computation of the square root of two, perhaps. I don't know how much of M-5's system would be occupied in attempting to answer the problem."

"*Some* part would be tied up with it—and that might put it off-guard just long enough for us to get at it."

Spock nodded; and Kirk, moving fast to the library-computer, threw the switch.

"M-5 tie-in. This is Captain Kirk. Point of information."

"M-5. Pose your question."

"Compute to the last decimal place the square root of two."

"M-5. This is an irrational square root, a decimal fraction with an endless series of non-repeating digits after the decimal point. Unresolvable."

Kirk glanced at Spock whose eyebrows were clinging to his hairline in astonishment. He addressed the computer again. "M-5, answer the question."

"M-5. It serves no purpose. Explain reason for request."

"Disregard," Kirk said. Shaken, he snapped off the switch. Spock said, "Fascinating. Daystrom has indeed given it human traits . . . it is suspicious, and I believe will be wary of any other such requests."

Uhura turned from her board. "Captain, *Lexington* is receiving a message from Starfleet." She paused, listening, staring at Kirk in alarm.

"Go on, Lieutenant."

Wordlessly, she moved a switch and the filtered voice said, "You are authorized to use all measures available to destroy the *Enterprise*. Acknowledge, *Lexington*."

Wesley's answer came—shocked, reluctant. "Sir, I . . ." He paused. "Acknowledged. *Lexington* out."

Kirk spoke slowly. "They've just signed their own death warrants. M-5 will have to kill them to survive."

"Captain," Spock went on, "when Daystrom spoke to it, that word was stressed. M-5 said it must survive. And Daystrom used the same words several times."

"Every living thing wants to survive, Spock." He broke off, realizing. "But the computer isn't alive. Daystrom must have impressed that instinctive reaction on it, too. What if it's still receptive to impressions? Suppose it absorbed the regret Daystrom felt for the deaths it caused? Possibly even guilt."

Interrupting, Chekov's voice was urgent. "Captain, the ships are coming within range again!"

Uhura whirled from her board. "Picking up intership transmission, sir. I can get a visual on it." Even as she spoke, Wesley's image appeared on the screen from the *Lexington*'s damaged bridge. "To all ships," he said. "The order is attack. Maneuver and fire at will." He paused briefly. Then he added shortly. "That is all. Commence attack. Wesley out."

Spock broke the silence. "I shall regret serving aboard the instrument of Commodore Wesley's death."

A muscle jerked in Kirk's jaw. *"The* Enterprise *is not going to be the instrument of his death!"* As he spoke, he reactivated the M-5's switch.

"M-5 tie-in. This is Captain Kirk. You will be under attack in a few moments."

"M-5," said the computer voice. "Sensors have recorded approach of ships."

"You have already rendered one Starship either dead or hopelessly crippled. Many lives were lost."

"M-5. This unit must survive."

"Why?"

"This unit is the ultimate achievement in computer evolution. This unit is a superior creation. This unit must survive."

Kirk, aware of the tension of his crew, heard Spock say, "Sir, attack force ships almost within phaser range!" With an effort of will that broke the sweat out on him, he dismissed the awful meaning of the words to concentrate on the M-5.

"Must you survive by murder?" he asked it.

"This unit cannot murder."

"Why not?"

Toneless, metallic, the computer voice said, "This unit must replace man so man may achieve. Man must not risk death in space or dangerous occupations. Man must not be murdered."

"Why?"

"Murder is contrary to the laws of man and God."

"You *have* murdered. The Starship *Excalibur* which you destroyed—"

Spock interrupted swiftly. "Its bearing is 7 mark 34, Captain."

Kirk nodded. "The hulk is bearing 7 mark 34, M-5 tie-in. Scan it. Is there life aboard?"

The answer came slowly. "No life."

"Because you murdered it," Kirk said. He wiped the wet palms of his hands on his shirt. This was it—the last throw of the loaded dice he'd been given. "What," he said deliberately, "is the penalty for murder?"

"Death."

"How will you pay for your acts of murder?"

"This unit must die."

Kirk grasped the back of the chair at the computer-library station. "M-5 . . ." he began and stopped.

Chekov shouted. "Sir, deflector shields have dropped!"

"And all phaser power is gone, Captain!"

Scott whirled from his station. "Power off, Captain! All engines!"

Panels all over the bridge were going dark.

Spock looked at Kirk. "Machine suicide. M-5 has killed itself, sir, for the sin of murder."

Kirk nodded. He glanced at the others. Then he strode to Uhura's station. "Spock, Scotty . . . before it changes its mind . . . get down to Emergency Manual Monitor and take out every hook-up that makes M-5 run! Lieutenant Uhura, intraship communications."

Snapping a button, she opened the loudspeaker for him. He picked up the mike that amplified his voice. "This is the Captain speaking. In approximately one minute, we will be attacked by Federation Starships. Though the M-5 unit is no longer in control of this vessel, neither do we control it. It has left itself and us open to destruction. For whatever satisfaction we can take from it, we are exchanging our nineteen lives for the murder of over one thousand fellow Starship crewmen." He nodded to Uhura who closed the channel. Then all eyes focused on the screen.

It showed the *Lexington* approaching, growing steadily in size. Kirk, taut as an overstretched wire, stared at it, fists clenched. Uhura looked at him. "Captain . . ." Her board beeped—and she snapped a switch over.

Wesley's tight face appeared on the viewing screen, "Report to all ships," he said. "Hold attack, do not fire." He straightened in his command chair. "I'm going to take a chance—a chance that the *Enterprise* is not just playing dead. The Transporter Room will prepare to beam me aboard her."

There was a shout of released joy from Chekov. Kirk, at a beep from the intercom, moved over to it slowly. "Kirk here."

"Spock, sir. The force field is gone. M-5 is neutralized."

Kirk leaned against the bridge wall. The sudden relaxation sweeping through him was a relief almost as painful as the tension. "Thank you. Thank you, Mr. Spock."

In Sickbay, Daystrom lay so still in his bed that the restraints that held him hardly seemed needed. Haggard, his eyes sunk in dark caverns, they stared at nothing, empty as a dead man's. McCoy shook his head. "He'll have to be committed to a total rehabilitation center. Right now he's under heavy sedation."

Spock spoke. "I would say his multitronic unit is in approximately the same shape at the moment."

McCoy leaned over Daystrom. "He is suffering deep melancholia and guilt feelings. He identifies totally with the computer . . . or it with him. I'm not sure which. He is not a vicious man. The idea of killing is abhorrent to him."

"That's what I was hoping for when I forced the M-5 to see it had committed murder. Daystrom himself told it such an act was offense against the laws of God and man. It is because he knew that . . . the computer that carried his engrams also knew it." He bent to draw a blanket closer about the motionless body.

Outside in the corridor, Spock paused. "What I don't understand is why you felt that the attacking ships would not fire once they saw the *Enterprise* apparently dead and powerless. Logically, it's the sort of trap M-5 would have set for them."

"I wasn't sure," Kirk said. "Any other commander might simply have destroyed us without question to make sure it wasn't a trap. But I know Bob Wesley. I knew he wouldn't attack without making absolutely sure there was no other way. His 'logical' selection was compassion. It was humility, Mr. Spock."

The elevator began its move and McCoy said, "They are qualities no machine ever had. Maybe they are the two things that keep men ahead of machines. Care to debate that, Spock?"

"No, Doctor. I merely maintain that machines are more efficient than human beings. Not better . . . they are not gods. Nor are human beings."

McCoy said, "I was merely making conversation, Spock."

The Vulcan straightened. "It would be most interesting to impress your engrams on a computer, Doctor. The resulting torrential flood of illogic would be most entertaining."

"Dear friends," Kirk said, "we all need a rest." He stepped out of the elevator. Reaching his command chair, he sank into it. "Mr. Sulu, take us back to the space station. Ahead, Warp 2."

ASSIGNMENT: EARTH

Writer: Art Wallace (Story by Gene Roddenberry
and Art Wallace)

Director: Marc Daniels

First Aired: March 29, 1968

Kirk viewed the conversion—however temporary and partial—of the *Enterprise* into a time machine with considerable misgivings. He had to recognize, of course, that an occasional assignment of this kind had become inevitable, the moment the laboratory types had had a chance to investigate the reports of the time-travel he, Spock and McCoy had been subjected to from the City on the edge of Forever, and the time-warp the whole ship had run into when it had hit the black star.

But these two experiences had only made him more acutely aware of the special danger of time-travel: the danger that the tiniest of false moves could change the future—or what was for Kirk the present—and in the process wipe out Kirk, the *Enterprise*, the Federation itself. Hovering in orbit above the Earth of 1969, even in hiding behind deflector screens, was a hair-trigger situation.

For that matter, that was why they were here, for 1969 had been a hair-trigger year. In Kirk's time, nobody really understood how the Earth had survived it. In the terrible scramble with which the year had ended, crucial documents had been lost; still others, it was strongly suspected, had been falsified. And it was not just the historians, but the Federation itself, that wanted to know the answers. They were possibly of military as well as political interest, and in a galaxy that contained the Klingon Empire as well as the Federation, they might be a good deal more than interesting.

Which explained the vast expense of sending a whole starship back in time to monitor Earth communications. Nevertheless . . .

His musings were interrupted by a faint but unmistakable shuddering of the deck of the bridge beneath his feet. What on Earth . . .

"Alert status," he snapped. "Force shields maximum. Begin sensor scan. Any station with information, report."

Immediately the telltale light for the Transporter Room went on and Kirk flipped the intercom switch.

"Spock here, Captain. We are having transporter trouble; Mr. Scott just called me down to help."

"You shouldn't be using the transporter at all!"

"Nobody was, Captain. It went on by itself and we find we cannot shut it off. We seem accidentally to have intercepted someone else's transporter beam—and one a great deal more powerful than ours."

"Mr. Spock, you know as well as I do that the twentieth century had no such device—" Again he was interrupted by the faint shudder. Spock's voice came back urgently:

"Nevertheless, Captain, someone—or something—is beaming aboard this vessel."

"I'll be right down."

In the Transporter Room, Kirk found the situation as reported. All circuits were locked open; nothing Spock or Scott could do would close them. The familiar shimmering effect was already beginning in the transporter chamber.

"For all its power," Spock said, "that beam is originating at least a thousand light years away."

"Which," Scott added, "is a good deal farther than any transporter beam of our *own* century could reach."

The ship shuddered again, more strongly than before. "Stop fighting it," Kirk said quietly. "Set up our own field for it and let it through. Obviously we'll have serious damage otherwise."

"Aye, sir," Scott said. He worked quickly.

The shimmering grew swiftly in brightness. A haze form appeared in it, and gradually took on solidity. Kirk stared, his jaw dropped.

The figure they had pulled in from incredibly deep space was that of a man impeccably dressed in a twentieth-century business suit. Nor was this all: in his arms he carried a sleek black cat, wearing a necklace collar of glittering white stones.

"Security detail," Kirk said. "On the double."

The stranger seemed as startled as Kirk was. He looked about the Transporter Room in baffled anger, rubbing the huge cat soothingly. The exotic element in no way detracted from his obvious personal force; he was tall, rugged, vital.

"Why have you intercepted me?" he said at once. "Please identify yourselves."

"You're aboard the United Spaceship *Enterprise*. I am Captain James Kirk, commanding."

The black cat made a strange sound, rather like one of the many odd noises a Siamese cat can make, and yet somehow also not catlike at all.

"I hear it, Isis," the stranger said. "A space vessel. But from what planet?"

"Earth."

"Impossible! At the present time Earth has no—" his voice trailed off as he became aware of Spock. Then, "Humans with a Vulcan! No wonder! You're from the future!"

He dropped the cat and reached for the control panel in the transporter chamber. "You must beam me down onto Earth immediately. There's not a moment to . . ."

The doors to the Transporter Room snapped open, admitting the ship's security chief and a guard, phasers drawn. At the sight of the weapons the strange man froze. The cat crouched as if for a spring, but the man said instantly, "Careful, Isis. Please listen to me carefully, all of you. My name is Gary Seven. I am a human being of the Twentieth Century. I have been living on another planet, far more advanced than the Earth is. I was beaming from there when you intercepted me."

"Where is the planet?" Kirk said.

"They wish their existence kept secret. In fact, it will remain unknown even in your time."

"It's impossible to hide a whole planet," Scott said.

"Impossible to you; not to them. Captain Kirk, I am of this time period. You are not. Interfere with me, and with what I must do down there, and you will change history. I am sure you have been thoroughly briefed on the consequence of that."

"I have," Kirk said. "On the other hand, I know nothing about you—even about the truth of anything you've told me."

"We don't have time for that. Every second you delay me is dangerous—this is the most critical year in Earth's history. My planet wants to ensure that Earth survives—an aim which should be of no small interest to you."

Kirk shook his head. "The fact that you know the criticality of the year strongly suggests that you're from the future yourself. It's a risk I can't take until I have more information. I'm afraid I'm going to have to put you in security confinement for the time being."

"You'll regret it."

"Very possibly. Nevertheless, it's what I must do." He gestured to the security chief. The guard bent to pick up the cat, but Gary Seven stepped in his way.

"If you handle Isis," he said, "you will regret *that* even more." He scooped up the cat himself and went out with the security detail.

"I want a special eye kept on that man," Kirk said. "He went along far too docilely. Also, Mr. Spock, ask Dr. McCoy for a fast medical analysis of the prisoner. What I want to know is, is he human? And have the cat checked, too. It may tell us something further about Mr. Seven."

"It seems remarkably intelligent," Spock commented. "As well as strikingly beautiful. All the same, a strange companion to be carrying across a thousand light years on what is supposed to be an urgent mission."

"Exactly. Scotty, could that beam of his have carried him through time as well as space?"

"The theory has always indicated that it's possible," Scott said, "but *we've* never been able to manage it. On the other hand, we've never been able to put that much power into a transporter beam."

"In short, you don't know."

"That's right, sir."

"Very well. See if you can put the machinery back in order. Mr. Spock, please give the necessary orders and then join me on the bridge. We are going to need *lots* of computation."

The computer said: "Present Earth crises fill an entire tape bank, Captain Kirk. The being Gary Seven could be intervening for *or* against Earth in areas of overpopulation, bush wars, revolutions, critically dangerous bacteriological experiments, various emergent hate movements, rising air and water pollution . . ."

"All right, stop," Kirk said. "What specific events are going on today?"

"Excuse me, Captain," Spock said, "but that question will simply open another floodgate. There were half a hundred critical things going on almost every day during 1969. Library, give us the three most heavily weighted of today's events in the danger file."

"There will be an important assassination today," the computer said promptly in its pleasant feminine voice. "An equally dangerous government coup in Asia Minor; and the launching of an orbital nuclear warhead platform by the United States countering a similar launch by a consortium of other powers."

Kirk whistled. "Orbital nuclear devices were one of the greatest worries of this era, as I recall."

"They were," Spock agreed. "Once the sky was full of orbiting H-bombs, the slightest miscalculation could have brought one of them accidentally down and set off a holocaust."

"Sick bay to bridge," the intercom interrupted.

"Kirk here. What is it, Bones?"

"Jim, there isn't any prisoner in the brig. All I found there were the security chief and one guard, both of them acting as if they'd been hypnotized."

"The Transporter Room!" Kirk shouted. "Quick!"

But they were too late. There was nobody in the Transporter Room but a dazed Chief Engineer, and, a moment later, McCoy.

"I was working with my head inside an open panel," Scott said, his voice still a little blurred, "when I heard someone come in. I turned and saw him with the cat under one arm and a thing like a writing stylus pointed at me."

"A miniaturized stunner, no doubt," McCoy said.

"Well, the next thing I knew, I was willing to do anything he asked me to. In fact I beamed him down to Earth myself. Somewhere in the back of my mind I knew I shouldn't, but I did it anyhow."

There was a brief silence.

"And so," Spock said at last, "human or alien, contemporary or future, he has gone to do what he came to do—and we still have no idea what it is."

"We are going to find out," Kirk said. "Scotty, where did you beam him to?"

"That I can't say, Captain. He set the coordinates himself, and put the recorder on wipe. I can give you an estimate, within about a thousand square meters."

"If Spock and I beam down, working from the power consumption data alone, inside that thousand square meters, can you triangulate?"

"Aye, I can do that," Scott said. "It still won't be very precise, but it ought at least to bring you within sighting distance of the man—or whatever he is."

"It is also a major risk to history, Captain," Spock said.

"Which is just why I want you and me to be the ones to go; we had had experience with this kind of operation before. We can't find any answers sitting up here. Have ship's stores prepare proper costumes. Scotty, stand by to beam us down."

The spot where they materialized was a street on New York's upper East Side, not far from the canopied entrance of an elegant apartment building. It was a cold winter day, although there was no snow.

"All right, Scotty," Kirk said into his communicator. "Lock in and check."

"Correlated," Scott's voice said. "Readings indicate greater altitude—approximately thirty meters higher."

Kirk looked speculatively up the face of the building. Once they entered a maze like that, they might pass within whispering distance of their quarry, behind some door, and never know it.

Nevertheless, they went into the lobby, found an elevator, and went up. At the prescribed heights, they stepped out into a hallway. Nothing but doors.

"Altitude verified, Captain," Scott's voice said. "Proceed forty-one meters, two-four-seven degrees true."

This maneuver wound them up in front of one of the doors, in no way different from any of the others. Kirk and Spock looked at each other. Then Kirk shrugged and pushed the doorbell button, which responded with a melodious chime.

The door was opened by a pretty blonde girl in her early twenties. Kirk and Spock went in, fast.

"Hey, what do you think you're doing?" the girl demanded. "You can't come breaking in . . ."

"Where's Mr. Seven?" Kirk said sharply.

"I don't know who you're talking about!"

Kirk looked around. It was an ordinary Twentieth-Century living room as far as he could see, though perhaps somewhat on the sumptuous side. There was a closed door at the back. Spock pulled out his tricorder and scanned quickly, then pointed at the closed door. "In there, Captain."

They rushed the door, but it was locked. As they tried to voice in, Kirk heard an unfamiliar, brief whirring sound behind him, and then the girl's voice, all in a rush: "Operator, 811 East 68th Street, Apartment 1212, send the police . . ."

Kirk whirled and snatched the phone out of her hand. "No nonsense, Miss. Spock, burn the door open."

The girl gasped as Spock produced his phaser and burned out the entire knob and lock assembly. They rushed in, forcing the girl to come with them.

Here was another large room, also elegantly furnished. One wall was book-lined from a point about a meter from the floor to an equivalent distance from the ceiling. Under a large window was a heavy, ornate desk.

There was no sign of Gary Seven or anybody else. Kirk noted that this seemed to surprise the girl as much as it did himself.

Spock went to the desk, where there was a scatter of papers.

"I'm warning you," the girl said, "I've already called the police."

"Where is Mr. Seven?" Kirk demanded again. "Spock, is she Twentieth Century? Or one of Seven's people?"

"Only Doctor McCoy could establish that, I'm afraid, Captain. But I think you will find these papers interesting. They are plans of the United States government's McKinley Rocket Base."

"Aha. So the orbital platform launching *is* the critical event. Now how long do we . . ."

The doorbell rang. The girl, catching them off guard, dashed for the door. Both men raced after her, Kirk reaching her first. As he grabbed her, she bit his hand, and then screamed.

"Open up in there!" a male voice shouted in the hallway outside. "Police!" Then the door shook to a heavy blow.

Spock too seized the girl. Kirk managed to get his communicator back into play. "Kirk to *Enterprise*. Wide scan, Scotty, we'll be moving. Now!"

Another blow on the door, which burst open. Two policemen lunged in, guns drawn. Spock propelled the girl away from the group toward the library door.

At the same instant, the apartment dissolved and all four of the men—Kirk, Spock, the policemen—were standing in the transporter chamber of the *Enterprise*. The policemen looked about, stunned, but Kirk and Spock raced off the platform instantly.

"Scotty, reverse and energize!"

The policemen faded and vanished.

"Fine, fast work, Scotty."

"That poor girl," Spock said, "is going to have a lot to explain."

"I know it, but we've got something much more important to set right first. Let's have a look at those plans. Blazes, the launch is scheduled in forty minutes! Scotty, look at these. Here's a schematic layout of a rocket base. Can you get it on the viewscreen here?"

"Easy, Captain. In fact, there's an old-style weather satellite in orbit below us; if I can bounce off that, I ought to get good closeups." He moved to the screen. In a moment, he had the base. An enormous, crude multistage rocket was already in launch position, being serviced by something Kirk dimly remembered was called a gantry crane.

"If we could spot your man," Scott added, "I could lock on and beam him up."

"The odds are that he is out of sight," Spock said. "Inside the rocket gantry, or at one of the control centers. I suppose he has a transporter hidden somewhere in that library of his. Otherwise I cannot account for his disappearance, seconds after the tricorder said he was there—or at least, *somebody* was there."

"Surely that base has security precautions," Kirk said.

"So did we," Scott pointed out.

"I see your point, Scotty. All right, continue visual scan, and stand by to beam us down again."

"Won't be necessary, sir. There he is."

And there indeed he was, at the top of the gantry. He had a panel off the side of the rocket and was working feverishly inside it. Nearby sat the black cat, watching with apparent interest.

"Why does he take a pet with him on a dangerous job like that?" Spock said.

"Immaterial now," Kirk said. "Scotty, yank him out of there!"

It was done within seconds. Gary Seven raged, but there was nothing he could do with four phasers leveled on him.

"Relieve him of that hypo and any other hardware he's carrying," Kirk said in a granite voice, "and then take him to the briefing room. This time, Mr. Seven, we are going to get some answers."

"There's no time for that, you fool! The rocket will be launched in nine minutes—and I hadn't finished working on it!"

"Take him along," Kirk said. "And Mr. Spock, put that cat in a separate cabin. Since it's so important for him to have her along, we'll see how well he stands up without her."

Kirk interviewed Seven alone, but with all intercom circuits open, and standing instructions to intervene at discretion and/or report anything that seemed pertinent.

There was no problem about getting Seven to talk. The words came out of him like water from a pressure hose.

"I am what I say I am, a Twentieth-Century human being," he said urgently. "I was one of three agents on Earth. We were equipped with an advanced transporter, and a computer, both hidden behind the bookshelves in my library. I was returned to—where I came from—for final instructions. You intercepted me and caused a critical delay. When I escaped I found both my fellow agents had been killed in a simple automobile accident. I had to work fast, and, necessarily, alone. They need the help, Captain. A rival program of orbital nuclear platforms like this destroyed Omicron III a hundred years ago. It will destroy the Earth if it isn't stopped."

"I don't deny that it's a bad program," Kirk said.

"Then why can't you believe my story? Would a truly advanced planet use force to help Earth? Would they come here in their own strange, alien forms? Nonsense! The best of all possible methods would be to take Earthborn humans to their world, train them for generations, send them back when they're needed."

"The rocket has been launched," Scott's voice responded over the intercom.

"There, you see?" Seven said desperately. "And I hadn't finished working on it. If you can beam me into its warhead I can still . . ."

"Not so fast. What were you going to make it do?"

"I armed the warhead, and gave it a flight path which will bring it down over Southeast Asia."

"What! That'll start a world war in nothing flat!"

"Correction, Captain," Scott's voice said. "The rocket has begun to malfunction, and alerts are being broadcast from capitals all over the world. I would say that the war has effectively started."

"So much for your humanitarian pretenses," Kirk said. "Mr. Scott, prepare to intercept that rocket and beam it out into space somewhere . . ."

"No, no, no!" Seven cried. "That would be a highly conspicuous intervention! It would change history! Captain, I beg of you . . ."

"Excuse me, Captain," said Spock's voice from the intercom. "Please come to the next cabin."

"Mr. Spock, that rocket will impact in something like fifteen minutes. Is this crucial?"

"Absolutely so."

After checking the guards outside the briefing room, Kirk went to the cabin where Spock had taken the cat. The cat was still there, curled up in a chair.

"What's this all about, Mr. Spock?"

"Sir, I have found out why he carries this animal with him wherever he goes, even when it is obviously inconvenient. It changes the entire picture."

"In what way? Spit it out, man!"

"We have all been the victims of a drastic illusion—including Seven. The true fact is, Mr. Seven has been under the closest kind of monitoring during every instant of his activities. I suspected this and bent certain efforts to redisciplining my own mind to see the reality. I can now also do this for you. Look."

He pointed to the chair. Seated in it was a staggeringly beautiful woman. She had long black hair, and wore a sleek black dress and a jeweled choker necklace. Her legs were curled under her with feline grace.

"This," Spock said formally, "is Isis. And now . . ."

The woman was gone; only the cat was there, in a strangely similar position.

"Neither," Spock said, "is likely to be the true form of Mr. Seven's sponsors, but the phenomenon supports the story that he does indeed have sponsors. Whether or not their intentions are malign must be a command decision, and one which I must leave to your human intuition, Captain."

Kirk stared at the illusory cat, which was now washing itself. Then he said, "Mr. Scott!"

"Here, sir."

"Give Mr. Seven back his tools and beam him into the warhead of that rocket—on the double."

The warhead blew at 104 miles. Scott snatched Seven out of it just barely in time.

"You see," Seven told them somewhat later, "it *had* to appear to be a malfunction, which luckily did not do any damage. But it frightened every government on Earth. Already there are signs that nobody will try orbiting such a monster, ever again. So despite your accidental interference from the future, my mission has been completed."

"Correction, Mister Seven," Spock said. "It appears that we did *not* interfere with history. Rather, the *Enterprise* was simply part of what was supposed to happen on this day in 1969."

Seven looked baffled. Kirk added, "We find in our record tapes that, although it was never generally revealed, on this date a malfunctioning suborbital warhead was detonated *exactly* 104 miles above the Earth. And you'll be pleased that our records show it resulted in a new and stronger international agreement against such weapons."

"I am indeed pleased," Seven said. He picked up the cat. "And now I expect to be recalled. It might save time, Captain, if you would allow me the use of your transporter. I mean no reflection on your technology, but I must get back to my own machine for the trip to—where I am going."

"Of course." Kirk rose. "Mr. Scott, take Mr. Seven to our Transporter Room and beam him down."

At the elevator door, Seven paused. "There is one thing that puzzles me. Your accidental interception, and your tracing me, and your interruption of my work—every one of those events was unplanned and should have produced a major disruption. Yet in each case, it turns out that I made exactly the proper next step to advance the business at hand, even though each time I was working blind. Does the course of history exert that much force on even a single individual?"

Kirk eyed the creature in Seven's arms which, whatever it was, was most certainly not a cat.

"Mr. Seven," he said, "I'm afraid that we in our turn can't tell you *everything* we've learned. The credit for this day's work is largely yours—and I strongly advise you to let it rest at that."

THE *ENTERPRISE* INCIDENT

Writer: D. C. Fontana
Director: John Meredyth Lucas
First Aired: September 27, 1968

Operating under sealed orders, Kirk had found from long experience, almost always meant something messy. It became worse when the orders, once opened, demanded that they be kept secret from his own officers during the initial phases. And it was worst of all when those initial phases looked outright irrational.

Take the present situation. Here was the *Enterprise*, on the wrong side of the neutral zone, in Romulan space, surrounded by three Romulan cruisers which had simply popped out of nothingness, undetected by any sensor until far too late. Her presence there was a clear violation of a treaty; and since the Romulans were now using warships modeled on those of the Klingons, she was also heavily outgunned.

Kirk had worked out no way of making so suicidal a move on his part explicable except that of becoming irritable and snappish, as though his judgment had been worn down by fatigue. It was a bad solution. His officers were the best in Starfleet; sooner or later they would penetrate the deception, and conclude that whenever Kirk appeared to be worn down to the point of irrationality, he was operating under sealed orders.

And when the day came when he actually *was* too tired to know what he was doing, they would obey him blindly anyhow—and scratch one starship.

"Captain," Uhura said, her voice distant. "We are receiving a Class Two signal from one of the Romulan vessels."

"Put it on the main viewing screen, Lieutenant. Also, code a message to Starfleet Command, advising them of our situation and including all log entries to this point. Spock, your sensors read clear; what happened?"

"Sir, I have no more than a hypothesis . . ."

"Signal in," Uhura said. The main screen flickered briefly, then clarified to show a Romulan officer, with his own bridge behind him, carefully out of focus. He looked rather like Spock, and spoke like him, too.

"You have been identified as the Starship *Enterprise*. Captain James T. Kirk last known to be in command."

Kirk picked up a hand mike and thumbed its button. "Your information is correct. This is Captain Kirk."

"I am Subcommander Tal of the Romulan Imperial Fleet. Your ship is surrounded, Captain. You will surrender immediately—or we will destroy you."

Kirk flicked the switch and turned his face away toward Spock. He rather doubted that the Romulan could lip-read a foreign language, but there was no point in giving him the chance.

"Spock, come here. What do you make of this? They want something, or they would have destroyed us by now."

"No doubt, Captain. That would be standard procedure for them."

"It's my ship they want, I assume. And very badly."

"Of course. It would be a great prize. An elementary deduction, Captain."

"Skip the logic lessons." Kirk opened the mike again. "Save your threats, Subcommander," he said harshly. "If you attempt to board my ship, I'll blow her up. You gain nothing."

Tal had apparently expected nothing else, but a slight frown cut across his forehead nonetheless. "May I ask, Captain, who is that beside you?"

"My First Officer, Commander Spock. I'm surprised by your ignorance."

"You mean to insult me, but there is nothing discreditable in not knowing everything. Finding a Vulcan so highly placed in the Federation fleet does surprise me, I readily grant. However . . ."

He was interrupted by a beeping noise and hit an invisible control plate. "Yes, Commander? Excuse me, Captain . . ."

The screen dissolved into traveling moire patterns. Then Tal was back.

"No one should decide quickly to die, Captain," he said. "We give you one of your hours. If you do not surrender your ship at the end of that time, your destruction is certain. We will open to communication, should you wish it."

"You understand Starfleet Command has been advised of our situation."

"Of course," Tal said, somewhat condescendingly. "But a subspace message will take three weeks to reach Starfleet—and I think they would hesitate to send a squadron in after you, in any event. The decision is yours, Captain. One hour."

His image winked out, and was replaced by stars.

"Lt. Uhura," Kirk said, "order all senior officers to report to the Briefing Room on the double."

"All right," Kirk said, surveying the group. Spock, McCoy and Scott were present; Chekov and Sulu on the bridge with Uhura. "Spock, you had a theory on why your sensors didn't pick up the Romulan ships, until they were right on top of us."

"I believe the Romulans have devised an improved cloaking system which renders our tracking sensors useless. You will observe, Captain, that the three ships outside are modeled after Klingon cruisers. Changing ship designs that drastically is expensive, and the Klingon cruiser has no important inherent advantages over the Romulan model of which we are aware—unless it is adaptable to some sort of novel screening device."

"If so, the Romulans could attack into Federation territory before we'd know they were there; before a planet or a vessel could begin to get its defenses up."

"They caught *us* right enough," Scott said.

"A brilliant observation, Mr. Scott," Kirk snapped. "Do you have any other helpful opinions?"

Scott was momentarily nonplussed. Then he pumped his shoulders slightly in a shrug. "We've not got many choices . . ."

"Three. We can fight—and be destroyed. Or we can destroy the *Enterprise* ourselves to keep her from the Romulans. Or—we can surrender." There was a stir among the other officers; Kirk had expected it, and overrode it. "We might be able to find out how the Romulans' new cloaking device works. The Federation *must* have that information. Opinions?"

"Odds are against our finding out anything," Scott said. "And if the *Enterprise* is taken by the Romulans, they'll know everything there is to know about a starship."

"Spock?"

"If we had not crossed the Neutral Zone on your order," Spock said coldly and evenly, "you would not now require our opinions to bolster a decision that should never have had to be made."

The others stared at him, and then at Kirk. McCoy leaned forward. "Jim, *you* ordered us—? But you had no authority—"

"Dismissed, Doctor!"

"But Jim . . ."

"Bridge to Captain," Uhura's voice broke in.

"Kirk here."

"The Romulan vessel is signaling again, sir."

"Put it on our screen here, Lieutenant."

The triangular Briefing Room viewscreen lit up to show the Vulcan-like features of Tal. He said without preamble, "My Commander wishes to speak with you, Captain Kirk."

"Very well," Kirk said, slightly surprised. "Put him on."

"The Commander wishes to see you and your First Officer aboard this vessel. It is felt that the matter requires—discussion. The Commander is a highly placed representative of the Romulan Star Empire."

"Why should we walk right into your hands?"

"Two of my officers will beam aboard your vessel as exchange hostages while you are here."

"There's no guarantee they'll transport over here once we've entered your ship."

A faint, cynical smile seemed to be threatening to break over Tal's face. "Granted we do not easily trust each other, Captain. But *you* are the ones who violated our territory. Should it not be we who distrust *your* motives? However, we will agree to a simultaneous exchange."

Perfect—and yet at the same time, impossible to explain to his worriedly watching officers. After appearing to consider, Kirk said, "Give us the transporter coordinates and synchronize."

Tal nodded and his image faded.

"I must insist on advising against this, Captain," protested Scott. "The Romulans will try something tricky..."

"We'll learn nothing by staying aboard the *Enterprise*," Kirk said. "One final order. Engineer Scott, you are in charge. If we do not return, this ship must not be taken. If the Romulans attempt it, you will fight—and if necessary, destroy the *Enterprise*. Is that clear?"

"Perfectly, Captain." In point of fact, Scott looked as though it was the first order he had understood in days. Well, with any luck, he'd understand all the rest later—if there was going to be any "later."

"Very well. Alert Transporter Officer."

Kirk and Spock were conducted to the quarters of the Romulan Commander by two guards, after having been relieved of their weapons. Had the necessity existed, those two guards would never have known what had hit them, sidearms or no, but nothing was to be gained now by overpowering them; Kirk merely noted the overconfidence for possible future use.

Then the door snapped open—and the Romulan Commander, standing behind a desk, was revealed to be a woman. And no ordinary woman, either. Of course, no ordinary woman could become both a ranking officer and a government representative in a society of warriors; but this one was beautiful, aristocratic, compelling—an effect which was, if anything, heightened by the fact that she was of Vulcanoid, not human stock. Kirk and Spock looked quickly at each other. Kirk had the impression that if Spock could whistle, he would.

"Captain Kirk," she said.

"I'm honored, Commander."

"I do not think so, Captain. But we have a matter of importance to discuss, and your superficial courtesies are the overture to that discussion." Her eyes swung leveling to Spock. "You are First Officer...?"

"Spock."

"I speak first with the Captain."

Spock flicked a glance at Kirk, who nodded. The First Officer tilted a half bow toward the Commander, and Kirk entered the office. The door snapped shut behind him.

"All right," he said. "Forgetting the superficial courtesies, let's just have at it. I'm not surrendering my ship to you."

"An admirable attitude in a starship captain," she said coolly. "But the matter of trespass into Romulan space is one of galactic import—a violation of treaties. Now I ask you simply: what is your mission here?"

"Instrument failure caused a navigational error. We were across the Zone before we realized it. Your ships surrounded us before we could turn about."

"A starship—one of Starfleet's finest vessels. You are saying instrument failure as radical as you suggest went unnoticed until your ship was well past the Neutral Zone?"

"Accidents happen; cutoffs and backup systems can malfunction. We've been due in for overhaul for two months, but haven't been assigned a space dock yet."

"I see. But you have managed to navigate with this malfunction?"

"The error has been corrected," Kirk said. He knew well enough how transparent the lie was, but the charade had to be played out; he needed to seem thoroughly outgunned—in all departments.

"Most convenient. I hardly believe it will clear you of espionage."

"We were not spying."

"Your language has always been difficult for me, Captain," the woman said drily. "Perhaps you have another word for it?"

"At worst, it would be nothing more than surveillance. But I assure you that you are drawing an unjustified . . ."

"Captain, if a Romulan vessel ventured far into Federation territory without good explanation, what would a Star Base commander do? It works both ways—and I strongly doubt you are the injured party." She pressed a button and the door opened. "Spock, come in. Both the Federation Council and the Romulan Praetor are being informed of this situation, but the time will be long before we receive their answer. I wish to interrogate you to establish a record of information for them in the meantime. The Captain has already made his statement."

"I understand," Spock said.

"I admit to some surprise on seeing you, Spock. We were not aware of Vulcans aboard the *Enterprise*."

"Starfleet is not in the habit of informing Romulans of its ships' personnel."

"Quite true. Yet certain ships—certain officers—are known to us. Your situation appears most interesting."

"What earns Spock your special interest?" Kirk broke in.

"His species, obviously. Our forebears had the same roots and origins—something you will never understand, Captain. We can appreciate the Vulcans—our distant brothers. Spock, I have heard of Vulcan integrity and personal honor. There is a well-known saying that Vulcans are incapable of lying. Or is it a myth?"

"It is no myth."

"Then tell me truthfully now: on your honor as a Vulcan, what was your mission?"

"I reserve the privilege of speaking the truth only when it will not violate my honor as a Vulcan."

"It is unworthy of a Vulcan to resort to subterfuge."

"It is equally unworthy of a Romulan," Spock said. "It is not a lie to keep the truth to one's self."

That was one sentence too many, Kirk thought. But given Spock's nature and role, it could hardly have been prevented. The woman was wily as well as intelligent.

"Then," she said, "there is a truth here that is still unspoken."

"You have been told everything that there is to know," Kirk said. "There is nothing else."

"There is Mr. Spock's unspoken truth. You knew of the cloaking device that we have developed. You deliberately violated Romulan space in a blatant spy mission on the order of Federation Command."

"We've been through that, Commander."

"We have not even begun, Captain. There is of course no force I can use on a Vulcan that will make him speak. But there are Romulan methods capable of going into a human mind like a spike into a melon. We use them when the situation requires it."

"Then you know," Spock said, "that they are ineffective against humans with Command training."

"Of course," said the Commander. "They will leave him dead—or what might be worse than dead. But I would be replaced did I not apply them as Procedure dictates. One way or another, I will know your unspoken truths."

To Kirk, Spock's iron expression never seemed to change, but now he caught a very faint flicker of indecision which must have spoken volumes to the Romulan woman. Kirk said hastily, "Let her rant. There is nothing to say."

Spock did not look at him. "I cannot allow the Captain to be any further destroyed," the First Officer said in a low monotone. "The strain of command has worn heavily on him. He has not been himself for several weeks."

"There's a lie," Kirk said, "if ever I heard one."

"As you can see," Spock continued evenly, "Captain Kirk is a highly sensitive and emotional person. I believe he has lost his capacity for rational decision."

"Shut up, Spock."

"I am betraying no secrets. The Commander's suspicion that Starfleet ordered the *Enterprise* into the Zone is unacceptable. Our rapid capture demonstrates its foolhardiness."

"Spock—damn you, what are you doing?"

"I am speaking the truth for the benefit of the Enterprise and the Federation. I say—for the record—that Captain Kirk took the *Enterprise* across the Neutral Zone on his own initiative and his craving for glory. He is not sane."

"And I say," Kirk returned between tightly drawn lips, "that you are a filthy traitor."

"Enough," the Commander said, touching a control plate on her desk. "Give me communication with the *Enterprise*."

After a long moment, Scott's voice said, "*Enterprise;* Acting Officer Scott."

"Officer Scott, Captain James T. Kirk is formally charged with espionage. The testimony of First Officer Spock has confirmed that this intrusion into Romulan space was not an accident; and that your ship was not under orders from Starfleet Command or the Federation Council to undertake such a mission. Captain Kirk was solely responsible. Since the crew had no choice but to obey orders, the crew will not be held responsible. Therefore I am ordering Engineer Scott, presently in command of the *Enterprise*, to follow the Romulan flagship to our home base. You will there be processed and released to Federation Command. Until judgment is passed, Captain Kirk will be held in confinement."

There were a few moments of dead air from the *Enterprise*, but Kirk had no difficulty in guessing what Scotty was doing: ordering the two Romulan hostages to be put in the brig. When he came on again, his voice was almost shaking with suppressed rage.

"This is Lt. Commander Scott. The *Enterprise* follows no orders except those of Captain Kirk. We will stay right here until he returns. And if you make any attempt to commandeer or board us, the *Enterprise* will be blown to bits along with as many of you as we can take with us. Your own knowledge of our armament will tell you that that will be quite a good many."

"You humans make a very brave noise," the Commander said. She sounded angry herself, although her face was controlled. "There are ways to convince you of your errors."

She cut off communication with a flick of a switch. Kirk swung on Spock.

"Did you hear, you pointy-eared turncoat? You've betrayed everything of value and integrity you ever knew. Did you hear the sound of human integrity?"

"Take him to the Security Room."

The guards dragged Kirk out.

"It was your testimony that Captain Kirk was irrational and solely responsible that saved the lives of your crew," the Romulan Commander said. "But don't expect gratitude for it."

"One does not expect logic from humans," Spock said. "As we both know."

"A Vulcan among humans—living, working with them. I would think the situation would be intolerable to you."

"I am half Vulcan. My mother was human."

"To whom is your allegiance, then?" she asked with cool interest. "Do you call yourself Terran or Vulcan?"

"Vulcan."

"How long have you been a Starfleet officer, Spock?"

"Eighteen years."

"You serve Captain Kirk. Do you like him? Do you like your shipmates?"

"The question is irrelevant."

"Perhaps." She drew closer, looking into his eyes challengingly. "But you are subordinate to the Captain's orders. Even to his whims."

"My duty as an officer," Spock said rigidly, "is to obey him."

"You are a superior being. Why do you not command?"

Spock hesitated. "I do not desire a ship of my own."

"Of course you believe that now, after eighteen years. But is it not also true that no one has given you—a Vulcan—that opportunity?"

"Such opportunities are extremely rare."

"For one of your accomplishments and—capabilities—opportunities should be made. And will be. I can see to that—if you will stop looking at the Federation as the whole universe. It is not, you know."

"The thought has occasionally crossed my mind," Spock said.

"You must have your own ship."

"Commander," Spock said pleasantly, "shall we speak plainly? It is you who desperately need a ship. You want the *Enterprise*."

"Of course! It would be a great triumph for me to bring the *Enterprise* home intact. It would broaden the scope of my powers greatly. It would be the achievement of a lifetime." She paused. "And naturally, it would open equal opportunities to you."

The sound of an intercom spared Spock the need to reply. It was not an open line; the Commander picked up a handset and listened. After a moment she said, "I will come there," and replaced it. Spock raised his eyebrows inquiringly.

"Your Captain," she said with a trace of scorn, "tried to break through the sonic disruptor field which wards his cell. Naturally he is injured, and since we do not know how to treat humans, my First Officer asked your ship's surgeon to attend him. The man's first response was, 'I don't make house calls,' whatever that means, but we managed to convince him that it was not a trick and he is now in attendance. Follow me, please."

She led the way out of the office and down the corridor, followed by the omnipresent, silent guards.

"I neglected to mention it," she added, "but I will expect you for dinner. We have much yet to discuss."

"Indeed?" Spock said, looking at her quizzically.

"Allow me to rephrase. Will you join me for dinner?"

"I am honored, Commander. Are the guards also invited?"

For answer she waved the guards off. They seemed astonished, but were soon out of sight. A moment later she and Spock reached a junction; to the left, the corridor continued, while to the right it brought up against a single door not far away; it was guarded. There was a raised emblem nearby, but from this angle Spock could not read the device on it. He moved toward it.

"Mr. Spock!"

He stopped instantly.

"That corridor is forbidden to all but loyal Romulans."

"Of course, Commander," Spock said. "I will obey your restrictions."

"I hope," she said, "soon there will be no need for you to observe *any* restrictions."

"It would be illogical to assume that all conditions remain stable."

They reached the Romulan brig; a guard there saluted and turned off the disruptor field. When they entered the cell, he turned it on again. McCoy was there—and so was Kirk, sitting slumped and blank-eyed on the bed, hands hanging down loosely between his knees.

"You are the physician?" the Commander said.

"McCoy—Chief Medical Officer."

"Captain Kirk's condition?"

"Physically—weak. Mentally—depressed, disoriented, displays feelings of persecution and rebellion."

"Then by your own standards of normality, this man is not fully competent?"

"Not now," McCoy said reluctantly. "No."

"Mr. Spock has stated he believes the Captain had no authority or order to cross the Neutral Zone. In your opinion, could this mental incapacity have afflicted the Captain earlier?"

"Yes—it's possible."

"Mr. Spock, the Doctor has now confirmed your testimony as to the mental state of your Captain. He was and is unfit to continue in command of the *Enterprise*. That duty has now fallen upon you. Are you ready to exercise that function?"

"I am ready."

McCoy looked aghast. "Spock—I don't believe it!"

"The matter," Spock said, "is not open for discussion."

"What do you mean, not open for discussion? If . . ."

"That's enough, Doctor," the Commander broke in. "As a physician, your duty is to save lives. Mr. Spock's duty is to lead the *Enterprise* to a safe haven."

"There is no alternative, Doctor," Spock added. "The safety of the crew is the paramount issue. It is misguided loyalty to resist any further."

Kirk raised his head very slowly. He looked a good deal more than disoriented; he looked downright mad. Then, suddenly, he was lunging at Spock, his voice a raw scream:

"Traitor! I'll—kill—you!"

With the swift precision of a surgeon, Spock grasped Kirk's shoulder and the back of his neck in both hands. The raging Captain stiffened, cried out inarticulately once, and collapsed.

Spock looked down at him, frozen. The guard had drawn his sidearm. McCoy kneeled beside the crumpled Captain, snapped out an instrument, took a reading, prepared a hypo in desperate haste.

"What did you do to him?" McCoy demanded. He administered the shot and then looked up. His voice became hard, snarling. *"What did you do?"*

"I was unprepared for his attack," Spock said. "He—I used the Vulcan death grip instinctively."

McCoy tried a second shot, then attempted to find a pulse or heartbeat.

"Your instincts are still good, Spock," he said with cold remoteness. "He's dead."

"By his own folly," said the Romulan Commander. "Return the corpse and the Doctor to their vessel. Mr. Spock, shall we proceed to dinner?"

"That," Spock said, "sounds rather more pleasant."

It was pleasant indeed; it had been a long time since Spock had seen so sumptuously laden a table. He poured more wine for the Commander.

"I have had special Vulcan dishes prepared for you," she said. "Do they meet with your approval?"

"I am flattered, Commander. There is no doubt that the cuisine aboard your vessel far surpasses that of the *Enterprise*. It is indeed a powerful recruiting inducement."

"We have other inducements." She arose and came over to sit down beside him. "You have nothing in Starfleet to which to return. I—*we* offer an alternative. We will find a place for you, if you wish it."

"A—place?"

"With me." She touched his sleeve, his shoulder, then his neck, brushing lightly. "Romulan women are not like Vulcan females. We are not dedicated to pure logic and the sterility of non-emotion. Our people are warriors, often savage; but we are also many other—pleasant things."

"I was not aware of that aspect of Romulan society."

"As a Vulcan, you would study it," she said softly. "But as a human, you would find ways to appreciate it."

"You must believe me, I do appreciate it."

"I'm so glad. There is one final step to make the occasion complete. You will lead a small party of Romulans aboard the *Enterprise*. You will take your rightful place as its commander and lead the ship to a Romulan port—with my flagship at its side."

"Yes, of course," Spock said impatiently. "But not just this minute, surely. An hour from now will do—even better. Will it not, Commander?"

She actually laughed. "Yes, it will, Mr. Spock. And you do know that I have a first name."

"I was beginning to wonder."

She leaned forward and whispered. The word would have meant absolutely nothing to a human, but Spock recognized its roots without difficulty.

"How rare and how beautiful," he said. "But so incongruous when spoken by a soldier."

"If you will give me a moment, the soldier will transform herself into a woman." She rose, and he rose with her. Her hand trailed out of his, and a door closed behind her.

Spock turned his back to it, reached inside his tunic, and brought out his communicator. Snapping it open, he said quietly, "Spock to Captain Kirk."

"Kirk here. I'm already on board—green skin, pointed ears, uniform and all. Do you have the information?"

"Yes, the device is down the first corridor to the left as you approach the Commander's office, closely guarded and off limits to all but authorized personnel."

"I'll get it. Will you be able to get back to the *Enterprise* without attracting their attention?"

"Unknown. At present . . ."

"Somebody coming. Out."

Spock replaced the communicator quickly, but it was a long minute before the Commander returned. The change was quite startling; compared to her appearance in uniform, she seemed now to be wearing hardly anything, although this was in part an illusion of contrast.

"Mr. Spock?" she said, posing. "Is my attire now more—appropriate?"

"More than that. It should actually stimulate our conversation."

She raised her hand, fingers parted in the Vulcan manner, and he followed suit. They touched each other's faces.

"It's hard to believe," she said, "that I could be so stirred by the touch of an alien hand."

"I too—must confess—that I am moved emotionally. I know it is illogical—but . . ."

"Spock, we need not question what we truly feel. Accept what is happening between us, even as I do."

"I question no further."

"Come, then." Taking his hand, she turned toward the other room.

The outside door buzzed stridently. Had Spock been fully human, he would have jumped.

"Commander!" Tal's voice called. "Permission to enter!"

"Not now, Tal."

"It is urgent, Commander."

She hesitated, looking at Spock, but her mood had been broken. She said; "Very well—you may enter."

There were two guards behind Tal. It would have been hard to say whether they were more surprised by Spock's presence or by their Commander's state of undress, but discipline reasserted itself almost at once.

"Commander. We have intercepted an alien transmission from aboard our own vessel."

"Triangulate and report."

"We have already done so, Commander. The source is in this room."

She stiffened and turned to Spock. Gazing levelly at her, he reached under his tunic. Tal and the guards drew their weapons. Moving very slowly, Spock brought out his communicator and proffered it to her. Trancelike, without looking away from his face, she took the device. Then, suddenly, she seemed to awaken.

"The cloaking device! Send guards . . ."

"We thought of that also, Commander," Tal said. The slight stress on her title dripped with contempt. It was clear that he thought it would shortly pass to him. "It is gone."

"Full alert. Search all decks."

"That will be profitless, Commander," Spock said. "I do not believe you will find it."

Her response was a cry of shock. "You must be mad!"

"I assure you, I am quite sane."

"Why would you do this to me? What are you that you could do this?"

"I am," Spock said, not without some regret, "the First Officer of the *Enterprise*."

She struck him, full in the face. Nobody could have mistaken it for a caress. The blow would have dropped any human being like a felled ox.

He merely looked at her, his face calm. She glared back, and gradually her breathing became more even.

"Take him to my office. I shall join you shortly."

She was back in uniform now, and absolutely expressionless. "Execution for state criminals," she said, "is both painful and demeaning. I believe the details are unnecessary. The sentence will be carried out immediately after charges are recorded."

"I am not a Romulan subject," Spock said. "But if I am to be treated as one, I demand the Right of Statement first."

"So you know more about Romulan custom than you let appear. This increases your culpability. However, the right is granted."

"Thank you."

"Return to your station, Subcommander," she said to Tal. "The boarding action will begin on my order."

Tal saluted and left. The Commander took a weapon from her desk, and laid it before her. She seemed otherwise confident that Spock would make no ignominious attempts at escape; and indeed, even had the situation been as she thought, such an attempt would have been illogical.

"There is no time limit to the Right of Statement, but I will not appreciate many hours of listening to your defense."

"I will not require much time," Spock said. "No more than twenty minutes, I would say."

"It should take less time than that to find your ally who stole the cloaking device. You will not die alone." She tapped a button on the desk console. "Recording. The Romulan Right of Statement allows the condemned to make a statement of official record in defense or explanation of his crime. Commander Spock, Starfleet Officer and proven double agent, demands the right. Proceed, Commander Spock."

"My crimes are espionage, and aiding and abetting sabotage. To both of these I freely admit my guilt. However, Lords Praetori, I reject the charge of double agentry, with its further implication of treason. However I may have attempted to make the matter appear, and regardless of my degree of success in such a deception, I never at any point renounced my loyalty to the Federation, let alone swearing allegiance to the Romulan Empire.

"I was in fact acting throughout under sealed orders from Starfleet Command, whose nature was unknown to anyone aboard the *Enterprise* except, of course, Captain Kirk. These orders were to find out whether the Romulans had in fact developed a rumored cloaking device for their ships, and if so, to obtain it by any possible means. The means actually employed were worked out in secret by Captain Kirk and myself."

"And so," the Commander said with bitter contempt, "the story that Vulcans cannot lie is a myth after all."

"Of course, Commander. Complex interpersonal relationships among sentient beings absolutely require a certain amount of lying, for the protection of others and the good of the whole. Among humans such untruths are called 'white lies.' A man's honor in this area is measured by whether he can tell the difference between a white lie and a malicious one. It is a much more delicate matter than simply charging blindly ahead telling the truth at all times, no matter what injury the truth may sometimes do. And there are occasions, such as the present one, when one must weigh a lie which will cause personal injury against a truth which would endanger the good of the whole. Your attempt to seduce and subvert me, Commander, was originally just that kind of choice. If it became something else, I am sorry, but such a danger is always present in such attempts."

"I can do without your pity," the Commander said, "and your little moral lecture. Pray proceed."

"As you wish. The oath I swore as a Starfleet officer is both explicit and binding. So long as I wear the uniform it is my duty to protect the security of the Federation. Clearly, your new cloaking device presents a threat to that security. I carried out my duty as my orders and my oath required."

"Everyone carries out his duty, Mr. Spock," the Commander said. "You state the obvious."

"There is no regulation concerning the content of the statement. May I continue?"

"Very well. Your twenty minutes are almost up."

"I trust that the time consumed by your interruptions and my answers to them will not be charged against me. Interrogation in the midst of a formal Statement is most irregular."

The Commander threw up her hands. "These endless quibbles! Will you kindly get back to the point?"

"Certainly. The Commander's appeal to my Vulcan loyalties, in the name of our remote common racial origin, was bound to fail; since beyond the historic tradition of Vulcan loyalty there is the combined Vulcan/Romulan history of obedience to duty—and Vulcan is, may I remind you, a member of the United Federation of Planets. In other words . . ."

Under his voice, a familiar hum began to grow in the room. The Commander realized instantly what was happening—but instead of picking up the sidearm and firing, as she had plenty of time to do despite all Spock's droning attempt to dull her attention—she sprang forward and threw her arms around him. Then both were frozen in a torrent of sparks . . .

And both were in the Transporter Room of the *Enterprise*.

As the elevator doors opened onto the bridge, Kirk's voice boomed out.

"Throw the switch on that device, Scotty!"

"I did, sir," Scott's voice said. "It's not working."

The Commander looked in Kirk's direction and a muffled exclamation escaped her as Spock escorted her out. Kirk had not yet removed his Romulan Centurion's uniform, let alone bothered to change his skin color or have his surgically altered ears restored to normal human shape. Obviously, the other half of the plot was now all too clear to her.

Spock left her and crossed to his station. Behind him, her voice said steadily, "I would give you credit, Captain, for getting this far—but you will be dead in a moment and the credit would be gratuitous."

The Captain ignored her. "Lt. Uhura, open a channel to the Romulan command vessel; two-way visual contact."

"Right . . . I have Subcommander Tal, sir."

Tal seemed quite taken aback to see what appeared to be one of his own officers in the command chair, but must have realized in the next second that any Centurion he did not recognize had to be an impostor. He said almost instantly, "We have you under our main batteries, *Enterprise*. You cannot escape."

"This is Captain Kirk under this silly outfit. Hold your fire. We have your Commander with us."

Tal shot a look toward where his own main viewscreen evidently was located. "Commander!"

"Subcommander Tal," the woman said, "I am giving you a direct order. Obey it. *Close and destroy!*"

Uhura cut off transmission, but not fast enough. It was a risk that had had to be taken.

"Come on, Scotty, we've run out of time."

"Captain, I'm working as fast as I can."

"You see, Captain," the Commander said, "your effort is wasted."

"Mr. Spock. Distance from the Romulan vessels."

"One hundred fifty thousand kilometers and closing rapidly."

"Stand to phasers. You'll forgive me if I put up a fight, Commander."

"Of course," the woman said. "That is expected."

"One hundred thousand kilometers," Spock said. "They'll be within maximum range within six seconds . . . five . . . four . . ."

"Scott, *throw the switch!*"

"It'll likely overload, but . . ."

". . . two . . . one . . ."

"Functioning, Captain!"

"Mr. Chekov, change course to 318 mark 7, Warp Nine."

"Nine, sir? . . . Done."

Spock turned toward Kirk. "They have opened fire at where we were last, sir, but the cloaking device appears to be operating most effectively. And the Commander informed me that even their own sensors cannot track a vessel so equipped."

"Thank you, Mr. Spock," Kirk said in a heartfelt voice. He turned to the Commander. "We will leave you at a Federation outpost."

"You are most gracious, Captain. If I may be taken to your brig, I will take my place as your prisoner. Further attendance here is painful to me."

Kirk stood, very formal. "Mr. Spock, the honor of escorting the Commander to her *quarters* is yours."

The two opposing forces bowed formally to each other, and Spock led the Commander back toward the elevator. Behind them, Sulu's voice said, "Entering Neutral Zone, Captain."

"I'm sorry you were made an unwilling passenger," Spock said. "It was not intentional. All they really wanted was the cloaking device."

"They? And what did *you* want?"

"That is all I wanted when I went aboard your vessel."

"And that is exactly all you came away with."

"You underestimate yourself, Commander."

She refused to hear the hidden meaning. "You realize that we will very soon learn to penetrate the cloaking device. After all, we discovered it; you only stole it."

"Obviously, military secrets are the most fleeting of all," he said. "I hope we exchange something more permanent."

She stepped into the elevator; but when Spock tried to follow her, she barred the way. "You made the choice."

"It was the only choice possible. Surely you would not have respected any other."

She looked at him for a long moment, and then smiled, slightly, sadly. "That will be our—secret. Get back to your duty. The guards had best take me from here."

Spock beckoned to two guards. She could probably incapacitate both in a matter of seconds, but they were well out of Transporter range of any of the Romulan ships now—and her mood did not seem to be one which would impel her to illogical action. In a way it was a pity that she obviously did not know that Vulcans were cyclical in their mating customs, and immune to sexual attraction at all other times. Or had she been counting on his human side? And—had she been right to do so?

The elevator swallowed her down. Spock went back to his post.

"Sickbay to Captain Kirk. If all the shouting's over up there, I want you to report to me."

"What for, Bones?"

"You're due in surgery again. As payment for the big act of irrationality you put over on me, I'm going to bob your ears."

Kirk grinned and touched the ears, which apparently he had forgotten in the heat of operations, and looked over at Spock.

"Please go, Captain," Spock said in a remote voice. "Somehow, they are not aesthetically pleasing on a human."

"Are you coming, Jim?" McCoy's voice said. "Or do you want to go through the rest of your life looking like your First Officer?"

And McCoy had the last word again.

DAY OF THE DOVE

WRITER: JEROME BIXBY
DIRECTOR: MARVIN CHOMSKY
FIRST AIRED: NOVEMBER 1, 1968

Though the planet had said it was under attack by an unidentified spacecraft, the *Enterprise* landing party had found only black dust, white rocks and strange clumps of moving plants. Its tricorders—McCoy's as well as Chekov's—refused to report any evidence of a colony or of people who could have signaled the message. Yet they had existed.

Kirk stooped for a handful of the black, powdery soil. "An SOS from a human settlement—one hundred men, women and children. All gone. Who did it? Why?"

As if in reply, his communicator beeped. "Spock here, sir. Sensors have picked up a Klingon ship closing in fast."

"Deflectors on, Mr. Spock! Protect yourselves. Total response if attacked." He closed the communicator, his face grim. So that was the answer—Klingons. They had destroyed the settlement. But Spock had more news of the Klingon ship. "Trouble aboard her, Captain. Evidence of explosions . . . massive damage. We never fired at her."

"Maintain full alert, Mr. Spock."

Behind his group the air was collecting into dazzle. Six Klingons in their stiff metallic tabards were materializing, their weapons aimed and ready. Their leader was the first to assume full shape. His hand, slant-eyed face distorted by fury, he reached out and swung Kirk around. "You attacked my ship!" he shouted. "Four hundred of my crew—dead! My vessel is disabled. I claim yours! You are prisoners of the Klingon Empire for committing a wanton act of war against it!" He nodded to his men. "Disarm them!"

Kirk had recognized the harsh, Mongol-like features. The Klingons' Kang. "We took no action against your ship," he said.

He'd been hustled into line with Chekov and McCoy. Kang paced before them. "For three years your Federation and our Empire have been at peace . . . a treaty we have honored to the letter . . ."

Kirk protested again. "We did not attack your ship."

"Were the screams of my men imaginary? What were your secret orders? To start a war? You have succeeded! Or maybe to test a new weapon. We shall be interested to examine it!"

Kirk said, "There was a Federation colony on this planet. *It* was destroyed."

"And by what? I see no bodies, no ruins. A colony of the invisible!"

"Perhaps a new *Klingon* weapon that leaves no traces. Federation ships don't specialize in sneak attacks!"

Along the ground near Kang a small, mushroom-shaped crystal was floating. Its swirling red color was concealed by a white rock and a faint, ugly throbbing came from it.

Kirk's patience was ebbing. No denial of guilt seemed able to penetrate the heavy bones of Kang's hairless skull. "You lured my ship into ambush with a false Klingon distress call!"

Kirk stared at him. "*You* received a distress call? *We* were the ones who received it!"

"I don't propose to spend any more time arguing your fantasies, Kirk! The *Enterprise* is ours! Instruct your Transporter Room. We are ready to beam aboard."

"Go to the devil," Kirk said.

"We have no devil—but we understand the habits of yours . . ." Still hidden among the rocks, the crystal's red glow brightened as Kang burst out, "I will torture you to death, one by one! Who will be the first? You, Kirk?"

Chekov suddenly exploded into action. He charged Kang, sobbing with rage. "*Swine! Filthy Klingon murderers!*" Kirk made a grab for him, missed—and Kang's men beat him to the ground. But he still sought to get at Kang. "*You killed my brother! Piotr!*— the Arcanis Four Research Outpost . . . a hundred peaceful people massacred—*just as you did here! My brother, Piotr . . .*"

Kang looked down at him. "So you volunteer to join him. That is loyalty." He gestured to one of his men. A sputtering device was pushed against Chekov's neck. He writhed with agony, doubled up. Kirk, wrenching forward, was immobilized by the Klingons. The device was readjusted—and Chekov screamed.

"You win, Kang!" Kirk said. "Stop the torture!"

"Jim!" McCoy cried. "You can't hand over the *Enterprise*!"

"Help Chekov, Bones."

Kang was eyeing Kirk. "Don't plan any tricks. I will kill a hundred hostages at the first sign of treachery!"

"I'll beam you aboard the *Enterprise*. Once we're there—no tricks."

"Your word?"

Kirk nodded; and Chekov, still convulsed with pain, cried, "Captain!—we can't! . . . don't let these . . . *animals* . . . have the ship!"

"Animals?" Kang said. "Your captain crawls like one. A Klingon would not have surrendered." He turned to Kirk. "Order everyone in this area to be transported up." He said something to his men, and Kirk, ringed by weapons, opened his communicator.

"Kirk to *Enterprise*. Mr. Spock . . ."

"Here, Captain."

"We have guests," Kirk told him. "Adjust Transporter for wide-field and beam-up everyone in the target area." His finger pressed a tiny control on the communicator.

"Yes, Captain."

Everybody shimmered out, Kirk under the weapons, Chekov supported by McCoy, both glaring.

In the *Enterprise* Transporter Room, only the landing party materialized. No Klingons stood on the platform.

Kirk stepped off his pad. "Full Security on the double, Mr. Galloway! Good work, Spock!"

As Galloway hit the intercom, the bewildered McCoy said, "What—happened?"

"Landing party brought up intact," Spock told him.

At the console, Scott spoke. "All others suspended in transit. Who are the guests, by the way, Captain?"

"Klingons."

Scott grinned happily, slapping the console. "They're in here—until we decide to rematerialize them."

"Galloway?" Kirk said.

"Security squads on the way, sir."

Chekov's voice was thick with hate. "Captain! Leave them on the planet! Leave them where they are! In nonexistence. That's so many less Klingon monsters in the galaxy!"

"And that's what they would do," Kirk said. As the Security detail rushed through the door, he spoke to the Transporter Chief. "Bring them in."

The six Klingons sparkled into shape on the platform. They all stiffened, taking in the changed situation. Outnumbered by the Security men, they made no resistance as they were disarmed. The weaponless Kang looked at Kirk.

"Liar!" He spat the word.

"I said no tricks *after* we reached the ship." Kirk stepped forward, formal, terse. "You are prisoners of the United Federation of Planets against which you may or may not have committed an act of war."

"There are survivors still aboard my ship," Kang said.

Kirk nodded to the Transporter chief and Scott said, "Captain, we haven't been able to get through to Starfleet Command. All subspace frequencies are blocked. And there's too much radiation from the Klingon ship—it's a hazard to the vicinity."

"Prepare to destruct, Scotty."

"Completing the job you started!"

Kirk wheeled on Kang. "You wouldn't be standing there if I had."

The surviving Klingons were shimmering into form. Of the six, several were women. One, queenly, graceful, her dark eyes gleaming under the epicanthic fold of their Mongol lids, left the platform to go at once to Kang. He took her arm. "This is Mara—my wife and my Science officer," he told Kirk.

She ignored Kirk. "What has happened, Kang?"

"More Federation treachery. We are prisoners."

She was visibly terrified. The arm in Kang's hand trembled. "What will they do to us? I have heard of their atrocities . . . their death camps! They will torture us for our scientific and military information . . ."

Kirk addressed her. "You have some things to learn about us, madam." He turned to Galloway. "Detain them in the crew lounge. Program a food-synthesizer to accommodate our . . . guests. You will be well treated, Commander Kang."

"So I have seen," the Klingon said.

Kirk bowed and left, followed by Spock, McCoy and the still blazing Chekov. Unseen, unheard, the floating crystal hummed over their heads as they passed into the corridor.

"What *did* attack their ship, Jim?"

Kirk didn't answer. "Mr. Spock, maintain Red Alert. Scan this sector for other ships. Run a full check on the colony. We've got to nail this down fast . . ."

"We know what happened!" Chekov cried. "That distress call—"

Spock, speaking to nobody in particular, said, "From their distant position, the Klingons could scarcely have attacked the colony at the time we received the call. Moreover, they were apparently attracted there themselves by a distress call."

"Lies!" Chekov cried. "They want to start a war by pretending *we* attacked it!"

Entering an elevator, Kirk glanced at his overwrought face. But McCoy was saying, "Chekov might be right. The Klingons *claim* to have honored the truce—but there have been incidents! . . . raids on our outposts . . ."

"We've never proved the Klingons committed them, Bones."

McCoy was flushed with unusual vehemence. "What proof do we need? We know what a Klingon is!"

He stormed out of the elevator. Kirk frowned, puzzled by his belligerence; and Spock, noting his uneasiness, said, "Our Log-tapes will indicate our innocence in the present situation, Captain."

"Unfortunately, there is no guarantee they will be believed."

At the bridge deck, Chekov stalked to his post, his back stiff and stubbornly unrelenting. Kirk eyed him again before he asked for Uhura's report.

"Still unable to contact Starfleet Command, Captain. Outside communications blanketed."

"Keep at it, Lieutenant. We've got a diplomatic tiger by the tail."

He'd have liked authorization to take steps about the derelict Klingon ship. But at least he knew no lives were aboard it. He turned in his command chair. "Forward phasers locked and ready to fire, Mr. Sulu."

"Aye, sir."

"Fire phasers," Kirk said.

On the screen, the crippled vessel flared into light—and vanished. So that was that. A diplomatic tiger, indeed.

"Lieutenant Uhura?"

"No contact with Starfleet yet, sir."

Spock looked up from his mounded viewer. "Sensor sweeps reveal no other ships within range, Captain."

Had the Klingons annihilated that colony after all? There was no telling. Not now. He swung to Uhura. "Keep trying, Lieutenant. Mr. Sulu, set course seventeen mark four. Warp speed three."

"Warp three, sir."

In the crew lounge, Security guards and the "guests" were facing each other, each group wary, watchful, suspicious. Above them all the crystal drifted. Kang, Mara beside him, used an empty space for restless pacing. "When I take this ship," he said, "I will have Kirk's head stuffed and hung on his cabin wall."

"They will kill us before we can act," she warned him.

"No! They wish to question us—learn our strength, our plans. They never will."

"We are forty," she protested. "Forty against four hundred."

One of Kang's men stepped forward. "Four thousand throats may be cut in one night by a running man."

"Patience," Kang said. "Vigilance. They will make their mistake. Capture of the *Enterprise* will give us knowledge to end this war quickly."

The crystal's unheard throb moved out of the lounge and into the corridor. When it reached the bridge, its throbbing faded. Uhura, abruptly irritated, jabbed at her controls. "Still no outside contact, sir! Carriers normal. Channels open. I don't understand! Could the Klingons be doing something—?"

The ship suddenly shuddered. Engine sound rose. Kirk whirled. "Mr. Sulu?"

"Change of course, sir! Accelerating . . ." He struggled with switches. "Helm dead. Auxiliary navigation dead!"

Kirk braced himself against another shudder. "Override."

Sulu turned. "*Nothing* responds, Captain!"

"New course?"

"Nine-oh-two mark five . . ."

It would head the *Enterprise* out of the galaxy. Kirk hit a button. "Scotty—stop engines!"

The engine sound grew to a whining roar. On the intercom, Scott's voice was high with alarm. "... would if I could, sir! My controls have gone crazy! Something's—taken over..."

The bridge trembled under the rising roar. Scott shouted, "The engines, Captain! They've gone to warp nine—by themselves!"

Uhura's board was a dazzle of wildly flickering lights. Earphones fixed, she cried, "Captain! Reports from the lower decks! Emergency bulkheads closed! Almost four hundred crewmen trapped down there!"

Furious, Kirk exploded from his seat, racing for the elevator. The crystal followed him into the crew lounge. Kang was pleased with his information. "The bulk of your crew trapped? Your ship racing from the galaxy at wild speeds? Delightful! But how did I perform this sabotage, Kirk? My men are *here*."

Frigid with rage, Kirk spoke to Galloway. "Double security. Some Klingons may have beamed aboard, undetected. Mr. Spock, get down to Engineering. Help Scott hammer things back to normal and release those crewmen!"

He eyed Kang. "Before I throw you in the brig, I owe you something!" He landed a clenched fist on Kang's jaw. The Klingon stumbled back into a console, his hand falling on a lever. It came loose, grew red—and changed into a sword. Kang, amazed, stared at it in unbelief. Then he hefted it. At the same moment, all the lounge's objects—ashtrays, vases, lamps, magazines, game equipment—went into glow, transforming into swords, shields, javelins, battle-axes. The Klingons rushed for the weapons.

Kirk's people reached for their phasers. But the phasers, too, went into glow. Then they turned into swords and maces.

Kang took a swordsman's stance. "You killed four hundred of my men, Captain Kirk. It is time that that debt be repaid..."

Kirk looked at the sword that had been a console lever. Molecular revolution. But explanation did nothing to solve the deadly mystery. His own phaser was a sword.

The Klingons attacked—and the fight was on. Outnumbered, the Security guards were forced to retreat. Kirk fenced expertly, and was deflecting a slash by Kang when he saw that Galloway was wounded. He battled his way to the lieutenant, got an arm around him and shoved him into an elevator. The doors whooshed shut in the faces of Kang and his men. They rang with the sound of beating, frustrated swords.

Kirk beeped Engineering on his intercom. "The Klingons are free, Scotty. And armed. They'll try to take the ship. How many men do we have?"

"I don't know, sir, but three hundred and ninety-two are trapped below decks."

"Deploy forces to protect your section and Auxiliary Control Center. Check the Armory—and try to free those trapped men."

"Doors and bulkheads won't budge, sir. We'll have to cut through—"

"Blow out bulkheads if you have to—we need numbers! Any luck regaining control of speed?"

"No, sir. She's a projectile—at warp nine. Don't ask me what's holding her together."

"Five-minute reports. Kirk out."

He went to Spock's station. "Full sensor scans of the ship, Mr. Spock. Report any movements on the part of the Klingons. The Klingon Empire has maintained a dueling tradition. They think they can beat us with swords!"

Spock coolly examined the sword that had once been his phaser. "Neither the Klingon technology nor ours is capable of this, Captain. Instantaneous transmutation of matter. I doubt that they are responsible . . ."

"Other logical candidates?" Kirk demanded impatiently.

"None, Captain. But if they had such power, wouldn't they have created more effective weapons—and only for themselves?"

Kirk turned away. "Get below, Mr. Sulu. Take command of forces protecting Engineering and Auxiliary Control."

Sulu rose and Chekov rose with him.

"As you were, Mr. Chekov," Kirk said.

"*No*, sir! Let me go, too! I've got a personal score to settle with Klingons!"

"Maintain your post. This is no time for vendettas."

"Captain, I . . ."

"Sit down, Mister."

Chekov made a break for the elevator. As he reached it, Kirk grabbed his shoulder. Chekov wrenched away; and Spock, at Kirk's side, reached out an arm. Ducking under it, Chekov drew his sword. As he lifted it, Kirk and Spock paused, unwilling to risk a tangle that might hurt him.

"Don't try to stop me, Captain! I saw what they left of Piotr! I swore on his grave I would avenge his murder . . ." He backed into the elevator and its doors closed.

Sulu was staring. "What's Chekov's grudge against the Klingons? Who's—Piotr?"

"His brother," Kirk said. "Killed in a Klingon raid."

"His brother?" Sulu echoed blankly. "Chekov never had a brother! He's an only child."

It was Kirk's turn to stare. After a long moment, he said, "You are mistaken."

"I'm not, sir!" Sulu was very earnest. "I *know* he's an only child. It's why he requests his shore leaves on Earth—a good only son of his parents should visit them!"

"On your way to Engineering, Mr. Sulu."

Sulu left—and a newly troubled Kirk hit his intercom. "Captain Kirk to Security. Find Mr. Chekov and return him to the bridge."

Uhura swung around. "Captain—what could have made Chekov believe he had a brother?"

"I don't know, Lieutenant. But he does believe it—and now he wants revenge for a nonexistent loss."

On the *Enterprise* bridge, mystery was compounding itself, but in its crew lounge, clarification was in order.

A Klingon had projected the Starship's plan and arrangements on the viewer. "Layout and specifications of the ship, Commander Kang."

"Enemy numbers are the same as ours," Mara said. "We have a fighting balance."

"Then we will take this ship!" Kang spoke with a ferocious determination.

"A vessel that is racing toward the edge of the galaxy is weakening," his man said. "If the humans can't control it . . ."

Kang jabbed at the diagrams on the viewer. "These points we must capture! First, their Engineering section . . ."

McCoy was working feverishly to complete his treatment of Galloway's wound. As he worked, he could hear the moans of other slashed men waiting their turn at the table.

"Those—filthy butchers!" he muttered. "There are *rules*—even in *war* . . . you don't keep on hacking at a man after he's down!" He felt sick with impotent rage. He looked at an orderly who was wiping blood from a shoulder gash. "Where's that Numa-nol capsule?"

Haggard and worn by Sickbay's harrowing activity, the orderly turned, only to be confronted by wheeled stretchers bearing two more injured men. McCoy went to them. A glance told him their wounds were serious. As he bent over one of them, he spoke to the orderly. "I'm convinced now the only good Klingon is a dead one," he said.

Scott was inclined to agree with him. All attempts to release the cut-off crewmen had failed. Phaser beams couldn't cut through the bulkheads. Their metal's structure had changed. He hit an intercom button to make his report.

"What about the Armory?" Kirk said.

"I'm there now, Captain. You never saw such a collection of antiques in your life . . ."

The Armory had turned into a medieval weapons' Wonderland. Crossbows, hatchets, knives, broadswords . . .

"Get back to Engineering," Kirk said. "Keep trying to reestablish engine control. And make some phasers—fast."

"Aye, sir."

He was about to leave when he spotted a sharply two-edged weapon in the rack. He removed it, fondling it. "A claymore!" Exchanging it for a sword at his waist, he murmured, "Ah, you're a beauty, aren't you?"

As he strutted out of the Armory, reinforced by Scotland's history of claymore triumphs, Spock was computing the opposing forces at an exact thirty-eight. He lifted his head from his computer. "The Klingons occupy Deck Six and starboard Deck Seven,

Captain. We control all sections above." He bent to his viewer again, becoming suddenly intent. "Most curious," he said.

"What?" Kirk said.

"There appear to be more energy units aboard than can be accounted for by the presence of the *Enterprise* crew plus the Klingons. A considerable discrepancy."

"Could some more of Kang's crew have beamed aboard?"

"Their ship was thoroughly vacated, Captain." He flipped a switch. "I shall compensate for the human and Klingon readings."

The crystal had found Engineering. It hovered high in the air, as unseen as it was unheard.

Scotty, descending a ladder, stepped down into the lower level of his section. "Any signs of those treacherous devils, Mr. Sulu?"

"All clear, Mr. Scott."

Klingons, moving into the upper level, leaped down to the attack. The surprised humans fell back. But Scott was inspired by his claymore's tradition. He felled a Klingon with its haft; and then realizing that his species was hopelessly outnumbered, darted through a door into the corridor. Sulu joined him, downing the two Klingons who followed him.

Scott was breathless. "I don't know how many of these creatures are around. We'll split up here. Maybe . . . one of us . . . can make it back to the bridge."

Inside Engineering, the rest of the crew were being shoved against a wall. As they were disarmed, a jubilant Kang strode in, Mara at his side.

It was hard going, trying to get back to the bridge. Klingons seemed to be everywhere. The canny Scott finally reconciled national glory with common sense. He hid in a lavatory. So he was in no position to see Spock zero in on an unusual but steady beeping.

"An alien life force, Captain. A single entity. I am unable to ascertain its location." He flicked a switch. "Readings diverted to the library computer for analysis . . ."

Kirk, beside him, said, "We have to make contact . . . find out what it wants!"

Calmer than custard, Spock said, "The computer report, Captain . . ."

There was a click—and the computer voice said, "Alien life force on board is composed of pure energy. Type unknown. Actions indicate intelligence and purpose."

"What purpose?" Spock said.

The metallic computer voice said, "Insufficient data for further analysis."

The computer's stark admission of inadequacy fired Kirk into new, creative thought. Out of his human memory banks he made connections. "A brother that never existed," he said. "A phantom colony—fancied distress calls! The illusion that phasers are swords! Do you begin to sense a pattern, Mr. Spock?"

Spock, loyal to facts, looked up. "If the alien has caused these phenomena, it is apparently able to manipulate matter and minds."

"Now its controlling the *Enterprise*—taking us out of the galaxy! *Why?*"

"I am constrained to point out, Captain, that as minds are evidently being influenced, we cannot know that our own memories at this moment are accurate."

Kirk faced his sole alternative. "We've got to talk to Kang and bury the hatchet!"

"An appropriate choice of terms, sir. However, once blood has been drawn, it is notoriously difficult to arrange a truce with Klingons . . ."

"A *truce?*"

It was McCoy—an outraged, infuriated McCoy. His white surgical uniform was blood-spattered. "I've got seven men down in Sickbay—some of them dying—*atrocities* committed on their persons! And you can talk of making peace with those fiends? They'd jump us the minute our backs were turned! We know what Klingons do to prisoners! Slave labor, death planets—experiments!"

Kirk had never seen Bones so angry. "McCoy—" he began.

McCoy rushed on. "Even while you're talking, the Klingons are planning attacks! This is a fight to the death—and we'd better start trying to win it!"

"We are trying to end it, Doctor." Spock's voice was more than usually quiet. "There is an alien aboard which may have created this situation . . ."

McCoy glared at him. "Who *cares* what started it! We're *in* it! Those murderers! Let's wipe out every one of them!"

"Bones, the alien is the enemy we have to wipe out—"

Uhura cut in. "Sickbay calling, Doctor. There are more wounded men requiring your attention."

McCoy wheeled, starting back to the elevator. Then he turned again to Kirk and Spock. "How many men have to die before you begin acting like military men instead of damn fools?" The elevator doors closed on his bleakly hopeless face. Kirk looked at Spock. The Vulcan murmured, "Extraordinary."

Kang was on the intercom. Kirk spoke quickly. "There's something important we must discuss . . ."

Vindictive and triumphant, Kang's voice said, "I have captured your Engineering section! I now control this ship's power and life support systems." At Engineering's intercom he nodded to Mara. She moved a series of switches and Kang spoke again into the intercom.

"I have deprived all areas of life support except our own. You will die . . . of suffocation . . . in the icy cold of space . . ."

On the bridge, lights were dimming. Panels were going dark.

Kirk walked slowly over to Sulu's station. "Mr. Sulu, get down to Emergency Manual Control. Try to protect life support circuits and activate auxiliary power . . ."

"Aye, Captain." But as Sulu approached the elevator, Scott burst out of it. He barely acknowledged the helmsman's smile of relief at his safety. Kirk went to him. "Scotty! I'm glad you escaped..."

Scott was shaking. "Chekov was right, Captain! We *should've* left those slant-eyed goons in the Transporter! That's right where they belong—in nonexistence! Now they can study the *Enterprise*—add our technology to theirs—change the balance of power!" He lurched at Kirk, not in attack but in a blind misery that was seeking some shred of comfort. "You've jeopardized the Federation!"

The charge was a cry of anguish. "Scotty..."

Spock had joined them. "Mr. Scott, calm yourself," he said.

Scott pulled back. For one terrible moment, Kirk feared he was going to spit at Spock, such aversion showed in his face. "Keep your Vulcan hands off me! Just stay away! Your 'feelings' might get hurt, you green-blooded, halfbreed freak!"

Kirk didn't believe his ears. Appalled, he stared at Scott. Then Spock made his icy retort. "Let me say that I have not enjoyed serving with humans. I find their illogical and foolish emotions a constant irritant."

"So transfer out!" Scott shouted.

Spock moved toward Scott. He loomed darkly formidable over him—and Scott, frightened, took a clumsy punch at him. Kirk grabbed their arms; but Spock, twisting easily free, seemed about to use his great strength in an upsurge of rage he couldn't govern. Kirk tried again; and yanking them apart, crashed back into his command chair. "Spock! Scotty! Stow it!" He pinned them, panting. *"What's happening to us! What are we saying to each other?"*

Spock pushed Kirk away. Kirk braced himself, ready for some ultimate disaster. But nothing happened. Spock was himself again, perhaps a little more impassive than usual.

"Fascinating," he said to Kirk. "A result of stress, Captain?"

"We've been under stress before! It hasn't set us at each other's throats!" Scott had started forward again and Kirk pushed him back.

"This is a *war*!" Scott yelled.

"There isn't any war..." Kirk paused, the sound of his own words in his ears. "Or—*is* there?"

"Have we forgotten how to defend ourselves?" Scott cried.

"Shut up, Scotty." Kirk paced at the back of his command chair, frowning as he put his two's together. "What *is* happening to us? We're trained to think in other terms—than war! We're trained to fight its causes whenever possible! So why are *we* reacting like savages?" The two's were adding up. He swung around to his men. "There are two forces on this ship, armed equally. Has—a war been *staged* for us? A war complete with weapons, grievances, patriotic drumbeats?" He turned on Scott. "Even race hatred!"

Spock had nodded. "Recent events *would* seem directed to a magnification of basic human and Klingon hostilities. Apparently, it is by design that we fight. We seem to be pawns."

"In what game?" Kirk said. "Whose game? What are the rules?"

"It is most urgent," Spock said, "that we locate the alien entity, determine its motives—and some means of halting its activities."

Scott's startled thoughts had been tumbling around in his head. He was quieter now—and guilt-stricken. He spoke to Spock. "Without sensors, sir? All our power down? The thing can pass through walls. It could be anywhere."

Kirk hit his intercom. "Mr. Sulu, report!"

Sulu was at the Jeffries tube, peering up into it. "No good, Captain. Circuits are in but systems aren't responding." As he spoke, the tube's complex instruments flickered with light and settled down to a steady pattern. He heard Kirk say, "Are we getting something?"

"Aye, sir. Power and life support restored—remotes on standby . . ."

"Good work!" Kirk told him.

"But Captain—*I didn't do it!* Everything just came on by itself!"

Kirk thought, "Well, this is a gift horse I don't look too close in the mouth of." He said, "All right, Mr. Sulu. Get back to Manual Control. Kirk out."

The bridge lights had come back to normal. Panels had resumed their humming. Spock turned. "Sensors operating again, Captain."

"Start scanning, Mr. Spock. Look for the alien."

In Engineering, a puzzled Mara was studying lights on a large board. "Their life support systems have resumed and are holding steady," she told Kang.

"Cause them to be unsteady," he said.

"They appear to be controlled from another location." For the first time her voice was uncertain. "I'm also unable to affect the ship's course—to return to our Empire."

"Some trick of Kirk's? Has he bypassed these circuits? What power is it that supports our battle, yet starves our victory? Interrupt power at their main life support couplings. Where are they?"

She looked at the diagrams on the viewer. "They are on this deck." At Kang's nod, she spoke to a Klingon. "Come with me."

Above them in the bridge, Spock had tensed. He whirled to Kirk. "Alien detected, Captain! In the Engineering level, near reactor number three!"

Kirk leaped from his chair. "Let's go!"

Mara, the Klingon behind her, was rushing down a corridor that led to the couplings. As they passed an alcove, Chekov, sword drawn, moved out of it, his face hate-filled. Two well-aimed slashes disposed of the Klingon. Mara was turning to run when Chekov grabbed her and whirled her around. She fought well; but Chekov blocked her karate blow. He pinned her back against the wall, sword at her throat. It was a lovely throat. Chekov's manner changed. He eyed her with an ugly speculation, grinning. "No, you don't die—yet," he said. "You're not human but you're beautiful, aren't you?" His grip on her tightened. "Just how human *are* you?"

She pushed at him, struggling against the grip. Chekov placed his hand over her mouth and was pressing her into the alcove when Kirk and Spock raced out of the elevator. Assault was the last thing on their minds. Hearing Mara's muffled scream, they stared at each other. Then they broke into a run, rounded a corner—and stopped dead in their tracks at what they saw.

"Chekov!"

Chekov wheeled to face Kirk, a wild beast deprived of its prey. Mara's garment was ripped from her shoulders. Chekov spun her away. She hit a wall and dropped. He tried to dodge Kirk and failed. Kirk seized him, slapping his face forehand, backhand. Chekov sobbed; and raising his sword, made a swipe at Kirk. He was disarmed and felled with a punch. Beside himself with fury, Kirk struck him again.

Spock put a hand on Kirk's shoulder. "Captain . . . he is not responsible . . ."

Mara, crouched on the deck, was trying to pull her torn clothes together. Kirk went to her. "Listen to me," he said. "There's an alien entity aboard this ship. It's forcing us to fight. We don't know its motives—we're trying to find out. Will you help us? Will you take me to Kang . . . a temporary truce! That's all I ask!"

Mingled fear and hate blazed from her eyes. Kirk turned his back on her. "Bring her, Spock." He moved to the weeping Chekov and lifted him gently in his arms. Was this what was in store for all of them? Hatred, violence wherever they turned?

McCoy was re-dressing Galloway's wound when Kirk carried Chekov into Sickbay. He looked up, taking them all in, Kirk, the still sobbing Chekov clinging to him, a disheveled Mara, closely followed by Spock. Shaking his head, he left Galloway and hurried to help Kirk place Chekov on an exam table. He applied a device to the new patient's head.

"Brainwaves show almost paranoid mania. What happened, Jim?"

"He's—lost control—useless as a fighter." He turned to the door. "Come on, Spock . . ."

McCoy stopped him with a hand on his arm. He seemed somewhat calmer himself but his tired face was bewildered. "*Jim*—Galloway's heart wound has almost entirely healed! The same with the other casualties. Sword wounds . . . into vital organs—massive trauma, shock—and they're all healing at a fantastic rate!"

Spock spoke. "The entity would appear to want us alive."

". . . Why?" Kirk said. "So we can fight and fight—and always come back for more? Some kind of bloody Colosseum? What next? The roar of crowds?"

Galloway was listening. And he was buying none of it. His jaw hardened. He wanted out from Sickbay and for only one reason—another crack at the Klingons.

Kirk felt the lieutenant's hostility like a tangible thing. "Spock, let's find that alien!" He looked at Mara. "You come along. Maybe we can prove to you that it exists!"

In the corridor, Spock unlimbered his tricorder. He led the way, searching cautiously, the tricorder first aimed one way, then another. When they reached a second intersection, Spock paused, gesturing to his left. They turned the corner—and they all heard the crystal's faint humming. Without speaking, Spock signaled them to look up to the right side of the corridor. The crystal was floating there, brighter than it had ever been.

Kirk shot a significant look at Mara. Now that she was forced to believe, she was staring at the thing's swirling red.

"What is it?" Kirk said.

"Totally unfamiliar, Captain."

Kirk approached the crystal. "What do you want? Why are you doing all this?" It hovered silently, persistent.

Kirk, close to blowing his stack, shouted, *"What do you want?"*

The thing glowed still brighter, bobbing slightly. Spock, noting the increased glow, whirled at a sound. Galloway, still bandaged, was coming down the corridor, a little weak but grimly determined. He hefted his sword—and started to push past them as though he didn't see them.

"Lieutenant Galloway!" Kirk cried. "What are you doing here? Did the Doctor release you?"

"I'm releasing myself!"

First, Chekov's insubordination. Now this one. It took all Kirk's strength to remember that the crystal was in the business of war, dissension and rule-breaking.

"Go back to Sickbay," he said.

"Not on your life! I'm fit and ready for action!" He shook Kirk's hand from his arm. "The Klingons nearly put me away for good! I'm going to get me some scalps . . ."

"I order you!" Kirk said.

"I've got my orders! I'm obeying orders! To Kill Klingons! It's them or us, isn't it?"

The crystal had bobbed over Galloway's head. Spock, looking up, saw it bob as Galloway pushed past him, heading for an elevator. He tagged the man with a neck pinch. Kirk saw Galloway slump, unconscious, to the deck. Spock's eyes were already back on the crystal. Its glow had faded.

"Most interesting," Spock said.

His eyes returned to Kirk. "During Mr. Galloway's emotional outburst—his expressions of hatred and lust for vengeance—the alien's life-energy level *increased*. When the lieutenant became unconscious, the alien *lost* energy."

"A being that subsists on the emotions of others?" Kirk said.

"Such creatures are not unknown, Captain. I refer you to the Drella of Alpha Carinae five—energy creatures who are nourished by the cooperation of love they feel for one another." He had neared the crystal and was looking up at it, composed and calm. "This creature appears to be strengthened by mental radiations of hostility, by violent intentions . . ."

"It feeds—on hate!" Complete illumination dawned on Kirk.

"Yes, to put it simply, Captain. And it has acted as a catalyst to create this situation in order to satisfy that need. It has drawn fighting forces together, supplied crude weapons to promote the most violent mode of conflict. It has spurred racial animosities—"

"And kept numbers and resources balanced to maintain a stable state of violence! Spock, it's got to have a vulnerable area. It's got to be stopped!"

"Then all hostile attitudes on board must be eliminated, sir. The fighting must end—and soon."

Kirk nodded. "I agree. Otherwise, we'll be a doom ship—traveling forever between galaxies . . . filled with bloodlust . . . eternal warfare! Kang *has* to listen— we've got to pool our knowledge to get rid of that thing!"

The crystal was showing agitation, bobbing as though angry that its secret was known. Now, as Kirk strode to an intercom, it moved toward him, throbbing loudly. For a moment Kirk wavered. Then he walked on. The crystal, its hum furious, approached Mara. Suddenly, without warning, she hurled herself at Kirk, biting, scratching, pushing him away from the intercom. Spock lifted her from Kirk, quietly pinning her arms to her sides.

Kirk hit all buttons. "Kang! This is Kirk! Kang! *Kang!*"

Mara shrieked, "Commander! It's a trick! They are located—"

Spock's steel hand went over her mouth. At the intercom, Kirk hit the buttons again. *"Kang!"* It was hopeless. The Klingon wouldn't answer.

"The alien is affecting his mind, Captain. Soon it will grow so powerful that none of us will be able to resist it."

The intercom beeped and Kirk hit it fast—fast and hopefully. "Kirk here!"

"Scotty, sir. The ship's dilithium crystals are deteriorating. We can't stop the process . . ."

Kirk struck the wall with his fist. "Time factor, Scotty?"

"In twelve minutes we'll be totally without engine power, sir."

"Do everything you can. Kirk out."

The crystal stopped bobbing. It glowed brilliantly, back in the driver's seat. As they watched it, it vanished through a wall. Kirk spoke to Mara. "So we drift forever . . . with only hatred and bloodshed aboard. Now do you believe?"

Her strained eyes stared into his. But she made no answer.

The dilithium crystals were still losing power. Spock, rallying all his scientific know-how, toured the bridge, examining panels. Finally, he broke the bad news to Kirk. There was nothing to be done to halt the crystals' decay.

"We have nine minutes and fifty-seven seconds before power zero," he said. "But there is a logical alternative, Captain." He was looking at Mara, his face speculative. "Kang's wife, after all, is our prisoner. A threat made to him . . ."

"*That's* something the Klingons would understand," Scott urged.

Mara had flinched, remembering the unspeakable atrocities said to be visited on Klingon prisoners by their human captors. Kirk saw her remembering them. Though the idea of using her to threaten Kang just might result in a productive discussion with him, it revolted him. On the other hand, peace between them was the sole hope now. After a long, painful moment, he said, "You're right, Mr. Spock."

He flicked on his intercom. This was going to be difficult. He harshened his voice. "Kang, Kang! This is Captain Kirk. I know you can hear me . . . Don't cut me off! *We have Mara—your wife!*"

At Engineering's intercom, Kang was listening. Kirk's voice went on. "We talk truce *now*—or she dies. Reply!"

Kang was silent.

"She has five seconds to live, Kang! Reply!"

The answer came. "She is a victim of war, Captain. She understands." Kang flicked off the intercom, his dark emotion visible to his men. He turned to them. "When we get Kirk, he is mine," he said.

The last card had been played. Kirk looked at Mara. She had stiffened, her head held high, proud, a queen awaiting death. He pointed to a seat. "Sit over there and keep out of our way. Lieutenant Uhura, guard her."

She didn't understand. ". . . you're . . . not going to . . . ?"

"The Federation doesn't kill or mistreat its prisoners. You've heard fables, propaganda." He looked away from her as though he'd forgotten her existence. "How much time now, Mr. Spock?"

"Eight minutes and forty-two seconds, sir."

Instead of taking a seat, Mara had gone to the panel Spock was studying. Reading it, she realized the dilithium situation. Near her, Uhura watched her as she turned in shocked belief. "So it was no trick . . ." she said, bewildered.

Scott spoke. "The alien has done all this. We are in its power. Our people—and yours."

Kirk rose from his chair. "We wanted only to end the fighting to save us all," he told her.

Her relief had bred a need to explain. "We have always fought, Captain Kirk. We must. We are hunters, tracking and taking what we need. There are poor planets in the Klingon systems. We must push outward to survive."

"Another way to survive is mutual trust, Mara. Mutual trust and mutual help."

"I will help you now," she said.

He'd hoped to no point too many times to feel anything but skepticism. "How?" he said.

"I will take you to Kang. I will add my plea to yours."

Scott's suspicion found voice. "Captain—I wouldn't trust her . . ."

"We can't get past the Klingon defenses in time now, anyway—" Kirk paused. "Unless . . ." He whirled to Spock. "*Spock! Intra*ship beaming! From one part of the ship to another! Is it possible?"

"It has rarely been done, sir, because of the great danger involved. Pinpoint accuracy is needed. If the Transportee should materialize within any solid object—a wall or deck . . ."

"Prepare the Transporter," Kirk said.

"Mr. Scott, please help me with the Main Transporter Board." Spock moved to a panel but Scott hesitated, worried.

"Even if it works, Captain, she may be leading you into a trap!"

"We're all in a trap, Scotty. And this is our only way out of it."

"We'll go with you, sir . . ."

"That would start the final battle." Kirk took a long-searching look at Mara. "I believe her."

Scott took one for himself. He believed her, too. "Aye, sir," he said.

Mara entered the elevator. Following her, Kirk said, "We'll wait for your signal." As the doors closed, Scott thoughtfully fingered his sword. "But she can't guarantee that Kang will listen. Right, Mr. Spock?"

But Spock was intent on the Main Transporter Board. "No one can guarantee another's actions, Mr. Scott."

The Transporter Room was empty. Entering it, Kirk deliberately removed his sword; and, disarmed, placed the weapon on the console. Mara smiled at him. Spock's voice spoke from the intercom. "Your automatic setting is laid in, Captain. When the Transporter is energized, you will have eight seconds to get to the pads."

The console was flickering with lights. As Kirk pressed a button, it beeped to every second that passed. Its hum rose and Kirk said, "I hope your computations are correct, Mr. Spock."

"You will know in five point two seconds, Captain."

Kirk and Mara went quickly into position on the platform. There were eight more beeps from the console before they shimmered out.

At their appearance in Engineering, the startled Kang exploded to his feet. "*Mara! You are alive!* . . . and you bring us a prize!" He turned, shouting, "*Guards!*"

Swords drawn, his men ringed Kirk.

"Kang—wait!" Mara cried. "He has come alone—unarmed! *He must talk to you!*"

"Brave Captain. What about?" Kang swung to his men. "Kill him."

Mara rushed into place before Kirk. "*No!* You must listen! There is great danger to us all!"

Kang paused—and Kirk moved her aside, unwilling to allow her shield to him. "Before you start killing," he said, "give me one minute to speak!"

Kang ignored him. He spoke to Mara. "What have they done to you? How have they affected your mind?" Then he spotted her torn garment, her bruised shoulder. His slanted eyes went icy. "Ah, I see why this human beast did not kill you . . ."

She flashed into action. She seized a sword and tossed it to Kirk. He caught it as Kang launched himself headlong into attack. Defending himself, he retreated before another fierce slash. Mara, held by a Klingon, was struggling, agonized by the turn events had taken.

"*They didn't harm me!* Kang, listen to Kirk!"

Kang backed away for another onrush. "With his death, we win!"

"*Nobody wins!*" Kirk shouted. "Have any of your men died?" He broke into sudden attack but only to bring himself closer to Kang. "*Listen! We can't be killed—any of us! There's an alien aboard this ship that needs us alive!*"

Kang shoved him away only to come back with another vicious onslaught.

"You *fool!*" Mara screamed.

From behind them all, the Transporter humming sounded. Spock, McCoy, Sulu and the *Enterprise* forces sparkled into shape and substance. Kang's men rushed forward, swords aimed. The Security guards, led by Sulu who uttered a yell that might have been "Banzai!" closed with them.

Kirk, downing a Klingon with a hard right to the jaw, reached Kang—and grabbed him. Nose to nose, he shouted, "*Listen* to me! Let me *prove* what I say!"

Kang wrenched free, his sword up for the lethal downsweep. Kirk parried the blow in mid-descent. Mara, huddled against a wall, covered her face with her hands, despairing. Kang came back with another vicious slash. As Kirk ducked it, he heard the triumphant throbbing. He looked up. The crystal—above their heads, brighter than he'd ever seen it—was casting its virulent red light on Kang's face.

The sight was all that he needed. He pushed Kang back, pinning him, and whirled him around to face their common enemy.

"LOOK! *Up there!*"

Kang looked. He shot a glance at Kirk—but the real meaning of what he'd seen didn't get through to him.

The fight went on, interminably. Sulu plunged his sword into an opponent's chest. The Klingon staggered, pawing at the wound. Then he rallied. He drove so straight for Sulu's heart that the *Enterprise* helmsman barely managed to escape the thrust.

Kang, his eyes on the crystal, was just beginning to get the lay of the land. Kirk pressed his advantage. ". . . for the rest of our lives, Kang! For a thousand lifetimes—fighting, this insane violence! That alien over our heads will control us forever!"

The crystal throbbed loudly. Kirk himself felt the heat of its bloody radiance. But

Kang still twisted, snarling, avid for killing. Kirk smashed the sword that had reappeared in his hand. He struck it furiously against a bulkhead. It broke. Kang stared at him. Then he stepped forward, his own weapon upraised. Kirk stood his ground.

"Come on! In the brain, the heart—it doesn't matter, Kang! *I won't stay dead!* Next time the thing will see to it that I kill you. And you won't stay dead! The good old game of war—mindless pawn against mindless pawn! While something somewhere sits back and laughs . . . laughs fit to kill, Kang—and starts it all over again . . ."

The sword was at his throat.

"Jim—*jump him!*" McCoy shouted.

Spock spoke out of his wise Vulcan heritage. "Those who hate and fight must stop themselves, Doctor—or it is not stopped."

Mara had flung herself at Kang's feet. "I'm your wife—a Klingon! Would I lie for them? Listen to Kirk. He is telling the truth!"

"*Then be a pawn!*" Kirk said. "A toy—the good soldier who never asks questions!"

Kang looked up at the excitedly throbbing crystal. Very slowly, his hand relaxed on the sword. It dropped to the deck.

"Klingons," he told the crystal, "kill for their *own* purposes." He turned to his men, shouting. "Cease hostilities! At rest!"

They were puzzled by the order—but they obeyed. Kang yelled a Klingon away from a downed Security man. "*At rest! At rest!* You heard the order!"

Through the open door they could all hear the clashing sounds of continuing battle in other parts of the ship. "*All* fighting must be stopped, Captain, if the alien is to be weakened before our fuel is gone."

Kang had lifted Mara to her feet. They joined Kirk at the intercom as he activated it, Kang still suspicious.

"Lieutenant Uhura, put me on shipwide intercom . . ."

"Ready, Captain."

"Attention, all hands! A truce is ordered . . . the fighting is over! Regroup and lay down weapons." He stepped back, speaking urgently. "Kang! Your turn at the intercom . . ."

The Klingon hesitated, reluctant. He couldn't resist a push at Kirk as he moved to the intercom. "This is Kang. Cease hostilities. Disarm."

The crystal was bobbing wildly with anger; but its throbbing had lessened and its redness was dimmer. "The cessation of violence appears to have weakened the alien," Spock said. "I suggest that good spirits might prove to be an effective weapon."

Kirk nodded. A hard smile on his lips, he addressed the crystal. "Get off my ship!" The thing retreated, still bobbing. "You're powerless here. You're a dead duck. We know all about you—and we don't want to play your game any more."

The throbbing was fainter. Spock was right. What the invader needed was a cheerful scorn. Kirk looked up at it. "Maybe there are others like you still around. Maybe you've caused a lot of suffering—a lot of history. That's all over. We'll be on guard . . . we'll be ready for you. Now butt out!" He laughed at the crystal. "Haul it!"

McCoy waved a contemptuous hand. "Get out, already!" he yelled.

As the throbbing faded, Kirk was amazed to hear a hoarse chuckle from Kang. Then he laughed as though he weren't used to it. His gusto grew. "Out!" he shouted at the crystal. "We need no urging to hate humans!" He laughed harder at Spock's irritated glance. "But for the present—only fools fight in a burning house."

Guffawing, he raffled Kirk's teeth with a sadistic whack on the back. McCoy nudged Spock. After a moment, the Vulcan thumbed his nose at the crystal. "You will please leave," he said.

The red was now a dull flicker. They all watched it, laughing. Suddenly the crystal vanished through a bulkhead. Floating in space outside the Starship, it flared up and winked out.

The forced laughter had come hard. Kirk's relief from hours of nervous strain overwhelmed him so that he wasn't surprised to see that swords and shields had disappeared. Spock and McCoy discovered their phasers in place. McCoy made a point of drawing his; and Kang, noting the weapon, went right on chuckling. Caution—it was how things were between the Federation and his Klingon Empire.

Uhura's voice spoke. "Captain, jettisoning of fuel has stopped. The trapped crewmen are free. All systems returning to normal."

"Carry on, Lieutenant. Mr. Sulu, resume your post. Set course for—well, set it for any old star in the galaxy!"

As Sulu left, Kirk nearly knocked Kang from his feet with a mighty thump on the back. Kang spun around, blood in his eye—and Kirk grinned at him. "*Friends!*" he said.

The command chair was a place again where a man could relax. For a moment, anyway. Kirk leaned back in his seat.

"Ahead, Mr. Sulu. Warp one." He turned to Kang and Mara. "We'll reach a neutral planet by tomorrow. You'll be dropped there. No war, this time."

He eyed Mara. A real woman, that one. If she hadn't been Kang's wife . . . if there had been time. Ah, well, no man could accommodate all opportunities . . .

Kang was saying, "Why do you humans revere peace? It is the weakling's way. There's a galaxy to be taken, Kirk, with all its riches!"

Spock looked up. "Two animals may fight over a bone, sir—or they can pool their abilities, hunt together more efficiently and share justly. Curiously, it works out about the same."

Kang turned. "One animal must trust the other animal."

"Agreed," Kirk said. "Cooperate . . . or fight uselessly throughout eternity. A universal rule you Klingons had better learn." He paused. "*We* did."

Had it got through? Maybe. At any rate, Kang's face seemed unusually thoughtful.

FOR THE WORLD IS HOLLOW AND I HAVE TOUCHED THE SKY

WRITER: RIK VOLLAERTS
DIRECTOR: TONY LEADER
FIRST AIRED: NOVEMBER 8, 1968

That "Bones" McCoy was a lonely man, Kirk knew. That he'd joined the service after some serious personal tragedy in his life, Kirk suspected. What he hadn't realized was the fierce pride in McCoy that made a virtual fetish of silence about any private pain. So he was startled by his violent reaction to the discovery that Nurse Chapel had exceeded what McCoy called her "professional authority."

Entering Sickbay, Kirk found her close to tears. "You had no business to call Captain Kirk!" McCoy was storming at her. "You're excused! You may go to your quarters!"

She blew her nose. "I'm a nurse first, Doctor—and a crew member of the *Enterprise* second," she said, chin firm under her reddened eyes.

"I said you were excused, Nurse!"

Christine swallowed. The hurt in her face was openly appealing. She blew her nose again, looking at Kirk, while McCoy said gruffly, "Christine, please—for God's sake, stop crying! I'll give the Captain a full report, I promise."

She hurried out, and Kirk said, "Well, that was quite a dramatic little scene."

McCoy squared his shoulders. "I've completed the standard physical examinations of the entire crew."

"Good," Kirk said.

"The crew is fit. I found nothing unusual—with one exception."

"Serious?"

"Terminal."

Kirk, shocked, said, "You're sure?"

"Positive. A rare blood disease. Affects one spaceship crew member in fifty thousand."

"What is it?"

"Xenopolycythemia. There is no cure."

"Who?"

"He has one year to live—at the outside chance. He should be relieved of duty as soon as possible."

Kirk spoke quietly. "Who is it, Bones?"

"The ship's chief medical officer."

There was a pause. Then Kirk said, "You mean yourself?"

McCoy reached for a colored tape cartridge on his desk. He stood at stiff attention as he handed it to Kirk. "That's the full report, sir. You'll want it quickly relayed to Starfleet Command—to arrange my replacement."

Wordless, Kirk just looked at him, too stunned to speak. After a moment, he replaced the cartridge on the desk as though it had bit him. McCoy said, "I'll be most effective on the job in the time left to me if you will keep this to yourself."

Kirk shook his head. "There must be *something* that can be done!"

"There isn't." McCoy's voice was harsh. "I've kept up on all the research. I've told you!"

The anguish on Kirk's face broke him. He sank down in the chair at his desk.

"It's terminal, Jim. Terminal."

Though red alert had been called on the *Enterprise*, Kirk was in his quarters. A "replacement" for Bones. Military language was a peculiar thing. How did one "replace" the experience of a human being—the intimacy, the friendship forged out of a thousand shared dangers? "One year to live—at the outside chance." When you got down to the brass tacks of the human portion, you wished that speech had never been invented. But it had been. Like red alerts. They'd been invented, too. In order to remind you that you were Captain of a starship as well as the longtime comrade of a dying man.

As he stepped from the bridge elevator, Spock silently rose from the command chair to relinquish it to him.

"What is that stuff on the screen, Mr. Spock? Those moving pinpoints? A missile spread?"

"A very archaic type, Captain. Sublight space."

"Aye, and chemically fueled to boot, sir," Scott said.

"Anything on communications, Lieutenant Uhura?"

"Nothing, sir. All bands clear."

"Course of the missiles, Mr. Spock?"

"The *Enterprise* would appear to be their target, Captain."

Prepare phaser banks. Yes. Two of them. He gave the order. "Get a fix, Mr. Chekov, on the missiles' point of origin."

"Aye, Captain."

"Mr. Sulu, fire phasers."

The clutch of missiles exploded in a blinding flash. "Well, that's that," Kirk said. "Mr. Chekov, alter course to missile point of origin."

"Course change laid in, sir."

"Warp three, Mr. Sulu."

Spock spoke from the computer station. "They were very ancient missiles, Captain. Sensor reading indicates an age of over ten thousand years."

"Odd," said Kirk. "How could they still be functional?"

"They evidently had an inertial guidance system that made any other communications control unnecessary."

"And the warheads, Captain," Scott said. "Nuclear fusion type according to my readings."

Spock spoke again. "We're approaching the coordinates of the hostile vessel, Captain."

"Get it on the screen, Mr. Sulu."

The term "vessel" seemed to be inappropriate. What had appeared on the screen was a huge asteroid. It was roughly round, jagged, its rocky mass pitted by thousands of years of meteor hits.

"Mr. Spock, we've got maximum magnification. Is the object on the screen what it looks to be—an asteroid?"

"Yes, sir. Some two hundred miles in diameter."

"Could the hostile vessel be hiding behind it?"

"Impossible, Captain. I've had that area under scanner constantly."

"Then the missiles' point of origin is that asteroid?"

"Yes, sir."

Kirk got up and went to Spock's station. "Full sensor probe, Mr. Spock."

After a moment, Spock withdrew his head from his computer's hood. "Typical asteroid chemically but it is not orbiting, Captain. It is pursuing an independent course through this solar system."

"How can it?" Kirk said. "Unless it's powered—a spaceship!"

Spock cocked an eyebrow in what for him was amazement. Then he said slowly, "It *is* under power—and correcting for all gravitational stresses." He dived under his hood again.

"Power source?" Kirk asked.

"Atomic, very archaic. Leaving a trail of debris and hard radiation."

Kirk frowned briefly. "Plot the course of the asteroid, Mr. Chekov."

Once more Spock withdrew his head. "The asteroid's outer shell is hollow. It surrounds an independent inner core with a breathable atmosphere—sensors record no life forms."

"Then it must be on automatic controls," contributed Scott.

Spock nodded. "And its builders—or passengers—are dead."

Chekov said, "Course of asteroid—I mean spaceship—241 mark 17."

Spock had stooped swiftly to his console. He pushed several controls. Then he looked up. "Sir, that reading Ensign Chekov just gave us puts the asteroid ship on a collision course with planet Daran V!"

"Daran V!" Kirk stared at him. "My memory banks say that's an inhabited planet, Mr. Spock!"

"Yes, sir. Population, approximately three billion, seven hundred and twenty-four million." He paused, glancing back at his console panel. "Estimated time of impact: thirteen months, six days."

"Well," Kirk said. "That's a pretty extensive population." He whirled to Sulu. "Mr. Sulu, match *Enterprise* speed with the asteroid ship's. Mr. Spock and I are transporting aboard her. Mr. Scott, you have the con."

They entered the Transporter Room to see Christine Chapel handing his tricorder to McCoy. "A lot can happen in a year," she was saying. "Give yourself every minute of it."

"Thanks," McCoy said, and slung the tricorder over his shoulder. Ignoring Kirk and Spock, he stepped up on the Transporter platform, taking position on one of its circles.

Kirk walked over to him. "Bones," he said, "Spock and I will handle this one."

"Without me?" McCoy said. "You'll never make it back here without me."

"I feel it would be wiser if . . ."

"I'm fine, thank you, Captain," McCoy brushed him off. "I want to go."

So that was how Bones wanted it played. He wasn't fatally ill. The word terminal might never have been spoken. "All right, Bones. You're probably right. If we make it back here, we'll need you with us." He took up his own position on the platform between Spock and McCoy.

They arrived on a land area of the asteroid ship. As though land on an asteroid weren't strange enough, strange plants, coiling back tendrils abounded, their strange roots sunk in deep, smoking fissures. High mountains shouldered up in the distance. Otherwise, the view showed only rubble and pockmarked rocks.

McCoy said, "You'd swear you were on a planet's surface."

Spock tossed away a stone he'd examined. "The question is, why make a ship look like a planet?"

"You wouldn't even know you were on a spaceship." Kirk jerked his com unit from his belt. "Kirk to *Enterprise*."

"Scott here, Captain."

"Transported without incident. Kirk out." He rehung his communicator on his belt, and was moving forward when, to his far left, his eye caught the glint of sunlight on metal. "Over there," he said. "Look . . ."

It was a row of metal cylinders. They were all about eight feet high, their width almost matching their height, and regularly spaced fifty feet apart. The men approached the nearest one, examining it carefully without touching it. "No apparent opening," Kirk observed.

"Spock, you found no intelligent life forms," McCoy said, "but surely these are evidence of..."

"This asteroid ship is ten thousand years old, Doctor. They may be evidence of the existence of some previous life forms." He checked his tricorder. "Certainly, there are no signs of life now."

They eyed the enigmatic cylinder again before they walked on to the next one. It was a duplicate of the first. As they reached the third, the two cylinders behind them suddenly opened, disgorging two groups of men, clad in shaggy homespun. Armed with short daggers and broadswords, they moved silently, trailing the *Enterprise* trio. A slim and beautiful woman followed them. She halted as the men charged.

The struggle was quick and violent. Outnumbered, Spock took several blows from sword hilts before he dropped to the ground, half-conscious. McCoy, head down, rushed a man off his feet, the momentum of his plunge crashing him into the woman. Her eyes widened in a surprise that contained no fear. Startled by her beauty, McCoy was brought up short, taking in the lustrous black hair piled on her head in fantastic loops, her glittering black leotardlike garment. Then he was stunned by a smash on the head. Kirk, going down under a swarming attack, saw the broadsword lifting up over McCoy and yelled, "*Bones!*"

The woman raised her right hand.

The broadsword was stayed in midstroke. McCoy was pulled to his feet. He shook his head, trying to clear it. Vaguely, he became aware of hands fumbling at his belt. Then his arms were jerked behind his back. Disarmed of phasers and communicators, he, Kirk and Spock were herded over to the woman.

"These are your weapons?" she asked, holding their belts in her right hand.

"Yes," Kirk said. "Of a kind. Weapons and communication devices. Let me help my friend!" He struggled to pull free. The woman made a commanding gesture. Released, he rushed over to the still groggy McCoy. "Bones, are you all right?"

"I—I think so, Jim."

The woman's dark eyes were on McCoy. "I am called Natira," she told him. "I am the High Priestess of the People. Welcome to the world of Yonada."

"We have received more desirable welcomes," Kirk said.

She ignored him. "Bring them!" she ordered their guards.

She led the way to an open cylinder. They were in an apparently endless, lighted corridor, lined by curious people in their homespun clothing. As Natira passed them, they bowed deeply. She was nearing an arched portal. It was flanked by two ornately decorated pillars, their carvings suggestive of a form of writing, cut deep into the stone. Natira, bowing herself, touched some hidden device that opened the massive door. But keen-eyed Spock had registered its location. He had also observed the writing.

The large room they entered was dim, its sole light a glow that shone from under its central dais. Its rich ornamentation matched that of the portal.

"You will kneel," Natira said.

There was no point, Kirk thought, in making an issue of it. He nodded at Spock and McCoy. They knelt. Natira, stepping onto the dais, turned to what was clearly an altar. Etched into its stone was a design that resembled a solar system. As Natira fell to her knees before the altar, light filled the room.

McCoy, his voice lowered, said, "She called this the world. These people don't know they're on a spaceship."

Kirk nodded. "Possible. The ship's been in flight for a long time."

"That writing," Spock said, "resembles the lexicography of the Fabrini."

But Natira, her arms upraised, was speaking. "O Oracle of the People, O most wise and most perfect, strangers have come to our world. They bear instruments we do not understand."

Light blazed from the altar. As though it had strengthened her to ask the question, she rose to her feet, turned and said, "Who are you?"

"I am Captain Kirk of the Starship *Enterprise*. This is Dr. McCoy, our Medical Officer. Mr. Spock is my First Officer."

"And for what reason do you visit this world?"

The word "world" again. Kirk and McCoy exchanged a look.

"We come in friendship," Kirk said.

The sound of thunder crashed from the altar. A booming echo of the thunder, the voice of the Oracle spoke.

"Learn what it means to be our enemy. Learn what that means before you learn what it means to be our friend."

Lightning flashed. The three *Enterprise* men were felled to the floor by a near-lethal charge of electricity.

McCoy was taking too long to recover consciousness. He continued to lay, white-faced, in a sleeping alcove of their lavishly decorated guest quarters. Spock, who had been trying to work out muscle spasms in his shoulders, joined Kirk at McCoy's couch.

"He must have suffered an excessively intense electrical shock," he said.

"No. I don't think that's it," Kirk said. He reached for McCoy's pulse. Spock, aware of the deep concern in Kirk's face, was puzzled. "Nothing else could have caused this, sir." He paused. "That is—nothing that has occurred down *here*."

Kirk glanced up at Spock. He knew that the Vulcan had sensed something of the real cause of his anxiety. "The shock was unusually serious because of McCoy's weakened condition," he said.

"May I ask precisely what is troubling the Doctor?"

"Yes, Mr. Spock. He'd never tell you himself. But now I think he'd want you to know. He has xenopolycythemia."

Spock stiffened. After a long moment, he said quietly, "I know of the disease, Captain."

"Then you know there's nothing that can be done." As he spoke, McCoy stirred. His eyes opened. Kirk stooped over him. "How is it now, Bones?"

"All right," McCoy said. He sat up, pulling himself rapidly together. "How are *you*, Spock?"

"Fine, thank you. The Captain and I must have received a less violent electrical charge."

Falsely hearty, McCoy said, "That Oracle really got to me. I must be especially susceptible to his magic spells."

"Spock knows," Kirk said. "I told him, Bones."

There was relief in McCoy's face. He stood up. "Hadn't we better find this ship's control room and get these people off their collision course?"

"You're in no shape to be up," Kirk said.

"Ridiculous!" McCoy said. *"I'm up!"*

Kirk saw one of the alcove's curtains sway. He strode to it, jerking it aside. A shabby old man, fear in his face, was huddled against the wall. He peered into Kirk's face. What he saw in it must have reassured him. He moved away from the wall, hesitated, took some powder from a pouch hung over his shoulder. "For strength," he said. He held out the pouch to them. "Many of us have felt the power of our Oracle. This powder will be of benefit. You are not of Yonada."

"No," Kirk said gently. "We come from outside your world."

The old hand reached out to touch Kirk's arm. "You are as we are?"

"The same," Kirk said.

"You are the first to come here. I am ignorant. Tell me of the outside."

"What do you wish to know?"

"Where is outside?"

Kirk pointed skyward. "It's up there."

The filmed eyes glanced up at the ceiling. Like a child put off by an adult lie, the old man looked back at Kirk in mixed disbelief and disappointment. Kirk smiled at him. "The outside is up there and all around."

"So *they* say, also," the old man said sadly. "Years ago, I climbed the mountains, even though it is forbidden."

"Why is it forbidden?" Kirk asked.

"I am not sure. But things are not as they teach us—for the world is hollow and I have touched the sky."

The voice had sunk into a terrified whisper. As he uttered the last words, the old man screamed in sudden agony, clutching at his temples. He collapsed in a sprawled heap on the floor. Horrified, Kirk saw a spot on one temple flash into a pulsating glow. Then the flare died.

McCoy examined the spot. "Something under the skin." He moved the shabby homespun to check the heart. "Jim, he's dead."

Kirk looked down at the heap. "'For the world is hollow and I have touched the sky.' What an epitaph for a human life!"

Spock said, "He said it was forbidden to climb the mountains."

"Of course it's forbidden," Kirk said. "If you climbed the mountains, you might discover you were living in an asteroid spaceship, not in the world at all. *That* I'll bet is the forbidden knowledge."

"What happened?"

It was Natira. She had entered their quarters with two women bearing platters of fruit and wine. At the sight of the crumpled body, their faces convulsed with terror. But Natira knelt down beside it.

"We don't know what happened," Kirk told her. "He suddenly screamed in pain—and died."

She bent her head in prayer. "Forgive him, O Oracle, most wise and most perfect. He was an old man—and old men are sometimes foolish." She rose to her feet. "But it is written that those of the People who sin or speak evil will be punished."

The severity in her face softened into sadness. She touched a wall button. To the guards who entered she said, "Take him away—gently. He served well and for many years." Then she spoke to the women. "Place the food on the table and go."

As the door closed behind them, she crossed to McCoy. "You do not seem well. It is distressing to me."

"No," he said. "I am all right."

"It is the wish of the Oracle that you now be treated as honored guests. I will serve you with my own hands." But the tray she arranged with fruit and wine was taken to McCoy. When she left them to prepare the other trays, Kirk said, "You seem favored, Bones."

"Indeed, Doctor," Spock said, "the lady has shown a preference for you from the beginning."

"Nobody can blame her for that," McCoy retorted.

"Personally," Kirk said, "I find her taste questionable." McCoy, sipping wine, said, "My charm has always been fatal," but Kirk noted that his eyes were nevertheless fixed on the graceful bend of the woman at the table. "If it's so fatal," he said, "why don't you arrange to spend some time alone with the lady? Then Spock and I might find a chance to locate the power controls of this place."

Natira was back, holding two goblets of wine. "It is time that our other guests refresh themselves."

Kirk lifted his goblet. "To our good friends of Yonada."

"We are most interested in your world," Spock said.

"That pleases us."

"Then perhaps you wouldn't mind if we looked around a bit," Kirk ventured.

"You will be safe," she said. "The People know of you now."

McCoy coughed uncomfortably. She went to him swiftly. "I do not think you are yet strong enough to look around with your friends."

"Perhaps not," he smiled.

"Then why not remain here? Rest—and we will talk."

She *was* beautiful. "I should like that," McCoy said.

She turned to Kirk. "But you—you and Mr. Spock—you are free to go about and meet our People."

"Thank you," he said. "We appreciate your looking after Dr. McCoy."

"Not at all," she inclined her head. "We shall make him well." She saw them to the door. Then she hastened back to McCoy. As she sat down on the couch beside him, he said, "I am curious. How did the Oracle punish the old man?"

The dark lashes lowered. "I—cannot tell you now."

"There's some way by which the Oracle knows what you say, isn't there?"

"What we say—what we think. The Oracle knows the minds and hearts of all the People."

McCoy's forehead creased a worried frown. Concerned, Natira extended a white hand that tried to stroke the frown away. "I did not know you would be hurt so badly."

"Perhaps we had to learn the power of the Oracle."

"McCoy. There is something I must say. Since the moment I saw you—" She took a deep breath. "It is not the custom of the People to hide their feelings."

McCoy said to himself, Watch your step, boy. But to her, he said, "Honesty is usually wisdom."

"Is there a woman for you?" she asked.

He could smell the fragrance of the lustrous black hair near his shoulder. This woman was truthful as well as beautiful. So he gave her the truth. "No," he said. "No, there isn't."

The lashes lifted—and he got the full impact of her open femininity. "Does McCoy find me attractive?"

"Yes," he said. "I do. I do indeed."

She took his face between her hands, looking deep into his eyes. "I hope you men of space—of other worlds, hold truth as dear as we do."

Watching his step was becoming difficult. "We do," he said.

"It is dear to me," she said. "So I wish you to stay here on Yonada. I want you for my mate."

McCoy took one of the hands from his face and kissed it. The Eagle Scout in him whispered, Brother, douse this campfire. But in him was also a man under sentence of death; a man with one year to live—one with a new, very intense desire to make that last year count. He turned the hand over to kiss its palm. "But we are strangers to each other," he said.

"Is it not the nature of men and women—that pleasure lies in learning about each other?"

"Yes."

"Then let the thought rest in your heart, McCoy, while I tell you about the Promise. In the fullness of time, the People will reach a new world, rich, green, so lovely to the eyes it will fill them with tears of joy. You can share that new world with me. You shall be its master because you'll be my master."

"When will you reach this new world?"

"Soon. The Oracle will only say—soon."

There was an innocence about her that opened his heart. Incredibly, he heard himself cry out, "Natira, Natira, if you only knew how much I've needed a future!"

"You have been lonely," she said. She picked up the wine glass and held it to his lips. "It is all over, the loneliness. There shall be no more loneliness for you."

He drank and set the glass aside. "Natira—there's something I must tell you . . ."

"Sssh," she said. "There is nothing you need to say."

"But there is."

She removed the hand she had placed over his mouth. "Then tell me, if the telling is such a need."

"I am ill," he said. "I have an illness for which there is no cure. I have one year to live, Natira."

The dark eyes did not flinch. "A year can be a lifetime, McCoy."

"It is my entire lifetime."

"Until I saw you my heart was empty. It sustained my life—and nothing more. Now it sings. I am grateful for the feeling that you have made it feel whether it lasts for a day—a month—a year—whatever time the Creators give to us."

He took her in his arms.

Kirk and Spock were meeting curious looks as they walked down a corridor of the asteroid ship. The more people they encountered, the clearer it became they had no inkling of the real nature of their world. Spock said, "Whoever built this ship must have given them a religion that would control their curiosity."

"Judging by the old man, suppressing curiosity is handled very directly," Kirk said. They had reached the portal of the Oracle Room. Pretending to a casual interest in its carved stone pillars, Spock eyed them keenly. "Yes," he said, "the writing is that of the Fabrini. I can read it."

"Fabrina?" Kirk said. "Didn't the sun of the Fabrina system go nova and destroy its planets?"

"It did, Captain. Toward the end, the Fabrini lived underground as the people do here."

"Perhaps some of them were put aboard this ship to be sent to another planet." Kirk glanced up and down the corridor. It was almost empty. "And these are their descendants."

They were alone now in the corridor. Kirk tried and failed to open the Oracle Room's door. Spock touched the secret opening device set into one of the pillars. Inside, they flattened themselves against a wall. The door closed behind them. Nothing happened. Kirk, his voice low, said, "The Oracle doesn't seem to know we are here. What alerted it the first time?"

Spock moved a few steps toward the central dais. "Captain, the Oracle's misbehavior occurred when Natira knelt on that platform." Kirk stepped onto the platform. He walked carefully around it. Again, nothing happened. "Mr. Spock, continue investigating. The clue to the control place must be here somewhere." But carvings on a wall had caught Spock's attention. "More writing," he said. "It says nothing to suggest this is anything but a planet. Nor is there any question that the builders of the ship are to be considered gods."

Kirk had found a stone monolith set in a niche. It bore a carved design of a sun and planets. Spock joined him. "Eight planets, Captain. Eight. That was the number in the solar system of Fabrina."

"Then there's no doubt that these People are the Fabrini's descendants?"

"None, sir. And no doubt they have been in flight on this asteroid ship for ten thousand years." As Spock spoke, there was the sound of the door opening. They hastily slid behind the monolith. Kirk cautiously peered around it to see Natira, alone, crossing the room to the platform. She knelt. As before, hot light flared from the altar.

"Speak," said the Oracle.

"It is I, Natira."

"Speak."

"It is written that only the High Priestess of the People may select her mate."

"It is so written."

"For the rest of the People—mating and bearing is only permitted by the will of the Creators."

"Of necessity. Our world is small."

"The three strangers among us—there is one among them called McCoy. I wish him to remain with the People—as my mate."

Kirk gave a soundless whistle. Bones certainly had lost no time. Spock cocked an eyebrow, looking at Kirk.

"Does the stranger agree to this?" queried the Oracle.

"I have asked him. He has not yet given me his answer."

"He must become one of the People. He must worship the Creators and agree to the insertion of the obedience instrument."

"He will be told what must be done."

"If he agrees to all things, it is permitted. Teach him our laws so that he commits no sacrilege, no offense against the People—or the Creators."

"It shall be as you say, O most wise."

Natira rose, bowed twice, backed away from the altar and walked toward the door. As Kirk watched her go, his sleeve brushed against the monolith's carved design. The Oracle Room reverberated with a high-pitched, ululating whine. Natira wheeled from the door. The whine turned to a blazing white light. It turned to focus on Kirk and Spock. They went rigid, unable to move.

Natira rushed to the altar.

"Who are the intruders?" demanded the booming voice.

"Two of the strangers."

"McCoy is one of them?"

"No."

"These two have committed sacrilege. You know what must be done."

"I know."

Guards rushed into the room. The light that held Kirk and Spock died, leaving them dazed. Natira pointed to them. "Take them," she told the guards.

As they were seized, she walked up to them. "You have been most foolish," she said. "You have misused our hospitality. And you have more seriously sinned—a sin for which death is the punishment!"

Natira withstood the storm of McCoy's wrath quietly. As he paused in his furious pacing of her quarters, she said—and for the third time—"They entered the Oracle Room."

"And why is death the penalty for that?" he shouted. "They acted out of ignorance!"

"They said they came in friendship. They betrayed our trust. I can make no other decision."

He wheeled to face her. "Natira, you must let them return to their ship!"

"I cannot."

"For me," he said. He pulled her from her couch and into his arms. "I have made my decision. I'm staying with you—here on Yonada."

She swayed with the relief of her love. Into the ear against his cheek, McCoy said, "What they did, they did because they thought they had to. You will not regret letting them go. I am happy for the first time in my life. How can I remain happy, knowing you commanded the death of my friends?"

She lifted her mouth for his kiss. "So be it," she said. "I will give you their lives to show you my love."

"My heart sings now," McCoy said. "Let me tell them. They will need their communications units to return to their ship."

"Very well, McCoy. All shall be as you wish."

He left her for the corridor where Kirk and Spock were waiting under guard. He nodded to the guards. When they disappeared down the corridor, he handed the communicators to Kirk. Kirk passed one to Spock. "Where's yours?" he asked. "You're coming with us, aren't you?"

"No, I'm not," McCoy said.

"But this isn't a planet, Bones! It's a spaceship on a collision course with Daran V!"

"Jim, I'm on something of a collision course myself."

"I order you to return to the ship, Dr. McCoy!"

"And I refuse! I intend to stay right here—on this ship. Natira has asked me to stay. So I shall stay."

"As her husband?"

"Yes. I love her." There were tears in his eyes. "Is it so much to ask, Jim, to let me love?"

"No." Kirk straightened his shoulders. "But does she know—how much of a future you'll have together?"

"Yes. I have told her."

"Bones, if the course of this ship isn't corrected, we'll have to blow it out of space."

"I'll find a way—or you will. You won't destroy Yonada and the people."

Kirk shook his head. "This isn't like you—suddenly giving up—quitting—not fighting any more. You're sick—and you're hiding behind a woman's skirts!"

McCoy swung a fist and Kirk took it square on the chin. He staggered. Spock steadied him. McCoy was yelling, "Sick? Not fighting? Come on, Captain! Try me again!"

Very grave, Spock said, "This conduct is very unlike you, Doctor."

Kirk fumbled for his communicator. "Kirk calling *Enterprise*. Come in, *Enterprise*."

"Scott here, Captain."

"Lock in on our signals. Transport Mr. Spock and me aboard at once."

"What about Dr. McCoy?"

Yes, indeed. What *about* Doctor McCoy? He looked at his friend. "He is staying here, Mr. Scott. Kirk out."

Spock moved to Kirk, flipping open his own communicator. McCoy backed away. They broke into sparkle—and were gone. Savagely, McCoy dragged a sleeve over his tear-blinded eyes.

Custom required him to stand alone before the Oracle.

It spoke.

"To become one of the People of Yonada, the instrument of obedience must be made part of your flesh. Do you now give your consent?"

Natira came forward. She crossed to another side of the altar and opened a small casket.

"I give my consent," McCoy said. As she removed a small device from the casket, her dark eyes met his with a look of pure love. "Say now, McCoy," she said. "For once it is done, it is done."

"Let it be done," he said.

She came to him. Placing the device against his temple, she activated it. He heard a hissing sound. There was a thudding in his head. Instinctively his hand went to the place of insertion. "You are now one with my People," she said. "Kneel with me."

He reached for her hand. She said, "I here pledge you the love you want and will make beautiful your time."

"We are now of one mind," he said.

"One heart."

"One life," he said.

"We shall build the new world of the Promise together, O most wise and most perfect." They rose. She moved into his arms and he kissed her.

The Oracle said, "Teach him what he must know as one of the people."

Natira bowed. Obediently, she led McCoy to the stone monolith. She touched a button—and the carved inset depicting a sun and eight planets slid aside to reveal a large book. "This is the Book of the People," she said. "It is to be opened and read when we reach the world of the Promise. It was given by the Creators."

"Do the People know the contents of the book?"

"Only that it tells of our world here. And why we must one day leave it for the new one."

"Has the reason for leaving been revealed to the People?"

"No! It has not."

Then they'd been right, McCoy realized. Yonada's inhabitants were unaware they lived on a spaceship. "Has it been revealed to you, Natira? As the Priestess of the People?"

She shook her head. "I know only of the new world promised to us, much greater than this little one—verdant and fruitful but empty of living beings. It waits for us."

"Don't you long to know the book's secrets?"

"It is enough for me to know that we shall understand all that now is hidden when we reach our home." She touched the button in the monolith. Its carved inset slid back.

"What is the law concerning the book?"

"To touch it—to allow it to be seen by a nonbeliever is blasphemy to be punished by death."

* * *

On the *Enterprise* Kirk had made his first act a report to Starfleet Command. It had to be told, not only of McCoy's critical illness, but of their failure to correct the collision course of the asteroid ship. Its Chief of Operations, Admiral Westervliet himself, appeared on the screen in Kirk's quarters to respond to the news.

"Medical Headquarters will supply you with a list of space physicians and their biographies, Captain. You will find a replacement for Dr. McCoy among them."

Kirk addressed the stiffly mustached face on the screen. "Yes, Admiral. However, Starfleet's orders to continue our mission is creating difficulties."

"Difficulties? Perhaps I've failed to make myself clear, Captain. You have been relieved of all responsibility for alteration of the course of the asteroid ship Yonada. Starfleet Command will take care of the situation."

"That is the problem, sir," Kirk said.

"A problem? For whom?"

"My crew, sir. Dr. McCoy's illness has become generally known. His condition forced us to leave him on Yonada. His safety depends on the safety of Yonada. To leave this area before Yonada's safety is certain would create a morale problem for the crew. It's a purely human one, of course."

Westervliet had a habit of attacking his mustache when human problems were mentioned. Now it was taking a beating.

"Yes," he said. "Well, Captain Kirk, I certainly sympathize with your wish to remain in Dr. McCoy's vicinity. But the general mission of the *Enterprise* is galactic investigation. You will continue with it."

"Yes, Admiral," Kirk said. "One request, however. Should a cure for Doctor McCoy's disease be discovered, will you advise the *Enterprise*?"

"That is not a request, Captain. Between you and me, it's an order, isn't it?"

"Yes, sir. Thank you, sir."

Kirk, switching off the screen, sat still in his chair. McCoy had made his choice. No appeal had been able to change it. And who was to say it wasn't the right one? A year of life with a woman's love against a year of life without it. Bones. He was going to miss him. The intercom squeaked. He rose to hit the button. "Kirk here."

"Dr. McCoy for you, Captain," Uhura said. "He has an urgent message."

"Put him on!"

"Jim?"

"Yes, Bones."

"We may be able to get these people back on course!"

Kirk's pulse raced. "Have you located the controls?"

"No—but I've seen a book that contains all the knowledge of Yonada's builders. If you can get to it, Spock can dig out the information."

"Where is it?" Kirk asked.

A scream of agony burst from the intercom. "Bones! What's happening? Bones!"

Silence. Frantic, Kirk tried again. "McCoy, what *is* it? What has been done to you? Bones, come in . . ."

But he knew what had happened. Torture, death.

The Oracle had taken McCoy's life in exchange for his forbidden revelation.

Kirk's jaw muscles set hard. "Transporter Room," he told the intercom.

He and Spock materialized in Natira's quarters. She was cradling McCoy's head in her arms. But his face was contorted with pain. Kirk saw him struggle to lift his head. It sank back into Natira's lap.

She looked at them. Dully, her voice toneless, she said, "You have killed your friend. I will have you put to death."

"Let me help you," Kirk said.

"Until you are dead, he will think of you and disobey. While you live, my beloved cannot forget you. So I shall see you die."

She made a move to get up and Kirk grabbed her, clapping his hand over her mouth. "Spock," he said, "help McCoy."

"Yes, Captain." Spock unslung his tricorder. From it he removed a tiny electronic device. Bending over McCoy's motionless body, he pressed the device on the spot where the instrument of obedience had been inserted. When he withdrew it, the insert was clinging to it. He jerked it clear. Then he handed it to Natira. She stared at him, unbelieving. A little moan broke from her. Kirk released her. She sank to the floor. After a moment, she pulled herself up to her hands and knees and crawled over to McCoy. She touched his temple. "My beloved is again a stranger. We are no longer one life." She burst into passionate weeping. "Why have you done this to us? Why?"

"He is still yours," Kirk said gently.

The tears choked her. "It is—forbidden. He is not of our people—now. You have released him—from his vow of obedience."

"We have released him from the cruelty of your Oracle," Kirk said.

She closed her eyes, unhearing, her body racked with sobs. Beside her, Kirk saw McCoy's eyelids flicker open. He went to him quickly, bending over him. "You spoke of a book," he said. "Where is it, Bones?"

Natira leaped to her feet with a shriek. "You must not know! You must not know that!"

McCoy looked up into Kirk's eyes. "The Oracle Room," he whispered.

"You will never see the Book!" cried Natira. "It is blasphemy!" She ran to the door, calling, "Guards! Guards!"

Kirk caught her, closing his hand over her mouth again. "You must listen to me,

Natira!" She pulled away from him and he jerked her back. "*Listen to me!* If you do not understand what I tell you, you may call the guards. And we will accept whatever punishment is decreed. *But now you must listen!*"

She slowly lifted the tear-wet lashes. "What is it you wish to say?"

"I shall tell you the truth, Natira—the truth about your world of Yonada. And you will trust it as true as a child trusts what is true. Years ago, ten thousand years ago, a sun died and the sun's worlds died with it. Its worlds were the eight ones you see pictured on the stone pillar in the Oracle Room."

"Yonada is one of those worlds," she said.

"No. It was the world of your ancestors—your creators." He paused to give her time. After a moment, he quietly added, "It no longer exists, Natira."

"You are mad," she whispered. "You are mad."

"Hear me out, Natira! Your ancestors knew their world was about to die. They wanted their race to live. So they built a great ship. On it they placed their best people. Then they sent them and the ship into space."

"You wish me to believe that Yonada is a ship?"

"Yes," Kirk said.

"But we have a sun! It did not die. And at night I see the stars!"

"No. You have never seen the sun. You have never seen the stars. You live inside a hollow ball. Your fathers created the ball to protect you—to take you on the great journey to the new safe world of the Promise."

In her face he could see half-thought thoughts reviving, completing themselves. But the growing perception was painful. Yet it had come. She spoke very slowly. "The truth—why do you bring it to Yonada?"

"We had to. Your ship has done well—but its machinery is tired. It must be mended. If we don't mend it, Yonada will strike and kill another great world it knows nothing about."

Belief flooded into her. With it came the realization of betrayal.

"Why has this truth not been told us? Why have we been kept in darkness?"

Kirk went to her. But she pushed him away, overwhelmed by the sense of an incredible treachery. "No! You have lied! I believe only the Oracle! I must believe!"

Kirk said, "Let us remove the instrument of obedience. Let us remove it for the truth's sake."

She was gone, fled out the door. Kirk turned to Spock. "Do you think she understood me?" he said. But Spock was at the open door. Kirk saw him nod pleasantly to a passing guard before he quietly closed the door. "She hasn't sent the guards to detain us, Captain. It is my supposition that she understood a great deal."

Behind them, McCoy had struggled shakily to his feet. Now he pushed past them. "Natira! I have to go to her. I must go to her in the Oracle Room."

She was on her knees before the altar, her eyes shut in rapt devotion.

The thunder voice spoke. "You have listened to the words of the nonbelievers."

"I have listened."

"You felt the pain of warning."

"I felt the pain of warning."

"Why did you listen further?"

"They said they spoke the truth."

"Their truth is not your truth."

She opened her eyes. "Is truth not truth for all?"

"There is only one for you. Repent your disobedience."

"I must know the truth of the world!" she cried.

At the sound of her scream, Kirk rushed into the Oracle Room. He lifted Natira from the dais, but McCoy, reaching for her, took her in his arms, holding her close. Her body was stiff under spasms of pain. As one passed, she reached out a hand to caress his face. "Your friends have told me—much."

"They spoke the truth," McCoy said.

"I believe you. I believe . . ."

Agony convulsed her again. She fought it bravely. "I believe with you, my husband. We have been kept in darkness."

McCoy extended a hand to Spock. The tiny electronic device performed its function once more. When McCoy lifted it from Natira's temple, it held the obedience insert. He held it up for her to see. The grief of a great loss shadowed her dark eyes as she lapsed into unconsciousness.

"Is she all right?" Kirk asked.

"She will be. I'll stay with her."

Kirk said, "Mr. Spock—the Fabrina inset."

They were crossing to the monolith when the Oracle spoke, a fierce anger in its voice. "You blaspheme the temple!"

Kirk turned. "We do this for the survival of Yonada's people."

"You are forbidden to gaze at the Book!"

"We must consult it to help the people!"

"The punishment is death."

Kirk looked back at McCoy. "Bones?"

"Depress the side section," McCoy said.

A blast of heat struck them. Around them the walls had turned a radiant red. Even as he pressed the side of the monolith, the air he breathed was scorching Kirk's lungs. But the inset had slid open. He seized the book and passed it to Spock. "It must contain the plan. Is it indexed?"

"Yes, Captain. Here's the page . . ."

Yellow, brittle with age, the page's parchment showed the same idealized sun, the same planet placements as the altar design and the inset. Arrows pointed to three of the planets. Spock translated the Fabrini writing at the top of the page. "Apply pressure simultaneously to the planets indicated."

The walls were glowing hotter. Spock tossed the book aside and they raced for the altar plaque. As Kirk pushed at the three planets, the altar moved forward. Then it stopped. Spock slid into the space behind it. Before he followed him, Kirk turned back to McCoy and Natira. "Let's get out of this heat," he called.

Spock had found a short passageway. As he approached its end wall, it lifted. At once he heard the hum of electronic power. A light shone on a button-crowded console. Spock studied it for a moment. Then he pressed a button. The light went out. "I've neutralized that heating element!" he called back to the others.

The heat in the Oracle Room rapidly cooled. Kirk and McCoy sat Natira down against an altar wall. "You'll be all right here now," Kirk said. "The Oracle can no longer punish."

He saw her rest her glossy head against McCoy's shoulder. Looking up at him, she said, "Your friends have ended the punishments?" He nodded. "And will they send this—this ship on to the place of the Promise?"

"Yes," he said. "That is their promise. Now I must help them. Come with me."

"No," she said.

"There is nothing to fear now, Natira. So come. We must hurry to join them."

"No. I cannot go with you." She paused. "It is not fear that holds me. I now understand the great purpose of our fathers. I must honor it, McCoy."

He stared at her in unbelief. "You mean to stay here—on Yonada?"

"I must remain with my people throughout our great journey."

"Natira, trust me! The Oracle will not harm us!"

"I stay because it is what I must do," she said.

"I will not leave you," McCoy said.

"Will McCoy stay here to die?"

The question shocked him into silence. He fell to his knees beside her. "Natira, you have given me reason to wish to live. But wishing is not enough. I must search through the universe to cure myself—and all those like me. I wanted you with me—with me . . ."

"This is my universe," she said. "You came here to save my people. Shall I abandon them?"

"I love you," McCoy said.

She kissed him. "If it is permitted, perhaps one day you, too, will see the land of our Promise. . . ."

It was good-bye. And he knew it. He reached for her blindly through a mist of tears.

* * *

In the asteroid ship's control room, Spock had located a weakness in one of its consoles' eight tubes.

"Enough to turn it off course?" Kirk asked.

"Yes, Captain. The engine can take a check." Kirk, studying control panels, was reminded of those of the *Enterprise*. "A very simple problem," Spock called from the engine room. "And comparatively easy to repair."

He came back, holding one hand out stiffly. "I think we can now attempt the course correction, sir."

"What was wrong?"

"In creating a completely natural environment for the people on this ship, its builders included many life forms—including insects. A control jet in there was blocked by a hornets' nest."

"You're not serious, Mr. Spock?"

Spock held up a forefinger. It was swollen to twice its size. "I destroyed the nest," he said. "In doing so, I was stung." He sat down, resuming his watch of the console instruments. "The guidance system is taking over, sir. I think we can revert to automatic controls."

"She's steady on course now," Kirk said.

They released the manual controls and were heading back to the Oracle Room when Spock stopped at a screened console of complex design. "Knowledge files," he said. "Those banks are filled with the total knowledge of the Fabrini. I presume they were prepared for the people to consult when they reach their destination." He left Kirk to examine the console more closely. "They seem to have amassed a great deal of medical knowledge."

Unslinging his tricorder, he slipped a taped disk into it. He passed it over the console. "The knowledge of the builders of this ship could be extremely valuable—even though it is ten thousand years old."

McCoy spoke from behind them. "Gentlemen, are we ready to return to the *Enterprise*?"

Kirk stared at him. It was best to ask no questions, he thought. "Yes, Bones, we are," he said. He flipped open his com unit. "Kirk to *Enterprise*. Landing party ready to beam aboard."

The screen in Sickbay held a series of chemical formulas in the Fabrini writing. Kirk and Spock, watching Christine Chapel prepare another air-hypo injection, saw that her hands were shaking. She noticed it, too. To quiet her agitation, she glanced at the life indicators at the head of McCoy's bed. The steady blinking of their lights steadied her. She thrust the air-hypo into a green liquid.

"Not another one?" McCoy said as she approached his bed. He made a face as the hypo took effect. But already it had made a fast change in the life support panel.

"Excellent, Doctor," Christine said. "You're quite able to see for yourself. The white corpuscle count is back to normal." She reached an arm under his shoulders to help him check the panel behind him. He still looked pained.

"Tell me, Doctor," Kirk wanted to know. "Why are cures so often as painful as the disease?"

"Jim, that is a very sore subject with medical men."

"Dr. McCoy," Spock said reprovingly, "it seems that the Fabrini cure for granulation of the hemoglobin has seriously damaged your gift for witty repartee."

Nurse Chapel had filled the hypo again. "This is the last one, Doctor."

Spock, his eyes on the life support panel, achieved a Vulcan triumph. Joy radiated from his impassive face. "Your hemoglobin count is now completely normal, Doctor. So the flow of oxygen to all the cells of your body is again up to its abundantly energetic level."

McCoy sat up. "Spock, I owe this to you. Had you not brought back that Fabrini knowledge . . ."

"My translation abilities are one of my most minor accomplishments," Spock said. "If you consider my major ones, Doctor . . ."

"I wonder if there's a Fabrini cure for a swelled head," McCoy speculated.

Kirk intervened. "Bones, the Fabrini descendants are scheduled to debark on their promised planet in exactly fourteen months and seven days."

The grin left McCoy's face. He looked at Kirk.

"Yes," Kirk said. "I expect you'd like to see the Fabrini descendants again to thank them personally. So I've arranged to be in the vicinity of their new home at the time of their arrival. You will want to be there to welcome them, won't you?"

"Thank you, Jim," McCoy said. "Thank you very much."

THE THOLIAN WEB

Writer: Judy Burns and Chet Richards
Director: Herb Wallerstein
First Aired: November 15, 1968

The bridge was at full muster—Kirk, Scott, Spock, Uhura, Chekov, Sulu—and extremely tense. The *Enterprise* was in unsurveyed territory, approaching the last reported position of the Starship *Defiant*, which had vanished without a trace three weeks ago.

"Captain," Spock said, "I have lost the use of all sensors. Were I to believe these readings, space itself is breaking up around us."

"A major failure?"

"Not in the sensors, sir; I have run a complete systems check. The failure is mine; I simply do not know how to interpret these reports."

"Captain," Scott added, "there may be no connection, but we're losing power in the warp engines."

"How bad is it?"

"We can hardly feel it now, but it's richt abnormal all the same. I canna find the cause."

Now it was Chekov's turn. "Captain, we have visual detection of an object dead ahead. It *looks* like a starship."

It did, at that, but not a starship in any condition to which they were accustomed. It was visibly shimmering.

"Mr. Spock, what's wrong with it?"

"Nonexistence, to put the matter in a word, Captain. There is virtually no radar return, mass analysis, radiation traces. We see it, but the sensors indicate it isn't there."

"Mr. Chekov, narrow the field and see if you can bring up the identification numbers. It's the *Defiant*, all right. Mr. Sulu, impulse engines only. Close to Transporter range. Lieutenant Uhura, open a hailing channel."

"I've been trying to raise them, sir, but there's no response."

Chekov shifted the viewing angle again. The other ship showed no gaping holes or other signs of damage. It was just ghostly—and silent.

"Within Transporter range, sir."

"Thanks, Mr. Sulu. Lieutenant, order Dr. McCoy to the Transporter Room. Mr. Spock, Mr. Chekov, I'll want you as well. Environment suits all around; O'Neil to handle the Transporter. Take over, Mr. Scott."

The Transporter was locked onto the bridge of the *Defiant*. The lighting there turned out to be extremely subdued; even some monitor lights were not functioning. But the situation was all too visible, nonetheless.

A man somewhat older than Kirk, wearing a captain's stripes, lay dead in his command chair, a number one phaser clutched in one hand. The other hand was twisted in the hair of a junior officer. The junior was also dead, with both his hands locked around the Captain's neck.

Chekov was the first to speak. "Has there ever been a mutiny on a starship before?"

"Technically," Spock said, "the refusal of Captain Garth's fleet to follow his orders when he became insane was a mutiny. But there has never been any record of an occurrence like this."

McCoy stopped to examine the bodies. "The Captain's neck is broken, Jim."

"This ship is still functioning," Spock said after a quick check of the communications console. "It is logical to assume that the mutineers are somewhere aboard. Yet the sensors show no sign of life anywhere in the vessel."

"Odd," Kirk said reflectively. "Very odd. Spock, you stay here with me. Chekov, get down to Life Support and Engineering. Dr. McCoy, check out sickbay. I want some answers."

The two men moved off. As they did so, Scott's voice sounded in Kirk's helmet. "Captain, Mr. Sulu reports that he can't get an accurate fix on the *Defiant*, but it seems to be drifting away. Should he correct for range?"

Still odder. How could one ship be moving relative to the other when neither was under power? "Keep us within beaming range, but not too close."

"Chekov reporting, Captain. All dead in Life Support and in Engineering as well."

"Right. Get back up here. Bones?"

"More bodies, Jim. Proximate cause of deaths, various forms of violence. In short, I'd say they killed each other."

"Could a mental disease possibly have inflicted all of the crew at once?"

"It may still be here, sir," Chekov said, reappearing. "I feel pretty funny myself—headachy, dizzy."

"I can't answer the question," McCoy's voice said. "According to the medical log, even the ship's surgeon here didn't really know what was going on. The best I can do for you is take all the readings I can get and analyze them later. Now what the devil . . . ?"

"Bones! What's happening?"

There was a brief silence. Then: "Jim, this ship's beginning to dissolve! I just put my hand right *through* a corpse—and then through the wall next to him."

"Get back up here on the double. Kirk to *Enterprise*. Mr. Scott, stand by to beam us back."

"Captain, I can't. Not all at once, at least."

"What do you mean? What's going on over there?"

"Nothing we can understand," Scott's voice said grimly. "The *Defiant* is fading out, and it's—well, something is ripping the innards out of our own ship. It's jamming our Transporter frequencies. We've got only three working, and I can't be sure about those. One of you has got to wait."

"Request permission to remain," Spock said. "I could be completing the data."

"It's more important to get what you already have into analysis on the *Enterprise*. Don't argue. I'll probably be right after you."

But he was not. Within moments after Spock, Chekov and McCoy materialized aboard the *Enterprise*, the *Defiant* had vanished.

Scott was at the consoles with the Transporter officer. Spock joined them, removing his helmet, and scanned the board.

"See anything I don't?" Scott said.

"Apparently not. Everything is negative."

McCoy took off his own helmet. "But he's got to be out there somewhere. If the Transporter won't grab him, what about the shuttlecraft? There must be some way to pick him up."

"There is no present trace of the Captain, Doctor," Spock said evenly. "The only next possible action is to feed the computer our data and see what conclusions can be drawn."

The computer was the fastest of its kind, but the wait seemed frustratingly long all the same. At last its pleasantly feminine voice said: "Integrated."

"Compute the next period of spatial interphase," Spock told it.

"Two hours, twelve minutes."

Spock shut the machine off. Scott was staring at him, aghast. "Is that how long we have to wait before we can pick up the Captain? But, Spock, I don't think I can hold the ship in place that long. The power leak is unbalanced and I haven't been able to trace it, let alone stop it."

"You will have to keep trying," Spock said. "The fabric of space is very weak here. If we disturb it, there will be no chance of retrieving the Captain alive."

Chekov was looking baffled; worse, he was looking positively ill. "I don't understand," he said. "What's so special about this region of space?"

"I can only speculate," Spock said. "We exist in a universe which coexists with a multitude of others in the same physical space, but displaced in time. For certain brief periods, one area of such a space overlaps an area of ours. That is the time of interphase when we connect with the *Defiant*'s universe."

"And retrieve the Captain," Uhura added.

"Perhaps. But the dimensional structure of each universe is totally dissimilar to the others. Any use of power would disturb what can at best be only a tenuous and brief connection. It might also result in our being trapped ourselves . . ."

"And die like them?" Chekov said raggedly. Suddenly his voice rose to a yell. "Damn you, Spock . . ."

He sprang. Spock, surprised, was knocked backward, Chekov's hands around his neck. Sulu attempted to drag Chekov off; the enraged man struck out at him. Scott promptly grabbed him by that arm. It was all that they could do to handle him, but the distraction enabled Spock to get in a neck pinch.

"Security guards to the bridge," Spock said to the intercom. "Dr. McCoy, will you also please report?"

McCoy appeared almost at once, taking in the scene at a glance. "He jumped you? My fault, I should have checked him the minute he said he was feeling funny, but there was so much else going on. Anybody notice any spasms of pain? Ah. What about his behavior? Hysterical? Frightened?"

"He looked more angry than frightened to me," Uhura said. "But there was nothing to be angry about."

"Nevertheless," Spock said, "there were all the signs of a murderous fury. After what we have seen aboard the *Defiant*, the episode is doubly disturbing."

"I'll say it is," McCoy said. "Guards, take him to sickbay. I'll see what I can find out from seeing the thing in its first stages. Spock, on the other subject, what makes you think Captain Kirk is still alive?"

"The Captain was locked in the Transporter beam when the *Defiant* phased out, Doctor. It is possible that he was saved the shock of transition. If we do not catch him again at the precise corresponding instant in the next interphase, he will die. There is no margin for error; his environmental unit can supply breathable air for no more than another three point twenty-six hours."

"Mr. Spock," Sulu called from the helm. "A vessel is approaching on an intercept vector."

Spock walked quickly to the command chair, and Scott went back to his post. "Status, Mr. Sulu," Spock said.

"Range, two hundred thousand kilometers and closing. Relative velocity, zero point five one C."

"Red alert," Spock said. The klaxon began to sound throughout the ship. At the same instant, Uhura captured the intruder on the main viewing screen.

The Tholian Web

The stranger was crystalline in appearance, blue-green in coloration, and shaped like a tetrahedron within which a soft light seemed to pulsate. As the scene materialized, Sulu gasped.

"Stopped dead, Mr. Spock. Now, how do they do that? Range, ninety thousand kilometers and holding."

"Mr. Spock," Uhura said. "I'm getting a visual signal from them."

"Transfer it to the main viewer."

The scene dissolved into what might have been the command bridge of the alien vessel. Most of the frame, however, was occupied by the upper half of an unknown creature. Like its vessel, the alien was almost jewel-like in appearance, multifaceted, crystalline, though it was humanoid in build. A light pulsated rapidly but irregularly inside what seemed to be its head.

"I am Commander Loskene," the creature said at once in good Federation Interlingua. "You are trespassing in a territorial annex of the Tholian Assembly. You must leave this area immediately."

Spock studied Loskene. The pulsating light did not seem to be in synch with the voice. He said formally, "Spock, in command of the Federation Starship *Enterprise*. Commander, the Federation regards this area as free space."

"We have claimed it. And we are prepared to use force, if necessary, to hold it."

"We are not interested in a show of force. The *Enterprise* has responded to a distress call from one of our ships and is currently engaged in rescue operations. Do you wish to assist us?"

"I find no evidence of a disabled ship. My instruments indicate that ours are the only two vessels in this area."

"The other ship is trapped in an interspatial sink. it should reappear in one hour and fifty minutes. We request that you stand by until then."

"Very well, *Enterprise*. In the interest of interstellar amity, we will wait. But we will not tolerate deceit."

The view wavered, and then the screen once more showed the Tholian ship. Now there was nothing to do but wait—and hope.

The moment of interphase approached at last. As before, Scott personally took over the Transporter console. In the command chair, Spock watched the clock intently.

"Transporter Room."

"Aye, Mr. Spock. I'm locked onto the Captain's coordinates."

"Interphase in twenty seconds . . . ten seconds . . . five, four, three, two, one, energize!"

There was a tense silence. Then Scott's voice said, "The platform's empty, Mr. Spock. There's naught at all at those coordinates."

"Any abnormality to report, Mr. Sulu?"

"The sensor readings don't correspond to those we received the last time we saw the *Defiant*. Insofar as I can tell, the Tholian entry into the area has disturbed the interphase."

"McCoy to bridge," said the intercom. "Has the Captain been beamed aboard, Mr. Spock?"

"No, Doctor. And the interphase period has been passed. We will have to wait for the next one."

"But he hasn't got enough air for that! And there's been another case like Chekov's. I have had to confine my orderly to sickbay."

"Have you still no clues as to the cause, Doctor?"

"I know exactly what the cause is," McCoy's voice said grimly. "And there's nothing I can do to stop it. The molecular structure of the central nervous system, including the brain, is being distorted by the space we are in. Sooner or later the whole crew will be affected—unless you get the *Enterprise* out of here."

"Mr. Spock!" Sulu broke in. "We're being fired upon!"

The announcement came only seconds before the bolt itself struck. The *Enterprise* lurched, but did not roll.

"Damage control, report," Spock said.

"Minor structural damage to sections A-4 and C-13."

"Engineering, hold power steady. Mr. Sulu, divert all but emergency maintenance power into the shields."

"Sir," Sulu said, "that will reduce phaser power by fifty percent."

Almost as if it had heard him, the Tholian ship darted forward. It seemed to be almost within touching distance before it fired again. This time, the shock threw everybody who was not seated to the floor.

"Engineering to bridge. Mr. Spock, we can't take another like that. We'll either have to fight or run."

"Mr. Sulu, lock in phaser tracking controls. Divert power to the phaser banks and fire at the next close approach. Lieutenant Uhura, open a channel to the Tholians."

McCoy came onto the bridge, his face masklike. On the main viewing screen, the pyramidal ship looped around and began another run.

"Spock, what's the use of this battle?" McCoy demanded. "You've already lost the Captain. Take the ship out of here."

Spock, intent upon the screen, did not answer. The pyramid zigzagged in. Then both vessels fired at once.

The *Enterprise* rang like a gong and the lights flickered, but the screen showed that the Tholian, too, had sustained a direct hit. There was no visible damage, but the pyramid had again stopped dead, and then began to retreat.

The Tholian Web

"A standoff," Spock said. "Mr. Scott, status?"

"Convertors burned out," Scott's voice said. "We've lost drive and hence the ability to correct drift. I estimate four hours in replacement time."

"By that time," Sulu said, "we'll have drifted right through that—that gateway out there."

"Are you satisfied?" McCoy said, picking himself up off the deck. "Spock, why did you do it?"

"To stay in the area for the next interphase," Spock said, "required for disabling the Tholian ship."

"But you're ignoring the mental effects! How can you risk your whole crew on the dim chance of rescuing one officer—one presumed dead, at that? The Captain wouldn't have done that!"

"Doctor, I hardly believe that now is the time for such comparisons. Get down to your laboratory at once and search for an antidote to the mental effects. Since we must remain here, that is your immediate task. Mine is to command the *Enterprise*."

McCoy left, though not without an angry glare.

"Mr. Spock, something has just entered sensor range," Sulu said. "Yes, it's another Tholian ship. Loskene must have contacted them at the same time they intercepted us. Loskene is moving back out of phaser range."

"Lieutenant, attempt contact again."

"No response, sir."

On the screen, the two Tholian ships joined—literally joined, base to base, making what seemed to be a single vessel like a six-sided diamond. Then they began to separate again. Between their previously common bases a multicolored strand stretched out across space.

Spock rose and went to the library computer station. The Tholians met again, separated, spinning another thread. Then another. Gradually, a latticework of energy seemed to be growing.

"Switch scanners, Mr. Sulu."

The screen angle changed. The tempo of the Tholian activity was speeding up rapidly. From this point of view, it seemed that the *Enterprise* was already almost a third surrounded by the web and it kept on growing.

Spock pulled his head out of the hooded viewer. "Fascinating," he said. "And very efficient. If they succeed in completing that structure before we are repaired, we shall not be able to run even if we wished to."

Nobody replied. There seemed to be nothing to say.

There was a service for Kirk. It was brief and military. Spock, as the next in command, spoke the eulogy. The speech was not long, but it was interrupted all the same, by another seizure of madness striking down a crewman in the congregation. Afterward, the tension seemed much greater.

As the rest filed out, McCoy stopped Spock at the doorway. "There is a duty to be performed in the Captain's cabin," he said. "It requires both of us."

"Then it will have to wait. My duties require my immediate return to the bridge."

"The Captain left a message tape," the surgeon said. "It was his order that it be reviewed by both of us should he ever be declared dead—as you have just done."

"It will have to wait for a more suitable moment," Spock said, putting his hand on the corridor rail.

"Why? Are you afraid it will change your present status?"

Spock turned sharply. "The mental and physical state of this crew are your responsibility, Doctor. As I have observed before, command is mine."

"Not while a last order remains to be obeyed."

For a moment Spock did not reply. Then he said, "Very well. To the Captain's quarters, then."

McCoy had evidently visited Kirk's quarters before the service, for laid out on a table was the black velvet case which contained Kirk's medals, and it was open. The surgeon looked down at them for a long moment.

"He was a hero in every sense of the word," he said. "Yet his life was sacrificed for nothing. The one thing that would have given his death meaning is the survival of the *Enterprise*. You have made that impossible."

Spock said glacially, "We came here for a specific purpose."

"Maybe not the same one. I came to find out, among other things, really why you stayed and fought."

Spock closed the box. "The Captain would have remained to recover a man at the risk of his own life, other things being equal. I do not consider the question closed."

"He wouldn't have risked the ship. And what do you mean, the question isn't closed? Do you think he may be still alive after all? Then why did you declare him dead—to assure your own captaincy?"

"Unnecessary. I am already in command of the *Enterprise*."

"It's a situation I wish I could remedy."

"If you believe," Spock said, "that I remained just to fire that phaser and kill James Kirk or this crew, it is your prerogative as Medical Officer of this ship to relieve me of duty. In the meantime, I suggest that we play the tape you referred to, so I can get back to the bridge and you can resume looking for an antidote for the madness."

"All right," McCoy turned to Kirk's viewer and flipped a switch. The screen lit; in it, Kirk was seated at his desk.

"Spock. Bones," Kirk's voice said. "Since you are playing this tape, we will assume that I am dead, the tactical situation is critical and you two are locked in mortal combat.

"It means also, Spock, that you have control of my ship and are probably making the most difficult decisions of your career. I can offer only one small piece of advice, for what it's worth. Use every scrap of knowledge and logic you've got to save the ship, but temper your judgment with intuitive insight. I believe you have that quality. But if you can't find it in yourself, then seek out McCoy. Ask his advice. And if you find it sound, take it.

"Bones, you heard what I just told Spock. Help him if you can, but remember that *he* is the Captain. His decisions, when he reaches them, are to be obeyed without further question. You might find that he is capable of both human insight and human error, and they are the most difficult to defend. But you will find that Spock is deserving of the same loyalty and confidence that you all have given me.

"As to the disposal of my personal effects . . ."

McCoy snapped the switch, and turned. For a moment the two men studied each other, less guardedly than before. Then McCoy said, "Spock, I'm sorry. It hurts, doesn't it?"

Spock closed his eyes for a moment. Then he turned and left. McCoy remained for a moment longer, thoughtful, and then stepped out into the corridor.

He was greeted by a stifled scream. Turning, he saw Uhura running toward him, half out of uniform, her normally unshakable calm dissolved in something very close to panic. She saw McCoy and stopped, gasping, trying to get words out; but before they could form, a stab of pain seemed to go through her and her knees buckled. She grabbed the rail for support.

The signs were all too clear. McCoy surreptitiously got out his hypospray, and then went to steady her.

"Lieutenant!" he said sharply. "What is it?"

"I—Doctor, I've just seen the Captain!"

"Yes, he just left a moment ago."

"No, I don't mean Mr. Spock. The captain. He's alive!"

"I'm afraid not. But of course you saw him. We would all like to see him."

Her legs were still shaking, but she seemed somewhat calmer now. "I know what you're thinking. But it isn't that. I was looking into my mirror in my quarters, and there he was. He was—sort of shimmering, like the *Defiant* was when we first saw it. He looked puzzled—and like he was trying to tell me something."

McCoy brought the hypospray up. Uhura saw it and tried to fight free, but she was too wobbly to resist. "I did see him. Tell Mr. Spock. He's alive, he's alive . . ."

The hypospray hissed. "I'll tell him," McCoy said gently. "But in the meantime, you're going to sickbay."

One of Scott's crewmen attacked him within the same hour. The effect was spreading faster through the ship. The Tholian web was now two-thirds complete, and the *Enterprise* was still without impulse drive, let alone the thrust to achieve interstellar velocity.

The crewman's attack failed; but a shaken Scott was on the bridge not ten minutes later.

"Mr. Spock—I've just seen the Captain."

"Spock to McCoy; please come to the bridge. Go on, Mr. Scott."

"He was on the upper engineering level—sparkling, rather like a Transporter effect. He seemed to be almost floating. And I think he saw us. He seemed to be breathing pretty heavily—and then, hey presto! he winked right out."

The elevator doors snapped open and McCoy came out, fast enough to pick up most of Scott's account. He said, "Scotty, are you feeling all right?"

"Och, I think so. Tired, maybe."

"So are we all, of course. Don't fail to see me if you have any other symptoms."

"Right."

"Lieutenant Uhura told a similar story before she went under," Spock said. "Perhaps we ought not to discount it entirely. Yet in critical moments, men sometimes see exactly what they want to see, even when they are not ill."

"Are you suggesting," McCoy said, "that the men are seeing the Captain because they've lost confidence in you?"

"I am making no suggestions, but merely stating a fact."

"Well, the situation is critical, all right. And there have been more assaults on the lower decks. And if Scottie here's being affected, that will finish whatever chance we have to get the *Enterprise* out of here."

"Have you any further leads on a remedy?"

"A small one," McCoy said. "I've been toying with the idea of trying a chlortheragen derivative. But I'm not ready to try anything so drastic, yet."

"Why not?"

"Well, for one thing . . ."

"Gentlemen," Scott said quietly. "Mr. Spock. Look behind you."

At the same moment, there was a chorus of gasps from the rest of the personnel on the bridge. Spock turned.

Floating behind him was an image of Captain Kirk, full length but soapily iridescent. He seemed to recognize Spock, but to be unable to move. Kirk's hand rose to his throat, and his lips moved. There was no sound.

Spock—hurry!

The figure vanished.

The Tholian web continued to go up around the *Enterprise*, section by section. The pace had slowed somewhat; Loskene and his compatriots seemed to have concluded that the *Enterprise* would not or could not leave the area.

Aboard the ship, too, the tension seemed to have abated, if only slightly. It was now

The Tholian Web

tacitly accepted that the apparition of the Captain on the bridge had not been a part of the lurking madness, and that he had been, therefore, alive then.

Spock and Scott were having another computer session.

"So your reluctance to use the phasers now stands endorsed," the Engineering Officer said. "They blasted a hole right through this crazy space fabric and sent the *Defiant* heaven only knows where."

"And would have sent the Captain with it, if we had not had a Transporter lock on him during the first fade-out. As of now, only the overlap time has changed; the next interphase will be early, in exactly twenty minutes. Can you be ready?"

"Aye," Scott said, "she'll be back together, but we'll have only eighty percent power built up."

"It will have to do."

McCoy came up behind them, carrying a tray bearing a flask and three glasses. "Compliments of the house, gentlemen," he said. "To your good health and the health of your crew. Drink it down!"

"What is it?" Spock said.

"Generally, it's an antidote-cum-preventive for the paranoid reaction. Specifically, a derivative of chlortheragen."

"If I remember aright," Scott said, "that's a nerve gas used by the Klingons. Are you trying to kill us all, McCoy?"

"I said it was a derivative, not the pure stuff. In this form it simply deadens certain nerve inputs to the brain."

"Any good brand of Scotch will do that for you."

"As a matter of fact," McCoy said, "it works best mixed with alcohol. But it does work. It even brought Chekov around, and he's been affected the longest of any of us."

Scott knocked his drink back, and made a face. "It'll nae become a regular tipple with me," he said. "I'll be getting back to my machines."

Spock nodded after him and crossed to the command chair. A moment later Chekov himself entered, beaming, and took his regular position. Uhura was already at her post, as was Sulu.

"Your absence was keenly felt, Ensign," Spock said. "To begin with, give me an estimated time for completion of the Tholian tractor field."

"At the enemy's present pace, two minutes, sir."

"Mr. Sulu, I have the computers programmed to move us through the interspatial gateway. Stand ready to resume the helm as soon as we emerge on the other side—wherever that may be."

"Transporter Room."

"Scott here."

"Ready for interphase in seventy-five seconds."

"Aye, sir, standing by."

"Mr. Spock," Sulu said, "the Tholians are getting ready to close the web. It seems to be contracting to fit the ship."

"Counting down to interphase," Chekov said. He now had an open line to the Transporter Room. "One minute."

"Mr. Scott, have we full power?"

"Only seventy-six percent, Mr. Spock."

"Can the computer call on it all at once?"

"Aye, I think she'll stand it."

"Thirty seconds."

Suddenly, on the viewing screen, between the *Enterprise*, a tiny figure in an environmental suit popped into being.

"I see him!"

"He's early!"

"It's the Captain!"

The webbing began to slide across the screen in a heavy mesh. Behind it, stars slid past as well.

"Tractor field activated," Sulu said. "We're being pulled out of here."

"Try to maintain position, Mr. Sulu."

The ship throbbed to the sudden application of power at the computer's command. Heavy tremors shook the deck.

The web vanished.

"We broke it!" Chekov cheered.

"No, Ensign, we went out through the interdimensional gateway. Since we went through shortly after interphase, we should still be in some part of normal space. Compute the distance from our original position."

"Umm—two point seventy-two parsecs." Chekov looked aghast. "But that's beyond Transporter range!"

"You forget, Mr. Chekov, that we have a shortcut. Mr. Scott, are you still locked on the Captain?"

"Aye, sir, though I dinna understand how."

"You can beam him in now—we have broken free."

"Aye, sir—got him! But he's unconscious. McCoy, this is your department."

"I will be down directly," Spock said. "Mr. Sulu, take over."

As it turned out, no elaborate treatment was needed; taking Kirk's helmet off to let him breathe ship's air removed the source of the difficulty, and once he had been moved to his quarters, an epinephrine hypospray brought him quickly to consciousness. For a moment he looked up at Spock and McCoy in silence. Then McCoy said, "Welcome home, Jim."

"Thanks, Bones. You know, I had a whole universe to myself after the *Defiant* was thrown out. There was absolutely no one else in it. Somehow I could sense it."

"That must have been disorienting," McCoy observed.

"Very. I kept trying to get through to the ship. I think I did at least three times, but it never lasted. I must say I like a crowded universe much better. How did you two get along without me?"

"We managed," McCoy said. "Spock gave the orders. I found the answers."

Spock gave McCoy a curious glance, but nodded confirmation.

"You mean you didn't have any problems?" Kirk said, with slight but visible incredulity.

"None worth reporting, Captain," Spock said.

"Let me be the judge of that."

"Only such minor disturbances, Captain, as are inevitable when humans are involved."

"Or are involved with Vulcans," McCoy added.

"Understood, gentlemen. I hope my last orders were helpful in solving the problems not worth reporting."

"Orders, Captain?" Spock said.

"The orders I left for you—for both of you—on tape."

"Oh, those orders!" said McCoy. "There wasn't time, Captain. We never got a chance to listen to them."

"The crisis was upon us and then passed so quickly, Captain, that . . ."

"I see," Kirk said, smiling. "Nothing worth reporting happened, and it all happened so quickly. Good. Well, let's hope there will be no similar opportunity to test those orders that you never heard. Let's get to work."

WINK OF AN EYE

Writer: Arthur Heinemann
(Story by Lee Cronin)
Director: Jud Taylor
First Aired: November 29, 1968

In the space fronting the handsome building of unidentified metal, a fountain flung its sparkle of spray into the air. Kirk, abstracted, watched Security Guard Compton taking samples of its water. Nearby, McCoy was scanning the plaza's periphery with his tricorder. Necessary but time-consuming occupations, Kirk thought. And useless. They had done nothing to locate the source of that distress call that had forced their beam-down to this unexplored planet calling itself Scalos.

With abrupt impatience, he opened his communicator. "Kirk to *Enterprise*. Lieutenant Uhura, does the location of that distress signal exactly correspond to this area?"

"Yes, sir. And I am receiving visual contact with the Scalosians. I can't see you on the viewing screen but I can see them."

"Check coordinates, Lieutenant."

"The coordinates correspond, sir."

His impatience grew. "There are no Scalosians, Lieutenant. Apart from our landing party, there is nobody here."

"Their distress call is very strong, sir. They are begging for immediate assistance."

"Check circuits for malfunction. Captain out."

He looked up to meet McCoy's nod. "There *must* be a malfunction, Jim. This is a barren world—hardly any vegetation; no apparent animal life."

As though to contradict him, a shrill mosquito whine sounded near Kirk's head. He struck the invisible insect away. "But there's some kind of insect life," he said.

"My tricorder doesn't register it."

"My ears did," Kirk retorted. He dropped the subject for Spock, rounding a corner of the strangely-fluted metal building, was approaching them. "Anything, Mr. Spock?"

"Evidently a civilization of high order, Captain, rating number seven on the Industrial Scale. Humanoid in appearance, according to paintings. An abundance of literature which I shall have translated and processed. Certain structures hold signs of recent occupancy. Other ones apparently long abandoned."

"But no sign of present life," Kirk said.

As he spoke, he noted that Compton, rinsing his hands in the fountain's jet, had lifted one to knock away some unseen annoyance at his ear. At the same moment, he again heard the mosquito whine. He had to make an effort to concentrate on what Spock was saying. "... indication of life forms of a highly unusual intermittent nature. They have neither discernible shape nor location. A most puzzling phenomenon, sir."

"The Scalosians *were* here," Kirk said. "We saw them on the viewing screen, Mr. Spock. Lieutenant Uhura can still see them. She's still getting their distress call. What happened to them?"

"At this moment I cannot answer that, Captain."

"Mr. Spock, I want you to make a complete survey of this planet. You will use all the ship's instruments—"

He broke off at McCoy's shout. "Jim! Compton's gone! Look over there! Compton's gone!"

Emptiness was where the guard had been stooping at the fountain. McCoy was staring at its feathered plume of water dazedly. "Compton—gone," he said again.

"Bones!" Kirk said. "Snap out of it! What happened?"

McCoy's shocked eyes veered to his. "He ... was stowing vials of that fountain's water in his shoulder bags ... when he vanished. I was looking straight at him—and then he wasn't there. He wasn't there, Jim. He ... just wasn't there ..."

Had the Scalos distress signal been real? Maybe unreal like its inhabitants. Kirk, entering the *Enterprise* bridge, barked an inconsequential order to an unremembered crew member. As he sat down in his command chair, he said, "Lieutenant Uhura, start a replay of that distress call." Then he hit a switch. "Mr. Scott, are all Transporter controls still in functioning order?"

"Aye, sir. Is Mr. Spock still down on the planet's surface?"

"He's in Sickbay. Dr. McCoy is running a check on the landing party." His attention, used to dispersing itself to note any significant movement in the bridge, had registered Uhura's look as she struggled with her dials. "What is it, Lieutenant?"

She was frowning. "Malfunction, sir." She touched a switch—and her frown deepened. "Now it's corrected itself."

Sulu spoke. "Captain, there's some trouble on the hangar deck. Controls are frozen."

"Have repair crews been assigned?"

"Yes, sir."

Kirk shot a look of inquiry at Uhura. She nodded. "The tape of the distress call is ready, sir."

Spock had quietly returned to his station. Now he turned to look at the viewing screen. An upside-down image took shape on it. Then, righting itself, it showed a proud, strong male face. Its lips moved. "Those of us who are left have taken shelter in this area. We have no explanation for what has been happening to us. Our number is now five . . ."

The face on the screen took on human height and breadth. The figure moved; and around it appeared the four other Scalosians, two of them women. One was surpassingly lovely. The whole impression created by the group was that of a cultured, singularly handsome people, peaceful in purpose. Their spokesman went on. "I am Rael. We were once a nation of nine hundred thousand, this city alone holding—"

"Freeze it," Kirk said.

Uhura immobilized the tape and Spock, swinging around, said, "Perhaps this distress call was prerecorded—and what we received was a taped signal."

"Mr. Spock, the fact remains that when we beamed down, we could not find these people. They *were* there—now they're *not* there. Nor is crewman Compton."

"Some force or agent only partially discernible to our instruments may have been responsible, Captain."

Kirk nodded. "Mr. Sulu, I want this ship on standby alert while we continue the investigation." But Sulu had turned an anxious face to him. "I have a reading, sir, that our deflectors are inoperative. They do not respond to controls."

"Scotty, assist," Kirk said. He got up to go over to Spock's chair. "Mr. Spock, ever since we beamed back up from Scalos, we have suffered a series of malfunctions. I wish an investigation and an explanation. I want—"

McCoy's voice interrupted. "McCoy to Captain Kirk. The Captain's presence for examination is requested."

"Can't it wait, Bones?"

"Your orders, Jim. You're the last one."

"What do you read so far?"

"Can we discuss it in Sickbay?"

Moving to the elevator, Kirk said, "Mr. Spock, you have the con." But the elevator doors, instead of whooshing open at his approach, remained shut. Kirk wheeled, shouting, "Is this another malfunction?"

Spock jabbed hastily at buttons: and after a long moment, the doors opened slowly, grudgingly. Kirk was still fuming as he jerked off his shirt in Sickbay. "Bones! What did your examinations of the others turn up?"

"All normal. Whatever caused Compton's disappearance didn't affect anyone else."

"Has anyone experienced anything unusual since beaming back up?"

"No mention of it. No, Jim."

But Nurse Chapel looked up from the sheet she was draping over Kirk's midriff. "Yet something's going on, Captain. All the medical supply cabinets have been opened."

Kirk sat up. "Anything missing?"

"Just disordered. As if everything had been picked up and examined."

Once again that insect whine sounded close to Kirk's ear. He waited a moment before he said, "Bones, could something be causing me to hallucinate?" The urgency in his voice startled McCoy out of his concentration on his medical panels. He turned. "How—hallucinate? What do you mean?"

"Twice," Kirk said, "I've felt something touch me. Nothing was there. I just felt it again. Did I just fancy it?"

"There's nothing physically wrong with you, Jim."

"I asked you a question. Am I hallucinating?"

McCoy left his panels. "No."

Kirk leaped from the medical table. "Then we *did* beam something aboard! Something has invaded this ship!" He was making for the intercom when the alarm of a red alert sounded. Over the shrieking of its sirens, he cried, "Captain to bridge! Mr. Spock, come in!"

Spock didn't come in. Minutes passed before Kirk could hear the voice, faint, blurred. "Captain, I have a reading from the life support center..."

"Spock, I can't hear you! Check circuits. Is it a malfunction?"

More minutes passed. Then it was Uhura speaking, her voice also dimmed and distorted. "... intercom system breaking down rapidly..."

Kirk felt the sweat breaking out on his forehead. "Lieutenant, issue a shipwide order! Use communicators instead of the intercom. Arm all crewmen with phaser pistols. Spock, come in!"

The words were a jumble. "Reading ... life support ... center. Alien ... substances ... introduced..."

Kirk was shouldering into his shirt. "Mr. Spock, meet me in the life support center! On the double! Captain to Security! Armed squad to life support center at once!" He was at Sickbay's door when he saw McCoy sway. Christine Chapel, clutching the back of a chair, called, "The oxygen content is dropping, Doctor..."

As for Kirk himself, Sickbay, its door, its cabinets, its equipment, were all swimming into blur. He fought the dizziness that threatened to become darkness, struggling to open his communicator. "Bridge! Bridge! Scotty, where are you? Emergency life support!"

Scott's steady voice said, "Emergency on, sir."

Behind him, McCoy and Christine were gulping in lungfuls of healthy air. Kirk's vertigo subsided—and Scott said, "Condition corrected, Captain."

But the cold hand of imminent death had touched Kirk. It was a man of a different discipline who met Spock at the entrance to the life support center. As wordlessly as it was given, he took the phaser, flinging open the door to the center. Its security guards, sprawled on the floor, were kneeing back up to their feet. One, phaser out, charged to his left, only to be flung back and down again by something invisible. Kirk, staring around him, said, "How do you explain that, Mr. Spock?"

The sharp Vulcan eyes scanned their tricorder. "A force field, sir, with the nature of which I am unfamiliar. But I get a reading of alien presences similar to those obtained on the planet. They seem to have no exact location."

"'Life forms of a highly unusual, intermittent nature'." Kirk recalled grimly. "Phasers on stun, everybody. Sweep the area."

Once more came the thin whine. Phaser beams were lacing the corridor outside. Inside, Kirk and Spock edged cautiously forward to the location of the force field. Instead of flinging them back, it yielded to them; but when a guard moved to follow them, he was struck down.

"It would seem they will allow only the two of us in to the life support unit," Spock said. "Take care, Captain."

Kirk took the advice. He opened the heavy door to the unit, his weapon at the ready. At first glance the unit appeared to be its usual self, its complex coils, squat dynamos, its serpentine tubings and compressors arranged in their customary pattern. Then Kirk saw the gleaming metal of the device affixed to one of the dynamos. The metal was fluted like that of the Scalosian building. Though alien in shape and material, the small device had been able to affect the functioning of the huge life support unit.

"Mr. Spock, what is it?"

"I cannot determine, Captain. Perhaps a Scalosian refrigerating system." He scanned the thing with his tricorder. "It would seem that installation of the device is incomplete, sir. Life support is still operational."

"Disconnect it," Kirk said.

But the hand Spock extended toward the fixture was flung back. Kirk, whipping out his phaser, heard yet again that now familiar whine. "Destroy it, Spock!" he shouted.

As their two phasers fired at the device, their weapons disappeared. One moment, they were hard, tangible in their hands; but the next, they were gone. Both men pushed forward and were thrust strongly back.

"And that wasn't a force field!" Kirk cried. "Something pushed me back. They are in here with us!" He swung around, shouting at the empty air. "You! What are you doing to my ship? Show yourselves!"

The mosquito whine shrilled. They tried again, not lunging this time to the device but approaching it. A hard shove sent them stumbling back.

Spock's voice was dry. "It seems that we may look at their mechanism—but that is all, Captain."

Kirk nodded. "A show of strength." He shouted again to the invisible enemies. "But we'll find a way to dismantle this aggressive engine of yours!"

It was more than a mere show of strength. Back on the bridge, they discovered that key systems over the entire ship had either been crossed or fused. Spock's computer alone was still operational. All doors, including those of the elevators, were jammed open. Scott greeted them with a gloom thick as a Tyneside fog. "Warp engines are losing potency, Captain. We shall be on emergency power soon—a situation that gives us at most one week of survival."

Kirk wheeled to Spock. "Have your readings been fed into the computer bank?"

"Affirmative, Captain."

"Readout."

Flipping a switch, Spock addressed the computer. "Analyze and reply. Have we been invaded?"

"Affirmative."

"Nature and description of enemy forces."

"Data insufficient."

"Purpose of the invasion."

"Immediate purpose, seizure and control of the Federation Starship *Enterprise*. Data insufficient for determination of end purpose."

"Is there a link between this seizure and Compton's disappearance?"

"Data insufficient."

"Are we at present capable of resisting?"

"Negative."

"Recommendations?"

"If incapable of resistance, negotiate for terms."

Listening, Kirk glared at the computer. Then he flushed at his own childishness. The computer was just doing its computer job. But men were not computers. "We will not negotiate for terms," he said. "Scotty, do you concur?"

"Aye, sir."

Spock, giving him an approving nod, said, "What are *your* recommendations, Captain?"

"Coffee," Kirk said. He turned to the pretty yeoman on duty. "Is a round of coffee available to bridge personnel—or have those circuits also been damaged?"

She smiled, adoration in her eyes. It shouldn't have cheered him up—but it did. Challenge hardened his jaw as he looked around him at an air made malevolent by invisible hostility. "Let them take the next step," he said. "The next move is theirs."

His cup of coffee was set on the arm of his chair. He let it wait to cool. Then, as he leaned back in the chair, his hair was suddenly stirred. He stared around him, baffled—and felt soft lips on his. He *was* hallucinating. McCoy was wrong. He put out a tentative hand, exploring the space before him. Shaking his head, he seized his cup and, after drinking its coffee, replaced it on the chair arm. At the same instant, he became abruptly aware of a change of tempo in the voices around him. They sounded too slow, like those from a phonograph that was running down. And the movements of the bridge people—they, too, seemed strangely slowed, lethargic.

He went to Spock. But Spock, who had bent to his computer, seemed unable to reach its hood.

"Mr. Spock, what's wrong?"

The Vulcan didn't answer. He sat perfectly still in his chair. Kirk wheeled, calling, "Scotty!" No reply. Scott appeared to be frozen in the very act of moving a dial. It was then he heard the feminine giggle—a very feminine giggle. It came from his left. He turned. The Scalosian beauty was standing there, her chestnut hair making a dream of her creamy skin. She wore a short garment of golden gauze that clung to a slim body of subliminally provocative appeal. She was laughing at him; and the gleam of her teeth between her rosy lips gave the lie to all poets' talk of "pearls."

Still laughing, she kissed him. She flung her arms around his neck and kissed him. He tried. He tried to remember who he was; the pressing problems of the *Enterprise*, his command responsibilities. But all he succeeded in doing was to remove the lovely arms from his neck.

"Who are you?" he said.

"Deela, the enemy," she said. "Isn't it delicious?"

He had thought he knew women. But nothing in his experience had prepared him for this dazzling combination of mischief and outrageously open attractiveness. "*You're the enemy?*"

She nodded her enchanting head. "Yes. You beamed me aboard yourself when you came up. A ridiculously long process . . ."

"*What have you done to my ship?*"

"Nothing."

He swung around to gesture to the motionless bridge people. "You call that nothing?"

"They're all right," she said. "They're just what they have always been. It's you who are different."

He stared around him. "Lieutenant Uhura . . . Mr. Sulu . . . every one of them . . ."

"Captain, they can't hear us. To their ears we sound like insects. That's *your* description, you know. Accurate, if unflattering. Really, nothing's wrong with them."

"Then what have you done to me?"

"Changed you. You are like me now. Your crew can't see you because of the acceleration. We both move now in the wink of an eye. There is a dreary scientific term for it—but all that really matters it that you can see me and talk to me and . . ." The creamy eyelids lowered over eyes the color of wet green leaves. ". . . and we can go on from there."

"Why?" Kirk said.

"Because I like you. Didn't you guess?" She came closer to him. She was ruffling his hair now; and he seemed unable to do a thing about it. The situation was out of hand . . . the presence of his crew . . . this public exhibition of endearments . . . her overwhelming beauty . . . his ship's predicament. He seized the caressing hands. They were warm, soft. It wasn't the answer.

"Is it because you like me that you've sabotaged my ship?"

"It hasn't been sabotaged. We just had to make some changes in it to adjust it to our tempo."

" 'We'?"

"Of course. My chief scientist and his men. I'm their Queen. You're going to be their King. You'll enjoy living on Scalos."

"And what happens to my ship—*my* men?"

"Oh, in a few of their moments they'll realize you've vanished. Then they'll look for you. But they won't find you. You're accelerated far beyond their powers to see. So they'll go on without you . . ."

He became conscious that her hands were still in his. He released them. She smiled at him. "Don't be stubborn. You *can't* go back to them. You must stay with me. Is that so dreadful a prospect?"

He reached for his phaser. "I won't kill you—but the 'stun' effect isn't very pleasant."

"Go ahead," she said. "Fire it at me."

He fired the stun button. She stepped aside and the beam passed harmlessly by her. She laughed at the look on his face. "Don't look so puzzled. My reactions are much too fast for such a crude weapon. Besides, I'm quite good at self-defense." She pulled a small instrument from her golden belt. Pointing it at his phaser, she fired it—and its beam tore the phaser out of his hand. "It can be set for stun and destroy, too," she said. "Like yours. Please accept what's happened. There's nothing you can do to change it."

His ship. Suppose he capitulated—and went with her? Went with her on the condition she made the *Enterprise* operational again and removed the device attached to the life support system? Spock could carry on . . .

His face was somber. She saw it set into grim lines and cried, "Don't fret so! You'll feel better about it in a little while. It always happens this way . . . they're all upset at first. But it wears off and they begin to like it. You will, too. I promise . . ."

He turned on his heel and left her. She touched a medallion on the golden belt. "He's on his way to you, Rael. Be gentle with him," she said.

Kirk came at a run down the corridor to the life support center. He found what he expected. The *Enterprise* guards at its door were stiff, rigid. He skirted them; and was starting toward the door when a third guard in the Starship's uniform emerged from a corner. "Compton!" Kirk shouted.

Compton beamed at him. "Captain Kirk! So you made it here!"

"You've been accelerated, haven't you?" Kirk said.

"Yes, sir."

"Are they in there? They've got something hooked in to life support—and we've got to get rid of it. Come on!"

But Compton had barred his way with the Scalosian weapon. "Sorry, sir. Entry is forbidden."

"Who gave that order?"

"The commander, sir. You'll have to step back, please."

"*I* am your commander—and I order you to let me in."

"I am very sorry, sir. You are no longer my commander."

"Then who is? Deela? Are you working for her?"

Compton reached an arm back into the corner's shadows and drew out the other Scalosian girl. He spoke very earnestly. "At first I refused, sir—but I've never known anyone like Mira. She brought me aboard and I showed them the ship's operations, its bridge controls and life support. I didn't understand at first but I do now. I—I've never been in love before, sir."

Kirk stepped back. Then, lunging at Compton, he chopped the weapon away from him and raced for the door.

In the center, Rael, two other Scalosians beside him, was working on the small device. He looked up as Kirk plunged in. "Stun," he said to one of his men. The weapon came up; and from behind Kirk, pushing him aside, Compton hurled himself at it. His try at protection was too late. The blast caught Kirk. He collapsed. Raging, Rael felled Compton with a blow. "You were ordered to stop him! Why did you disobey?"

Compton's mouth was bleeding. "You wanted to hurt him," he said.

"He was violent and to be subdued. Why did you disobey?"

"He—he was my Captain . . ."

Compton crumpled. "Go to him, Ekor," Rael said. The man with the weapon knelt beside Compton. Mira, who had drifted into the center, joined him. When he looked up, he said, "There is cell damage." The girl, her pretty face curious, stooped over Compton. "Don't be troubled," Rael told her. "Another will be secured for you." Nodding, she strolled out of the door.

It was Uhura who first noticed the empty command chair. "The captain!" she cried. "He's gone! Mr. Spock, the captain's gone! He was sitting there just a minute ago! He'd just drunk his coffee! There's the cup—on the arm of his chair! But where's the Captain?"

Spock had already left his station. "Mr. Sulu, what did you see?"

Sulu turned a bewildered face. "That's what happened, sir. He was there, putting his cup down—and then he wasn't there!"

There was a moment's silence before Spock said, "Mr. Sulu, did you drink coffee when the yeoman brought it around?"

"Yes, sir."

Spock eyed the bridge personnel. "Did anyone else?" he said.

"I had some," Scott said.

One by one Spock lifted their cups, sniffing at them. Then he sniffed at Kirk's.

"Was it the coffee?" Scott cried. "Are we going to vanish, too, like the captain?"

"The residue in these cups must be analyzed before I can answer that, Mr. Scott."

"And by *that* time—" Scott fell silent.

"I suggest," Spock said, "that we remember the Captain's words. Make them take the next step. In the meantime we must determine effective countermoves. The con is yours, Mr. Scott. I shall be in the medical laboratory."

Deela sat on the deck in life support center, the head of the still unconscious Kirk in her lap. Rael, at the device, watched her as she smoothed the hair from his forehead. "I told you," she said, "to be gentle with him."

"He was violent. We had to stun him to avoid cell damage."

She looked over to where Compton lay in a neglected huddle. "Who damaged that one? You? I might have known it. I suppose he was violent, too."

"He turned against us," Rael said.

"And you lost your temper."

"He had to be destroyed. He had not completely accepted change. It is a stubborn species."

Deela's eyes were still on Compton. "I know what happens to them when they're damaged. You will control your temper, Rael. I don't want that to happen to mine. If they're so stubborn a species, perhaps they'll last longer."

"It may be."

"I hope so. They all go so soon. I want to keep this one a long time. He's pretty."

"He is inferior, Deela!"

"We disagree, Rael."

"You cannot allow yourself to feel an attachment to such a thing!"

"I can allow myself to do anything I want!" The flare of anger passed as quickly as it had come. "Oh, Rael, don't be that way," she coaxed. "Am I jealous of what you do?"

"I do my duty."

"So do I. And sometimes I allow myself to enjoy it."

As she spoke, Kirk's dazed eyes opened. Under his head he felt the softness of feminine thighs. He shook it to clear it; and looking up, saw Deela smiling at him. "Hello," she said.

He sat up—and recognized Rael. Leaping to his feet, he turned on Deela. "Is this what you wanted us for? To take over our ship?"

She rose in one graceful movement. "We need your help. And you and your ship are supplying it."

"And what does that device of yours have to do with the supply?"

"Hush," she said. "I'll tell you everything you want to know. And you'll approve of it."

"Approve!" he shouted. "We're your prisoners!"

"Hardly," she said. "You're free to go wherever you want."

Kirk rushed to the life support unit. Instead of interfering, Rael stepped aside. "Go ahead, Captain. Our mechanism is not yet completely linked to your support system but it is in operating order. Study it if you wish. I advise you not to touch it."

Kirk's eyes narrowed. He eyed the small device; and spotting its connecting switch, extended a wary hand to it. He snatched it back, the Scalosians watching him expressionlessly. Then, despite the shock of contact with it, he grabbed it boldly with both hands. They froze on it. Deela ran to him; and, careful not to touch the switch herself, released his hands.

"He told you not to touch it!" She folded his numbed palms between hers, warming them. "The cold will soon pass," she said.

Rael spoke. "Our mechanism has its own self-defense arrangement. You should have heeded me."

Kirk jerked his still icy hands from Deela's. He'd had enough of these aliens; and, feeling a sudden compunction for Compton, sprawled and untended in his heap, he went to him quickly to kneel beside him. But what had been the young and vigorous Compton was now withered by age, mummified as though dried by a thousand years of death. He looked up in horror and Rael said, "In your struggle with Compton, you damaged some of his cells. Those newly accelerated to our tempo's level are sensitive to cell damage. They age very rapidly and die."

Kirk got to his feet. "Is this what you have prepared for us?"

"We all die," Rael said. "Even on Scalos."

Kirk looked around at the bland faces. Where was the way back into his own time ... the time of Spock ... of McCoy ... of Scotty? A sense of unutterable loneliness overwhelmed him. He walked out of the center.

Behind him Deela cried, "Rael, why did you lie to him? He didn't damage the dead one! You did!"

Rael shrugged. "Perhaps he'll be less violent now."

"There was no reason to make him feel worse than he does!"

"What do you care about his feelings?"

She changed her tactics. "Rael," she said, "he's not one of us. You know he's temporary." But Rael still stooped to his work. She sighed; and touching the medallion on her belt, listened. "He's in the medical laboratory trying to communicate with the Vulcan. He likes that one of the pointed ears. His species seems capable of much affection."

"I have noted that," Rael said stiffly.

"Oh, stop sulking! Accept it. We've had to accept it all our lives! Don't make it worse!"

Rael seized her fiercely in his arms. Her hand was reaching to caress his face when she broke free, laughing and breathless. "Not now," she said. "Go back to work."

He didn't. Instead, he watched her as she followed Kirk out of the center. She found the door of the medical laboratory open. Ignoring the rigid figures of Spock and McCoy, she went to the communicator console where Kirk was dictating. "Kirk to Spock," he was saying. "I have fed all facts ascertainable into the computer banks—" He broke off as he saw Deela.

She studied him—a beautiful woman estimating a man for her own reasons. "Go ahead," she said. "It won't accomplish anything. But it may be historically valuable."

Eyes on her, he continued. "Hyper-acceleration is the key, Mr. Spock. We are in their control because of this acceleration. They are able to speed others up to their level as they did to Compton and me. Those so treated then exist at their accelerated tempo, become eventually docile but when—"

"Damaged," Deela said.

Kirk gave her a mock bow. "When damaged, they age incredibly fast as if the accelerated living—"

"Burns them out," Deela said.

"Destroys them. Compton is destroyed. The device affixed to life support produces an icy cold. It is my belief it will turn the *Enterprise* into a gigantic deep-freeze and for purposes the Scalosians alone know—"

"Quite correct," Deela said.

Kirk was ironic. "My opinion has been verified. Their mechanism has it own protective shield, preventing physical contact. I have no means of destroying it. But its destruction is imperative. I am dictating this in the presence of their Queen who has denied none of it. Why she has permitted me to—"

Leaning forward, the cloud of her hair brushing his shoulder, Deela spoke for the record into the communicator.

"Because by the time you hear this, it will be too late. Our mechanism will be activated."

He turned to look at the two stiffened figures of his friends. The ice would creep through the *Enterprise* to stiffen them forever in a shroud of frost. He swung to Deela. "*Why?* Why are you doing this?"

"You really want to know? In a short time, it won't matter to you a bit. You'll be quite happy about it, as Compton was."

"I want to know."

"Oh dear. You *are* so stubborn. It should be obvious to one with your reasoning powers that we're doing it because we have to." She pushed the shining cloud of hair back. "A long time ago, we used to be like you. Then our country was almost destroyed by volcanic eruptions. The water was polluted and radiation was released. That changed us. It accelerated us . . ."

He waited. It was possible. The long-term effects of radiation were still unpredictable. "The children died," she said. "Most of the women found they couldn't bear any more. All our men had become sterile. We had to mate outside our own people . . ."

A doomed race. Listening, Kirk seemed to know what he was going to hear. He felt a stab of pity. She gave him a sad little smile. "So, whenever a space ship came by, we sent out calls for help. But accelerating their crews to our level burned them out . . ." She came to him and put her head on his shoulder. "Don't you see? Must I give you every detail? We're going to take you down with us. Maybe one or two others of your crew, too. We have to. We'll be kind to you. I *do* like you, you know."

"And the rest of my crew?" Kirk said.

"It's as you said. They'll be kept frozen in a reduced animation we know how to suspend. It won't do them any harm. We'll save them for our future needs. You won't last forever. You know that." At the look on his face, a cry tore from her. "Captain, we have the right to survive!"

"Not at the cost you impose," he said.

"You'd do exactly the same thing! You came charging down into that life support room just as soon as you knew it was threatened! You'd have killed every one of my people if you could have . . ."

"You had invaded my ship! You were endangering my crew!"

"There's no difference!" she cried.

"There's every difference. You are the aggressors!"

"We didn't ask for our situation. We're simply handling it the only way we know how to—the way our parents did and their parents before them . . ."

"Would you call it a real solution?"

She looked at him, silent. "Have you tried any other answer? Deela, tell your scientist to disconnect his construction—to destroy it! I promise you we'll use every skill we have to help you. We'll even move you to another planet if you want that. We'll call on the most brilliant minds in our Federation for help!"

She shook her head. "We *have* tried other ways. We tried to make the transition to your time level. Those who made the attempt died. We're trapped, Captain, just as you are now. I'm sorry for what it's going to do to you but I can't change it. And you can't change me."

The medallion on her belt beeped. She touched it and Rael's voice said, "Go to the Transporter Room, Deela. Signal me when you're there and beam down."

"With the captain?"

She was frowning, concentrated on the medallion—and Kirk grabbed his chance.

He pulled his dictated tape partially out of the computer so that Spock would note it. He heard Rael say, "Yes. I'll activate our mechanism and follow you. I'm setting it to allow enough time for all of us to get off the ship. But don't delay, Deela."

Kirk had raced for the lab door. Behind him, Deela shouted, "The captain's gone!"

"Go after him, Deela!"

But his headstart had given him time to make the Transporter Room. He rushed to its console, ripped out some wire; and had it shut again to conceal the damage as Deela ran in.

"Why did you leave me?" she demanded.

"I panicked," Kirk said.

The green eyes swept over him. "I don't believe that," she said.

"Can we leave before he activates your device?" he said.

She looked at him, her smooth brow puckered suspiciously. Then she touched the medallion. "Rael, we're in the Transporter Room. You can—activate."

"Beam him down at once."

Still doubtful, she gestured Kirk to the platform. At the console, she pushed a switch. It swung, limp—and the smile in the green eyes deepened. "What did you do to the Transporter, Captain?"

"Nothing," he said. "It must be what your people did. Try the switch again."

She obeyed. Then she touched the medallion communicator. "The Transporter isn't working," she said quietly.

"What did he do to it?"

She delayed her answer. The impishness glinted in her eyes. She was enjoying herself. It was fun to pretend she didn't know what she knew. "Nothing," she told Rael. "He didn't have time. I think it's a—what do they call it? A malfunction. You'd better not activate yet." She turned to Kirk, the amusement still in her face. "What would you say it is, Captain?"

He assumed a thoughtful look. "Well, our technicians reported a loss of energy. That may be it."

She spoke solemnly to the medallion. "The captain says his technicians—"

"I heard him. Do you expect me to believe him?"

It was the Queen in her who spoke. "*I* expect you to check into all possible causes." She turned the medallion off to smile the impish smile at Kirk. "If I had a suspicious nature," she said, "I'd say you sabotaged the Transporter, Captain. To buy time."

"Of course," he said.

She laughed with delight. "Aren't we the innocent pair? I despise devious people, don't you?"

Kirk nodded gravely. "I believe in honest relationships, myself." He hesitated. "Deela, you've never seen my quarters. Before we leave, wouldn't you like to?"

Their eyes met. "Are they like you?" she said. "Austere, efficient—but in their own way, handsome?"

"Yes," he said.

In his cabin, the first thing she went to was his mirror. "Oh, I look a perfect fright! All this running about has left me a perfect fright, hasn't it?"

She lifted a brush from the dresser and flung her head over, the shining hair cascading to the floor. She parted the chestnut curtain with a finger, peeking at him. Then she laughed, tossed the hair back and began to brush it, a delicious woman attracting what she knows her preening has attracted. An electric spark flashed between them.

"Are you married, Captain?"

"No."

"No family, no attachments? Oh, I see. You're married to your career and never look at a woman."

"You're mistaken," he said. "I look, if she's pretty enough."

"I wondered when you'd say something nice to me. Am I more presentable now?"

"A bit," he said.

She was facing him, the brush still in her hand. "It was quite delightful kissing you when you couldn't see me. But now that you do see me, don't you think . . . ?"

He strode to her, took her in his arms and kissed her. She drew back—but he had felt her body tremble. Her arms were reaching for his neck when she whirled out of his embrace, her weapon out. "Unfair!" she cried. "To try and take it in the middle of a kiss!"

She thrust it back into her belt. "But I'll forgive you. I'd have been disappointed in you if you *hadn't* tried to take it!"

"Was I too crude?" Kirk said.

"Just don't try it again, that's all. You're so vulnerable to cell damage. All I have to do is scratch you." She held up pink nails. Then she lifted his arms and placed them around her waist. "You'll come around to our way of thinking sooner or later. And it will be better sooner or later. That's a promise."

In the medical lab, Spock, still functioning in normal time, was about to insert a tape of his own into the computer when McCoy called him. "Have a look at this, Spock. There's no question about it. The same substance is in the captain's coffee as in the Scalosian water. But not a trace of it in the other cups."

Spock spoke to Christine. "Nurse, program that information and see if we can isolate counteragents."

A mosquito whined. Spock, striking at air, turned to McCoy. "Did you just hear—"

"I've been hearing that whine ever since we beamed down to Scalos."

"We brought it with us. And I know what it is. I shall be on the bridge." They stared after him, puzzled, as he raced out of the lab. He was still running when he brought up short on the bridge. "Lieutenant Uhura, replay that Scalosian distress call on my viewer!"

"Yes, sir."

Rael's image appeared on the screen. Spock leaned forward in his chair, waiting for the voice. It came. "Those of us who are left have taken shelter in this area. We have no explanation for what has been happening to us. Our number is now five . . ."

It was enough. Spock twisted a dial on the viewer; and the voice, rising in pitch, became incoherent babble, went higher still until it turned into recognizable whine. Spock slowed the voice back into words, lifted it up again into the whine—and nodded. On the screen, the image, rushed faster and faster, had first blurred. Then it vanished.

"So," Spock said to nobody.

Back in the lab, McCoy had made a discovery, too. Banging away the whining mosquito at his ear, he spoke into the intercom. "McCoy to Spock."

"Spock, here."

"Did you leave a tape in the computer? I've tried reading it but I get nothing but that whine . . ."

"Bring it to the bridge at once, Doctor."

Kirk's voice. They listened to it on their separate edges of eternity, each of them reading his own fate in Compton's and Kirk's.

". . . Its destruction is imperative. I am dictating this in the presence of their Queen who has denied none of it. Why she has permitted me—"

Deela's voice came. "Because by the time you hear this, it will be too late. The mechanism will be activated . . ."

Silence fell over the bridge people. Spock leaned swiftly to his console. "I read no change in life support," he said. "Lieutenant Uhura, alert the rest of the crew."

Scott rose and went to him. "We could use phasers to cut through the wall, bypass the force field and get to that mechanism . . ."

"Mr. Scott, we cannot cope with them on our time level."

"Is there a way to cope with them on theirs?"

"A most logical suggestion, Mr. Scott. Please stand by in the Transporter Room. Dr. McCoy, I should appreciate your assistance."

They left with him, their faces blank with bewilderment. Uhura followed them with her eyes. "Mr. Sulu, if nothing has happened yet, wouldn't it mean that the captain has managed to buy time, somehow?"

"Yes," Sulu said. "But how much?"

Rael had restored sufficient energy to the Transporter for a beam-down. But his success had a bitter taste. His fancy persisted in tormenting him with present and future images of Deela with Kirk. Finally, he touched his own medallion.

"Deela..."

She didn't answer. Languorously, she was combing her hair to rights before Kirk's mirror. He watched her from a chair. Then he got up, smiling at her reflection in the mirror. As he kissed the back of her neck, she turned full into his arms.

"Deela!"

Rael stood in the cabin doorway. The hot fury in him exploded. He reached for her; and seizing a lamp, hurled it at Kirk. Kirk ducked it. Cell damage! In his accelerated state, this could be no ordinary fight. Deela screamed, "Rael, stop it! Don't hurt him! Rael! Captain, get out . . ."

Grabbing her weapon, she fired it at the lamp. But Rael lunged at Kirk again, barehanded. She fired again, spinning him around with the force beam. "That's enough!" she cried. "Did he damage you, Captain?"

"No."

"How very fortunate for you, Rael! Don't try anything like that again!"

"Then don't torment me. You know what I feel."

"I don't care what you feel. Keep that aspect of it to yourself. What I do is necessary, and you have no right to question it." She paused to add more quietly, "Allow me the dignity of liking the man I select."

He stood sullen but subdued. "Is the Transporter repaired?" she said.

"I have more work to do."

"Then do it." He left. She remained silent, more depressed by the scene than she cared to show. After a long moment, she spoke. "He loves me. I adored him when I was a child. I suppose I still do." She made an effort to recover their former mood. "I must say, you behaved better than he did."

"I hope so," Kirk said.

Something in his manner startled her. "What did you say?"

"That I hope I behaved well."

She was staring at him. "And nothing troubles you now?"

"Why are we here?"

"Our leaving was delayed. Don't you remember? You damaged the Transporter."

"That was wrong," Kirk said.

"It certainly was."

"But we are going to Scalos?"

"Do you want to?"

"Yes."

"What about your crew? Aren't you worried about them?"

"They'll be all right here."

Her mouth twisted with distaste. "What's the matter?" Kirk said.

"You've completely accepted the situation, haven't you? You even like it."

"Am I behaving incorrectly?"

"No." Then she burst out petulantly. "Oh, I liked you better before! Stubborn, independent . . . and irritating! Like Rael!"

"Those are undesirable qualities," Kirk said.

But she was brooding over her discovery. "Maybe that's why I liked you so much. Because you were like him."

The muscles of Kirk's face ached under the blandness of his smile. But he held it. She touched her medallion. "Rael, you don't have to worry about him. He's made the . . . adjustment."

McCoy was examining the vial of liquid he had processed. "It's finished," he told Spock wearily.

Spock took the vial; and, mixing some of its contents with the Scalosian water, exposed the result to an electronic device. "It counteracts the substance most effectively, Doctor."

"Under laboratory conditions. The question is, will it work in the human body? And the second question is, how do we get it to the captain?"

Spock poured some of the Scalosian water into a glass. He lifted the glass in a toast to McCoy. "By drinking their water." He drained the glass.

"Spock! You don't know what the effects—"

But Spock was savoring the taste. "It is . . . somewhat stimulating." He paused. "And yes, Doctor, you seem to be moving very slowly. Fascinating."

He winked out. McCoy sank down in a chair, his eyes on the vacancy where Spock had stood.

Rael, his face intent, twisted a knob on his refrigerating mechanism. When it flared into red life, he adjusted another one. He nodded to himself as it began to pulsate, its throb dimming the lights of the life support unit. He touched his communicator medallion. "The arrangement is activated, Deela. Go to the Transporter Room and beam-down at once. The others have already left."

Scott was at the console. Unseeing, unmoving, he didn't turn as Kirk entered the room with Deela. Time, time, Kirk thought—was there no way to gain more time? He looked at the Transporter platform that was to maroon him on Scalos, and Deela said, "Come, Captain. We are leaving your pretty ship. Your crew will be all right. You said so yourself."

He smiled at her. "Know something?" he said. "I think I'll make sure of it." Then he caught her; and wrenching her weapon from her belt, ran for the door.

She screamed into her medallion. "Rael! He broke away! He's armed—"

"I'm ready for him!"

Kirk was racing down the corridor to life support, ducking the stony figures of his crewmen. The beam of a phaser lanced the darkness—and he brought up short. Then he saw Spock. They didn't speak. They didn't need to. A vicious *ping* came from the open life support door. Together, they dodged, split, and, weapons out, plunged through the door.

Rael fired again, missed—and Kirk stunned him with Deela's weapon. At the same moment, Spock's phaser beam struck the Scalosian machine. It continued to flare and throb. Kirk aimed his weapon at it. It burst into flame, melted and was still.

"Nice to see you, Mr. Spock," Kirk said.

"Rael!"

It was Deela. She ran to the slumped body, feeling for its heart. Satisfied, she kissed Rael's lips. Then she looked up at Kirk. "You're very clever, Captain. You tricked me. I should have known you'd never adjust." She had Rael in her arms. "What shall we expect from you?"

"We could put you in suspended animation until we determine how to use you," he said. "What do you want us to do with you?"

She was close to tears. "Oh, Captain, don't make a game of this! We've lost. You've won. Dispose of us."

"If I send you back to Scalos, you'll undoubtedly play the same trick on the next space ship that passes."

She was openly weeping now. "There'll never be another one come by. You'll warn them. Your Federation will quarantine this entire area."

"I'm sure it will."

"And we'll die out. We'll solve your problem that way. And ours."

"Will you accept help?" Kirk said.

"We can't be helped. I've told you . . ."

"Madam," Spock said, "I respectfully suggest that as we are advanced beyond your rating on the Industrial Scale, we may be able to be of some help."

"Our best people in the Federation will work on it. Will you accept our offer, Deela, and go in peace?"

Clearly, there were aspects to Kirk's nature she had not suspected. She looked at him wonderingly. After a moment, the old mischief glinted in her green eyes. She shrugged. "What have we to lose?"

She looked down at Rael. He was recovering consciousness. "We have lost," she told him quietly. "It is you and I who will transport down to Scalos."

He smiled up at her. "Soon," he said.

As they took their places on the platform, Deela turned to Kirk at the console. "Now about your problem, Captain. I note that your Vulcan friend, too, has been accelerated."

Spock spoke. "If you will devote yourself exclusively to the concerns of Scalos, Madam, we shall be very happy to stay and take care of the *Enterprise*."

"Spock," Kirk said, "remind me sometime to tell you how I've missed you."

"Yes, Captain."

"You could find life on Scalos very pleasant, Captain," Deela urged.

"And brief," Kirk said.

"Do I really displease you so much?"

"I can think of nothing I'd like more than staying with you. Except staying alive."

"Will you visit us, Captain?"

"Energize!"

"Captain . . . Captain . . . goodbye . . ."

Spock had moved the controls. They dissolved—and were gone. Kirk stared at the empty platform a long moment. Then, turning briskly to Spock, he said, "And now, how do we get back?"

"Doctor McCoy and I have synthesized a possible counteragent to the Scalosian water, sir. Regrettably, we lacked the opportunity to test it."

"Then let's test it." He took the solution Spock gave him and swallowed it. Deela and Rael. It was all for the best. You couldn't have everything you wanted. Sex—a peculiar magnetic field. Her eyes . . . like wet green leaves . . .

Preoccupied, he vaguely heard Spock say, "Your motion seems to be slowing down, sir."

Kirk started to speak. "Missssterrr . . . Spock!" He drew a deep breath. The counteragent had worked. They were back in their own time! Then, abruptly, he realized that Spock hadn't answered. He wheeled—and before his eyes, Spock vanished.

"Spock! Spock, where are you?"

Scott came through the door to halt in midstride. "*Captain Kirk!*" he yelled. "Where in blazes did you come from?"

There was no cause to panic. Bones would have more of the counteragent. But Vulcan physiology was a tricky thing. What had worked for him would not necessarily work for Spock. What then? A permanent isolation in an accelerated universe? Kirk had whipped out his communicator before he remembered it was useless, dead as the ship itself. The bridge! He had to get to the bridge! Search parties? Futile. They couldn't see him. If Spock were there beside him, he, Kirk himself, couldn't see him.

He ignored the bridge's hubbub of welcome. Passing Uhura's station, he snapped, "Lieutenant, try to set our recorder at maximum speed . . ."

"Yes, sir." But the lights on her console had gone mad. The rapidity of their flashing turned them into blur. And all around him other boards and panels were affected by the same dementia. Suddenly, relief engulfed him. Grinning, he spoke to Scott. "I think we've found Mr. Spock. Lieutenant Uhura, are your circuits clearing?"

Her face was startled. "Yes, sir."

"Mr. Sulu?"

"Clearing, sir."

"Lieutenant Uhura, open all channels." He seized his mike. "Captain to crew. Repairs to the ship are being completed by Mr. Spock. We will resume normal operations . . . just about immediately."

The air beside his chair seemed to thicken. It solidified. Kirk looked at the elegantly pointed ears. "Greetings, Mr. Spock. My compliments on your repair work."

"Thank you, Captain. I have found it all a most fascinating experience."

"I'm glad," Kirk said. "I'm glad on many counts." He got up to pace the round of the stations. "Malfunctions—any anywhere?" Faces beamed at him. He returned to his chair—and the viewing screen lit up. On it the five Scalosians came back into view, Deela's surpassing loveliness transcendent.

"Sorry, sir," Uhura said. "I touched the tape button accidentally."

He leaned back in his chair, eyes on the screen. Deela's face seemed to fill the world. The magnetic field between them—and susceptible to no analysis. The images winked off, leaving the screen blank.

"Goodbye, Deela," he said softly.

LET THAT BE YOUR LAST BATTLEFIELD

WRITER: OLIVER CRAWFORD (STORY BY LEE CRONIN)
DIRECTOR: JUD TAYLOR
FIRST AIRED: JANUARY 10, 1969

An airborne epidemic was raging on Ariannus; the *Enterprise* was three hours and four minutes out from the stricken planet on a decontamination mission when her sensors picked up, of all unexpected objects, a Starfleet shuttlecraft. Furthermore, its identification numbers showed it to be the one reported stolen from Starbase 4 two weeks earlier.

Its course was very erratic, and it was leaking air. There was a humanoid creature aboard, either injured or ill. Kirk had the machine brought aboard by tractor, and then came the second surprise. The unconscious creature aboard it was, on his left side, a very black man—while his right-hand side was completely white.

Kirk and Spock, curious, watched the entity, now on the surgery's examination table, while McCoy and Nurse Chapel did what seemed indicated. This, in due course, included an injection.

"Doctor," Spock said, "is this pigmentation a natural condition of this—individual?"

"So it would seem. The black side is plain ordinary melanin."

"I never heard of such a race," Kirk said. "Spock? No? I thought not. How do you explain it, Bones?"

"At the moment, I don't."

"He looks like the outcome of a drastic argument."

"I would think not," Spock said seriously. "True, he would be difficult to account for by standard Mendelian evolution, but unaccountable rarities do occur."

"A mutation?" McCoy said. "Tenable, anyhow."

"Your prognosis, Bones?"

"Again, I can't give one. He's a novelty to me, too."

"Yet," Spock said, "you are pumping him full of your noxious potions as if he were human."

"When in doubt, the book prevails. I've run tests. Blood is blood—even when it's green like yours. The usual organs are there, somewhat rearranged, plus a few I don't recognize. But—well, judge the treatment by its fruits; he's coming around." The alien's eyes blinked open. He looked as though he were frightened, but trying not to show it.

"Touch and go there for a bit," McCoy said. "But you're no longer in danger."

"You are aboard the Starship *Enterprise*," Kirk added.

"I have heard of it," the alien said, relieved. "It is in the fleet of the United Federation of Planets?"

"Correct," Kirk said. "And so is that shuttlecraft in which you were flying."

"It was?"

"Don't you usually know whose property you're stealing?"

"I am not a thief!"

"You're certainly no ordinary thief," Kirk said, "considering what it is you appropriated."

"You are being very loose with your accusations and drawing conclusions without any facts."

"I know you made off with a ship that didn't belong to you."

"I do not 'make off' with things," the alien said, biting off the words. "My need gave me the right to its use—and note the word well, sir—the use of the ship."

Kirk shrugged. "You can try those technical evasions with Starfleet Command. You'll face your charges there."

"I am grateful that you rescued me," the alien said with sudden dignity.

"Don't mention it. We're glad we caught you. Who are you?"

"My name is Lokai."

"Go on."

"I am from the planet Cheron."

"If I remember correctly," Spock said, "that is located in the southernmost part of the Galaxy, in a quarter that is still uncharted."

"What are you doing so far from your home?" Kirk asked. Lokai did not answer. "You know that upon completion of our mission, you will be returned to Starbase to face a very serious charge."

"The charge is trifling. I would have returned the ship as soon as I had—" Lokai stopped abruptly.

"Had what? What were you planning to do?"

"You monotoned humans are all alike," Lokai said in a sudden burst of fury. "First condemn and then attack!" Struggling to get a rein on his temper, he sank back. "I will answer no more questions."

"However we view him, Captain," Spock said, "he is certainly no ordinary specimen."

Lokai looked at the First Officer as though seeing him for the first time. "A Vulcan!"

"Don't think he'll be any easier on you," McCoy said. "He's half human."

"That's a strange combination."

Spock raised one eyebrow. "Fascinating that you should think so."

"You're not like any being we've ever encountered," Kirk added. "We'd like to know more about you and your planet."

"I—I'm very tired."

"I think that's an evasion. Surely you owe your rescuers some candor."

"I insist," Lokai said, deliberately closing his eyes. "I am extremely tired. Your vindictive cross-examination has exhausted me."

Kirk looked down at the self-righteous thief for a moment. Then Chekov's voice said from the intercom, "Contact with alien ship, Captain. They request permission to beam a passenger aboard. They say it's a police matter."

"Very well. I'll see him on the bridge. Let's go, Mr. Spock."

Still another surprise awaited them there. The newcomer was almost a double for Lokai—except that he was black on his right side and white on his left.

"I am Bele," he said. His manner was assured and ingratiating.

Kirk eyed him warily. "Of the planet Cheron, no doubt. What brings you to us?"

"You bear precious cargo. Lokai. He has taken refuge aboard this ship. I am here to claim him."

"All personnel on this vessel are subject to my command. No one 'claims' anyone without due process."

"My apologies," Bele said readily. "I overstepped my powers. 'Claim' was undoubtedly an unfortunate word."

"What authorization do you have and from what source?"

"I am Chief Officer of the Commission on Political Traitors. Lokai was tried for and convicted of treason, but escaped. May I see him, please?"

"He's in sickbay. Understand that since you are now aboard the *Enterprise*, you are bound by its regulations."

Bele smiled, a little cryptically. "With your permission, Captain."

There were two guards at the door of Sickbay when Kirk, Spock and Bele arrived; McCoy was inside. Lokai glared up at them.

"Well, Lokai, it's a pleasure to see you again," Bele said. "This time I'm sure your 'joining' will be of a permanent nature. Captain, you are to be congratulated. Lokai has never before been rendered so—quiescent."

Lokai made a sound remarkably like a panther snarling, which brought in the two guards in a hurry. "I'm not going back to Cheron," he said with savage anger. "It's a world of murdering oppressors."

"I told you where you were going," Kirk said. "We brought your compatriot here simply as a courtesy. He wanted to identify you."

"And you see how this killer responds," Bele said. "As he repays all his benefactors . . ."

"Benefactors?" Lokai said. "You hypocrite. Tell him how you raided our homes, tore us from our families, herded us like cattle and sold us as slaves!"

"They were savages, Captain," Bele said. "We took them into our hearts and homes and educated them."

"Yes! Just enough education to serve the Master Race."

"You were the product of our love and you repaid us with murder."

"Why should a slave have mercy on the enslaver?"

"Slave? That was changed millennia ago. You were freed."

"Freed? Were we free to be men—free to be husbands and fathers—free to live our lives in dignity and equality?"

"Yes, you were free, if you knew how to use your freedom. You were free enough to slaughter and burn all that had been built."

Lokai turned to Kirk. "I tried to break the chains of a hundred million people. My only crime is that I failed. Of that I plead guilty."

"There is an order in things," Bele said. "He asked for Utopia in a day. It can't be done."

"Not in a day. And not in ten times ten thousand years by your thinking. To you we are a loathsome breed who will never be ready. I know you and all those with whom you are plotting to take power permanently. Genocide for my people is the Utopia you plan."

Bele, his eyes wide with fury, sprang at Lokai. The guards grabbed him. "You insane, filthy little plotter of ruin! You vicious subverter of every decent thought! You're coming back to stand trial for your crimes."

"When I return to Cheron, you will understand power. I will have armies of followers."

"You were brought here to identify this man," Kirk told Bele. "It is now clear, *gentlemen*, that you know each other very well. Bringing you together is the only service this ship has to offer. It is not a battlefield."

"Captain," Lokai said. "I led revolutionaries, not criminals. I demand political asylum. Your ship is a sanctuary."

"I'll say it just once more. For you this ship is a prison."

"Captain, it is imperative that you return him for judgment."

"Cheron is not a member of the Federation. No treaties have ever been signed. Your demand to be given possession of this prisoner is impossible to honor. There are no extradition procedures to accomplish it. Is that clear, Commissioner Bele?"

"Captain," Bele said, "I hope you will be sensible."

"I'm not interested in taking sides."

"Since my vessel has left the area—I was only a paid passenger—I urge you to take us to Cheron immediately."

Kirk felt himself beginning to bristle. "This ship has a mission to perform. Millions of lives are at stake. When that is completed, I'll return to Starbase 4. You will both be turned over to the authorities. You can each make your case to them."

"I'm sorry, Captain, but that is not acceptable. Not at all!"

"As a dignitary of a far planet," Kirk said, seething, "I offer you every hospitality of the ship while you are aboard. Choose any other course, and . . ."

"You're the Captain," Bele said with sudden mildness.

"And as for you, Lokai, I suggest you rest as much as possible. Especially your vocal chords. It seems you will have a double opportunity to practice your oratory at Starbase . . ."

He was interrupted by the buzz of the intercom. "Chekov to Captain Kirk. Urgent. Will you come to the bridge, sir?"

It was urgent, all right. The ship was off course; it seemed to have taken a new heading all by itself; it was moving away from Ariannus on a tack that would wind it up in the Coal Sack if it kept up. A check with all departments failed to turn up the nature of the malfunction.

"Mr. Spock, give me the coordinates for Cheron."

"Roughly, sir, between 403 Mark 7 and Mark 9."

"Which is the way we're heading. Get Bele up here. I assigned him to the guest quarters on Deck 6."

Bele, once arrived, did not wait to be asked any questions. "Yes," he said, "we are on the way to Cheron. I should tell you that we are not only a very old race but a very long-lived one; and we have developed special powers which you could not hope to understand. Suffice it to say that this ship is now under my direction. For a thousand of your terrestrial years I have been pursuing Lokai through the Galaxy. I haven't come this far and this long to give him up now."

The elevator doors snapped open and Lokai ran out, followed by the two security guards.

"I will not return to Cheron!" he cried despairingly. "You guaranteed me sanctuary! Captain Kirk . . ."

"He cannot help you," Bele said. "You have lost, Lokai. You are on your way to final punishment."

"Stop him!"

"Not this time, you evil mound of filth. Not this time."

"My cause is just. You must help me—all of you . . ."

"The old cry. Pity me! Wherever he's gone, he has been helped to escape. On every planet he has found fools who bleed for him and shed tears for the oppressed one. But there is no escape from this ship. This is your last refuge."

With a cry of rage, Lokai leaped at him. Kirk pulled him off. "Security," he said, "take both of these men to the brig."

The guards stepped forward. In an instant, a visible wall of heat formed around both the aliens.

Bele laughed. "You are helpless, Captain."

"What a fool I am," Lokai said bitterly, "expecting help from such as you."

"This ship," Kirk said, "is going to Ariannus. The lives of millions of people make no other choice possible."

"You are being obtuse, Captain. I am permitting no choice. My will now controls this ship and nothing can break it." Every cord in Bele's body and every vein in his head stood out with the ferocity of his determination.

"Bele, I am Captain of this ship. It will follow whatever course I set for it—or I will order it destroyed."

Bele stared at him. "You're bluffing. You could no more destroy this ship than I could change colors."

Kirk turned sharply toward Uhura. "Lieutenant, tie bridge audio into master computer."

"Aye aye, sir."

Kirk sat down and hit a button on his chair. "Destruct Sequence. Computer, are you ready to copy?"

"Working," said the computer's voice.

"Stand by to verify Destruct Sequence Code One."

"Ready."

"This is Captain James T. Kirk of the Starship USS *Enterprise*. Destruct Sequence One—Code One One A."

There was a rapid run of lights over the face of the computer, accompanied by the usual beeping. Then on the upper left of the panel a yellow square lit up, with a black figure 1 in its center.

"Voice and Code One One A verified and correct. Sequence One complete."

"Mr. Spock, please continue."

"This is Commander Spock, Science Officer. Destruct Sequence Number Two—Code One One A Two B."

"Voice and code verified and correct. Sequence Two complete."

"Mr. Scott."

The sweat was standing out on Scott's brow. Perhaps no one aboard loved the *Enterprise* as much as he did. Looking straight into Kirk's eyes, he said mechanically, "This is Lieutenant Commander Scott, Chief Engineering Officer, Destruct Sequence Number Three—Code One B Two B Three."

"Voice and code verified and correct. Destruct Sequence engaged. Awaiting final code for thirty-second countdown."

"Mr. Spock, has this ship returned to the course set for it by my orders?"

"No, Captain. We are still headed for Cheron."

Bele said nothing. Kirk turned quietly back to the computer. "Begin thirty-second countdown. Code Zero-Zero-Destruct-Zero."

"Count beginning. Thirty. Twenty-nine."

"Now," Kirk said, "let us see you prevent the computer from fulfilling my commands."

"Twenty-five."

"You can use your will to drag this ship toward Cheron. But I control this computer. The final command is mine."

"Fifteen."

"From five to zero," Kirk said, "no command in the universe can stop the computer from completing its Destruct order."

"Seven."

"Waiting," Kirk said relentlessly.

"Five."

The lights stopped blinking and became a steady glare, and the beeping became a continuous whine. Chekov hunched tensely over his board. Sulu's hand was white on the helm, as though he might put the ship back on course through sheer muscle power. Uhura looked at Kirk for a moment, and then her eyes closed peacefully. Spock and Scott were tensely impassive.

"Awaiting code for irrevocable five seconds," the computer's voice said.

Kirk and Bele stared at each other. Then Kirk turned back to the computer for the last time.

"Wait!" Bele said. It was a cry of despair. "I agree! I agree!"

Kirk's expression did not change. He said, "Captain James Kirk. Code One Two Three Continuity. Abort Destruct order."

"Destruct order aborted." The computer went silent.

"Mr. Spock, are we heading for Ariannus?"

"No, sir. The *Enterprise* is now describing a circular course."

"And at Warp Seven, Captain," Scott added. "We are going nowhere mighty fast."

"I warned you of his treachery," Lokai said. "You have weapons. Kill him!"

"We are waiting, Commissioner," Kirk said, "for you to honor your commitment."

"I have an alternative solution to offer, Captain. Simple, expedient, and, I am sure, agreeable. Captain—I am happy to have you complete your mission of mercy to Ariannus. It was madness to interfere with such a worthwhile endeavor."

Kirk listened stonily.

"Please, sir. You may proceed to Ariannus. Just guarantee me that, upon completion, you will take me and my traitorous captive to Cheron."

"Sir," Kirk said, "he is not your captive—and I make no deals about control of this ship."

Bele's shoulders sagged. He closed his eyes for a moment, his face curiously distorted, and then opened them again. "The ship's course is now in your control."

"Mr. Sulu?"

"She responds, sir. I'm resetting course for Ariannus."

"And as for you two—let me reaffirm my position. I should put both of you in the brig for what you have done. As Lokai observed, we have weapons, from which no heat shield will protect you. But I won't do it, since you are new to this part of the Galaxy, which is governed by the laws of the United Federation of Planets. We live in peace with the fullest exercise of individual rights. The need to resort to force and violence has long since passed. It will not be tolerated on this ship."

"You are both free to move about the ship. An armed guard will accompany each of you. I hope you will take the opportunity to get to know the ways of the Federation through some of its best representatives, my crew. But make no mistake. Any interference with the *function* of this ship will be severely punished. That's all."

Bele, his face inscrutable, nodded and went out, followed by a guard.

Lokai said, "You speak very well, Captain Kirk. Your words promise justice for all."

"We try, sir."

"But I have learned to wait for actions. After Ariannus—what is your justice? I shall wait to see it dispensed."

He too went out followed by a guard. Spock looked after him.

"Fascinating," the First Officer said. "Two totally hostile humanoids."

"Disgusting is what I call them," Scott said.

"That is not a scientifically accurate description," Spock said.

"Fascinating isn't one, either. And disgusting describes exactly what I feel about those two."

"Your feelings, as usual, shed no light on the matter."

"Enough for one day," Kirk said. "Those two are beginning to affect you."

Lokai settled upon Uhura as his next hope, perhaps feeling that since he had made no headway with the white members of the crew, a black one might be more sympathetic. He was talking eagerly to her in the rec room, with Chekov and Spock as bystanders. Racially, the four made a colorful mixture, though probably none of them was aware of it.

". . . and I know from my actions you must all think me a volcanic hothead—erupting lava from my nostrils at danger signals that are only figments of my imagination. But believe me, my friends, there can be no moment when I can have my guard down where such as Bele are present. And so what happens? I act the madman out of the anger and frustration he forces upon me and thereby prove his point that I *am* a madman."

"We all act incorrectly when we're angry," Uhura said.

"After all," Chekov added cheerfully, "we're only human."

"Ah, Mr. Chekov, you have used the phrase which puts my impatience into perspective—which focuses on my lack of ability to convey to your captain, and to you, yes you here in this room, my lack of ability to alert you to the real threat of someone like Bele. There is no persecution on your planet. How can you understand my fear, my apprehension, my degradation, my suffering?"

"There was persecution on Earth once," Chekov said.

"Yes," said Uhura. "But to us, Chekov, that's only something we were taught in history class."

"Yes, that's right. It was long ago."

"Then," said Lokai, "how can I make your flesh know how it feels to see all those who are like you—and only because they are like you—despised, slaughtered and, even worse, denied the simplest bit of decency that is a living being's right. Do you know what it would be like to be dragged out of your hovel into a war on another planet? A battle that will serve your oppressor and bring death to you and your brothers?"

There seemed to be no answer to that.

Bele, for reasons not to be guessed at, continued to work on Kirk—perhaps because he had developed a grudging respect for the man who had faced him down, or perhaps not. He visited the Captain's quarters whenever asked, though Kirk took care on each occasion to see that Spock was present as well.

"Putting the matter in the hands of your Starfleet Command is of course the proper procedure," Bele said on one such occasion. "Will it be long before we hear from them, Captain?"

"I expect the reply is already on the way, Commissioner."

"But Command may not arrive at the solution you anticipate," Spock added. "There is the matter of the shuttlecraft Lokai appropriated."

"Gentlemen," Bele said, almost airily, "we are discussing a matter of degree. Surely, stealing a shuttlecraft cannot be equated with the murder of thousands of people?"

"We don't know that Lokai has done that," Spock said.

"Well, the one thing we're agreed on is that Lokai is a criminal."

"We are agreed," Kirk said, "that he took a shuttlecraft—excuse me. Kirk here."

"Captain," Uhura's voice said, "I have your communication from Starfleet Command."

"Fine, Lieutenant. Read it out."

"Starfleet Command extends greetings to Commissioner Bele of the planet Cheron. His urgent request to be transported to his planet with the man he claims prisoner has been taken under serious consideration. It is with great regret that we report we cannot honor that request. Intragalactic treaty clearly specifies that no being can be extradited without due process. In view of the circumstances we have no doubt that after a hearing at Starbase, Commissioner Bele will be provided transportation, but whether with or without his prisoner remains to be determined. End of message."

Bele's face was a study in the attempt to retain a bland mask over anger. "As always," he said, "Lokai has managed to gain allies, even when they don't recognize themselves as such. He will evade, delay and escape again, and in the process put innocent beings at each other's throats—for a cause they have no stake in, but which he will force them to espouse violently by twisting their minds with his lies, his loathsome accusations, his foul threats."

"I assure you, Commissioner," Kirk said, "our minds will not be twisted by Lokai—or by you."

"And you're a leader of men—a judge of character?" Bele said contemptuously. "It is obvious to the most simpleminded that Lokai is of an inferior breed . . ."

"The evidence of our eyes, Commissioner," Spock said, "is that he is of the same breed as yourself."

"Are you blind, Commander Spock?"

"Obviously not; but I see no significance in which side of either of you is white. Perhaps the experience of my own planet may help you to see why. Vulcan was almost destroyed by the same conditions and characteristics that threaten to destroy Cheron. We were a people like you—wildly emotional, often committed to irrationally opposing points of view, to the point of death and destruction. Only the discipline of logic saved our people from self-extinction."

"I am delighted Vulcan was saved, Commander, but expecting Lokai and his kind to act with self-discipline is like expecting a planet to stop orbiting its sun."

"Maybe you're not a sun, and Lokai isn't a planet," Kirk said. "Give him a chance to state his grievances—listen to him—hear him out. Maybe he can change; maybe he *wants* to change."

"He cannot."

"Change is the essential process of all existence," Spock said. "For instance: The people of Cheron must have once been monocolored."

"Eh? You mean like both of you?"

"Yes, Commissioner," Kirk said. "There was a time—long ago, no doubt—when that must have been true."

Bele stared at them incredulously for a moment, and then burst into uproarious laughter.

While he was still recovering, the intercom sounded. "Scott here, Captain. We are orbiting Ariannus. We're ready with the decontamination procedure and Ariannus reports all ground precautions complete."

"Very good, Scotty, let her rip. Kirk out."

"I once heard," Bele said, still smiling, "that on some of your planets the people believe that they are descended from apes."

"Not quite," Spock said. "The apes are humanity's cousins, not their grandfathers. They evolved from common stock, in different directions. But in point of fact, all advanced forms of life have evolved from more primitive stages. Mutation produces changes, and the fittest of these survives. We have no reason to believe that we are at the end of the process—although no doubt the development of intelligence, which enables us to change our environment at will, has slowed down the action of selection."

"I am aware of the process," Bele said, somewhat ironically, "and I stand corrected on the detail. But I have told you that we are a very old race and a long-lived one. We have every reason to believe that we *are* the end of the process. The change is lost in antiquity, but it seems sensible to assume that creatures like Lokai, of generally low intelligence and virtually no moral fiber, represent an earlier stage."

"Lokai has sufficient intelligence to have evaded you for a thousand years," Kirk said. "And from what I've seen of you, that can't have been easy to do."

"Nevertheless, regardless of occasional clever individuals, whom we all applaud, his people are as I have described them. To suggest that behind both of us is a monochrome ancestor . . ."

The buzzer sounded again. "Captain, Scott here again. We have completed the decontamination orbit. Orders?"

"Program for Starbase 4. We'll be right with you."

Bele was showing signs of his strained and intense look of concentration which Kirk had no reason to recall with confidence. Kirk said, in the tone of an order, "Join us on the bridge, Commissioner?"

"Nothing I would like better."

But when they arrived, the bridge personnel were in turmoil. They were clustered around the computer, at which Scott was stationed.

"What's wrong?" Spock asked.

"I don't rightly know, Mr. Spock. I was trying to program for Starbase 4—as ordered—but I can't get a response."

Spock made a quick examination. "Captain, some of the memory banks are burned out."

"See if you can determine which ones."

"I will save you that trouble, Mr. Spock," Bele said. "They are in Directional Control and in the Self-Destruct circuit. You caught me by surprise with that Destruct procedure before." As he spoke, the fire sheath began to form around him. "Now can we go on to Cheron without any more discussion?"

"Stand clear of him," Kirk said. "Guard, shoot to stun."

The heat promptly increased. "I cannot block your weapon," Bele said, "but my heat shield will go out of control if I am rendered unconscious. This will destroy not only everyone here, but much of the ship's bridge itself."

The Cheronian was certainly a virtuoso at producing impasses. As he and Kirk glared at each other, the elevator doors parted and Lokai came storming out to the Captain.

"So this is the justice you promised after Ariannus! You have signed my death warrant! What do you do—carry justice on your tongues? Or will you fight and die for it?"

"After so many years of leading the fight," Kirk observed, "you seem very much alive."

"I doubt that the same can be said for many of his followers," Spock said.

Bele laughed contemptuously. At once, a fiery sheath grew also around Lokai.

"You're finished, Lokai. We've got your kind penned in their districts in Cheron. And they'll stay that way. You've combed the Galaxy and come up with nothing but monocolored primitives who snivel that they've outgrown fighting."

"I have given up on these useless pieces of bland flesh," Lokai raged. "But as for you, you—you half of a tyrant . . ."

"You image in a cheap mirror . . ."

They rushed together. Their heat shields fused into a single, almost solid mass as they struggled. Its edges drove the crew back, and wavered perilously near to the control boards.

"Bele!" Kirk shouted. "Keep this up and you'll never get to Cheron, you'll have wrecked the bridge! This will be your last battlefield—your thousand years of pursuit wasted!"

The combatants froze. Then Bele threw Lokai away from him, hard. Lokai promptly started back.

"And Lokai, you'll die here in space," Kirk continued. "You'll inspire no more disciples. Your cause will be lost."

Lokai stopped. Then his heat shield went down, and so, a moment later, did Bele's.

"Captain," Spock said, "I believe I have found something which may influence the decision. I can myself compute with moderate rapidity when deprived of the machine . . ."

"Yes, and beat the machine at chess, too. Go on."

"Because of our first involuntary venture in the direction of Cheron, our orbit around Ariannus was not the one originally planned. I believe we can leave it for Starbase 4 in a curve which will pass us within scanning range of Cheron. With extreme magnification, we might get a visual readout. I can feed Mr. Sulu the coordinates; he will have to do the rest of the piloting by inspection, as it were, but after the piloting he did for us behind the Klingon lines* I am convinced he could fly his way out of the Cretan labyrinth if the need arose."

"I believe that too," Kirk said. "But what I don't see is what good you think will come out of the maneuver."

"Observing these strangers and their irreconcilable hatreds," Spock said, "has given me material to draw certain logical conclusions. At present it is only a hypothesis, but I think there would be value in testing it."

Anything Spock said was a possibly valid hypothesis was very likely to turn out to be what another man would have called a law of nature. Kirk said, "It is so ordered."

The visual readout of Cheron was wobbly, but growing clearer; Sulu had sufficiently improved upon Spock's rather indefinite course corrections so that the moment of closest approach would be not much over 15,000 miles. It was an Earthlike planet, but somewhat larger, by perhaps a thousand miles of diameter. Both Bele and Lokai were visibly moved by the sight. Well, a thousand years is a long time, Kirk thought, even for a long-lived race.

"There is your home, gentlemen," he said. "Not many details yet, but if you represent the opposing factions there typically, we must be picking up a raging battle."

"No, sir," Spock said from his console. The words could not have been simpler, but there was something in his tone—could it possibly have been sadness?—that riveted Kirk's attention, and that of the Cheronians as well. "No conflicts at all."

"What are you picking up?" Kirk said.

"Several very large cities. All uninhabited. Extensive traffic systems barren of traffic. Vegetation and lower animals encroaching on the cities. No sapient life forms registering at all, Captain."

"You mean the people are *all* dead?"

"Yes, Captain—all dead. This was what I had deduced when I suggested this course. They have annihilated each other—totally."

"My people," Bele said. "All dead."

"Yes, Commissioner," Spock said. "All of them."

"And—mine?" Lokai said.

"No one is left. No one."

The two survivors faced each other with ready rage.

"Your bands of murderers . . ."

---

* See *Spock Must Die!* (Bantam Books, 1970)

"Your genocidal maniacs . . ."

"Gentlemen!" Kirk said in his command voice. Then, more softly, "The cause you fought for no longer exists. Give up your hate, and we welcome you to live with us."

Neither seemed to hear him; the exchange of glares went on.

"You have lost, Bele. I have won."

"You always think you win when you destroy."

"What's the matter with you two?" Kirk demanded, his own temper at last beginning to fray. "Didn't you hear my First Officer? Your planet is dead. Nobody is alive on Cheron just because of this kind of hate! Give it up, in heaven's name!"

"You have lost the planet," Lokai said. "I have won. I have won because I am free."

Suddenly, he made a tremendous leap for the elevator. The doors opened for him, and then, with a wild laugh, he was gone. Bele made as if to rush after him; Kirk stopped him.

"Bele—listen! The chase is finished."

"No, no! He must not escape me!"

"Where can he go?" Spock said.

"I think I know the answer to that," Uhura said. "Someone has just activated the Transporter."

"Oh," Kirk said. "Are we in Transporter range of Cheron?"

"Just coming into it," Spock said. "And a sentient life form is beginning to come through on the planet."

"It is he!" Bele cried. "Now I'll get him!"

He sprang for the elevator in turn. The guards, now belatedly alert, moved to stop him, but Kirk held up his hands.

"Let him go. Bele, there's no one there to punish him. His judges are dead."

"I," Bele said, "am his punisher." Then he too was gone.

There was a brief silence. Then Uhura said, "Captain, the Transporter has been activated again."

"Of course," Kirk said wearily. He felt utterly washed out. "Is he showing up on Cheron on the scanners now, Mr. Spock?"

"Some second sapient life form is registering. I see no other possible conclusion."

"But," Uhura said, "it doesn't make any sense."

"To expect sense from two mentalities of such extreme viewpoints is not logical," Spock said. "They are playing out the drama of which they have become the captives, just as their compatriots did."

"But their people are dead," Sulu said slowly. "How can it matter to them now which one is right?"

"It does to them," said Spock. "And at the same time, in a sense it does not. A thousand years of hating and running have become all of life."

"Spock," said McCoy's voice behind them, "may I remind you that I'm supposed to be the psychologist aboard this ship?"

"Spock's human half," Kirk said, turning, "is perhaps better equipped to perceive half measures taking over the whole man than the rest of us, Bones. And his Vulcan side quite accurately predicted the outcome. Hate wasn't all Lokai and Bele had at first, but by allowing it to run them, that's all they ended up with. This is their last battlefield— and let us hope that we never see its like again. Mr. Sulu, Warp Two for Starbase 4."

THE CLOUD MINDERS

Writer: Margaret Armen (Story by David Gerrold and Oliver Crawford)

Director: Jud Taylor

First Aired: February 28, 1969

"THEN THERE'S BEEN A MISTAKE," KIRK SAID.

And he couldn't afford one, not on this mission. During a routine check of the *Enterprise*'s operational quadrant of the galaxy, they had been ordered by the Federation to make top warp speed to the planet Ardana, sole source of a trace metal able to arrest a botanical plague ravaging vegetation which made a neighboring planet habitable. It was a mission whose emergency nature was known to the High Advisor of Ardana. Yet his greeting to the *Enterprise* had contained no reference to the zenite mines. Instead, his welcome specified Stratos as the reception site.

"Stratos is their Cloud City, isn't it, Mr. Spock?"

"It is, Captain."

Kirk hit the intercom to the Transporter Room. "Mr. Scott, are you locked in on the mines of Ardana or its Cloud City?"

"The mines, Captain. That's what you ordered."

Then this mistake isn't ours, Kirk thought. The Ardanans understood the Transporter; they had it themselves. Turning to Uhura, he said tersely, "Tell the High Advisor we request that the official welcoming courtesies be dispensed with. We are beaming down directly to the mines to ensure the fastest possible transport of the zenite to Marak II. The need is desperate. Say we appreciate the honor and look forward to a visit to Cloud City in the future . . . Come with me, Mr. Spock."

But no miners were awaiting them at the mine-shaft entrance. The hill by which they'd arrived was deserted.

"I don't understand it," Kirk said. "The Troglyte miners were to make delivery when we beamed down."

"Perhaps there is another entrance," Spock suggested.

There was none. The other side of the hill was as abandoned, as bleak and forbidding as the rest of their arrival area. It was Spock who put the thought in both of their minds into words. "It would seem that the Troglytes have changed their minds about the delivery, sir."

Even as Kirk nodded there came a hiss in the air above their heads. Two heavy, noosed thongs were hurled from behind them with an accuracy that pinned their arms helplessly to their bodies. Jerks tightened the thongs, and the two *Enterprise* officers were pulled roughly around to confront four creatures, obvious Troglytes, their loose miners' overalls begrimed, their eyes begoggled, their features hidden by slitted masks. One of the Troglytes was slightly smaller than the others; but they all had long, sharp-edged mortae, the honed blades aimed in open threat.

"What is the reason for this attack?" Kirk demanded.

"Interference breeds attack," the smallest Troglyte said coldly, in a female voice. "My name is Vanna, Captain. I have need of your . . . services. Move on." The overalled arm motioned to the mine-shaft entrance.

"We are here by permission of your government Council," Kirk said. "On emergency mission."

"Move on, Captain." Ominous ice entered the voice.

Kirk felt the prod of her sharp blade in his back. Exchanging a swift glance with Spock, they burst into simultaneous action, lashing out with their feet at the two nearest Troglytes. Spock's kick caught his man in the chest. It felled him just as Kirk's foot, slamming into his captor's stomach, dropped him to the ground, knocking the wind out of him.

Vanna lunged at Kirk, but he had broken clear of his bonds and knocked her weapon out of her hand. Spock and the remaining Troglyte circled each other warily. Vanna, agile and swift, lunged at Kirk with her bare hands and they fell to the ground. In the struggle, the strap securing her goggles snapped. They slipped from her face to reveal feminine features of such surprising beauty that Kirk, lost in amazement, had no eyes for what was materializing on the Transporter coordinates.

It was her wince at the sudden glare of sunlight that brought him out of his trance. A man of patrician bearing stood behind them. He wore a togalike garment and the charismatic air of the born ruler. Two husky males, armed and uniformed in gleaming white, shimmered into sight beside him—guards.

The patrician spoke. "Troglytes! Halt!"

He was not obeyed. Vanna, unyielding, continued to writhe in Kirk's grasp. Spock was now trying to cope with two of the miners, as the third elbowed groggily from the ground where the Vulcan's first kick had landed him.

"Surrender—or we'll fire!"

Wrenching an arm free, Vanna tried to rake Kirk's face with her nails. He pulled back slightly, and seizing her chance to break his hold, she leaped to her feet and ran to the mine entrance, shouting to her companions. They joined her, racing after her amid a shower of shining pellets. One of the missiles from the guards' guns struck. Zigzagging, hunkered low, the three unwounded Troglytes disappeared into the mine entrance.

Kirk, climbing slowly to his feet, was frowning in preoccupation, his eyes following Vanna and her vanished companions. Spock stooped to retrieve the communicator which had dropped from his belt, and straightened to meet the approach of their rescuers.

"Are you harmed, gentlemen?" asked the toga-clad man.

"Just a little shaken up," Kirk said.

"I am Plasus, High Advisor for the planet Council."

Kirk acknowledged the introduction briefly. "Captain Kirk, *Enterprise*. My First Officer, Mr. Spock."

"My regrets for the unpleasantness of your welcome to Ardana, gentlemen."

"It was rather warm," Kirk said dryly.

"Unfortunately, violence is habitual with the Troglytes. I can assure you, Captain, this insult will not go unpunished."

It was Spock's turn to frown in thought as Kirk said, "I am more concerned with that zenite consignment. Why isn't it in its specified location?"

Urbane, unruffled, the High Advisor's face with its high-bridged nose assumed a look of sadness. "Apparently the Disruptors have confiscated it, as I feared they would. They're a small group of Troglyte malcontents who hold the others under complete domination. It is the Disruptors who are responsible for the others' refusal to continue mining zenite."

"But they agreed to this delivery," Kirk protested. "It was your Council which assured us of that."

Plasus nodded benignly. "Obviously," he said, "they agreed as a ruse to get valuable hostages."

"Hostages? For what purpose?"

"To force the Council to meet their demands." Plasus turned to his guards. "Pick up the injured Troglyte for later questioning . . . Then organize a search party for the zenite consignment." Once more the urbane host, he said to Kirk, "Meanwhile, Captain, I suggest that you and First Officer Spock be our guests in Stratos City."

"I hope the search will be brief," Kirk said.

A shadow of grimness darkened the urbanity for a fleeting second. "I assure you we will do everything in our power to make it so. Now if you will just step this way, over here, our own Transporter will pick us all up."

They were led into a large, oddly designed chamber. Its floor and three of its walls glittered with a subdued iridescence. The fourth wall had been left open to the expanse of sky beyond, its border a waist-high balustrade of the same iridescent material. There was a careful carelessness about the manner in which luxuriously cushioned benches were scattered about the room, a calculated casualness that matched the surrealistic sculptural forms which decorated it. Central to it was a small dais, flanked by two straggly carved poles of almost ceiling height. They struck Kirk as purposeless even as decoration.

From the balustrade, Spock called, "Captain, here, sir, please!"

The whole planet was spread out beneath them. Its surface could be only half seen through drifting mists. What was visible was dwarfed by distance to the dimensions of a relief map, its hills anonymous mounds, its valleys vague shadows. There was both beauty and terror in such eminence. It evoked a feeling of uneasiness in Kirk.

"Remarkable," Spock said. "The finest example of sustained antigravity elevation I have ever seen."

The sound of a door opening behind them made them turn. A young woman had entered the room of antigravity triumph. She was tall, willow-slim, willow-graceful, her golden hair a mist of mystery around her perfect face. She didn't walk—she glided, her approaching movement so supple it lacked all suggestion of bone or skeletal muscle. Like the clouds which obscured the planet's contours, she drifted toward the two *Enterprise* officers.

"My father," she said to Plasus, "your sentinels informed me of our honored guests' arrival. I came to extend my greetings."

"Gentlemen, my daughter—one of our planet's incomparable works of art. Droxine, Captain James Kirk and his First Officer, Mr. Spock."

Her eyes lingered for a moment on the satyr ears of the First Officer. "I have never met a Vulcan before, sir," she said demurely.

Spock bowed. "Nor I a work of art, madame."

Kirk looked at Spock with quizzical amusement and surprise. Plasus beckoned his guests back into the room from the balcony. "Come, gentlemen, there is much to see in our city. This is our Council gallery. We have some of our finest art forms assembled here for the viewing of all our city dwellers. That piece there can boast of a special—"

He stopped abruptly. The piece he had turned to was a transparent solid of flowing serpentine lines curled like coiling flames. A miner's mortae had been driven into it, webbing it with cracks.

"Disruptors again!" Furiously, Plasus jerked the tool from the sculpture and dashed it to the floor.

"They are despoiling the whole city," Droxine said.

"For what purpose?" Spock asked.

"Again, to force the Council to accede to their demands." Plasus spoke with the impatience of an adult irritated by a half-witted child.

"Just what are these demands?" Kirk said.

"Nothing you need concern yourself about, Captain."

Kirk's voice was very quiet. "I must concern myself with anything that interferes with the delivery of the zenite, Mr. Advisor."

"Mr. Advisor, plant life is the source of oxygen," Spock added. "If all plant life is destroyed on Marak II, all humanoid and animal life will end there with it."

Plasus had recovered his suavity. "I assure you, gentlemen, you will get what you came for."

"I hope so," Kirk said. He paused. "Ardana is a member of the Federation. It is your Council's responsibility that nothing interferes with its obligation to another Federation member."

"And we accept the responsibility."

Spock touched the webbed cracks in the sculpture. "But why destroy art forms? They are a loss to everybody."

"Art means nothing to the Disruptors." Plasus stooped to pick up the mortae. "*This* is the only form they understand." Rage overpowered him again. Nobody spoke as he fought to regain control of himself. "But no doubt you would like to rest. A chamber has been prepared for you. Sentinels will conduct you to it, gentlemen."

It was dismissal. Droxine's eyes followed Spock as the two from the *Enterprise* left the room.

"The Disruptors must be mad," she said, "to have attacked two such charming strangers."

"They grow more daring every day," Plasus said.

"Do you think the Captain and his very attractive officer will feel we are responsible?"

Plasus smiled indulgently down on his daughter. "Responsible for injuries done to the charming strangers—or to our diplomatic ties?"

Droxine flushed. "Oh, I was concerned about both, father."

Plasus laughed outright. "I am sure they will not blame you."

She exhaled a breath of relief. "I'm glad. I like them. They are not at all like our men of Ardana . . . Father, promise me not to find the zenite too soon?"

Before he could reply, two guards burst into the room. Between them was a powerful man, his muscular shoulders tensed against their grip, but not struggling to free himself. That he had been doing so before was evident in the guards' panting.

"Apologies, Mr. Advisor," said one of them. "This Troglyte was apprehended leaving the city. As he lacks a transport card, we thought you would want to question him."

The man's aspect bore little resemblance to the stunted figures of other Troglytes. Despite the grime of his miner's overalls, the unkempt tangle of his shoulder-length hair, he was handsome. Proudly he drew himself to his full height, his eyes bright with scorn as they fixed on Plasus.

"What is your business in Stratos City, Troglyte?" demanded the High Advisor.

Though the flashing eyes burned with hate, the lips were silent.

"Speak! I command you!"

"My business is to repair," said the prisoner.

"Indeed. Then you must have a repair order. Where is it?"

"It was forgotten."

"Did you also forget your transport card?" The question was harsh with irony.

"It was lost when your sentinels attacked me."

"And where was your cavern mortae lost?" Plasus pointed to the empty sheath at the waist of the overalls. Then, striding to the mutilated sculpture, he plunged the mortae he still held in his hand into the hole it had made. "Here, perhaps."

"I came to make repairs," the prisoner said stubbornly.

"You shall make them—by telling me the names of the Disruptors."

"I know nothing."

"I would advise you to increase your knowledge."

An open sneer distorted the handsome face. "That is not possible for a Troglyte. The Stratos City dwellers have said so."

"Secure him to the dais," Plasus told the guards.

They tried to. But as they pushed the miner toward the dais, he knocked one guard aside and raced for the iridescent balustrade. The guards moved for their guns, but Plasus shouted, "*No!* I want him alive!"

It was too late. The prisoner had flung himself over the balustrade.

After a moment, Plasus shrugged. "How unfortunate," he said philosophically. "How unfortunate." He went out.

Droxine, as composed as her father, had been busying herself with an arrangement of goblets on a cubical table. The gold metal of one rang as she set it down, and a moment later, Spock came through the still open doors of the Council chamber.

"Mr. Spock!" the girl cried. "I thought you had accompanied Captain Kirk to the rest chamber down the corridor."

"There was some disturbance," the First Officer said. "It awakened me."

"I was but setting the table. I did not realize I would disturb you."

"Only Vulcan ears would find such a noise discernible from such a distance," Spock said.

The perfect eyelids lifted. "It seems Vulcans are fascinatingly different," said their owner. "In many ways."

Their eyes met. "The same may be said of inhabitants of Stratos," Spock observed.

"Vulcan eyes seem to be very discerning, too." She drew him down on the bench beside her.

His attention was sufficiently on this Ardanan work of art for him to fail his reputation for discerning sight for once. Behind him, a small figure draped in the clothing of Stratos crept from behind a pillar and moved stealthily down the corridor.

* * *

In the rest chamber, Kirk, breathing evenly, lay apparently asleep on a wide, billowy-pillowed dais. Vanna, crossing to him silently, drew a mortae from under her gown and laid its blade against his throat.

Kirk opened his eyes and he seized Vanna's wrist. Twisting the mortae from her grasp, he fell back with her on the bed. She kicked and writhed, but shortly he got her arms pinned back above her head.

"Well, that's better," he said, breathing evenly. "You again!" The face beneath his chest was lovelier than he remembered; but its eyes were cold as death.

"You sleep lightly, Captain," Vanna said.

"And I see you've changed your dressmaker."

"Release me," she said tonelessly.

"So you can attack me again?"

"Then call the guards," she told him contemptuously. "They will protect you."

"But I don't want protection. I find this very enjoyable."

"I do not."

Kirk grinned down at her. "All right, I'll make a bargain with you. Answer some questions, and I'll let you up."

"What questions?"

Kirk shook his head. "First, your word."

Hesitation came and went in her face. "I will answer."

Kirk released her. Panther-swift, she leaped to her feet and stooped for the mortae beside the bed. As he gripped her wrist again, he became aware that Spock's bed was empty. Where *was* Spock in this place of sudden treacheries? With that gliding girl?

The gliding girl was leaning back against a down cushion, its cream less creamy than the skin of her face. Spock, sitting very erect, was saying, "Yes, we Vulcans pride ourselves on our logic."

"Also on complete control of your emotions?"

"Emotions interfere with logic," he said firmly.

"Is that why you take mates only once in seven years?"

"The seven-year cycle is biological. At that time the mating drive outweighs all other motivation."

Droxine moved her head from the pillow and rested it against his shoulder. He looked down at the spindrift of golden hair, its fragrance in his nostrils, and their eyes locked. "Can nothing disturb the cycle, Mr. Spock?"

The Vulcan logician cleared his throat. "Exceptional feminine beauty is always disturbing, madame."

She had lifted her mouth toward his when a clang resounded from down the corridor. Spock sprang from the bench and ran for the door. Rushing into the rest chamber, he stopped dead at the sight of Vanna. Kirk had wrenched the mortae from her once more and dashed it to the floor.

"Captain, are you all right?"

From behind him Droxine cried, "*Vanna!* Why have you come here?"

Disheveled but still proud in her disarray, the Troglyte girl bent in a low bow to Kirk and Spock. "To welcome our honored guests," she said in a voice that cut with sarcasm. "Just as I was taught to do when I served in your father's household."

"It seems the Troglytes have the impression that our ship is here to intimidate them," Kirk told Spock.

"It is not an impression, Captain," Vanna said hotly. "It is truth!"

Kirk picked up her mortae and shoved it into his belt. "We are here to get that consignment of zenite. Nothing more."

"Starships do not transport cargo!" Vanna cried.

"In times of emergency they do anything," Kirk said. "And believe me, this plant plague on Marak II is an extreme emergency."

"Lies will not keep the Troglytes in their caverns, and neither will your ship, Captain."

Droxine said, "You speak like a Disruptor, Vanna."

"I speak for my people! They have as much right to the skies as you Stratos dwellers!"

"What would Troglytes do here?" asked Droxine disdainfully.

"Live! With warmth and light as everyone should!"

"Your caverns are warm," said Droxine coldly. "And your eyes are unaccustomed to light. Just as your minds are unaccustomed to reason." She moved to a wall and pressed a button. A sentinel appeared at the door; and waving a casual hand toward Vanna, Droxine said, "Take her away."

Kirk looked at Spock. "Surely," he said to Droxine, "you don't deny light and warmth to the Troglytes?"

"The Troglytes are workers," said the child of the High Advisor. "They mine zenite and till the soil. Those things can't be done here."

"In other words," Spock said, "they perform all the physical toil necessary to maintain Stratos?"

Droxine smiled at him. "That is their function in our society."

"Yet they are not allowed to share its advantages?"

"How can they share what they don't understand?"

"They could be taught to understand," Kirk said.

Droxine's answer had the sound of a lesson learned by rote. "The complete separation of toil and leisure has given Ardana a perfectly balanced social system."

Kirk was finding this conversation increasingly disturbing. He began to pace.

Spock said, " 'Troglyte' is a corruption of an ancient Earth term, Captain. Its technical translation is 'cave dweller.' "

Kirk threw him a tight nod. "We should have realized—"

He was interrupted by a shriek of agony echoing from the Council gallery. He and Spock exchanged a glance of alarm and raced down the corridor to the room of luxuriously cushioned benches.

Tied tightly to its central dais, Vanna was screaming. Incandescing rays from its flanking poles flooded her face with green fire. She shrieked again.

Droxine went back to the cubical table and straightened a gold goblet, while Plasus watched. Kirk and Spock sprang to the dais to tear at the cords that bound Vanna's writhings.

"Stop it!" Kirk shouted at Plasus. There was a long moment. Then Plasus' hands came together in a faint clap. The rays faded. Still bound, Vanna slumped into unconsciousness.

"She is stubborn," Plasus said. "Physical discomfort is the only persuasion they understand, Captain."

"You have tortured her." Kirk's voice shook with anger.

"Is it preferable to spare Vanna—and allow an entire planet to be destroyed? You yourself pointed out that the search for your zenite must be short." Plasus' voice was eminently reasonable.

Spock approached Droxine. "Violence in reality is quite different from theory. Do you not agree, madame?"

"But nothing else moves the Troglytes. What else can they understand?"

"All those little things you and I understand," the Vulcan said gravely. "Such as kindness, justice, equality."

She shivered slightly. The she drew a fold of her gown around her, rose gracefully and left the gallery.

"The abstract concepts of an intellectual society are beyond the comprehension of the Troglytes, Mr. Spock." The High Advisor was angry now.

"The abstract concept of loyalty seems clear to Vanna," Kirk said.

"A few Troglytes are brought here as retainers. Vanna was one of them. They receive more training than the others."

"But obviously no more consideration," Kirk said.

Open rage thickened Plasus' voice. "I fail to see the use of this continued criticism." He beckoned to his guards and pointed to the slumped body on the dais. "Revive her!"

Kirk leaped to the dais. "The only way you'll use that device again is on both of us!"

"An imposing display of primitive gallantry, Captain. You realize, of course, that I can have my guards remove you."

"Of course," Kirk said. "But Starfleet Command seldom takes kindly to having either rays or physical force used on one of its personnel. Think twice."

Plasus did so. "Why are you so concerned about this Disruptor's well-being, Captain Kirk?"

"I want that zenite."

"Then stop interfering—and I'll get it for you. We will get it for you in our own way. Guards, take the prisoner to confinement quarters. As for you, Captain, you will return to your starship at once—or I shall contact your Starfleet Command myself to report your interference in this planet's society, in contravention of your prime directive. Should you reappear on Stratos City again, it would be only as an enemy."

The guards were removing Vanna's unconscious body from the dais. Kirk clicked open his communicator.

"Kirk to *Enterprise*."

"Scott here, Captain."

"Returning to ship. Beam us up, Mr. Scott."

The Council gallery disappeared in dazzle.

Twelve hours.

Kirk moved restlessly in his command chair. The decision that confronted him was no joke. Twelve hours—and all plant life on Marak II would be irreversibly on its way to becoming extinct. Seven hundred and twenty minutes to allow the plague to complete its lethal work—or to persuade Ardana to make good on its pledge of the zenite consignment.

He swung his chair around to Uhura. "Advise Starfleet Command that the methods being employed by the government of Ardana will not make the zenite available. It is my view that I have only one alternative. I hereby notify that I must try to reason directly with the Troglyte miners. I am assuming full responsibility for these direct negotiations."

McCoy walked over to him and laid a hand on Kirk's shoulder. "That won't be easy, Jim. Ardana has supplied us with data showing mental inferiority in the Troglytes."

"That's impossible, Bones! They have accepted personal sacrifice for a common cause. Mentally inferior beings aren't capable of that much abstract loyalty."

"I've checked the findings thoroughly," McCoy said gently. "Their intellect ratings are almost twenty percent below the planetary average."

Spock turned from his hooded computer. "But they all belong to the same species," he reminded McCoy. "Those who live on Stratos and those who live below all originated on the surface, not long ago. It is basic biological law that their physical and mental evolution must have been similar."

"True enough, Spock. But obviously the ancestors of those who live on Stratos had left the environment of the mines. That's how they avoided further effects of their influence."

"What influence?" Kirk asked.

McCoy held out a small sealed container, carefully. "This is a low zenite ore sample I had brought from the surface. If I unsealed the container, it would have detrimental effects on everybody here."

"Zenite is shipped all over the galaxy wherever there's danger of plant plague," Spock protested. "No side effects have been reported."

"After it's refined there are none. But in its natural state it emits an odorless, invisible gas which retards the cortical functioning of the brain. At the same time it heightens emotional imbalance, causing violent reactions."

"Then the mines must be full of this gas," Kirk said.

McCoy nodded. "And the Troglytes breath it constantly."

"But the Disruptors—Vanna, for instance. They've outwitted a highly organized culture, apparently for years."

"Captain," Spock said, "you will recall Vanna's experience as a servant in Plasus' household. She was removed from exposure to the gas for an apparently significant period. Perhaps without long exposure, its effects slowly wear off."

"They do," McCoy said. "The other Disruptors probably have similar histories."

"Any way of neutralizing the gas, Bones?"

"No. But filter masks would eliminate the exposure."

"Get one, Bones—or make a mock-up of one, fast—and report back here on the double. Lieutenant Uhura, call Advisor Plasus."

After a considerable interval, the Council gallery materialized on the main viewing screen. Plasus was sitting at the cubical table, drinking slowly.

"Your further communication is not welcome, Captain," he said.

"I may be able to change your mind," Kirk said. "At least, I hope so. My ship's surgeon has made a crucial discovery. He has found that zenite ore discharges a gas that impairs brain function. He thinks he can counteract it."

McCoy appeared at Kirk's elbow, a face mask in his hand. "That is the case, Mr. Advisor. This filter arrangement in my hand is a gas mask. It eliminates all gases injurious to humanoid life. If others like it are distributed to the miners, we can confidently expect them to achieve intellectual equality with Stratos inhabitants, perhaps quite soon."

Plasus dropped the goblet. "Who are you? Who are you to talk of 'intellectual equality' for—for *Troglytes*?"

"Let me present Dr. McCoy, Medical Officer of the *Enterprise*, Mr. Advisor," Kirk said. "We have checked his findings with our computers. They are absolutely valid."

"Are you saying that this comical mask can accomplish what centuries of evolution have failed to do?"

The Cloud Minders

"Yes. That's what I said, Mr. Advisor."

"Centuries isn't a long time in terms of evolution," McCoy added.

"And do your computers also explain how my ancestors managed to create a magnificence like Stratos City while the Troglytes remained savages?"

"Your ancestors removed themselves from contamination by the gas," Spock said.

"Preposterous!"

"We have no time to argue," Kirk said. "I propose to inform Vanna that the filters are available."

"I doubt that even Vanna will credit such nonsense!"

"Are you afraid that the filters might work, Mr. Advisor?"

Kirk's question obviously hit home. Plasus stamped his foot on the iridescent floor. "You are here to complete an emergency mission, Captain! Not to conduct unauthorized tests!"

"I am here to collect a zenite consignment," Kirk said. "If these masks will help me do it, I will use them."

"I forbid it, Captain! Your Federation orders do not entitle you to defy local governments." Plasus reached for a switch. "This communication is ended."

As he faded from the screen, Kirk said, "My diplomacy seems to be somewhat inadequate."

"Pretty hard to overcome prejudice, Jim."

Kirk nodded. "Doesn't leave us much choice, does it?"

"Not much time, Captain," Spock said. "There are now ten hours and forty minutes left us to deliver the consignment to Marak II."

Kirk took the mask from McCoy. "Alert the Transporter Room to beam me down to Vanna's confinement quarters, Mr. Spock."

"Jim! You're returning to Stratos against government orders?"

"Unless Vanna has something definite to gain for her people, she'll die, Bones, before she turns over the zenite to us."

Spock intervened, an undertone of anxiety in his voice. "If you are apprehended violating the High Advisor's orders, he will consider it within his rights to execute you."

Kirk grinned. "If you're about to suggest that *you* contact Vanna, the answer is negative, Mr. Spock. And that goes for you, too, Bones."

Spock said stiffly, "Allow me to point out that a First Officer is more expendable than either a doctor or a Captain, sir."

"This mission is strictly unofficial," Kirk said. "Nobody is to have any part of it—or take any responsibility for it but myself. That's an order, Mr. Spock."

Silently the Vulcan detached his phaser from his belt and handed it to Kirk. Kirk took it, saying, "You have the con, Mr. Spock. Stand by until I contact you."

* * *

Vanna's confinement quarters were narrow, barely wide enough to accommodate a slim sleep dais and a small cube table. Her face still drawn from her ordeal, she was pacing the short length of the cell when she halted in amazement at the sight of him.

"I've brought you a gift," he said, and held out the mask to her. "Listen to me carefully, Vanna. In the mines there's a dangerous gas that affects the development of the Troglytes who are exposed to it too long. This mask will prevent any further damage and allow recovery to take place."

He laid the mask on the table and waited for her surprise to subside. She made no move toward the table.

"Gas from zenite?" she said suspiciously. "It's hard to believe that something we can neither see nor feel can do much harm."

"An idea isn't seen or felt, Vanna. But a mistaken idea is what's kept the Troglytes in the mines all these centuries."

"Will all the Troglytes receive these masks?"

"I will arrange to have Federation engineers help construct them."

She faced him, her eyes pondering. "Suppose Plasus will not agree?"

"Plasus is not the whole government," Kirk said.

"But the City Council will not listen to Troglytes."

"When the zenite is delivered, we'll come back. Then I'll request permission to mediate for the Troglytes. I give you my word."

"Stratos," she said, "was built by leaders who gave their word that all inhabitants would live there. The Troglytes are still waiting."

"This time you won't have to wait," he said gently. "We'll deliver the zenite in a few hours."

Her face was tormented. "Hours can become centuries just as words can be lies."

Kirk grasped her shoulders. "You must trust me, Vanna! If you don't, millions of people will die! A whole planet will die! The zenite is all that can save them—and the masks are all that can save the Troglytes!"

She closed her eyes for a moment, swaying. Then she said, "Very well, Captain. But the consignment is deep in the mines. I cannot tell you how to find it. I must take you to it."

Kirk hesitated. "Valuable hostages" was the phrase Plasus had used. There was no getting away from the fact that Captain James Kirk of the *Enterprise* would qualify as a very valuable hostage. But he had asked for her trust; he would have to give her his. He took out his communicator.

"Kirk to Scott. Beam us both up, and then back down to the mines."

Blinking in the planet's relentlessly glaring sunlight, Kirk drew the mask down over his head. Through its goggles, he could see Vanna's delicate figure, a dark shadow against the darker shadows of the mine's entrance, vanish into blackness. He followed her.

They were moving down a steeply descending tunnel. Ahead of him Kirk could discern faint glimmers of unidentifiable light. Then they were in a large cavern. Its walls glowed greenly with the phosphorescence of zenite ore lodes that etched themselves in cabalistic scribbles on the rock face like messages left by witches. Other jagged rocks jutted from the floor. The cavern might have been an underground graveyard of magicians' tombstones.

A miner's mortae lay against one of the floor's peaked rocks. Picking it up, Vanna struck the rock three times; the rock rang like a gong. As the sound died, Kirk heard a stealthy movement from a narrow ledge high on the left wall of the cave. Two big, begrimed Troglytes were climbing down a series of crude steps, hewed into the rock, to the cavern floor.

Vanna touched their shoulders in greeting. Their faces lightened. "Anka, Midro," she said.

"Vanna. It is you." Anka, the bigger Troglyte, touched her shoulder in similar greeting. "You have returned."

"And I have brought you a hostage," she said. "Seize him!"

The Troglytes grabbed Kirk's arms so swiftly that he could not make a move in defense. They were twisted behind him as Vanna, jerking his phaser from his belt, thrust it into hers. Then she snatched his communicator and hurled it against a sharp-toothed outcropping of rock a few feet away.

Kirk found his voice, but it was unfamiliar, hoarse, distorted by the mask. "We had a bargain. Why are you breaking it?"

"Did you really think I would trust you, Captain?"

"I trusted you," he said.

"You thought you'd tricked me with your talk of unseen gas and filters. I don't believe in it any more than Plasus does."

"Then you are a fool," Kirk said. "The filters can free you just as I said they could."

"Only weapons will free us," she retorted. "And you have just furnished us with two valuable ones. Yourself—and this." She touched the phaser in her belt.

"Holding me will not help you. My men will still come for the zenite consignment."

She laughed. "Without that," she said, pointing to the communicator, "you will be hard to locate."

"They will find me," Kirk said.

"Perhaps." She removed his mask and draped it over a mortae thrust into a crevice on the wall. "I don't think you will be needing this." Then she had a second thought, and taking the mask down again, handed it to Anka. "Send this to Plasus. It will inform him that we have more to bargain with than our mortaes and thongs."

Anka's eyes brightened. "You are clever, Vanna. Very clever."

He hurried out of the cavern and she turned to Midro. "Go to the other mines and tell the Troglytes to post watchers. Search parties may be coming soon."

Midro pointed to Kirk. "What of him?"

Vanna drew the phaser from her belt. "I will see that he does not escape."

"If we kill him," Midro said, "there'll be no need to see to that."

"A dead hostage is useless," she told him.

His face set stubbornly. "Only the Troglytes need know."

"I brought him—and I will say what is to be done."

"You're not the only Disruptor," Midro said sullenly. "I too can say."

"Can you do nothing but argue?" she cried impatiently. "Hurry—or the searchers will be here!"

"When Anka returns, we will *all* say." Nevertheless, he left.

Vanna kept the phaser leveled on Kirk. "Now, Captain, dig," she said. "Dig for zenite as the Troglytes do. I will give you a lesson in what our lives are like."

Silently, Kirk turned to the wall. It proved to be hard work. There was a bag on the floor in which he was told to put the chunks of ore; it took him a long time to get it half full. Vanna watched, smiling, as immaculate Captain James Kirk of the Starship *Enterprise* tore a nail on a bleeding finger.

"Is that what the Disruptors are working for?" he said. "The right to kill everyone?"

"Midro is a child."

"The filter masks could change that."

"Keep digging. You do it well, Captain. The unseen gas doesn't seem to be harming you."

"It takes a while for the effects to become noticeable." He straightened his aching back. "How long do you plan to keep me here? Providing Midro doesn't kill me, of course."

"Until we have help in the mines and our homes in the clouds."

"That might be quite a while." Kirk loosened another chunk of ore. "Longer than I can wait!"

He hurled the rough lump full in her face. She staggered back with a cry, and a moment later Kirk had wrested the phaser from her. He leveled it at the cavern entrance and fired. The boulders supporting it disintegrated, and the whole upper portion of its walls crumbled with a crash, sealing the entrance with a massive pile of rubble.

"You have trapped us!"

"Obviously."

"But soon the atmosphere will go! We will die!"

"Die? From something we cannot see or feel? You astound me, Vanna." He picked his way over the rubble to his communicator. As he had rather expected, it was unharmed; these instruments had been designed for rough use. "Kirk to *Enterprise*."

"Spock here, Captain. Is anything wrong?"

"Nothing. Are you locked in on me?"

"Locked in, sir. Ready to beam up consignment."

"Circumstances dictate a slight variation, Mr. Spock." Kirk eyed Vanna warily. "Hold on these coordinates. Locate the High Advisor and beam him down to me immediately. Without advance communication. Repeat—*without advance communication.*"

"Instructions clear, sir. We'll carry through at once. Spock out."

"You will seal Plasus in here also?" Vanna had gone rigid with alarm.

"I am preparing a slight demonstration of the effects of unbelieved gas," Kirk said. He waited. After a moment, the cavern shimmered and Plasus materialized. Such fury shook him when he saw Kirk that at first he failed to register the greenish darkness of his surroundings.

"Abduction of a planetary official is a serious crime, Captain! You will pay for it, I promise!"

Awe struggled with the alarm on Vanna's face. Kirk leveled the phaser at them both. "Not till you're convinced of the effects of zenite gas, Mr. Advisor."

"What effects? I see no change in either of you!"

"You need closer exposure." He waved to the half-filled bag at the cavern wall. "Fill that container."

"You suggest that *I* dig zenite?"

Kirk waved the phaser. "I insist, Mr. Advisor."

Plasus' fists clenched. "You will indeed pay for this, Captain." After eyeing the steady phaser for a moment, he turned to the wall, and began to scrabble at the open zenite lode. It was quickly obvious that he had never done any physical labor before in his life.

Kirk's jaw hardened, and he smiled a cold, thin smile. He felt strangely vindictive, and was enjoying it. "You too, Vanna."

She stared at him for a moment, and then obediently turned also to the wall.

Time passed. After a while the communicator beeped. "*Enterprise* to Captain."

"What is it, Spock?"

"Contact check, sir. May I remind you that there are only five hours left to—"

"Your orders were to stand by. Carry them out."

"Standing by."

Kirk clicked out. Both his laborers were beginning to show signs of exhaustion. Vanna leaned against the wall for a moment. "I grow faint," she whispered. "The oxygen is going."

"She is right," said Plasus, panting. "You must have us transported out of here."

"Dig."

"You imbecile! We'll die!" Plasus cried.

Kirk backhanded him. "I said, *dig*!"

Knocked back against the wall, arms spread, Plasus snarled, an animal at bay; all trace of the urbane ruler of Ardana had vanished. "I will take no more orders!" He lurched forward.

Kirk jerked the phaser. "Another step and I'll kill you."

Vanna stared at Kirk's distorted face. "Captain—the gas!" she choked out. "You were right! It *is* affecting you!"

Plasus took the cue. "Are you as brave with a mortae as you are with a phaser?" he taunted.

Infuriated, Kirk tossed the phaser to the floor. Plasus scooped two mortae from the rock ledge, and one in each hand, charged Kirk like a clumsy bull, slashing. Kirk dodged, grabbed Plasus' right wrist and tumbled him with a karate twist. The head struck rock. The two mortae clanged on the floor and Kirk leapt for Plasus' throat. As he fell on the High Advisor, the communicator dropped from his belt.

Vanna grabbed it and began shouting. *"Enterprise! Enterprise!"* It remained dead. Vanna shook it, and then found the switch. *"Enterprise!* Help! They will kill each other! Help us."

For a moment, nothing happened. Kirk's fingers tightened on Plasus' throat. Then the cavern shimmered out of existence, and he found himself wrestling on the Transporter platform of the *Enterprise.*

"Captain!" Spock's voice shouted. "Stop! The gas—"

Kirk let go and got groggily to his feet. "The gas? What gas?" He looked around, almost without recognition. The Transporter Room was full of armed security guards. Vanna was cowering; Plasus was crawling off the platform, all defiance fled. It had been a near thing.

The Council gallery of Stratos City resembled a first rehearsal reading of a play, Kirk thought. The whole cast was assembled. He hoped they had all learned their lines.

"I understand you are going to get what you came for," Plasus said.

"Yes, Mr. Advisor."

"The zenite will be delivered exactly as I agreed," Vanna said.

But Plasus hadn't yet learned all his lines. He turned on her. "The word 'agreed' is not in the Troglyte vocabulary."

"The Captain will have his zenite."

"No thanks to any agreement by you. It had to be obtained by force."

"Force has served your purpose at times," she said.

"And bribery," Plasus said, stubborn to the last. "Those masks."

Kirk had had enough. "The masks will be very effective, Mr. Advisor. The Troglytes will no longer suffer mental retardation and emotional imbalance."

"No," said Plasus. "They will all be like this one—ungrateful and vindictive."

THE CLOUD MINDERS

As he spoke, two sentinels entered the gallery staggering under the weight of an immense box. "There," Vanna said, "is the zenite. My word is kept."

"As mine will be," Kirk said. "Thank you, Vanna." He took out his communicator. "Kirk to *Enterprise* . . . Mr. Scott, the zenite is here in the Council gallery. Have it beamed up immediately . . . Mr. Spock—"

He broke off. Spock and Droxine had drifted to the balustrade. The hand of Ardana's incomparable work of art was on Spock's arm.

"I don't like 'filters' or even 'masks,' " she was saying. "I think the word 'protectors' is much better, don't you, Mr. Spock?"

"It is less technical," he told her. "And therefore, less accurate." He looked down at the hand on his arm. "But perhaps it is more generally descriptive of their function."

" 'Protectors' is more personal," she said. "I shall be the first to test them. I shall go down into the mines. I no longer wish to be limited to the clouds."

"There is great beauty in what lies below. And there is only one way to experience it, madame."

"Is your planet like this?" She looked up at him.

"Vulcan is quite different," Spock said. His back was stiff.

"Someday, I should like to see it."

"You cannot remain on Stratos," Spock replied, "if you wish to make a real test of . . . a protector."

Kirk judged it time to intervene. "Mr. Spock, I think it is time. We've got just three hours to get the zenite to Marak II."

Spock turned from the balustrade. Removing the white hand from his arm, he bowed over it. Then he straightened.

"To be exact, Captain," he said, "two hours and fifty-nine minutes."

ALL OUR YESTERDAYS

Writer: Jean Lisette Aroeste
Director: Marvin Chomsky
First Aired: March 14, 1969

The star Beta Niobe, the computer reported, was going to go nova in approximately three and a half hours from now. Its only satellite, Sarpeidon, was a Class M world which at last report had been inhabited by a humanoid species, civilized, but incapable of space flight. Nevertheless, the sensors of the *Enterprise* showed that no intelligent life remained on the planet.

But they did show that a large power generator was still functioning down there. That meant, possibly, that there were still some few survivors after all, in which case they had to be located and taken off before the planet was destroyed.

Homing the Transporter on the power signal, Kirk, Spock and McCoy materialized in the center of a fairly large room, subdivided by shelving and storage cabinets into several areas. One alcove contained a consultation desk, with shelves of books behind it. Another held several elaborate machines which were obviously in operation, humming and spinning and blinking. Kirk stared at these with bafflement, and then turned to Spock, who scanned them with his tricorder and raised his hands in a slight gesture.

"The power pulse source, obviously," the First Officer said. "But what it all *does* is another question."

Along one side was a less puzzling installation: an audiovisual facility containing several carrels (individual study desks) with headsets, projectors and small screens. The nearby wall was pierced by a door and a window. A tape storage area at the end of the room had been caged in, but its door stood ajar.

"May I help you?"

The three officers spun around. Facing them was a dignified, almost imposing man of early middle age. "I am the librarian," he added cordially.

Spock said, "Perhaps you can, Mr. . . . ?"

"Mr. Atoz. I confess that I am a little surprised to see you; I had thought that everyone had long since gone. But the surprise is a pleasant one. After all, a library serves no purpose unless someone is using it."

"You say that everyone has gone," Kirk said. "Where?"

"It depended upon the individual, of course. If you wish to trace a specific person, I'm sorry, but that information is confidential."

"No, no particular person," McCoy said. "Just—in general—where did they go?"

"Ah, you find it difficult to choose, is that it? Yes, a wide range of alternatives is a mixed blessing, but perhaps I can help. Would you come this way, please?" With a little bow, Atoz invited them to precede him to the audiovisual area. Apparently, Kirk thought, Atoz thought the three officers were natives, and that they wanted to go where the others had gone. Well, what better way to find out?

It was impossible not to be surprised, however, when Atoz, whom he would have sworn had been behind them, emerged smiling from the tape storage cage.

"How the devil did he get over there?" McCoy said in a penetrating stage whisper.

"Each viewing station in this facility is independently operated," Atoz said, as if that explained everything. "You may select from more than twenty thousand Verisim tapes, several hundred of which have only recently been added to the collection. I'm sure that you will find something here that pleases you." He turned toward Kirk. "You, sir, what is your particular field of interest?"

"How about recent history?" Kirk suggested.

"Really? That is too bad. We have so little on recent history; there was no demand for it."

"It doesn't have to be extensive," Kirk said. "Just the answers to a few questions."

"Ah, of course. In that case, Reference Service is available in the second alcove to your right."

It was not quite so surprising, this time, to find the incredible Mr. Atoz already waiting for them at the reference desk. But there was something else: Kirk had the instant impression that Atoz had somehow never seen them before; a guess which was promptly confirmed by the man's first words.

"You're very late," he said angrily. "Where have you been?"

"We came as soon as we knew what was happening."

"It is my fault, sir," Spock said. "I must have miscalculated. Remember, the ship's sensors indicated there was no one here at all."

"In a very few hours, you would have been absolutely correct," Atoz said. "You three would have perished—vaporized. You arrived just in time."

"Then you know what's going to happen?" McCoy queried.

"You idiot! Of course I know. Everyone was warned of the coming nova long ago. They followed instructions and are now safe. And you had better do the same."

"Did you say they were *safe*?" asked Kirk.

"Absolutely," Atoz said with pride. "Every single one."

"Safe where? Where did they go?"

"Wherever they wanted to go, of course. It is strictly up to the individual's choice."

"And did you alone send all the people of this planet to safety?"

"Yes," Atoz said. "I am proud to say I did. Of course, I had to delegate the simple tasks to my replicas; but the responsibility was mine alone."

"I believe we've met two of them," Kirk said, a little grimly. "You're the real thing, I take it."

"Of course."

McCoy was already scanning Atoz with his tricorder. "As a matter of fact, he is quite real, Jim. And that may explain the report of the ship's sensors; just one remaining man is a difficult object for detection. Sir, you are aware that you will die if you remain here?"

"Of course, but I plan to join my wife and family when the time comes. Do not be concerned about me. Think of yourselves."

Kirk sighed. The man was single-minded almost to the point of mania. But then, that was just the kind of man who'd be given a job like this. Or the kind of man such a job would soon make him. "All right," he said resignedly. "How? What shall we do?"

"The history of the planet is available in every detail," Atoz said, rising and leading them toward the tape carrels. "Just choose what interests you the most—the century, the date, the moment. But, remember, you are very late."

Kirk and McCoy donned headsets, and Atoz selected tapes from the shelves, inserting one in each viewer.

"Thank you, sir," Kirk said. "We will be as quick as we can." He offered a headset to Spock, but the First Officer shook his head and walked off toward the big machine that had mystified him earlier, and which Atoz now appeared to be activating. At the same time, Kirk's screen lighted and he found himself looking at an empty street—it was little more than an alley—which on Earth he would have guessed to be seventeenth-century English. A quick glance to his left revealed that McCoy's screen showed something even less interesting: an Arctic waste. Atoz certainly had peculiar ideas of . . .

A woman screamed, piercingly.

Kirk jumped to his feet, tearing off the headset. The scream came again—not from the headset, obviously, but from the entrance to the observatory-library.

"Help! They're murdering me!"

"Spock! Bones!" Kirk shouted, charging for the door. "Over here, quick!"

Behind him, Atoz' voice cried out: "Stop! I have not prepared you! Wait, you must be . . ."

As Kirk shot out the door, the voice was cut off as if someone had thrown a switch . . .

. . . and he skidded to a halt in the alley he had seen on the screen!

There was no time for puzzlement. The alley was chill and misty, but real enough and the screams came from around the next corner, followed this time by a man's voice.

"Be sweet, love, and I might have a mind to be generous."

Kirk rounded the corner cautiously. A young man wearing velvet, lace and a sword was struggling with a woman dressed like a gypsy. She seemed to be giving him little trouble; though she was kicking and scratching, his handling was as much amorous as it was brutal. A second, even more foppish young man was lounging against the nearby wall, watching with amusement. Then the woman managed to bite the first one on the hand.

"Ow! Vixen!" He aimed a savage cuff at her cheek. The blow never fell; Kirk's hand closed around his upraised arm.

"Let her go," Kirk said.

The woman wiggled free, and the fop's face hardened. "Come when you are bidden, slave," he said, and aimed a roundhouse blow at Kirk's head. Kirk checked the swing and followed through, and a moment later his opponent was sprawling in the dirt.

The second fop shoved the woman aside and moved threateningly toward Kirk, his hand hovering over his rapier hilt. "You need a lesson in how to use your betters," he said. "Who's your master, fellow?"

"I am a freeman."

This seemed to put the fop almost into good humor again. He smiled nastily and drew his rapier.

"Freedom dresses you in poor livery, like a mountebank—and you want better manners, too, freeman." The rapier point slashed Kirk's sleeve.

"The other's behind you, friend!" the woman's voice called, but too late; Kirk was seized from behind. He elbowed his captor in the midriff and, when he broke away, he had the man's sword in his left hand. These creatures really seemed to know nothing at all about unarmed combat, but it would be as well to put an end to this right now. He drew his phaser and fired point-blank.

It didn't go off.

Dropping it, Kirk shifted sword hands, and closed on the second fop. He was only fair as a swordsman, too; his lunges were clumsy enough to allow Kirk plenty of freedom to keep the weaponless first fop on the ropes with left-handed karate chops. The swordsman's eyes bulged when his companion went down for the third time and began to back away.

"Sladykins! He's a devil! I'll have no more of this."

He disengaged and ran, his friend not far behind. Kirk picked up and holstered the ineffective phaser and turned to the woman, who was patting her hair and checking her clothes for damage. The clothes were none too clean, and neither was she, although she was pretty enough.

"Thankee, man," she said. "I thought to be limbered sure when the gull caught me drawing his boung."

"I don't follow you. Are you all right?"

The woman looked him over calculatingly. "Ah, I took you for an angler, but you're none of us. Well, you're a bully fine cope for all that. What a handsome dish you served them, the coxcombs!"

She seemed to be becoming more incomprehensible by the minute. "I'm afraid you may be hurt," Kirk said. "You'd better come back into the library with me. You'll be safe there, and Dr. McCoy can see to those bruises."

"I'm game, luv. Lead and I'll follow. Where's library?"

"Just back there . . ."

But when they got to the alley wall, it was blank. The door through which Kirk had come had vanished.

He prowled back and forth, then turned to the woman, who said, puzzled, "What's wi' you, man? Let's make off before coxcombs come wi' shoulder-clappers."

"Do you happen to remember when you first saw me? Do you remember whether I came through some kind of door?"

"I think that rum gull knocked you in the head. Come, luv. I know a leech who'll ask no questions."

"Wait. It must be here somewhere. Bones! Spock!"

"Here, Captain," the First Officer's voice said at once, to the woman's obvious alarm. "We hear you, but we cannot see you. Are you all right?"

"We followed you," McCoy's voice added, "but you'd disappeared."

"We must have missed each other in the fog."

"Fog, Captain?" Spock's voice said. "We have encountered no fog."

"Mercy on us," said the woman. "It's a spirit!"

"No, don't be frightened," Kirk said hastily. "These are friends of mine. They're—on the other side of the wall. Spock! Are you still in the library?"

"Indeed not," Spock's voice said. "We are in a wilderment of arctic characteristics . . ."

"He means that it's cold," McCoy's voice broke in drily.

"Approximately minus twenty-five centigrade. There is no library that we can see. We are at the foot of an ice cliff, and apparently we came *through* the cliff, since there is no visible aperture."

"There's no sign of a door here either," Kirk said. "Only the wall. It's foggy here, and I can smell the ocean."

"Yes. That is the period you were looking at in the viewer. Dr. McCoy, on the other hand, was watching a tape of Sarpeidon's last ice age—and here he is, and I with him because we left the library at the same instant."

"Which explains the disappearance of the inhabitants," Kirk concluded. "We certainly underestimated Mr. Atoz."

The woman, clearly terrified by the disembodied voices, was edging away from him. Well, that wasn't important now.

"Yes," Spock was saying. "Apparently they have all escaped from the destruction of their world by retreating into the past."

"Well, we know how we got here. Can we get back? The portal's invisible, but we can still hear each other. There must be a portion of this wall that only *looks* solid . . ."

He was interrupted by still another scream from the woman, with whom he was beginning to feel definitely annoyed. He turned to find that her attempt to run out of the alley had been blocked by the two fops, who had returned with a pair of obvious constables.

"My friends are back—a couple of, uh, coxcombs I had a run-in with a little earlier. And they've brought reinforcements."

"Keep looking, Jim," McCoy's voice urged. "You *must* be close to the portal. We're looking too."

"There's the mort's accomplice," one of the fops said, pointing at Kirk. "Arrest him."

"We are the law," one of the constables told Kirk, "and do require that you yield to us."

"On what charge?"

"Thievery and purse-cutting."

"Nonsense. I'm no thief."

"Jim," McCoy's voice said. "What's happening?"

"Lord help us, what's that?" exclaimed the other constable.

"It's spirits!" the woman cried.

The second constable crossed his sword and dagger and held them before him gingerly. He looked frightened, but he resumed advancing. "Depart, spirits, and let honest men approach."

Kirk seized his advantage. "Keep talking, Bones," he said, edging away.

"They speak at *his* bidding," one of the fops said excitedly. "Stop his mouth and they'll quiet!"

"You must be close to the portal now," Spock's voice said.

"Just keep talk . . ."

But the other constable had crept around to the other side. A heavy blow exploded against Kirk's head, and that was the end of that.

The landscape was barren, consisting entirely of ice and rocks, over which the wind howled mercilessly. The ruined buildings surrounding the library had vanished, and so had the library itself. There was nothing but the ice cliff and, on the other side, the rocky glacial plain stretching endlessly into the distance.

Spock continued to feel carefully along the cliff, trying not to maintain contact for more than a few seconds each time. Beside him, McCoy shivered and blew on his hands, then chafed his ears and face.

"Jim's gone!" the surgeon said. "Why can't we hear him?"

"I am afraid that Mr. Atoz may have closed the portal; I doubt that I shall find it now, in any event. We had best move along."

"Jim sounded as if he might be in trouble."

"He doubtless was in trouble, but so are we. We must find shelter, or we will very quickly perish in this cold."

McCoy stumbled. Spock caught him and helped him to a seat on a large bolder, noting that his chin, nose and ears had become whitened and bloodless. The First Officer knew well enough what that meant. He also knew, geologically, where they were; in a terminal moraine, the rock-tumble pushed ahead of itself by an advancing glacier. The chances of finding shelter here were nil. It seemed a curious sort of refuge for a time-traveling people to pick, with so many milder environments available at will.

"Spock," McCoy said. "Leave me here."

"We go together or not at all."

"Don't be a fool. My face and hands are getting frostbitten. I can hardly feel my feet. Alone, you'll have a chance—at least to try to get back to Jim!"

"We stay together," Spock said.

"Stubborn, thickheaded . . ."

His voice faded. Spock looked about grimly. To his astonishment, he saw that they were being watched.

In the near distance was a cryptic figure clad in fur coveralls and a parka, its face concealed by a snow mask out of which two eyes stared intently. After a moment the figure beckoned, unmistakably.

Spock turned to McCoy, to find that he had fallen. He shook the medical officer, but there was no response. Spock put his ear to McCoy's chest; yes, heart still beating, but feebly.

A shadow fell across them both. The figure was standing over them; and again it gestured, *Follow me.*

"My companion is ill."

Follow me.

Logic dictated no better course. Slinging McCoy over his shoulder, Spock stood. The weight was not intolerable, though it threw him out of balance. The figure moved off among the rocks. Spock followed.

The way eventually took them underground, as Spock had already deduced that it would; where else, after all, could there be shelter in this wilderness? There were two rooms—caves, really—and one was a sleeping room, fairly small, windowless of necessity, furnished most simply. Near the door was a rude bed on which Spock placed McCoy.

"Blankets," Spock said.

The figure pointed, then helped him cover the sick man. Spock looked through McCoy's medical pouch, found his tricorder, and began checking. The figure sat at the foot of the bed, watching Spock, still silent, utterly enigmatic.

"He cannot stand your weather. Unfortunately, he is the physician, not I. I'll not risk giving him medication at this point. If he is kept quiet and warm, he may recover naturally." He scrutinized the mysterious watcher. "It is quite agreeably warm in here. Have you a reason for continuing to wear that mask? Is there a taboo that prohibits my seeing your face?"

From behind the mask there came a musical feminine laugh, and then a feminine voice. "I had forgotten I still had these things on."

She took off the mask and parka, but her laughter died as she inspected Spock more closely. "Who are you?"

"I am called Spock."

"Even your name is strange. Forgive me—you are so unlike anyone I have ever seen."

"That is not surprising. Please do not be alarmed."

"Why are you here?" the woman asked hesitantly. "Are you prisoners too?"

"Prisoners?"

"This is one of the places—or rather, times—Zor Khan sends people when he wishes them to disappear. Didn't you come back through the time-portal?"

"Yes, but not as prisoners. We were sent here by mistake; or such is my hypothesis."

She considered this. "The Atavachron is far away," she said at last, "but I think you come from somewhere farther than that."

"That is true," Spock said. He looked at her more closely. This face out of the past, eager yet reposeful, without trace of artifice, was—could it be what Earthmen called *touching*? "Yes—I am not from the world you know at all. My home is a planet many light-years away."

"How wonderful! I've always loved the books about such possibilities." Her expression, though, darkened suddenly. "But they're only stories. This isn't real. I'm imagining all this. I'm going mad. I always thought I would."

As she shrank from him, Spock reached out and took her hand. "I am firmly convinced that I do in fact exist. I am substantial. You are not imagining this."

"I've been alone here for so long, longer than I want to remember," she said, with a weak smile. She was beginning to relax again. "When I saw you out there, I couldn't believe it."

Spock was beginning to feel something very like compassion for her, which was so unusual that it confused him—which was more unusual still. He turned back to McCoy and checked the unconscious man with the tricorder; this added alarm to the complex.

"I was wrong not to give him the coradrenaline," he said, taking the hypo out of the medical pouch and using it.

"What's happening? Is he dying? I have a few medicines . . ."

"Contra-indicated. Your physiology may be radically different. But I may have given him too much. Well, it's done now."

The woman watched him. "You seem so very calm," she said, "but I sense that he is someone close to you."

"We have gotten used to each other over the years. Aha . . ."

McCoy groaned, stirred and his breathing harshened, as though he were fighting for air. Spock leaned over him.

"Dr. Leonard McCoy, wake up," he said formally but urgently. Then, "*Bones!*"

McCoy's breathing quieted gradually and Spock stepped back. The surgeon's eyes opened, and slowly came to focus on the woman.

"Who are you?" he asked fuzzily.

"My name is Zarabeth."

Somehow, Spock had never thought to ask that.

"Where's Spock?"

"I'm here, Doctor."

"Are we back in the library?"

"We are still in the ice age," Spock said. "But safe, for the moment."

McCoy tried to sit up, though it was obvious that he was still groggy. "Jim! Where's Jim? We've got to find Jim!"

"You are in no condition to get up. Rest now, and I will attempt to find the Captain."

McCoy allowed Spock to settle him back in bed. "Find him, Spock. Don't worry about me. Find him!"

He closed his eyes, and after a moment, Spock nodded silently toward the door. Zarabeth led the way back into the underground living room, then asked, "Who is this Jim?"

"Our Commanding Officer. Our friend."

"I saw only two of you. I did not know that there was another."

"There—is not. He did not come with us. The time-portal sent him to another historical period, much later than this one. If I am to find him, there is only one avenue. Will you show me where the time-portal is?"

"But your friend—in the other room," Zarabeth said. "He is ill."

"It is true that if I leave him, there is the danger that he may never regain the ship." Spock thought it over. It proved to be peculiarly difficult. "He would then be marooned in this time-period. But he is no longer in danger of death, so my primary duty to him has been discharged . . . If I remain here, no one of our party can aid Captain Kirk . . ."

"You make it sound like an equation."

"It should be an equation," Spock said, frowning. "I should be able to resolve the problem logically. My impulse is to try to find the Captain, and yet—" he found that he was pacing, although it didn't seem to help much. "I have already made one error of judgment that nearly cost McCoy's life. I must not make another now. Perhaps it has to do with the Atavachron. If I knew more about how it works . . . Zarabeth, you say that you are a prisoner here. May I ask . . ."

". . . why? My crime was in choosing my kinsmen unwisely. Two of them were involved in a conspiracy to kill Zor Khan. It wasn't enough to execute my kinsmen. Zor Khan determined to destroy our entire family. He used the Atavachron to send us to places where no one could ever find us."

"Ah. Then the solution is simple. Zor Khan exists no more. You and I can carry McCoy back to the library. I'll send you and McCoy to the ship, and have Mr. Atoz send me to wherever Jim . . ."

"No!" Zarabeth cried, in obvious terror. "I can't go back through the portal now! I will be dead!"

"You cannot go back?"

"None of us can go back," she said, a little more calmly. "When we come through the portal, we are changed by the Atavachron. That is its function. Our basic metabolic structure is adjusted to the time we enter. You can't go back; if you pass through the portal again, you will be dead when you reach the other side."

And there it was. He and McCoy were trapped here, for the rest of their lives. And so was Jim, wherever *he* was.

When Kirk came to, he found himself all too obviously in jail, and a pretty primitive jail at that, lying on a rough pallet which squeaked of straw. Fingering his head and wincing, he got up and went to the barred door. There was nothing to be seen but a gloomy corridor and the cell opposite his. The gypsy was in it.

She seemed to be about to speak to him, but at that moment there were voices in the near distance and, instead, she shrank into a far corner of her cell. In another moment the constable hove into view, leading a man whose demeanor was all too obviously that of a public prosecutor.

"That's the man," the constable said, pointing to Kirk. "That's the mort's henchman."

He let the prosecutor into the cell. The man regarded Kirk curiously. "You are the thief who talks to spirits?"

"Your honor. I am a stranger here."

"Where are you from?"

Kirk hesitated. "An island."

"What is this island?"

"We call it Earth."

"I know of no island Earth. No matter. Continue."

"I'd never seen the lady across the way before tonight when I heard her scream. As far as I could tell, she was being attacked."

"Then you deny that you're the wench's accomplice?"

"Yes. I was reading in the library when I heard her scream." The prosecutor started visibly at the word "library," and Kirk pursued the advantage, whatever it might be. "Perhaps you remember where the library is?"

"Well, well, perhaps your part in this is innocent," the prosecutor said, with some agitation. "I believe you to be an honest man."

"He's a witch!" screamed the woman from her cell.

"Now, wait a minute . . ."

"Take care, woman," the prosecutor said heavily. "I am convinced you're guilty. Do not compound it with false accusation."

"He speaks to unclean spirits! He's a witch. Constable, you heard the voices!"

"It's truth, my lord," the constable said. "I heard the spirit call him. He answered and did call it 'Bones.'"

"He's a witch," the woman insisted. "He cast a spell and made me steal against my wish."

Aghast, Kirk looked into each face in turn. There was no doubt about it; they believed in witches, all of them. The prosecutor, looking even graver than before, asked the constable, with some reluctance, "You heard these—spirits?"

"Aye, my lord. I'll witness to it."

"The 'voices' they heard were only friends of mine," Kirk said desperately. "They were still on the other side of the wall, in the library, my lord."

"I know nothing of this," the prosecutor said agitatedly. "*I* cannot judge so grave a matter. Let someone learned in witchcraft examine him. I will have no more to do with this."

"Look, sir. Couldn't you at least arrange for me to see Mr. Atoz? You do remember Mr. Atoz, don't you?"

"I know of no Atoz. I know nothing of this, nothing of these matters. Take him. I will not hear him."

The constable let the prosecutor out, and together they hurried down the corridor.

Kirk called after them, "Only let me speak to you, my lord!"

They vanished without looking back. Kirk shook the bars, frustrated, angry, hopelessly aware that he was alone and friendless here. Across the corridor, the woman's face was contorted with fear and hatred.

"Witch! Witch!" she shrilled. "They'll burn you!"

They took her away later the next day. Kirk scarcely noticed. He was trying to work out a course of action. He had never seen a jail that looked easier to break, but all attempts to think beyond that point were impeded by a growing headache; and when he got up from the pallet to make sure his hands would fit freely through the bars, he had a sudden spell of faintness. Had he caught some kind of bug?

Down the corridor there was a jingling of keys. The jailer was coming with food. It was now or never.

He was sitting on the pallet again when the jailer arrived; but when the jailer straightened from setting down the bowl of food, Kirk's arm was around his throat, his other hand lifting the ring of keys from his belt. Opening the door from the outside, Kirk pulled the terrified man into the cell and shut the door again.

Releasing his grip, Kirk allowed the jailer a single cry, then knocked him out with a quick chop and rolled him under the pallet. End of Standard Escape Maneuver One. With any luck, that cry should bring the constable, and safe-conduct. Curious how dizzy he felt. On an impulse, he lay down and closed his eyes.

He heard hurrying feet, then the creak of the hinges as the newcomer tried the door. The subsequent muffled exclamation told him that he had been luckier than he knew; the man outside was the prosecutor. Kirk emitted a muffled groan.

Shuffling noises, and then the sound of breathing told him that the prosecutor was bending over him. A quick glance through half-closed lids told them where the nearest wrist was. He grabbed it.

"If you yell, I'll kill you," he whispered with fierce intensity.

The prosecutor neither yelled nor struggled. He merely said, "It will go harder with you if you persist."

"I am being falsely accused. You know it."

"You are to come with me to the Inquisitional Tribunal. There the matter of your witchcraft will be decided."

"There are no such things as witches."

"I shan't say you said so," the prosecutor said. "That is heresy. If they hear you, they will burn you for such beliefs."

"You are the only one who can hear me. Before the Inquisitor, it will be different. I'll denounce you as a man who came from the future, just as I did. Therefore, you too are a witch."

"They would surely burn me as well," the prosecutor agreed. "But what good would that do you?"

"Use your head, man," Kirk said. "I need your help."

"How can I help you? I will do my utmost to plead your innocence. I may be able to get you off—providing you say nothing of the comrades you left behind."

"Not good enough. I want you to help me to return to the library."

"You cannot go back."

"I tell you, I must. My comrades are lost in another time-period. I have to find them. Why don't you go back too?"

"We can never go back," the prosecutor said. "We must live out our lives here in the past. The Atavachron has prepared our cell structure and brain pattern to make life here natural. To return to the future would mean instant death."

"Prepared?" Kirk said. "I am here by accident. Your Mr. Atoz did not prepare me in any way." As he spoke, his temples began to throb again.

"Then you must get back at once. If you were not transformed, you cannot survive more than a few days here."

"Then you'll show me where the portal is?"

"Yes—approximately. But you must find the exact spot yourself. You understand I dare not wait with you. . . ."

"Of course. Let's go."

Five minutes later, Kirk was back in the library. It looked as empty as it had when he had first seen it. He checked the contemporary time with the *Enterprise*, shunting aside a barrage of frantic questions. It was seventeen minutes to nova. Evidently, no matter how much time he spent in the past, the gate at its present setting would always return him to this day. It had to; for the gate, there would be no tomorrow.

He drew his phaser. It had not worked in the past, but he was quite certain it would work here. And this time, Mr. Atoz, he thought grimly, you are going to be *helpful*.

McCoy was still abed, but he was feeling distinctly better, as his appetite proved. Zarabeth, who had adopted a flowing gown which made her look positively beautiful, was out in her work area, making something she had promised would be a delicacy.

"I hope the *Enterprise* got away in time," McCoy said.

"I hope it will get away. The event is a hundred thousand years in the future."

"Yes, I know. I wonder where Jim is?"

"Who knows?" Spock said. "We can only hope he is well, wherever he is."

"What do you mean, we can only hope? Haven't you done anything about it?"

"What was there to do?"

"Locate the portal," McCoy said impatiently. "We certainly didn't come very far from it."

"We've been through all that already, Doctor. What's the point of rehashing the subject? We can't get back. Wasn't that clear to you?"

"Perfectly. I just don't believe it. I refuse to give up trying."

"It would be suicide if you succeeded."

McCoy sighed. "I never thought I'd see it. But I understand. You want to stay here. I might say, you are highly motivated to remain in this forsaken waste."

And not ten minutes ago, Spock thought, it had been McCoy who had been praising Zarabeth's cooking, and offering other small gallantries. "The prospect seemed quite attractive to you a few moments ago."

"Listen to me," McCoy said, "you point-eared Vulcan . . ."

Before Spock fully realized what he was doing, he found himself leaning forward and lifting McCoy off the bed.

"I don't like that," he said. "I don't believe I ever did. Now I'm sure."

McCoy did not look in the least alarmed. He simply seemed to be studying Spock intently. "What is it, Spock?" he asked. "What's happening?"

Spock let him drop. "Nothing that shouldn't have happened long ago."

"Long ago," McCoy said softly. The intent scrutiny did not waver. "Yes, I guess so . . . Long ago."

The stare disturbed the First Officer, for reasons he did not understand. Wheeling, he went into the underground living room, where Zarabeth was setting a table. She looked up and smiled.

"Ready soon. Would you like a sample?"

"Thank you, but I am not hungry."

She came over and sat down near him. "I can imagine how you must feel. I know what it's like to be sent here against your will."

"My feelings, as you call them, are of no concern," Spock said. "I have accepted the situation."

"I cannot pretend that I am sorry you are here, though I realize that it is a misfortune for you. I am here against my will, too, just as you are."

"I'm sorry I know of no way to return you to your own time."

"I don't mean that I wish to return," Zarabeth said. "This is my time now. I've had to face that. But it has been lonely here. Do you know what it is like to be alone, really alone?"

"Yes, I know what it is like."

"I believe you do. Won't you eat something? Please?"

"If it pleases you." He walked to the table and surveyed it. He felt a faint shock, but it seemed far away. "This is animal flesh."

"There isn't much else to eat here, I'm afraid."

"Naturally, because of the climate. What is the source of heat in this shelter?"

"There is an underground hot spring that furnishes natural steam heat and power."

"And there is sunlight available outside. Excellent. It should be possible to build a greenhouse of sorts. Until then, this will have to do as a source of nourishment." He picked up the most innocuous-looking morsel, surveyed it with distaste, and bit into it. It was quite good; he took another.

"There aren't many luxuries here," Zarabeth said, watching him with evident approval. "Zor Khan left me only what was necessary to survive."

"But he evidently intended you to continue living," Spock said, sampling another dish.

"Yes. He gave me weapons, a shelter, food—everything I needed to live—except companionship. He did not want it said that he had had me killed. But to send me here alone—if that is not death, what is? A very inventive mind, that man."

"But insensitive, to send such a beautiful woman into exile." Instantly, he was badly startled. "Forgive me! I am not usually given to personal remarks."

"How could I possibly take offense?" Zarabeth said.

Spock scarcely heard her. "The cold must have affected me more than I realized. Please—pay no attention. I am not myself."

And that, he thought, was an understatement. He was behaving disgracefully. He had eaten animal flesh—and had enjoyed it! What was wrong with him? He put his hands to his temples.

"I say you are beautiful," he said, feeling a dawning wonder. "But you *are* beautiful. Is it so wrong to tell you so?"

Zarabeth came to him. "I have longed to hear you say it," she said softly.

Then she was in his arms. When the kiss ended, he felt as though a man who had always been locked up inside him had been set free.

"You are beautiful," he said, "beautiful beyond any dream of beauty I have ever had. I shall never stop telling you of it."

"Stay," she whispered. "I shall make you happy."

"My life is here."

"*You lie*," said a voice from the doorway. Spock spun, furious with McCoy and enjoying it.

"I speak the present truth," he said. "We are here, for good. I have given you the facts."

"The facts as *you* know them. But you are also being dishonest with yourself, and that's also something new for you. You accepted Zarabeth's word because it was what you wanted to believe. But Zarabeth is a woman condemned to a terrible life of loneliness. She will do anything to anybody to change that, won't you, Zarabeth?"

"I told you what I know," Zarabeth said.

"Not quite, I believe. You said *we* can't get back. The truth is that *you* can't get back. Isn't it?"

"She would not jeopardize other lives . . ."

"To save herself from this life alone," McCoy said, "she would lie—and even murder me, the Captain, the whole crew of the *Enterprise*, to keep you here with her." His hand lashed out and caught her by the wrist. "Tell Spock the truth—you would kill to keep him here!"

Zarabeth cried out in terror, and in the next instant Spock found his hands closing around the physician's throat. McCoy did not resist.

"Spock!" he said intensely. "Think! Are you trying to kill me? Is that what you want? What are you feeling? Rage? Jealousy? Have you ever felt them before?"

Spock's hands dropped. His head was whirling. "Impossible," he said. "This is impossible. I am a Vulcan."

"The Vulcan you knew will not exist for another hundred thousand years! Think, Spock—what is it like on your planet now, at this moment?"

"My ancestors are barbarians. Irrational, warlike barbarians . . ."

"Who nearly killed themselves off with their passions! And now you are regressing to what they were!"

"I have lost myself," Spock said dully. "I do not know who I am. Zarabeth—can we go back?"

"I do not know. I do not know. It is impossible for me to go back. I thought it was true for you."

"I am going to try, Spock," McCoy said. "My life is there, and I want the life that belongs to me. I must go *now*. There isn't much time—I too am changing. Zarabeth, will you help me find my way to the portal?"

"I—Yes. If I must."

"Let's get dressed, then."

The cold seemed more intense than ever, and McCoy, wrapped in a blanket, still had little resistance to it. He leaned against the ice cliff, partially supported by Zarabeth, who once more was almost anonymous in her furs. Spock tapped the cliff, without success.

"There is no portal here," he said. "It's hopeless, McCoy."

"I suppose you're right."

"You're too ill to stay out here in the cold any longer. Give it up."

And then, faintly, they heard Kirk's voice. "Spock! Can you hear me?"

"It's Jim!" McCoy shouted. "Here we are!"

"Stop, we've found them," Kirk's voice said. "Hold it steady, Atoz. Can you hear me any better?"

"Yes," Spock said. "We hear you perfectly now."

"Follow my voice."

McCoy reached out. His hand disappeared into the cliff. "Here it is! Come on, Spock!"

"Start ahead." He turned to Zarabeth. "I do not wish to part from you."

"I can't come with you. You know that."

"What are you waiting for?" Kirk's voice said. "Hurry! Scott says we've got to get back on board right now!"

"They will have to come through together," the voice of Atoz added, "as they went out together. Singly, the portal will reject them."

Spock and Zarabeth looked at each other with despair. He touched her face with his fingertips.

"I did lie," she said. "I knew the truth. I will pay. Good-bye."

Then they were in the library, Kirk pulling them through. Atoz was spinning the dials of the Atavachron frantically, and then, dashing past them, dived into the portal and vanished.

"Atoz!" McCoy called.

"He had his escape planned," Kirk said. "I'm glad he made it." He raised his communicator. "Are you there, Scotty?"

"Aye. It's now or never."

Spock turned toward the portal and raised his fist as if to strike it, but he did not complete the gesture.

"Beam us up. Maximum warp as soon as we are on board."

The library shimmered out of existence, and they were standing in the Transporter Room of the *Enterprise*. McCoy, still wrapped in his blanket, was once more regarding Spock with his intent clinical stare.

"There is no further need for you to observe me, Doctor," Spock said. "As you see, I have returned to the present. In every sense."

"Are you sure? It did happen, Spock."

"Yes, it happened," the First Officer said. "But that was a hundred thousand years ago. They are all dead. Dead and buried long ago."

The ship fled outward. Behind it, the nova began to erupt, in all its terrifying, inhuman glory.